BLACKWELL STUDIES IN GLOBAL ARCHAEOLOGY

Series Editors: Lynn Meskell and Rosemary A. Joyce

Blackwell Studies in Global Archaeology is a series of contemporary texts, each carefully designed to meet the needs of archaeology instructors and students seeking volumes that treat key regional and thematic areas of archaeological study. Each volume in the series, compiled by its own editor, includes 12–15 newly commissioned articles by top scholars within the volume's thematic, regional, or temporal area of focus.

What sets the *Blackwell Studies in Global Archaeology* apart from other available texts is that their approach is accessible, yet does not sacrifice theoretical sophistication. The series editors are committed to the idea that usable teaching texts need not lack ambition. To the contrary, the *Blackwell Studies in Global Archaeology* aim to immerse readers in fundamental archaeological ideas and concepts, but also to illuminate more advanced concepts, thereby exposing readers to some of the most exciting contemporary developments in the field. Inasmuch, these volumes are designed not only as classic texts, but as guides to the vital and exciting nature of archaeology as a discipline.

1. Mesoamerican Archaeology: Theory and Practice
    Edited by Julia A. Hendon and Rosemary A. Joyce

2. Andean Archaeology
    Edited by Helaine Silverman

3. African Archaeology: A Critical Introduction
    Edited by Ann Brower Stahl

4. Archaeologies of the Middle East: Critical Perspectives
    Edited by Susan Pollock and Reinhard Bernbeck

5. North American Archaeology
    Edited by Timothy R. Pauketat and Diana DiPaolo Loren

6. The Archaeology of Mediterranean Prehistory
    Edited by Emma Blake and A. Bernard Knapp

7. Archaeology of Asia
    Edited by Miriam T. Stark

Forthcoming:
Archaeology of Oceania: Australia and the Pacific Islands
  Edited by Ian Lilley

Historical Archaeology
  Edited by Martin Hall and Stephen Silliman

Classical Archaeology
  Edited by Susan E. Alcock and Robin G. Osborne

Archaeology of Asia

Edited by

Miriam T. Stark

Blackwell
Publishing

© 2006 by Blackwell Publishing Ltd

BLACKWELL PUBLISHING
350 Main Street, Malden, MA 02148-5020, USA
9600 Garsington Road, Oxford OX4 2DQ, UK
550 Swanston Street, Carlton, Victoria 3053, Australia

First published 2006 by Blackwell Publishing Ltd

1   2006

Library of Congress Cataloging-in-Publication Data

Archaeology of Asia / edited by Miriam T. Stark.
    p.   cm.—(Blackwell studies in global archaeology)
  Includes bibliographical references and index.
  ISBN-13: 978-1-4051-0212-4 (hardcover : alk. paper)
  ISBN-10: 1-4051-0212-8 (hardcover : alk. paper)
  ISBN-13: 978-1-4051-0213-1 (pbk. : alk. paper)
  ISBN-10: 1-4051-0213-6 (pbk. : alk. paper)

  1. Asia—Antiquities.   2. Asia—Civilization.   3. Archaeology—Asia.
  4. Social archaeology—Asia.   I. Stark, Miriam T.   II. Series.

DS11.A72 2005
950′.1—dc22

                                                    2004024918

A catalogue record for this title is available from the British Library.

Set in 10/12½ pt Plantin
by SNP Best-set Typesetter Ltd, Hong Kong
Printed and bound in Great Britain
by TJ International Ltd, Padstow, Cornwall

The publisher's policy is to use permanent paper from mills that operate a sustainable forestry policy, and which has been manufactured from pulp processed using acid-free and elementary chlorine-free practices. Furthermore, the publisher ensures that the text paper and cover board used have met acceptable environmental accreditation standards.

For further information on
Blackwell Publishing, visit our website:
www.blackwellpublishing.com

Contents

Series Editors' Preface

This series was conceived as a collection of books designed to cover central areas of undergraduate archaeological teaching. Each volume in the series, edited by experts in the area, includes newly commissioned articles written by archaeologists actively engaged in research. By commissioning new articles, the series combines one of the best features of readers, the presentation of multiple approaches to archaeology, with the virtues of a text conceived from the beginning as intended for a specific audience. While the model reader for the series is conceived of as an upper-division undergraduate, the inclusion in the volumes of researchers actively engaged in work today will also make these volumes valuable for more advanced researchers who want a rapid introduction to contemporary issues in specific sub-fields of global archaeology.

Each volume in the series will include an extensive introduction by the volume editor that will set the scene in terms of thematic or geographic focus. Individual volumes, and the series as a whole, exemplify a wide range of approaches in contemporary archaeology. The volumes uniformly engage with issues of contemporary interest, interweaving social, political, and ethical themes. We contend that it is no longer tenable to teach the archaeology of vast swaths of the globe without acknowledging the political implications of working in foreign countries and the responsibilities archaeologists incur by writing and presenting other people's pasts. The volumes in this series will not sacrifice theoretical sophistication for accessibility. We are committed to the idea that usable teaching texts need not lack ambition.

Blackwell Studies in Global Archaeology aims to immerse readers in fundamental archaeological ideas and concepts, but also to illuminate more advanced concepts, exposing readers to some of the most exciting contemporary developments in the field.

Lynn Meskell and Rosemary A. Joyce

Figures

Tables

Notes on Contributors

Francis Allard (Ph.D., 1995, University of Pittsburgh) is an Assistant Professor in the Department of Anthropology at Indiana University of Pennsylvania. His research has focused primarily on the emergence of complex societies in China and the archaeology of Eurasian pastoralist societies. Since 2001, he has directed the Khanuy Valley Project on Early Nomadic Pastoralism in Mongolia. Some recent publications include "Recent Archaeological Research in the Khanuy Valley, Central Mongolia" (in *Beyond the Steppe and the Sown: Integrating Local and Global Visions*, Brill Academic Publishers, In press), "Lingnan and Chu during the First Millennium B.C.: A Reassessment of the Core-Periphery Model" (in *Early Guangdong, Between China and Southeast Asia. Archaeological and Textual Evidence*, Harrassowitz Publishers, In press), "A Xiongnu Cemetery found in Mongolia" (*Antiquity* 2002), and "Mortuary Ceramics and Social Organization in the Dawenkou and Majiayao Cultures" (*Journal of East Asian Archaeology* 2001).

Chunag Amartuvshin (Ph.D., 2004, Mongolian Academy of Sciences) is a research archaeologist at the Institute of Archaeology in Ulaanbaatar, Mongolia. He has codirected both survey and excavation projects across the Mongolian steppe to better understand early transitions to mobile herding and the organization of small-scale political groups during the Bronze Age. Some of his recent publications include "Archaeological Monuments of Egiin Gol Valley" (coauthored with Tsagaan Torbat and Ulambayar Erdenebat; Institute of Archaeology, 2003) and "A Study of the Slab Burials of Egiin Gol" (in *Collected Papers of the First Mongolian–Korean Academic Symposium*, Academy of Sciences, 2003).

Peter Bellwood (Ph.D., 1980, Cambridge University) is a Professor in the Department of Anthropology and Archaeology at the Australian National University. He has written four books that deal in part with archaeology in the East Asian region – *Man's Conquest of the Pacific* (1978); *The Polynesians* (1987); *Prehistory of the Indo-Malaysian Archipelago* (1997); and *First Farmers: The Origins of Agricultural*

Societies (2004). His books have been translated into Japanese, Russian, French, and Indonesian. He has also recently co-edited *Examining the Farming/Language Dispersal Hypothesis* (with Colin Renfrew, 2003) and *Southeast Asia: From Prehistory to History* (with Ian Glover, 2004). He is Secretary-General of the Indo-Pacific Prehistory Association and Editor of its Bulletin. He has worked throughout island Southeast Asia and Polynesia, and is currently involved in archaeological field research in the Philippines and Vietnam.

Xingcan Chen (Ph.D., 1991, Institute of Archaeology, Chinese Academy of Social Sciences) is a Professor in Archaeology and Assistant to the Director of the Institute of Archaeology, Chinese Academy of Social Sciences. He has carried out many archaeological projects in China, and codirects the Yi-Luo River Archaeological Survey in central China. His research interests include history of Chinese archaeology, ethnoarchaeology, settlement archaeology, Chinese Neolithic culture, and the development of early Chinese civilization. Some of his recent publications include *State Formation in Early China* (co-edited with Li Liu, Duckworth Publishers, 2003), *Archaeology Essays* (Wenwu Press, Beijing, 2002, in Chinese), and *The History of Chinese Prehistoric Archaeology (1895–1949)* (Sanlian Press, Beijing, 1997, in Chinese).

Gary W. Crawford (Ph.D., 1979, University of North Carolina) is a Full Professor in the Department of Anthropology, University of Toronto at Mississauga. He specializes in the paleoethnobotany of China, Japan, Korea, and eastern North America. His Asian research has focused on agricultural origins and intensification in the Yellow River system in North China and among the Ainu in Hokkaido, Japan. Some of his recent publications include "Agricultural Origins in the Korean Peninsula" (with Gyoung–Ah Lee, *Antiquity* 2003), "Late Neolithic Plant Remains from Northern China: Preliminary Results from Liangchengzhen, Shandong" (with Anne Underhill, Zhijun Zhao, Gyoung-Ah Lee, Gary Feinman, Linda Nicholas, Fengshi Luan, Haiguang Yu, Hui Fang, and Fengshu Cai, *Current Anthropology*, In press), and *Human Evolution and Prehistory* (with W. Haviland and S. Fedorak, Nelson, a division of Thomson Canada, 2005).

Ian C. Glover (Ph.D., 1972, Australian National University) is Emeritus Reader in Southeast Asian Archaeology at the Institute of Archaeology, University College London. He has undertaken excavations in East Timor, Sulawesi, Western Thailand, and Central Vietnam on periods ranging from Late Pleistocene cave deposits, Iron Age cemeteries, and the emerging Cham Civilization of Central Vietnam. He has published widely on the early technologies of bronze, iron, and glass, the effects of inter-regional trade in South and Southeast Asia, and the relationship between archaeology and nationalism. Some of his recent publications include *Southeast Asia: from Prehistory to History* (co-edited with Peter Bellwood, Routledge/Curzon, 2004), "The Late Prehistoric to Early Historic Earthenware of Central Vietnam" (in *Earthenware in Southeast Asia*, Singapore University Press, 2003), and "Letting the Past Serve the Present: Some Contemporary Uses of Archaeology in Viet Nam" (*Antiquity* 73, 1999).

Junko Habu (Ph.D., 1996, McGill University) is an associate professor at the Department of Anthropology, University of California-Berkeley. Her research focuses on Japanese prehistory and hunter-gatherer archaeology. She has recently published the following volumes: *Ancient Jomon of Japan* (Cambridge University Press, 2004); *Beyond Foraging and Collecting: Evolutionary Change in Hunter-Gatherer Settlement Systems* (co-edited with Ben Fitzhugh, Kluwer Academic/Plenum, 2002); and *Subsistence-Settlement Systems and Intersite Variability in the Moroiso Phase of the Early Jomon Period of Japan* (International Monographs in Prehistory 2001).

William Honeychurch (Ph.D., 2004, University of Michigan) is a postdoctoral researcher at the Smithsonian Institution, Department of Anthropology. He has codirected a number of archaeological field projects in northern Asia to study the sociopolitical networks and long-distance interactions of nomadic states and empires. He has authored a number of publications with Mongolian and American colleagues including: "Survey and Settlement in Northern Mongolia: the Structure of Intra-Regional Nomadic Organization" (in *Beyond the Steppe and the Sown*, E. J. Brill, forthcoming) and "Chemical Analysis of Prehistoric Mongolian Pottery" (*Arctic Anthropology* 1999).

David N. Keightley (Ph.D., 1969, Columbia University) is Professor Emeritus of History at the University of California-Berkeley. Some of his publications include *Sources of Shang History: The Oracle-Bone Inscriptions of Bronze Age China* (University of California Press, 1978), *The Origins of Chinese Civilization* (ed., University of California Press, 1983), and *The Ancestral Landscape: Time, Space, and Community in Late Shang China (ca. 1200–1045 B.C.)* (Institute of East Asian Studies, 2000). He has published numerous articles on Neolithic and Bronze-Age China, with particular attention to the Shang dynasty. Many of the roots of East Asian culture – in Japan, Korea, Southeast Asia, as well as China – can be traced back to the Neolithic-to-Bronze-Age transition in China, the period when the first written records appear. It is to the analysis and characterization of that seminal culture that Keightley has devoted his scholarly career.

Li Liu (Ph.D., 1994, Harvard University) is a Lecturer in Archaeology at La Trobe University and codirects the Yi-Luo River Archaeological Survey in central China. Her research interests include settlement archaeology, zooarchaeology, Neolithic China, and state formation in China. Some of her recent publications include: "Settlement Patterns and Development of Social Complexity in the Yiluo Region, North China" (coauthored with Xingcan Chen, Yun Kuen Lee, Henry Wright, and Arlene Rosen, *Journal of Field Archaeology* 29, 2002); "The products of minds as well as of hands:" Production of Prestige Goods in the Neolithic and Early State Periods of China" (*Asian Perspectives* 42, 2003); *The Chinese Neolithic: Trajectories to Early States* (Cambridge University Press, 2004); and *State Formation in Early China* (co-edited with Xingcan Chen, Duckworth Publishers, 2003).

Koji Mizoguchi (Ph.D., 1995, Cambridge University) is an Associate Professor of Archaeology at the Graduate School of Social and Cultural Studies, Kyushu

University, Japan. His current research interests include: (1) mortuary archaeology of the Yayoi period of Japan, (2) transformations in social structures and the conception of time, and (3) modernity, its transformation and archaeology. Some of his recent publications include: *An Archaeological History of Japan, 30,000 B.C. to A.D. 700* (University of Pennsylvania Press, 2002), and "Identity, Modernity, and Archaeology: The Case of Japan" (in *A Companion to Social Archaeology*, Blackwell, 2004).

Kathleen D. Morrison (Ph.D., 1992, University of California-Berkeley) is Professor of Anthropology and Director of the Center for International Studies at the University of Chicago. Her research interests include colonialism and imperialism, environmental change and landscape anthropogenesis, and the intersections of anthropology, history, and natural science in South Asia and western North America. She is the author of *Fields of Victory: Vijayanagara and the Course of Intensification*, 1995, Contributions of the University of California Archaeological Research Facility (Repr. 2000, Munshiram Manoharlal, New Delhi) and *Oceans of Dharma: Landscapes, Power, and Place in Southern India* (in preparation). Some of her other recent publications include *Empires: Perspectives from Archaeology and History* (co-edited with Susan E. Alcock, Terence N. D'Altroy, and Carla Sinopoli, Cambridge University Press, 2001) and *Forager-Traders in South and Southeast Asia: Long-Term Histories* (co-edited with Laura L. Junker, Cambridge University Press, 2002).

Sarah Milledge Nelson (Ph.D., 1973, University of Michigan) is a Professor at the University of Denver. Her research interests involve the explanation of culture change from the appearance of pottery to the formation of the state, especially the problems of the origins of agriculture, the distribution of the knowledge of bronze technology, and the archaeology of gender. She has written extensively on the archaeology of East Asia and has published two synthetic volumes: *The Archaeology of Korea* (Cambridge University Press, 1993) and *The Archaeology of Northeast China* (ed., Routledge, 1995). Some of her most recent publications include the following books: *Korean Social Archaeology: Early Villages* (Jimoondang Publishing, 2004); *Gender in Archaeology, Analyzing Power and Prestige* (Altamira Press, 2nd edition, 2004); and *Ancient Queens: Archaeological Explorations* (Rowan and Littlefield, 2003).

Yuri Pines (Ph.D., 1998, Hebrew University of Jerusalem) is the Michael William Lipson Senior Lecturer in Chinese Studies, the Hebrew University of Jerusalem. His research fields are China's pre-imperial history, historiography, and political thought. Some of his recent publications include: *The Foundations of Confucian Thought: Intellectual Life in the Chunqiu Period, 722–453 B.C.E.* (University of Hawai'i Press, 2002); "Disputers of the Li: Breakthroughs in the Concept of Ritual in Preimperial China" (*Asia Major Third Series*, 2000); "Friends or Foes: Changing Concepts of Ruler-Minister Relations and the Notion of Loyalty in Pre-Imperial China" (*Monumenta Serica* 50, 2002); "History as a Guide to the Netherworld: Rethinking the Chunqiu shiyu" (*Journal of Chinese Religions* 31, 2003); and "The Question of Interpretation: Qin History in Light of New Epigraphic Sources" (*Early China*, In press).

Himanshu Prabha Ray (Ph.D., 1984, Jawaharlal Nehru University) is an Associate Professor in the Centre for Historical Studies, Jawaharlal Nehru University. In her research she adopts an interdisciplinary approach for a study of seafaring activity in the Indian Ocean, the history of archaeology, and the archaeology of religion in South Asia. Her publications include: *Monastery and Guild: Commerce under the Satavahanas* (Oxford University Press, 1986); *The Winds of Change: Buddhism and the Maritime Links of Ancient South Asia (*Oxford India Paperbacks, 2000); *The Archaeology of Seafaring in Ancient South Asia* (Cambridge University Press, 2003); and several edited volumes: *Tradition and Archaeology* (with Jean-François Salles, Manohar, 1996); *Archaeology of Seafaring: The Indian Ocean in the Ancient Period* (Indian Council of Historical Research Monograph I, 1999); and *Archaeology as History in Early South Asia* (with Carla Sinopoli, Aryan Books International, 2004).

Gideon Shelach (Ph.D., 1996, University of Pittsburgh) is an Associate Professor in the Department of East Asian Studies, The Hebrew University. His research interests include the development of sedentary communities and emergent social complexity in Northeast China, social change and interregional interactions, and the formation of state-level systems. He has conducted archaeological work in China since 1994 and is part of the team of the Chifeng Regional Survey in Inner Mongolia. Some of his publications include *Leadership Strategies, Economic Activity, and Interregional Interaction: Social Complexity in Northeast China* (Kluwer Academic/Plenum Press, 1999), and "The Earliest Neolithic Cultures of Northeast China: Recent Discoveries and New Perspectives on the Beginning of Agriculture" (*Journal of World Prehistory* 14, 2000).

Carla M. Sinopoli (Ph.D., 1986, University of Michigan) is a Professor in the Department of Anthropology and Curator of Asian Archaeology at the Museum of Anthropology, University of Michigan. She has conducted archaeological research in India since 1983, focusing on the Vijayanagara Empire, and more recently, on the South Indian Iron Age and Early Historic periods. Her research interests include political economy of early states and empire, material culture theory, and ceramic analysis. Sinopoli is the author of several books. Three of her most recent publications are: *The Political Economy of Craft Production: Crafting Empire in South India, c. 1350–1650* (Cambridge University Press, 2003); *Archaeology as History* (co-edited with Himanshu P. Ray, Aryan Books, 2004), and *Empires* (co-edited with Susan Alcock, Terence N. D'Altroy, and Kathleen D. Morrison, Cambridge University Press, 2001).

Miriam T. Stark (Ph.D., 1993, University of Arizona) is an Associate Professor in the Department of Anthropology at the University of Hawaii-Manoa. She has conducted archaeological research in Southeast Asia since 1987, and currently codirects the Lower Mekong Archaeological Project in southern Cambodia. She has edited *Asian Perspectives* since 2000, and edited *The Archaeology of Social Boundaries* (Smithsonian Institution Press, 1998). Some of her recent publications include: "Pre-Angkorian and Angkorian Cambodia" (in *A Cultural History of Southeast Asia: From Earliest Times to the Indic Civilizations*, Routledge/Curzon Press, 2004); "OSL and Radiocarbon Dating of a Pre-Angkorian Canal in the Mekong Delta, Southern

Cambodia" (coauthored with Paul Bishop and David C. W. Sanderson, *Journal of Archaeological Science* 31, 2003); and "Current Issues in Ceramic Ethnoarchaeology" (*Journal of Archaeological Research* 11, 2003).

Anne P. Underhill (Ph.D., 1990, University of British Columbia) is an Associate Curator in the Department of Anthropology at The Field Museum (Chicago, Illinois) and adjunct Associate Professor, University of Illinois-Chicago and Northwestern University. Her research has focused on the Neolithic and early Bronze Age of China on the topics of craft production, settlement patterns, mortuary analysis, agriculture, and ceramic ethnoarchaeology. She is the American director of a long-term collaborative research project with Shandong University in southeastern Shandong province that has involved both systematic regional survey and excavation. Some of her recent publications include: "Early State Economic Systems in China" (coauthored with Hui Fang, in *Archaeological Perspectives on Political Economies*, University of Utah Press, 2004); "Ceramic Ethnoarchaeology in China: Evaluation of Archaeological Criteria for Identifying Variation in Organization of Production" (*Journal of Archaeological Method and Theory* 19, 2003); *Craft Production and Social Change in Northern China* (Kluwer Academic Press, 2002); and "Regional Survey and the Development of Complex Societies in Southeastern Shandong, China" (coauthored with Gary Feinman, Linda Nicholas, G. Bennett, Hui Fang, Fengshi Luan, Haiguang Yu, and Fengshu Cai, *Antiquity*, 2002).

Part I

Introduction

1

Contextualizing an Archaeology of Asia

Miriam T. Stark

This volume offers an archaeology of Asia whose geographic coverage ranges from the equator to the upper latitudes, and from the South China Sea to the lakes of eastern Kazakhstan. For many readers picking up this book, their first question is likely, "Why Asia?" The answer is fourfold: Asia is vast; it is diverse; its history merits comparison with other regions of the world; and for the last century Western archaeologists have largely ignored Asia's archaeology. The primary goal of this volume is to bring to the fore Asia's past as part of world archaeology by including case studies on subjects of global archaeological interest.

Asia is vast in geographic, demographic, economic, and political terms. Physically, Asia constitutes the world's largest landmass, contains a large percentage of the world's population, and all of the world's institutionalized religions. Three of the world's four most populous countries today (China, India, Indonesia) are found in Asia. Countries across the region are becoming the world's economic and political superpowers, and these developments represent the endpoints of millennia-long histories. The region's geographic size is so large, and the internal divisions (particularly between South, East, and Southeast Asia) so pronounced that a single volume can only hope to capture a sense of its history.

The Asian land mass also encompasses extraordinarily high social, ethnolinguistic, and ecological variability. Ecologically, the region stretches from the arctic to the equatorial. Its multiple social histories intersect and overlap, and ethnolinguistic groups span large areas. Studying ancient Asia requires the use of multiscalar approaches that transcend both neoevolutionary frameworks that archaeologists so commonly embrace, and also modern nation-state boundaries that blur the borders of ancient polities and interactional networks. Even today, Asia's industrial centers and high-tech cities exist alongside lowland peasant farmers and upland swidden cultivators. These farming communities continue to trade with small-scale forest foragers across parts of India, and nomadic pastoralists in western China. Coastal strandlopers across Southeast Asia barter with settled villagers, and both struggle with pirates in the Southeast Asian seas. Such relationships between groups practicing different economic strategies have deep historical roots, as state economies across ancient Asia were founded on the coexistence of forest and maritime foraging strategies with agrarian economies.

In many respects, Asia is unique. This is clear through its archaeological record, which contains distinctive hominoid and hominid varieties during the Pleistocene, unusual subsistence adaptations from the Holocene, and singular complex polities from the last three millennia that lack analogues elsewhere in the world. This record challenges neoevolutionary frameworks that continue to dominate Americanist research on emergent complexity, despite nearly 30 years of critique. The early Holocene transition to sedentary agricultural life, for example, took varied forms across Asia and occurred at very different points in time (Underhill and Habu, this volume). In addition, myriad forms of foraging (for example, hunting, gathering, maritime and pastoral nomadism) persisted across Asia and many evolved in lockstep with ancient states (Morrison, this volume).

Asia's archaeological record is also known for some "firsts." The geographer Carl Sauer (1952), for example, was one of the first scholars to recognize Asia as a hearth for the origins of agriculture: some of the world's earliest domesticated plants are found in Asia (Crawford, this volume). The world's earliest pottery technologies also appeared more than 12,000 years ago among complex Jomon hunter-gatherers in Japan (Underhill and Habu, this volume). Asia is also the linguistic and genetic origin area for populations that settled island archipelagoes across the entire Pacific Ocean (Bellwood, this volume). Yet Asia's uniqueness does not render it incomparable to developments elsewhere in the Old and New Worlds, and under-standing Asia's ancient histories is integral to explaining developments across the Eurasian continent.

Several discrete writing systems functioned across Asia by ca. 3500 B.P. (Keightley, this volume), and some of the world's largest early states and empires emerged in ancient China (Shelach and Pines, this volume; Allard, this volume). Complex polities arose along the region's coasts, in conjunction with far-flung trade overland, and maritime networks and ideological movements that spread from South Asia to the eastern most reaches of the region (Ray, this volume). Early states appeared in most of Asia's river deltas and fertile river valleys, and many South Asian states developed into empires (Sinopoli, this volume). States also developed along the borders of Asia's empires, among sedentary farmers and among pastoralist nomads (Honeychurch and Amartuvshin, this volume). Linking farmers with pas-toral nomads and foragers (Morrison, this volume), these systems merged coastal and inland regions and moved goods, animals, and people thousands of kilometers within Asia, and from Asia westward.

The foregoing discussion has emphasized Asia's size, its diversity, and its unique-ness; yet the region's archaeological sequence also merits comparison with other parts of the world. The Asian archaeological record is a fundamental aspect of organizational and environmental changes since the Pleistocene, and thousands of trained archaeologists study and manage its cultural heritage. Despite the acceler-ation in the pace of Asian archaeology since the 1960s, however, results of this research remain largely inaccessible to the Western archaeological world in part for linguistic reasons. A burgeoning Asian archaeological literature is regularly published in more than ten languages, and Asia's archaeological past remains a foreign country to most archaeologists trained in Europe and North America. Even archaeologists working within different Asian countries have difficulty reading across their national boundaries.

Those of us who have had the opportunity to work in Asian archaeology are constantly impressed by the amount and intensity of research undertaken in the region, and by how little of that work is visible in the western-language literature. Asia's huge geographic scale, its historical importance to cultural developments in the West, and its overwhelming cultural diversity make it a rich source of comparative material on subjects ranging from the origins of agriculture to state formation. Growing numbers of archaeologists and historians now acknowledge Asian archaeology's relevance to world archaeology, and increased numbers of Western archaeologists have launched research projects in Asia in the last 15 years. Yet continued difficulties in accessing the Asian archaeological literature were a central reason for the construction of this volume.

Chapter topics for the volume were selected with dual objectives in mind: the first was to foreground some of the more noteworthy aspects of the archaeological sequence and of the rich datasets that are available for study. The second was to provide comparative information on social issues for archaeologists working elsewhere in the world. Space constraints, relative to the size of the landmass that this volume showcases, require a light touch rather than an in-depth exploration. We encourage readers to use this volume as a springboard for learning more about Asian archaeology, and for incorporating Asian material into their comparative research worldwide.

Goals of This Volume

This volume is not designed to serve as an introductory text to the archaeology of specific subregions in Asia; myriad textbooks and summaries have been published that provide chronological frameworks and culture histories to subregions within Asia. For China, key English-language texts include Barnes (1999), Chang (1986), Li (1986), and Nelson (1995). Several summaries are also available in English on different aspects of Japanese archaeology, including Barnes (1999), Farris (1998); Hudson (1999); Imamura (1996) and Mizoguchi (2002). Western archaeological coverage of Korea is less intensive than that of Korea or Japan, but two volumes – one by Barnes (2000) and the other by Nelson (1993) – are especially useful. The number of English-language volumes published on South Asia is enormous, but two books by Allchin and Allchin (1993, 1997) and one by Khanna (1992) are good starting points. Textbooks on Southeast Asian archaeology have been divided neatly into the insular (Bellwood 1997) and the mainland (Higham 1989, 1996, 2002) regions.

This volume is also not intended to provide a comprehensive background to social theory in Asian archaeology. Instead, this volume samples Asian archaeological

research on "social archaeology." Readers who judge Asian archaeology theoretically impoverished do so by imposing their Western ideas on Asian archaeology and
run the risk of intellectual ethnocentrism. Social approaches in Asian archaeology
take different forms than those employed in the West, and Asian archaeology has
multiple indigenous intellectual traditions that contrast markedly with those found
in Euroamerican archaeology. Epistemological, cultural, and sociopolitical reasons
underlie these differences, and the fact that nationalism and heritage management
concerns guide regional archaeological traditions across Asia is paramount (Glover,
this volume; Nelson, this volume; Mizoguchi, this volume; Sinopoli, this volume).
This is especially clear in the case of Chinese archaeology, which until recently
employed a Marxist evolutionary framework to interpret state formation (Li and
Chen, this volume; von Falkenhausen 1993:846–7). Asian archaeology's historiographical orientation (von Falkenhausen 1993, 1995) and its emphasis on identity
politics have thus far precluded concern with several topics (for example, gender
and power) that are currently in favor with Euroamerican archaeologists.

Although some of Asia's leading archaeologists and scholars have contributed
studies to this volume, publication constraints preclude involvement in this volume
by many of Asia's important scholars; we owe them a great intellectual debt, and
their work is cited throughout the volume. This volume's chapters draw from
authors' own research and articulate that research into broader issues. Four substantive themes structure the volume from the mid-Holocene onward: (1) sociopolitics of archaeology, (2) formative developments across the region, (3) case studies
in emergent complexity, and (4) the nature of ancient states. At least one methodological thread, which focuses on the interdependency of texts and archaeological
remains, also weaves together several of the volume's chapters. Discussion of these
themes helps strengthen the comparative framework for understanding archaeological practice in various areas of Asia, and to trace divergent trajectories in the
history of the discipline.

Sociohistorical Contexts of Asian Archaeology

Like other areas throughout the world, several regional traditions in Asian archaeology have colonial roots. Asian archaeology must thus be understood first within
its historical, social, and cultural contexts. The book's first section, accordingly, uses
case studies of archaeological practice in Asia to examine the complex relationship
between archaeology, heritage management, and national identity. The strong historical tradition in East Asia has a time-depth of two millennia and flavors Asian
archaeological traditions like that of China. The countries of Southeast Asia were
subjected to strong cultural influences from the maritime countries of Western
Europe, and most came under their direct political control at various times from
the late 16th to the 19th century. Scholarly interest in the past of these countries,
and especially archaeological research into their past, developed from the mid 19th
century and was strongly influenced by the traditions and concerns of the various
colonizing countries.

The first chapter in this section, by Ian Glover, discusses the influence of colonialism in the history of archaeological research across Southeast Asia with an emphasis on Vietnam, Thailand, and Indonesia. He points out the differential impact of colonialist archaeology and its consequences in these countries, and explores how, and where, current archaeological research bears the imprint of Western thought through its theory and practice. Comparisons are drawn between this dynamic in Southeast Asian archaeology and East Asian archaeology. Only through such analysis can we understand the role of science – and Western empiricist research – within an Asian context.

That archaeology is also political practice is clearly illustrated in the following chapter on the "Two Koreas" by Sarah Nelson. Twentieth-century Cold War history has affected the nature and scope of archaeological work in the Korean peninsula, as archaeological traditions in North and South Korea diverged sharply after World War II. Nelson argues that South Korean archaeology's dual focus on chronology building and identifying ethnic groups is related to its search for a national identity.

This section's last chapter, by Koji Mizoguchi, explores the relationship between sociopolitics and historical identity construction in Japanese prehistoric archaeology. Following World War II, scholars studied the Yayoi period to understand the failure of Japan as a modern nation-state. One reason behind the current widespread public interest in Jomon archaeology, Mizoguchi argues, lies in the close association of Jomon archaeology with the roots of Japanese identity. These three examples, drawn from different parts of Asia, illustrate the historical and political embeddedness of archaeological practice and provide the necessary foundation for studying particular developments in the Asian sequence.

Formative Developments in Ancient Asia

Asia's uniqueness is one pillar of the rationale for this volume. Research in the last several decades has firmly established East and South Asia as one of the world's most important regions for formative developments. This is especially clear in the origins of plant and animal domestication, which occurred more than 9,000 years ago. Because some of the earliest dates for domesticated plants derive from east-central China and their antiquity rivals those of the Near East, Gary Crawford's chapter focuses on East Asia as its case study. Not only was domestication early in East Asia, however; the timing and directionality of the adoption of domestication varied and brought with it a range of consequences. This chapter summarizes our current knowledge regarding the origins of plant and animal domestication in East Asia, and examines reasons why the timing of the adoption varied from one region to the next.

Asia has also experienced diasporas in its 1.8 million year sequence of human history; the origins and spread of agriculture across the region provides an excellent example. As Peter Bellwood explains in his chapter, the consequences of early agricultural development in several regions of Asia included population growth, the geographic expansion of food-producing populations into areas previously used by foragers and nomads, and the expansion of language families. Bellwood examines evidence from archaeology, linguistics, and biological anthropology, and argues that agriculturalist expansion lies at the root of many of the world's major language families (although farmers may not always have replaced foragers in the biological sense). History, environmental variations, and prior cultural configurations dictated many of the outcomes, some of which played a fundamental role in the large-scale genesis of human cultural and biological patterning from mid-Holocene period onward.

Emergent Complexity in Asia

Ancient Asia is perhaps best renowned for its early complex societies, and organizational shifts in that direction occurred as early as the mid-Holocene. The paper by Anne Underhill and Junko Habu investigates the economic and sociopolitical organization of early sedentary communities in East Asia with a focus on the Chinese Neolithic (ca. 8000–2000 B.C.), on Jomon-period Japan (ca. 14,500–400 B.C.), and Chulmun-period Korea (ca. 6000–1300 B.C.). Their study demonstrates how the emergence of complex societies involved an increase in vertical inequality and an increase in heterogeneity. Such changes included increased variety in subsistence strategies, production of valued goods by craft specialists, the development of social inequality, and material evidence for the elaboration of rituals. Evidence from each region exists for increased inter-community interaction, some competitive and some peaceful, that lead to the formation of regional polities. Such changes directly or indirectly laid the foundation for the development of more complex societies that emerged in some regions during the later prehistoric period.

This volume's chapters describe many early states that arose in several parts of Asia, while leaving some areas (like the Indus valley) that have been the subject of extensive research to other publications. Multiple pulses of state formation characterized Asia over a 3,000-year period, involving the emergence, collapse, and regeneration of complex polities built on elements of preceding states. The Mongol empire was one of Asia's latest pre-industrial states, and its expansion to Western Europe's margins made it one of the most successful empires in recent world history.

Writing is commonly associated with state formation across the Old World, yet some of Asia's earliest writing systems preceded state formation. This is evidently the case in China, where writing first appeared in the Late Neolithic, where writing became firmly linked to power and authority. David Keightley's chapter summarizes our knowledge of the origins of writing in China, and explores the social, religious, and political significance of early Chinese writing systems. He argues that these writing systems were not linked simply to ritual and shamanism as had been previously proposed, but also to high status. He also raises the possibility that only some elites were literate, and that writing was used as performance and for registry rather than documentation.

The chapter by Li Liu and Xingcan Chen focuses on social and political changes that accompanied (or instigated) technological transformations associated with the adoption of metallurgy, and specifically bronze metallurgy. Because the earliest dates for bronze metallurgy in Asia derive from China, China forms the case study for studying sociopolitical change from the Neolithic to Bronze Age. Although archaeological evidence suggests that complex societies developed in several regions in Neolithic China, many of these entities collapsed ca. 4000 B.P. This variable trajectory forms the basis for discussion and analysis in this chapter. Examining a range of archaeological data permits the investigation of dynamics of social and economic change, and also the roles that actors and factions played in these processes. This chapter examines settlement patterns, variability in political formations, and the development of complex polities in northern China. Their comprehensive review of sociopolitical change in ancient China that emphasizes ancestor cults and prestige goods production provides a compelling alternative to both standard Chinese (Marxist) approaches and Western neoevolutionary models.

The scale and longevity of some Asian states, and particularly the Chinese states, makes them distinctive worldwide. So, too, does their demographic scale and monumental achievement. Yuri Pines and Gideon Shelach combine archaeological and documentary data to explore power, identity, and ideology in the core of one such Asian megastate: the Qin dynasty. In so doing, they challenge the accepted view of cultural continuity in China. Their examination of the Qin also identifies a social and political Bauplan of the Chinese state that subsequent civilizations emulated for two millennia. The Qin state, they argue, emerged through peer-polity interaction, in which elites were able to successfully manipulate the ruling ideology.

Crossing Boundaries and Ancient States

The monumentality of ancient states invariably draws archaeologists to study their cores rather than their peripheries, and most Asian archaeologists are no exception. Yet it is at the margins of some of Asia's early states – and particularly at the edges of empire – that we see the most interesting developments of secondary states, both sedentary and nomadic. It is also along the peripheries of ancient Asian states that foraging strategies, whether land-locked or maritime, apparently developed and thrived. As several authors in this volume illustrate, Asian political and economic formations do not conform to conventional models that archaeologists apply elsewhere, and thus compel revision.

Francis Allard's chapter focuses on developments along the southern boundary of Han China. Imperial China began with the founding of the Qin dynasty in 221 B.C. (see chapter 10). This short-lived dynasty established the foundations for the unified and homogeneous Han dynasty that followed (ca. 206 B.C.–A.D. 220). The expansionist Han empire exceeded the Roman empire in scale, and rivaled that of Alexander the Great. The Han empire effectively Sinicized much of what is now considered China. Although substantial research has been undertaken on the archaeology of the Han empire within the borders of present-day China, less attention has been paid to the archaeology of its peripheries. Yet one hallmark of the Han dynasty involved the expansion of trade and empire to its north, south, and west along the Silk Route. This chapter explores the archaeology of the Han empire's southern periphery, from what are now the southwest provinces of Yunnan and Guangxi to the Chinese border with northern Vietnam. It reviews the history of research in this region, discusses the nature of archaeological data from a series of excavated sites, and offers new theoretical frameworks that deepen our under-standing of this region and polity.

Such developments occurred not only along China's southern borders, but also along its western and northern borders during periods of successive state forma-tion. William Honeychurch and Chunag Amartuvshin focus on archaeological evidence for complex polities that developed on the northeast Asian steppe in conjunction with some of China's largest early empires, from the Xiongnu polity (third century B.C. to A.D. second century) to the rise of the Mongol empire. They use these case studies to examine structural influences of mature state systems on neighboring regions and models for interregional interaction. The historical trajec-tories of these steppe polities, which flourished along the margins of China, com-plement our extant knowledge of state formation in East Asia.

Not only did states form along the margins of other states; populations con-tinued, or turned to, foraging–trading strategies as these states emerged. Kathleen Morrison's paper discusses the complex, long-term historical ecology of foraging in South and Southeast Asia, and focuses on the integration of foraging strategies with agriculture, wage labor, tribute relations, and pastoralism in a succession of world systems. Asian foraging strategies must be viewed as particular relations of humans to the natural world, as relations of power and affinity, and sometimes as interde-pendence with others. Case studies from India provide some examples of historic-ally situated tactics deployed within contexts of specific local ecologies, polities, exchange networks, and cultural frameworks.

Several chapters in the volume illustrate how some of Asia's earliest states linked populations within and across political boundaries perhaps as much through ideo-logical power as political force. By the mid-first millennium B.C., religious ideolo-gies tied to South Asian states also spread through missionaries and traders who traversed the desert expanses of the Asian steppe and sailed across the Bay of Bengal into the South China Sea. Himanshu Ray's chapter examines the nature, diffusion, and impact of Buddhism as it moved ever eastward into Southeast and East Asia. Emerging during the "Axial Age" (*sensu* Eisenstadt 1986), Buddhism became Asia's premier religious ideology and shaped social and political structures from the bottom up rather than through political hegemony. As it moved across the Asian continent, Buddhism evolved into different forms to accommodate local cultures, and today remains dominant in much of East and Southeast Asia. That Buddhism traveled along commercial maritime and terrestrial routes but operated indepen-dently of the mercantile system suggests an intriguing kind of mutualism.

Several of the volume's chapters focus on the archaeological record for selected empires that arose across Asia by the first millennium A.D. East and South Asian imperial case studies described in this volume were large states containing diverse ethnic compositions that were forged through conquest and coercion (following Sinopoli's [2001] definition), but they varied greatly in their duration and their territorial scope. Carla Sinopoli's chapter focuses on archaeological evidence for several early historic period South Asian empires: their expansion, consolidation, and collapse. She has selected case studies that linked South Asia to neighboring polities in all directions: the Achaemenid and Seleucid empires, the Mauryan empire (which stimulated the spread of Buddhism eastward), the Kushana empire (with roots in Central Asia), and the Satavahana empire (of peninsular India). These varied in the degree of imperial control that penetrated local political, economic, and social structures. The Kushana imperial hegemony she describes, for example, bears some parallels to the Han example of Sinicization that Allard (this volume) documents. Combining settlement pattern data and other lines of archaeological evidence with documentary data provides a useful chronicle of the changing landscape of imperial politics and administration, economy, and military organization.

Concluding Thoughts

This volume's range of topics, geographic scale, and time depth vary greatly, yet some methodological and theoretical issues surface in multiple case studies. The first concerns the interdependency of texts (from oracle bones, royal annals, literary sources, and religious texts to monumental inscriptions) and archaeological remains. That archaeologists must critically engage the documentary record has been emphasized in calls for "source-side criticism" (see also Feinman 1997; Stahl 1993; Wylie 1985). Case studies throughout Asia also highlight this need to avoid privileging documentary sources over other kinds of data, to evaluate the authenticity of sources and the social contexts in which they were written (Sinopoli, this volume; Stark and Allen 1998) but also to understand their contexts of recovery (Morrison and Lycett 1997). Writing in ancient states, as David Keightley (this volume) points out, was not always intended to produce documentary records. Such issues become important in this volume's chapters on the Qin dynasty (Shelach and Pines), on the expansionist Han empire (Allard), and on a plethora of South Asian examples (Sinopoli).

Many chapters in this volume also challenge the sharp division between East and West imposed largely by a 19th- and 20th-century Western intellectual tradition. Asia's variability in ancient sociopolitical trajectories, for example, eludes the application of more conventional models of emergent political complexity that use as their baseline examples from the New World or the Near East (Underhill and Habu, this volume). It also resists the conventional dichotomization between despotic Asian states and democratic Western civilizations (Shelach and Pines, this volume).

This volume was entitled "An Archaeology of Asia" to indicate its necessary incompleteness: a single book cannot hope to capture the entire spectrum of theoretical approaches that characterize Asian archaeology today. The keyword in understanding Asia's archaeology is diversity: in climate, geography, language, genetics, and the variety of social formations which emerged, collapsed, and regenerated in the last three millennia. This vast array of developments across Asia rippled out in all directions to neighboring regions to affect their respective histories. This volume's chapters seek to illustrate some ways that, at different points in the prehistoric past, the region's diversity was counterbalanced by unifying threads – economic, social, ideological – that linked linguistically distinct populations, and moved their goods and political systems across terrestrial and maritime landscapes. Studying these threads in the archaeological past creates a distinctive cultural mosaic that we know today as Asia, and enriches our understanding of developments across the Old World during the last 12,000 years.

ACKNOWLEDGMENTS

I would like to thank Rosemary Joyce and Lynn Meskell for inviting me to edit a volume in their Global Archaeology series. This volume has suffered from a remarkable number of medical (and other) events that caused delays in its publication process, and I am grateful to both Blackwell Publishers and to my contributors (scattered across all the world's continents) for their patience and perseverance. I also thank the University of Hawaii-Manoa Department of Anthropology, which provided critical infrastructural support and resources during the project.

REFERENCES

Allchin, Bridget, and Raymond Allchin, 1993 The Rise of Civilization in India and Pakistan. Cambridge: Cambridge University Press.
—— 1997 Origins of a Civilization: The Prehistory and Early Archaeology of South Asia. Cambridge: Cambridge University Press.
Barnes, Gina Lee 1999 Rise of Civilization in East Asia: The Archaeology of China, Korea and Japan. London: Thames and Hudson.
—— 2000 State Formation in Korea: Historical and Archaeological Perspectives. Honolulu: University of Hawaii Press.
Bellwood, Peter 1997 The Prehistory of the Indo-Malaysian Archipelago, 2nd edition. Honolulu: University of Hawaii Press.
Chang, Kwang-chih 1986 Archaeology of Ancient China. 4th edition. New Haven: Yale University Press.
Eisenstadt, Samuel, ed. 1986 The Origins and Diversity of Axial Age Civilizations. New York: State University of New York Press.
Falkenhausen, Lothar von 1993 On the Historiographical Orientation of Chinese Archaeology. Antiquity 67:839–49.
—— 1995 The Regionalist Paradigm in Chinese Archaeology. In Nationalism, Politics, and the Practice of Archaeology. Philip L. Kohl and Clare Fawcett, eds. Pp. 198–217. Cambridge: Cambridge University Press.
Farris, William Wayne 1998 Sacred Texts and Buried Treasures: Issues in the Historical Archaeology of Ancient Japan. Honolulu: University of Hawaii Press.

Feinman, Gary M. 1997 Thoughts on New Approaches to Combining the Archaeological and Historical Records. Journal of Archaeological Method and Theory 4:367–77.

Higham, Charles 1989 The Archaeology of Mainland Southeast Asia, from 10,000 B.C. to the Fall of Angkor. Cambridge: Cambridge University Press.

—— 1996 The Bronze Age of Southeast Asia. Cambridge: Cambridge University Press.

—— 2002 Early Cultures of Mainland Southeast Asia. Bangkok: River Books.

Hudson, Mark J. 1999 Ruins of Identity: Ethnogenesis in the Japanese Islands. Honolulu: University of Hawaii Press.

Imamura, Keiji 1996 Prehistoric Japan: New Perspectives on Insular East Asia. Honolulu: University of Hawaii Press.

Khanna, Amar Nath 1992 Archaeology of India. New Delhi: Clarion Books.

Li, Xueqin 1986 Eastern Zhou and Qin Civilizations. K. C. Chang, trans. New Haven: Yale University Press.

Mizoguchi, Koji 2002 An Archaeological History of Japan: Self and Identity from 30,000 B.C. to A.D. 700. Philadelphia: University of Pennsylvania Press.

Morrison, Kathleen D., and Mark T. Lycett 1997 Inscriptions as Artifacts: Precolonial South India and the Analysis of Texts. Journal of Archaeological Method and Theory 4(3/4):215–37.

Nelson, Sarah Milledge 1993 The Archaeology of Korea. Cambridge: Cambridge University Press.

—— 1995 The Archaeology of Northeast China. London: Routledge Press.

Sauer, Carl O., ed. 1952 Agricultural Origins and Dispersals. New York: American Geographic Society.

Sinopoli, Carla 2001 Empires. In Archaeology at the Millennium. T. Douglas Price and Gary M. Feinman, eds. Pp. 439–71. New York: Kluwer/Plenum.

Stahl, Ann Brower 1993 Concepts of Time and Approaches to Analogical Reasoning in Historical Perspective. American Antiquity 58:235–60.

Stark, Miriam T., and S. Jane Allen 1998 The Transition to History in Southeast Asia: An Introduction. International Journal of Historical Archaeology 2(3):163–75.

Wylie, Alison 1985 The Reaction Against Analogy. In Advances in Archaeological Method and Theory. Volume 8. Michael B. Schiffer, ed. Pp. 63–111. New York: Academic Press.

Part II

Contexts of Asian Archaeology

2

Some National, Regional, and Political Uses of Archaeology in East and Southeast Asia

Ian C. Glover

This chapter examines some of the ways that the style and practice of archaeology, and the conclusions reached, are influenced by the political – using the term in a very broad sense – framework of the cultures in which they work and especially the links between ethnic and linguistic affiliation, national political identity, origins of the nation-state and the archaeological remains within its boundaries. Such issues are not, of course new to archaeological discourse (e.g., Diaz-Andreu and Champion 1996; Kohl and Fawcett 1995; Meskell 2002), and increasing numbers of publications focus explicitly on East Asia (e.g., Habu and Fawcett 1999; Han 2004; Ikawa-Smith 1999; Kaner 1996; Li 1999; Pai 1999, 2000; Pak 1999) and Southeast Asia (e.g., Bray and Glover 1987; Glover 1986, 1993, 1999, 2001; 2003; 2004; Han 2004). Archaeology often has a political function in building nation-states, and examples from East and Southeast Asian archaeology are similar to those documented more fully for Europe and the Mediterranean.

East and Southeast Asia are my primary concern here; I find remarkable similarity, however, in the issues and arguments, despite markedly divergent social, temporal, and economic conditions in the world's nations over the past 170 years or so during which we can recognize something like archaeological studies. I will try to isolate these briefly before turning to East and Southeast Asia.

- As pre-state polities, whether modern or ancient, have struggled to define geographic and ethnic–cultural boundaries and assert national sovereignty from a single political center, appeal is regularly made to a real or imagined past to support the new structure, to give it time-depth, to link it with a heroic past, and often with an ethnic or linguistic group deemed to be ancestral to the dominant lineage or ethnic group.
- In so doing, the emphasis is usually placed on some past community or ruling dynasty responsible for constructing surviving and monumental structures and/or establishing a real or imagined empire.

- In this process, emphasis is often placed on a past – real or imagined – dominant ethnic or linguistic group within the new state territory to establish such continuities.
- Creating a national identity includes both a definition of differences between one's own community and others and the unique content of the national culture.
- Emphasizing real or imagined links and continuities to past greatness has not been confined to Western states nor to modern times.

Similar patterns are evident across ancient East and Southeast Asia. In late second millennium B.C. China, the usurping Zhou Dynasty continued to practice rituals of the preceding Shang rulers in order assert legitimacy (Li 1999:604). In the early second millennium A.D., the Khmer rulers at Angkor manipulated lineage connections and inscribed these on stone stele in order to claim descent from previous rulers and legitimize their reigns – a practice which still bedevils epigraphic and historical studies in Cambodia. In northern Vietnam, the Le Dynasty, having freed themselves from Chinese rule, collected, and perhaps displayed, ancient bronze drums surviving from the Dong Son Culture (a period that preceded the Chinese invasions of the early centuries of A.D.) to stress their connection with the heroic Lac Viet peoples of antiquity (Ha Van Tan, p.c., 1995). Likewise in China, in the early second millennium A.D. the rulers of the Southern Song Dynasty collected and treasured the ritual vessels of the Shang and Zhou rulers, already some 1,500 to 2,000 years old by then. The classification of these bronze vessels, which is still used, was established in the Song Dynasty on the basis of the transmitted ritual classics (von Falkenhausen 1993:842–3). The following section reviews some relationships between nationalism and archaeology across East Asia, and summarizes related research in Southeast Asia.

Ideology, Nationalism, and Archaeology in the Peoples' Republic of China

Archaeological research in China began with the excavations between 1927 and 1938 by Li Ji and his colleagues at Yinxu near Anyang. This was thought to be the location of the last Shang capital of the late second millennium B.C., and the spectacular results in the form of royal burials with human sacrifices, inscribed tablets, and a wealth of bronze ritual vessels convincingly showed how archaeology substantiated historical texts and legitimized the discipline by refuting revisionist historians of the early first Republic of the "Doubters of the Old" school (von Falkenhausen 1993:840).[1] From this time onwards, Chinese archaeology has remained historiographical and even today as in earlier dynastic times, serves to propagate official government interpretations of historical events. An independent, questioning tradition of archaeology, might have developed from the work of Li Ji and his colleagues, but the Japanese invasions and civil war followed leading to the establishment, under Mao Zedong, of the Peoples' Republic of China in 1949.

Between 1949 and 1979, China was deeply centralized and governed under a distinctive form of Marxist ideology and administrative structures (Tong 1995). From 1949–59, Soviet Russian ideas and practices were generally followed, but with the ideological break with the USSR archaeology in China was dominated by the directives of Mao Zedong. Slogans such "Eliminate Bourgeois Ideology and Foster Proletarian Ideology," or "Let the Past Serve the Present" guided the nation's archaeologists. The government did encourage archaeology to the extent that it showed the emergence of a unique Chinese society in the their homeland through the well-established stages from primitive promiscuous bands via matrilineality to patrilineality; from Savagery, Barbarism, Feudal Society to Civilization and so on – stages first proposed by Lewis Henry Morgan, borrowed by Engels and systematized in the Soviet Union. Many sites were excavated, often with spectacular and huge quantities of finds, but beyond description and listing; "naked artefactology" as Bulkin et al. (1982:274) referred to such a stage in Soviet archaeology, there was little attempt to learn something new about the past. Rather the finds were used to demonstrate the truth of well-accepted doctrines such as unilineal evolution, the class struggle in ancient society, the inevitable demise of capitalism and, importantly, the unique originality of Chinese society.

Paleolithic research was under the control of the Institute of Vertebrate Paleontology, and relatively free of political thought control. Virtually all work from the Neolithic through the great historic civilizations (Han to Qing), however, was organized, funded, and controlled by the Institute of Archaeology (*Kaogu Yanjiusuo*) of the National Academy of Social Sciences under its formidable Director, Xia Nai,[2] the State Bureau of Cultural Relics (*Guojia Wenwuju*) and to a lesser extent by the Department of Archaeology of Peking University. Virtually all reports appeared in two publications from these institutions, *Kaogu* and *Wenwu*. Emphasis was put on a single origin of Chinese civilization in the loess lands along the Huang He (Shanxi and Shaanxi Provinces). Developments in other regions were always represented to be later than, and dependent on, this "Nuclear Area." This bias was also taken up by overseas-based archaeologists such as the very influential K. C. Chang, and is found in the earlier editions of his influential *The Archaeology of Ancient China* (1963, 1968 and 1977) and only modified in the 4th edition (1986) after mainland Chinese archaeologists had themselves changed their position in the light of new dating evidence and a more relaxed administrative framework.

The Cultural Revolution from 1966–76 brought most archaeological work to a standstill with enormous destruction to museums, sites, and collections through the "Four Olds" campaign. With the re-establishment of some sort of order under Deng Xiao Peng, archaeological research was encouraged again with less emphasis on central planning as resources and decision-making were handed to provincial museums, institutes, and universities.

The past decades have seen substantial changes in how archaeology has been used to support national history in China (von Falkenhausen 1993, 1995). As resources and decision-making in the cultural sphere decentralized from Beijing to the provinces, archaeologists throughout China have been competing to add their parts to the "national story." This change partly reflects the enormous quantities of data acquired that cannot be fitted into the mononuclear thesis of Chinese cultural evolution, and it partly reflects administrative changes and the relative freedom of thought in the post-Mao era. Historians and archaeologists now compete, argue and disagree, provided their conclusions do not contribute to any ideas that might lead to the fragmentation of the Chinese nation-state.

Here we can see an interesting difference to the way regional ethnic and linguistic archaeology in post-Franco Spain as undertaken in Catalonia, Galicia, and the Basque territories, are giving explicit support to political divisions which might lead up to the dissolution of the unitary Spanish state (Diaz-Andreu 1995). In China, by contrast, archaeologists seem to be eager to promote their own provinces' contributions to a coherent national identity to which all subscribe. This sometimes leads to seemingly irresolvable contradictions, such as when different provinces lay claim to be the unique site of a historical polity such as Wu, or the prehistoric culture known as Jin, and other times give quite different archaeological assemblages the same name, or very similar ones different names in their eagerness to lay claim to their origins (von Falkenhausen 1995:205–10).

Archaeology in other Chinese provinces such as Taiwan, however, has contributed to another discourse. All agree politically that Taiwan is a province of China, albeit with temporarily quite different governments. Yet, the last fifty years of physical, social, economic, and political separation has led the two entities to have quite distinct identities, and now perhaps national archaeological histories. In K. C. Chang's (1969) published thesis on Taiwan in prehistory the prehistoric cultures of Taiwan are clearly interpreted as resulting from an agricultural expansion from a "nuclear area" of northern China: this was characterized as the "Lungshanoid Horizon." However, by the 2002 Indo Pacific Prehistory Congress (IPPA) in Taipei, sites that Chang had labeled Lungshanoid had become ancestral, or proto–Austronesian settlements. The pottery and stone tools had not changed, but shifting political priorities in Taiwan found it convenient to emphasize the island as the homeland of the Austronesian peoples (which it may well be) and to downplay earlier connections to the Chinese mainland. Actually this brings us to ask when and how early Chinese cultural materials in the island should be classified. The Austronesian origins in Taiwan, both in the past and the present were a *leitmotif* running through much of the conference which was exceptionally well funded by the popularly-elected government of Taiwan. The sense was that Taiwan was being re-positioned a little further away from the mainland and moved out into the Pacific closer to its Austronesian neighbors.

The history of the National Palace Museum collections also provides an instructive example of the political use of archaeology. Possession of the imperial collections of antiquities served to legitimize traditional Chinese rulers in much the same way as the Crown Jewels and Royal Regalia have done for English monarchs over centuries in the British Isles. When the English kings traveled the country the regalia went with them. The English, for example, all know the story of how the usurping King John had, in the 13th century, lost his crown jewels in the Wash – a flood-prone shallow sea on the east coast of the country – and in so doing, made it clear to the people that he had lost the "Mandate of Heaven." Doing so cleared the way for the return of his half-brother King Richard. So when the Chinese government moved, the palace collections went along, and this tradition continued under the Republic. Faced with the Japanese invasion of China and capture of Peking (Beijing) in 1937, the palace collections went to the capital of the Republic of China at Nanking (Nanjing), and from there to Chunking in the west where the collections were hidden safely until 1945. With the defeat of the nationalist government of Chiang Kai-Shek in 1949, the collection moved to a new magnificent museum in Taiwan. The National Palace Museum collections have since remained in Taiwan as imperial collections from the palace in Peking. The presence in Taiwan of the funerary material of the Shang rulers excavated at An-yang by the archaeologist Li Chi provide support for the Taiwan government's claim – especially that of the former KMT regime – to be the legitimate rulers of China.

The Politics of Origins in Korea

Until archaeological methods of studying the past were introduced by colonizing Japanese from late in the 19th century, Korean history was entirely contained within the tradition of Chinese historiography; archaeological research, as known in the West, was barely known. Following the Japanese annexation of Korea, there arrived, together with the army, administrators, railway engineers and industrialists, numerous talented and energetic scholars from the Tokyo University Department of History who were not only well trained in classical Chinese history, but in the newly imported disciplines of geology, geography, paleontology, physical anthropology, and archaeology. Over the following two generations, they completely transformed the understanding of the physical nature of the country, knowledge of the past and, of course the political structure. Ancient sites were recorded, some (especially tombs) excavated, and intensive research was undertaken on the remains of the Han Commandery of Leleang in the northwest.

With the defeat of Japan and independence came the division of Korea into mutually antagonistic political bodies following a bitter war, and new directions of archaeology in the two Koreas (Nelson, this volume). Whatever their politics, Korean archaeologists, along with those in Japan, have been concerned, to a very great extent, with ethnogenesis – the origins of the Korean people. The distinctiveness and homogeneity of the Korean race and language is invariably stressed and a single origin has been sought amongst nomadic, proto-Tungusic-speaking peoples of Manchuria who are believed to have migrated into Korea sometime in the 2nd millennium B.C. displacing, or absorbing, a scattered population of fisher-farmers (Nelson 1995).

Pai attributes the rise of Korean nationalist historiography to the leaders of the anti-Japanese independence movement, one of whose aims was to raise national consciousness by drawing on new historical and archaeological research even though Japanese scholars undertook most of the latter. In Korea, as in Japan, the creation of a national story has demanded the integration of ancient textual sources with the results of ethnography and archaeology, and this has increasingly led to contradictions with the national story, and even conflict that in Korea is both extreme and specific.

Koreans believe that they have existed as one homogenous population since prehistoric times, and try to distance themselves from both Chinese and Japanese cultural history. Korea's myth of origin represents the people to be descended from a first ancestor, Tan'gun, born of a female bear and Hwan'tung, the son of heaven. Tan'gun founded the first Korean state of Kochoson in 2333 B.C., and his descendents established the historic dynasties of Puyo, Koguryo, Paekche, and Silla thus legitimizing the well-documented historic kingdoms (Pai 2000:57–60). This myth appears to be widely accepted as historical truth both in South and North Korea. Pai (2000:60) mentions that the North Korean, English Language paper, the *People's Daily*, reported on October 16, 1993, the discovery of bones in the tomb of Tan'gun in Kangdon-up with a headlines, "5000 year-long history and homogeneity of the nation corroborated," and "Tan'gun, founder of the ancient Korea, born in Pyonyang." The eighty-six bone fragments were identified as belonging to King Tan'gun and his Queen and subsequently dated to 5001 B.P. by electron paramagnetic resonance dating.

Such a myth, of course, fits uncomfortably with the concept of a migration of bronze-working Tungus from Manchuria in the second millennium B.C. It also fits uneasily with increasing evidence for a rich and earlier sequence of dated Korean Paleolithic and Neolithic cultures that extends back some forty thousand years, and with a quite different tradition derived from Chinese historiography deriving the mediaeval Yi dynasty of Korea from the Xia, Shang, and Zhou dynasties of early China. The conflicts, ambiguities, and contradictions involved in this wealth of data are elegantly analyzed by Pai (2000).

Ideology, Nationalism, and Archaeology in Japan

Clare Fawcett (1995) clearly articulates the interplay between ideology, nationalism, and archaeology in post-war Japan, a process always mediated by pragmatism, idealism, opportunism, and manipulation. Hudson (1999) on the other hand, focuses on ethnogenesis, the formation of the Japanese from about 400 B.C. – the Late Jomon Period – to the early medieval Period, ca. A.D. 1200 when, as he sees it the essential character of Japanese people, their language, and culture was established in something like a modern form – although there were many changes still to come. In contrast to the self-perception of most Japanese and Korean people who have a concept of a static, bounded, and closed culture already established during the Yayoi Period, Hudson sees Japanese culture as being always in a state of change, following Myers (1930:538).

Western-style archaeology was introduced to Japan by British and American natural scientists in the 1860s and developed a homegrown momentum in the 1890s. This period also witnessed the growth of an ultra-nationalistic ideology of kingship that depended on two eighth-century texts, *Kojiki* and *Nihon Shoki*, that emphasized the divine descent of the Emperors, "fathers of the Japanese people" who owed the Emperor absolute allegiance (Kita 1978:211). Rather than challenge this dominant ideology, Japanese archaeologists (although basically accepting this idea of descent from a common ancestor, Jimmu, the First Emperor) took refuge in minute description and artifact classification at the expense of synthesis and interpretation, as had the European prehistorian Oscar Montelius in the late 19th century (see Bulkin et al. 1982 for parallel case in Soviet archaeology). This characteristic still plagues Japanese archaeology today, as much on account of the expansion of salvage archaeology in the country, as stemming from a particular epistemology. However, there is a contradiction in this concept of a single closed descent group since most archaeologists recognize several quite separate strands in Japanese physical and cultural ancestry coming from the Ainu (Jomon) of the northern islands, China (Kumaso of southern Kyushu) and Korea (Yayoi). Misuse of the term Japan (Nihon) masks the ethnic and cultural diversity of the pre-modern islands to legitimize imperial rule (Hudson 1999:15).

Following defeat in the Pacific War, the first generation of Japanese archaeologists (many of them amateurs, teachers, or government servants working part-time) felt that they should study the past in order to present a history for the Japanese people independent of imperial mythology. Marxist approaches, for which physical remains of the past such as stone and metal tools, and ceramics, as well as technologies and subsistence strategies, are particularly well suited, strongly influenced many of these scholars, although such socialist tendencies did not appeal to the increasingly conservative, business class, and new political elites. Over the next 20 to 30 years, increasing concern for the destruction of the physical heritage of the past both encouraged and even forced public authorities at all levels to provide ever-increasing funds for rescue archaeology as opposed to research archaeology. By 1987 (to point to a single year), archaeologists excavated 21,755 sites in Japan of which only 409 were for research (Fawcett 1995:244).

Through this period, a broad concern for the uniqueness of the Japanese cultural tradition (*Nihonbunkaron* or *Bunkkaron*) was spreading through the nation and this lent itself to political manipulation. The idea that the Japanese people were homogenous, and had a unique and rich cultural legacy from the prehistoric Jomon period, if not from an earlier Paleolithic period, provided a form of intellectual defense against increasing Westernization of everyday life, and this culminated in the creation of a National Cultural Park at Asuka Mura near Nara (central Honshu). This, largely recreated archaeological complex, was portrayed as a typical homeland of the Japanese people and a symbol of national identity (Fawcett 1995:242). In this way, archaeology fed into a new sort of Japanese nationalism that focused on the uniqueness and cohesiveness of the Japanese people themselves rather than on the divine Emperor. Business, administrative, and political elites have strongly influenced the direction of archaeology in Japan through control of funding; they have, in a sense stuffed the mouths of the Marxists of the late 1940s–1950s with money, and bought a new past for the country.

Archaeology and Nationalism in Southeast Asia

In this section I examine some of the interconnections between archaeology, nationalism, and politics in Southeast Asia. Many more can be found in the literature, especially in the popular cultural journals and magazines, of these countries, and from the experiences of archaeologists working in these and other countries of Southeast Asia. In some earlier articles (Bray and Glover 1987; Glover 1986, 1993, 1999) I examined the distinctions between what has been called "colonialist, imperialist and nationalist archaeologies" as defined by Trigger (1984). I will not go over this ground again here, but merely reiterate the proposition that archaeology, and especially prehistoric archaeology, has, almost everywhere, arisen out of an attempt to satisfy nationalist aspirations (Trigger 1984:358–60).

In many newly independent countries, forms of nationalist archaeology are strongest amongst peoples who feel threatened, insecure, or deprived of their political rights by more powerful nations, or in countries where appeals for national unity are being made to counteract serious divisions along class or ethnic lines. Nationalist archaeology tends to emphasize the more recent past, and to draw attention to visible, monumental architecture and centralized political structures. Earlier prehistory, or the archaeology of small-scale preliterate communities, tends to be ignored by nationalist archaeology. The popularity of Classical and Islamic archaeology in Indonesia, the focus on the Late Bronze–Iron Age Dong Son Culture of northern Vietnam, on the archaeology of Sukhothai and Ayutthaya in Thailand, and on the Pagan period in Myanmar, are cases in point.

Some of the attitudes and procedures of "ethnic archaeology" mentioned earlier were also followed in the post-colonial states in Southeast Asia which, in many cases do not correspond to "natural" nations based on a common language, coherent cultural traditions, shared ethnicity, or long and centralized dynastic rule as was the case in northeast Asia. The borders, indeed the very existence of the great majority of nation-states in the region, were created as a result of competing spheres of influence of the European and American colonial powers in the 19th century. This is true even for Thailand, never a European colony but whose present borders were forced on to a modernizing monarchy by France and Britain at the beginning of the 20th century. Thus, the concept of delineated borders within which a single political body claims unique authority is, in Southeast Asia as in many other areas, a product of the 19th-century colonial experience. Archaeology, with history, plays a role in developing these discourses with the past in the service of the state and its ruling elite and thus writing history, or archaeology, in modern Southeast Asian countries is often problematic since it is yoked here, as in so many places, to the political demands of the present.

Western archaeologists tend to see nationalism in archaeology as a malign influence, perhaps because of their experience of the distortions and even falsification of the past by researchers working under totalitarian regimes such as Nazi Germany, Fascist Spain, or the Communist Soviet Union and its satellites, and this aspect is well to the fore in most of the articles in Kohl and Fawcett (1995). I, too, share this prejudice and I have several times characterized nationalism in archaeology as divisive and too easily leading to a serious lack of objectivity and distortions in the interpretation of the past. However, in the same volume, Trigger (1995:277–8) sees a more positive aspect in archaeological nationalism when it has helped to provide the basis for resisting colonial or dynastic oppression and creating a broader notion of popular sovereignty. And a perceptive article by Paz (1998) has also made me rethink my very negative view. Paz argues that despite the many excesses of nationalist archaeology, it can be a positive force helping to strengthen what may be rather recent and artificial national communities. Paz also argued that when a nation-state actively supports archaeology and provides resources and leadership this can lead to major advances in knowledge of the past that can be used for purposes other than the creation of xenophobic national and ethnic consciousness.

Mainland Southeast Asia

Vietnam

From the 1840s, France, following the example of Britain, was determined to acquire a colonial empire in the tropics in order to generate raw materials for her rapidly developing industries. The early years of French expansion and rule in Indochina, starting soon after the attack on Tourane (now Danang) in 1858, brought to the attention of French scholars the remains of much earlier civilizations. These scholars found the remains of the Cham people extending from around Hue, south to near Saigon, with its temples, sculpture and inscriptions, and, of course, the great monuments of Cambodia, especially around Tonle Sap – the Great Lake – particularly interesting. The monuments of Cambodia were re-discovered by Henri Mouhot in 1860 (Rooney 1998) as part of the French drive for a riverine route into South China, to bypass the British control of the Yangzi Valley trade, and the explorers and scholars of the Mission Pavie revealed the material framework of early historic Indochina.

A learned society on the model of the Royal Asiatic Society, the *Société des Etudes Indochinoises* was founded in Saigon in 1865 to provide a forum for colonials and administrators to learn about their new acquisition; however, it was only with the establishment of the *École Française d'Extrême-Orient* (EFEO) between 1898 and 1900 that a sustained archaeological program for the investigation of pre- and protohistory was possible. French scholars approached Indochina through their knowledge of India and China and, not surprisingly, paid most attention to the monuments of "advanced" civilizations, such as that of the Indianized Cham (2nd–15th centuries A.D.) of central and southern Vietnam.

The French scholars who had earlier introduced archaeology into Indochina were working within the liberal tradition of European scholarship and did not, I am sure, see their work as nothing more than an intellectual prop for a quite ruthless extractive colonial regime. Nevertheless, their work did lend a form of intellectual and scholarly legitimacy to the colonial regime and their interpretations were sometimes unashamedly colonialist in slant. When the Dong Son site in Than Hoa province first came to light in the 1920s its inhabitants were thought to be intrusive, too culturally advanced for native Southeast Asian peoples, and the Austrian ethnographer Robert Heine-Geldern (1937) derived them through a series of complex migrations in the first millennium B.C. from an ancestral homeland somewhere in Southern Russia. Bernard Karlgren (1942) the Swedish Sinologist, on the other hand derived the Dong Son cultural tradition from China – a view that is still disputed between Vietnamese and Chinese archaeologists (Han Xiaorong 2004). The Vietnamese themselves see in their Bronze Age, in what they call the Dong Dau, Go Mun, and Dong Son Cultures (from the late second to late first millennium B.C.) the first flowering of native Vietnamese genius, the creation of a territorial political state, or states, with high levels of technical and artistic skills.

The practice of modern archaeology was introduced to Indochina by those French scholars early in the 20th century, and was subsequently molded during the wars of liberation and unification within the framework of Russian Marxist–Leninist philosophy, put to the service of nationalism, and students were sent for training in China, Russia, and eastern Europe. Archaeology thus secured its place in rebuilding the national identity. The main focus of the new research of the 1950s and 1960s was to identify the ancestral cultures of the Lac Viet peoples in their homeland on the plains of the Red River Valley where the Dong Son Culture was seen as the "glorious product of the Vietnamese people before their subjection to Han Imperial hegemony." It is a paradox that a country materially so poor, barely recovering from many generations of war against the French, Japanese, Americans, and Chinese, has devoted so much attention to archaeology. But the past is a moral force in Vietnam, unequalled anywhere in the world except perhaps in Korea, and in the process of trying to reassert a Vietnamese national identity, archaeology has played an important part. President Ho Chi Minh took an active interest in prehistoric archaeology and often visited excavations even at the height of the wars and appointed Pham Huy Tong, a former secretary, to be director of the newly created National Institute of Archaeology. Following independence the Vietnamese were encouraged to see in their Bronze Age the first flowering of native Vietnamese genius, the creation of a territorial political state, or states, with high levels of technical and artistic skills equaling those of southern China.

Archaeology was thus used to show that the Vietnamese peoples had achieved political maturity and high standards of cultural expression before the Chinese invasions over 2,000 years ago. A recurrent theme in recent Vietnamese historical and archaeological writing has been its long resistance to Chinese cultural dominance. For instance, Van Trong (1979:6) asserted that the presence of imported bronzes from China in Dong Son assemblages "only heightens the vitality of the Vietnamese culture, an independent one, of deep and solid basis having resolutely refused to be submerged by Chinese culture while many other cultures were subjugated and annihilated." Ha Van Tan (n.d.), Director of the Institute of Archaeology in Hanoi, argued that Dong Son with its capital at Co Loa just outside present-day Hanoi was a centralized state, not just a confederacy of chiefdoms as is the perception of most foreign observers.

Vietnamese histories of the post-Dong Son period, at least those written until the last few years, tend to leap over what they call the "Feudal period" of Chinese imperial domination (2nd–10th centuries A.D.) and emphasize the ethnic, linguistic, and social continuities from the Dong Son to the medieval era of the independent Ly and Tran Dynasties (10th–14th centuries). Scholarly debate and inquiry, however, seem not to be stifled by this political framework and I have regularly been heartened to find that Vietnamese archaeologists disagree with each other just as much as we do in the West.

Further to the south in Indochina, pioneering French scholars had earlier revealed the ruined towers of the Cham peoples whose alien origins seem more secure; their language belonged to the Austronesian family, closely linked to the languages of northern Borneo and perhaps Sumatra. Their rulers at least, were heavily Indianized, built temples dedicated to Shiva, used Sanskrit for their inscriptions and gave themselves Indian names such as Bhadravarman, Rudravarman, and Indravarman. Likewise their cities were called Simhapura or Vijaya; their polities, Amaravati, Kauthara, and Paduranga.

The Cham, like their neighbours in Cambodia, provided the French a perfect example of how cultures could wither and decay without external stimulation. Inspired by the flowering of Indian Hindu culture in the early centuries of the Christian Era, it appeared to the French that the Cham and Khmer people had declined into a slothful apathy. Some Europeans were at first unwilling to accept that the "backward" native peoples they encountered in Indochina could have been responsible for the great temples of Cambodia and Champa and attributed them variously to Alexander the Great's Macedonians, to a lost legion of Trajan; or, more realistically as the result of stimulation and assimilation of tribal society following the arrival of more civilized Indian settlers.

However, recent archaeology in the ancient Cham territories (Glover and Yamagata 1995) shows that however Indianized was the Cham ruling elite, there was, beneath the Indianized veneer, a long continuity of culture tradition from a series of Neolithic, Bronze, and Iron Age cultures. The maritime trading traditions of the late prehistoric Iron Age Sa Huynh Culture (ca. 600 B.C.–A.D. 200) provided the basis for the subsequent historic kingdoms of Champa that were only subjugated by the expanding Dai Viet from the 15th century. Whether the recent interest in Cham archaeology, history, and culture will give encouragement to a resurgence of a local national identity and even a national movement must await the future – but we can be sure that such a development would not be welcomed in Hanoi.

Thailand

In Thailand, in contrast to the situation in the European-dominated territories of the region, an interest in prehistory was late in developing. Archaeology was, until the early 1960s, largely confined to art-historical studies of sculpture, temples, painting, and fine arts, and was mainly the prerogative of aristocratic, Western-educated Thais of the royal clan (Higham 1989:25–7; Peleggi 2001). This delayed start to prehistoric archaeology in Thailand can be explained by the fact that, alone of the Southeast Asian countries, the kingdom was never the colony of a Western power. Not having been subjected to alien rule with their political institutions overthrown, Thais could more easily than, say, Vietnamese or Indonesians, take their past for granted. Critical historiography in Thailand was not well developed, and the country was an agrarian, quasi-feudal kingdom. Nevertheless, as part of the process of modernization started by King Rama IV (Mongkut) in the mid-19th century the cyclical timeframe of Buddhist cosmology was slowly replaced by the Western concept of linear time and with it developed an interest in the history of the kingdom. Peleggi (2001:13–18) succinctly shows how the antiquarian interests of the princely clan led to the establishment of a museum based on the royal collections that, through a series of transformations, became the National Museums of today. Prince Damrong, younger brother of King Rama V, took it upon himself to search for and document the ancient cities of the Thai kingdoms and founded the Fine Arts Department, which is still the government authority responsible for documentation and conservation of the built heritage and much of the field archaeology, although in the past few years much of this is put out to commercial contract teams.

In the 1830s, Rama IV also brought to light at Sukhothai the Ramkhamhaeng inscription on a stone stele, now in the National Museum in Bangkok, which has long been regarded by scholars to date from the 13th century and to be the oldest record of the Thai language and culture in their present homeland, thus becoming the principal icon of national identity. The authenticity of this has however been much disputed in recent times. Pirya Krairiksk (1992)[3] was the first to question its antiquity and argued on epigraphic, linguistic, and contextual grounds that the inscription could not be earlier than the 15th century. It has also been suggested that the inscription had been made to the order of King Rama IV in order to demonstrate the antiquity and "modern" nature of the Thai Kingdom at a time when it was coming under pressure from Western colonial powers (see also Bernon and Lagirade 1994; Chamberlain 1991; Kaye 1990).

This royal concern with the past was limited to places, structures, and inscriptions that could be associated with the rather recent Thai past and it was not until the early 1960s that the systematic investigation of Thai prehistory was initiated by a series of joint field projects. Until about 1980 most sustained work in Thai prehistory was carried out by overseas researchers and was published in English, usually in international journals or monographs published overseas. During the subsequent 30 years Thailand underwent dramatic social and economic transformations. The country became more urbanized, secondary and tertiary education was extended widely and, following the political upheavals in neighboring countries and some within Thailand itself, a new generation of Thais has emerged who require new explanations of their past. With relatively few historical sources, many Thais have looked with enthusiasm to archaeology to provide them with this new understanding, but of course the questions they seek to answer from archaeology are not necessarily those favored by overseas archaeologists. In particular, as I understand it, few Thai archaeologists show an interest in generalized explanations couched in terms of evolutionary processes and not very much in comparative archaeology outside Thailand. In the past decade foreign archaeological investment in Thailand has been much reduced,[4] most local archaeologists[5] have forsaken research-oriented fieldwork and most resources devoted to archaeology in Thailand go into the reconstruction of the great temples and ancient cities of the Khmer, Sukhothai, and Ayutthaya phases of the Thai medieval period. This is archaeology in the service of both nationalism and business, for Thailand is a country where tourism is a major industry (Peleggi 2001).

Archaeology in Burma/Myanmar

Research archaeology is perhaps less well developed in Burma than elsewhere in Southeast Asia. This has not always been so, for research on prehistoric Burma started early; there was much pioneering and thoughtful research into the Paleolithic in Burma by geologists, especially T. O. Morris, in the late 19th century.[6] But it was not until the 1960s that U. Aung Thaw, trained at the School of Archaeology of the Archaeological Survey of India at Dehra Dun, brought modern field methods to the study of early Burma. His excavations at Beikthano, and speedy publication of his discoveries, remain a lonely beacon amid the rather gloomy scene of the archaeology of early Burma. The historian, Michael Aung Thwin has argued that, given the situation in Burma in the years following independence, "prehistory was a luxury the country could ill afford," and priority had to be given to the great monuments of the medieval period. But this was not inevitable and contrasts starkly with the situation in newly independent, and even more resource-poor North Vietnam after 1954. There Vietnamese archaeologists surveyed, recorded, excavated, and published more than in all the other newly independent countries of the regions put together. It was not really shortage of funds that held back Burmese archaeology, but a lack of vision on the part of the politicians and the nation's emerging leaders as to how archaeology could serve nation-building. A realization of the political (and financial) value of archaeology seems to have come only within the last decade or so with investment and resources put into the restoration – sometimes even re-invention – of the great monuments at Pagan and elsewhere as a glorification of Myanmar's "great and unique past."

Miksic (2002) recently considered the potential value of ancient Burmese cities to the tourist economy. Here he makes a not-too-hidden criticism of both government policies and the implementation of them during the reconstruction projects at Pagan and other historic sites in Burma. Inhabitants were cleared with little warning or compensation from their traditional homes while ambitious building and reconstruction work was undertaken with too few trained personnel, leading to a substantial lack of the "authenticity" that successful heritage sites require. At Pagan, for example, some ruined temples and stupas have been leased out to wealthy and powerful provincial families to rebuild as they please, as an act of merit with no regard for the original form.

Government acceptance that prehistoric archaeology, rather than the great Buddhist monuments, can contribute to linking the present to an earlier past – and to income from tourists – has appeared only in the last few years following the discovery of a Bronze Age cemetery at Nyaunggan in central Burma. The finds made there were thought to be significant enough for the Center for Historical Studies of Yangon University to arrange for an international group of archaeologists (in which I was fortunate enough to be included) to visit the site in early 1999, hold a two-day workshop on the discoveries and comparative perspectives, and to publish a book on this before the end of the year (Anon 1999). Perhaps Nyaunggan will be the "Ban Chiang of Burma" and stimulate, among the military elite and intellectuals of Burma, some feeling of national pride in their early indigenous, but non-Buddhist, cultural traditions.

Cambodia

Before World War II, research on the great historic monuments of the Khmer kingdoms was undertaken for the most part under colonial rule. Field archaeology is rather new to Cambodia, although very encouraging starts have been made in quite recent years by foreign teams and Cambodian archaeologists trained locally and overseas. It is too soon to see how the new information arising from these studies may be used in a nationalist discourse, however a very dramatic example of the opportunistic use of archaeological monuments can be seen in the row which arose in January–February 2003 between Cambodia and Thailand. It seems that a Thai "soap-opera" actress, Suwanan Konying, was alleged to have said that "Thailand should take back Angkor Wat," which had at various times been controlled by the Bangkok monarchy, but today is in Cambodia and appears on the national flag. She later denied having made this statement. Nevertheless this was reported in Phnom Penh on "Beehive Radio" and lead to serious riots, the partial destruction of the Thai Embassy, and the looting of many Thai-owned businesses and some US $42 million in damage. Thailand closed all borders with Cambodia, expelled the Cambodian ambassador, deployed warships, and demanded an apology from the Cambodian Prime Minister Hun Sen. But behind this is the suspicion that Cambodian politicians exacerbated, if not actually instigated, the incident for nationalist political reasons ahead of national elections (The Guardian February 2, 2003). The issue was still alive when I left Bangkok in April 2003.

Insular Southeast Asia

Indonesia

At a conference in Bern devoted to the cultural links between Europe and Indonesia I argued (Glover 1986) that archaeology, and especially prehistoric archaeology, was an alien European concept and practice introduced into Indonesia in the days of Dutch colonial hegemony and refurbished in a period of European and American intellectual dominance in the mid-20th century. I argued then that Indonesian prehistory as reflected, for example, in the books of van Heekeren (1957, 1958,

1972) or in the most recent regional prehistory by Peter Bellwood (1997), was an abstract mental construct, satisfying certain concerns of Western academics, but of no significance to more than a handful of Indonesians. Following from this was the implied conclusion that research into prehistory by the few Indonesians undertaking it was likely to be a derivative and sterile occupation with no roots in Indonesian culture, satisfying none of the desires many Indonesians have, to know more about the past of their own societies.

Even today European researchers have carried out a very large part of the investigations into Indonesia's prehistoric past. Peter Bellwood, a British-born, Cambridge-trained prehistorian now working from Australia, has presented the most authoritative interpretation of Indo-Malaysian prehistory (Bellwood 1997). Nothing comparable has yet been produced within Indonesia, and the many European contributions to Indonesian prehistory have not been very significant. Although we have constructed some sort of "Prehistory for Indonesia" it is for external consumption only and of little relevance to Indonesian interests in their own past, and could be placed into Trigger's category of "Imperialist Archaeology" (1984). I am still uncertain as to whether local researchers share this pessimistic and negative view of the state of Indonesian prehistory.

For an example of archaeology put to the service of reinforcing national and regional identities in Indonesia, we need only to look to the use of Srivijaya (Manguin 2000). The name of this early Indic kingdom was first recovered by the Dutch linguist Hendrik Kern (1913) from an inscription dated to 608 in the *Saka* Era (ca. A.D. 682) found at Kota Kapur on Bangka Island, and Georges Coedès (1968) subsequently developed the concept of a powerful Srivijayan maritime empire. Sumatran intellectuals soon incorporated the newly discovered glorious past of their native island into a quest for identity. By the 1930s this regional nationalism moved up to a national level and Mohammad Yamin argued that Srivijaya should be considered the first "Negara Indonesia" – a pan-Indonesia national state with the Javanese kingdom of Majapahit as the second national state, anticipating the emergence of the future Indonesia nation state.

Following Indonesia's independence in 1945, the concept of Srivijaya has been claimed back by the people of Palembang; this despite negative evidence from archaeology (Bronson and Wisseman 1976) and it is only in the past decade that more extensive excavations by a joint Indonesian–French team have established beyond reasonable doubt that Palembang was the center of an ancient polity named Srivijaya. Today visitors to Palembang are confronted with Srivijaya on almost every corner. The airport welcomes them to "Bumi Srivijaya," there are innumerable Toko Srivijaya, Toko Buku Srivijaya, Semen Srivijaya, Pupuk Srivijaya and even the local army corps is the Srivijaya Division.

The Philippines

Archaeology in the Philippines presents an instructive contrast. There is no evidence for pre-colonial powerful centralized kingdoms or states leaving behind inscriptions or other written documents,[7] no great standing indigenous monuments as witness of a great civilization to look back to – other than Spanish colonial forts and churches – fine tourist attractions, but culturally ambiguous and hardly the focus for sustained nationalist pride. And not surprisingly archaeology in the Philippines has been, until recently, amongst the most underdeveloped and backward in the region.

Summary and Conclusions

Benedict Anderson's (1991) examination of the politics of national origins in Europe and Asia emphasizes the link between nationalism and history. That these are linked in South and Southeast Asia's pasts is evident: 19th-century colonial administrations in India, Burma, the Netherlands' Indies, and Indochina appropriated the great monuments of decayed Indic civilizations to further legitimate their colonial rule (Anderson 1991:178–85). Substantial resources were put into clearing, excavating, and restoring great temples and "old sacred sites were incorporated into the map of colony, their ancient prestige draped around the mappers" (Anderson 1991:181–2). These reminders of vanished greatness were enthusiastically adopted by the first post-colonial regimes, to confer legitimacy and (an often fictitious) cultural continuity, and to raise revenue through cultural tourism.

In this chapter I have argued that archaeology can, and usually does, have a political function, and the uses to which the past has been, and is being, put in East and Southeast Asia are not so different from those found during the development of archaeology in Europe. Quite recently a distinguished Japanese prehistorian living and working in Canada commented that in East Asia archaeology is not a generalizing and comparative discipline such as anthropology, but is "national history or it is nothing" (Ikawa-Smith 1999:626) – a conclusion I have reluctantly come to accept.

Archaeology in the service of political nationalism, however, is a two-edged sword. It can be beneficial insofar as it encourages an interest in local origins and educates a people who may have few other sources of information on their more remote past to relate to their ancestors and take a pride in their achievements. But nationalist archaeology can easily lead to xenophobia and manipulation by unscrupulous politicians and a media looking for short-term advantages. Archaeologists working in a country with a strong nationalist historical tradition need to be aware of the problem and be ready to counter the misrepresentation of their researches by those with other agendas.

ACKNOWLEDGMENTS

Many colleagues have contributed ideas and suggestions to the material in this chapter, but I would especially like to thank David Blundell for his insight into the political aspects of archaeology in Taiwan.

NOTES

1   As a personal note I should mention that, as a graduate student at the Australian National University in the late 1960s I met Li Ji and heard him lecture on these literally "ground-breaking" excavations at Anyang.

2   Interestingly I found that Xia Nai had been a student of Egyptology at University College London, my own institution.

3   The first publication by Pirya Krairiksk was in Thai in 1986 in the journal *Muang Boran*. His paper in Chamberlain (ed.) (1991) is more accessible to non-Thai readers.

4   Only Charles Higham, of Otago University, New Zealand and Roberto Ciarla and Fiorella Rispoli of IsIAO, Rome seem to be maintaining active research programmes in Thailand at the start of the 21st century.

5   I must exclude the prehistorians of the Faculty of Archaeology, Silpakorn University, especially Dr Surapol Natapintu, Dr Rasmi Shoocondej, and Professor Phasook Indrawooth and Dr Sawang Lertrit, from this generalization.

6   See a recent issue of the journal *Asian Perspectives*, volume 40 (1) 2001, for a collection of articles that together provide a valuable overview of archaeological research in Burma/Myanmar.

7   The Laguna copper plate inscription in an early form of Kawi script dated to about A.D. 900, was found in 1990 east of Manila (Postma 1991). This is an exceptional find but despite its potential significance for the presence of a literate chiefly, if not state-level society in the Manila region it seems to be rather overlooked by Filipino archaeologists who tend to regard it as an import from Java despite convincing internal evidence from still-known place names for its authenticity.

REFERENCES

Anderson, Benedict 1991 Imagined Communities: Reflections on the Origin and Spread of Nationalism. Rev. edition. London: Verso.

Anon. 1999 Proceedings of the Workshop on Bronze Age Culture in Myanmar. Yangon: Universities Historical Center.

Bellwood, Peter 1997 Prehistory of the Indo-Malaysian Archipelago. 2nd edition. Honolulu: University of Hawaii Press.

Bernon, Olivier de, and F. Lagirade 1994 Review of "The Ram Khamhaeng Controversy." J. Chamberlain ed. Bulletin de l'École Française d'Extrême-Orient 81:390–95.

Bray, Warwick. M., and Ian C. Glover 1987 Scientific Investigation or Cultural Imperialism; British Archaeology in the 3rd World. Bulletin of the Institute of Archaeology (London) 24:109–25.

Bronson, Bennet, and Jan Wisseman 1976 Palembang as Srivijaya: The Lateness of Cities in Southern Southeast Asia. Asian Perspectives 19(2):220–39.

Bulkin, V. A., Leo S. Klejn, and G. S. Lebedev 1982 Attainments and Problems of Soviet Archaeology. World Archaeology 13(3):272–95.

Chamberlain, James R., ed. 1991 The Ram Khamhaeng Controversy: Collected Papers. Bangkok: The Siam Society.

Chang, Kwang-Chih 1969 Fengpitou, Tapenkeng and the Prehistory of Taiwan. Yale University Publication Series in Anthropology 73. New Haven: Yale University Press.

—— 1963–86 The Archaeology of Ancient China. New Haven: Yale University Press. (2nd edition 1968; 3rd edition 1977, 4th edition 1986).

Coedès, Georges 1968 The Indianized States of Southeast Asia. Honolulu: University of Hawaii Press.

Diaz-Andreu, Margarita 1995 Archaeology and Nationalism in Spain. *In* Nationalism, Politics, and the Practice of Archaeology. Philip L. Kohl and Claire Fawcett, eds. Pp. 39–56. Cambridge: Cambridge University Press.

Diaz-Andreu, Marguerita, and Timothy Champion, eds 1996 Nationalism and Archaeology in Europe. London: UCL Press.

Falkenhausen, Lothar von 1993 On the Historiographical Orientation of Chinese Archaeology. Antiquity 67:839–48.

—— 1995 The Regionalist Paradigm in Chinese Archaeology. *In* Nationalism, Politics, and the Practice of Archaeology. Philip L. Kohl and Claire Fawcett, eds. Pp. 198–217. Cambridge: Cambridge University Press.

Fawcett, Claire 1995 Nationalism and Postwar Japanese Archaeology. *In* Nationalism, Politics, and the Practice of Archaeology. Philip L. Kohl and Claire Fawcett, eds. Pp. 231–46. Cambridge: Cambridge University Press.

Glover, Ian C. 1986 Some European Contributions to the Prehistory of Indonesia: A Personal View. Indonesia Circle 40:5–16.

—— 1993 Other Peoples' Pasts – Western Archaeologists and Thai Prehistory. Journal of the Siam Society 81:45–53.

—— 1999 Letting the Past Serve the Present – Some Contemporary Uses of Archaeology in Viet Nam. Antiquity 73:594–602.

—— 2001 Archaeology, Politics and Nationalism in Southeast Asia. Hukay 3:37–65.

—— 2003 National and Political Uses of Archaeology in South-East Asia. Journal of Indonesian and Malay Studies 32(89):16–30.

—— 2004 European Archaeology in Southeast Asia – The Past, the Present and a Future? *In* Fishbones and Glittering Emblems – Southeast Asian Archaeology 2002. Anna Kallén and Anna Karlström, eds. Pp. 23–30. Stockholm: Museum of Far Eastern Antiquities.

Glover, Ian C., and Mariko Yamagata 1995 The Origins of Cham Civilization: Indigenous, Chinese and Indian Influences in Central Vietnam as Revealed by Excavations at Tra Kieu, Vietnam 1990 and 1993. *In* Archaeology in Southeast Asia, Hong Kong. C. T. Young and W. L. Li, eds. Pp. 145–70. Hong Kong: University Museum and Art Gallery.

Habu, Junko, and Claire Fawcett 1999 Jomon Archaeology and the Representation of Japanese Origins. Antiquity 73:58–79.

Ha Van Tan, n.d. From Pre-Dongson to Dongson. Paper presented at the conference, The High Bronze Age of Southeast Asia and South China, Hua Hin, Thailand, 14–19 January 1991.

Han, Xiaorong 2004 Who Invented the Bronze Drum? Nationalism, Politics, and a Sino-Vietnamese Archaeological Debate of the 1970s and 1980s. Asian Perspectives 43(1):7–33.

Heekeren, Hendrick Robert van 1957 The Stone Age of Indonesia. 2nd rev. edition 1972. The Hague: Nijhoff.

—— 1958 The Bronze-Iron Age of Indonesia. The Hague: M. Nijhoff.

Heine-Geldern, Robert 1937 L'art prébuddique de la Chine et de l'Asie du Sud–est et son influence en Océanie. Revue des Arts Asiatiques 11:17–206, 283–9.

Higham, Charles F. W. 1989 The Archaeology of Mainland Southeast Asia: From 10,000 B.C. to the Fall of Angkor. Cambridge: Cambridge University Press.

Hudson, Mark 1999 Ruins of Identity: Ethnogenesis in the Japanese Islands. Honolulu: University of Hawaii Press.

Ikawa-Smith, Fumiko 1999 The Construction of National Identity and Origins in East Asia: A Comparative Perspective. Antiquity 73:626–9.

Kaner, Simon 1996 Beyond Ethnicity and Emergence in Japanese Archaeology. *In* Multicultural Japan: Palaeolithic to Postmodern. Donald Denoon, Mark Hudson, Gavan McCormack, and Tessa Morris-Suzuki, eds. Pp. 46–77. Cambridge: Cambridge University Press.

Karlgren, Bernard 1942 The Date of the Early Dong-s'on Culture. Bulletin of the Museum of Far Eastern Antiquities 14:1–28.

Kaye, Lincoln 1990 Rock of Ages, Set Us Free. Far Eastern Economic Review, 8 November 1990, 36–7.

Kern, Hendrick 1913 Inscriptie van Kota Kapur (eiland Bangka: 608 Saka). Bijdragen tot de Taal-, Land-, en Volkenkund, 67:393–400.

Kita, Sadakichi 1978 Yamato minzokushi gaisetsu. *In* Nihon Minzoku Bunka Takei 5 Ueda Masa'aki, ed. Pp. 211–316. Tokyo: Kodansha (First pub. 1928).

Kohl, Philip L., and Claire Fawcett, eds 1995 Nationalism, Politics, and the Practice of Archaeology. Cambridge: Cambridge University Press.

Li Liu 1999 Who Were the Ancestors? The Origins of Chinese Ancestral Cult and Racial Myths. Antiquity 73:602–13.

Manguin, Pierre-Yves 2000 Welcome to Bumi Sriwijaya or the Building of a Provincial Identity in Contemporary Indonesia. *In* Indonésie: un demi-siècle de construction nationale. F. Blanchard Cavrac, S. Dovert, and F. Durand, eds. Pp. 199–214. Paris/Montréal: L'Harmattan Collection Recherches Asiatiques.

Meskell, Lynn 2002 The Intersections of Politics and Identity. Annual Review of Anthropology 31:279–301.

Miksic, John 2002 Early Burmese Urbanization: Research and Conservation. Asian Perspectives 40:88–107.

Myers, John L. 1930 Who were The Greeks? Berkeley and Los Angeles: University of California Press.

Nelson, Sarah 1995 The Politics of Ethnicity in Prehistoric Korea. *In* Nationalism, Politics, and the Practice of Archaeology. Philip L. Kohl and Clare Fawcett, eds. Pp 218–31. Cambridge: Cambridge University Press.

Pai, Hyung Il 1999 Nationalism and Preserving Korea's Buried Past: The Office of Cultural Properties and Archaeological Heritage Management in South Korea. Antiquity 73:619–25.

—— 2000 Constructing "Korean" Origins. A Critical Review of Archaeology, Historiography and Racial Myth in Korean State-Formation Theories. Cambridge: Harvard University Press.

Pak, Yangjin 1999 Contested Ethnicities and Ancient Homelands in Northeast Chinese Archaeology: The Case of Koguryo and Puyo Archaeology. Antiquity 73:613–18.

Paz, Victor 1998 Is Nationalism Detrimental to Archaeology? Hukay 1:17–25.

Peleggi, Maurizio 2001 The Politics of Ruins and the Business of Nostalgia. Bangkok: White Lotus.

Pirya Krairiksh 1991 Towards a Revised History of Sukhothai Art: A Reassessment of the Inscription of King Ram Khamhaeng. *In* The Ram Khamhaeng Controversy: Collected Papers. James Chamberlain, ed. Pp. 53–159. Bangkok: The Siam Society.

Postma, Antoon 1991 The Laguna Copper Plate Inscription. National Museum Papers (Manila) 2:1–25.

Rooney, Dawn 1998 In the Footsteps of Henri Mouhot: A French Explorer in 19th Century Thailand, Cambodia and Laos. SPAFA Journal 8:5–16.

Tong Enzheng 1995 Thirty Years of Chinese Archaeology (1949–1979). *In* Nationalism,

Politics, and the Practice of Archaeology. Philip L. Kohl and Claire Fawcett, eds. Pp. 177–97. Cambridge: Cambridge University Press.

Trigger, Bruce 1984 Alternative Archaeologies: Colonialist, Nationalist, Imperialist. Man 19:355–70.

—— 1995 Romanticism, Nationalism and Archaeology. *In* Nationalism, Politics, and the Practice of Archaeology. Philip L. Kohl and Clare Fawcett, eds. Pp. 263–79. Cambridge: Cambridge University Press.

Van Trong 1979 New Knowledge on Dong–s'on Culture from Archaeological Discoveries These Twenty Years. Recent Discoveries And New Views On Some Archaeological Problems in Viet Nam. Hanoi: Institute of Archaeology.

3

Archaeology in the Two Koreas

Sarah M. Nelson

The archaeology of the Korean peninsula has sometimes been treated as a pale reflection of archaeology in Japan and China, but this is an inaccurate assessment of both actual discoveries in Korea and the potential for Korean archaeology as comparative material. Korean sites are important in illuminating both general processes of cultural change and the history of the entire region. Korea's archaeology demonstrates specific ways of adapting to the particular environment of the Korean Peninsula, as well as change through time as it related to but differed from neighboring regions.

Like Japan and China, archaeology in Korea has been considered as merely producing refinements in the history as it is known from written documents. But in contrast, stages of evolution derived from Marxist theory have been applied in North Korea, and the anthropological tenor of Anglo-American archaeology also has adherents, especially in South Korea. Bands, tribes, chiefdoms, and states have all been described and argued over in South Korean archaeology. Although archaeology has taken divergent paths in the Democratic People's Republic of Korea (North Korea) and the Republic of Korea (South Korea) since the tragic division of the peninsula at the conclusion of World War II, the two polities share a much longer common history which forms the base of the archaeology practiced in both Koreas. Differences occur in archaeological interpretations, dating, and methodology in the two Koreas, but archaeological purposes are similar north and south, both rooted in the archaeology established by Japanese colonialism, and Korean responses to it.

Imperialism in the Korean peninsula included some intervention of Western powers, but true colonialism came from Japan. Korean archaeology was largely shaped by the experience of Japanese overlordship from 1910 to 1945. Archaeologists from Japan arrived in Korea even before the formal annexation, and explored not only the Korean peninsula, but most of Manchuria as well. Japanese archaeologists were particularly interested in tombs, but they also excavated fortresses, palaces, shell mounds, and other sites, intending to demonstrate the similarities of the peoples of Northeast Asia. From this experience arose the common themes of archaeology in the two halves of the peninsula: the coherence and identity of the Korean people, and self-reliance.

Because China has a long written history, which refers to regions on its borders as well as within China proper, archaeology in East Asia is generally seen as the handmaid of history, rather than as a discipline on its own. The disagreements in interpretation that arise, especially between the modern countries of China, Korea, and Japan, are therefore centered on how to interpret specific events and processes within East Asia, rather than being more widely comparative. Disagreements are often rooted in national pride, with territorial covert or overt implications. To understand how this has played out in Korea, it is necessary to understand the history of Korea in the 20th century, when archaeology began.

The Korean Peninsula as Political Football

The geography of the Korean peninsula has been described as creating both a bridge and a barrier between cultures and nations, and indeed it has performed both functions. Chinese culture was largely introduced to Japan through the Korean peninsula, acting as a bridge between China and Japan, but it was not a mere transmitter of Chinese culture to Japan. Korea's own forms of pottery, bronze and iron, rather than Chinese types, were initially introduced into the Japanese islands. On the other hand, there is no easy route down the peninsula, so the dissected topography has sometimes created a barrier to cultural exchange, or at least slowed the transmission of both cultures and peoples. For example, the Silla kingdom in the southeast corner was the last to adopt Buddhism and Chinese-introduced customs. The peninsular history, however, has certainly not been isolated from its neighbors on any side. The interaction with neighboring polities and cultures is reflected in built landscapes and artifacts, as well as in documents.

Korea was one of the last Asian countries to open its ports to ships from the West. Known as the "Hermit Nation" because of its closed-door policies, Korea did not have a trade treaty even with Japan until 1876, and a treaty between the United States and Korea was finally concluded in 1882, after military and other pressures had been brought to bear. During most of the historic period, Korea had been a sovereign nation but had played the role of "younger brother" to China's "elder brother," regardless of whether a native Chinese or a northern "barbarian" dynasty was ruling China. But beginning in the late 19th century, Japan waged a number of wars in and around the Korean peninsula to destabilize the power of China and itself acquire hegemony in East Asia. War between Japan and China in 1884–5, much of it fought in and around the Korean peninsula, left Korea unprotected. Japanese power moved in to pull the strings of the last kings of the Yi dynasty in Korea.

Borders were indefinite in the far north of China, which was the ancestral territory of the Manchu rulers of China, known as the Qing dynasty. In that circumstance Russia began colonizing these unprotected areas. Japan thereupon waged and won a war against Russia, leaving Korea as a Japanese protectorate. In 1910, Korea was formally annexed as a colony by Japan. This was not a happy event for Korea. The Japanese colonial powers wielded a heavy hand, forcing Koreans to take Japanese names and making children speak only Japanese in school. Both of these policies were deeply resented by the Korean people, and they still rankle even with generations who never knew Japanese rule. In 1932, Japan created the puppet state of Manchuria, with the "last emperor of China," Puyi, on the throne as the figurehead.

By 1941 much of the world was enmeshed in war, with German and Italian conquests in Europe and North Africa, and Japan rapidly gaining territory in the Pacific. Two sides formed. The Axis (Germany, Italy, and Japan) and the Allies (most of the rest of unoccupied Europe, America, China, and the Soviet Union). Although the Soviet Union never fought in the Pacific, when the Allies accepted Japan's surrender, it was decided that they would govern the part of Korea north of the 38th parallel, and the United States the south, until democratic elections could be held. Naturally, the Soviet military government backed the Communist cause in the north, and even brought in with them Koreans who had been schooled in Russian-held cities in Manchuria. Meanwhile, the American military government was trying to foster a democratic government in the south (Osgood 1954).

Before any local government could take hold, however, communist forces from the north invaded and swept over the south as far as a small region around the city of Pusan in the south. A three-year bloody war raged up and down the peninsula, with U.S. forces and others from the United Nations fighting on the side of the south, and Chinese troops weighing in on the side of the north. A truce was declared in 1953, but it was not a peace settlement. The truce line follows the battle lines along the contours of the hills, roughly the same division as the 38th parallel. This situation still exists.

The Beginnings of Korean Archaeology

Japanese surveyors and scholars were the first archaeologists in Korea. Japanese interpretations of their discoveries in Korea were slanted toward a nationalist policy that considered Koreans to be Japanese. This meant that the most interest and excavations were focused on the early historic period, in the first few centuries B.C. and A.D. These time periods are called Yayoi and Kofun in Japan. According to the Korean histories, the *Samguk Yusa* and *Samguk Sagi*, in Korea this period was called Three Kingdoms. (Archaeologists now refer to the earlier part as Proto-Three Kingdoms.) Tombs of nobles and rulers were excavated in Kyongju, the ancient capital of the Silla kingdom. Large burials near Pyongyang, where the Han Chinese commandery of Lelang flourished, were excavated and meticulously published. Tombs from the Koguryo kingdom of the early centuries A.D. were also explored. Japanese crews explored painted tombs on both sides of the Yalu River, especially north of the river near the (Chinese) city of Jian which was an earlier capital of Koguryo.

Inscribed stones and Buddhist monuments were also described and sometimes moved to new locations.

Neolithic sites were not entirely neglected. A few archaeologists were interested in the coastal shell mounds, comparing them to those of Jomon in Japan. Some of the more conspicuous shell mounds on the East Sea coast were excavated. Fujita Ryosaku (1933) noted that early pottery was sometimes plain and sometimes decorated with incised geometric designs. These came to be called in Korean Mumun, without decoration, and Chulmun, comb-marked, respectively. Fujita was concerned with the chronological order of Korean pottery styles, partly because pottery was believed at that time to have diffused across Central Asia to Korea and then to Japan. This notion was of course later overturned with radiocarbon dates, showing Jomon pottery in Japan to be the earliest in the world.

Because iron and bronze appear to have arrived in Japan at the same time, Japanese archaeologists interpreted the archaeology of Korea as having no separate Bronze and Iron Ages. A few coastal shell mounds proved to be Iron Age, and some dolmens and burials in large jars were excavated. Paleolithic sites were of little interest to Japanese archeologists at the time. Pleistocene sites were only found after the division of the peninsula into competing halves.

As noted above, Japanese imperialism of the 19th and early 20th centuries did not begin with the annexation of Korea. Encroachment on Russian and Chinese territories started even before the Sino-Japanese (1894–5) and Russo-Japanese (1904–5) wars. With success in these ventures, the Japanese built the South Manchurian railway, opening up the territory north of the Chinese heartland. This region was the ancestral home of the Manchu emperors, who for centuries had ruled China as the Qing dynasty. Japan looked to this area for its own antecedents, in the same way that Koreans did, so to excavate in "Manchuguo" was to explore their own ancestors.

Japanese interest in the archaeology, ethnography, folklore, and history of the newly conquered areas meant that archaeologists followed right behind the surveyors. However, even before the energetic surveys and excavations of Torii Ryuzo and Fujita Ryosaku among others, Russian and Chinese archaeologists, along with Europeans living in China, had also explored and sometimes published sites from this vast region now known as the Dongbei, or the Chinese Northeast (for discussions on the archaeology of this region, see Nelson 1997). As a result, sometimes the same site is found in the archaeological literature under multiple names. More often, the orthography of the local name written in various languages was different enough that the sites only seemed to be renamed each time they were recorded in a different language.

When Korea was annexed to Japan, "Korean studies became viewed as an extension of Manchurian history and geography" (Pai 2000:26), and the common origin of Japanese and Koreans was asserted, as noted above. Using Chinese histories that describe northeastern peoples from long ago, the current inhabitants were linked to these ancient tribes. Studies made by Russian ethnographers about the indigenous people speaking related languages grouped as "Tungusic" were used as a base for much Japanese scholarship in the area, along with ancient Chinese documents which were translated into Japanese and sometimes western languages as well.

Archaeology was used by Japanese scholars to verify several stances that upheld their colonial rule (Pai 1994). It was necessary to justify the takeover of Korea (which was, as we have seen, only a part of Japanese imperialism in Asia), and this was done in several ways. Especially it was asserted that Japanese and Koreans were the same "race" (*Nissen dosoron*). Thus, discovering the past of Japan was also to investigate Korea's past, and this concept supplied Japanese archaeologists with a reason to excavate on Korean soil.

In spite of this assertion of identity between Japanese and Koreans, Koreans were seen as inferior to the Japanese. Their cultural "backwardness" was blamed on their historical dependency on China, rather than on any "racial" traits (Pai 2000:37). One example of Korean lack of modern spirit (according to the Japanese) was the topknot riots of 1895. Under pressure from Japan to "modernize," the Korean king and his court sheared their previously uncut hair. An edict by the king demanded that other men do the same. Uncut hair in traditional Korea was symbolic of male adulthood and respect for parents and more remote ancestors. Men's hair was traditionally bound into a topknot and covered with a hat. In response to the edict, a few men in the countryside did cut their hair, but some of them were murdered by local farmers in horror at the sacrilege. Other men committed suicide rather than scissor their hair (Bishop 1898:359–70; Nelson 1998:111). Such an attitude contrasted markedly with the enthusiasm with which Japanese men were changing to western fashions of both clothing and hair styles. Thus for adhering to Confucian tradition, Korea was considered a backward culture in Japan.

Archaeology during the Japanese occupation was almost entirely carried out by Japanese archaeologists. The archaeologists themselves were educated in Japan, and they did not train Koreans to follow in their footsteps. Some Koreans were allowed to go to Japan for advanced schooling in other fields. A few amateur archaeologists were involved in the Japanese excavations, especially in Kyongju, the capital of ancient Silla, but on the whole, with the conquest by the Japanese, Korea was left at the conclusion of World War II with a scholarly deficit.

In the aftermath of World War II, museums, which had been established under Japanese rule, were being sponsored by the American military government, but few people in Korea had the expertise to run a museum. Arimitsu Kyoichi, a Japanese archeologist who was born in Korea, was asked by NATO forces to remain in Korea and help re-establish and reopen the National Museum in Seoul. His short memoir of that post-war year gives an insightful snapshot of the time (Arimitsu 1996). Arimitsu had worked in Korea since 1931, and had excavated widely around the peninsula, especially Neolithic sites. Living in Korea after the fall of Japan was difficult and even dangerous for the few Japanese that remained. The hostility toward Japanese was so marked that Arimitsu did not even attend the reopening of the museum on December 3, 1945. However, he managed to impart his knowledge and experience to Kim Chae-won, who became the first director of the Seoul National Museum. The military government asked Arimitsu to excavate two tombs in the

42   SARAH M. NELSON

Silla capital of Kyongju. With a Korean team, he excavated two high status tombs from the Silla period, containing gold crowns and bronze vessels with short inscriptions. This provided good training for Arimitsu's Korean crew in their future excavations, as well as additional artifacts for the museum. The two tombs were published by the Seoul National Museum in 1948, fulfilling the obligation to publish as well as to dig and conserve artifacts. The tombs were excavated from May 1 to May 25, 1946, followed by a ritual to close the excavation.

Thus with little training of its practitioners, Korean archaeology continued to operate on the principles established by Japanese archaeologists. One of the most important legacies was the concept of cultural properties. That is, antiquities are owned by the state, which has the responsibility for maintaining them, whether they are buildings, artifacts, or sites. This system continues to this day. The Office of Cultural Properties (*Munhwajai Kwalliguk*) remains a powerful force in Korean archaeology.

The designation of National Treasures was also established under the Japanese occupation, along the same lines as that created in Japan. Korean National Treasures include artifacts such as gold crowns and large Silla bronze bells, individual monuments like pagodas and bell towers, and architecture such as temples and fortresses. Other types of National Treasures can even be living people who preserve traditional arts in some way.

Although Korea was divided administratively between the United States and the Soviet Union along the 38th parallel in the aftermath of World War II, this division was never intended to be a permanent condition. However, the incursion of communist forces from the north that precipitated the Korean War ultimately resulted in a long-term division of the peninsula into a communist north influenced first by the Soviet Union and later by the People's Republic of China, and a market-economy south under the influence of the United States of America. The demarcation line between the two Koreas ran along the battle line when the cease-fire was signed in 1953, with a demilitarized zone two kilometers wide on either side of the line, and the truce village of Panmunjom in the middle, guarded by the United Nations. The result was that the truce line had more geographic integrity than the imaginary parallel, and included roughly the same amount of territory for each side.

Who Are the Koreans?

Koreans as a unified group of people with a common language, culture, and past is an unshakable tenet of archaeological interpretation throughout the peninsula. I have described this concept of an eternal Koreanness as a kind of "ethnicity" (Nelson 1993, 1995), but Hyung Il Pai (1999; Pai and Tangherlini 1998) refers to it as "race," a stronger term perhaps better reflecting the Korean perception of themselves. The Korean understanding is that genetic inheritance ("bones" in Korean metaphor, rather than "related by blood" as in Euro-America imagery) is a basic part of Koreanness. There is no possibility of *becoming* Korean, a person must be *born* Korean. The concept is also not the same as nationality – from the Korean perspective a person of Korean descent can be both an American citizen, for example, and a Korean. The Korean race, language, and culture are believed to go back to unimaginable antiquity, hence the connection with archaeology. It thus becomes important for archaeology in Korea to establish when this Koreanness was formed, and where it arose. To understand the arguments it is necessary to understand Korean points of view on their own past.

In Korea, divisions of the archaeological past are based on terminology derived from European archaeology. Thus time periods are designated as Paleolithic, Neolithic, Bronze Age, and Iron Age, rather than by any indigenous descriptions or place names. This scheme was adopted after the end of the Japanese occupation. Some inevitable distortion occurs with the application of the technological ages of Europe, as the Korean archaeological data are not so clearly unilinear. For this reason I have used other terms in describing stages in Korean archaeology (Nelson 1993), but they have not been widely adopted in Korea. Furthermore, technological change was probably *not* the driving force of increasing complexity in the peninsula (see Nelson 1999 for an example of other possible causes of increasing complexity). The terminology used in Korea reflects, however, the fact that archaeology has a historiographic orientation, rather than a comparative one. Considering archaeology as a contribution to history may be derived from the Japanese occupation, but it is also true of archaeology in China (Nelson 1995). Evolutionary political stages of band, tribe, chiefdom, and state are applied in South Korea, while the north still uses the standard Marxist terminology: matriarchal clan community, patriarchal clan community, slave society, and feudal kingdom (FLPH 1977).

Paleolithic sites are few relative to China and Japan, but they are increasingly being discovered. The earliest Paleolithic cave sites in North Korea are reported as being as old as half-a-million years, but this claim is generally not accepted in South Korea. Paleolithic in the south is represented by cave sites, open air sites near the surface, and deeply stratified sites. The most famous site of Chon'gongni was originally held to be Early Paleolithic, but scientific dating of the basalts now suggests that it is Middle to Late Paleolithic. Chon'gongni was the first site found in Korea with hand-axes, and much was made over this discovery as disproving the "Movius" line. Hallam Movius (1948) from Harvard had written that hand-axes (and subsequent formal tools) were found only in Europe, Africa, and India, and that chopper/chopping tools were found east of a line that includes the rest of Asia. Thus the discovery of hand-axes in Korea was heralded as proving that Asia was not so backward after all, even in the Paleolithic.

Even after the discovery of Paleolithic sites, a Mesolithic period was believed not to exist. The most common interpretation was that the Paleolithic people died out or moved away, leaving the peninsula empty of humans until the immigration of the pottery-making Paleoasiatics. In the last several years, with intense survey and excavation in the south, a great many early Holocene sites have been found. These prove to have a variety of lithic technologies, from stemmed points to microliths. Some sites with pottery, especially on the south coast, have pottery gradually added to a pre-pottery base, without much change in the lithics or bone tools.

The earliest pottery has been called Chulmun, which means comb-marked, and implies a relationship to the Siberian comb-marked pottery. This is a misnomer, for most Chulmun pottery was not decorated with a toothed implement, but with a variety of objects that can make marks in clay, from bird bones to fingernails. Since radiocarbon dating has been applied, we know that the earliest dated sites with pottery are not decorated with incising at all; the vessels are either plain or decorated with appliqué or carved stamps. Still, Jomon as used in Japan is also a misnomer – it means cord-marked, but the term covers all pottery from the beginning to the end of the period however it may be decorated. In Korea, even if the pottery is varied, settlements of the early village period are similar. Houses are small and semi-subterranean, with central hearths. They are grouped into small villages, sometimes with outdoor pits or hearths, but few other features. The subsistence base was thought to be fishing, hunting, and gathering, with shellfish collecting on the coasts. Recent flotation, however, has produced macroflora that demonstrate some cultivation of millets and other plants, gradually increasing through time (Crawford and Lee 2003).

The Mumun period introduced a number of new characteristics. These include new varieties of house styles, dolmens, rice cultivation, and eventually imported bronze artifacts. In North Korea it is claimed that this trend began as early as 2000 B.C., but the date commonly used in South Korea is closer to 1000 B.C. The dates are contested for a variety of reasons, including insufficient and contradictory evidence and preconceived ideas. The concepts are derived from documents, to be described later. It may also be correct that bronze is found in the north earlier than in the south. The first bronze objects found in North Korea are small knives with loop handles and buttons – objects that are found nearby in China. Later, daggers with bracket-shaped edges (Yoyong daggers) appear in the north and south, along with mirrors decorated with zigzag designs. These mirrors and daggers are found widely in the Liaoning Province of China, often as grave goods in stone slab coffins. Dolmens are also found in Liaoning. Thus it is not hard to perceive northern China as the source of the new traits in Korea. Rice was first domesticated in China, as well, and rice begins to appear in Korea along with the Mumun pottery. With all this evidence of influence from the Chinese northeast, it is curious that tripod pottery vessels were not part of the package. They were characteristic of northern China from the Peiligang culture of the earliest Neolithic through the Shang dynasty. Before everything is charged to diffusion or migration from the continent, the lack of tripods should give us pause (Nelson 1993, 1999).

Iron-working technology came into Korea along with the establishment of commanderies by the Han Dynasty of China in 108 B.C. The Han was the first real Chinese empire (in spite of all the hype about Qin Shi Huang Di and his pottery burial army, he and the Qin empire lasted just two generations.) The Han needed funding for their expansionist policies, so they declared a state monopoly on iron and salt. The Korean peninsula with its rich veins of iron ore must have looked very tempting. Battles were fought with the inhabitants, who, according to the Chinese histories, already lived in cities, were literate, rode horses, and used iron armor. When the peoples north of the Han River in central Korea were conquered, four commanderies were set up, and Chinese administrators were sent in to govern them, using some local leaders as well. The best known of these commanderies is Lelang, centered on the present city of Pyongyang, now the capital of North Korea.

In the south, tribes went their own way, and formed the Kingdoms of Silla in the southeast and Paekche in the southwest. Between these two polities were the loosely affiliated cities of Kaya. North of the Lelang commandery, another kingdom called Koguryo was forming. This was known as the Three Kingdoms period, traditionally from the first century B.C. to A.D. 668, when the Silla Kingdom, with the help of armies from Tang China, conquered the other two kingdoms and became United Silla. During this time, Buddhism was adopted in all kingdoms, schools were set up, and Chinese naming systems, calendars, and governance became the norm. Officially the Three Kingdoms are Silla, Paekche, and Koguryo. The Kaya people in the south between the kingdoms of Paekche and Silla never formed a larger polity, and were picked off one by one by Silla.

Purposes of Korean Archaeology

Based on the interest in confirming history, the main purpose of Korean archaeology both north and south is building chronology. Chronological studies are based largely on detailed studies of stylistic change, anchored only rarely in radiocarbon dates. A second aim is to identify ethnic groups, especially those named in the Chinese written record. For example, a Chinese history of Korea before the Three Kingdoms named three groups of people in the south of the Korean peninsula called Han (a different character from the Chinese Han): Chinhan, Pyonhan, and Mahan. The official name of the Republic of Korea in Korean is Tae Han Minguk, the great Han people; clearly the name still has resonance. The intent is to be able to recognize their ethnicity by specific artifact styles or other traits, especially those that are noted in the documents. For example, during the Three Kingdoms period, the region around the Han River was a continuous battle ground. It was occupied successively by Paekche, which was pushed south by Koguryo, then Silla which displaced Koguryo because of the former's need for a port on the Yellow Sea for better communication with the Tang Dynasty of China. The different pottery styles found in various fortresses, palaces, and tombs verify which kingdom was in control at the time, and tend to be used to date the structures.

These two goals of chronology and stylistic variation interlock. Thus, as we have seen, the appearance in the Korean peninsula of the so-called Yoyong (Liaoning) daggers is equated with the migration of people into Korea from the Liaodong Peninsula in the first millennium B.C. Stylistic markers also are seen to distinguish among the Three Kingdoms of Silla, Paekche, and Koguryo (first century B.C. to seventh century A.D. in the traditional dating). Thus time can be deduced from style. For example, the Paekche, Koguryo, and Silla kingdoms occupied the Han River region in succession, according to Korean histories. The style of sites, tombs, or artifacts allows an inference about the time frame of any Three Kingdoms site along the Han River.

These characteristics of Korean archaeology derive from the Japanese occupation, when the first serious archaeology was undertaken in the Korean peninsula. In spite of the anger which still smolders regarding the Japanese occupation of Korea, even with regard to the archaeological results from that period, the way archaeology is practiced has not moved far from that which was established by the Japanese. Japanese techniques were detailed and careful, and the publications (at least of sites considered important) were made to a high standard. This part of the legacy has been helpful in establishing post-colonial processes in Korea.

Since archaeology is treated as a historical science, its findings are used to discover the origin of this supposedly unified Korean people which existed from time immemorial. As noted above, that place of origin is assumed to be Liaoning. Another way that history is used is in relation to Japan. Just as Yoyong daggers and mirrors turned up in Korea and "evolved" into thin bronze daggers and more sophisticated mirrors, so these later daggers and mirrors are found in Japan, later to evolve into their own styles. But before metal from Korea is found in Japan, rice farmers appeared to create the Yayoi period. There was a time when rice was alleged to have arrived in Japan straight from southern China rather than through Korea.

While the Japanese position was that Korea and Japan are the same people, they rejected the idea of actual migration into the islands from the peninsula. The famous "horse riders" theory of the origin of the Kofun period asserts that the horses and riders came from "the continent," not Korea. One irony is that in modern times Koreans are seen as distinctly different from the Japanese (Pai 2000:57) on the one hand, but as contributing strongly to the creation of Japanese states and civilization on the other (Hong 1988, 1994).

As noted above, the concept of Koreans and Japanese as the same people dates to Japanese policy while they ruled Korea. Asserting that Japanese and Koreans were one people was a reason for Japan to justify the occupation of Korean territory. It is therefore unwelcome in post-colonial Korea, especially in its original form. Indubitable similarities between the Yayoi culture of Japan and Mumun in Korea are therefore interpreted as unidirectional influence from Korea to Japan. Likewise artifacts discovered in ruling class tombs in the two regions are believed to be related to peninsular influence on the islands of Japan.

Self-Reliance and Interpretations of Korean Archaeology

Self-reliance is *juch'e*, an important slogan in North Korea. While it is largely applied to the present (*juch'e* is cited as a reason that North Korea should produce nuclear weapons, for example), echoes can be found in the construction of the prehistoric past. As will be explained more fully below, this means denying any influence on the Korean peninsula from China at any time in the past, and glorifying the "pure Korean" legends of Tangun and later Kija, two controversial figures.

The Han Dynasty records (first century B.C. to third century A.D.) are quite specific and detailed about the establishment of four commanderies in the northern part of the Korean peninsula and nearby regions of Manchuria. In order to assert that this self-reliance was active in the past, the historicity of the commanderies must be denied. Unquestionably Chinese artifacts from tombs of the Han period near Pyongyang are explained away as merely imports, rather than as the accouterments of people of Chinese ethnicity who were members of the ruling elite, sent by the Han Dynasty to govern the Lelang colony in the Korean peninsula. *Juch'e* also requires the notion that all things were invented in the Korean peninsula. Especially in North Korea, outside influence is completely denied. In the south the same attitude infuses archaeology, but it manifests itself most vigorously with regard to Japan, rather than China. Supposed ancient invasions from the Japanese islands are rejected as mythical, and hotly contested with reference to a variety of archaeological evidence.

An important example of contention between Japan and Korea over the past is the history of a 6.39 meter high stele, erected in A.D. 414, inscribed on four sides in 1,775 Chinese characters (Kang 2001). This stele extols the conquests of King Kwanggaet'o, an early king of the northernmost of the Three Kingdoms of Korea, called Koguryo. The first capitals of this kingdom were north of the Amnok (Yalu) River, territory which is now part of China in the Korean Autonomous Province (Yanbian). The stele was rediscovered in the city of Jian, a former capital of Koguryo, in 1882 (note that this is before the Sino-Japanese War). Within a few years, a rubbing of all four sides of this tall stele was made by a Japanese officer and sent back to Japan for study. A translation of the inscription was read by scholars in Japan as confirming 8th century Japanese histories, especially *Nihon Shoki*. This document claimed that a Japanese colony called Mimana occupied southern Korea from A.D. 368 to 562. Some of the sentences on the stele are read as confirming the existence of Mimana and its hegemony over Silla and Paekche as well as its alliance with Koguryo. However, many of the characters are defaced, and the readings of other characters are questionable. Under these circumstances there is room for more than one interpretation (Grayson 1977). Recall that Korean archeology and history recognizes a group of city-states called Kaya.

Korean scholarly responses had to wait until after the conclusion of World War II and the Korean War truce. The responses when they came were often both scholarly and bitter. For example, Wontaek Hong writes that "the myth that Japan had a unified and powerful state as early as the third or fourth century, possessed a colony called Mimana on the southern tip of Korea, and controlled Paekche and Silla is based on anachronistic and incoherent bits and pieces of episodes and fantasies recorded in *Nihongi*" (Hong 1994:195). Hong asserts that the interpretation promulgated in Japanese writing, and cited in many Western texts (Hong 1994:21–8), is based on a single line of the Kwanggaet'o stele, with critical missing characters supplied by Japanese scholars to bolster their case. Some Koreans have charged that the characters were deliberately defaced, in order to make possible the favored Japanese reading. The rancor toward Japanese archaeology in the Korean peninsula runs deep, and is an attitude that tends to unify archaeology in the two Koreas more than any other factor. It is important to note, however, that changes in these attitudes are occurring in both Korea and Japan. More Japanese students are studying Korean archaeology in Korea, and more Korean archeology students are studying in Japan. Japanese museums no longer insist that there is no influence on their early history from the Korean peninsula, and meetings between Korean and Japanese archeologists are held annually.

Post-Korean War Archaeology in North Korea

Archaeology in the north followed Soviet models in interpretation, but Japanese field procedures were often used. Unfortunately, the standard of reporting in the north, including illustrating and map-making, never reached the high mark of that produced by Japanese archaeologists. Reportage tended to be prompt, however. Archaeological journals were founded, such as *Kogo Minsok* (Archaeology and Folklore) and *Kogohak Charyochip* (Archaeological Reports). In addition, detailed excavation reports appeared which were bound separately. North Korea uses only *han'gul*, an alphabetic script unique to Korea which was created for the Korean language. This script is logical (it can be learned in a few hours) and easy to read. However, it is hard to understand, because many loan words from Chinese have made their way into the Korean language. The number of words that sound alike with different meanings is legion. In scholarly writing in South Korea, the appropriate Chinese character, singular for the meaning although not the sound, is used instead of han'gul, making the meaning explicit. However, even in the south more and more is written in han'gul only.

A very helpful and complete bibliography of North Korean archaeology has been published in South Korea, arranged by journal issues, date of publication, author, and time period (Yi, Lee, and Shin 1989). A useful chart shows when specific authors were active in publication and presumably in excavation. More than 100 volumes and several hundred individual reports have been published on North Korean archaeology. The output has been uneven in time, however. Very little was published in the 1940s and early 1950s, understandable as a result of post-war turmoil. The most productive times were the 1960s and again in the 1980s. Sometimes excavations were reported jointly by North Korean and Russian archaeologists, appearing in Russian journals (see Chard 1960 for an English summary of some of these). The usual problem of orthography arises, with Korean transliterated into Russian and then into English, making site names not immediately recognizable.

Although sites from North Korea were published, they were inaccessible for an extended period. The reports that appeared in Russian were occasionally translated and summarized in English (e.g. Chard 1960), and a few scholars had direct access to North Korean reports and reported them in English also (Henthorn 1966, 1968). Some North Korean archaeology journals found their way to Japan, and could be copied there, or occasionally even were available for purchase. However, under the early South Korean military governments materials published in North Korea were prohibited in South Korea, so that knowledge within South Korea of the archaeology of North Korea was tragically limited. When I was given a government grant to do research in South Korea in 1983, I was allowed to read the North Korean site reports, but only in a library attic where North Korean books were kept under lock and key. I was not permitted to make any copies, although I was allowed to take notes.

In addition to the difficulty of obtaining them, reading North Korean site reports is often frustrating, since many details that would have been useful are omitted. On the other hand the locations of artifacts in the sites either appear on sketch maps or are generally described, following the Soviet practice of digging whole house floors rather than trenches only. Inferences about gender in regard to the locations of artifacts were sometimes made, for example stating that the "male" side of the house contained tools and weapons, while the "female" side had pots and spindle whorls. Neolithic sites were divided into the "matriarchal stage" and the "patriarchal stage," of which the latter is more developed, following Marxist thought.

An interest in faunal material prevailed in North Korean archaeology, so that papers on the domestication of pigs in the Neolithic, or the use of the horse in the Bronze Age, could be found in the pages of North Korean journals. Human osteology, however, was researched more in the Japanese period than in North Korean excavations.

Recalling that radiocarbon dating only appeared in the 1950s, it is not surprising that few of the earliest sites to be excavated were dated by this method. The lack of radiocarbon dates at later times may be simply a matter of expense, or perhaps may arise from a belief that such dates are unnecessary since the time period was known from historic documents (Nelson 1992). This latter attitude often prevails in South Korea as well, especially for sites of the Three Kingdoms period. One result of having few radiocarbon dates is that a discrepancy has arisen between the dating of time periods in North and South Korea, with South Korean dates being much more conservative. For example, the Bronze Age is estimated to have begun in North Korea around 2000 B.C. (FLPH 1977), while it is often dated 1000 B.C. or even later in the South. Of course, bronze could have arrived significantly earlier in the north, but it would be useful to have backing from radiocarbon dates to understand the process better.

Two figures that appear in various ancient documents, said to be important in the foundation of Korean states, are Kija and Tangun. They have quite different traditional backgrounds and impact the interpretation of Korean archaeological sites in different ways. Kija (Qizi in Chinese) is mentioned in documents from the Zhou Dynasty (founded around 1000 B.C.). Noted for his filial piety toward his ancestors the Shang kings, he was allowed to take a retinue of people, leave the central Chinese state and set up a state in the east called Choson (Chaoxian). Many Korean historians have fastened upon this as a record of an early state in the Korean peninsula. The problem for archaeology is that nothing that resembles artifacts of the Shang Dynasty has been found in Korea. Most notably no bronze vessels and no writing have been discovered, although such have been found in the district of Yan, in northeastern China.

Although Kija may have truly existed as a historical figure, Tangun is more problematical. The legend of Tangun involves his father, the sky god, marrying a she-bear who was turned into a human woman, giving Tangun mythic proportions.

Tangun was said to have ruled Ancient Choson (Ko Choson) for more than a thou-sand years, eventually becoming a god presiding over Chonji, the Heavenly Lake. This lake was formed in a huge volcanic crater of Mt. Paektusan on the border between North Korea and China. The current leader, Kim Jong-Il, has been mys-tically connected to Tangun by his purported birth near Paektusan. North Koreans excavated a joint burial of a man and a woman near Pyongyang in 1992, purported to be the grave of Tangun and his wife. The human bones are said to be very large. This interpretation has received much publicity, as proof of the historicity of Tangun, and by implication the inheritance of Kim Jong-Il.

Later historical dynasties have different kinds of archaeological problems. The kingdom of Koguryo began in territory that is now China, although hundreds of grave mounds have also been recorded south of the boundary river. After the fall of the Lelang colony, Koguryo established a new capital in Pyongyang, the present capital of North Korea as well. Burial mounds dot the hillsides nearby. It is one of these mounds that is purported to be the grave of Tangun. Since the earlier Koguryo capitals are found within the present boundaries of China, the official Chinese position is that Koguryo (Kaoguli in Chinese) was a Chinese kingdom, not a Korean one (Pak 1999).

A few joint excavations with Chinese and North Korean archaeologists took place in the Liaodong peninsula. However, problems of publication arose, and joint excavations have not been continued. These sites, being close to the Korean penin-sula, were of great interest in both Koreas, and it is a pity that more such cooper-ative archaeology ventures did not occur.

More European than American scholars have been permitted to visit North Korea. Eastern Europeans have been particularly welcomed. Visitors to the north are increasing, so that there will soon be a guidebook to museums and archaeo-logical sites in North Korea written in English. Some official exchanges with other archaeologists in the region have occurred, especially with archaeologists from Vladivostok in the Russian Far East. Similar Neolithic sites along the coast of the East Sea (called Sea of Japan on many English-language maps) have made this a productive exchange of information, but sites have not been excavated jointly.

Post-Korean War in South Korea

Although the American military government in the south helped re-establish the National Museum in Seoul and sponsored two excavations of Silla tombs, the inva-sion from the north temporarily put an end to such cultural interests. Interested members of the American military did report on some archaeological discoveries, however. One, Howard MacCord, noted the remains of houses and artifacts while digging foxholes near Chunchon, northeast of Seoul. After the truce, David Chase, another soldier stationed in Korea, reported on a survey of a stretch of the Han River conducted jointly with the National Museum. Chester Chard sent two of his students to South Korea in 1962 to survey and the next year to excavate at

Tongsamdong (Sample 1974; Sample and Mohr 1964). Greg Bowen, stationed near the demilitarized zone (DMZ), discovered a hand-axe from the Paleolithic site of Chonggongni while picnicking along the Hantan River in 1978. But on the whole Americans in Korea did not concern themselves with archaeology.

A few south Koreans became the "grandfathers" of Korean archaeology by earning doctorates abroad. Two prominent figures were Kim Won-yong and Sohn Pow-Key, both of whom earned Ph.D.s from American universities in the early days. However, neither of them studied archaeology. Kim earned his doctorate from New York University in Art History, and Sohn at University of California at Berkeley in History. Both returned to Korea and established lineages of graduate students who are still active in Korean archaeology, Kim at Seoul National University and Sohn at Yonsei University. Hwang Yong-hoon studied archaeology in Denmark and returned to found the archaeology department at Kyunghee University, and others went to England and France. Archaeology in South Korea thus tended to be eclectic with the first generation of trained archaeologists, and that tradition has continued to the present, with younger archaeologists having Ph.D.s from a dozen or so different American universities as well as others, especially Cambridge.

In spite of a fierce determination to do archaeology without foreign influence, the archaeologists in Korea welcomed Richard Pearson (Pearson and Im 1968) and were extraordinarily helpful to me when I arrived in 1970 with a recent MA from the University of Michigan and an interest in Korean archaeology. Two foreign dissertations came out of archaeological work in Korea in the early 1970s – Alex Townsend's (1975) and my own (Nelson 1973). Thus it would be quite unfair to say that foreigners were not welcome, but it is appropriate to note that foreigners who were overly dogmatic about their own perspectives were referred to as "emperors" behind their backs.

In the 1970s, new archaeological journals were founded, and archaeological societies were begun and flourished beginning in the 1970s and 1980s. Annual meetings put the archaeology on a professional footing. Archaeological departments were founded in most of the state universities, and most departments have a museum.

Museums and the Office of Cultural Properties also became training grounds for South Korean archaeologists. With industrialization and urbanization moving swiftly, survey and excavation work for archaeologists exceeded the number of trained archaeologists. For example, the city of Seoul doubled in size between 1970 and 1985, going from four-and-a-half million to nine million people in 15 years. When I was there in 1970–1, half of the city lacked piped-in water and sewage mains, but more people crowded in daily, erecting temporary shelters around doors and windows salvaged from their previous homes. Sites that were in the countryside in 1970, reachable only by dirt roads that sometimes resembled stream beds, had already been incorporated into the city of Seoul by 1978 when I next returned.

In the 1970s and 1980s, a generation of Korean archaeologists learned field methods from work they did surveying huge areas which would be inundated under lakes, for which dams were being constructed. The amount of information generated was overwhelming, hard for anyone to digest and synthesize. Leading up to the Seoul Olympics in 1988, the activity near Seoul was frenetic. Even fortresses from the Three Kingdoms period were discovered and excavated, as well as tombs, enlarging the understanding of that period by leaps and bounds.

Rapprochement

A fervent wish in South Korea is for reunification of the two Koreas. Many initiatives have begun, with the hope of this desired outcome. For example, some tourism from South Korea has been allowed into the Diamond Mountains, a scenic area not far north of the DMZ. The sightseers go by boat from the south, and must spend nights on the boat. They are not allowed to make any personal contacts with North Koreans.

Contacts between archaeologists of the north and south have also been established. A prominent South Korean archaeologist journeyed to Pyongyang recently, and was shown sites and museums. Joint conferences were discussed, to be held in both Pyongyang and Seoul.

Archaeology in the two Koreas has made considerable progress in the last half-century. When joint meetings can be held, and differences in approaches frankly discussed, it will be a great day for archaeology in the Korean peninsula.

REFERENCES

Arimitsu Kyoichi 1996 Archaeology and Museums in Korea between 1945 and 1946: A Personal Account. Han'guk Kogo Hakbo 34:7–27 (in Korean).

Bishop, Isabella Bird 1898[1970] Korea and her Neighbors. London: John Murray. Reprinted by Yonsei University Press, Seoul.

Chard, Chester 1960 Neolithic Archaeology in North Korea. Asian Perspectives 4:151–155.

Crawford, Gary, and Gyoung-Ah Lee 2003 Agricultural Origins in the Korean Peninsula. Antiquity 77:87–95.

FLPH (Foreign Languages Publishing House) 1977 The Outline of Korean History (Until August 1945). Pyongyang: Foreign Languages Publishing House.

Fujita Ryosaku 1933 Chosen Kokugaku Ryakushi (Historical sketch of the archaeology of Korea). Dolmen 4:13–17.

Grayson, James H. 1977 Mimana, a Problem in Korean Historiography. Korea Journal 7(8):65–69.

Henthorn, William E. 1966 Recent Archaeological Activity in North Korea (I): The Cave at Misongni. Asian Perspectives 9:73–78.

—— 1968 Recent Archaeological Activity in North Korea (II): The Shellmound at Sopo-hang. Asian Perspectives 11:1–18.

Hong, Wontaek 1988 Relationship between Korea and Japan in Early Period: Paekche and Yamato Wa. Seoul: Ilsimsa.

—— 1994 Paekche of Korea and the Origin of Yamato Japan. Seoul: Kudara International.

Kang, Hugh 2001 The Historiography of the Kwanggaet'o Stele. In History, Language, and Culture in Korea. Youngsoon Pak and Jaehoon Yeon, eds. Pp. 28–42. London: Saffron Press.

Movius, Hallam 1948 The Lower Paleolithic Cultures of South and East Asia. Transactions of the American Philosophical Society 38:329–420.

Nelson, Sarah M. 1973 Chulmun Period Villages on the Han River in Korea: Subsistence and Settlement. Ph.D. Dissertation, University of Michigan.

—— 1992 Korean Archaeological Sequences from the First Ceramics to the Introduction of Iron. In Chronologies in Old World Archaeology, vols I. and II. Robert W. Ehrich, ed. Vol. I pp. 430–38, vol. II pp. 418–24.

—— 1993 The Archaeology of Korea. Cambridge: Cambridge University Press.

—— 1995 The Politics of Ethnicity in Prehistoric Korea. In Nationalism, Politics, and the Practice of Archaeology. Philip L. Kohl and Claire Fawcett, eds. Pp. 218–31. Cambridge: Cambridge University Press.

—— 1997 The Archaeology of Northeast China: Beyond the Great Wall. London: Routledge.

—— 1998 Bound Hair and Confucianism in Korea. In Hair, Its Power and Meaning in Asian Cultures. Alf Hiltbeitel and Barbara Diane Miller, eds. Pp. 105–121. Albany: SUNY Press.

—— 1999 Megalithic Monuments and the Introduction of Rice into Korea. In The Prehistory of Food, Appetites for Change. Chris Gosden and Jon Hather, eds. London: Routledge.

Osgood, Cornelius 1954 Koreans and Their Culture. Tokyo: Charles E. Tuttle Co.

Pai, Hyung Il 1994 The Politics of Korea's Past: The Legacy of Japanese Colonial Archaeology in the Korean Peninsula. East Asian History 7:25–48.

—— 1999 The Colonial Origins of Korea's Collected Past. In Nationalism and the Construction of Korean Identity. Hyung Il Pai and Tim Tangherini, eds. Pp. 13–32. Korean Research Monograph Series. Berkeley: Center for Korean Studies, University of California.

—— 2000 Constructing "Korean" Origins. A Critical Review of Archaeology, Historiography and Racial Myth in Korean State-Formation Theories. Cambridge: Harvard University Press.

Pai, Hyung Il, and Timothy R. Tangherlini 1998 Nationalism and the Construction of Korean Identity. Korean Research Monograph 26. Berkeley: Institute of East Asian Studies.

Pak, Yangjin 1999 Contested Ethnicities and Ancient Homelands in Northeast China Archaeology: The Case of Koguryo and Puyo Archaeology. Antiquity 73:613–18.

Pearson, Richard J., and Im Hyo-jai 1968 Preliminary Archaeological Research on Cheju Island, Korea. Proceedings of the VII International Congress of Anthropological and Ethnographic Sciences 3:199–204.

Sample, Lillie Laetitia 1974 Tongsamdong: A Contribution to Korean Neolithic Culture History. Arctic Anthropology 11(2):1–125.

Sample, Lillie Laetitia, and Albert Mohr 1964 Progress Report on Archaeological Research in the Republic of Korea. Arctic Anthropology 2:99–104.

Townsend, Alex 1975 Cultural Evolution during the Neolithic Period in West Central Korea. Ph.D. Dissertation, University of Hawaii.

Yi Seonbok, Lee Kyodong, and Shin Jong-Won 1989 Bibliography of North Korean Archeology, Hanguk Kogohak 23:94–217.

FURTHER READING

Barnes, Gina L. State Formation in Korea. London: Curzon.

Kim, Jeong-hak 1972 The Prehistory of Kore. R. J. Pearson and K. Pearson, translators and eds. Honolulu: University of Hawaii Press.

Kim, Won-yong 1983 Recent Archaeological Discoveries in the Republic of Korea. Paris:
    UNESCO.
—— 1986 Art and Archaeology of Ancient Korea. Seoul: Taekwang Publishing Co.
Nelson, Sarah M. 2003 Korean Social Archaeology. Seoul: Jipmoon Press.
Pai, Hyung Il 1999 Japanese Anthropology and the Discovery of Prehistoric Korea. Journal
    of East Asian Archaeology 1:353–82.
—— 1999 Nationalism and Preserving Korea's Buried Past: The Office of Cultural Proper-
    ties and Archaeological Heritage Management in South Korea. Antiquity 73:619–25.

4

Self-Identification in the Modern and Post-Modern World and Archaeological Research: A Case Study from Japan

Koji Mizoguchi

Japanese later prehistory, dating roughly from 12,000 B.P. to A.D. 700, is commonly divided into three periods: Jomon, Yayoi, and Kofun (also see Crawford and Underhill, and Habu, this volume). Briefly stated, the Jomon (ca. 12,000 B.P.–400 B.C.) was a hunter-gatherer society; the Yayoi (ca. 400 B.C.–A.D. 250/300), an agrarian society that saw the initial development of social complexity and stratification; and the Kofun (ca. A.D. 250/300–600), a complex agrarian society that witnessed the construction of monumental keyhole-shaped tumuli and the foundations of an early state (e.g., Barnes 1993; Imamura 1996; Tsuboi 1992).

Interestingly, archaeological studies of these three periods have constituted three distinct domains, each of which has its own spatiality and is reproduced by drawing upon a distinct set of structuring principles. In that sense, these domains may be called "discursive spaces:" they played, and continue to play, a distinct role in self-identification in contemporary Japan (see Table 4.1). Here, "discursive space" is meant as a certain way of interpreting, discussing, and describing something – in this case, people's lives in a period in the past – that is inseparably connected to a certain set of material items – in this case, archaeological sites, features, artifacts, and the like reconstructed and represented in museums and in the form of publications and so on. Archaeology helps people form a cultural identity in Japan (e.g., Fawcett 1996) that seeks and praises Japan's uniqueness in terms of qualities such as harmony, cooperation, vertical social structure, and nonverbal communication. In this discourse, such qualities exist only in Japan (Fawcett 1996:74–5). However, the underpinning of the link between archaeology and Japanese identity is much more complicated. Not only is the linkage multifaceted, but it is also related to the spatio-temporal differences which the Japanese have experienced since the inception of their modernity.

Table 4.1. Three "archaeologies" and their characteristics

Archaeological period and dates	Discursive characteristics
Jomon (Hunter-Gatherer/Band-Tribal Society): ca. 12,000 B.P. (uncalibrated C14 dates)–500/400 B.C. (see below)	Eastern Japan-centered; archaeology of the domestic/shamanistic; articulated to female images epitomized by clay figurines; study of the origin of a "different" Japan (in contrast to agrarian Japan); affinity to Processual approaches
Yayoi (rice paddy-field agriculturalist/Tribal-chiefdom society): ca. 500/400 B.C.–250/300 A.D. (dated by datable artifacts shared with/imported from mainland Asia)	Western Japan-centered; archaeology of the political; articulated to male images epitomized by metal weapons/combat-related ritual items; study of the origin of agrarian Japan; affinity to Marxist/Post-processual approaches
Kofun (chiefdom-early state society): ca. 250/300 A.D. (see above)–600 A.D. (dated by written sources)	Study of imperial genealogy; affinity to Marxist/Post-processual approaches

Archaeological practice tries to make sense of the past and communicates this past in the present (e.g., Shanks and Tilley 1987a:7–28). We choose what to make sense of, and how to talk and write in order to make sense of it. And, by doing so, we identify what we are: we draw upon our experience and predict the outcome, and by monitoring the outcome we see how similar or different we and the others are, and decide how to act in future. In that sense, archaeology constitutes a field of self-identification, as do other domains of communicative action. It is natural to assume that the distinct discursive spaces – which the archaeological studies of the Jomon, Yayoi, and Kofun periods constitute – reflect three distinct axes of self-identification that coexist in contemporary Japanese society.

In this chapter, I will show how these axes of self-identification are interconnected to three distinct features of the discursive space of postwar Japan. Those features were shaped through the experience of the catastrophe brought about by the war and that of the subsequent Cold War. Situated in the Cold War equilibrium of politico-economic systems as a frontline nation against the Soviet Union, Japan was provided economic as well as militaristic protection by the United States, and enjoyed unprecedented economic growth. This historically contingent condition allowed some significant problems – notably the emperor system, regarded by many as having led to the devastation of World War II – to remain intact. Japan had to undergo rapid socioeconomic reconstruction from the ashes in order to function as a strategically important ally of the U.S. and Western Block. To ensure this was achieved, the emperor system (which had functioned to maintain the integration and order of pre-World-War-II Japanese society) had to be preserved (Mizoguchi, 2004). Naturally, critiques of the emperor system, whose legitimacy was heavily reliant upon the narratives of the continuity of the imperial genealogy from the deepest past in Japanese history, formed an important element of postwar Japanese archaeology. Archaeological research on the Yayoi and Kofun periods, which were characterized by increasing social complexity, social stratification, and the emergence of a supreme chief who was regarded as the predecessor of the ancient emperors, was expected to play a crucial role in the critique. Effectively, a significant objective of the study of the Yayoi and Kofun periods was to seek the roots of the ills of Japan that were yet to be overcome. In contrast, the Jomon period was tacitly regarded as the prehistory of Japan that preceded the imperial geneal-ogy and what are viewed as the Japanese people. In that sense, Jomon studies were regarded as irrelevant to understanding the ills of Japanese society. These different meanings attached to the Jomon, Yayoi, and Kofun periods constituted the charac-teristics of the three discursive spaces and their positionality in the general discur-sive space of postwar Japan.

What follows will also touch upon a phase – which began in the 1970s and con-tinues today – during which the conditions that supported the relative stability of the discursive space of postwar Japan are being eroded (Osawa 1998; Mizoguchi 2004). If we characterize the phase between the foundation of the modern Japanese nation-state in 1867 (the Meiji Restoration) and the 1970s as "the Modernity of Japan," the phase from the 1970s through to today would be characterized as the high-/late-/post-Modernity of Japan. It is during this time that the general discur-sive space of Japan is being fragmented – as is, naturally, the archaeological dis-cursive space embedded in it – and the self-identification of the Japanese people, including archaeologists, is facing an unprecedented challenge.

This chapter describes the character and transformation of the three archaeolo-gies, and seeks to elucidate both universal and unique aspects of the experience Japanese archaeology has undergone in the maturation of Modernity and the tran-sition to high-/late-/post-Modernity. In what follows, I do not impose artificial divi-sions between scholastic and popular discourse. Both are firmly embedded in the discursive space of contemporary society, and despite their different appearances, are structurally identical and constitute one another's content and state.

The Three Archaeological and Self-Images of the Japanese

Jomon archaeology/discursive space

The Jomon period, widely known by its very early use of pottery, began around 12,000 B.P. and ended around 400 B.C. (Imamura 1996:53–126; Mizoguchi 2002:49–115; Takahashi, Toizumi, and Kojo 1998). Despite its lengthy duration (perhaps the longest single archaeological age in world prehistory), the Jomon period is dominantly defined by its culture or "lifeways," not its society or history. How the Jomon hunter-gatherers acquired their foodstuffs, clothed themselves, buried their dead, and prayed for good fortune to natural spirits and ancestors has been the subject of detailed, and importantly synchronic, "reconstruction" (e.g., Izumi 1996). Despite having an enormously detailed pottery-based chronology, the period has never quite been historicized. Rather, the Jomon period tends to be treated in a tacit way as the "timeless past," either as a time that preceded the dawn of history of the "Japanese" and "Japaneseness" or a time when the authentic essence of Japaneseness was born.

The image of the timeless, static Jomon derives from two factors. First, the pace of social change and transformation in the Jomon period was much slower and more gradual than that in the Yayoi and Kofun periods. Second, the way in which Jomon archaeology is situated in the discursive space of Japanese archaeology, which has been formed through the history of the modernity of Japan, contributes to its perception as timeless and static in contrast to the historical, dynamic Yayoi and Kofun.

Previous reviews of Jomon archaeology illustrate how the Jomon sequence was in fact punctuated by "historical" episodes suggesting significant changes in the way society was organized and structured. Two significant episodes vividly illustrate the dynamism of Jomon history. The first is the later Initial Jomon, with the beginning of a sedentary way of life, and the emergence of stable, substantial settlements with a distinctive circular layout showing traces of long-term occupation (also see Underhill and Habu, this volume). The second is the Middle/Late Jomon, with the development of social integration, reflected by the formation of regional ritual centers located at roughly equal intervals through wide areas of the archipelago.

Most research on the later Initial and Middle/Late Jomon, however, has so far stopped short of situating them in their unique historical contexts or in a long-term transformational perspective. Instead, ranges of characteristics and traits are extracted from each of these historical phenomena, are given niches in a synchronic system of meanings, and are treated as the essences of "Jomon-ness," and hence, in some cases, the essence of Japaneseness. For example, Michio Okamura characterizes the Jomon "culture" by the traits he regards as significant in comparison to the "traditional Japanese way of life" (Okamura 1996:77–80). The Jomon culture is, in this case, tacitly recognized as the root of the traditional Japanese way of life and characterized as a timeless entity. The jacket of Okamura's recent book also bears the phrase: "the roots of our life reside here" (Okamura 2000), where "our life" is the traditional Japanese way of life, and "here" is (the synchronic discursive space of) the Jomon period. This synchronization of traits, originally embedded in a diachronic process and in constant transformation, constitutes one of the significant principles on which the reproduction of the discursive space of Jomon archaeology draws.

This habituated ignorance of history – in other words, the de-historicization of the Jomon period – seems to derive, partially but significantly, from the following historically contingent factors. Until the end of World War II, it was taken for granted, at least on the surface, that a new population, which was to become the ancestors of the imperial family and the Japanese people, arrived on the archipelago and either replaced or assimilated the aboriginal population (cf. Oguma 1995: Chapter 5; Teshigawara 1995:47). (To what extent this, as well as other historical narratives related to imperial mythology, was sincerely believed as historical fact is problematic, but it was treated as such. See Teshigawara 1995:78–9.) The population, speculated from the mythological description of the imperial chronicles Kojiki and Nihonshoki (cf. Aston 1972), brought with them agriculture, metallurgy, and other developed technologies. Therefore, the stone age people who left behind Jomon cultural remains were recognized as the indigenous population of Japan who persisted until the end of the Kofun period along its fringes (Teshigawara 1995:139). Until the establishment of the nationwide pottery chronological system in the 1930s (cf. Teshigawara 1995:134–43), the Jomon period was considered prehistoric (i.e., before the foundation of the imperial genealogy) and thereby excluded from the domain of historical research. Besides, the Jomon culture, in that paradigm, was the culture of the Other in the same way that the culture of the subsequent periods was the culture of the Same, i.e., the rice agriculture-based, "Japanese" culture. This division and the positionality attached to the Jomon archaeology in the prewar era of Japanese archaeology, as illustrated later, continue to function and influence the way the discursive space of contemporary Japanese archaeology is structured.

This constituted a significant background against which the strong inclination toward the synchronic reconstruction of lifeways is founded. Some constitutive elements of Euroamerican processual archaeology, such as the application of the "middle-range" research strategy and systemic thinking, also characterize conventional research on the Jomon period. This formed the background against which both the autonomous development and the introduction of the processual methods and perspectives took place relatively easily in the Jomon discourse. Site-catchment analysis is a notable example (e.g., Akazawa and Aikens 1986).

The above-mentioned factors can be arranged into sets of dichotomies that establish the boundary separating the discursive space of Jomon archaeology from that of the subsequent Yayoi period.

Jomon	Yayoi
static (timeless)	dynamic (historical)
pre-history of the Japanese	history of the Japanese
Other	Same
Nature	Culture

The Yayoi period, as the period that witnessed the introduction and establishment of rice agriculture-based lifeways, has long been regarded as the period when the basic elements of the Japanese way of life and the essence of the Japanese mentality were formed (e.g., Takakura 1995:13–15; Watsuji 1951:47–56). This perception, in addition to the factors mentioned above, has resulted in the Jomon period being treated as the "pre"-history of the Japanese, and hence, as the pool of non-historic, i.e., cyclical/repetitive, matters such as domestic and shamanistic activities.

The functions of symbolic items of the Jomon material culture tend to be understood in relation to the domestic or shamanistic. This contrasts with their Yayoi counterparts, whose functions are always connected to the political and economic. Clay figurines, whose mysterious appearance renders them as quintessentially Jomon, are understood to have been mobilized in rituals for the fertility and regeneration of subsistence resources by metaphorically referring to the childbearing ability of the female (Isomae 1987). However, in a number of cases, vast quantities of figurines were amassed, deliberately smashed, and deposited in ceremonial gatherings (e.g., Yamagata 1992). This normally leads to a range of possible interpretations, one being that rituals regularly conducted by mobilizing clay figurines at what were apparently regional ceremonial centers had political as well as shamanistic/religious purposes: the mobilization of clay figurines would have enhanced, structured, and reproduced intra- and intercommunal ties somewhat unintentionally through the mediation of ritual communication among those who gathered from a wider domain than that of a daily encounter.

Yayoi ritual items such as bronze bells, which from our modern perspective are as mysterious in their appearance and usage as Jomon clay figurines, are commonly interpreted as having functioned as political items. They are understood to have been strategically mobilized, that is, displayed at politico-ceremonial occasions (e.g., Fukunaga 1998:236–9) and deposited for the maintenance and enhancement of hierarchy, power, and intra- and intercommunal ties (Kobayashi 1967:208–35).

It should also be noted that the Jomon clay figurines are often analyzed as generally depicting female figures (e.g., Imafuku 1999:90; Isomae 1987), despite the fact that many of them cannot be sexed (Kobayashi 1990:15–16). What is contrasted to the strategic nature of the Yayoi knowledge here is the Jomon ritual knowledge that is literally "embodied" in the sexed body of the figurines. Combined with the fact that many Yayoi symbolic items are weapon-shaped, and hence easily linked to male activities, one might form further sets of dichotomies such as the following:

Jomon	Yayoi
female	male
figurines	bronze (weapon-shaped) ritual items
domestic/shamanistic	political
embodied knowledge	strategic knowledge

Various symbols of the sexes existed in the Jomon period, many of which depicted the male sexual organ (the so-called stone clubs or rods known as *sekibo* in Japanese (see Yamamoto 1995). Some depicted male and female sexual organs in one. Referring to these facts, some might say that it is overstated to say that the dichotomies between Jomon and Yayoi and between female and male constitute the boundary of Jomon discursive space. However, it appears undeniable that much more attention has been placed upon Jomon clay figurines in the representation of the Jomon in various media than on other Jomon symbolic items depicting sexual organs or sex characteristics. This attention has, to a considerable extent, been derived from the sex/gender of the figurines. Even if the contribution of the dichotomies between Jomon and Yayoi and between female and male to the boundary formation of Jomon discursive space were rejected, it would be accepted that the dichotomies between Jomon and Yayoi and between embodied and strategic knowledge and experience significantly constitute the boundary of Jomon discursive space.

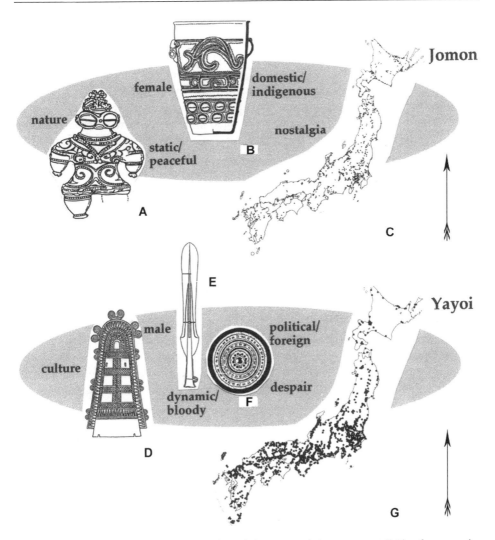

Figure 4.1 Linkage between the Jomon–Yayoi dichotomy and the east–west divide of present-day Japan. Note the dense distribution of Jomon sites in Eastern Japan (C) and Yayoi sites in Western Japan (G). (A: clay figurine after Ono et al. 1992:3; B: Jomon (Katsusaka style) pottery after Ono et al. 1992:53; C: Ono et al. 1992:84; D (bronze bell); and E (bronze spearhead-shaped ritual implement): Ono et al. 1992:143; F: imported early Han bronze mirror after Ono et al. 1992:138; G: Ono et al. 1992:131.)

Shifting our focus to spatiality, we can see that Jomon and Yayoi discursive spaces form distinct "stations" in the daily life of contemporary Japanese (see Figure 4.1). These stations are not only bounded by material media/residues of the practice of people in those periods and images attached to them, but also by actual spatial differences in contemporary society. While the majority of major Jomon sites with either monumental structures or reconstructed features (e.g., the San'naimaruyama site of Aomori, the Oyu site of Akita) are located in eastern Japan, most major Yayoi sites (e.g., the Yoshinogari of Saga, Ikegami-Sone sites of Osaka) are located in western Japan. This geographic division is partly related to real differences in the sociohistorical processes that structured society in those periods, but the fact in contemporary Japan that visible/visualized (by site reconstruction) traces of the life of the Jomon and Yayoi periods mark such a clear division between eastern and western Japan constitutes a firm base for the reality of the boundary between those stations. Moreover, this reality constitutes an epistemological base for the significance of those stations in the self-identification of contemporary Japanese.

The interconnected discursive layers of the Jomon–Yayoi division are, importantly, embedded in the East–West division constituted by the uneven distribution of wealth and social capital of modern Japan (Figure 4.1). The East, particularly the Tohoku (northeast) region, has suffered from a lack of commercial and industrial investment and from the long-term decline in rice growing which is, quite ironically (considering that rice growing was the definitive trait of the Yayoi sociocultural complex), the main source of wealth in the region. As the economic growth of postwar Japan has stagnated, it is only natural that the somewhat systemic interdependence between those discursive spaces should be changing. This is influenced by the profound changes affecting the value attached to the experience of those discursive spaces and to the discursive spaces themselves (cf. Akasaka 1996).

In these interconnections of Jomon and Yayoi discursive spaces, Jomon-related items and characters, regardless of material or imagery, have been negatively valued, while their Yayoi counterparts have been accorded positive meanings. It is widely accepted that the Japanese have toiled to achieve success in the postwar topography of international relations and the distribution of wealth by acquiring technologies and ideas from abroad, refining them, and re-exporting them. Economic success, which the majority of Japanese regard as characterizing postwar Japan as a nation-state, is widely believed to have been achieved by the intrinsic diligence of the Japanese, long nurtured through their involvement in labor-intensive rice paddy-field agriculture and by their diligent copying and refining of imported ideas (cf. Sahara 1987:328–30, esp. 329). A parallel between this and the characterization of the Yayoi period, constituted through the reproduction of the Yayoi discursive space, is obvious: the Yayoi discursive space has been the space in which the economic success of postwar Japan, most significantly enjoyed in the areas west of Tokyo, is assigned a cause and in which both the good and bad consequences of that success are determined in a generally positive manner. A commonly shared, but not necessarily explicitly expressed, feeling would be: "Although a number of mistakes have been made, we have achieved affluence and a measure of respect in the international community after a number of years of struggle diligently learning things from abroad and trying to make them better, as our Yayoi ancestors did."

Currently, however, the picture is changing. The kind of Jomon image now gaining popularity is, in a way, the mirror image of postwar Japan. Many traits, such as those mentioned above, long regarded as constituting the backbone of the success of postwar Japan, have become the targets of serious doubts amid the current economic difficulties; many of these traits have often been linked to the characteristics of the Yayoi culture. The appeal of Jomon-ness, signified by those on the opposite side of their Yayoi counterparts in the above-illustrated dichotomies, is currently growing (e.g., Akasaka 2000; Okamura 2000:118–29, 336–7).

Jomon	Yayoi
Eastern Japan	Western Japan
nostalgia	despair

An intriguing element of the growing interest in the Jomon period and Jomon-ness is that this phenomenon is related to changing public attitudes to the body and the mind. When Jomon-ness is depicted in such media as exhibition brochures and popular books (e.g., Organizing Committee of Jomon World '96, 1996), it is the embodied nature of Jomon knowledge and technology that is repeatedly emphasized. The embodied nature of Jomon knowledge and the foreign, hence discursive (because it has to be translated), hence modern (because modernity was imported into Japan in the wake of the Meiji Restoration, 1867) nature of Yayoi knowledge are rarely subject to explicit contrast, but the embeddedness of Jomon subsistence activities in the body of nature, often tacitly connected to the image of Jomon clay figurines such as the Japanese "mother goddess" (see, e.g., Isomae 1987), is often contrasted with destructive intervention in the body of nature by the Yayoi agriculturists.

Just as colonial encounters were often depicted as an encounter between a fully attired male figure and a naked female figure (see, e.g., Gregory 1994:124–33), Jomon-ness, it seems to me, has begun to be connected to the female body, into which Yayoi-ness, which has traditionally been linked to male images, has penetrated. Interestingly, one prominent theory on the emergence of the Yayoi agrarian society argues that a group of males introduced a wet rice agriculture-related sociotechnological complex from the Korean peninsula and married Jomon women (e.g., Komoto 1982). In this theory, this Korean/Yayoi male and Japanese/Jomon female union explains the persistence of many Jomon pottery traits into the initial/early Yayoi period. Such a scenario is unique in the discursive space of traditional modern Japan, in which masculinity plays such an important role. This approach adds a new layer of gender-related dichotomous contrasts to the archaeology-related discursive space of modern Japan, as follows:

Jomon	Yayoi
Eastern Japan	Western Japan
(female) body	(male) mind
(mother	father) (?)
idyllic	evil
nostalgia	despair
remedy for modernity	ills of modernity

Moreover, the increasing emphasis on the left-hand side of the dichotomies, I would argue, is further related to the coming of the social condition that can be described as high-/late-/post-Modern, to which we will return later. This attempt at mapping meanings and images in the archaeology-related discursive space of modern Japan can be carried on endlessly, but I will stop here. However, it should be noted that this discursive space, seen through the boundary between the Jomon and Yayoi, is multilayered; each layer constitutes, is embedded in, or is supported by its spatiality and the changing psyche of the modern Japanese.

Yayoi archaeology

The archaeology of the Yayoi period dates roughly between 400 B.C. and A.D. 275/300 (Imamura 1996:147–96; Mizoguchi 2002). Yayoi archaeology emphasizes technological advancement, increasing social complexity, and the ideological concealment of growing social stratification. At the same time, Yayoi archaeology, as mentioned, has been tacitly regarded as the archaeology of the earliest stage in the history of Japan.

The Yayoi is associated with the beginning of systematic rice agriculture in the archipelago. It is also associated with a rapid population increase, the emergence of competition over the control of agricultural surpluses, and the rise of a contradiction between the desire for family ownership and tribal egalitarianism (e.g., Kondo 1983). These consequences of the introduction of rice agriculture are traditionally argued to have resulted in rapid social stratification. Drawing on these views, one can identify the two dominant axes of Yayoi studies: (1) the study of the process through which intra- and intercommunal relations became stratified; and (2) the study of the ways in which emerging relations of dominance were ideologically naturalized. These studies constitute a distinct discursive space and draw heavily upon a Marxist framework, which was initially developed during prewar years to reveal the roots of the historical process towards Japanese imperialism and the devastation as its consequence (Teshigawara 1995:214–18; 247–58, esp. 252–8; Wajima 1955, 1973). This sociohistorical background, against which the Yayoi discursive space originated, makes Yayoi studies intrinsically politically motivated. The rice agriculturalist-oriented perspective, which constituted the backbone of the above-mentioned Marxist framework, has been criticized by scholars such as Yoshihiko Amino (e.g., 1996) for its ignorance of nonagricultural populations that played a role as important as that of the rice agriculturalist population and for its tacit contribution to the reproduction of the singularity/homogeneity/purity myth; however, it remains very much at the core of Yayoi discursive space.

Within this broad Marxist framework, the Yayoi period was (and still tacitly is) regarded as having been the crucial period in Japanese history when the basic characteristics of the ancient Japanese state was formed. Characteristics of the Yayoi period are also believed to have influenced the subsequent long-term historical process toward the formation and collapse of modern imperial Japan (cf. Watabe [1931]1972). Therefore, the study of the Yayoi period, particularly for those who were determined to do something good for the reconstruction of Japan during the postwar years, was the study of the seeds of Japan's failure as a modern nation-state. Using a Marxist perspective, archaeologists believed that investigating the origins of social inequality during the Yayoi period was deeply significant. They sought to understand this historical event by employing evolutionary (developmental) stages from primitive communism through ancient slavery and feudalism to capitalism, and argued that understanding the Yayoi was particularly important for deciding what strategy should be taken to lead a socialist revolution in Japan. According to the communist doctrine of the time, the strategy of a given country's socialist revolution had to be decided according to the country's own historical trajectory (Watabe [1931]1972). This discursive characteristic of the Marxist theory, explaining the present in terms of the past, made its advocates feel that the ills of the present had their roots at certain points in the past. Critiques of the past became critiques of the present through Yayoi archaeology, which can be described as a precursor of the critical social archaeology that emerged in the West in the 1980s (e.g., Shanks and Tilley 1987a, b).

This constituted the background against which the Japanese rejected both processual and post-processual developments from the West. On the one hand, the Euroamerican processual archaeological package appeared anti-historical to Japanese Marxist archaeologists, and hence, apolitical and reactionary. On the other, the significant characteristic of the post-processual approach (with its emphasis on critical political self-awareness), appeared very familiar.

The diachronic study of social change characterizes Yayoi archaeology, in contrast to the way the synchronic study of lifeways characterizes Jomon archaeology. Political awareness constitutes a backbone of the Yayoi archaeology. In contrast, it is the descriptive–positivistic attitude, which encourages the construction of increasingly fine-grained pottery chronological systems and the reconstruction as to how a settlement would have looked like at one point in its history, for instance, that characterizes the Jomon archaeology. Alternately, reconstructing how a settlement would have looked at one point in its history, for instance, characterizes Yayoi archaeology.

Yayoi archaeology, however, has another element: it also functions as a field in which a self-image of the Japanese was constituted and reproduced. The Yayoi period witnessed the introduction of bronze and iron products and their production technology as well as rice paddy-field agriculture. Bronze weapons, initially brought in from the Korean peninsula, were copied in short order and modified to become nonutilitarian weapon-shaped ritual items (e.g., Iwanaga 1994). The image of importing foreign ideas and modifying them to "Japanese versions," as mentioned above, fits well with the self-image of the Japanese from the end of World War II to the end of the economic peak of the 1980s, when the Japanese, and the Yayoi, discursive space mirrored the self image of the successful postwar Japanese. The masculine work ethic of postwar Japan also nicely dovetailed with the discourse in which objects related to male activities (e.g., bronze and iron weapons, weapon-shaped ritual items, and agricultural tools) and occupied a significant niche in the domains of production and ideology as well as the archaeological evidence of the social life of the period.

The previous section investigated how this positive picture in the constitution of the identities of the modern Japanese has changed in recent years. Here, I would like to add another possible cause of the downfall of the profile of the Yayoi discursive space: the historicity of the Yayoi discourse itself. Yayoi archaeology is the study of the history of the Yayoi society; it is an archaeology of change, in which past individuals are depicted as either knowledgeable actors or structural dupes, the former making history by inventing new ideological strategies and the latter being cheated and not making history at all. There is no sense of togetherness, solidarity, or fixity here. Instead, division is depicted, and in a way glorified, in the discursive space as the engine that made history move forward.

In the Jomon discursive space, in contrast, Jomon knowledge is depicted as a unifying force that can only exist in the form of embodied knowledge. That body was shared by everyone, and hence was the same, universal, and bound fragmented identities together. The Yayoi discursive space, in this way, has come to be viewed as the embodiment of high-Modern competitive fragmentation, a symptom of modern corporate culture, and, as a systemic reaction to it, the Jomon discursive space is currently gaining ground.

Kofun archaeology

The archaeology of the Kofun period, between ca. A.D. 275/300 and 600 (Mizoguchi 2002:197–225) is the archaeology of politico-historical processes and core and periphery relations centered on the emergent chiefs of the Kinai region of central Honshu Island. It is believed, with certain public skepticism and reservation, that the genealogy of the imperial family can be traced back to them.

This period arguably witnessed the formation of the early state of Japan (cf. Tsude 1992). With the Marxist-oriented political motivation shared with Yayoi archaeology, Kofun archaeology has focused on how the ancestors of the imperial family came to obtain their despotic power and extend their domain of control as far as the southern part of Kyushu in the west and the Tohoku region of the northeastern part of Honshu in the east (Tsude 1992:81–5). The Kofun period is also the "proto-historic" period in Japanese history: Japanese as well as Chinese documentary data provide fragmentary, biased, but invaluable pieces of information on mostly political events of the period (e.g., Aston 1972). Both Chinese and Japanese documents are regarded as having been biased toward the interests of the political authorities who ordered their production, but they are believed at least to reflect some elements of what actually took place. The Japanese documents, namely the Kojiki and the Nihonshoki (Aston 1972), are the chronicles of events related to the "reigns" of the successive paramount chiefs of the "Yamato court," and each of their burial mounds is claimed by the Imperial Household Agency to have been accurately identified. These "imperial mausoleums" are under the protection and care of the agency, and public access is normally strictly forbidden. In reality, however, from the examination of datable artifacts, the dates of some of these mausoleums have turned out to be much earlier or much later than the recorded reigns of the paramount chiefs claimed by the agency to be buried in them (e.g., Morita 1996).

The main trend of the study of the period has been dominated by analysis of the mounded tombs (e.g., Kondo and Fujisawa 1966). It has been argued that politico-historical processes of the period (i.e., changes in the relationships between the paramount chiefs and regional chiefs) are reflected by the shape, size, and various other traits of the mounded tombs. The majority are shaped like keyholes, in which supreme and local chiefs of various levels are supposed to have been buried (Tsude 1992:70–3). It is widely accepted that most of the "prestigious" goods buried with local chiefs and the methods by which they were buried were invented by the para-mount chiefs and then redistributed to the hands of the local chiefs (e.g., Kobayashi 1967:306–35).

Therefore, the study of the Kofun period has been, and still very much is, the investigation of the genealogical roots of the imperial family and the genesis of their "despotic rules" of the archipelago. In fact, an established methodology in Kofun archaeology, tracing the sequence of the largest tumuli of the archipelago and of individual regional units (e.g., Shiraishi 1999), is firmly based upon this premise. The series of the largest tumuli of the archipelago, many of them imperial mau-soleums, is viewed as a materialized genealogy of the imperial family, and variations in their size are studied as a sensitive indicator of variations in the political power and authority of the successive emperors (Shiraishi 1999). The same is presumed to apply to the study of the sequence of the burial mounds of the successive chiefs of a regional unit.

This obsession with tracing the sequence of the largest tumuli as a materialized genealogy of the ancient emperors and that of regional chiefs leads to a tendency to overlook the nuanced interdependence between the chiefs and the "common-ers," without whom the gigantic keyhole-shaped tumuli could not have been built. It was tentatively calculated to have taken 2,000 people 15 years and 8 months to construct the largest keyhole-shaped tumulus designated by the Imperial House-hold Agency as the mausoleum of the Emperor Nintoku (Obayashigumi 1986). At the same time, the population occupying the archipelago is inferred to have been around 6 to 7 million (Hirose 2002:2). State institutions such as a standing army did not exist at the time, and hence coercion would not have been the cause of the mobilization of that amount of labor. It is thus highly unlikely that the largest keyhole-shaped tumuli could have been constructed without some sort of willing-ness on the side of the commoners to be mobilized for their construction (Hirose 2002:28–9).

However, the factors that would have played a crucial role in creating the men-tality that would have compelled commoners to voluntarily engage in the con-struction of gigantic keyhole-shaped tumuli are, with some notable exceptions (e.g., Hirose 2002:7–17; Kondo 1983:167–74), rarely investigated. Instead, the author-ity of the paramount and local chieftains is considered a given. Under this para-digm, the daily life of commoners, in which the mentality enabling the construction of gigantic keyhole-shaped tumuli would have been formed, tends to be given less attention than it deserves, and the expansion of the distributional horizon of the keyhole-shaped tumulus is regarded as reflecting the expansion of the internally homogeneous realm of the authority and dominance of the supreme chief. Most archaeological research on Kofun focuses on the chiefs rather than the commoners.

These elite are assumed to have embodied the homogeneous political order covering the archipelago except for the Okinawan Islands and the lands north of present-day Iwate prefecture, where no keyhole-shaped tumuli were built. In other words, the formation of the distributional horizon of the keyhole-shaped tumulus, in this paradigm, is regarded as marking the formation of an internally homogeneous socio-political entity that can be called a people or folk (cf. Tsude 1998:119–26). The thesis of the internal homogeneity of the distributional horizon of the keyhole-shaped tumuli has recently been called into question (e.g., Hojo et al. 2000). However, in a perception tacitly shared by scholars and the general public, the homogeneity thesis lives on, and accordingly the basic shape of the domain of the Japanese people, whose existence has been perceived by many to be embodied by the emperor, is regarded as having already fully come into being in the Kofun period.

Although the profile of the imperial family is low-key in the domain of daily life in contemporary Japan, it is still attributed a role in symbolizing the integration and unity of the Japanese nation. (The Constitution states that the emperor is the symbol of the integration of the nation.) Besides, imperial mausoleums constitute an imposing element in the mental landscape of ordinary Japanese; a picture of the largest imperial mausoleum, the mausoleum of Emperor Nintoku (as claimed by the Imperial Household Agency) is a regular feature of primary school and middle school textbooks, and gives pupils the impression of the mysterious (because the social processes which made its construction possible/necessary are never explained in the textbooks) force of the past as well as that of the ancient imperial family. In that sense, the Kofun archaeology/discursive space has been, and still is, the locale where various opinions about and sentiments for and against the emperor system – which has been an ideological pillar, in both positive and negative terms, of modern Japan (cf. Mizoguchi 2004) – collide, and for that very reason, the prohibition by the Imperial Household Agency of access to the "imperial mausoleums" continues to stir a huge public row.

Post-Modern Difficulties and Japanese Archaeology

Three period-specific discursive spaces coexist within the discursive space of postwar Japanese archaeology, and these have been embedded in the historical trajectory of postwar Japan. Each space has a unique spatiality and a unique repository of feeling, attitudes, and language that have mediated the way people identify themselves and acquire a sense of security in the volatile, rapidly changing topography of the contemporary life-world. Though the positionality of each of these discursive spaces in relation to the others has changed over time, they continue to function as stable frameworks for the self-identification of the Japanese.

Lately, however, this stability appears to have been shaken, and that inevitably affects the way archaeology is interconnected with society. Increasing complexity in the formation of capitalist society has led to increasing segmentation and differentiation of new discursive spaces, and the way in which self-identity is constituted has undergone a drastic transformation as a systemic reaction to it. Socially shared values and norms have become increasingly relativized and fragmented as the scale and durability of sharable domains of experience continue to shrink (cf. Bauman 2000), and one's identification with such presuppositions as stable jobs, predictable life-courses, and so on is becoming increasingly difficult (Bauman 2000). The institutionalization of cultural resource management can be understood as being a part of the ongoing process, and the problems that have resulted exemplify the difficulties that the above-mentioned phenomena – which are described as late-/high-/post-Modern – have brought about.

Following the dramatic increase in large-scale developments, cultural resource management units, usually attached to local education boards, began to be organized back in the late 1960s and early 1970s, and archaeology became a stable "job," a domain of expert knowledge. This resulted in a rise in professionalism, in which "pragmatic" concerns – that is, how to retrieve as much information as possible in rescue contexts rather than how to consider and describe the character and the importance of a site from a wider, theoretically informed perspective – were given priority.

Each rescue context requires strong personal commitment, which is often challenging both physically and mentally. Moreover, it creates a sense of deep personal attachment to the site and the unique local circumstances under which the site is being rescue-excavated, and renders the narrative created out of the excavation inevitably local, personal, and different. The officers conducting such a rescue excavation must excavate and identify features and artifacts belonging to various periods over the long – often very long – history of the site, must maintain good human relations among diggers, and must complete the excavation on time. In addition, they must be ruthless managers and be extremely knowledgeable. Many of them have a hard time oscillating between these two "social persona" – the ruthless manager and the knowledgeable archaeologist – and they inevitably resort to the sincerest solution: to excavate the site at hand in the best possible way and do nothing more.

It means that one just concentrates on everyday details and keeps oneself away from thinking about wider and abstract issues that may be addressed by the outcomes of the excavation. This has eroded the mentality of doing archaeology in the interests of posterity. Such a future-oriented inclination used to focus the intentions of individual archaeologists who worked in a domain yet to be professionalized. As illustrated in this chapter, the practice of archaeology (particularly in the Marxism-inspired Yayoi and Kofun discursive spaces) was about investigating the past for the construction of a better future, and archaeologists maintained a sense of undertaking a collective project by experiencing the reality of working to construct a socialist Japan.

Professionalization, ironically, has replaced the future-oriented mentality with a present, everyday-oriented one and led to the fragmentation of archaeology as a field of practice/praxis and the fragmentation of the identity of the archaeologist. Together with the erosion of the reality and persuasiveness of the Marxist project (cf. Mizoguchi 1997, 2004), the segmentation and differentiation of each excavation site as a field of the life-world experience has resulted in the fragmentation of the objective of the practice of archaeology, and many archaeologists, particularly those who worked in the domain of rescue archaeology, came to feel that they did not know what they were working for. And, in such a situation, it becomes difficult to maintain a sense of security in living in one's own life-world and maintaining one's identity.

It is natural for the fragmented self to seek transcendental entities. By comparing oneself to the transcendental (which is perceived to offer oneself as well as others their roots and existential base), one regains a stable self-identity. The inflation of the narratives of the extremes, such as the oldest and the largest in the archaeological discourse since the 1980s, can be understood as such a move, and it was this trend that gave rise to scientifically baseless theses such as that the "Jomon hunter-gatherer culture" had advanced enough to develop urban settlements such as the San'nai-Maruyama of Aomori prefecture and deserved to be called the Jomon "civilization" (Organizing Committee of the Jomon World '96 Exhibition 1996).

The increasing popularity of Jomon archaeology as the study of the roots of Japaneseness, as illustrated above (Akasaka 2000; Okamura 2000), can also be understood to be a systemic reaction to a situation. For the purpose of seeking an image that is difficult to fragment and relativize (i.e., the body), and the stable existential base (i.e., embodied knowledge), the Jomon discursive space, in comparison to the Yayoi and Kofun discursive spaces, is better suited. By indulging in this illusory act of mending a fragmented self-identity, people, including archaeologists, might be trying to cope with the above illustrated difficulties, which can be characterized as late-/high-/post-Modern difficulties.

Conclusions

This chapter has argued that archaeology, with its unique disciplinary characteristics of being embedded in materiality and spatiality, constitutes a unique discursive space in contemporary society in which people acquire their self-identity and sense of security of living in their life-world. The positionality of the archaeological discursive space within the general discursive formation of a given society, it has also been shown, changes as the structure of the latter changes through time.

In the case of Japanese archaeology, the archaeological discursive space is subdivided into three period-specific discursive spaces, each of which has functioned as a unique space and repository of resources for the self-identification of the modern Japanese. All Japanese have tried, and continue to try, to find the roots of something they recognize to be the source of their identity in one of those discursive spaces. The manner in which the theories and methods developed in the Western world are introduced and rejected has also been determined by the positionality of each of those discursive spaces, constituted through the unique historical trajectory of modern Japanese archaeology.

As the above-mentioned late-/high-/post-Modern difficulties – particularly the endless fragmentation and relativization of social values and norms – deepen, archaeology increasingly becomes mobilized for drawing dividing lines between groupings of various types, most often "ethnic identity"-based groupings. Those dividing lines, in actuality, tend to be drawn along the lines of the politico-economic disputes of the present. However, those lines, being connected to the past, are authenticated by and contribute to the perpetuation of conflicts and human misery. A fundamental problem with the effort to remedy the situation is that the act of drawing those dividing lines itself is a systemic reaction to the increasing difficulty of self-identification. We cannot live our social lives without knowing who we are, and self-identity and a feeling of security in living in a society are acquired by developing a connection to the history, that is, the narrative of the continuation, of society.

If we are to be sufficiently self-critical to avoid unwittingly committing ourselves to inflicting harm on others in the form of discrimination (by accepting the fateful interdependence between self-identification and the past), we archaeologists, who are directly reproducing discursive spaces for self-identification in the present, must theorize the way the interdependence between self-identification and the past is made fateful. The foregoing was such an attempt, and I hope it has shown the potential of the theorization and historicization of modern Japanese archaeology in investigating the nature of the fateful interdependence between archaeology and self-identification in the present.

REFERENCES

Akasaka, Norio 1996 Tohoku-gaku e (Towards the construction of the Tohoku studies) 1 and 2 (in Japanese). Tokyo: Sakuhinsha.
—— 2000 Tozai nanboku ko: Ikutsumono Nihon he (Of east–west/south–north divides: toward multi-faceted Japan) (in Japanese). Tokyo: Iwanami.
Akazawa, Takeru, and Melvin Aikens 1986 Prehistoric Hunter-Gatherers in Japan: New Research Methods. Bulletin of Tokyo University Museum, 27. Tokyo: University of Tokyo Press.
Amino, Yoshihiko 1996 Emperor, Rice and Commoners. In Multicultural Japan: Palaeolithic to Postmodern. Donald Denoon, Mark Hudson, Gavan McCormack, and Tessa Morris-Suzuki, eds. Pp. 235–44. Cambridge: Cambridge University Press.
Aston, W. G., trans. 1972 Nihongi: Chronicles of Japan from the Earliest Times to A.D. 697. Tokyo: Charles E. Tuttle Co.
Barnes, Gina L. 1993 China, Korea, and Japan: The Rise of Civilization in East Asia. London: Thames and Hudson.
Bauman, Zygmunt 2000 Liquid Modernity. Cambridge: Polity Press.
Fawcett, Clare 1996 Archaeology and Japanese Identity. In Multicultural Japan: Palaeolithic to Postmodern. Donald Denoon, Mark Hudson, Gavan McCormack, and Tessa Morris-Suzuki, eds. Pp. 60–77. Cambridge: Cambridge University Press.
Fukunaga, Shin'ya 1998 Dotaku kara dokyo e (From the bronze bells to bronze mirrors) (in Japanese). In Kodai kokka ha koshite umareta (The emergence of Japanese ancient state). Hiroshi Tsude, ed. Pp. 217–75. Tokyo: Kadokawa.

Gregory, Derek 1994 Geographic Imaginations. Oxford: Blackwell.

Hirose, Kazuo 2002 Zenpo-koen fun to Yamato seiken (The keyhole-shaped tumulus and the Yamato court) (in Japanese). *In* Nihon kodai oken no seiritsu (The formation of the ancient kingship of Japan). Kazuo Hirose and Yoshinao Kojita, eds. Pp. 1–31. Tokyo: Aoki.

Hojo, Yoshitaka, Koji Mizoguchi, and Y. Murakami Yasuyuki 2000 Kofun jidai zo wo minaosu (Social structure and social change in the formative phase of the mounded-tomb period of Japan: a new perspective) (in Japanese). Tokyo: Aoki.

Imafuku, Rikei 1999 Jomon bunka wo taigen suru dainino dogu (Jomon nonfunctional tools as the symbols of the Jomon culture) (in Japanese). *In* Saishin Jomon-gaku no sekai (Latest outcomes of Jomon studies). Tatsuo Kobayashi, ed. Pp. 84–95. Tokyo: Asahish-inbunsha.

Imamura, Keiji 1996 Prehistoric Japan: New Perspectives on Insular East Asia. Honolulu: University of Hawaii Press.

Isomae, Jun'ichi 1987 Dogu no yoho ni tsuite (The usage of Dogu clay figurines) (in Japanese). Kokogaku kenkyu (Quarterly of archaeological studies) 34(1):87–102.

Iwanaga, Shozo 1994 Nihon-retto san seido buki rui shutsugen no koko-gaku teki igi (Archaeological significance of the beginning of bronze weapon making in Japanese archipelago) (in Japanese). Kobunka danso (Journal of the society of Kyushu prehistoric and ancient culture studies) 33:37–60.

Izumi, Takura, ed. 1996 Jomon doki shutsugen (The emergence of the Jomon pottery) (in Japanese). Tokyo: Kodansha.

Kobayashi, Tatsuo, ed. 1990 Jomon dogu no sekai (The world of Jomon Dogu type clay figurines) (in Japanese). Kikan kokogaku (Archaeology quarterly) 30 (Special issue).

Kobayashi, Yukio 1967 Jyookoku no shutsugen (The emergence of the queendom [The Yamatai state]) (in Japanese). Tokyo: Bun'eido.

Komoto, Masayuki 1982 Yayoi bunka no keifu (Sociocultural ancestry of the Yayoi culture) (in Japanese). *In* Noko bunka to kodai shakai (Agrarian culture and ancient society). Anon., ed. Pp. 48–56. Tokyo: Yusankaku.

Kondo, Yoshiro 1983 Zenpo-koen-fun no jidai (The age of the keyhole-shaped tumuli) (in Japanese). Tokyo: Iwanami.

Kondo, Yoshiro, and Choji Fujisawa, eds. 1966 Nihon no koko-gaku (Archaeology of Japan) 1 and 2 (in Japanese). Tokyo: Kawadeshobo-shinsha.

Mizoguchi, Koji 1997 The Reproduction of Archaeological Discourse: The Case of Japan. Journal of European Archaeology 5(2):149–65.

—— 2002 An Archaeological History of Japan, 30,000 B.C. to A.D. 700. Philadelphia: University of Pennsylvania Press.

—— 2004 Modernity, Identity, and Archaeology. *In* A Companion to Social Archaeology. Lynn Meskell and Robert Preucel, eds. Oxford: Blackwell.

Morita, Katsuyuki 1996 Sin'ike-iseki (Shin'ike site) (in Japanese). *In* Dai 40 kai maizo-bunkazai kenkyu shukai: Kokogaku to jitsunendai (Proceedings of Japanese Association for Field Archaeology, the 40th annual meeting: approaches to chronometric dates in Japanese archaeology) 1. Meeting Organizing Committee, ed. Pp. 19–28. Takatsuki: Japanese Association for Field Archaeology.

Obayashigumi 1986 Fukugen to Koso: Rekishi kara mirai he (Reconstruction and imagination: from history to the future) (in Japanese). Tokyo: Tokyo-shoseki.

Oguma, E. 1995 Tanitsu-minzoku shinwa no kigen (The myth of the homogeneous nation) (in Japanese). Tokyo: Shin'yosha.

Okamura, Michio 1996 Jomon bunka toha nandaroka (What is the Jomon culture?) (in Japanese). *In* Jomon no tobira (The Jomon world '96). Organizing Committee of the Jomon World '96 Exhibition, ed. Pp. 72–81. Tokyo: Organizing Committee of the Jomon World '96.

—— 2000 Jomon no seikatsu-shi (The life of the Jomon people) (in Japanese). Tokyo: Kodansha.

Ono, Akira, Hideji Harunari, and Shizuo Oda, eds. 1992 Atlas of Japanese Archaeology (in Japanese). Tokyo: Tokyo University Press.

Organizing Committee of the Jomon World '96 Exhibition, ed. 1996 Jomon no tobira (The Jomon world '96). Tokyo: Organizing Committee of the Jomon World '96.

Osawa, Masachi 1998 Sengo no shiso kukan (The discursive space of post-world-war-II Japan) (in Japanese). Tokyo: Chikuma shobo.

Sahara, Makoto 1987 Taikei Nihon no rekishi 1: Nihonjin no tanjo (A new history of Japan) 1 (in Japanese). Tokyo: Shogakukan.

Shanks, Michael, and Christopher Tilley 1987a Re-Constructing Archaeology: Theory and Practice. Cambridge: Cambridge University Press.

—— 1987b Social Theory and Archaeology. Cambridge: Polity Press.

Shiraishi, Taichiro 1999 Kofun to Yamato seiken (The Kofun tumulus and the Yamato polity) (in Japanese). Tokyo: Bungeishunju.

Takahashi, Ryuzaburo, Takeshi Toizumi, and Yasushi Kojo 1998 Archaeological Studies of Japan: Current Studies of the Jomon Archaeology (in English). Nihon kokogaku (Journal of the Japanese Archaeological Association) 5:47–72.

Takakura, Hiroaki 1995 Kin'in kokka gun no jidai (The age of the states given golden seals from the Han Dynasty of China) (in Japanese). Tokyo: Aoki.

Teshigawara, Akira 1995 Nihon kokogaku no ayumi (A history of Japanese archaeology) (in Japanese). Tokyo: Meicho Shuppan.

Tsuboi, Kiyotari, ed. 1992 Archaeological Studies of Japan. Acta Asiatica: Bulletin of the Institute of Eastern Culture 63 (special issue).

Tsude, Hiroshi 1992 The Kofun period and State Formation. *In* Archaeological Studies of Japan. Theme issue. Acta Asiatica 63:64–86.

—— 1998 Kodai kokka no taido (The emergence of the ancient state of Japan) (in Japanese). Tokyo: Nihon hoso shuppan kyokai.

Wajima, Seiichi 1955 Hattatsu no shodankai (Stages in the development of Japanese archaeology). *In* Nihon kokogaku koza (Seminar in Japanese archaeology) 2. Tsugio Mikami, ed. Pp. 22–36. Tokyo: Kawade shobo.

—— 1973 Nihon kokogaku no hattatsu to kagaku teki seishin (The development of Japanese archaeology and scientific attitude) (in Japanese). Okayama: Publication committee.

Watabe, Yoshimichi 1972[1931] Nihon genshi-kyosan shakai no seisan oyobi seisanryoku no hatten (Productive activities of Japanese primitive communistic societies and the development of the force of production) (in Japanese). *In* Rekishi kagaku taikei (Important works in Japanese historical science) 1. Hidesaburo Hara, ed. Pp. 121–59. Tokyo: Azekura Shobo.

Watsuji, Tetsuro 1951 Shinko Nihon kodai bunka (The ancient culture of Japan). Tokyo: Iwanami.

Yamagata, Mariko 1992 The Shakado Figurines and Middle Jomon Ritual in the Kofu Basin. Japanese Journal of Religious Studies 19(2/3):129–38.

Yamamoto, Teruhisa 1995 Sekibo (Stone club/rod) (in Japanese). *In* Jomon bunka no kenkyu (Studies in the Jomon culture) 9. Sinpei Kato ed. Pp. 170–80. Tokyo: Yusankaku.

Part III

Formative Developments

5

East Asian Plant Domestication

Gary W. Crawford

The oldest substantial record of potential agriculture in East Asia is in both North and South China from 7000 to 6000 B.C., and an understanding of the relationship between people and their environs during and preceding this period is a priority for current research. For now, such research is only beginning. The traditional link between archaeology, history, and art in East Asia has deprived the field of important interdisciplinary scientific research. There are, of course, exceptions to this generalization but it is important to keep it in mind when assessing research, or lack of it, on domestication and agricultural origins in East Asia.

Considering that the number of plants cultivated in East Asia (China, Korea, Japan, and Russian Far East) ranks second only to Southeast Asia (Zeven and Zhukovskiæi 1975), investigating the origin of these crops and their agricultural context is a complex matter. A significant number of these plants, including some of the world's most important crops (e.g. rice and soybean) (Table 5.1), were domesticated in this vast region, yet we know little of their history. Domestication is, of course, fundamental to agricultural origins but it is also a "clear and dominant feature of the conceptual landscape between hunting-gathering and agriculture" (Smith 2001:27). This chapter, then, is about the evidence for domestication, including its context, rather than agricultural origins specifically. It complements more detailed discussions of East Asian cultigen history (Chang 1983; Crawford 1992; Ho 1977; Li 1983). Despite intensive archaeological research exploring the complex cultural history of East Asia, archaeologists are still delineating the appropriate questions concerning domestication and early food–resource production in East Asia. Current issues include the domestication and evolution of indigenous crops, early post-Pleistocene events, the role of low-level food production, and agricultural intensification. Korea and Japan in the Early and Middle Holocene are important to investigate in their own right and are discussed here from the perspective of low-level resource–food production and expansion of intensive agriculture.

The Crops

East Asia is a center of diversity for most crops grown there (Table 5.1). Such centers indicate that a crop has a long history in a region, but not necessarily that its origins can be found there. The concept of a "center" can be misleading though. Most crops in Table 5.1 are either "oligocentric," that is, with "a definable center of origin, wide dispersal, and one or more secondary centers of diversity," or non-centric, suggesting "domestication over a wide area" (Harlan 1992:139). Many of the wild counterparts of plants in Table 5.1 are so widespread that the present distribution of these plants does not help delineate the location of their early management and domestication. Furthermore, each crop has an independent history and may have had multiple origins (Harlan 1992:155).

Research on plant domestication in East Asia has emphasized rice, consequently reinforcing a stereotype that rice is central to East Asian agriculture (Figure 5.1). Rice is one of many grains important in the region, and for a variety of reasons rice has become culturally significant in East Asia despite its temporal and regional economic variance. Domesticated rice belongs predominantly to two subspecies (Table 5.1). They are distinct to the extent that they do not readily hybridize. Japonica rice is East Asian, and DNA analysis of 28 archaeological rice specimens in China links them all to japonica (Sato 2002). Little is known about the original distribution of indica rice (see Crawford and Shen 1998 for a detailed discussion), however historic references to indica rice in China indicate it was not significant until about A.D. 1000 (Ho 1977:446). The Yangzi River basin has gained acceptance in recent years as the region where people domesticated rice (Crawford and Shen 1998). Rice is unique among the world's primary food grains because of its wetland adaptation. Paddy fields are complex structures designed to direct and control the flow of water through the paddies, mimicking rice's natural habitat. Rice is still grown in natural, seasonally inundated wetlands in parts of Asia today, so paddy fields are not essential for rice production (White 1989). In fact, in flood-prone areas rice is the *only* crop that can be grown. Rice can be grown in dry fields and, although its productivity in such fields is relatively low, this may well have been an important strategy in some areas. Annual wild rice is well adapted to the annual monsoon-influenced rise and fall of water levels at the edges of rivers, lakes, and marshes in the Yangzi River. Abundant natural stands can still be found in these settings but, unlike domesticated rice, the seeds do not ripen synchronously and when they do ripen, they disarticulate almost immediately (White 1989).

Two other prominent crops in East Asia, six-row barley and bread wheat (Table 5.1), were introduced from the Near East. Barley has not been confirmed in the early archaeological record in eastern China. Research at the Fengtai and Arhetela sites document barley becoming significant in western China during the Bronze Age some time between 2000 and 800 B.C. (Zhao 2004). In China today barley is primarily a fodder crop, with wheat being the second most significant crop, important even in rice growing areas. The rice–wheat combination has become critical to the Chinese agricultural economy. Bread wheat, but not barley, appears in eastern

Table 5.1. Examples of managed and domesticated plants in East Asia

Use	Common Name	Scientific Name	Native Distribution
Tree fruit	chestnut	*Castanea crenata*	Japan
		C. motissima	China
	Chinese bayberry	*Myrica rubra*	S. China
	hawthorn	*Crataegus*	China
	hazelnut	*Corylus* (4 species)	E. Asia
	jujube	*Ziziphus jujuba*	China
	litchi	*Litchi chinensis*	China
	mandarin orange	*Citrus reticulata*	China
	paper mulberry	*Broussonetia payrifera*	China
	peach	*Prunus persica*	China
	persimmon	*Diosporus kaki*	E. Asia
Grains	barley (six-row)	*Hordeum vulgare*	Near East
	barnyard millet	*Echinochloa crus-galli*	China, Korea, Japan
	broomcorn millet	*Panicum miliaceum*	China
	buckwheat	*Fagopyrum esculentum*	S. China
	chenopod	*Chenopodium* spp.	China, S. China
	foxtail millet	*Setaria italica*	China
	Job's tears	*Coix lacryma-jobi*	SE Asia
	rice	*Oryza sativa* spp. *japonica*	Yangzi River Basin
	rice	*O. sativa* spp. *indica*	S. China, S. Asia
	wheat (bread)	*Triticum aestivum*	Near East
	wild rice	*Zizania latifolia*	N. China
Legumes	azuki	*Vigna angularis*	E. Asia
	mungbean	*Vigna radiata*	S. Asia
	soybean	*Glycine max*	E. Asia
Roots, tubers	burdock	*Arctium major*	Japan/China?
	Ginseng	*Panax quinquefolia*	China
	lotus root	*Nelumbo nucifera*	E. Asia/Japan
	turnip	*Brassica rapa*	N. China
	radish	*Raphanus sativus*	E. Asia
	prickly water lily	*Euryale ferox*	E. Asia
	yam	*Dioscorea japonica*	Japan
	yam	*D. opposita*	S. China
Greens, bulbs	beefsteak plant	*Perilla frutescens*	E. Asia
	Chinese cabbage	*Brassica chinensis*	N. China
	knotweeds	*Polygonum* spp.	E. Asia
	onion	*Allium* (9 species)	E. Asia
Beverage	broomcorn millet	*Panicum miliaceum*	China
	foxtail millet	*Setaria italica*	China
	rice	*Oryza sativa* spp. *japonica*	Yangzi River Basin
	tea	*Camellia sinensis*	S. China
Oil	beefsteak plant	*Perilla frutescens*	E. Asia
	hemp	*Cannibis sativa*	Asia
	rapeseed (canola)	*Brassica campestris*	N. China
	sesame	*Sesamum indicum*	Africa/S. Asia?
	soybean	see legumes	
Technology	lacquer tree	*Rhus verniciflua*	E. Asia
	paper mulberry	*Broussonetia payrifera*	E. Asia
	hemp	*Cannibis sativa*	Asia
	bottle gourd	*Lagenaria siceraria*	Africa, Asia
Other	hops	*Humulus lupulus*	E. Asia
	water chestnut	*Trapa natans*	E. Asia

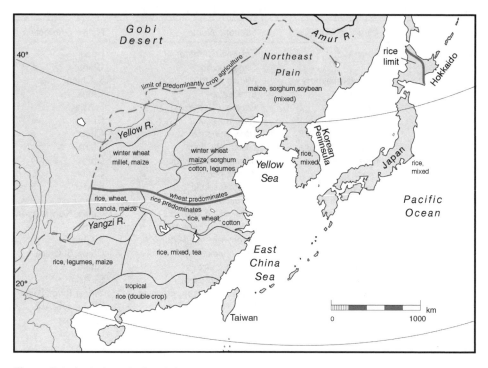

Figure 5.1 Agriculture in East Asia

China by the Late Neolithic dating to between 2600 and 1900 B.C. (Crawford, et al. n.d.). All the bread wheat recovered from contexts before A.D. 1500 in East Asia is small-seeded, possibly derived from small shot-wheat in Pakistan. Small-seeded varieties are also short, so the plants are adapted to the monsoonal climate of much of East Asia. Under high winds and heavy rain, short wheat will not tangle and therefore remains easy to harvest. Two genotypes of barley are present in East Asia indicating at least two separate introductions from the West (Takahashi 1955).

Barnyard millet (Table 5.1) is the only crop in northeast Asia for which flotation sampling has produced a record of evolution from a wild to a cultigen phenotype (Crawford 1983, 1997). Barnyard grass (wild barnyard millet) seeds are common in late Early Jomon deposits (4000–3500 B.C.) at the Hamanasuno site, Hokkaido. Seeds indistinguishable from the larger-seeded barnyard millet, a cultigen, are evident by the end of the Middle Jomon (about 2500 B.C.) at the nearby Usujiri B site. Broomcorn and foxtail millet are the two most significant grains in the early history of northern China yet no sequence evidencing their domestication has been found yet. Archaeologists have just begun looking for plant remains at sites in China where the crops may have been undergoing domestication. Missing from the earliest reports of domesticated millet in China are the criteria for their identification as millet as well as their domesticated status. Until these criteria are reported, we need to be cautious about subsistence interpretations. The ancestor of foxtail millet is green foxtail grass (*Setaria italica* subsp. *viridis*). The ancestor of broomcorn millet is not known; however, a weedy form (*Panicum miliaceum* subsp. *ruderale*) grows throughout Eurasia (Sakamoto 1987). Its possible role in broomcorn millet's lineage still needs to be explored.

Five grains have glutinous (sticky) varieties in East Asia and nowhere else: barley, broomcorn and foxtail millet, Job's tears, and rice (Sakamoto 1996). Dietary preferences are likely responsible for the selection of sticky or glutinous grains (Sakamoto 1996), and a single recessive gene is responsible for the glutinous starch in these grains. Glutinous foxtail millet is used for making wine and millet cakes in central Taiwan (Fogg 1983). The recognition of glutinous grains in the archaeological record is problematic, but would be useful in discerning when such customs as wine and cake making developed.

Two legumes, soybean and azuki (red) bean, figure prominently in East Asian history and cuisine. Wild soybean grows throughout East Asia (Hymowitz and Singh 1987; Yamaguchi 1992). Cultigen soybean seed size and shape are extremely variable but seeds of all landraces are larger than their wild counterpart, *Glycine soja*. Modern domesticated azuki beans are also larger than the seeds of their wild relative (*Vigna angularis* ssp. *nipponensis*). The main distinctions between wild and cultigen azuki and soybean is that cultigen pods are indehiscent and do not release their seeds naturally. Wild pods spring apart and distribute their seeds some distance from the plant; wild soybean is a vine while domesticated soybean is not. Both traits will be difficult to recognize in the archaeological record. The oldest archaeological examples of cultigen-size soybean date to about 1000 B.C. and are from the Daundong site, South Korea (Crawford and Lee 2003). They are associated with intermediate-size azuki beans. So far only wild size soybean has been found in the Yellow River basin archaeological record (Crawford, et al. n.d.). In China, only a few azuki beans have been found at one site – the Late Neolithic Liangchengzhen site – and they are similar to the examples from Korea (Crawford et al. n.d.); many archaeological examples are reported from Korea and Japan (Crawford 1992; Crawford and Lee 2003).

Other cultigens in the local archaeological record are hemp, beefsteak plant, and bottle gourd. Hemp has been identified in archaeological contexts in East Asia, and it has many uses including fiber, drug, oil, and food. Beefsteak plant is known mainly from Japanese and Korean archaeological contexts, but at least one example, from the Erlitou period (ca. 1900–1500 B.C.) Zaojiaoshu site, is from China. Its ancestor is also found throughout East Asia. It is an oil and medicinal plant whose leaves are used for food. Bottle gourd was a crop in the later prehistory of East Asia and has an early association with people there, seeds having been recovered from Middle Holocene sites in Japan and China (Crawford 1992). Wild bottle gourd seems to be extinct but it likely originated in Africa and found its way naturally to Asia following ocean currents (Heiser 1989). How and when it was domesticated in Asia is still unknown.

Root crops are also important in East Asia (Table 5.1) but so far no archaeological examples have been identified. Wild yams are distributed widely and at least two species were domesticated, one in China and one in Japan. Domesticated yam tubers grow shallower and are thicker than wild tubers (White 1989).

Tree fruit production is an important characteristic of East Asian agriculture (Table 5.1). The lifespan of nut trees and their ease of harvesting may mitigate against their domestication (Harris 1977) but the fact remains that many trees were effectively domesticated. They were likely domesticated after agriculture began. In the Near East domesticated tree fruit appears after other crops were domesticated (Spiegel-Roy 1986). Trees that respond well to vegetative reproduction (grafting), such as hazel, are quicker to domesticate than are others (Spiegel-Roy 1986). Dioecious species, with separate male and female plants, can be bred to reduce the number of male plants; thorniness is reduced; bitterness is eliminated; and self-fertility can develop (Spiegel-Roy 1986).

The Early Evidence

The Early Neolithic in North China is simply the time when the first substantial communities with pottery are visible in the archaeological record (see Underhill and Habu, this volume). Chinese archaeology tends to assume Early Neolithic communities are on the path to agriculture, and may even be called agricultural, with no supporting evidence. The traditional approach in Japan and Korea is to assume that substantial communities with pottery are, to the contrary, *not* nascent agricultural communities despite evidence, discussed later in this chapter, that this, too, is a significant oversimplification. Villages developed and expanded, apparently independently, on the central loess plateau and in northeast China. Clusters of pit houses are the first evidence for these communities (Chang 1986). Pit houses do not necessarily mean settlements are year-round, although they indicate substantial sedentism. The pit houses of the Nivkh in the lower Amur River and northern Sakhalin, for example, were only winter residences (Black 1973), so pit houses provided a number of options, including year-round residences. The Peiligang and Cishan sites along the Yellow and Wei Rivers and the Xinglongwa and Zhaobaogou sites near Inner Mongolia characterize the Early Neolithic in the north (Figure 5.2). Xinglongwa is partially surrounded by a ditch, the earliest known in China. Pit house construction and the ditch mean that anthropogenic habitats ideal for pioneering weeds were developing. Old pit house sites were used as gardens by native people in the U.S. Southeast (Waslekov 1997). We have no idea yet whether people who lived in early pit house communities in Asia were taking advantage of such habitats but it would be surprising if they were not. Millet remains have been recovered from the loess plateau sites but not yet from the northeast China Early Neolithic. Only nut remains have been found at Xinglongwa (Shelach 2000). Locality 1 (ca. 8000–7000 B.P.) at another Xinglongwa culture site, Xinglonggou, has produced a high density of broomcorn and foxtail millet with smaller relatively elongate grains compared to those from Locality 2, a 4000 B.P. Xiajiadian culture occupation. Locality 1 remains may represent an early domesticated form (Zhao 2004). Recently, Zhao Zhijun has collected flotation samples from another Xinglongwa culture site so we will soon be able to evaluate the paleoethnobotany of this culture.

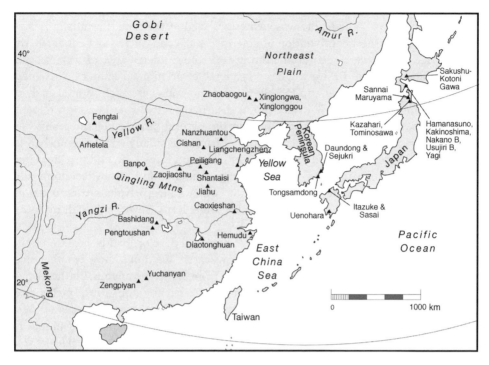

Figure 5.2 Map of East Asia with sites mentioned in the text

Changing relationships between plants and people hypothesized for the Early Neolithic are easier to discern at sites such as Banpo, characteristic of the North China Middle Neolithic. The millets here are domesticated rather than undergoing domestication. The perimeter of Banpo was surrounded by a ditch even larger than the one at Xinglongwa, perhaps 5 to 6 meters wide and about as deep. Food reserves were stored in large pits sometimes up to two meters deep. Some structures appear to be animal pens; people raised dogs and pigs. Plant remains include broomcorn and foxtail millet, hemp, and jujube. Exchange and alliances probably played an important role in providing access to regionally variable resources. Many landraces of the Yangshao crops likely developed and valued seeds of special landraces may have been important exchange items. Special types of foxtail millet were exchanged among groups in central Taiwan in the 1970s as part of rituals or peaceful meetings (Fogg 1983:106).

Research in South China emphasizes rice. Unfortunately, the literature is rife with unsubstantiated claims of early domestication. Zengpiyan cave (11,000 B.P.) has been assumed to have evidence of pig domestication and rice agriculture but recent research indicates that the occupants had no domesticated plants or animals. In particular, flotation samples document the collection of a range of wild plants, none of them small grain plants (Zhao 2003). The oldest directly-dated rice grains have been found in two areas: the Yangzi River drainage basin (6500 B.C.); and to the north in Henan at Jiahu (6000–7000 B.C.) (Crawford and Shen 1998). Some of the best evidence for early rice is from the Pengtoushan and Bashidang sites on the Liyang Plain near Dongting Lake. Both sites belong to the Pengtoushan culture (7500 to 6100 B.C.). Village life was well established at the time. Bashidang is surrounded by the earliest combination of defensive walls and ditches in China. Nearly 15,000 rice grains were recovered from a 100 square meter area of waterlogged deposits. The rice from Bashidang has considerable variation so cannot be assigned to a rice subspecies (Zhang and Pei 1996), and the grains are slightly smaller than modern domesticated rice. Wild rice grains disarticulate freely and have prominent awns, and both these characteristics help in the natural dispersal of the grains. So far, no description of rachis remains or awns from Bashidang and Pengtoushan is available. Three other wetland plants – water chestnut, lotus root, and prickly water lily – may have been used by the Bashidang residents and all are economically important in the area today. Water chestnut (water caltrop) fruits are reported at Bashidang and some pottery bowls are shaped like lotus leaves, although no lotus remains have been found.

How people domesticated rice and first came to develop paddy fields are still problems to be resolved by interdisciplinary research. We don't know whether rice was grown in managed habitats or harvested from natural wetlands by the Pengtoushan residents. Sickle harvesting would help select for non-brittle rachis rice plants, whatever the habitat. Once water flow and containment systems were developed, rice selection could be particularly rapid. The history of these techniques is poorly known. The first written reference to paddy fields is relatively late (Ho 1977). However, rice paddies date to as early as 2500 B.C. at the Caoxieshan site where numerous paddies and an irrigation system have been uncovered (Liu 2000). Paddy fields and water management systems are evident in Korea during the Early and Middle Mumun periods (Kwak 2000; Lee and Lee 2001), ca. 3500–2000 B.C., so rice paddy fields seem to have a much longer history than written records suggest.

While the domesticated status of rice from the Pengtoushan culture is open to question, the best example of an early group reliant upon domesticated rice is represented by the Hemudu site, part of a culture thriving near the mouth of the Yangzi River. The earliest rice-growing group there dates to 5000–4500 B.C. (Zhejian Provincial Museum 1978). The site is located in a wetland on the south side of Hangchou Bay not far from Shanghai (Chang 1986). During the excavation, a thick layer of complete rice plants was discovered in the waterlogged soils near the houses. Once exposed to air, the plant remains were impossible to preserve but many grains were recovered. Some of the rice glumes have awns so have a wild trait, but most glumes have no awns indicating that they are from cultigen rice. Dogs, pigs, water buffalo, bottle gourd, water chestnut, and rice are all evidenced here.

Low-Level Food–Resource Producers

The sparse data related to the subsistence-economy during the shift from the Upper Palaeolithic to Neolithic agriculture in China currently frustrates efforts to understand how agriculture began there. What we do know about the shift elsewhere may inform our hypothesis building. The archaeological record immediately after the

Palaeolithic in the Near East, the Epi-Palaeolithic, is characterized by intensification of animal and plant use and the first pit house communities. The material
culture excludes pottery. The earliest domesticated plants appear at the end of this
period but several thousand years passed before the emergence of balanced agricultural societies (Smith 1998, 2001). In Mexico, the earliest domesticated cucur-
bit appears by 9000–8000 B.C. in a seasonal encampment, but village agricultural
people are not evident until about 2500 B.C. (Smith 2001:19). In eastern North
America the relatively mobile Paleo-Indian culture was eventually superseded by
Archaic cultures who, west of the Appalachians, settled into river valleys and highlands alike, exploiting a variety of resources from smaller territories than their
predecessors had. Several local plants were being domesticated by 3000 B.C., long
before pottery and the widespread adoption of village life. Three to four millennia
later, agricultural communities were widespread (Fritz 1990; Smith 2001). Low-
level food–resource-producing societies appear to be common, and are so long
lasting that they ought to be considered stable adaptations and should be studied
in their own right rather than being considered on the way *to* agriculture or *from*
hunting and gathering (Smith 2001).

Precious little is known about adaptations in North China and Korea immediately after the Palaeolithic. Pottery is becoming increasingly evident in the archaeological record at the end of the Pleistocene in Japan, China, and the Russian Far
East (Yasuda 2002). Little is known about human and environmental relationships
or subsistence at the time. Virtually no archaeological data of any sort have yet to
be recovered from the period from about 10000 B.C. to 7000 B.C. in Korea and
North China. One exception appears to be the Nanzhuangtou site, an occupation
near Baiyangdian Lake in North China (Wang 1999:96). The site has the oldest
pottery in North China, dating to 9000–8000 B.C. None of the plant remains from
Nanzhuangtou has been identified.

One site in South China – the Diaotonghuan site near Dongting Lake – has substantial evidence that rice exploitation was underway by 10000 B.C. (see Underhill
and Habu, this volume), although the rice was not domesticated (Zhao 1998). Diaotonghuan differs from floodplain sites such as Pengtoushan and Bashidang in being
a small shelter under an arch of rock 60 meters above the Dayuan Basin. The bot-
tomlands of Dayuan Basin would have been wetlands during the Early Holocene,
providing an appropriate habitat for wild rice. Small silica bodies (phytoliths) that
develop in structural support cells of the rice plant are found in the soils at Diaotonghuan (Zhao 1998). Rice phytoliths have distinct shapes that can be linked to
specific parts of the rice plant and rice chaff phytoliths are common in the Diaotonghuan sediments. Rice would not grow at the site because of its elevation unless
people were trying to grow it as a dry crop; people probably brought the rice grains
to the site from the lowland. Rice phytoliths occur in deposits that are older than
10000 B.C. and their morphology is identical to that of wild rice. Phytoliths resem-
bling those from domesticated rice are common after 8000–7000 B.C. At the onset
of rice domestication then, Diaotonghuan was used by a small group of people
with little opportunity to produce anthropogenic communities. A similar site is
Yuchanyan, where a few undated rice husks and some phytoliths have been recovered

and are associated with an Upper Palaeolithic assemblage typical of the region. The rice appears to be wild except for missing awns (Yuan 2002). The sample is undated and too small to provide much insight on rice domestication, but the potential for learning more about early rice exploitation at these sites is tantalizing.

Pit house communities appear by 10000 B.C. in southwestern Japan as part of a long unbroken archaeological sequence starting at the beginning of the Upper Palaeolithic (Imamura 1996). One of the earliest villages so far discovered anywhere in East Asia is the Uenohara site in Kyushu, an Initial Jomon pit house community dating to 10000–7500 B.C. By 6500 B.C., villages were common throughout Japan as they were in north and central China; however, nothing yet suggests these early village residents of the Japanese islands were developing crops. Relatively intensive agriculture is not known in Japan before roughly 400 B.C. at the earliest (Crawford 1992). Japan, therefore provides an important comparative counterpoint to China.

During the Early Jomon period beginning about 4500 B.C., villages were common and often large, particularly in northeastern Japan. Stone tool technology included flaked stone, as well as grinding and polishing, to make a variety of tools. Material culture in general is not particularly different from that of North China. Over the ensuing millennia, Jomon material culture became more elaborate. Middle Jomon pottery in the north included the tall cylindrical pots of their predecessors, but people were making use of a broad range of pottery forms. Population density was relatively high and probably within the range of what we might expect for agricultural populations. By 2500 B.C., Jomon peoples had sizeable, complex villages and large communal buildings are found at some sites. An example is the Sannai Maruyama site in Aomori Prefecture. Distinct activity precincts include dwelling areas and a cemetery, as well as a communal structure. Missing is extensive evidence of obvious crops, although plants such as bottle gourd are present. Azuki is also reported and it is well north of its modern range. Walnut dominates the pollen assemblage.

For many decades, scholars have debated whether Jomon people were agricultural (Crawford 1992). In fact, the debate is so explicit that the phrase "Jomon hunter-gatherers" is used by some rather than simply "the Jomon" (see Underhill and Habu, this volume). This forces the view that the Jomon must be categorized as either agricultural or hunter-gatherer and furthermore, that researchers must make a choice. However, another theoretical view holds that economies lie along a continuum from hunting and gathering to intensive agriculture and that a binary opposition is untenable (Smith 2001). More to the point, then, is where along the continuum from hunting and gathering to agricultural intensification are Jomon cultures? Research in Hokkaido helps clarify the issue of northeastern Jomon subsistence (Crawford 1983, 1997, 2000; Crawford and Bleed 1998; Crawford et al. 1978). This investigation also suggests what may await investigators when early sites in China such as Nanzhuangtou are extensively sampled for plant remains. The research explores what we now know is one of the longest-lasting, low-level food-producing adaptations in the world. For several years, our team carried out flotation at the Hamanasuno, Usujiri B, Hakodate Airport, Nakano B, and Yagi sites in southwestern Hokkaido (Crawford 1983). The sites are Initial through Middle

Jomon (ca. 7000–2500 B.C.). Similar extensive sampling of the Middle Jomon Tomi-nosawa and Late Jomon Kazahari occupations in Aomori Prefecture provides insight from northern Honshu (D'Andrea 1992; D'Andrea et al. 1995).

Walnut remains are common in the Initial and early phases of the Early Jomon in southwestern Hokkaido (6700–4000 B.C.). Nuts are often assumed to have been the most important food source of the Jomon; many archaeologists feel that nuts were a staple food while others believe that nut domestication was taking place (Hudson 1999; Nishida 1983). Nut exploitation strategies can be conducive to agricultural origins (Gardner 1997), and nuts, without doubt, are nutritious and can be harvested in large quantities. They are particularly high in fat for example, and fat is a precious resource in late winter and early spring in regions with long winters. Successful, long-term use of nuts is constrained by a number of factors (Gardner 1997:173). Nut trees do not produce the same quantities of nuts (masts) year after year; they require plenty of work to process; and nut mast is also sensitive to weather conditions. Nut trees do not need to be genetically altered to change their productivity: people can clear vegetation around the nut trees; with more sunlight, more nuts are produced. People were probably well aware that nut trees are more productive on forest edges and in clearings than in the shaded forest. Once people began to reproduce some tree species vegetatively, their fruit production would have been more predictable and productive.

By the end of the Early Jomon in southwestern Hokkaido nearly all the plants represented at these sites flourished in disturbed habitats. Nuts become rare in the record indicating that alternate resources were available. Nearly 200 kinds of plants are represented in flotation samples from the Hokkaido and Aomori Early and Middle Jomon. However, only 15 kinds of plants dominate the carbonized seed assemblages. People were primarily interested in collecting small grains and leafy greens of barnyard grass, chenopod, dock (*Rumex* sp.), and knotweed. Fleshy fruits include elderberry (*Sambucus*), grape (*Vitis*), a wild kiwi (*Actinidia*), and udo (*Aralia cordata*). Sumac (*Rhus*) seeds also appear in a variety of contexts in these archaeological sites. In some parts of the world sumac is used as a spice or beverage, and lacquer is made from the sap of a sumac, *Rhus vernicifera*. The earliest lacquer in the world comes from the town of Minamikayabe in southwestern Hokkaido where six red lacquer items from the Kakinoshima site have been AMS dated to 9000 B.C. The evidence of sumac in the archaeological record in Minamikayabe could reflect lacquer production in the area, although the seeds are not part of the lacquer production process. Sumac, a perennial, flourishes in disturbed, sunny locations. One small pit structure, H. 74 at Hamanasuno, had a high concentration of sumac seeds in a fill deposit near the floor.

Disturbed habitats are precisely what we would expect to find in and around large villages. Tree removal, house construction, and similar activities all have important impacts on the local ecology. These impacts are referred to as anthropogenic, some of which may be intentional while others not. Such impacts are often beneficial to people, primarily by enhancing spatial heterogeneity, biodiversity, and productivity (Crawford 1997; Smith and Wishnie 2000). From intentional burning to large-scale construction, such ecosystem engineering is an important aspect of human adaptation, even in small-scale communities (Smith and Wishnie 2000). Weedy plants, for example, are extremely productive in open, sunny areas. Jomon peoples took advantage of the plants and animals in these anthropogenic habitats, and they therefore had an impact on the local environment and in turn, took advantage of the impacts. This kind of reciprocity between people and their environment was probably common long before the shift to low-level food production. We cannot rule out the purposeful choice people may have made in order to increase the local environmental productivity. This may have been an important step in the evolution of domesticated organisms in East Asia. At least one grass, barnyard millet, shows evidence of having been domesticated in this setting in northern Japan. A variety of grasses other than barnyard grass is common in nearly all the sites, including a few examples of wild foxtail grass. Barnyard grass seeds increase in size by about 20 percent over the 1,500 year period between the Early and Middle Jomon (Crawford 1983, 1997). By the end of the Middle Jomon barnyard grass seeds are indistinguishable from barnyard millet, an important economic plant in Medieval Japan. Buckwheat, indigenous to southern China (Ohnishi 1995), may also be present during the Early Jomon in Hokkaido. However, only one buckwheat grain may date that early. It may have been traded from southwestern Japan where pollen evidence suggests the crop was grown. Similar research needs to be undertaken in the Chinese early Neolithic.

A project similar to the one in northeastern Japan is investigating the paleoethnobotany of early South Korea (Crawford and Lee 2003). The Chulmun culture flourished in the Korean Peninsula from at least 6000 B.C. to 1500 B.C. Chulmun people lived in pit house villages and their economy was based largely on hunting, gathering, and fishing. Shell mounds are common along the coast. So far, little evidence for high population densities and social complexity has been found in the Korean Chulmun, suggesting Chulmun subsistence was not as productive as that of the Jomon. Research in the early Korean sequence is just beginning but preliminary data indicate that subsistence in the early Chulmun had some similarities to that of the Early Jomon. At the 5000 B.C. Sejukri shell midden researchers have recovered quantities of charred nuts as well as small seeds (Crawford and Lee 2003).

Archaeologists should base their models of plant use on systematically collected plant remains. Unfortunately, all too often such reconstructions are speculative or informed by indirect evidence. A good example is the Tongsamdong site, South Korea, where a coastal, maritime adaptation during the middle Holocene has been modeled from data collected in the 1960s. The animal remains are primarily maritime, dominated by sea bream (Sample 1974:93). Although innovations in stone technology partway through the sequence suggested an economic shift, that may have included crops, subsistence interpretations ignored plants completely. Gyoung-Ah Lee returned to Tongsamdong in 2000 when the site was once again being excavated. A soil sample she took from the floor of a Middle Chulmun pit house contained a high density of both broomcorn and foxtail millet. Specimens have been directly AMS dated to 3400 B.C. and confirm the association of crops with the Middle Chulmun (Crawford and Lee 2003). Low-level food production at Tongsamdong therefore involved at least two millets.

Intensification

The initial development of agriculture may be followed by a significant commitment to the new ecology. Social change may be rapid: community structures change; social hierarchies develop; population growth increases; and warfare becomes common. Health may actually decline. Resource output increases and risk reduction may also result (Fritz 1992; Gallagher and Arzigian 1994). Resources may change because of exchange and procurement of resources from outside the region. Migration may also be a factor. In the Near East, agriculture initially developed along at least two trajectories (Smith 1998). Eventually, the two systems blended. The resulting system was more productive and probably more resilient, at least initially, than either ancestral system on its own. In other areas, a productive crop evolved after other crops were domesticated. In the New World, corn evolved later than many of the earliest crops. In East Asia, agricultural intensification occurs but the mechanisms for this process are not well understood. In China, substantial changes begin at least by the third millennium B.C., in Korea 1,500 years later, and in Japan 1,200 years after that. China is the least well known of the three.

In North China, the material cultural diversity of the Yangshao and Dawenkou is superseded by the Late Neolithic Longshan culture ca. 2500 B.C. Longshan is generally viewed as ancestral to state societies in North China and was well on the way to having a form of centralized authority. Earthen walls surround a few Longshan sites; cemeteries contain clusters of burials probably representing differential power; and craft specialization is evident. Population growth increased (Liu 1996:267). Rapid settlement nucleation during the subsequent Erlitou period appears to correlate with changes in resource procurement and craft specialization (Liu 1996; Underhill 2002). Intensified agriculture was one important factor enabling these developments (Chang 1986:250), but in reality we actually know very little about Longshan subsistence. Several archaeological projects are addressing the issue. Excavations at Liangchengzhen and Shantaisi involve substantial soil flotation programs (Crawford et al. 2001; Crawford et al. 2005). Millet appears to be the primary grain of the preceding Yangshao and Dawenkou. Our preliminary results indicate rice was becoming significant, particularly to eastern Longshan people. Wheat is probably an addition to the crop complex (Crawford et al. 2001; Crawford et al. n.d.), and the new combination of crops likely played a role in agricultural intensification. Domestic animals are an unknown aspect of intensification because of their long-time presence in the Neolithic economy; fodder production and availability may also be a factor. Through the Shang and Zhou periods agriculture continued to develop. By 1000–500 B.C. barley, wheat, rice, soybean, beefsteak plant, melon, and gourd were all common. None were domesticated in the Yellow River basin.

In Korea, a sequence of crop introductions with intervening periods of little change is being documented (Crawford and Lee 2003). People in the Korean Peninsula and Japan eventually adopted agriculture largely based on Chinese systems, although potentially local azuki, barnyard millet, and soybean were grown along with Chinese crops. By 2000 B.C., rice appears to have been added to the suite of crops (Crawford and Lee 2003). Intensive agriculture did not develop until the beginning of the Bronze Age Mumun period between 1500 and 1000 B.C.; Mumun people made a significant investment in rice, bread wheat, soybean, azuki, and hemp production. Soybean and azuki bean origins are still unclear. Early Chinese records mention that soybean was a gift from the northeast China–Korean Peninsula region (Ho 1977). The Korean soybeans dating to about 1000 B.C. are the oldest yet discovered. Mumun ridged, dry fields, and paddy fields have been excavated in the southern Korean Peninsula. Intensification in Korea involved new crops, new production strategies, and significant technological and cultural change underlying the eventual development of state society there.

Intensified agriculture in southwestern Japan was not a unilineal development from local agriculture. Changes seen almost a millennium earlier in Korea were impacting the southern Japanese archipelago by 400–300 B.C. The Yayoi culture – known for its metallurgy, intensive agriculture, and more centralized sociopolitical organization – began replacing the Jomon in Kyushu. Cultigens were not new to Kyushu where rice is AMS dated to 900–800 B.C. and soybean to 760–550 B.C. at the Sasai site (Takano and Komoto 2004), but the Yayoi signaled a new era of balanced agriculture. The Itazuke site has evidence of well-engineered drainage systems that maintained paddy fields. Ditches and earthworks served as defensive structures around these densely populated communities. Crops included rice, millet, wheat, barley, soybean, azuki bean, hops, bottle gourd, peaches, and persimmons.

The Yayoi transformation moved northeastward until all but Hokkaido, the northernmost prefecture, was part of the Yayoi world by 100 B.C. In southwestern Japan, the Yayoi developed mainly through migration but northeastern Jomon people appear to have adopted aspects of Yayoi life including intensive agriculture. As in Kyushu, crops were not entirely new to northeastern Japan because the oldest directly dated rice, foxtail millet, and broomcorn millet in Japan are from Late Jomon contexts (900 B.C.) at the Kazahari site in Aomori Prefecture. On the northern frontier, people experimented with paddy field agriculture but any success they had was short-lived. Dry field production was eventually the system of choice. This form of agriculture continued into recent centuries in Hokkaido where the Ainu practiced a mixed economy of agriculture, hunting, fishing, and gathering. Soil samples from the Sakushu-Kotoni-Gawa site in Sapporo dating to A.D. 700 to 900 contain the largest collection of cultigen remains yet documented in any detail in East Asia. By A.D. 700, millets, beans, hemp, barley, and wheat were grown in northern Honshu and Hokkaido. A small number of rice, melon, and safflower seeds suggest these resources were imported. The wheat grown in Japan until at least the 16th century was all the small-grained type.

Discussion

Over many millennia in East Asia, several hundred plants were domesticated. Grains, "root" crops, tree fruit, and legumes are among the significant resource categories, each requiring somewhat different interactions with people to be domesticated. Little is known about the archaeological record in China and the Korean Peninsula between the end of the Palaeolithic and 6500 B.C. when significant developments in the relationships between plants and people must have been taking place. So far, it appears that at least rice was being used in China before incontrovertible evidence of its domestication appears. The same is probably true for millet in China. Between 6500 and 6000 B.C., millet and rice had become significant resources and mixed procurement strategies (hunting, gathering, fishing, agriculture) were on the way to being well established in several regions in China. Anthropogenic habitats are prominent by then, given the structure of Neolithic sites.

Nothing is known about the early stages of foxtail and broomcorn millet domestication. In fact, southwestern Hokkaido, Japan is the only locale where wild millet is superseded by domesticated millet. Paleoethnobotany in Japan and Korea exemplifies the potential for research in China. Much more is known about low-level food–resource production during the Jomon than anywhere else in East Asia. Not only do we need comprehensive paleoethnobotanical research on occupations in China pre-dating 6500 B.C., but intensive research on resource exploitation and habitat reconstruction will be required to assess issues around agricultural origins.

Jomon plant resource procurement was based on a relatively stable agricultural ecology with anthropogenic resources and a few crops. The Initial and Early Jomon, with their narrowing exploitation territories, use of anthropogenic and aquatic resources, degree of sedentism, and substantial non-portable technology including pottery and grinding stones, are similar to cultures at the dawn of agriculture in North China. However, subsistence evolution diverged significantly from the trajectory taken in China where agriculture blossomed in the Middle Holocene. Instead, Jomon economies persisted in an "in between" state (Smith 2001). This was due to the success of Jomon strategies rather than to any failure to intensify food production. Korea is another case where hints of evidence for anthropogenesis during the Early Chulmun have been found and where two Chinese millets appear by 3600 B.C. The Chulmun adaptation was relatively stable until 1500 B.C. when agricultural intensification began.

Several features appear to be common to domestication around the world (Cowan and Watson 1992; Smith 1998). Seed plants were the first to be domesticated, the ancestors of these plants having been resources before they were domesticated, and affluent people in large, permanent communities near rivers and lakes were the first to domesticate plants. Another factor is lack of security in the environment, especially marked seasonality. Most of these characteristics should apply to the 10000 and 7000 B.C. period in much of China and Korea. Insecurity is likely due to marked seasonality in East Asia. In the north, the lean times were the winters; in the south, regular, severe flooding along the Yangzi would have brought about lean times as it does today in parts of Southeast Asia. Storable, productive resources such as rice and millet would have brought added security.

Until comprehensive, interdisciplinary archaeological research results in systematically collected, accurately dated assemblages of plant remains from the Early Neolithic in China, we will know little about the first stages of domestication there.

For now, we can only speculate about the initial processes of domestication, the sequence of plants to be domesticated, how they were domesticated, if there were crops that were domesticated and failed to have any longevity, and what the spatial variation of domestication was. We are only now beginning to study the intensification of agriculture in East Asia.

REFERENCES

Black, Lydia 1973 The Nivkh (Gilyak) of Sakhalin and the Lower Amur. Arctic Anthropology X(1):1–110.

Chang, Kwang-Chih 1986 The Archaeology of Ancient China, 4th edition. New Haven: Yale University Press.

Chang, Te-Tzu 1983 The Origins and Early Cultures of the Cereal Grains and Food Legumes. In The Origins of Chinese Civilization. David N. Keightley, ed. Pp. 65–94. Berkeley CA: University of California Press.

Cowan, C. Wesley, and Patty Jo Watson 1992 Some Concluding Remarks. In The Origins of Agriculture: An International Perspective. C. Wesley Cowan and Patty Jo Watson, eds. Pp. 207–12. Washington and London: Smithsonian Institution Press.

Crawford, Gary W. 1983 Paleoethnobotany of the Kameda Peninsula Jomon. Volume 73. Ann Arbor, Michigan: Museum of Anthropology, University of Michigan.

—— 1992 Prehistoric Plant Domestication in East Asia. In The Origins of Agriculture: An International Perspective. C. Wesley Cowan and Patty Jo Watson, eds. Pp. 7–38. Washington and London: Smithsonian Institution Press.

—— 1997 Anthropogenesis in Prehistoric Northeastern Japan. In People, Plants, and Landscapes: Studies in Paleoethnobotany. Kristen Gremillion, ed. Pp. 86–103. Tuscaloosa: University of Alabama Press.

—— 2000 43rd Parallels. Rotunda 33(2):30–7.

Crawford, Gary W., and Peter Bleed 1998 Scheduling and Sedentism in the Prehistory of Northern Japan. In Identifying Seasonality and Sedentism in Archaeological Sites: Old and New World Perspectives. Thomas Rocek and Ofar Bar-Yosef, eds. Boston: Peabody Museum, Harvard University.

Crawford, Gary W., and Gyoung-Ah Lee 2003 Agricultural Origins in the Korean Peninsula. Antiquity 77(295).

Crawford, Gary W., and Chen Shen 1998 The Origins of Rice Agriculture: Recent Progress in East Asia. Antiquity 72(278):858–66.

Crawford, Gary W., William H. Hurley, and Masakazu Yoshizaki 1978 Implications of Plant Remains from the Early Jomon, Hamanasuno Site. Asian Perspectives 19(1):145–55.

Crawford, Gary W., Jian Leng, and Gyoung-Ah Lee 2001 Paleoethnobotany in Northern China and Southern Korea During the Neolithic/Bronze Periods. Society for American Archaeology, New Orleans LA, 2001. Unpublished MS.

Crawford, Gary W., Anne Underhill, Zhijun Zhao, Gyoung-Ah Lee, Gary Feinman, Linda Nicholas, Fengshi Luan, Haiguang Yu, Hui Fang, and Fengshu Cai In press Late Neolithic Plant Remains from Northern China: Preliminary Results from Liangchengzhen, Shandong. Current Anthropology 46.

D'Andrea, A. Catherine 1992 Palaeoethnobotany of Later Jomon and Yayoi Cultures of

Northeastern Aomori and Southwestern Hokkaido. Ph.D. Dissertation, University of Toronto.

D'Andrea, A. Catherine, Gary W. Crawford, Masakazu Yoshizaki, and T. Kudo 1995 Late Jomon Cultigens in Northeastern Japan. Antiquity 69(262):146–52.

Fogg, Wayne 1983 Swidden Cultivation of Foxtail Millet by Taiwan Aborigines: A Cultural Analog of the Domestication of *Setaria italica* in China. *In* The Origins of Chinese Civilization. David N. Keightley, ed. Pp. 95–115. Berkeley CA: University of California Press.

Fritz, Gayle J. 1990 Multiple Pathways to Farming in Precontact Eastern North America. Journal of World Prehistory 4(4):387–435.

—— 1992 "Newer," "Better" Maize and the Mississippian Emergence: A Critique of Prime Mover Explanations. *In* Late Prehistoric Agriculture: Observations from the Midwest. William I. Woods, ed. Pp. 19–43. Springfield: Studies in Illinois Archaeology No. 8. Illinois Historic Preservation Agency.

Gallagher, James P., and Constance Arzigian 1994 A New Perspective on Late Prehistoric Agricultural Intensification in the Upper Mississippi River Valley. *In* Agricultural Origins and Development in the Midcontinent. William Green, ed. Pp. 171–88. Iowa City: Report 19, Office of the State Archaeologist, The University of Iowa.

Gardner, Paul 1997 The Ecological Structure and Behavioral Implications of Mast Exploitation Strategies. *In* People, Plants, and Landscapes: Studies in Paleoethnobotany. Kristen J. Gremillion, ed. Pp. 161–78. Tuscaloosa: University of Alabama Press.

Harlan, Jack R. 1992 Crops and Man. Madison: American Society of Agronomy.

Harris, David R. 1977 Alternative Pathways Toward Agriculture. *In* Origins of Agriculture. Charles A. Reed, ed. Pp. 179–243. The Hague: Mouton.

Heiser, Charles 1989 Domestication of Cucurbitaceae: *Cucurbita* and *Lagenaria*. *In* Foraging and Farming. David R. Harris and Gordon C. Hillman, eds. Pp. 471–80. London: Unwin Hyman.

Ho, Ping-Ti 1977 The Indigenous Origins of Chinese Agriculture. *In* The Origins of Agriculture. C. A. Reed, ed. Pp. 413–84. Chicago: Mouton.

Hudson, Mark 1999 Ruins of Identity: Ethnogenesis in the Japanese Islands. Honolulu: University of Hawaii Press.

Hymowitz, T., and R. J. Singh 1987 Taxonomy and speciation. *In* Soybeans: Improvement, Production, and Uses. James R. Wilcox, ed. Pp. 23–48. Agronomy. Madison: American Society of Agronomy.

Imamura, Keiji 1996 Prehistoric Japan: New Perspectives on Insular East Asia. Honolulu: University of Hawaii Press.

Kwak, Jong-Chul 2000 Prehistoric Wet-Field Rice Agriculture in Korea. *In* Ancient Rice Agriculture in Korea (the National Museum of Korea Symposium proceedings). National Museum of Korea, ed. Pp. 69–107. Seoul: National Museum of Korea.

Lee, Sankil, and Gyoung-Ah Lee 2001 Current Research on Agricultural Sites in Korea. Pp. 1–11. Paper presented at the 2nd Meeting of the Osaka Joint Research Task Committee on Exchange Between Korean Peninsula and Japan, Osaka, Japan.

Li, Hui-Lin 1983 The Domestication of Plants in China: Ecogeographic Considerations. *In* The Origins of Chinese Civilization. David N. Keightley, ed. Pp. 21–63. Berkeley CA: University of California Press.

Liu, Li 1996 Settlement Patterns, Chiefdom Variability, and Development of Early States in Northern China. Journal of Anthropological Archaeology 15(3):237–88.

Liu, Zhiyi 2000 Thoughts about the Domestication of Rice. Agricultural Archaeology (Nongye Kaogu) 1(1):122–28.

Nishida, Masaki 1983 The Emergence of Food Production in Neolithic Japan. Journal of Anthropological Archaeology 2:305–22.

Ohnishi, Ohmi 1995 Discovery of New *Fagopyrum* Species and Its Implication for the Study of Evolution of *Fagopyrum* and of the Origin of Cultivated Buckwheat. http://soba.shinshu-u.ac.jp/contents/contents.html.

Sakamoto, Sadao 1987 Origin and Dispersal of Common Millet and Foxtail Millet. Japan Agricultural Research Quarterly 21(2):84–9.

—— 1996 Glutinous-Endosperm Starch Food Culture Specific to Eastern and Southeastern Asia. *In* Redefining Nature: Ecology, Culture, and Domestication. R. F. Ellen and Katsuyoshi Fukui, eds. Pp. 215–31. Oxford: Berg.

Sample, T. 1974 Tongsamdong: A Contribution to Korea Neolithic Culture History. Arctic Anthropology 11(2).

Sato, Yoichiro 2002 Origin of Rice Cultivation in the Yangtze River Basin. *In* The Origins of Pottery and Agriculture. Yoshinori Yasuda, ed. Pp. 143–50. New Delhi: Roli Books Pvt. Ltd.

Shelach, Gideon 2000 The Earliest Neolithic Cultures of Northeast China: Recent Discoveries and New Perspectives on the Beginning of Agriculture. Journal of World Prehistory 14(4):363–413.

Smith, Bruce D. 1998 The Emergence of Agriculture. New York: Scientific American Library.

—— 2001 Low-Level Food Production. Journal of Archaeological Research 9(1):1–43.

Smith, Eric Alden, and Mark Wishnie 2000 Conservation and Subsistence in Small-Scale Societies. Annual Reviews of Anthropology 29:493–524.

Spiegel-Roy, P. 1986 Domestication of Fruit Trees. *In* The Origin and Domestication of Cultivated Plants. Claudio Barigozzi, ed. Pp. 201–11. Developments in Agricultural and Managed-Forest Ecology 16. New York: Elsevier.

Takahashi, Ryuhei 1955 The Origin and Evolution of Cultivated Barley. Advances in Genetics 7:227–66.

Takano, Shinji, and Masayuki Komoto 2004 14C Dating Based upon Prehistoric Seeds from Kyushu. *In* Prehistoric and Ancient Botanical Remains in Kyushu and East Asia. Masayuki Komoto, ed. Pp. 145–9, vol. 2. Kumamoto: University of Kumamoto, Faculty of Letters.

Underhill, Anne P. 2002 Craft Production and Social Change in Northern China. New York: Kluwer Academic/Plenum Publishers.

Wang, Haining 1999 Early Pottery in China: A Review of Archaeological and Environmental Data from Eight Sites, Ph.D. Dissertation, Southern Illinois University at Carbondale.

Waslekov, Gregory 1997 Changing Strategies of Indian Field Location in the Early Historic Southeast. *In* People, Plants, and Landscapes: Studies in Paleoethnobotany. Kristen J. Gremillion, ed. Pp. 179–94. Tuscaloosa: University of Alabama Press.

White, Joyce C. 1989 Ethnoecological Examples on Wild and Cultivated Rice and Yams in Northeastern Thailand. *In* Foraging and Farming. David R. Harris and Gordon C. Hillman, eds. Pp. 152–8. London: Unwin Hyman.

Yamaguchi, Hirofumi 1992 Wild and Weed Azuki Beans in Japan. Economic Botany 46:384–94.

Yasuda, Yoshinori 2002 Origins of Pottery and Agriculture in East Asia. *In* The Origins of Pottery and Agriculture. Yoshinori Yasuda, ed. Pp. 119–42. New Delhi: Roli Books Pvt. Ltd.

Yuan, Jiarong 2002 Rice and Pottery 10,000 Yrs. B.P. at Yuchanyan, Dao County, Hunan Province. *In* The Origins of Pottery and Agriculture. Yoshinori Yasuda, ed. Pp. 157–66. New Delhi: Roli Books Pvt. Ltd.

Zeven, A. C., and P. M. Zhukovskiæi 1975 Dictionary of Cultivated Plants and their Centers of Diversity Excluding Ornamentals, Forest Trees, and Lower Plants. Wageningen: Center for Agricultural Publishing and Documentation.

Zhang, Wenxu, and Anping Pei 1996 Analysis of Ancient Rice from Bashidang in Mengxi, Lixian County. *In* Origin and Differentiation of Chinese Cultivated Rice. Xiangkun Wang and Chuanqing Sun, eds. Pp. 47–53. Beijing: China Agricultural University Press.

Zhao, Zhijun 1998 The Middle Yangtze in China is One Place Where Rice was Domesticated: Phytolith Evidence from Diaotunghuan Cave, Northern Jiangxi. Antiquity 278:885–97.

—— 2003 Study of Plant Remains. *In* Zengpiyan: A Prehistoric Site in Guilin. C. Institute of Archaeology, ed. Pp. 286–96, 342–4. Beijing: The Cultural Relics Publishing House.

—— 2004 Tanxun Zhongguo Beifang Han Zuo Nongye Qiyuan de Xin Xiansuo (Seeking new clues about the origins of dry farming in Northern China). Zhongguo Wenwu Bao (Cultural relics newsletter of China) November 11, 2004.

Zhejian Provincial Museum, Natural History Section, 1978 A Study of Animal and Plant Remains Unearthed at Hemudu. Archaeology (Kaogu) 1:95–111.

6

Asian Farming Diasporas? Agriculture, Languages, and Genes in China and Southeast Asia

Peter Bellwood

With the arrival of farming in a new landscape, human populations are given the wherewithal for rapid demographic growth, as we can see so clearly in recent situations of agricultural colonization in Australia and many regions of North America. Did similar "diasporas" happen in the deeper past, when agriculture was first developed in different regions around the world? The documentation required to assess this hypothesis for any region will be drawn from the disciplines of archaeology, comparative linguistics, and human biology (including genetics). When the origin patterns and directions of flow that can be derived independently from these three disciplines are compared, then the histories of human populations can begin to be understood.

The archaeological record can reveal to us the directions and tempos of spread of agriculture-related material culture and domesticated species, identifying homelands and peripheries. One agricultural homeland was of course located in the central part of China, in the middle and lower Yangzi and Yellow Valleys, during the early Holocene (see Crawford, this volume). Another, marginal for this chapter, was located in New Guinea.

Figure 6.1 presents an archaeological view of the expansion of one major crop, domesticated rice (*Oryza sativa*), from a Yangzi Basin homeland (for details see Bellwood 1997, 2005: Fig. 6.1). The dates are derived from the archaeological record. Similar maps could doubtless be prepared for many other items of material and economic culture – cord-marked and red-slipped pottery, stone adzes with quadrangular and trapezoidal cross-sections, spindle whorls, domesticated pig and dog bones, and so forth. Some of these items are discussed in more detail from a Southeast Asian perspective below.

But in this introductory section I wish to drive home the concept that this chapter is about people, not rice grains or stepped adzes. If we wish to understand how people moved in prehistory, then single-minded devotion to the archaeological record alone is not going to get us very far. Material culture and crops can be

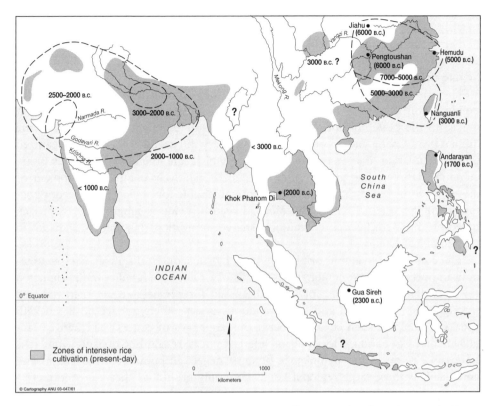

Figure 6.1 The origins and spread of domesticated rice (*Oryza sativa*) in Asia, showing the Yangzi homeland, radiocarbon dated arrivals of rice in various regions, and the distribution of intensive rice cultivation today (from Bellwood 2005, Figure 6.1); drafted by Jenny Sheehan (ANU)

exchanged between groups who share no close common linkages of linguistic or genetic descent. So can languages, but the linguistic record at the language family level offers us a phylogenetic perspective on a huge geographic scale that we can, with care, equate with the movements and diversification patterns of ancient populations. The long-distance movements of languages in pre-state circumstances can be argued to have been associated very closely with movements of their native speakers, i.e. "people." The archaeological record is more equivocal in this regard. The genetic record, that many might assume will hold the answers, is in fact fraught with much disagreement, as we will see.

East Asian Language Families and Their Histories

In the ethnographic record of Asia, and throughout history, we meet "peoples" as named ethnic groups with identifying languages, cultures, and histories. Some are very small, for instance groups of Punan hunters and gatherers in Borneo, others are vast in number, such as the Cantonese or the Thais. Archaeologists are unable to trace such ethnolinguistic groups backwards into prehistory because a major part of their essential definition will always be *linguistic*, and without translatable writing we simply cannot read the presence of a particular ancestral language in the pre-literate past.

There is another way of considering the rather difficult topic of ethnic (or ethnolinguistic) prehistory. This is to take a broader comparative approach, one that opens up the possibility of great insight into major population expansions in the human past. Living and recorded languages carry the useful ability to be organized into much larger *language families*, within which the member languages share common descent. Languages, since most exist relatively complete as spoken or otherwise recorded entities, are rather more amenable for phylogenetic reconstruction than the fragmentary archaeological record, using a subgrouping approach based on the identification of uniquely shared innovations (similar to cladistics in the biological sciences).

The concept of a shared origin, followed by subsequent dispersal, is of tremendous importance for human linguistic prehistory. Language families both originated (as proto-languages, a concept to be discussed further below) and then radiated through space and time, and such radiations must somehow have occurred with speakers. Whether such speakers learnt the languages of concern as "native" languages or by secondary learning of lingua francas is another question, but it is impossible to avoid the significance of some degree of population movement and contact. It is these large regional language family groupings that are of interest – how did they originate?

In order to answer such questions we must compare the historical conclusions drawn from the linguistic record with the independent conclusions from the archaeological and genetic records. The emphasis here is on comparison rather than circular reconstruction – the subject matters of linguistics, archaeology, and human genetics are entirely independent of each other and the comparisons only become circular if inferences from one discipline are applied uncritically to another.

It is also necessary to note that the geographic boundaries of cultures, languages, and genes need not always coincide (although sometimes, as on isolated islands, they probably did). For instance, Malaysian Negrito hunter-gatherers and the inhabitants of Angkor both spoke related Austroasiatic languages 800 years ago; Javanese rice farmers and Philippine Negrito hunters both speak related Austronesian languages today. Yet these pairs of populations are quite different in human biology, history, and material culture. Genes, languages, and material cultures may or may not have varied together in past circumstances – working out why there should be correlations here, non-correlations there, is part of the excitement of understanding history, especially history as it has impacted upon the creation of the contemporary world.

Since this chapter is written for an archaeological readership, it is necessary to explain briefly how the data of comparative linguistics and human genetics can inform about the human past. Unlike archaeology and paleoanthropology, that both work directly on the surviving traces of the past, comparative linguists and geneticists draw essentially on data from the present – living languages (or recent records for those no longer spoken) and samples of hair, saliva, and blood from living peoples. True, ancient inscriptions and ancient DNA from bone can add a few clues, but these sources are scarce or non-existent for the subject matter of this chapter. The essence for linguists and geneticists is, of course, comparison of modern data drawn from modern or recent populations, combined with backwards projection to reconstruct the natures, geographic locations, and chronologies of source configurations, both for the proto-language ancestors of extant language families, and for mitochondrial DNA and Y chromosome lineages.

Linguists have long realized that the languages of Asia fall into a number of families, each defined internally by widely shared lexical and grammatical retentions from a common ancestor, and none overlapping to any great extent with others, except via processes of post-dispersal borrowing and contact. In other words, language families are "genetic" entities that have internal shared ancestries and histories of radiation from homeland areas. They have not formed through convergence of genetically unrelated languages, but instead enshrine records of gradual yet increasing *overall* diversification through time. "Diversification" in this sense refers to time depth of genetic differentiation between the languages and subgroups within the family. It has nothing to do with sheer number of languages spoken or with the complexities of borrowed lexicon, and is not normally affected by the expansion of the major languages of nation-states and empires, unless (and this can be quite important) these expansions have totally erased entire previous linguistic landscapes.

The informed comparison of languages within families allows them to be classified into subgroups, and in turn the subgroups can be arranged into phylogenetic hierarchies in terms of their time depths of origin (a subgroup being a set of languages that shares a set of unique and commonly-inherited, not borrowed, defining features). The subgrouping structure within a language family can throw direct light on two issues of enormous importance for prehistory: *homeland location*, and the history of *phylogenetic differentiation*, the latter reflecting directly the geography of spread of the subgroups concerned. This, at least, is the theory, but as we will see, actual definition of homelands and phylogenies can sometimes be fraught with problems, especially if major language replacement occurred in later history, or if the early movements of proto-languages were unusually rapid and widespread, leading to rake-like rather than hierarchical phylogenetic structures and thus the absence of an identifiable geographic origin.

In addition, linguistic comparison (unlike radiocarbon dating) does not yield precise time depth, despite claims concerning glottochronology, a dating method based on purported rates of language change through time. However, if ancestral proto-languages can be reconstructed from cognate lexical items that reveal unequivocal traces of shared descent, by virtue of undergoing regular sound changes, then vocabularies of ancestral lexicon and their attached meanings can be revealed. These vocabularies can be very convincing for cultural cognates with stable meanings that are spread over very large areas. Proto-lexicons can, in turn, be compared with the archaeological record of different times and places. For instance, concepts such as *rice, pig, metal, pottery, weaving,* and *meeting/community house* can exist in proto-languages and the archaeological record alike. Such material concepts have origins and dates – none are cultural universals. Locating their appearances in archaeological time, geographic space, and in proto-language lexicons can be very informative.

One very important result of this kind of reconstruction, crucial for this chapter, is that with little doubt the ancestral proto-languages of all the major existing Asian language families had terms for *crops* and *domestic animals* in their vocabularies. This is an observation worth noting and it is not a result of pure coincidence. The early speakers of Sino-Tibetan languages did not spread as hunters, and neither did the Austronesians. Neither did their primary spreads occur within the time span covered by historical states and empires, despite the more recent spreads of individual languages such as Vietnamese and Thai (as opposed to the Austroasiatic and Tai language families). These language family spreads were neither Palaeolithic, nor were they early historical – mighty empires had rather little effect on language maps, except in core heartlands. The in-between time span, essentially the Neolithic in archaeological terms, is the focus of interest here and was indeed, in my view, the most crucial period in Holocene prehistory for the creation of ensuing human diversity.

Early Farmers and the Dispersal of Language Families

Before we head into the linguistics and Neolithic archaeology there is a hypothesis that requires introduction. The farming–language dispersal hypothesis as developed by Colin Renfrew and myself (for details see Bellwood 2005; Bellwood and Renfrew 2002; Diamond and Bellwood 2003) suggests that the *foundation* dispersals of many of the major language families of tropical and temperate latitudes occurred consequent upon the establishment of reliable agricultural (and especially agropastoral) economies and increasing population densities in and around agricultural homeland areas. As a result of these increasing population densities, some degree of centrifugal movement would have been inevitable in non-circumscribed situations. The hypothesis has now been applied to many parts of the world. The rationale behind the hypothesis is as follows:

1. Situations of early agricultural development will have tended to encourage outflows of languages, cultures, and genes in situations where early farmers had a demographic advantage (i.e. greater population densities) over surrounding and contemporary populations of hunters and gatherers.
2. The foundation spreads of language families, in many cases occurring long before history and over vast extents, and in sociocultural situations of small-scale preliterate farming societies, *required population movement as a major driving force*. Language shift doubtless worked to a degree on a local scale, but it could never have propelled, for instance, the foundation Sino-Tibetan languages across the vast stretch of territory from northeast China to Tibet, Burma, and

northern India, or Austronesian languages across the even more vast extent of ocean and islands from Taiwan to Madagascar and Easter Island. The corpus of recorded language-spread situations in history is extremely large, and supports this perspective strongly (Bellwood 2005). There are no recorded situations of language shift, whether through elite dominance or any other mechanism, that could conceivably explain such large-scale dispersals (virtually trans-continental in many cases) in the absence of any substantial factor of population movement.

3. Such outward flows from agricultural heartland areas will have tended to continue as long as demographic gradients falling off centrifugally were maintained, even though antecedent populations, whether hunter-gatherers or other preceding groups of less numerous/less aggressive farmers, can always be expected to have given rise to at least *some* substratum effects. In addition, antecedent hunter-gatherers might sometimes have adopted agriculture and the languages of incoming farmers, and then might have undergone expansion in their own right. Preceding groups of agriculturalists could also have adopted the languages of different incoming farming populations, as must presumably have happened amongst some original Khmer speakers of Thailand who adopted Thai, and amongst many southern Chinese minority groups who adopted Sinitic languages. Obviously one needs to incorporate concepts of language shift and contact-induced change in any global class of explanation, such as that represented by the farming–language dispersal hypothesis. But such concepts alone cannot explain everything, especially if they are not tied to an importation of target languages in the first place by processes of population movement.

The farming–language dispersal hypothesis is not acceptable to all scholars, as several of the chapters in Bellwood and Renfrew 2002 will indicate. Some linguists claim that language shift has been more important than native-speaker movement as the driver of language spread, others believe that factors other than early agriculture were the drivers. Disputes about the origin regions and mutation dates of mtDNA and Y chromosome lineages abound. Multidisciplinary hypotheses on this world-wide scale are impossible to "prove," but proof is not the aim. We are more concerned with overall "goodness of fit."

The Chinese and Southeast Asian language families

Within the Asian region of concern there are three language families that appear to represent a primary dispersal of agricultural populations through landscapes that were mostly occupied previously by hunting and gathering groups. These are the Sino-Tibetan, Austroasiatic, and Austronesian families. In addition, Japanese evidently spread to Japan with Yayoi rice farmers, replacing the languages of Jomon "hunter-gatherers" (Hudson 1999; Crawford, this volume, on the nature of the Jomon economy), and a similar case for Neolithic spread could perhaps be made for Korean. One might make similar cases for the Dravidian and even the Indo-Aryan languages of South Asia, but these are debates for other venues. The present day distributions of these language families are shown in Figure 6.2.

The Austroasiatic language family, the most widespread and also the most geographically fragmented in Mainland Southeast Asia and eastern India, includes approximately 150 languages in two major subgroups; Mon-Khmer of Southeast Asia, and Munda of northeastern India. The Mon-Khmer subgroup is the largest and contains Mon, Khmer, Vietnamese, and, besides many other tribal languages, the far-flung outliers of Khasi in Assam, the Aslian languages of Malaya, and Nicobarese. The Munda languages of Bihar, Orissa, and West Bengal are even more far-flung, and the very disjointed distribution of this family today suggests that it represents the oldest major language dispersal recognizable in Southeast Asia, one overlain by many expansive languages of civilizations, such as Burmese, Thai, and Malay.

An observation of great interest is that the reconstructed vocabulary of Proto-Austroasiatic suggests a knowledge of rice cultivation (Higham 2002b; Mahdi 1998; Sagart 2003). The possibility that Austroasiatic languages were once spoken very widely in southern China, with linguistic traces even as far north as the Yangzi River (Norman and Mei 1976), is also worthy of note. The homeland of Austroasiatic is not clear owing to massive overlying expansion of other language families, but most linguists suggest southern China or northern Mainland Southeast Asia. Peiros and Schnirelman (1998) suggest a homeland near the middle Yangzi.

Of the other Southeast Asian language families, Hmong-Mien is the one most likely to have originated closest to the central Yangzi early rice zone (discussed below), although the actual dispersal of this group as hill tribes into Southeast Asia has been relatively recent and due in part to pressure from the Chinese state. Peiros (1998:160) suggests that a combined Austroasiatic–Hmong-Mien grouping could have a glottochronological age of about 8,000 years, but whether Austroasiatic and Hmong-Mien are indeed related genetically is a matter for linguists to decide – the prospect is at least interesting since such genetic relationship would automatically imply propinquity of homeland.

The Tai languages are, as a group, not of great antiquity, with a diversification history dating within the past 4,000 years according to Peiros (1998). Their homeland lies in the southern Chinese provinces of Guizhou and Guangxi, and probably Guangdong as well prior to Han Chinese expansion (Ostapirat 2004). The spread of Thai into Thailand and Laos has occurred in recent historical times and cannot be attributed to Neolithic dispersal.

As far as these three language families are concerned, we can perhaps hypothesize on linguistic grounds that, around 6000 B.C., ancestral Hmong-Mien languages were located to the immediate south of the middle Yangzi, with early Austroasiatic languages further to the southwest and early Tai languages to the southeast. In the first instance, only the Austroasiatic group underwent expansion, with Hmong-Mien and Tai presumably remaining relatively circumscribed.

Sino-Tibetan is a little more difficult. In recent years, linguists have given some remarkably divergent opinions on the its homeland. Van Driem (1999) favors Sichuan, Matisoff (1991) prefers the Himalayan Plateau, but Janhunen (1996:222) presents in my view the most likely homeland hypothesis by associating the early

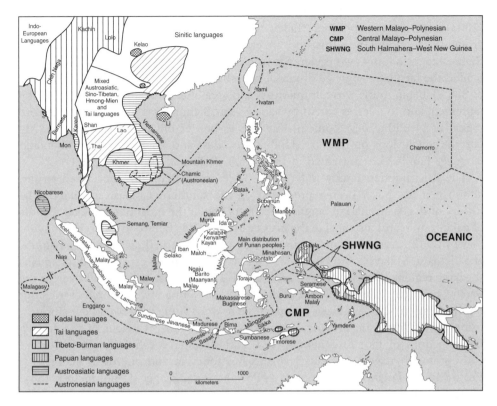

Figure 6.2 Present-day language family distributions in China, Southeast Asia, and New Guinea (from Bellwood 2004a, Figure 1.1); drafted by Jenny Sheehan (ANU)

Sino-Tibetan languages with the Yellow River Neolithic (Yangshao culture). This is partly based on archaeological reasoning, but it does recognize the powerful continuity in central Chinese material culture from Neolithic times onwards into the Shang Dynasty. Norman (1988:17) merely states that the homeland is unknown, but notes that, on the way to the Yellow River, the early Sino-Tibetan languages borrowed from early Hmong-Mien and early Austroasiatic languages, thus implying a slightly southerly origin. This is quite likely, given that Proto-Sino-Tibetan also has strong reconstructions for rice cultivation (Sagart 2003).

Of all the recent hypotheses, that of van Driem (1999, 2003) is perhaps the most detailed and lucid. Van Driem refers to the whole language family as Tibeto-Burman and sources it to Sichuan, from where the oldest movements took place into the Himalayas and northern India. Soon after this, other groups (Northern Tibeto-Burmans) spread with Neolithic cultures into the Yellow River Basin. The Sinitic languages later developed from the more easterly of these populations.

Clearly, the range of views here is extremely varied. Sino-Tibetan subgrouping is rake-like rather than tree-like in structure (Peiros 1998), a possible indicator of a fast and widespread early radiation, similar to that reconstructed for the Malayo-Polynesian languages within Austronesian (see below). As already noted, such fast radiations do not lend themselves to homeland identification, and van Driem (2003) uses the metaphor of "fallen leaves" to describe the Sino-Tibetan sub-grouping situation. Given this, and the erasure of much early patterning caused by Sinitic expansion, my own preference would be to move straight into the reasoning behind the farming–language dispersal hypothesis. This would place the homeland of Sino-Tibetan in the agricultural heartland area of central China, as preferred by Janhunen, and to a lesser extent by van Driem (Sichuan is a little west of the core region of Neolithic development, but it does border on the middle Yangzi). My current conclusions on the homelands of the East and Southeast Asian mainland language families are presented in Figure 6.3 (Bellwood 2004b: Map 1.1).

The Austronesian family is far more widespread than any considered so far, although it has never been represented on the southern Chinese mainland. The history of the Austronesian languages reflects one of the most phenomenal records of colonization and dispersal in the history of mankind (Bellwood 1997; Blust 1995; Pawley 2002). Austronesian languages are now spoken in Taiwan, parts of southern Vietnam, Malaysia, the Philippines, and all of Indonesia except for the Papuan-speaking regions in and around New Guinea. They are also spoken right across the Pacific, to Easter Island. Because of the wealth of comparative research carried out on the Austronesian languages it is possible to draw some very sound conclusions, using purely linguistic evidence, concerning the region of origin of the family, the directions of its subsequent spread, and also the vocabularies of important early proto-languages, particularly Proto-Austronesian and one of its successors, Proto-Malayo-Polynesian. The Malayo-Polynesian languages do not include those of Taiwan, but incorporate the vast remaining distribution of the family from Madagascar to Easter Island.

The reconstruction of overall Austronesian linguistic prehistory which is most acceptable today, and which fits best with all independent sources of evidence, is that favored by the linguist Robert Blust (1995, 1999). Reduced to its essentials, this reconstruction favors a geographic expansion beginning in Taiwan, the location of Proto-Austronesian and of the majority of the primary subgroups of Austronesian. Subsequent Malayo-Polynesian dispersal then encompassed the Philippines, Borneo, and Sulawesi, and finally spread in two branches, one moving west to Java, Sumatra, and the Malay Peninsula, the other moving east into Oceania. The Proto-Austronesian vocabulary located on Taiwan indicates an economy well suited to marginal tropical latitudes with cultivation of rice, millet, sugarcane, presences of domesticated dogs, pigs and possibly water buffalo, and the use of canoes. The vocabulary of Proto-Malayo-Polynesian, perhaps of northern Philippine genesis, adds a number of tropical economic indicators that are not well attested in the earlier Proto-Austronesian stage. These include taro, breadfruit, banana, yam, sago, and coconut, and their presences reflect the shift away from rice towards a greater dependence on tubers and fruits in equatorial latitudes (Blust 1995; Zorc 1994).

One point to note concerns the shape of the Austronesian family tree. As discussed by Blust (1993) and Pawley (1999), the early Malayo-Polynesian languages spread very far very quickly, before linguistic differentiation was able to proceed very far. As an example, the oldest Malayo-Polynesian language in western Oceania

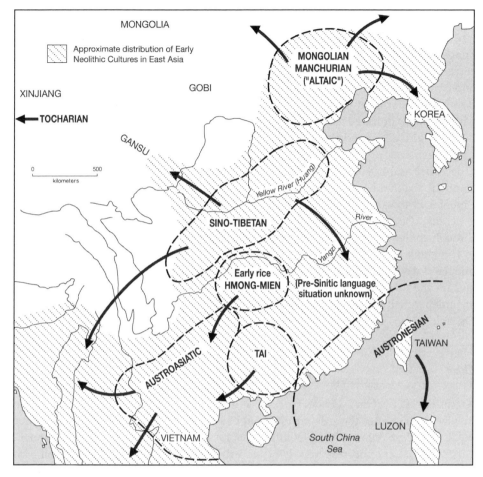

Figure 6.3 Suggested homelands for the major language families of China and Southeast Asia (Bellwood 2005, Figure 10.8A); drafted by Jenny Sheehan (ANU)

(Proto-Oceanic, probably located in the Bismarck Archipelago) contained almost the same basic vocabulary as did Proto-Malayo-Polynesian itself, located perhaps in the northern Philippines almost 5,000 km away. Such rake-like phylogenies have been discussed above, and in the Malayo-Polynesian case they are a very strong indicator of a rapid foundation spread, at least from the northern Philippines to the central Pacific.

Early Agriculture in China and Southeast Asia

Nowhere in Southeast Asia is there currently any hard evidence for any form of food production (as opposed to potential resource management) before 3000 B.C. This is significant, given that rice was well-domesticated by at least 6000 B.C. along the Yangzi, as were the two Asian millets (foxtail and broomcorn) along the Yellow River (Figure 6.1). Why it took so long for farming to spread from central China into Southeast Asia is not currently understood. Possible reasons could include hunter-gatherer resistance, day length factors slowing down the spread of cultivated cereals that were sensitive to latitude, or just simple lack of data (the tropics are often not kind to the archaeological record, and maybe some basic variety of farming is older than we think). Once on the move, however, Neolithic complexes with pottery, polished stone adzes, shell ornaments, spindle whorls, barkcloth beaters, and presumed-domesticated bovids, pigs, and dogs replaced the older hunter-gatherer archaeological complexes of the early and mid-Holocene with orderly precision, generally moving down a north–south axis from southern China through Mainland Southeast Asia towards Malaysia, and through Taiwan and the Philippines towards Indonesia (although spindle whorls and bovid bones do not generally occur in the Neolithic of Island Southeast Asia). Within Indonesia, through the equatorial zone, the spread of agricultural populations was converted to run along a latitudinal axis out of the Borneo–Sulawesi–Moluccas region, on the one hand westwards into western Indonesia, the Malay Peninsula and Madagascar, and on the other hand eastwards into Oceania (Bellwood 1997). The presence of an independent focus of early food production in New Guinea complicates the Oceanic story, but lies outside the focus of this chapter.

China

As discussed by Gary Crawford (this volume), the archaeological record of the Yellow River points towards an oldest appearance of the Neolithic prior to 6500 B.C. The oldest Yellow River Neolithic sites formed a continuum with four internal clusters, two centered respectively around the major sites of Cishan and Peiligang (Figure 6.4), with two smaller groups in the Wei and upper Han valleys. Southerly sites, for instance Lijiacun in the upper Han valley, often contain small quantities of rice as well as millet. Jiahu in Henan, a site located in the Huai basin with a material culture very close to that of the Peiligang culture, is especially important because it actually appears to have had a rice-based economy dated to between 7000 and 6000 B.C. Jiahu renders completely untenable the idea that the millets and rice were domesticated by separate communities living in splendid isolation.

In the Yangzi basin, the agricultural economy seems to have been based primarily on rice by at least 7000 B.C., for instance at the sites of Pengtoushan and Bashidang (Figure 6.4). New Chinese discoveries, so far unpublished, indicate that sites of similar age exist also in the lower Yangzi, in the vicinity of the famous Middle Neolithic site of Hemudu. Although no fields have survived from earliest Neolithic times, new discoveries at Chengtoushan and Caoxieshan, near Pengtoushan, have yielded remains of small bunded rice fields dating from about 4500–3000 B.C., these being so far the oldest actual rice field remains discovered in China (He 1999).

Thus, by 6500 B.C., perhaps 3,000 years before any evidence appears for agriculture in Southeast Asia, or for that matter in India (east of the Indus region),

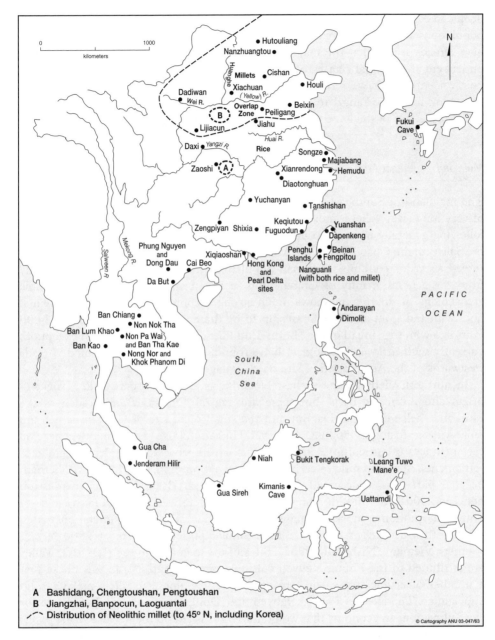

Figure 6.4 The homelands of rice and foxtail millet cultivation in East Asia, together with archaeological sites mentioned in the text (Bellwood 2005, Figure 6.3); drafted by Jenny Sheehan (ANU)

people in central China were developing intensive agricultural systems with growing populations and, most probably, increasing propensities for population outflow. We have already noted that the major language families of eastern Asia all evidently underwent their initial phases of evolution within or very close to their modern political entity that we term "China." The heartland of East Asian agriculture, stretching from the Yangzi to the Yellow drainage basins, probably witnessed the initial dispersals of the ancestors of almost half of the world's modern population.

Mainland Southeast Asia

The mainland of Southeast Asia consists of upland terrain separated by a number of very long river valleys, most rising in the eastern fringes of the Himalayas and following generally in north–south directions. These rivers include the Irrawaddy, the Salween, the Chao Phraya, the Mekong, and the Red (Hong), and all must have served as major conduits of human population movement in the past, especially from the general vicinity of China. Thus, it is not surprising that the Neolithic archaeology of this region shows much stronger connections with China than it does with India, an axis of relationship to be dramatically overturned after 2,000 years ago with the spread of the Hindu–Buddhist civilizations. The main exception, currently with little archaeological background, would be the presumed spreads westwards of the Austroasiatic (Munda) languages.

In northern Vietnam, the earliest Neolithic is a little obscure with respect to origin and economic basis, but there are coastal "Neolithic" sites such as the estuarine shell midden at Da But and the small open site of Cai Beo which are reliably dated to about 4500 B.C. However, Higham (2002a) notes that they have no certain traces of agriculture, and may thus have been essentially hunter-gatherer settlements. Apart from these early and somewhat puzzling sites, northern Vietnam became part of a widespread Mainland Southeast Asian Neolithic expression between 2500 and 1500 B.C., an expression characterized by a distinctive style of pottery decoration comprising incised zones filled with stamped punctations, often made with a dentate or shell-edge tool. Similar pottery appears by 2000 B.C. in southern Vietnam (Nishimura 2002). Sites of this complex in the Red River Valley are attributed to the Phung Nguyen cultural complex, and it is in this phase that a number of artifact types with strong southern Chinese parallels make a solid appearance. The sites of Phung Nguyen and Dong Dau have good evidence for rice cultivation, an economy that would have flourished on the fertile alluvial plains of the Red River. Cattle, buffalo, and pigs might have been domesticated during the late Neolithic, but precise data are not available.

Firm data for a spread of rice agriculture by 2500 B.C. are even more clearly attested for Thailand. As in northern Vietnam, the oldest pottery on the Khorat Plateau of northeastern Thailand and in the lower Chao Phraya Basin has zoned incision infilled with punctation, widespread between 2500 and 1500 B.C. at sites such as Nong Nor, Khok Phanom Di, Non Pa Wai, Tha Kae, and Ban Chiang. The economic record for the Thai Neolithic is especially rich (Higham 2002a) and many sites have evidence for rice cultivation, especially in the form of husk temper in pottery. In northeastern Thailand, Ban Chiang has rice remains that may predate 2500 B.C., but in the drier southern part of the Khorat Plateau the first agricultural sites seem to postdate 1500 B.C. Domestic animals include pig and dog from an early date, but at Khok Phanom Di (2000–1500 B.C.) only the dog is likely to have been domesticated, together possibly with a species of jungle fowl. Domesticated cattle (probably of gaur or banteng ancestry) were present by at least 1500 B.C. in northeastern Thailand, at Non Nok Tha, Ban Lum Khao, and Ban Chiang.

In southern Thailand and Malaysia, the majority of archaeological assemblages come from cave locations, a circumstance which doubtless biases the record. But what can be stated from these caves is that there was a very marked shift in cave usage from Hoabinhian into Neolithic times, from habitation to burial functions. This is expectable if the arrival of agriculture promoted a sedentary lifestyle in villages as opposed to a mobile lifestyle using temporary camps in caves. Peninsular Neolithic pottery is quite distinctive and contains vessel tripods with perforations to allow hot air to escape during firing, so far found in about 20 sites down almost the whole length of the 1,600 km long peninsula, from Ban Kao in western Thailand to near Kuala Lumpur (Bellwood 1993; Leong 1991). These represent a very consistent tradition of pottery manufacture, perhaps first developed in central Thailand at about 2000 B.C. Gua Cha in Kelantan also has fine incised pottery with zoned punctation, like that discussed above with respect to Vietnam and Thailand, here dating to about 1000 B.C. (Adi 1985). However, south of central Thailand there is no direct archaeological evidence for rice at this date, so the nature of the economy remains something of a mystery.

Summarizing the Neolithic record for the Southeast Asian mainland, we have indications of the spread of a well-defined incised and stamped pottery style associated with rice cultivation in southern China, Vietnam, and Thailand, between 2500 and 1500 B.C. A contemporary but slightly different style of tripod pottery spread down the Malay Peninsula after 2000 B.C., with a presence of rice being uncertain. These spreads appear to have been rapid, extensive, and with little sign of continuity from local Hoabinhian forebears. The question remains, if there was a wave of advance of farmers out of southern China at this time, did it occur down the major rivers, around the Vietnam coastline, or by both routes? Only future research is likely to answer this question.

Taiwan and Island Southeast Asia

We now move southeast to the island chains that festoon the coastline of Southeast Asia. The oldest Neolithic culture in Taiwan, the Dapenkeng, spread all round the coastline of Taiwan after 3500 B.C., with a cord-marked and incised pottery style so homogeneous that spread with a new population from Fujian replacing or assimilating the earlier Changbinian (a facies of the Hoabinhian) seems assured (Bellwood 2000). Close relationships occur with slightly older Fujian pottery assemblages from sites such as Keqiutou and Fuguodun, the latter on Jinmen (Quemoy)

Island (Chang 1995). As a result of recent excavations in Taiwan, the Dapenkeng culture is known to have had rice production, pearl shell reaping knives, spindle whorls and barkcloth beaters (Tsang 2004) by at least 3000 B.C.

By 2000 B.C., the Dapenkeng pottery style had evolved into various regional cord-marked or red slipped expressions, and it was at this point, perhaps a millennium after farmers first arrived in Taiwan, that agriculture spread south into the Philippines and eventually Indonesia. In the Philippines, northern Borneo, and many regions of eastern Indonesia the oldest Neolithic pottery is characterized by simple forms with plain or red slipped surfaces, often stamped with dentate patterns or circles. This phase dates overall between 2000 and about 500 B.C., and can be traced onwards into Oceania after 1400 B.C. in the form of the Lapita cultural complex of the western and central Pacific, and contemporary settlements in the Mariana Islands. As a result of recent research in the Batanes Islands and the Cagayan Valley of northern Luzon (Bellwood et al. 2003; Ogawa 2002), the origins of this red slipped pottery can perhaps be traced to Taiwan during the early second millennium B.C., precise links being as yet uncertain although the best candidates currently lie in pottery assemblages of this date found along the eastern coast of the island. Rice occurs in the pottery from Andarayan in northern Luzon, and as impressions in the pottery from Bukit Tengkorak in Sabah, at dates between c.1600 and 500 B.C. (Doherty et al. 2000:152; Snow et al. 1986).

The extent of human movement through this zone of red slipped pottery at about 1300 B.C. can be illustrated by the obsidian carried 3,500 km from a source on New Britain in the Bismarck Archipelago into Bukit Tengkorak (Bellwood and Koon 1989). Other assemblages with similar red slipped pottery, so far without rice, come from northern Sulawesi, the northern Moluccas, and eastern Java, dated in the first two cases to about 1500 B.C. onwards. They occur with polished stone adzes, shell beads and bracelets, and bones of pig and dog, none of these (apart from shell beads) being present in any older assemblages in eastern Indonesia or the Pacific Islands beyond New Guinea.

The implication of all this archaeological material is that a marked cultural break with the preceramic lithic industries of the Indonesian region occurred across a very large area, possibly commencing by 2000 B.C. in the Philippines and appearing in the Moluccas and Bismarcks, close to New Guinea, by about 1300 B.C. Archaeological assemblages with related forms of red slipped and stamped or incised pottery, shell artifacts, stone adzes, and bones of pigs and dogs thus spread over an area extending almost 10,000 km, from the Philippines, through Indonesia, and then via the Lapita complex into the western islands of Polynesia in the central Pacific. The economy driving this expansion was strongly maritime in orientation, but these people were also farmers with domesticated animals. We have no evidence that any of them grew rice in the equatorial islands of eastern Indonesia or in Oceania, and it seems that this subtropical cereal faded from the economic repertoire as people moved south (Dewar 2003). In equatorial latitudes rice was replaced by tubers and fruits such as yams, taro, coconut, breadfruit, bananas, pandanus, canarium nuts, and many others, all originally domesticated in the tropical regions from Malaysia through to Melanesia (Lebot 1999). Neolithic populations domesticated or acquired these crops as they moved southwards and eastwards through the islands, and some might have been domesticated independently in and around the island of New Guinea, where evidence for swamp drainage and presumably an independent agricultural tradition in the highlands dates back to beyond 6,000 years ago (Denham et al. 2003).

Meanwhile, it needs to be noted that the red slipped pottery horizon does not appear in western Indonesia, where the Neolithic archaeological record is unfortunately still almost non-existent. Most early pottery assemblages in western Borneo and Java tend to have cord-marked or paddle-impressed surface decoration without red slip (except in East Java). In Borneo, research by Karina Arifin in Kimanis Cave in East Kalimantan indicates that some sherds of this kind of pottery contain rice impressions. Similar rice impressions occur in pottery in the Niah Caves in Sarawak (Beavitt et al. 1996) and in the cave of Gua Sireh near Kuching, here with an actual rice grain embedded in a sherd dated to about 2200 B.C. by AMS radiocarbon (Bellwood et al. 1992). My impression from these data, still admittedly faint and unconfirmed by any coherent information from Java or Sumatra, is that a paddle-impressed style of pottery with widespread evidence of rice spread from the Philippines, where similar impressed pottery occurs in Palawan, through Borneo and presumably into western Indonesia, after 2500 B.C. This spread was apparently independent of that which carried red slipped pottery and a non-cereal economy eastwards into the Pacific.

Relating Archaeology and Languages

The data reviewed so far suggest the following inferences based on the comparative linguistic and archaeological data sets:

1. Linguistically, a series of language families with foundation agricultural and domestic animal vocabularies evolved in halo-like fashion around central China, with extensions into the northern fringes of Southeast Asia and Taiwan. Three of these language families (Austroasiatic, Sino-Tibetan, and Austronesian) underwent major expansions long before history began, in the latter case with very firm phylogenetic reconstructions indicating spread southwards from Taiwan into Indonesia and Oceania. Linguistic dating estimates for these families, albeit rather impressionistic, indicate ages generally between 7,000 and 4,000 years ago – certainly post-hunter-gatherer and pre-Iron Age in cultural terms. Numerous linguistic hypotheses suggest that these families share basal genetic relationships, implying their derivations from regions quite close together in space (for example, Benedict 1975; Blust 1996; Reid 1996; Sagart et al. 2004). However, I would not be so unwise as to claim that all relationships are *genetic*; arguments for early borrowing also are numerous. The suggestion here is that early forms of the major families – Sino-Tibetan,

Austroasiatic, Hmong-Mien, Austronesian, and Tai – were at one time located sufficiently close together for some degree of sharing of heritage, both genetic and areal.

2. Archaeologically, rice and millet cultivation in central China have a lead of about 3,000 years over evidence for any form of agriculture in other regions (excluding New Guinea and Pakistan). By 3000 B.C. there was a spread of Neolithic cultures through the mainland and islands of Southeast Asia, in radio-carbon terms decreasing in age southwards toward Malaysia and southwards and eastwards into Island Southeast Asia and the Pacific (Spriggs 2003). The northerly cultures grew rice, whereas those along the equator in Island Southeast Asia depended on fruits and tubers. Related pottery and other artifact forms suggest ultimate origins for these complexes in the southern China–Taiwan region. As far as Austronesian is concerned, a standstill of about 1,000 years in Taiwan, before Neolithic cultures spread further into the Philippines, is documented by both the archaeological and the linguistic records (the latter reflecting the above-described rake-like phylogeny of the Malayo-Polynesian languages).

At this point, it would take a very determined skeptic indeed to suggest that these patterns are totally unrelated and coincidental. The suggestion that early agricul-tural economies, and foundation languages at the bases of language families, spread hand in hand is a very powerful one in the situations discussed above. But there is still the litmus test of human biology – did farming and languages just spread through entirely unmoving communities, formerly hunter-gatherer, who all decided to adopt the new forms? Or did the farming and languages spread with actual farmers and native speakers of the languages? I strongly favor the latter as the main process, but not always the only one (Bellwood 1991, 1996, 2001a, 2001b, 2005).

The Witness of Human Biology

The genetic field of research is a little more complex to follow than that of lin-guistics, partly because of a division into studies based on analysis of sexually recombining genes within the cell nucleus, versus studies based on the non-recombining genetic systems contained within mitochondrial DNA (mtDNA – inherited exclusively through females) and on part of the Y chromosome (inherited through males). Analysis of geographic clines in the frequencies of recombining genes, such as those that determine blood groups and serum proteins, informed much of the early work on European and Asian genetic history (e.g. Cavalli-Sforza et al. 1994). But most research nowadays is focused on the non-recombining systems. In these, the occurrence of occasional nucleotide mutations allows geneti-cists to reconstruct (often with considerable disagreement, as techniques improve and evolve) the homelands and chronologies of specific mtDNA and Y chromo-some lineages. Whether the histories of mtDNA and Y chromosome lineages can be considered equivalent to the histories of whole human populations is an issue that leads to much debate (one might ask in like vein if the history of a word can also be the history of a language family, or the history of an artifact type can be that of a whole culture – the answer will of course be situational and subject to contingency). Genetic analysis is just starting to make inroads into Asian population history, but sometimes gives results that conflict with what appear to be clear conclusions from archaeology and linguistics (e.g., Bellwood 2003; Oppenheimer and Richards 2001; Young 2004).

Prior to the development of modern mtDNA and Y chromosome studies, genetics added rather little to the general picture of Asian prehistory, apart from plotting the distributions of certain genetic markers located in blood (Kirk et al. 1986). These had the benefit of distinguishing Asian-Pacific populations into loosely Mongoloid and Australomelanesian clinal nodes of variation, an impression reinforced by multivariate analysis of skull characteristics (Pietrusewsky 2004). The skeletal record from archaeology indicates that, through Southeast Asia generally, the Mongoloid populations are the most recent of the two (Bellwood 1997), but there are also regions where such separation is not evident (e.g. Bulbeck 2004 for Malaysia), implying that regional continuity has to be taken seriously, as well as population replacement. Turner (1995) also claims dental continuity in Southeast Asia since the Pleistocene, although this need not rule out Holocene population movements emanating from within the general area of southern China, since like can of course replace like. Indeed, other paleoanthropological data support some degree of population replacement in the Chinese Neolithic. Brown (1998), for instance, claims that Mongoloids only appeared in China during the Neolithic, replacing older non-Mongoloid populations (see also Kamminga and Wright 1988).

None of this paleoanthropological material is, of course, very specific in terms of the linguistic and archaeological populations discussed above. Nowadays, all eyes are on human genetics because it is possible to sample populations selected according to ethnolinguistic criteria. Population-specific genetic testing suggests, for instance, relatively close relationships in blood genetic markers between Malaysian Semai and Cambodian Khmer, both Austroasiatic speaking populations (Saha et al. 1995). On a broader scale, Karafet et al. (2001), using Y chromosome haplotypes, note relatively deep-seated differences between Northeast Asians (including Chinese) and Southeast Asians, although whether this reflects population differentiation since about 6000 B.C. is not clear. Many geneticists have recently discussed the origins of Austronesian-speaking populations, coming into disagreement in the process but generally reinforcing the possibility of a language and population homeland in Taiwan, combined with considerable amounts of population mixing in Island Southeast Asia (Capelli et al. 2001; Cox In press; Hurles 2002; Karafet et al. 2005; Melton et al. 1998; Merriwether et al. 1999; Young 2004), and possibly also with continuing new genetic lineage formation through mutation as the population spread ever further towards the Pacific.

The impression is hard to resist, however, that the genetic data are not yet equal in coverage to the data from linguistics and archaeology. Genetic data are spotty at best, and often hard to interpret owing to uncertainties over mutation rates through time, over possibilities of lineage loss or expansion owing to a range of stochastic factors (such as founder effects), and over the role of natural selection, especially disease, in determining lineage frequencies. Perhaps the most positive statement in favor of the reconstruction presented in this chapter comes from the Y chromosome research of Peter Underhill and colleagues (2001). They identify an East Asian cluster of Y chromosome lineages, termed M122 (part of their larger East Asian Group VII, and now more commonly termed lineage O3 in the genetic literature), and suggest that its distribution.

> . . . may reflect the impact of millet and rice agriculture on East Asian Mongoloid demographic history . . . displacing to a great extent all other NRY [non-recombining Y chromosome] variants with a clinal frequency from the expected China area of origin. (Underhill et al. 2001, p. 55)

They go on to compare this early agricultural population expansion with that of the Bantu speakers in Africa, another of the world's great early farming diasporas. The moral to be drawn from all this is that, on the broad scale, the impacts of Neolithic population expansion in East Asia can be seen in the genetic record. But on the narrow scale, life is often more complex, as was the impact in local population terms of the recent European colonial era. Barring genocide or extinction, the genes of every population will live on into future generations, long after their original cultures and languages might have been irrevocably replaced.

ACKNOWLEDGMENTS

Andy Pawley kindly checked some of my linguistic terminology, but is not responsible for anything stated above. Jenny Sheehan in the Cartography Unit, Research School of Pacific and Asian Studies at ANU, drew the maps.

REFERENCES

Adi Haji Taha 1985 The Re-Excavation of the Rockshelter of Gua Cha, Ulu Kelantan, West Malaysia. Kuala Lumpur: Federation Museums Journal 30.

Beavitt, Paul, Edmund Kurui, and Gillian Thompson 1996 Confirmation of an Early Date for the Presence of Rice in Borneo. Borneo Research Bulletin 27:29–37.

Bellwood, Peter 1991 The Austronesian Dispersal and the Origin of Languages. Scientific American 265(1):88–93.

—— 1993 Cultural and Biological Differentiation in Peninsular Malaysia: The last 10,000 Years. Asian Perspectives 32:37–60.

—— 1996 The Origins and Spread of Agriculture in the Indo-Pacific Region. In The Origins and Spread of Agriculture and Pastoralism in Eurasia. David Harris, ed. Pp. 465–98. London: University College Press.

—— 1997 Prehistory of the Indo-Malaysian Archipelago, 2nd edition. Honolulu: University of Hawaii Press.

—— 2000 Formosan Prehistory and Austronesian Dispersal. *In* Austronesian Taiwan. David Blundell, ed. Pp. 337–65. Berkeley CA: Phoebe A. Hearst Museum of Anthropology.

—— 2001a Early Agriculturalist Population Diasporas? Farming, Languages and Genes. Annual Review of Anthropology 30:181–207.

—— 2001b Archaeology and the Historical Determinants of Punctuation in Language Family Origins. *In* Areal Diffusion and Genetic Inheritance: Problems in Comparative Linguistics. Alexandra Aikhenvald and Robert Dixon, eds. Pp. 27–43. Oxford: Oxford University Press.

—— 2004a The Origins and Dispersals of Agricultural Communities in Southeast Asia. *In* Southeast Asia: From Prehistory to History. Ian Glover and Peter Bellwood, eds. Pp. 21–40. London: RoutledgeCurzon.

—— 2004b Examining the Language/Farming Dispersal Hypothesis in the East Asian Context. *In* The Peopling of East Asia: Putting Together Archaeology, Linguistics and Genetics. Laurence Sagart, Roger Blench, and Alicia Sanchez-Mazas, eds. Pp. 17–30. London: Routledge/Curzon.

—— 2005 First Farmers: The Origins of Agricultural Societies. Oxford and Malden MA: Blackwell.

Bellwood, Peter, and Peter Koon 1989 Lapita Colonists Leave Boats Unburned. Antiquity 63:613–22.

Bellwood, Peter, and Colin Renfrew, eds. 2002 Examining the Language/Farming Dispersal Hypothesis. Cambridge: McDonald Institute for Archaeological Research.

Bellwood, Peter, R. Gillespie, Gillian Thompson, I. Wayan Ardika, and Ipoi Datan 1992 New Dates for Prehistoric Asian Rice. Asian Perspectives 31/2:161–70.

Bellwood, Peter, Janelle Stevenson, Atholl Anderson, and Eusebio Dizon 2003 Archaeological and Paleoenvironmental Research in Batanes and Ilocos Norte Provinces, Northern Philippines. Bulletin of the Indo-Pacific Prehistory Association 23:141–61.

Benedict, Paul King 1975 Austro-Thai Language and Culture. New Haven: HRAF Press.

Blust, Robert 1993 Central and Central-Eastern Malayo-Polynesian. Oceanic Linguistics 32:241–93.

—— 1995 The Prehistory of the Austronesian-Speaking Peoples: A View from Language. Journal of World Prehistory 9:453–510.

—— 1996 Beyond the Austronesian Homeland: The Austric Hypothesis and Its Implication for Archaeology. *In* Prehistoric Settlement of the Pacific. Ward Goodenough, ed. Pp. 117–40. Philadelphia: American Philosophical Society.

—— 1999 Subgrouping, Circularity and Extinction. *In* Selected Papers from the Eighth International Conference on Austronesian Linguistics. Elizabeth Zeitoun and Paul J-K. Li, eds. Pp. 31–94. Taipei: Academia Sinica, Institute of Linguistics.

Brown, Peter 1998 The First Mongoloids? Acta Anthropologica Sinica 17(4):260–75.

Bulbeck, David 2004 Indigenous Traditions and Exogenous Influences in the Early History of Peninsular Malaysia. *In* Southeast Asia: An Archaeological History. Ian Glover and Peter Bellwood, eds. Pp. 314–36. London: RoutledgeCurzon.

Capelli, Cristian, James Wilson, Martin Richards, Michael Stumpf, Fiona Gratrix, Stephen Oppenheimer, Peter Underhill, Pascali Vincenzo, Ko Tsang-Ming, and David Goldstein 2001 A Predominantly Indigenous Paternal Heritage for the Austronesian Speaking Peoples of Insular South East Asia and Oceania. American Journal of Human Genetics 68:432–43.

Cavalli-Sforza, Luigi Luca, Paolo Menozzi, and Alberto Piazza 1994 The History and Geography of Human Genes. Princeton: Princeton University Press.

Chang, Kwang-Chih 1995 Taiwan Strait Archaeology and Proto-Austronesian. *In* Austronesian Studies Relating to Taiwan. Paul Jen-kuei Li, Ho Dah-An, Huang Ying-Kuei, Tsang Cheng-Hwa, and Tseng Chiu-vu, eds. Pp. 161–84. Taipei: Institute of History and Philology, Academia Sinica.

Cox, Murray In press Indonesian Mitochondrial DNA and its Opposition to a Pleistocene-era Origin of Proto-Polynesians in Island Southeast Asia. Human Biology.

Denham, Timothy, Simon Haberle, Carol Letnfer, Richard Fullagar, Julie Field, Michael Therin, Nicholas Porch, and B. Winsborough 2003 Origins of Agriculture at Kuk Swamp in the Highlands of New Guinea. Science 301:189–93.

Dewar, Robert 2003 Rainfall Variability and Subsistence Systems in Southeast Asia and the Western Pacific. Current Anthropology 44:369–88.

Diamond, Jared, and Peter Bellwood 2003 Farmers and their Languages: The First Expansions. Science 300:597–603.

Doherty, Christopher, Paul Beavitt, and Edmund Kurui 2000 Recent Observations of Rice Temper in Pottery from Niah and Other Sites in Sarawak. Bulletin of the Indo-Pacific Prehistory Association 20:147–52.

Driem, George van 1999 A New Theory on the Origin of Chinese. Bulletin of the Indo-Pacific Prehistory Association 18:43–58.

——— 2003 Tibeto-Burman Phylogeny and Prehistory: Languages, Material Culture and Genes. *In* Examining the Language/Farming Dispersal Hypothesis. Peter Bellwood and Colin Renfrew, eds. Pp. 223–49. Cambridge: McDonald Institute for Archaeological Research.

He Jiejun 1999 Excavations in Chengtoushan in Li County, Hunan Province, China. Bulletin of the Indo-Pacific Prehistory Association 18:101–4.

Higham, Charles F. W. 2002a Early Cultures of Mainland Southeast Asia. London: Thames and Hudson.

——— 2002b Languages and Farming Dispersals: Austroasiatic Languages and Rice Cultivation. *In* Examining the Language/Farming Dispersal Hypothesis. Peter Bellwood and Colin Renfrew, eds. Pp. 223–32. Cambridge: McDonald Institute for Archaeological Research.

Hudson, Mark 1999 Ruins of Identity. Honolulu: University of Hawaii Press.

Hurles, Matthew 2002 Can the Hypothesis of Language/Agriculture Co-Dispersal be Tested with Archaeogenetics? *In* Examining the Language/Farming Dispersal Hypothesis. Peter Bellwood and Colin Renfrew, eds. Pp. 299–309. Cambridge: McDonald Institute for Archaeological Research.

Janhunen, Juha 1996 Manchuria: An Ethnic History. Helsinki: Suomalais-Ugrilainen Seura.

Kamminga, Johan, and Richard Wright 1988 The Upper Cave at Zhoukoudian and the Origin of the Mongoloids. Journal of Human Evolution 17:739–67.

Karafet, Tatiana, J. Lansing, Alan Redd, Joseph Watkins, S. Surata, W. Arthawiguna, Laura Mayer, Michael Bamshad, Lynn Jorde, and Michael Hammer 2005 Balinese Y-chromosome Perspective on the Peopling of Indonesia: Genetic Contributions from Pre-Neolithic Hunter-gatherers, Austronesian Farmers, and Indian Traders. Human Biology 77:93–113.

Karafet, Tatiana, Liping Xu, Ruofu Du, William Wang, Shi Feng, R. S. Wells, Alan J. Redd, Stephen L. Zegura, and Michael F. Hammer 2001 Paternal Population History of East Asia. American Journal of Human Genetics 69:615–28.

Kirk, Robert L., Derek F. Roberts, and G. F. de Stefano 1986 Human Genetic Diversity in South-East Asia and the Western Pacific. *In* Genetic Variation and its Maintenance.

D. F. Roberts and G. F. de Stefano, eds. Pp. 111–33. Cambridge: Cambridge University Press.

Lebot, V. 1999 Biomolecular Evidence for Plant Domestication in Sahul. Genetic Resources and Crop Evolution 46:619–28.

Leong Sau Heng 1991 Jenderam Hilir and the Mid-Holocene Prehistory of the West Coast Plain of Peninsular Malaysia. Bulletin of the Indo-Pacific Prehistory Association 10:150–60.

Mahdi, Waruno 1998 Linguistic Data on Transmission of Southeast Asian Cultigens to India and Sri Lanka. *In* Archaeology and Language II. Roger Blench and Matthew Spriggs, eds. Pp. 390–415. London: Routledge.

Matisoff, James 1991 Sino-Tibetan Linguistics: Present State and Future Prospects. Annual Review of Anthropology 20:469–504.

Melton, Terry, Stephanie Clifford, Jeremy Martinson, Mark Batzer, and Mark Stoneking 1998 Genetic Evidence for the Proto-Austronesian Homeland in Asia. American Journal of Human Genetics 63:1807–23.

Merriwether, D. Andrew, Jonathan Friedlaender, Jose Mediavilla, Charles Mgone, Fred Gentz, and Robert Ferrell 1999 Mitochondrial DNA Variation is an Indicator of Austronesian Influence in Island Melanesia. American Journal of Physical Anthropology 110:243–70.

Nishimura, Masanari 2002 Chronology of the Neolithic Age in the Southern Vietnam. Journal of Southeast Asian Archaeology 22:25–57.

Norman, Jerry 1988 Chinese. Cambridge: Cambridge University Press.

Norman, Jerry, and Tsu-lin Mei 1976 The Austroasiatics in Ancient South China: Some Lexical Evidence. Monumenta Serica 32:274–301.

Ogawa, Hidefumi 2002 Chronological Study on the Red-Slipped Pottery of the Lal-lo Shell Middens. Journal of Southeast Asian Archaeology 22:59–80.

Oppenheimer, Stephen, and Martin Richards 2001 Fast Trains, Slow Boats, and the Ancestry of the Polynesian Islanders. Science Progress 84:157–81.

Ostapirat, Weera 2004 Kra-dai and Austronesians. *In* The Peopling of East Asia: Putting Together Archaeology, Linguistics and Genetics. Laurence Sagart, Roger Blench, and Alicia Sanchez-Mazas, eds. Pp. 107–31. London: Routledge Curzon.

Pawley, Andrew K. 1999 Chasing Rainbows: Implications of the Rapid Dispersal of Austronesian Languages for Subgrouping and Reconstruction. *In* Selected Papers from the Eighth International Conference on Austronesian Linguistics. E. Zeitoun and P. J-K. Li, eds. Pp. 95–138. Taipei: Institute of Linguistics, Academia Sinica.

—— 2002 The Austronesian Dispersal: Languages, Technologies and People. *In* Examining the Language/Farming Dispersal Hypothesis. Peter Bellwood and Colin Renfrew, eds. Pp. 251–74. Cambridge: McDonald Institute for Archaeological Research.

Peiros, Ilya 1998 Comparative Linguistics in Southeast Asia. Pacific Linguistics Series C-142. Canberra: Australian National University.

Peiros, Ilya, and Victor Schnirelman 1998 Rice in Southeast Asia. *In* Archaeology and Language II. Roger Blench and Matthew Spriggs, eds. Pp. 379–89. London: Routledge.

Pietrusewsky, Michael 2004 The Physical Anthropology of the Pacific, East Asia and Southeast Asia. *In* The Peopling of East Asia: Putting Together Archaeology, Linguistics and Genetics. Laurence Sagart, Roger Blench, and Alicia Sanchez-Mazas, eds. Pp. 201–29. London: Routledge Curzon.

Reid, Laurence 1996 The Current State of Linguistic Research on the Relatedness of the Language Families of East and Southeast Asia. Bulletin of the Indo-Pacific Prehistory Association 15:87–92.

Sagart, Laurence 2003 The Vocabulary of Cereal Cultivation and the Phylogeny of East Asian Languages. Bulletin of the Indo-Pacific Prehistory Association 23:127–36.

Sagart, Laurence, Roger Blench, and Alicia Sanchez-Mazas, eds. 2004 The Peopling of East Asia: Putting Together Archaeology, Linguistics and Genetics. London: Routledge Curzon.

Saha, N., J. Tay, Y. Liu, et al. 1995 Population Genetic Study Among the Orang Asli (Semai Senoi) of Malaysia. Human Biology 67:37–57.

Snow, Brian E., Richard Shutler, Richard Nelson, J. S. Vogel, and J. Southon 1986 Evidence of Early Rice Cultivation in the Philippines. Philippine Quarterly of Culture and Society 14:3–11.

Spriggs, Matthew 2003 Chronology of the Neolithic Transition in Island Southeast Asia and the Western Pacific. Review of Archaeology 24/2:57–80.

Tsang Cheng-hwa 2004 Recent Discoveries of the Tapenkeng Culture in Taiwan. *In* The Peopling of East Asia: Putting Together Archaeology, Linguistics and Genetics. Laurence Sagart, Roger Blench, and Alicia Sanchez-Mazas, eds. Pp. 63–74. London: Routledge Curzon.

Turner, Christy G. 1995 Shifting Continuity: Modern Human Origin. *In* The Origin and Past of Modern Humans as Viewed from DNA. S. Brenner and K. Hanihara, eds. Pp. 216–43. Singapore: World Scientific.

Underhill, Peter, G. Passarino, A. Lin, P. Shen, Marta Lahr, Robert Foley, P. J. Oefner, and Luigi L. Cavalli-Sforza 2001 The Phylogeography of Y Chromosome Binary Haplotypes and the Origins of Modern Human Populations. Annals of Human Genetics 65:43–62.

Young, Emma 2004 Last of the Great Migrations. New Scientist 182:38–41.

Zorc, David 1994 Austronesian Culture History through Reconstructed Vocabulary, Austronesian Terminologies: Continuity and Change. Andrew Pawley and Malcolm Ross, eds. Pp. 541–95. Pacific Linguistics Series C, No. 12794. Canberra: Australian National University.

Part IV

Emergence and Development of Complex Asian Systems

7

Early Communities in East Asia: Economic and Sociopolitical Organization at the Local and Regional Levels

Anne P. Underhill and Junko Habu

Recent archaeological discoveries in East Asia have made archaeologists re-evaluate traditional interpretations of the development of prehistoric human societies in a cross-cultural context. This chapter demonstrates the considerable regional variability in subsistence strategies, settlement patterns, and social organization that existed among early communities in East Asia. The invention of pottery probably occurred in more than one region of East Asia during the terminal Pleistocene, possibly triggered by different causes. Subsequently, diverging paths between regions began to emerge during the early Holocene. By the mid-Holocene, differences between the agriculture-based systems in China and hunting–gathering systems in Japan and Korea became evident. Variability in subsistence practices also resulted in the varying degree of residential mobility.

This chapter reveals significant diversity in East Asia in the process by which economic and sociopolitical complexity emerged. For China, two dimensions of social complexity will be examined: increasing heterogeneity (horizontal or non-vertical differentiation), and increasing vertical inequality (McGuire 1983). Evidence for increasing heterogeneity, such as the onset of craft specialization, begins at relatively early dates in more than one region, while evidence of increasing vertical inequality, found primarily in burial sites, is reported from later periods.

For Japan and Korea, increasing heterogeneity, such as the development of long-distance trade, can be observed, but evidence of vertical social inequality is limited. Furthermore, the degree of economic complexity in these two regions did not necessarily develop unilinearly from simple to complex. This pattern is especially evident in the Jomon of northeastern Japan, where organizational complexity in subsistence and settlement reached its high point during the Middle Jomon period, followed by a decline.

The diverging patterns of Neolithic China and the Jomon–Chulmun, as well as regional and temporal variability within each culture, pose the question of how and why these differences occurred. We suggest that the rich data from China, Korea, and Japan can contribute significantly to our understanding of the mechanisms of long-term change in early communities.

Although a large number of publications in Chinese, Korean, and Japanese are available, we have tried to cite references readily available in English. With the wealth of materials in Chinese, Japanese, and Korean, Underhill, a specialist in the archaeology of China, is the primary author of the first section (The Neolithic Period in China). Habu, a specialist in Japanese archaeology, is the primary author of the second section (Jomon and Chulmun: Development of Complex Hunter-Gatherer Cultures and Their Regional Variability).

The Neolithic Period in China

Numerous and diverse Neolithic cultures developed all over China (Barnes 1993; Chang 1986; Debaine-Francfort 1999; Murowchick 1994). Most archaeological fieldwork has taken place in the eastern half of China. The Chinese mainland and adjacent islands (including Hong Kong and Taiwan) cover an enormous area and diverse environmental zones (Ren et al. 1985). The environmental zones in eastern China alone range from frigid forested areas in the far north to humid, tropical areas in the south. In eastern China there are six major cultural areas: (1) the central Yellow River valley; (2) the northeast; (3) the lower Yellow River valley; (4) the central Yangzi River valley; (5) the lower Yangzi River valley; and (6) southernmost China (Figure 7.1). The prehistoric cultures that developed in China from ca. 8000 to 2000 B.C. are traditionally described as "Neolithic," meaning that farming was the main method of subsistence for a community, there was sedentism rather than seasonal mobility, and people relied on pottery vessels for the preparation and consumption of food, as well as on ground stone tools. In the first three areas of northern China, millet became an important crop. In areas 4–6, rice became the basis of agricultural systems. It will be seen that the complex of features associated with Neolithic societies such as farming, pottery production, and ground stone tools varied by region and developed at different rates.

Changing lifeways during the late Pleistocene and early Holocene periods in north and south China

Archaeological research on the transition from the late Pleistocene period to the early Holocene shows that people in more than one area developed new strategies of getting food, tools for daily use, and shelter in response to changing environmental conditions and increased inter-community social interactions. It will be important to more thoroughly investigate the full range of subsistence strategies and settlement organization on a seasonal basis in each major area. Diverse subsistence practices, craft production, and social organization are evident even for this early period.

In northern China it has been profitable to not only study plant and animal remains but also to consider a range of factors affecting degree of sedentism. In the

Figure 7.1 Cultural areas discussed in the text

central Yellow River valley of northern China (Figure 7.1, area 1), more reliable water sources, methods for storing food, and diverse sets of stone tools allowed people to live in some locations for longer periods of time (Madsen et al. 1996). Also, new studies of stone tools provide clues about subsistence practices. Stone tools at sites in Ningxia province dated to ca. 9600 B.C. or older are suitable for grinding plants (Elston et al. 1997). Microlithic technologies have been identified at a range of sites in several areas of north and south China (Lu 1998). These small blade tools probably had several different functions. Microblades from late Pleistocene sites in Shandong province in the lower Yellow River valley (Figure 7.1, area 2) probably represent a hunter–gatherer–fisher economy (Luan 1996; Shen 2003).

Another likely sign that people in some areas were residing in one location for longer periods of time each year is domestication of the dog. Dogs probably were domesticated from wolves, to aid in hunting and to protect living areas (see Underhill 1997). Evidence for domesticated dogs is reported for the site of Nanzhuangtou, located in central Hebei province (at the northern edge of area 1). Evidently the deposits in question from this open-air site date to ca. 8000 B.C. (Yuan and Flad 2002). It appears that in both China and the Near East, the dog is the earliest domesticated animal (see Bar-Yosef and Meadow 1995:57).

Nanzhuangtou and a roughly contemporary site called Hutouliang to the northeast contain the earliest known ceramics from northern China. At Nanzhuangtou some sherds have plain surfaces, and others are incised (see Guo and Li 2000). The low-fired pottery from these sites is reported as dating between 9000 and 8000 B.C. (Chang 1999; Cohen 1998:25; Yan 2000:6, 12). It is likely that pottery was invented in northern China prior to the onset of plant cultivation. People may have invented pottery independently in China as early as in Japan and the Russian Far East (see the discussion below). There may have been different factors that inspired people to independently invent pottery. One must consider other kinds of materials available in these areas for making containers to store, cook, and serve food (such as wood, reeds, gourds, or soft stone). Although increased reliance on pottery vessels probably was linked to increased sedentism, the associated foods could have varied by area (Shelach 2000:378; Underhill 1997:116). At Nanzhuangtou the presence of pottery and grinding stones probably indicates greater reliance on plant foods.

Important changes in social and economic organization continued to take place in northern China from ca. 8000–6300 B.C. It is likely that as hunter-gatherer peoples experimented with cultivated plants and became more reliant on them, they became more sedentary in order to protect their plants during harvesting (Lu 2002:11). Increased sedentism in East Asia probably then fostered greater elaboration in treatment of the dead. As scholars have noted for the Near East, ritual expressions of territoriality and ancestral ties to land are linked to increased sedentism (Bar-Yosef and Belfer-Cohen 1991). The earliest formal burials in northern China date to late Pleistocene deposits at the cave site of Zhoukoudian near Beijing (area 1), sometime between 18,000–10,000 B.C. (see Underhill 1997:117). Recently another very early burial dated by radiocarbon to ca. 7500 B.C. was found near Beijing. The intricate shell necklace around this adult female's neck indicates elaboration in mortuary ritual, and a relatively warm climate is indicated by the particular species represented (Hao et al. 2001).

In southern China the sequence in which plant cultivation and pottery developed is beginning to be understood. Evidence for early rice cultivation, in the form of phytoliths (microscopic silica bodies of plants) and macrobotanical remains, from a few cave sites in the lower Yangzi River valley (area 5) and in the central Yangzi River valley (area 4), has been debated (see Chen 1999; Cohen 1998; Lu 1999; Yan 1999, 2000; Yuan 2000; Crawford, this volume). People may have continued to rely on wild rice for longer periods of time in some areas.

Other kinds of remains demonstrate diversity in subsistence practices during this early period. The presence of bone harpoons at Xianrendong in the lower Yangzi River valley indicates fishing, while deer and other kinds of animal bone reveal the importance of hunting (Chen 1999:85). Archaeologists reported bones of domesticated pig at the cave site of Zengpiyan near Guilin, Guanxi, in southernmost China (area 6). A recent analysis (Yuan and Flad 2002) concludes that the initial dates for this context are much more recent than scholars had thought. Furthermore, there is insufficient evidence to conclude that pigs in this site were domesticated. Exploitation of riverine resources in southernmost China is inferred on the basis of bone tools suitable for fishing and mollusks (Cohen 1998:26).

In southern as well as northern China, the invention of pottery indicates that methods of food acquisition and preparation were diversifying. Thick-walled, impressed pottery was found in a context with cultivated rice at the cave site of Yuchanyan in Hunan province, although the dates are debated (see Yan 2000; Yuan 2000). The earliest occupation could be ca. 9000 B.C. The earliest pottery at Diaotonghuan or Wangdong and Xianrendong also was low fired, with different kinds of surface finishes including incisions, linear impressions, and smoothing (Chen 1999; Zhang 2000:47). The earliest pottery at Zengpiyan cave may be as old as ca. 7500 B.C. (Lu 2003:138). Apparently, pottery older than 10,000 B.C. was found at a cave site called Miaoyan, located in the same area of Guangxi as Zengpiyan (Yan 2000:6, 12). The relatively early dates for these sites in both southern and northern China strengthen the argument that pottery vessels were independently invented in more than one region of East Asia. The invention of pottery most likely represents decreased residential mobility on a yearly basis, or longer stays during different seasons at specific locations. People in more than one part of China could have been motivated to invent a new kind of container that could efficiently cook grain or shellfish (Lu 1999, 2003:139; Underhill 1997:115–16).

No doubt there would have been more than one kind of social change as families in southern China lived in specific locations for longer periods of time each year. Here also, there is evidence for the emergence of funerary rituals. At the cave site of Zengpiyan, mourners placed red ochre over the flexed bodies of the deceased (see Chang 1986:102; Underhill 1997:140–1).

Growing communities with mixed economies, ca. 7000–5500 B.C.

Dramatic changes in economic and social organization are evident after 7000 B.C. in northern and southern China. There is considerable evidence for at least partial reliance on domesticated plants and/or animals in several areas. Most communities probably were inhabited for at least several months of the year. Since more floral and faunal remains are currently being collected during excavations, important insights about regional variation in early subsistence economies will be made in the next decade (Yuan 1999; Zhao 2001). Sites from this phase tend to possess more of the traits traditionally associated with Neolithic societies: farming, pottery production, ground stone tools, and long-term occupation of villages.

It is clear that communities of millet farmers developed in the central Yellow River valley (area 1) by ca. 6200 B.C. Domesticated millet has been found in abundance at Peiligang culture sites in this area, ca. 6200–5000 B.C., in Henan province. Related cultures such as Cishan and Laoguantai have been identified in neighboring areas. At several Peiligang sites, archaeologists found clear evidence for increased reliance on animal husbandry from the bones of domesticated dog, pig, cow, and chicken. Hunting and gathering continued to be important, judging from the bones of wild animals and remains of seeds and nuts in many sites. Because sites of the Peiligang and related cultures tend to be large, farming must have been a way of life for a substantial period of time. The site of Cishan, for example, is ca. 8 hectares (80,000 m^2) in size (Yan 1999:134). At Peiligang culture sites there are numerous semi-subterranean houses and storage pits (see Chang 1986; Cohen 1998; Underhill 1997; Yan 1999). Peiligang culture households made a variety of chipped (including sickles) and ground stone tools. The earliest painted pottery in northern China was found at the Baijia (Laoguantai culture) site in Shaanxi province (see Underhill 1997). It is likely that this more elaborate pottery was used for special purposes.

Peiligang culture sites also have formal cemeteries. Mourners prepared graves and interred pottery vessels, stone tools, and other artifacts for the deceased to use in the afterlife. This pattern represents the development of stronger beliefs about territoriality, familial ties to land (past, present, and future), and the importance of ancestors (Underhill 1997, 2002). Peiligang sites tend to have roughly 75–100 graves that are roughly equal in size, with little differentiation in the quality and quantity of interred goods (Henan Team 1995). Placement of graves in the same spatial areas over time indicates familial ties to the land from one generation to another (see Chen 2002; Henan Team 1995).

Communities in other parts of northern China probably also relied at least partially on millet. Millet has not been reported for Houli culture sites ca. 6300–5600 B.C. in north-central Shandong province (area 2), but it is likely given the presence of suitable plant processing tools and substantial settlement remains. Archaeologists did recover bones of domesticated dog and pig, as well as semi-subterranean houses and a pottery kiln (see Luan 1996; Underhill 1997). Kilns were used to fire pottery in China at a relatively early date, foreshadowing remarkably skilled production of earthenware during the late Neolithic period, especially in Shandong province (see Liu and Chen, this volume).

The Xinglongwa culture of northeast China, ca. 6200–5400 B.C. (area 3), provides some interesting contrasts to the two areas described above. Xinglongwa communities are comparable in size to Peiligang culture sites, and until recently it did not appear that households relied on farming (see Crawford, this volume), or that settlements were occupied year round. Plant cultivation cannot be assumed on the basis of any particular forms of artifacts. (A study of microscopic use-wear on stone tools formerly assumed to be hoes has shown that the tools must have had other functions [Wang 2002]. Many stone tools probably were used for hunting and processing meat, et cetera [Lu 1999:6; Shelach, 2000:386–7].)

There is amazing preservation of community organization at more than one Xinglongwa site. At three sites, several rows of houses, with about ten houses in each, were found, indicating that the settlements were carefully planned (Shelach 2000:398; Yan 1999). These communities also were surrounded by the earliest known ditch features in China that would have been suitable for containing animals or for protection against floods. Some of the structures at Xinglongwa sites are quite large (up to 140 m²), and at least some occur in the center of villages (Shelach 2000). Therefore they may be public, communal structures instead of residences – the first known structures of this kind in China. The Xinglongwa culture also is notable for producing the earliest jade ornaments as well as the earliest depictions of dragons in China (Shelach 2000; Underhill 1997:124). It appears that these ornaments are the earliest jade items produced anywhere in the world.

Some graves found at the Xinglongwa site are located in separate areas near residences, while others are under house floors. One unusually rich grave (unknown age and sex) contained jade items, pottery vessels, bone and shell items, and two complete pig skeletons (see Shelach 2000:402). The individual interred here could have had a distinct social role in more than one respect. Even in small-scale societies with limited social ranking, people may be categorized according to several factors such as age, gender, nature of kin group, and roles outside of the household (Paynter 1989).

It is likely that there was well-established rice cultivation at Pengtoushan culture communities (ca. 7000–5200 B.C.) in the central Yangzi River valley (area 4) in southern China (see Crawford and Shen 1998). There is an enormous quantity of rice grains (15,000) at the relatively late site of Bashidang located near Lake Dongting in Hunan province, more than at any other Neolithic site (Chen 1999:86). There was a well-established adaptation to this aquatic landscape judging from the discovery of two cultivated aquatic plants, water caltrop and lotus root.

A striking feature of Pengtoushan culture sites is the presence of extensive, well preserved settlement remains, including more than one style of house and numerous burials. The sites range in size from roughly 1 to 3 hectares (Chen 1999:86; Cohen 1998:26). For the first time, pile dwellings (raised houses on wooden posts) appear, a clever adaptation to an aquatic environment. In addition there are semi-subterranean and ground level houses (Chen 1999; Cohen 1998; Underhill 1997). At Bashidang archaeologists found a surrounding ditch interpreted as a moat, and the remains of what appears to be a surrounding wall. This trend of constructing surrounding ditches and walls intensifies in several regions during the later prehistoric period. Another significant find at Bashidang was a unique structure built on a platform that appears to have been used in public rituals. In the center of the floor was a wooden post set on top of a bovid mandible (Chen 1999:86).

Another exceptional early site with the remains of domesticated rice is Jiahu, classified as a Peiligang culture site. Jiahu is located in the upper Huai River valley (close to area 4) in southern Henan province. It differs greatly from other Peiligang sites. Palynological analysis shows that the Huai River valley had a warmer climate than it does today (Chen and Jiang 1997). Jiahu was occupied from as early as ca. 7000 B.C. to 5800 B.C. (Chen 1999:89; Henan Institute of Cultural Relics 1999). The settlement clearly was extensive, judging from the discovery of 45 houses, 300 pits, and 300 burials. By the middle and late phases at the site, there is evidence for community planning, with clusters of houses, burials, and production areas.

The craft goods found at Jiahu are exceptionally diverse and reveal a high level of workmanship, including painted pottery vessels (Henan Institute of Cultural Relics 1999). There is one simple pit kiln from the early phase of occupation at the site, evidently the earliest pottery kiln in China. The excellent preservation of organic remains at Jiahu revealed a variety of artifacts that provide important information about ritual life, most notably, several bone flutes. Most of these were recovered from burials, and they represent the earliest known musical instruments in China. Another very unusual type of artifact in burials was sets of turtle shells containing pebbles that some scholars have interpreted as divination equipment for shamans. A significant finding was incised symbols on several of the turtle shells, possibly part of the divination process (Li et al. 2003). The burials at Jiahu exhibit considerable variation in the quality and quantity of grave goods. Mourners probably aimed to distinguish ritual specialists (the individuals with the flutes) and incipient differences in household wealth. Other unusual grave goods include a number of small, perforated turquoise ornaments (Chen 1999:88; Henan Institute of Cultural Relics 1999:398).

Increased regional differentiation in economic and social systems, ca. 5500–4000 B.C.

During this phase, regional variation in subsistence methods, housing, and crafts became more pronounced in several areas of China. Social differentiation is evident in more areas on the basis of variation in craft goods and burial treatment. There has been extensive archaeological fieldwork, especially at Yangshao culture sites in the central Yellow River valley (area 1). Early Yangshao settlements based on millet farming flourished from ca. 5100–3700 B.C. There were diverse economic activities at these settlements, including the use of domesticated hemp for oil and fiber in clothing (Chang 1986:113–14). A number of ceramic spindle whorls for spinning thread have been found too.

There is much information available about settlement organization for the early Yangshao period. Many of these sites were occupied during the middle Yangshao phase as well, up to ca. 3500 B.C. Most sites range in size from ca. 3 to 6 hectares (Chang 1986:116–19), but Jiangzhai, an extensively excavated site, is ca. 18 hectares in size (Yan 1999:136). Early Yangshao settlements contain a variety of house styles, usually semi-subterranean (either round or square), and with wattle and daub walls and a thatched roof. Ground-level houses became more common during later phases of the Yangshao period, as evident from sites such as Jiangzhai (Xian Banpo Museum et al. 1988). It appears that there was frequent rebuilding of the perishable houses at Yangshao sites, given the complex sequence of occupation there. Some scholars argue that this pattern represented slash and burn farming techniques, requiring families to move frequently from their homes (Chang 1986:114), although ethnographic data from Taiwan and other areas show that swidden fields can be used for up to 20 years (see Underhill 1997:126).

Well-known sites in Shaanxi province such as Banpo and Jiangzhai are very similar in spatial layout. Typically these sites contain numerous houses and a small cluster of pottery kilns located within a circular, protective ditch. At Jiangzhai, the houses face a central plaza area. As seen at Xinglongwa (area 3), there also are a few large (over 100 m²) structures that probably were communal in function. At Jiangzhai there is also evidence of an inner wall or palisade, signaling concern with defense. At some early Yangshao sites the clustering of kilns and animal pens near houses could indicate some specialization of occupation by household and intra-community exchange of goods (Yan 1999:136–7). At some Yangshao sites, burials are located outside of the enclosed area in what appears to have been a shared village cemetery. At others, however, there also is a distinct spatial clustering of houses and burials. This pattern may symbolize extra-household social institutions such as lineages, where blood ties are traced through males or females, or clans, in which ties are more loosely reckoned (Chang 1986; Xian Banpo Museum et al. 1988; Yan 1999).

Early and middle Yangshao period sites contain three kinds of graves: single graves, multiple graves, and ceramic urns with infants and small children near houses (Chang 1986; Wang 1987; Zhang 1985). There is also variation in body treatment; there are both primary and secondary burials. At some sites there are a small number of graves (single and multiple) that appear richer than others. There is considerable debate about the relative status of young males versus females at sites such as Yuanjunmiao. There also are debates about the relative social standing of people in primary versus secondary burials. Wang (1987:15) argues that individuals in secondary burials actually had positions of higher prestige than people in primary burials. Why different customs coexisted needs to be investigated further. Liu (2000) demonstrates that numerous secondary collective burials at sites indicate different offerings to groups of ancestors over time.

There is a similar pattern of an emerging, mixed subsistence economy and the development of distinct local traditions in other areas of northern China ca. 5500–4000 B.C. Beixin culture villages in the lower Yellow River valley (area 2) were based on millet farming (Luan 1996). Bones from a variety of domesticated animals and fish have been reported as well, including domesticated water buffalo (Underhill 1997).

In northeast China (area 3), there is direct evidence for millet farming and pig domestication at Xinle culture (ca. 5500–4800 B.C.) sites (Underhill 1997). Similarly, analysis of stone tools from the Zhaobaogou culture (ca. 5400–4500 B.C.) indicates agricultural tasks (Wang 2002). Zhaobaogou sites are comparable in size to villages from the central Yellow River valley and include some large structures that could have functioned as public buildings. Zhaobaogou culture sites are also noted for intricately designed pottery vessels (evidently incised) and the first known human figurines (of stone and clay) in China (Shelach 2000). As Shelach notes, craft specialists, including potters, probably developed at an early date in China. It is important to keep in mind that specialized production can be small in scale (see Costin 1991).

In southern China there also were well-established villages during the period ca. 5500–4500 B.C. Several sites from the Zaoshi culture (ca. 5700–400 B.C.) in the central Yangzi River valley (area 4) yielded domesticated rice as well as water buffalo, cow, and pig. The most famous site from this period is located in the lower Yangzi River valley (area 5). At the waterlogged site of Hemudu, ca. 5000–4500 B.C., in northern Zhejiang, rice and other aquatic domesticated plants such as water caltrop, lotus root, and gourd were preserved (see Underhill 1997). There were extensive remains of raised wooden houses (pile dwellings), wooden artifacts (including agricultural tools and a boat oar), finely incised bone and ivory orna-ments, fragments of reed mats, and the earliest known lacquer container (a wooden container covered with a special kind of tree resin). Musical instruments – bone whistles – also were recovered (Liu and Zhao 1993). The wooden houses were in effect long houses, similar to those currently used in some areas of Southeast Asia by extended families (Yan 1999:135). On the southernmost mainland and Taiwan (area 6), coastal fishing peoples from the Dapenkeng culture after ca. 5000 B.C. may have grown root crops such as taro, although this kind of plant is extremely difficult to identify in archaeological sites. A distinctive form of artifact found that is also known from ancient sites in Oceania is the grooved stone bark (tapa) beater for extracting fiber (Chang 1999:54; Underhill 1997).

Increased inter-community interaction and the emergence of regional polities, ca. 4000–2600 B.C.

Fundamental changes in regional organization began to take place after 4000 B.C. in China. It is likely that regional polities such as chiefdoms developed in more than one area, judging from the emergence of settlement hierarchies, in which relatively large centers were surrounded by smaller, presumably subsidiary, communities (see Earle 1991). On the basis of the large quantity of sites, population densities increased in several areas. Greater similarities in styles of artifacts from different sites indicate that there were more frequent interactions between communities (Chang 1986). The challenge that remains is to identify the specific nature of these interactions, both competitive and peaceful. Settlement remains and burials from more than one area reveal more pronounced differences in wealth and social posi-tion. There is also some evidence for inter-community violence. Common patterns that emerge are the importance of public rituals, elaboration of ideology sym-bolized by craft goods, and concern with ancestors. It is likely that an important component of leadership in more than one region was ties to the supernatural (Chang 1983). At present there is more information available about northern cul-tures than southern cultures.

A huge ritual complex, about 8 by 10 km², was discovered at the late Hongshan period (ca. 3500–3000 B.C.) site of Niuheliang in western Liaoning province (area 3; Barnes and Guo 1996; Chang 1986; Nelson 1995a, 1995b; Sun and Guo 1990; Yan 1999). It contains stone platforms interpreted as altars, stone foundations that could have been temples, and parts of a large clay statue of an adult female, including the head, with inlaid jade eyes, that could represent a goddess. In addition there are other female clay models, some of which look pregnant and probably symbolized fertility. Chen (1990) suggests that the small figurines were used by shamans in rituals. In certain areas of the temple complex are a few stone-lined graves of varying sizes. Some contain ornate jades, including a distinctive, "pig-dragon" shape. In areas with temples and tombs, there also were hundreds (or thousands, according to some counts; Nelson 1995b:13) of painted ceramic cylinders with no base. Not surprisingly, the incredible site of Niuheliang has sparked debate about the nature of Hongshan society.

The essence of the debate is the nature of social hierarchy during the late Hongshan period. Nelson (1995b) argues that the stone-lined graves at Niuheliang were constructed to display the elite status of a minority of individuals. Also, these elites managed the production of the fine craft goods found at the temple complex. In other words, there was a stratified society. Another possibility is that the regional ceremonial center was constructed to honor certain key ancestors (such as male and female founding ancestors) who were important to a multi-community social group such as a lineage. Since there are few traces of residential life at the site, people from surrounding areas may have had access to the center for periodic ceremonies (Chen 1990). Skilled crafts people in more than one community could have contributed the fine jades and pots. As Shelach (1999:83–4) points out, emerging leadership roles in northeast China probably were linked to communal ritual.

A remarkable ceremonial feature of a different kind was found at another site in northern China, at the middle Yangshao period (ca. 3700–500 B.C.) site of Xishuipo in northeastern Henan (area 1). Although multiple burials continued to be the dominant form of mortuary ritual in this area, one individual was singled out for special treatment. Grave M45 of an adult male was flanked by life-sized, intricately shaped images made from clam shells, apparently representing a tiger on the right and a dragon to the left (Chang 1999; Puyang CPAM et al. 1988). The adult male lay at the southern end of the grave; three other skeletons of youths (male and female, ages 12–16) were carefully placed in the east, west, and north corners. These people may have been sacrificed to accompany the deceased to the afterlife. Feng (1990) proposes that the location of the grave was calculated according to the position of the sun during the spring and fall equinox. Therefore the animals could be figures the ancient people associated with constellations. Emerging leadership roles in this area seem linked to specialized knowledge of the heavens, and this distinctive adult male could have been a shaman (Chang 1999).

There was significant differentiation in the size of middle and late phase Yangshao settlements. Settlement hierarchies have been identified from systematic survey and reconnaissance (Liu 1996; Liu and Chen 2000). In the Yi-Luo River valley, Yangshao sites range in size from less than one hectare to about 75 hectares, which formed a two-tiered settlement hierarchy (Liu 1996:254). There is a three-tiered hierarchy in the Lingbao region of western Henan. There is an unusually large settlement (about 90 hectares) called Beiyangping located between two tributaries, while most sites range in size from about 2 hectares to 36 hectares (Henan Institute of Cultural Relics et al. 1999; Henan Team et al. 1995). Several social, economic, and ideological factors may have motivated people to establish larger, denser settlements and new forms of political organization. Changing social relations are also evident from new kinds of architectural remains at late Yangshao sites. At Xishan near the modern city of Zhengzhou, archaeologists discovered a settlement surrounded by a wall of rammed earth (National Bureau 1999). This kind of site became more common in northern China during the succeeding Longshan period (ca. 2600–1900 B.C.), indicating increasing concern with protection of resources (Liu and Chen, this volume).

In two culture areas lying to the east, however, there is more evidence for social hierarchy. The Dawenkou culture, primarily restricted to Shandong province (area 2), dates from ca. 4100–2600 B.C. Reconnaissance surveys reveal that at least two-tiered settlement hierarchies had emerged in more than one region of Shandong. For example, late Dawenkou sites in central Shandong range in size from ca. 80 hectares to ca. 1 hectare (X. Zhang 1997:62). It is likely that as some communities were able to accumulate more wealth than others, raiding was a growing problem. At the site of Dadunzi in northern Jiangsu, archaeologists found a skeleton with a projectile point in the femur (see Underhill 2002:42).

There is marked differentiation among individual burials, for both males and females, dating to the late Dawenkou period after ca. 3000 B.C. (Chang 1986; Pearson 1988; Underhill 2000, 2002). Labor-intensive craft goods found in graves include ceramics (some wheel thrown) and items made of exotic materials, such as carved ivory cylinders inlaid with turquoise and jade items (tool forms such as axes often with no sign of use). Probably both raw materials and finished objects were exchanged between settlements. The large amount of pottery vessels for food preparation and consumption, including drinking cups, has prompted scholars to propose that feasting took place during some funerals (Allard 2001; Fung 2000; Keightley 1985; Pearson 1988; Underhill 2002). Emerging social inequality may have been linked to the ability of ambitious or charismatic individuals backed by their lineage branch members to gain control of a food surplus, which they used to attract followers and labor by sponsoring feasts in public contexts, including funerals. It has been proposed that this caused diversification in production of elaborate pottery vessels for feasting and mortuary ritual (Underhill 2002). Economic power in this area may have included control over domesticated pigs as a form of wealth (Kim 1994).

There is clear evidence for social hierarchy at the later Liangzhu culture sites in the lower Yangzi River valley near Lake Tai (area 5), ca. 3300–2200 B.C., primarily from burials. Little is known about Liangzhu settlements. In one area, archaeologists discovered clusters of sites that seem to indicate groups of settlements sharing a ritual center (Fei 1995). Remains of houses have been difficult to find. It is possible that some elites lived on large earthen mounds, since a large structure was found at the site of Mojiaoshan, with a total site area of 30 hectares (Zhejiang Province Institute 2001).

Elite graves from the Liangzhu culture are known primarily for their large quantities of diverse jade objects, although they also contain finely made pottery vessels (Chang 1986; Huang 1992). Liangzhu burial sites typically are human-made mounds above the floodplain, containing a small quantity of rich graves. At the Fuquanshan site near Shanghai, there were also special rituals for high status individuals. There was more than one stone altar and sediments of burnt earth suggestive of sacrificial offerings involving burning (CPAM of Shanghai 2000). One grave contained a female sacrificial victim, another likely indicator of the high status of the deceased. In addition to numerous jades, there were exquisitely incised pottery vessels and carved elephant ivory objects.

These incredibly rich graves have prompted many debates about the degree of social inequality and nature of society during the Liangzhu period (CPAM of Shanghai 2000). The unusual jade shapes found in elite Liangzhu burials, especially those incised with the *taotie* animal-mask design, may indicate that emerging leadership roles developed from acquisition of ideological power through special connections to the gods and ancestors (Chang 1986, 1989, 1999). Cemeteries such as Fuquanshan could have been ceremonial loci for all households in a region belonging to different branches of the same descent group. High-ranking individuals may have controlled labor within their own descent groups to build the earthen mounds. Since numerous graves also contain symbolic jade weapons such as *yue* "battle-axes," it is likely that another characteristic of high rank was leadership in military affairs. Leaders also may have managed production and exchange of jade objects (Liu 2003). Nephrite could have been acquired from nearby areas during the Liangzhu period, judging from the recent discovery of a nephrite source near Lake Tai (Wen and Jing 1992:270).

It appears that similar social, political, economic, and ideological changes took place in southern China after 4000 B.C. Information is rapidly accumulating about later cultural phases of the middle Yangzi River valley (area 4), such as Daxi and Qujialing, where rice became the staple food (Chang 1986, 1999; Underhill 1997; C. Zhang 1997). Although few house remains have been recovered, it is known that houses were built with organic materials such as bamboo, other woods, reeds, and clay. Late phase burials at Qujialing culture (ca. 3000–2500 B.C.) sites contain elaborate, thin-walled and painted vessels (Hunan Museum 1979).

In southernmost mainland China and Taiwan (area 6), there were a variety of economic and social systems after ca. 3500 B.C. Communities from the Shixia culture of southern Guangdong relied largely on rice, but peoples in Taiwan probably relied on root crops until ca. 2,000 B.C. (Underhill 1997). In Hong Kong and other parts of southernmost China, lifeways in fishing villages similar to those known in historic times probably had great antiquity (see Meacham 1994). The styles of some artifacts from late Neolithic sites in south China appear similar to those known from earlier periods in more northerly regions (Chang 1986). This kind of pattern might partially be explained by the common human desire to acquire special goods from "foreign" or outside areas, or to copy them. Objects can acquire different meanings in their new cultural contexts.

Diverse economic and social systems developed in several areas of China during the early and mid Neolithic period. There was considerable regional variation in subsistence systems, house styles, craft production, and ritual. At the same time, several common trends can be noted: successful adaptation to different local environments, early use of ceramic food containers, eventual development of fully sedentary communities, production of goods for ritual purposes as well as daily use, increased interaction between communities, and marking the status of a minority of individuals in mortuary ritual. More intensive investigation of individual regions will reveal in more detail how and why different kinds of social, economic, ideological, and political changes took place. In several areas, there is abundant evidence for the development of social hierarchies, including regional polities – a trend that continues during the succeeding Longshan period (Liu and Chen, this volume). Qualities of leadership probably included managing labor, communicating with the supernatural, coordinating defense, and managing interactions with people from outside areas. The cultures of prehistoric Japan and Korea form an interesting contrast to those of China, in more than one respect.

Jomon and Chulmun: Development of Complex Hunter-Gatherer Cultures and their Regional Variability

As discussed above, agricultural economies in China developed steadily from the early to mid-Holocene. In contrast, early inhabitants of the Korean peninsula and the Japanese archipelago did not rely on cultivated plants until approximately 1300 B.C. (Korea) or later (Japan): these people developed unique hunter-gatherer cultures. They are called the Chulmun culture (ca. 6000–1300 B.C.) on the Korean peninsula and the Jomon culture (ca. 14,500–400 B.C.) on the Japanese archipelago. Evidence of plant cultivation does exist, but none of the cultigens seem to have been staple food (Crawford, this volume).

The Chulmun and Jomon periods are divided into several sub-periods on the basis of typological chronology of pottery. Calibrated dates for the four Chulmun sub-periods are shown in the far right column of Table 7.1. For the six Jomon sub-periods, both conventionally accepted uncalibrated 14C dates and calibrated dates are listed in the table, since Japanese archaeologists have been slow in adopting calibrated dates, and the use of uncalibrated dates still dominates the field of Jomon archaeology[1] (see Habu 2004:26–7). Since this table is based on a limited number of 14C dates, many of which were measured during the 1960s and 1970s when accuracy and precision were still low, the absolute chronology for the Jomon and Chulmun periods needs to be refined in the near future. The issue of the reservoir effect further complicates this problem (e.g., M. Imamura et al. 1999).

Although the Jomon and Chulmun are considered to have been hunter-gatherer cultures, the presence of pottery, polished stone axes, and seemingly sedentary vil-

Table 7.1. Approximate dates for the six Jomon and four Chulmun sub-periods

Sub-period	Jomon		Chulmun***
	Uncalibrated 14C B.P.*	Calibrated B.C.**	Calibrated B.C.
Final	3000–2300 B.P.	1300–400 B.C.	N/A****
Late	4000–3000 B.P.	2600–1300 B.C.	2000–1300 B.C.
Middle	4700–4000 B.P.	3700–2600 B.C.	3500–2000 B.C.
Early	6000–4700 B.P.	5000–3700 B.C.	5000–3500 B.C.
Initial	9500–6000 B.P.	9100–5000 B.C.	N/A****
Incipient	13,800?–9500 B.P.	14,500?–9100 B.C.	6000?–5000 B.C.

* Partially modified from dates for the Kanto region listed in Keally and Muto (1982).
** For the methods of calibration, see note 1 at the end of this chapter.
*** From Im (1997).
**** Not applicable (the Chulmun period consists of only four sub-periods: Incipient, Early, Middle, and Late).

lages have made Korean and Japanese archaeologists claim that these cultures were the equivalent of the Neolithic in Europe, China, and other places. In addition, food storage, subsistence intensification, elaboration in rituals and crafts, and long-distance trade also characterize the Jomon and Chulmun cultures. These characteristics qualify the two cultures to be called "complex" (Price and Brown 1985) or "affluent" (Koyama and Thomas 1981) hunter-gatherer cultures.

The definition of "complexity" in hunter-gatherer archaeology differs among researchers (e.g., Habu et al. 2003, Price and Brown 1985). In the following discussion, cultural complexity refers to complexity in both (1) economic and (2) sociopolitical organization. The former refers to organizational complexity in subsistence and settlement, which can be measured by the degree of the incorporation of various "logistical" strategies (i.e., intensive exploitation of remotely located resources by specially organized task groups [Binford 1980]). Typically, logistically organized subsistence systems are also characterized by food storage and low residential mobility. The latter, complexity in sociopolitical organization, refers to the degree of vertical and horizontal social differentiation (i.e., both social inequality and heterogeneity; cf. McGuire 1983), as well as the degree of the integration of the differentiated parts (Fitzhugh 2003).

It should be noted that regional and temporal variability in these two cultures is quite large. Thus, not all of these "complex" features can be found when we look at Jomon or Chulmun cultures of a given region at a given time. In fact, the production and use of pottery may be the only common characteristic of all Jomon and Chulmun sub-cultures. In particular, a rapid increase in the number of excavated Jomon sites over the past several decades has contributed significantly to our understanding of this variability. Characteristics of six Jomon sub-periods are outlined in such English references as Habu (2004) and K. Imamura (1996). The number of excavated Chulmun sites is much smaller, but W.-Y. Kim (1986), J.-J. Lee (2001), and Nelson (1993) provide succinct summaries of the current status of Chulmun archaeology.

As space is limited, the remainder of this chapter focuses on two issues in Jomon and Chulmun archaeology: (1) early pottery production and its implications, and (2) regional and temporal variability in economic and sociopolitical organization. Locations of Jomon and Chulmun sites mentioned in the text are shown in Figure 7.2.

Early pottery excavated on the Japanese archipelago and the Korean peninsula

The origin of pottery in East Asia is a hotly debated topic. During the 1960s, "linear relief" pottery excavated from Fukui Cave, Japan, was dated to 12,700 ± 500 uncal. B.P. [GaK-950 1σ:13,900–12,300 B.C.] (N. Watanabe 1966). This pottery was identified as the oldest evidence of pottery made as containers. It was regarded to be the oldest until recently, when pottery from the Gasya site in the Amur River Basin, Russia, was dated to 12,960 ± 120 uncal. B.P. [LE-1781 1σ:14,050–13,200 B.C.] (Zhushchikhovskaya 1997). This discovery was followed by a series of reports of early pottery from the Amur River region, including that from the Khummi site dated to 13,260 ± 100 uncal. B.P. [AA-13392, 1σ:14,300–13,650 B.C.] (Kuzmin and Keally 2001).

In 1999, plain pottery recovered from the Odai Yamamoto I site (Odai Yamamoto I Site Excavation Team 1999) in northern Honshu, Japan, was dated to 13,780 ± 170 uncal. B.P. [NUTA-6510 1σ:14,900–14,250 B.C.]. This discovery pushed back the estimated date of the beginning of the Jomon period to approximately 14,500 B.C.[2]

The causes and consequences of this early onset of pottery production have been hotly debated. Traditionally, Japanese archaeologists have assumed that the adoption of pottery was related to changes in target resources from large terrestrial mammals to mid-sized mammals (mainly boar and sika deer), plants, and marine food, and that these changes were caused by the warming climate at the end of the Pleistocene. However, if the Odai Yamamoto I date is accurate, it implies that the earliest pottery production on the Japanese archipelago took place prior to the warming trend. It should also be noted that there is a gap of over 5,000 years between the emergence of pottery (ca. 14,500 B.C.) and the shift in subsistence focus from terrestrial mammals to plants and marine resources (ca. 9000 B.C. or later; see below). In addition, the amount of pottery in Incipient Jomon artifact assemblages is usually relatively small (e.g., Senpukuji Cave, Kamikuroiwa Rockshelter, the Hanamiyama site). These lines of evidence indicate that the beginning of pottery production was not the direct cause of the development of Jomon cultural complexity, although it does not negate the possibility that it was a condition of the subsequent developments.

The discovery at the Odai Yamamoto I site by no means implies that pottery production originated in northern Japan. Given the fact that many early pottery sites are located in the Amur River region, and given the presence of early pottery in China (see above), many scholars believe that the origins of pottery production can be traced back before Odai Yamamoto I, possibly somewhere in China or Northeast Asia.

Figure 7.2 Prefectures and regions of Japan, and Jomon and Chulmun sites discussed in the text

In the Korean peninsula, raised-design (*Yungkimun*) pottery excavated from Locality B of the Osan-ni site is commonly cited as the oldest pottery (Han 1995; Nelson 1993; but see Im 1997).[3] The pottery is associated with 7,050 ± 120 uncal. B.P. [KSU-515 1σ:6020–5790 B.C.]. Five other 14C dates from Osan-ni, which are obtained from Layer V of Locality A, range from 7,120 ± 700 uncal. B.P. [KSU-492 1σ:7000–5300 B.C.] to 5,740 ± 210 uncal. B.P.[KSU-620 1σ:4810–350 B.C.]. Bowls with small flat bases and stamped decorative patterns were recovered from this layer (Nelson 1993:67–8). Because relatively few Incipient Chulmun sites have been excavated, our knowledge of the Incipient Chulmun culture is still limited. It is likely that future excavations will reveal the presence of earlier pottery, and thus will fill in the gap between the oldest pottery in Korea and that found in neighboring regions.

Regional and temporal variability in economic and sociopolitical organization

While terminal Pleistocene cultures in Japan (and possibly China and Korea) are characterized by an early emergence of pottery production, subsequent cultural developments in East Asia showed marked differences between regions. Rather than adopting agriculture as a new form of subsistence strategy, the Jomon people in Japan and the Chulmun people in Korea chose to develop logistically organized hunting–gathering strategies, with a focus on intensive exploitation of plant food and marine resources. This pattern is especially evident in the Middle Jomon culture of eastern Japan (the northeastern half of the Japanese archipelago), which was associated with a large number of dwellings, specialized subsistence strategies (i.e., subsistence strategies that focused on bulk exploitation of a limited number of resources, particularly plant food), and varying degrees of sedentism.

Japanese archipelago

Initial Jomon (ca. 9100–5000 B.C.): By the beginning of the Initial Jomon period, a shift in target resources from terrestrial mammals to plant and marine resources began to take place. An increase in the importance of plant food can be inferred through changes in stone tool assemblages (i.e., an increase in plant-food-processing tools, such as grinding stones and stone mortars). The appearance of shell-middens, such as Natsushima, signals the onset of intensive utilization of marine resources. Nevertheless, many Initial Jomon settlements are still small, associated with only a few pit-dwellings and usually with no storage facilities.

The Initial Jomon period was also the time when certain differences between eastern and western Japan began to develop. Regional variability in pottery styles emerged. Density of Initial Jomon sites in eastern Japan is clearly higher than that in western Japan (Koyama 1978).

Early Jomon (ca. 5000–3700 B.C.): A fair number of relatively large Early Jomon settlements have been reported in eastern Japan (e.g., Sannai Maruyama, Itoi Miyamae, Akyu, Nakanoya Matsubara). Many of them are associated with storage pits. This indicates that relatively sedentary settlement systems supported by logistical subsistence strategies were well established by the end of the Early Jomon period.

Because of the presence of large settlements, many archaeologists have suggested that the Early Jomon people in eastern Japan were fully sedentary, with each group occupying a single village throughout the year. However, Habu's (2001) analysis of regional settlement patterns in the Kanto and Chubu regions indicates that not all the Early Jomon people were fully sedentary. At most, they were likely to have been only seasonally sedentary. In addition, towards the end of the Early Jomon, some groups may have been quite mobile, with very few logistical strategies. These results question the validity of the traditional assumption of Early Jomon full sedentism in eastern Japan. They also indicate that Jomon subsistence-settlement systems may have been quite fluid, frequently moving between the high and low ends of the residential mobility scale depending on changes in natural and cultural environments, population density, and other factors.

As a hypothetical scenario, Habu (2002) suggests that a change from relatively sedentary to mobile settlement systems in the Kanto region at the end of the Early Jomon period triggered a large-scale population movement to the Chubu region. This may have led to the development of highly specialized subsistence-settlement systems during the Middle Jomon period.

Reports of ceremonial artifacts and features from the Early Jomon period are more common than in the Initial Jomon period, but are still relatively small in number. Ceremonial features made of a large number of stones are reported from such sites as Wappara and Akyu.

In western Japan, discoveries of large Early Jomon settlements are less common than in eastern Japan. Population estimates by Koyama (1978, 1984) indicate that Early Jomon population density in western Japan was much lower than that in eastern Japan.

Middle Jomon (ca. 3700–2600 B.C.): The Middle Jomon period in eastern Japan is known for an abundance of extremely large settlements (e.g., Sannai Maruyama, Miharada, Takanekido, Sannomaru). In the Kanto and Chubu regions, high site density and an abundance of so-called chipped stone axes have been noted. Scholars have suggested that these chipped stone axes were used as hoes for plant cultivation, but many others believe that their primary function was to collect wild plant roots. These lines of evidence strongly suggest that Middle Jomon people in eastern Japan adopted highly specialized subsistence strategies, presumably with low residential mobility and high logistical mobility (*sensu* Binford 1980).

The Middle Jomon of eastern Japan is also known for an abundance of artistic pottery and an increase in ritual artifacts including clay figurines, large stone rods, and large jade beads. Scholars suggest that a mass of clay figurines is associated only with a limited number of sites (e.g., Shakado). Several archaeologists have also suggested the possibility that different types of ceremonial artifacts are associated with different houses (e.g., Mizuno 1963). This may indicate an emergence of a certain type of social differentiation (although not necessarily vertical). The presence of jade bead production sites near jade sources implies the emergence of craft specialists. All of these lines of evidence indicate that Middle Jomon societies in eastern Japan were likely to have been characterized by increasing heterogeneity. Despite these characteristics, no clear evidence of social stratification has been reported. Thus, it is likely that the nature of social complexity of this period was more horizontal than vertical.

Unlike in eastern Japan, changes from the Early to the Middle Jomon periods in western Japan seem to have been more gradual. Population estimates by Koyama (1978, 1984) show little changes in Kinki, Chugoku, Shikoku, and Kyushu.

Nevertheless, evidence of subsistence intensification can be observed at several sites. For example, excavation of the Awazu shell-midden revealed intensive processing of acorns and horse chestnuts in the fall and freshwater shellfish in the spring (Matsui 1999). Reports of ceremonial artifacts and features are present, but not abundant.

Late and Final Jomon (2600–400 B.C.): The Late and Final Jomon periods in eastern Japan are generally characterized by a decrease in the relative frequency of large settlements and site density, and by an increase in ceremonial artifacts and features, and sophistication of crafts, including lacquerware production. The former seems to indicate a decrease in organizational complexity in subsistence and settlement. However, a variety of new items began to be systematically traded. These include natural asphalt and probably salt (Habu 2004:chapter 6). In the Tohoku region, the development of ceremonial sites away from settlements, such as the Komakino stone circle, can be noted. Increased variability in burial types is also apparent (Habu 2004:chapter 6; Ikawa-Smith 1992). A small number of Late Jomon child burials are associated with grave goods, which may indicate the emergence of hereditary social inequality (Nakamura 2000).

It is important to note that the development of Late and Final Jomon social complexity in eastern Japan occurred *after* the apparent decrease in organizational complexity in subsistence and settlement. In other words, the case of Jomon in eastern Japan demonstrates that the development of economic organization and sociopolitical organization did not go hand in hand.

Two possible explanations for this incongruity can be proposed. First, it can be argued that the development of Middle Jomon economic complexity provided the initial kick to trigger the development of social complexity. Alternatively, one can also argue that the decline of specialized subsistence systems resulted in a more hierarchical social structure in order to cope with economic difficulties. These two hypotheses are not necessarily contradictory; indeed the combination of these two scenarios is a possibility.

The incongruity between declining organizational complexity in subsistence-settlement systems and increasing social complexity in eastern Japan is not observable in western Japan. In the Kinki, Chugoku, Shikoku, and Kyushu regions, site density increased steadily from the Middle through to the Late and Final Jomon (Koyama 1978, 1984). Although the overall density was much lower than in eastern Japan, no decline in site size and density is observed.

Korean peninsula

In contrast to an abundance of Jomon data, the amount of available data from Chulmun sites is still relatively small. As a result, the present picture of Chulmun subsistence, settlement and society is very fragmentary.

Many scholars have labeled Chulmun subsistence as a "broad-spectrum economy," because Chulmun hunter-gatherers appear to have exploited a wide variety of food resources (e.g., J.-J. Lee 2001). However, given the signs of organizational complexity in subsistence and settlement as discussed above, it is more likely that Chulmun subsistence strategies focused on bulk-exploitation of a limited number of resources, probably either plant or marine food. The lack of extremely large settlements and relatively low site density may indicate that the degree of subsistence specialization of the Chulmun period in general was roughly comparable to that of the Jomon period in western Japan.

Korean archaeologists have discussed characteristics of subsistence, settlement, and social organization of the Early to Late Chulmun periods in the context of regional differences. Many archaeologists suggest that Early to Late Chulmun people on the southeastern coast were less residentially mobile than those in other regions. This is because, in this region, a large number of shell-midden sites have been identified (e.g., Tongsam-dong, Yondae-do, Sangnodae-do, Yokji-do), for which year-round occupation was assumed. Over the last decade, however, a significant number of inland sites have been excavated in southern Korea (J.-J. Lee 2001:81). This has led to discussions on the relationship between coastal and inland areas, including a possible population movement from the coast to inland in the beginning of the Middle Chulmun period (J.-J. Lee 2001:80).

Among shell-midden sites in southern Korea, Tongsam-dong provides a series of 14C dates from the Early to Late Chulmun periods (Nelson 1993:64–5) along with rich faunal data (e.g., Sample 1974). More recently, Crawford and G.-A. Lee (2003) reported the recovery of broomcorn millet (*Panicum miliaceum*) and foxtail millet (*Setaria italica*) from the floor of a Middle Chulmun pit dwelling at Tongsam-dong. According to these authors, the foxtail millet grains are AMS dated to 3360 B.C., thus confirming their Middle Chulmun association. Crawford and Lee suggest that these crops supplemented, rather than altered, hunting-gathering Chulmun lifeways. At the same time, these scholars suggest that nuts may have become less important over time as grain plants came into use.

Representative Early to Late Chulmun sites in the central-western part of the Korean peninsula include the Amsa-dong, Misa-ri (Seoul National University Museum 1997:42–51), Kungsan-ni, and Chitam-ni (Chit'ap-ri). Excavations of Amsa-dong have revealed the presence of at least 20 pit-dwellings (Nelson 1993:79–80). Acorn remains (*Quercus*) have been recovered from both Amsa-dong and Misa-ri (J.-J. Lee 2001:76). These lines of evidence seem to suggest logistically organized settlement systems, but systematic regional settlement pattern analyses have yet to be conducted.

Discoveries of burials and ceremonial sites have been scarce (Nelson 1993). One of the few exceptions is the secondary burial recovered from the Late Chulmun Hupo-ri site on the east coast of southern Korea. The burial was associated with approximately 40 skeletal remains of both men and women, and was accompanied by a large number of polished stone axes (J.-J. Lee 2001:84; Nelson 1993:95). Given the elaboration of the polished stone axes, this burial seems to reflect the development of complex rituals by the Late Chulmun, but it does not imply vertical social inequality.

Concluding Remarks

The archaeological record outlined above provides excellent data for examining the mechanisms of long-term change in economic and sociopolitical complexity. Formerly, archaeologists tended to interpret long-term change from the perspective of unilinear cultural evolution, assuming that the degree of economic and sociopolitical organization changed gradually from simple to complex. According to this perspective, a transition from non-food-producing to food-producing economies, as well as a shift from mobile to fully sedentary lifeways, must have occurred as soon as certain conditions were met. When aberrations were detected, often they were explained from the perspective of either environmental determinism or classical Marxism. For example, the development of affluent Jomon and Chulmun hunter-gatherers was explained as the result of extremely rich natural environments (i.e., abundant natural resources enabled Jomon and Chulmun peoples to develop unusually complex hunter-gatherer cultures). The decline of economic complexity at the end of the Middle Jomon period was explained either by a cooling climate, or by the imbalance between the growth of "forces of production" and the limitation of the natural environment.

Examination of long-term change in the Chinese Neolithic, Jomon, and Chulmun cultures indicates that the reality was far more complex. Developments of economic and sociopolitical organization did not necessarily go hand in hand, and different historical paths can be identified both between and within these regions. In China, for example, the domestication of the dog and the invention of pottery probably occurred before farming began. Distinctly different cultures developed, exhibiting regional variation in housing, rituals, and degree of social inequality.

These lines of evidence indicate that unilinear models of cultural evolution or environmental determinism do not sufficiently explain the observed variability. The adoption of an agricultural economy with fully sedentary communities and the development of marked social inequality did not occur everywhere in East Asia. Case studies from these regions also indicate that these key developments did not necessarily occur just because certain conditions were met. The new data generated from East Asia will allow archaeologists to propose new models of long-term change in subsistence, settlement, and society. The extremely rich settlement and burial data from these regions can be used to test theories regarding the causes and consequences of emergent cultural complexity. While such studies have just begun, they indicate that East Asia is an excellent field for study in order to understand the dynamics of long-term change in early communities.

ACKNOWLEDGMENTS

We thank Miriam Stark, Rosemary Joyce, and Lynn Meskell for the opportunity to write this chapter and for their constructive comments. We are very grateful to Li Liu and Xingcan Chen for their valuable comments, as well as additional references for China. We also thank Mark Hall, Holly Halligan, Minkoo Kim, and Tanya Smith for their comments on earlier versions of this chapter. Jill Seagard, Department of Anthropology, The Field Museum, prepared Figure 7.1. Any errors, of course, are our own.

NOTES

1   In this section, all the terrestrial and marine 14C dates from Jomon and Chulmun sites were calibrated using the OxCAL program and the calibration curves of Stuiver et al. 1998a for terrestrial samples and Stuiver et al. 1998b for marine samples. For each 14C date, the calibrated one-sigma (1σ) range (i.e., the range for 68 percent probability) is shown in square brackets. Because the calibration curve is not always smooth, sometimes the one-sigma range is split into two or more intervals. When the discussion refers to general estimates in uncalibrated B.P., rough estimates of calibrated dates are shown in parentheses.
2   It should be noted that a total of five 14C dates were obtained from carbonized adhesions on the surface of plain potsherds from Odai Yamamoto I. These dates range from 13,780 ± 170 to 12,680 ± 140 uncal. B.P. Since 13,780 ± 170 uncal. B.P. is the oldest among the five 14C dates, the absolute date estimate for the pottery assemblage requires further discussion.
3   Im (1997) suggests that pottery excavated from the Kosan-ni site on Cheju Island may be older.

REFERENCES

Allard, Francis 2001 Mortuary Ceramics and Social Organization in the Dawenkou and Majiayao Cultures. Journal of East Asian Archaeology 3(3–4):1–22.
Bar-Yosef, Ofer, and Anna Belfer-Cohen 1991 From Sedentary Hunter-Gatherers to Territorial Farmers in the Levant. In Between Bands and States. Susan Gregg, ed. Pp. 181–202. Center for Archaeological Investigations Occasional Paper No. 9. Carbondale: Southern Illinois University Press.
Bar-Yosef, Ofer, and Richard Meadow 1995 The Origins of Agriculture in the Near East. In Last Hunters. First Farmers. T. Douglas Price and Anne B. Gebauer, eds. Pp. 39–94. Santa Fe NM: School of American Research Press.
Barnes, Gina 1993 China, Korea, and Japan. The Rise of Civilization in East Asia. London: Thames and Hudson.
Barnes, Gina, and Dashun Guo 1996 The Ritual Landscape of "Boar Mountain" Basin: The Niuheliang Site Complex of North-Eastern China. World Archaeology 28(2):209–19.
Binford, Lewis R. 1980 Willow Smoke and Dogs' Tails. American Antiquity 45(1):4–20.
Chang, Kwang-chih 1983 Art, Myth, and Ritual. Cambridge: Harvard University Press.
—— 1986 The Archaeology of Ancient China. 4th Edition. New Haven: Yale University Press.
—— 1989 An Essay on Cong. Orientations 20(6):37–43.

—— 1999 China on the Eve of the Historical Period. *In* The Cambridge Ancient History of Ancient China. Michael Loewe and Edward Shaughnessy, eds. Pp. 37–72. Cambridge: Cambridge University Press.

Chen, Baozhang, and Qinhua Jiang 1997 Antiquity of the Earliest Cultivated Rice in Central China and Its Implications. Economic Botany 51(3):307–10.

Chen, Xingcan 1990 Feng Chan Wu Shu Yu Zu Xian Chong Bai (Bumper-harvest magic and ancestral worship: on the female figures from the Hongshan culture). Huaxia Kaogu 3:92–8.

—— 1999 On the Earliest Evidence for Rice Cultivation in China. Bulletin of the Indo-Pacific Prehistory Association 18:81–93.

—— 2002 Kaogu Suibi (Informal essays on Archaeology). Beijing: Wenwu Press.

Cohen, David 1998 The Origins of Domesticated Cereals and the Pleistocene-Holocene Transition in East Asia. The Review of Archaeology 19(2):22–9.

Costin, Cathy 1991 Craft Specialization: Issues in Defining, Documenting, and Explaining the Organization of Production. *In* Archaeological Method and Theory. Volume 3. Michael Schiffer, ed. Pp. 1–56. Tucson: University of Arizona Press.

CPAM of Shanghai 2000 Fuquanshan – Xinshiqi Shidai Yizhi Fajue Baogao (Report of the excavation of the Fuquanshan neolithic site). Beijing: Wenwu Press.

Crawford, Gary W., and Gyoung-Ah Lee 2003 Agricultural Origins in the Korean Peninsula. Antiquity 77(295):87–95.

Crawford, Gary W., and Chen Shen 1998 The Origins of Rice Agriculture: Recent Progress in East Asia. Antiquity 72:858–66.

Debaine-Francfort, Corrine 1999 The Search for Ancient China. New York: Harry N. Abrams.

Earle, Timothy, ed. 1991 Chiefdoms: Power, Economy, and Ideology. New York: Cambridge University Press.

Elston, Robert, Cheng Xu, David Madsen, Kan Zhong, Robert Bettinger, Jingzen Li, Paul Brantingham, Huiming Wang, and Jun Yu 1997 New Dates for the North China Mesolithic. Antiquity 71:983–5.

Fei, Guoping 1995 Zhejiang Yuhang Liangzhu Wenhu Yizhi Qun Kaocha Baogao (Report of investigations of groups of settlements of the Liangzhu Culture in Yuhang, Zhejiang). Dongnan Wenhua 2:1–14.

Feng, Shi 1990 Henan Puyang Xishuipo 45 Hao Mu de Tianwenxue Yanjiu (Astronomical research on tomb 45 at Xishuipo, Puyang, Henan). Wenwu 3:52–69.

Fitzhugh, Ben 2003 The Evolution of Complex Hunter-Gatherers on the Kodiak Archipelago. *In* Hunter-Gatherers of the North Pacific Rim. Junko Habu, James M. Savelle, Shuzo Koyama and Hitomi Hongo, eds. Pp. 13–48. Senri Ethnological Studies 63. Osaka: National Museum of Ethnology.

Fung, Christopher 2000 The Drinks are on Us: Ritual, Social Status, and Practice in Dawenkou Burials, North China. Journal of East Asian Archaeology 2(1–2):67–92.

Guo, Ruihai, and Li Jun 2000 Cong Nanzhuangtou Yizhi Kan Huabei Diqu Nongye He Taoqi De Qiyuan (The origins of farming and pottery in Northern China from the perspective of the Nanzhuangtou site). *In* Dao Zuo Taoqi He Dushi de Qiyuan (The origins of rice farming, pottery, and cities). Yan Wenming and Yasuda Yoshinori, eds. Pp. 51–63. Beijing: Wenwu Press.

Habu, Junko 2001 Subsistence-Settlement Systems and Intersite Variability in the Moroiso Phase of the Early Jomon Period in Japan. Ann Arbor: International Monographs in Prehistory.

—— 2002 Jomon Collectors and Foragers: Regional Interactions and Long-Term Changes in Settlement Systems among Prehistoric Hunter-Gatherers in Japan. *In* Beyond

Foraging and Collecting. Ben Fitzhugh and Junko Habu, eds. Pp. 53–72. New York: Kluwer Academic/Plenum Publishers.

—— 2004 Ancient Jomon of Japan. Cambridge: Cambridge University Press.

Habu, Junko, James M. Savelle, Shuzo Koyama, and Hitomi Hongo, eds. 2003 Hunter-Gatherers of the North Pacific Rim. Senri Ethnological Studies No. 63. Osaka: National Museum of Ethnology.

Han, Byongsam 1995 Kankoku no Kodai Bunka (Ancient cultures of Korea). Tokyo: Nihon Hoso Kyokai (Japan Broadcasting Corporation).

Hao, Shou-gang, Xue-Ping Ma, Si-Xun Yuan, and John Southon 2001 The Donghulin Woman from Western Beijing: 14C Age and An Associated Compound Shell Necklace. Antiquity 75:517–22.

Henan Institute of Cultural Relics 1999 Wuyang Jiahu (The Jiahu site in Wuyang). Volumes I and II. Beijing: Kexue Press.

Henan Institute of Cultural Relics, Institute of Archaeology, CASS, Sanmenxia City Cultural Relics Team, and Lingbao City Bureau of Cultural Relics 1999 Henan Lingbao Zhudingyuan Ji Qi Zhouwei Kaogu Diaocha Baogao (Report of surveys at Zhudingyuan and surrounding areas in Lingbao, Henan). Huaxia Kaogu 3:19–42.

Henan Team, Institute of Archaeology, and CASS 1995 Henan Jiaxian Shuiquan Peiligang Wenhua Yizhi (The Shuiquan site of the Peiligang culture at Jia county, Henan). Kaogu Xuebao 1:39–77.

—— 1999 Henan Lingbao Shi Beiyangping Yizhi Diaocha (Survey of the Beiyangping site in Lingbao, Henan). Kaogu 12:1–15.

Huang, Tsui-Mei 1992 Liangzhu – A Late Neolithic Jade-Yielding Culture in Southeastern Coastal China. Antiquity 66:75–83.

Hunan Provincial Museum 1979 Li Xian Mengxi Sanyuanguan Yizhi (The site of Sanyuanguan at Mengxi, Li county). Kaogu Xuebao 4:461–89.

Ikawa-Smith, Fumiko 1992 Kanjodori: Communal Cemeteries of the Late Jomon in Hokkaido. In Pacific Northeast Asia in Prehistory. C. Melvin Aikens and Song Nai Rhee, eds. Pp. 83–9. Pullman: Washington State University Press.

Im, Hyojai 1997 Sinsukki Sidae ui Siki-kupun (Chronology of the Neolithic period). In Hankuku-sa 2: Kusukki Munhwa wa Sinsukki Munhwa (Korean history volume 2: Palaeolithic and Neolithic cultures) (in Korean.) Hyojai Im, ed. Pp. 305–16. Seoul: Kuksa Pyonchan Wiwonwhae (National Institute of Korean History).

Imamura, Keiji 1996 Prehistoric Japan: New Perspectives on Insular East Asia. Honolulu: University of Hawaii Press.

Imamura, Mineo, Seichiro Tsuji, Hideji Harunari, Toyohiro Nishimoto, and Minoru Sakamoto 1999 Jomon Jidai no Koseido Hennen o Mezashite, II: Sojo o Riyoshita Nendai no Seimitsuka (Towards high precision dating of the Jomon period, part II: Refining the dates by using stratigraphic data). In Nihon Bunkazai Kagaku-kai Dai 16 kai Taikai Kenkyu Happyo Yoshi-shu (Abstracts of the papers presented at the 16th annual meeting of the Japanese Society for Scientific Studies on Cultural Properties). Pp. 88–9. Sakura: Nihon Bunkazai Kagaku-kai.

Keally, Charles T., and Yasuhiro Muto 1982 Jomon Jidai no nendai (Dating of the Jomon period). In Jomon Bunka no Kenkyu (Studies of the Jomon culture), Volume 1. Shinpei Kato, Tatsuo Kobayashi, and Tsuyoshi Fujimoto eds. Pp. 246–75. Tokyo: Yuzankaku.

Keightley, David N. 1985 Dead But Not Gone: The Role of Mortuary Practices in the Formation of Neolithic and Early Bronze Age Chinese Culture, ca. 8000 to 1000 B.C. Paper presented at the Conference on Ritual and the Social Significance of Death in Chinese Society, The Sun Space Ranch Conference Center. Oracle, Arizona, January 2–7, 1985.

Kim, Seung-Og 1994 Burials, Pigs, and Political Prestige in Neolithic China. Current Anthropology 35(2):119–41.

Kim, Won-Yong 1986 Art and Archaeology of Ancient Korea. Seoul: Taekwang Publishing.

Koyama, Shuzo 1978 Jomon Subsistence and Population. Senri Ethnological Studies 2:1–65.

—— 1984 Jomon Jidai (The Jomon period). Tokyo: Chuo Koron-sha.

Koyama, Shuzo, and David H. Thomas, eds. 1981 Affluent Foragers. Senri Ethnological Studies No. 9. Osaka: National Museum of Ethnology.

Kuzmin, Yaroslav V., and Charles T. Keally 2001 Radiocarbon Chronology of the Earliest Neolithic Sites in East Asia. Radiocarbon 43:1121–8.

Lee, June-Jeong 2001 From Shellfish Gathering to Agriculture in Prehistoric Korea: The Chulmun to Mumun Transition. Ph.D. Dissertation, University of Wisconsin-Madison.

Li, Xueqin, Garman Harbottle, Juzhong Zhang, and Changsui Wang 2003 The Earliest Writing? Sign Use in the Seventh Millennium B.C. at Jiahu, Henan Province, China. Antiquity 77:31–44.

Liu, Jun, and Zhao Zhongyuan 1993 Zhongguo Hemudu Wenhua (The Hemudu culture of China). Hangzhou: Zhejiang People's Press.

Liu, Li 1996 Settlement Patterns, Chiefdom Variability, and the Development of Early States in North China. Journal of Anthropological Archaeology 15(3):237–88.

—— 2000 Ancestor Worship: An Archaeological Investigation of Ritual Activities in Neolithic North China. Journal of East Asian Art and Archaeology 2(1–2):129–64.

—— 2003 "The Products of Minds as Well as of Hands:" Production of Prestige Goods in the Neolithic and Early State Periods of China. Asian Perspectives 42(1):1–40.

Lu, Tracey Lie-Dan 1998 The Microblade Tradition in China: Regional Chronologies and Significance in the Transition to Neolithic. Asian Perspectives 37(1):84–112.

—— 1999 The Transition from Foraging to Farming and the Origin of Agriculture in China. BAR International Series 774, Oxford.

—— 2002 A Green Foxtail (Setaria viridis) Cultivation Experiment in the Middle Yellow River Valley and Some Related Issues. Asian Perspectives 41(1):1–14.

—— 2003 New Archaeological Discoveries in South China. Bulletin of the Indo-Pacific Prehistory Association 23(1):137–40.

Luan, Fengshi 1996 Dong Yi Kaogu (Archaeology of the eastern Yi). Jinan: Shandong University Press.

Madsen, David, Robert Elston, Robert Bettinger, Xu Cheng, and Zhong Kan 1996 Settlement Patterns Reflected in Assemblages From the Pleistocene/Holocene Transition of North Central China. Journal of Archaeological Science 23:217–31.

Matsui, Akira 1999 Postglacial Hunter-Gatherers in the Japanese Archipelago: Maritime Adaptations. In Man and Sea in the Mesolithic: Coastal Settlement Above and Below Present Sea Level. Anders Fisher, ed. Pp. 327–35. Oxford: Oxbow Books.

McGuire, Randall 1983 Breaking Down Cultural Complexity: Inequality and Heterogeneity. In Advances in Archaeological Method and Theory. Volume 6. Michael Schiffer, ed. Pp. 91–142. New York: Academic Press.

Meacham, William, ed. 1994 Archaeological Investigations on Chek Lap Kok Island. Hong Kong Archaeological Society.

Mizuno, Masayoshi 1963 Jomon Bunka-ki ni okeru Shuraku Kozo to Shukyo Kozo (Settlement organization and religious structure during the Jomon period). In Nihon Kokogaku Kyokai Dai 29 kai Sokai Kenkyu Happyo Yoshi (Abstracts of the papers presented at the 29th general conference of the Japanese Archaeological Association). Pp. 11–12. Tokyo: Nihon Kokogaku Kyokai (Japanese Archaeological Association).

Murowchick, Robert, ed. 1994 Cradles of Civilization. China. Norman: University of Oklahoma Press.

Nakamura, Oki 2000 Saishu Shuryo-min no Fukuso Koi (Mortuary goods associated with hunter-gatherer burials). Kikan Kokogaku (Archaeology quarterly) 70:19–23.

Nelson, Sarah M. 1993 The Archaeology of Korea. Cambridge: Cambridge University Press.

—— 1995a The Archaeology of Northeast China. New York: Routledge.

—— 1995b Ritualized Pigs and the Origins of Complex Society: Hypotheses Regarding the Hongshan Culture. Early China 20:1–16.

Odai Yamamoto I Site Excavation Team, ed. 1999 Odai Yamamoto Iseki no Kokogaku Chosa [Archaeological research at the Odai Yamamoto I site]. Tokyo: Odai Yamamoto I Site Excavation Team.

Paynter, Robert 1989 The Archaeology of Equality and Inequality. Annual Review of Anthropology 18:369–99.

Pearson, Richard 1988 Chinese Neolithic Burial Patterns. Problems of Method and Interpretation. Early China 13:1–45.

Price, Douglas T., and James A. Brown 1985 Aspects of Hunter-Gatherer Complexity. In Prehistoric Hunter-Gatherers. T. Douglas Price and James A. Brown, eds. Pp. 3–20. Orlando: Academic.

Puyang CPAM, Puyang City Museum, and Puyang Cultural Work Team 1988 Henan Puyang Xishuipo Yizhi Fajue Jianbao (Short report on the excavation of the Xishuipo site at Puyang, Henan). Wenwu 3:1–6.

Ren, Mei'E, Renzhang Yang, and Haosheng Bao 1985 An Outline of China's Physical Geography. Beijing: Foreign Languages Press.

Sample, Lillie Laetitia 1974 Tongsamdong: A Contribution to Korean Neolithic Culture History. Arctic Anthropology 2:99–104.

Seoul National University Museum 1997 Cultural Relics in Seoul National University Museum [Palgul Yumul Dorok]. Seoul: Seoul National University Museum (in Korean with English title).

Shelach, Gideon 1999 Leadership Strategies, Economic Activity, and Interregional Interaction. Social Complexity in Northeast China. New York: Kluwer Academic/Plenum Publishers.

—— 2000 The Earliest Neolithic Cultures of Northeast China: Recent Discoveries and New Perspectives on the Beginning of Agriculture. Journal of World Prehistory 14(4):363–413.

Shen, Chen, Xing Gao, and Bing-hua Hu 2003 Shandong Xishiqi Yicun Yi Ji Dui "Fenghuangling Wenhua" de Zhongxin Renshi (Shandong microblade industries and re-evaluation of Fenghuangling culture). Acta Anthropologica Sinica 22:293–307.

Stuiver, M., P. J. Reimer, E. Bard, J. W. Beck, G. S. Burr, K. A. Hughen, B. Kromer, G. McCormac, J. van der Plicht, and M. Spurk 1998a INTCAL98 Radiocarbon Age Calibration, 24000–0 cal B.P. Radiocarbon 40(3):1041–83.

Stuiver, M., P. J. Reimer, and T. F. Braziunas 1998b High-Precision Radiocarbon Age Calibration for Terrestrial and Marine Samples. Radiocarbon 40(3):1127–51.

Sun, Ningdao, and Guo Dashun 1990 Liaoning Zhongda Wenhua Shiji (A record of important cultural finds from Liaoning). Shenyang: Liaoning Art Press.

Underhill, Anne 1997 Current Issues in Chinese Neolithic Archaeology. Journal of World Prehistory 11(2):103–60.

—— 2000 An Analysis of Mortuary Ritual at the Dawenkou Site, Shandong, China. Journal of East Asian Archaeology 1(3):93–127.

—— 2002 Craft Production and Social Change in Northern China. New York: Kluwer Academic/Plenum Publishers.

Wang, Ningsheng 1987 Yangshao Burial Customs and Social Organization: A Comment on the Theory of Yangshao Matrilineal Society and Its Methodology. David Keightley, trans. Early China 11–12:6–32.

Wang, Xiaoqing 2002 Shiqi Shiyong Henji Xianwei Guancha de Yanjiu: Cong Ju Jin 8200–6500 Nian Qian de Neimenggu Dongnan Bu Diqu Ziliao Wei Zongxin (Research on observations of microscopic usewear from stone tools: from materials dating to about 8200–6500 B.P. from Southeastern Inner Mongolia). Unpublished Postdoctoral Dissertation, Institute of Archaeology, Chinese Academy of Social Sciences.

Watanabe, Naotsune 1966 Jomon oyobi Yayoi Jidai no C14 Nendai (Radiocarbon dates of the Jomon and Yayoi periods in Japan). Daiyonki Kenkyu (Quaternary research) 5(3–4):157–68.

Wen, Guang, and Zhichun Jing 1992 Chinese Neolithic Jade: A Preliminary Geoarchaeological Study. Geoarchaeology 7(3):251–75.

Xian Banpo Museum, Shaanxi Province Institute of Archaeology, and Lintong County Museum 1988 Jiangzhai – Xinshiqi Shidai Yizhi Fajue Baogao (Report on the excavation of the Neolithic site of Jiangzhai). Volumes I and II. Beijing: Wenwu Press.

Yan, Wenming 1999 Neolithic Settlements in China: Latest Finds and Research. Journal of East Asian Archaeology 1(1–4):131–47.

—— 2000 Dao Zuo, Taoqi He Dushi de Qiyuan (The origins of rice farming, pottery and cities). In Dao Zuo, Taoqi He Dushi de Qiyuan. Yan Wenming and Yasuda Yoshinori, eds. Pp. 3–15. Beijing: Wenwu Press.

Yuan, Jiarong 2000 Hunan Daoxian Yuchanyan Yi Wan Nian Yiqian de Daogu He Taoqi (Rice and pottery from 10,000 years ago at Yuchanyang in Dao County, Hunan). In Dao Zuo, Taoqi He Dushi de Qiyuan (The origins of rice farming, pottery, and cities). Yan Wenming and Yasuda Yoshinori, eds. Pp. 31–41. Beijing: Wenwu Press.

Yuan, Jing 1999 Lun Zhongguo Xinshiqi Shidai Jumin Huoqu Rou Fan Ziyuan de Fangshi (On human meat acquisition patterns during the Neolithic period of China). Kaogu Xuebao 1:1–22.

Yuan, Jing, and Rowan Flad 2002 Pig Domestication in Ancient China. Antiquity 76:724–32.

Zhang, Chi 1997 The Rise of Urbanism in the Middle and Lower Yangzi River Valley. Bulletin of the Indo-Pacific Prehistory Association 16:63–7.

—— 2000 Jiangxi Wannian Zaoqi Taoqi He Dao Yi Ti Gui Shi Yicun (Rice phytolith remains and early pottery at Wannian in Jiangxi). In Dao Zuo, Taoqi He Dushi de Qiyuan (The origins of rice farming, pottery and cities). Yan Wenming and Yasuda Yoshinori, eds. Pp. 43–9. Beijing: Wenwu.

Zhang, Xuehai 1997 Dong Tu Gu Guo Tansuo (Discussion of ancient states in the east). Huaxia Kaogu 1:60–72.

Zhang, Zhongpei 1985 The Social Structure Reflected in the Yuanjunmiao Cemetery. Journal of Anthropological Archaeology 4:19–33.

Zhao, Zhijun 2001 Zhiwu Kaoguxue de Xueliao Dingwei Yu Yanjiu Neirong (The disciplinary position and research content of paleoethnobotany). Kaogu 7:55–71.

Zhejiang Province Institute of Archaeology 2001 Yuhang Miaojiaoshan Yizhi 1992–93 Nian de Fajue (Excavations from 1992–93 at the site of Miaojiaoshan in Yuhang). Wenwu 12:4–19.

Zhushchikhovskaya, Irina 1997 On Early Pottery-Making in the Russian Far East. Asian Perspectives 36(2):159–74.

8

Sociopolitical Change from Neolithic to Bronze Age China

Li Liu and Xingcan Chen

China is one of the oldest civilizations in the world. The transition from the Neolithic to the Bronze Age, accompanied by the sociopolitical change from prestate to state structure, took place during the early part of the second millennium B.C. This transition also roughly correlates with the rise of the first dynasty, the Xia (ca. 21st–16th century B.C.), as recorded in ancient texts. In the archaeological record we see the emergence of the first state-level society, known as the Erlitou culture (ca. 1900–1500 B.C.), centered in the Yiluo region of the middle Yellow River valley. This is the time when the Harappan civilization in the Indus valley had just collapsed, but Southeast Asia witnessed the emergence of complex societies characterized by bronze metallurgy and long-distance trade of valuables, and the Jomon people in Japan lived in large and complex villages and practiced hunting–gathering economy combined with low-level food production (see Crawford, and Underhill and Habu, this volume).

This technological, political, and historical transformation has been a focus of studies in Chinese archaeology and prehistory, and there are various views on related issues. Archaeologists in China, who are primarily historiographically orientated (von Falkenhausen 1993), are interested in finding correlations between archaeological remains and recorded historical events, especially the development of the Xia dynasty (Allan 1984; Lee 2002; Thorp 1991), rather than concerned with elaborating the sociopolitical configurations of these ancient societies. This approach is best reflected in the recently completed project sponsored by the state – the Xia Shang Zhou Chronology Project (Lee 2002). Such a research orientation resembles those of many other East Asian countries, such as Japan, Korea, and Vietnam (Ikawa-Smith 1999). On the other hand, it is historians who, in China, have done most of the interpretations of state formation, although they have not gone beyond the application of concepts derived from classical evolutionism and neoevolutionism (such as "tribal confederation," "military democratic formation," and "chiefdom") to textual and archaeological data (e.g., Li 1997; Xie 1996). The classical evolutionist approach in particular has dominated the field for decades, but there have been encouraging signs of incipient change in recent years. Several Sino-foreign collaborative research teams have conducted interdisciplinary projects in China since the 1990s, introducing new methods and theories to Chinese archaeology (Liu et al. 2002–4; Murowchick 1997; Murowchick and Cohen 2001; Sino-American Huan River 1998; The Chifeng Research Project 2003; Underhill et al. 1998; Underhill et al. 2002). By employing settlement archaeology, these projects focus on the long-term sociopolitical changes at the regional level, providing invaluable data for comparative study. Much of the discussion in this chapter draws information from the results of these projects.

Anthropological archaeologists in the West have proposed many theoretical models to explain social change, and we will employ some of these models in our discussion below. By doing so, we are hoping to make cross-cultural comparisons between China and other civilizations in the world.

The transition from the Neolithic to the Bronze Age in China was a long process which involved many competing parties and actors, as well as cycles of development and decline of many complex societies. Prior to the formation of states, many regional cultures of the Neolithic period developed into high levels of social complexity, which became widespread in both north and south China after 4000 B.C. (see Underhill and Habu, this volume). Such development, however, was not a homogenous process cross-regionally, but showed multiple trajectories leading to various outcomes in social formation. Some gave rise to early states, but others disappeared from the political landscape.

The causes for such diverse development, to some extent, may have related to the political strategies employed by elite groups. According to Blanton et al. (1996) and Feinman (1995), political strategies may be generally classified in two major types – network and corporate – which, however, are not mutually exclusive. Societies with network strategies emphasize the identification of elite individuals, both by special housing and burial structures and also by status-defining items of wealth, especially prestigious objects obtained through long-distance exchange. The elite individuals tend to form inter-group networks for exchange of politically charged valuables to negotiate power and status. Such an individualizing social formation may also be reinforced by ancestral ritual that legitimates the control of society by a limited number of high-ranking individuals or households. Corporate strategies, by contrast, characterize a group-oriented social formation, in which the importance of group definition was emphasized through investment in construction projects built by corporate labor, in which intra-group differentiation was minimal. Social integration may be emphasized through communal ritual based on broad themes such as fertility and renewal in society and cosmos (Blanton et al. 1996; Feinman 1995). Although in many mid-range political formations both strategies can be seen, this model emphasizes political actors, and is enlightening for our comprehension of sociopolitical variability among Neolithic societies in China.

The major sociopolitical change occurred in a rather confined area in the middle and lower Yellow River valley. In this region the late Neolithic societies are identified with the Longshan culture, often described as chiefdom-level societies (Liu

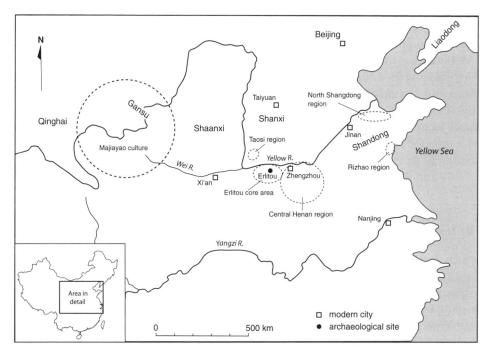

Figure 8.1 Major archaeological regions mentioned in the text

1996b; Underhill 1994), which gave rise to the earliest state centered at the Erlitou site in the Yiluo basin (Chang 1999; Liu and Chen 2003) (Figure 8.1). The Central Plains is also the region where the earliest dynasties, the Three Dynasties – Xia, Shang and Zhou (ca. 2100–221 B.C.) – as recorded in ancient texts, were established (Table 8.1).

There has been a major shift in regard to the role which various regional cultures played in the formation of early civilization or the state in China (see Liu and Chen 2001a). A traditional view, which has dominated Chinese thinking for many centuries and was commonly accepted by Chinese archaeologists before the 1980s, regards the Central Plains as the cradle of Chinese civilization, from which advanced cultural elements diffused outward to the periphery. This perspective is clearly reflected in the three editions of *Archaeology of Ancient China* by K. C. Chang published in 1963, 1968, and 1977, as von Falkenhausen (1995:198–9) observed. This viewpoint however was challenged by numerous archaeological discoveries in recent decades, which show that many Neolithic cultures in areas previously considered backward peripheries in fact evolved to advanced levels of social complexity comparable with that in the Central Plains. Interpretations of Neolithic social formation soon shifted from the traditional mono-centric model to propositions favoring multi-regional independent development (Su and Yin 1981; Wang 1997) and interregional interaction spheres (Chang 1986: 234–42), although the leading

Table 8.1. Chronology of major archaeological cultures in the Yellow River valley mentioned in this chapter

Chronology	Date (B.C.)	Upper Yellow river	Middle Yellow river	Lower Yellow river
	1045–771	Regional cultures	Western Zhou dynasty	Western Zhou dynasty
Bronze Age	ca. 1600/1500–1046	Regional cultures	Shang dynasty	Shang dynasty
	ca. 2000/1900–1600/1500	Qijia	Erlitou	Yueshi
	ca. 2600/2500–2000/1900	Banshan-Machang	Late Longshan	Longshan
Late Neolithic	ca. 3100/3000–2600/2500	Majiayao	Early Longshan	Late Dawenkou

role of the Central Plains in the processes toward civilization has by no means been neglected (Yan 1987; Zhang 2003).

The configuration of the early state in China is another issue currently under debate among Chinese specialists. Anthropologists have categorized early states in different parts of the world into various forms based on their sociopolitical characteristics. In recent years, several scholars have attempted to apply these generalizations to their interpretations of early Chinese civilization, using a cross-cultural comparative perspective, but opinions vary. Four models are most frequently used, based on such variables as political organization, urban structure, economic system, and territorial size. These models include city-states (Lin 1998; Yates 1997), segmentary states (Keightley 2000; Southall 1993:33), territorial states (Trigger 1999), and village states (Maisels 1987, 1990). These studies focus mainly on data from the Shang and Western Zhou dynasties (ca. 1600–770 B.C.), which represent more developed forms of states, but do not provide insights into the sociopolitical transition from pre-state to state in early China (Liu and Chen 2003). Our focus on the Longshan and Erlitou cultures in this chapter, therefore, aims to explain the related transitional processes.

The center–periphery relationship in the early state is a major concern in our discussion of state formation. Many archaeologists have applied World-Systems theory (Wallerstein 1974), although with extensive modifications (e.g., Blanton and Feinman 1984; Kohl 1987; Schneider 1991), to the study of economic and political interactions in complex societies from the multinational perspective (see Hall 2000b). A world-system is an inter-societal system marked by a self-contained division of labor. The core area exercises both political and economic control over surrounding peripheral regions, and extracts resources from the periphery via power and coercion. The periphery specializes in raw material production and becomes economically dependent on the core (Wallerstein 1974). The relationship between the core and periphery, according to this model, is superordinance-dependency (see Hall 2000a). Despite many deficiencies associated with the application of the world-systems concept to different case studies (e.g., Stein 1999), this theory provides a powerful analytic model for the study of the multi-regional economic–political system of the early state in China, especially if we take production and distribution of elite goods into account (cf. Blanton and Feinman 1984).

How ideology, economy, and politics interacted with one another in a society is crucial for understanding social processes. Two aspects are especially important in our discussion below: ancestral cults and prestige-goods production. Ancestral cults were one of the oldest religious forms in Neolithic China (Lee and Zhu 2002; Liu 2000a) and a significant characteristic of early Chinese dynasties (Keightley 1978). A prestige-goods system is characterized by specific political–economic structures in which the elite gains political advantage by exercising control over access to resources that can only be obtained externally (Frankenstein and Rowlands 1978:76–7). Such a system seems to have developed in some regions in Neolithic China, associated with interregional interactions among elite groups (Liu 2003). Ancestral cult ritual became closely intertwined with the production of prestige goods, particularly bronze vessels used in ancestral ceremonies, in the dynastic period (Chang 1983). It is critical, therefore, to understand the development of these particular cultural elements in relation to the process of state formation.

In this chapter we examine several developmental trajectories, from the Longshan culture of the late Neolithic to the Erlitou culture of the early Bronze Age, and such aspects as settlement pattern, prestige-goods production, and ritual practice. The geographic area is limited to the middle and lower Yellow River valley, since we see this region as the most dynamic area where social transformation took place. In the following pages, we will demonstrate that the Erlitou state was derived from a particular social system, characterized by inter-group competition and intra-group cooperation, which was only one of many Neolithic systems in the region. This earliest state then developed into a centralized political system, in which the control of prestige-goods production, especially bronze ritual objects, was the major driving force of political expansion. We argue that the sociopolitical change from chiefdoms to the early state occurred as multifaceted transformations, affected by environmental conditions, pre-existing political–economic systems, and ideology. The dynamics underlining state formation are best understood as change in political strategy, manifested by the development of a territorial state, or a "world system," which integrated the core and periphery into the first coherent political–economic entity centered in the middle Yellow River.

Longshan Settlement Patterns and Sociopolitical Organization

The settlement pattern approach is the broadest and most direct approach available to archaeologists for reconstructing patterns of regional organization, and has been applied to regions where social complexities developed at different levels (Billman and Feinman 1999). The use of this method in many parts of the world has proved to be highly effective for the understanding of social processes. Settlement archaeology in China has come a long way since the 1990s. Several projects using systematic regional survey methods have been carried out in the Yellow River region (for a review see Liu and Chen 2001c), and the results from these projects, together with data produced by traditional archaeological surveys conducted by Chinese archaeologists in the past decades, provide much information for further analysis of population change and social organization on a large spatial and temporal scale.

Longshan sites appear to cluster in areas with abundant arable land, within which people tended to choose residential locales near rivers offering easy access to water for domestic uses and transportation. Two patterns of settlement distribution are observable among ten site clusters in the middle and lower Yellow River valley. The first is the mono-centered system: each site cluster is dominated by one large center; the second pattern is the multi-centered system: in each cluster there are multiple centers of medium-sized sites spread out evenly over the landscape. The second pattern can be further characterized as two types: linear multi-centered and scattered multi-centered systems (Figure 8.2) (Liu 2004).

Mono-centered regional systems

A three- or four-tier settlement hierarchy coexisting with large regional centers is observed in Clusters 1, 2, 7, and 8 in the environmentally circumscribed regions (Figure 8.2). Minor centers were clustered around the major centers and, in turn, were closely surrounded by a lower level of settlements. The best examples of this form of settlement system are those from early Taosi and Rizhao clusters.

The Taosi cluster in south Shanxi is situated in the Linfen basin surrounded by mountain ranges in all directions (Figure 8.2: cluster 1). The Early and middle Taosi phase (ca. 2600–2300 B.C.) witnessed the rapid settlement nucleation centered at a walled site of Taosi (280 hectares) and the development of three-tiered site hierarchy. The rank-size curve shows a log-normal distribution (Figure 8.3A), suggesting a centralized political system. A palatial area (5 hectares) and an elite residential area (1.6 hectares) have been found in the southern section of this enclosure (Shanxi Team et al. 2003a), and the Taosi cemetery is characterized by hierarchically organized burial patterns and prestige goods (jade, finely made ceramics, stone, and, possibly, lacquer ritual paraphernalia, etc.) concentrated in a small group of elite individuals (Liu 1996a). Obtaining lithic material (hornfel) from the Dagudui quarry, 6 kilometers south of the site, Taosi was also a manufacturing center of stone artifacts, both tools and ritual paraphernalia such as chime stone. Craft production therefore may have played a major role in the development of this large regional center (Liu 2004).

In the Rizhao region in eastern Shandong, a group of Longshan sites (ca. 2600–2000 B.C.) is distributed around the major center, Liangchengzhen (246 hectares) in an area bounded by the ocean in the east and mountains in the west (Sino-American Collaborative Liangcheng 1997, 2002; Underhill et al. 1998; Underhill et al. 2002). Although the settlement data from the survey project have not been fully published, based on available information a four-tiered settlement

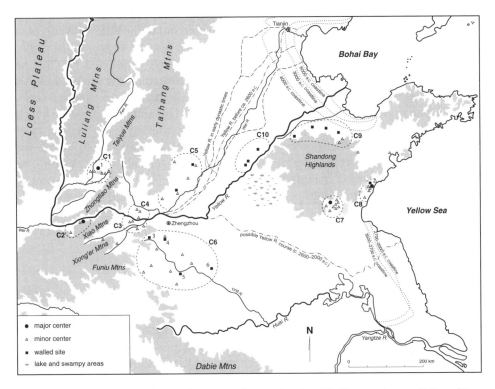

Figure 8.2 Distribution of Longshan site clusters in the Middle and Lower Yellow River region. Major sites: 1. Taosi; 2. Liangchengzhen; 3. Wangchenggang; 4. Guchengzhai; 5. Haojiatai; 6. Pingliangtai. Site clusters: C1. Taosi; C2. Western Henan; C3. Yiluo; C4. Qin River; C5. Northern Henan; C6. Central Henan; C7. Linyi; C8. Rizhao; C9. Northern Shandong; C10. Western Shandong

hierarchy and a log-normal rank-size curve can be observed, which however represents only the central portion of the regional settlement distribution (Figure 8.3B). The settlement nucleation happened rather suddenly since Liangchengzhen and its surrounding areas were barely populated prior to the Longshan period. Similar to Taosi, Liangchengzhen was also engaged in craft production, making both utilitarian and prestige goods, including stone tools (Bennett 2002), jades (Yin 1955: 58), and perhaps black egg-shell pottery goblets (Liu 1992; see also Liu 1996a:9–16) (more discussion below). However, the means of production and distribution of these goods remain to be investigated.

It is possible that Liangchengzhen developed into a large regional center probably because of its optimum location for easy access to raw lithic materials in the surrounding areas identified by the regional surveys (Sino-American Collaborative Liangcheng 1997:6), as well as to marine transportation which facilitated the flow of resources and craft products from and to other regions. This important regional function in craft production and distribution may have in turn stimulated the rapid growth of population as well as the hierarchical settlement system there.

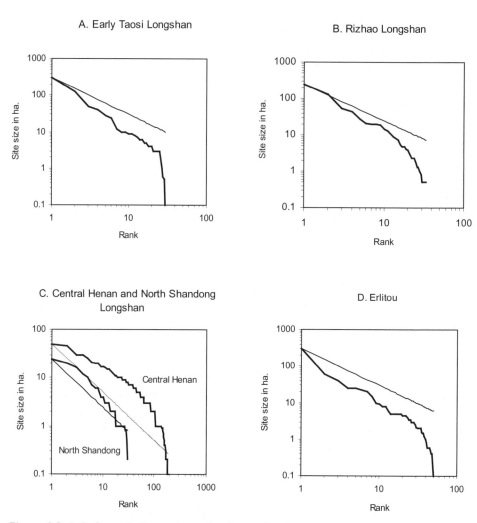

Figure 8.3 A, B, C, and D Comparison of rank–size distribution in Longshan and Erlitou cultures

These mono-centered settlement systems represent the most complex social systems in the region. However, they did not directly lead to the formation of early states. In the Rizhao region, the Longshan culture ended around 2000 B.C.; from then on the region was nearly depopulated for some thousand years before the Zhou dynasty (ca. 1000 B.C.). The Linfen basin during the late Taosi phase experienced a marked change in social organization. The large rammed-earth enclosure was destroyed; the palatial area of the early phase now became a craft production area, making stone and bone artifacts, particularly bone arrowheads; archaeological evidence of violence has been found, and elite tombs were broken into (Shanxi Team et al. 2003a, b). Moreover, as another regional center emerged at Fangcheng-Nanshi, the Linfen basin appears to have been dominated by two regional centers, leading to increased military competition between sub-regional polities for the rest of the Longshan period (Liu 2004). This situation finally changed when the Erlitou assemblages appeared there around 1800 B.C. South Shanxi then became the periphery of the first state centered at Erlitou in the Yiluo region (Liu and Chen 2001b).

Multi-centered competing regional systems

The second type of settlement distribution in the Yellow River basin is one showing coexistence of multiple medium-sized centers (no more than 100 hectares in size) (Zhao 2001:142–4) with or without rammed-earth enclosures in less circumscribed regions. Two sub-types, linear multi-centered and scattered multi-centered systems, developed in different geographic conditions.

Clusters 9 and 10 in northern and western Shandong are characterized by the distribution of several walled centers with a linear pattern in the semi-circumscribed regions (Figure 8.2). Each sub-regional settlement system exhibits two or three levels of settlement hierarchy, most centers were regularly spaced walled towns, about 40 kilometers in average distance between one another, and the rank-size distribution shows a convex curve (Figure 8.3C) (Liu 2000b). All these phenomena indicate inter-group political competition and independence (cf. Earle 1991:93), as well as territorial administration controlled by the local elites (cf. Johnson 1982:415; Renfrew 1975:14).

Clusters 5 and 6 in north and central Henan represent the scattered multi-centered systems. The centers, some of them walled, are spread out over the landscape, and the distances between centers are also regular. Most sub-clusters reveal a two-tiered settlement hierarchy, with only a few three-tiered, and the rank-size distribution is convex (Figure 8.3C). Evidence of inter-group conflict is present. Human sacrifices were practiced in some walled centers, such as Wangchenggang (Henan Institute 1992a). Skeletons with traits of scalping have also been found at Jiangou in southern Hebei (Longshan culture) and Dasima in Henan (Erlitou culture), suggesting that violent behavior became widespread in the Central Plains during the Longshan and Erlitou periods (Chen 2000; Yan 1982). These two clusters therefore are also characterized by competing relationships with a low level of integration among centers (Liu 1996b).

Cluster 6 in the Central Henan region is especially significant for understanding the political organization of the multi-centered settlement system. Four sub-regional centers were walled, including Wangchenggang (Henan Institute 1992a), Guchengzhai (Henan Institute 2002), Pingliangtai (Henan Institute 1983), and Haojiatai (Henan Institute 1992b). Differentiation in social status had developed within communities, as suggested by well-constructed buildings found inside walled enclosures. Some of these buildings were large in size and complex in structure, and some were associated with human sacrifice. These fortified sites were often equipped with such facilities as guardhouses, a drainage system (at Pingliangtai), and a palatial compound (at Guchengzhai), which are not seen in small villages.

Although residential areas have also been found outside the walled enclosures (e.g., Wangchenggang and Guchengzhai), a majority of the population of communities, including elite groups, likely resided within rammed-earth enclosures. The construction of rammed-earth walls and related facilities required great amounts of manpower, as well as certain forms of leadership, to mobilize the laborers who participated in communal productive activities at a regional level.

Multiple functions may have been associated with these sub-regional walled centers. The walls were probably built for defensive purposes as well as for flood control during a period of climatic fluctuation and social instability (Liu 2000b).

Cluster 3 in the Yiluo basin is similar to the clusters in north and central Henan in that multiple medium-sized centers, no more than 40 hectares (Zhao 2001:144), are scattered on the landscape, although none of them has walls (Liu 1996b; Liu et al. 2002–4). Considering that the earliest urban site developed at Erlitou in this region, it is particularly interesting to note that the settlement system here during the Longshan period appears a rather decentralized one.

It is notable that, similar to Liangchengzhen and Taosi, many centers in Henan also engaged in craft production. For example, evidence of pottery making was found at Pingliangtai (Henan Institute 1983), many stone tool blanks were discovered at Wangchenggang (Henan Institute 1992a), and fragments of crucibles were unearthed from Guchengzhai (Henan Institute 2002). In addition, many of these central places were situated in proximity to natural resources and near river channels, which provide water, lithic raw material, and means for transportation by boat; such locations facilitated craft production and distribution. These settlements may have developed into regional centers with greater population density than ordinary villages partially as the result of their elite groups' control of the manufacture of craft products, mainly utilitarian goods, which were distributed regionally.

Social organization appears to have been less integrated in a region including northern and central Henan and the Yiluo River valley, than in other settlement clusters during the Longshan period: the former case shows smaller sizes of centers, decentralized settlement systems, a lack of production and exchange of prestige items, and the absence of elaborate burials. However, it was from the variability of settlement patterns in this less integrated region that the early state arose, when the first phase of the Erlitou culture, the Xinzhai phase, was developed in the northwestern part of Central Henan before expanding to a broader region and establishing the first urbanism at Erlitou (Liu 1996b; Zhao 2002).

Longshan prestige-goods production

The production of prestige goods developing out of political strategies is associated with craft specialization . Therefore, variables in the production and distribution of prestige items can provide insights into the political structure of a given society (Brumfiel and Earle 1987; Costin 2001; Hayden 2001; Peregrine 1991).

Jade objects and fine ceramics were the major forms of prestige items in many Neolithic cultures in China. In the middle and lower Yellow River region, through which the Longshan culture was distributed, these two types of prestige goods were mainly found in Shandong and the Linfen basin in south Shanxi. In Shandong jades and fine pottery goblets made from "egg-shell" ware, often associated with rich burials, were status markers circulated regionally among elite individuals (Liu 1996a). It appears that Liangchengzhen may have been one of the locales for making jades and intensive use of egg-shell pottery, as suggested by semi-finished jade artifacts and a large quantity of egg-shell pottery sherds found at the center of the site (Liu 1992:29; Yin 1955:58; Yun and Mou 1992:28). At Taosi elite burials have yielded a large number of elite goods, including polychrome pottery, large-sized wooden–lacquer and stone ritual paraphernalia, alligator drums, and jades. Among these objects some were produced locally (e.g., chime stones, large cere-monial stone knives, and pottery), but others may have been obtained from distant places (e.g., alligator drums and jades).

Each of these two regions had its unique assemblages of prestige goods, likely associated with local ritual traditions. Concurrently, some prestige items, particu-larly jades with distinctive motifs and shapes, were widespread trans-regionally, probably resulting from interregional interaction among chiefly figures who were both ritually important and patrons of the arts and crafts. Such interaction pro-moted some elements of shared belief and of artistic styles, although these never formed a centralized system of prestige-goods production and distribution on a cross-regional scale (Liu 2003). Such locally oriented systems of production and distribution of prestige goods correspond to the segmentary political landscape of chiefdom societies during the Longshan period.

Longshan ritual and ideology

In the religious domain, communities of these two settlement systems seem to have had different emphases in ritual traditions. In Taosi and Shandong, cults addressed to the ancestors were more pronounced than those addressed to other deities. Ancestor venerations were directed to a limited number of individuals, and were conducted by specific kin groups. This individual-oriented ancestor worship became intertwined with hierarchical social systems, with much energy expended in the pro-duction of labor-intensive ritual–prestige items. As exemplified at Taosi in Shanxi and Chengzi in Shandong, the ancestors receiving long-term ritual offerings were individuals who held high ascribed social status and enjoyed political, religious, and economic prestige in certain prominent families and lineages. Living members of closely related kin groups likely conducted the ritual ceremonies. Ancestral ritual, therefore, became a part of political institutions, and reinforced the stratified, although still kinship-based, social systems (Liu 1996a, 2000a). In Shandong this tradition can be traced back to the Dawenkou culture (ca. 4100–2600 B.C.) (Fung 2000; Underhill 2000, 2002).

In Henan, on the contrary, no evidence for individual ancestral worship has been found, due to the lack of burials associated with material remains for ongoing ritual activities. However, some clues suggest that ritual practices held on the community level in this region may have been part of a long tradition which can be traced back to the Yangshao period. For example, a large public building (516 meters² for the entire structure) with possible ritual functions, dating to the middle Yangshao period, was found at Xipo in Lingbao (Ma 2003; Wei and Li 2002), and a middle Yangshao cemetery at Hongshanmiao in Ruzhou yielded more than 130 carefully arranged secondary collective burials (Henan Institute 1995). At a late Longshan culture site at Lutaigang in eastern Henan, two non-residential structures have been excavated. Structure I had two layers of walls – square-shaped outside and round-shaped inside (4.7 meters in diameter). Within the round-shaped walls, two paths arranged in a cross were found. Structure II consisted of eleven rammed-earth columns, arranged in a circle that was 4.4–4.5 meters in diameter. Ten small columns surround a central large column (1.48 meters in diameter). No domestic features or refuse have been found near either structure (Zhengzhou University 2000).

The shape of Structure I, square outside and round inside, apparently resembles the shape of jade *cong* tubes that have been found at many Neolithic sites in China (Huang 1992). This reoccurring design of square and round shapes symbolized heaven and earth in traditional Chinese cosmology, and the combination of the two shapes on one object has been interpreted by many archaeologists as an indicator of the connection between the two natural realms, heaven and earth, in religious practice (e.g., Chang 1989). This structure, therefore, may have been designed for the worship of heaven and earth (Liu 1997). Structure II, which is also unique in its design, has been interpreted as a locale for solar worship, as the coexistence of multiple suns was postulated in ancient China, and motifs of multiple suns were depicted on Yangshao ceramics dating to 3000–2500 B.C. (Liu 1997). These two structures were not associated with any particular residential features, and probably were constructed for communal ritual activities.

The contrast between these two social formations is clear. On the one hand, in Taosi and Shandong the practice of individual-oriented ancestral ritual supported individual elite groups' power acquisition in the ideological realm, and the social status of the elite was a major focus of concern. On the other hand, in central Henan, the group-oriented character of ritual activities seems to emphasize the whole community's interests, and elite individuals are not identified.

Political strategies of the Longshan elite

Interestingly, the differences in settlement pattern coincide with the dichotomy in political strategy, revealed in archaeological remains from these regions, which can be characterized as that between network and corporate strategies (Blanton et al. 1996; Feinman 1995), as discussed above. In the Taosi and Shandong regions, elaborate burials associated with exotic materials and labor-intensive products have been found. The production, redistribution, and exchange of prestige goods – such as alligator drums, jade objects, and elaborate ceramics – were carried out on a regular basis. Ancestral ritual was directed to individuals with high social status. The political–economic strategy was apparently focused on production and manipulation of prestige goods. The functions of such an economic system were intended to cement alliances between the leaders of different groups, and to attract and establish patronage relationships with headmen of smaller groups. This political strategy may have facilitated a steady expansion of political influence in the Rizhao and early Taosi regions, as revealed in the most integrated settlement patterns there. The elite groups in these two regions appear to have employed network strategies for creating and maintain power.

In contrast, in the Henan region, there is no evidence that prestige goods were produced and circulated regularly by local elites. Construction of town walls, which characterized the settlement system, was a communal activity undertaken by corporate labor, and was aimed at benefiting the entire community rather than a few high-status individuals or households. In this region military competition was a major force contributing to the sociopolitical systems. This sociopolitical formation therefore is best characterized as the corporate strategy.

Why did the Longshan societies in Shandong and early Taosi in southern Shanxi, which were characterized by network strategies, fail to develop into a state-level political organization? What dynamics were involved in the social transformation of corporate systems in the Central Plains? It is still difficult to provide conclusive answers to these questions, but examining some social and environmental factors may help us to comprehend the circumstances that gave rise to social change.

Although the production and distribution of prestige goods as an economic strategy can facilitate a rapid expansion of the sphere of political influence by establishing new channels for exchange, it suffers from high risks and instability. The chiefdom societies that mainly rely on this type of economic strategy are vulnerable to any kind of disruption in the exchange networks that provide the prestige goods needed to sustain the elite. As a result, some societies may cycle between periods of expansion and collapse (Earle 1987; Gilman 1987). This general tendency may explain the decline of the Longshan cultures in Shandong, as the societies concerned failed to adjust to changing social and natural environments.

Climatic fluctuations developed around 2000 B.C., with rising sea level, and generally cooler and dryer conditions (Shi et al. 1992; Zhao 1996). The rise of sea level may have led to marine transgression in the east coast. In colder–drier climatic episodes the reduction in vegetation cover would have led to more soil erosion, heavier sediment loads, and a flash flood regime in river systems in the loess regions (Quine et al. 1999). These conditions would have caused river flooding, especially the Yellow River's changing course, in the lowland regions. As a result, these natural disasters may have partially caused the cultural disruption evident at the end of the Shandong Longshan culture (Wang 1993, 1996, 1999). However, there are signs of gradual cultural decline occurring earlier in the late Longshan period, as the quality of finely made pottery deteriorated, and egg-shell pottery began to disappear (Luan 1993). It is likely that the slow cultural change was a consequence of social decisions made in response to environmental change. Environmental change may either promote opportunities for the elite to gain even more power, or devastate sociopolitical structures, if the elite fail to effectively respond to the external impact (cf. Rosen 1995). Weak coherence in the political and economic system of

individual-oriented political structures employing network strategies may have contributed to the decline of social complexity.

The centralized political system of the early Taosi phase broke down during the
late Taosi phase, as mentioned above. Although it is unclear how and why this region
lost its momentum toward further development into a higher level of social complexity, the highly circumscribed geological environment may have limited its
integration on a broader trans-regional basis.

The ultimate social change took place in the Henan region, and several phenomena during the third millennium B.C. may have been responsible. First, a
marked population movement from eastern and southeastern areas to central
Henan happened during the late fourth millennium and early third millennium
B.C., partially caused by the marine transgression on the east coast. This may have
led to population pressure and competition for limited resources there. Second,
climatic fluctuation may have caused the Yellow River to change its course
around 2600 and again around 2000 B.C., as well as causing floods of many other
rivers in the central Henan region (Liu 1996b, 2000b).

Longshan people in the Henan region responded to these social and environmental challenges in three ways. First, their communal ritual activities, focused on
worship of natural deities, may have been an ideological response to the environmental instability of the era. Second, the local elite groups competed for resources
and sought regional domination by intensive use of military force. Third, constructing town walls may have been communal projects to protect the communities from periodic floods as well as social rivals. These factors may account for the
practice of corporate strategies, expressed through group-oriented chiefdom organizations. As conflict between different ethnic or local groups was intensive, communities may have been forced to rely on local resources to maintain internal
solidarity against outsiders. Societies employing corporate strategies may have had
better potential to cope with social and environmental impacts. These situations
were perhaps the major forces contributing to the emergence of the state in Henan
rather than in Shandong. Furthermore, unlike the Taosi region, the less circumscribed environmental conditions in central Henan and the Yiluo basin would have
facilitated broader interaction with many neighboring polities, resulting in greater
political integration (Liu 1996b, 2000b). Several scholars have also suggested that,
compared with their neighboring cultures in the east and south which show more
mystical and transcendent characteristics, the Henan Longshan people appear to
have spent more energy on secular economic production than on religious activities. The this-worldly and realistic character of the Henan Longshan people may
provide some explanations for the cultural endurance and further social development shown in this region (Shao 1996; Zhao 1999).

The Erlitou State

The Erlitou culture, centered on the type-site of Erlitou in the Yiluo basin, has been
the focus of attention in debates concerning development of the earliest state in

ancient China. On the one hand, many archaeologists and historians, especially those whose early education was received in China, argue that the Erlitou culture was a state-level society and represents a later part of the Xia dynasty (e.g., Chang 1999:71–3; Du 1991; Gao et al. 1998; Li 1997; Song 1991; Wang 1998; Zhao 1987; Zou 1980). These scholars tend to believe that the coincidence in time and space between the archaeological Erlitou culture and the textually recorded Xia dynasty is sufficient to prove the historical link between the two. On the other hand, with few exceptions agreeing with the viewpoints of Chinese scholars (e.g., Childs-Johnson 1988, 1994), many Sinologists in the West question that the Erlitou culture represented a state-level polity, and are particularly skeptical about the reliability of textual information and thus the historical connection between the Erlitou and the Xia (e.g., Allan 1984, 1991; Bagley 1999:130–1; Keightley 1983; Linduff 1998:629; Railey 1999:178–86; Thorp 1991). The debates about Erlitou and the Xia are likely to continue for some time, unless an inscribed object bearing the name "Xia" is discovered at Erlitou. Nevertheless, we can still use archaeological data to study the level of social complexity in the Erlitou polity, regardless of its historical identity.

Some 38 calibrated radiocarbon dates derived from Erlitou sites in Henan (Institute of Archaeology 1991) and results from the recently accomplished "Xia Shang Zhou Chronology Project" (Lee 2002) indicate that the Erlitou culture flourished during a period between 1900 and 1500 B.C. (Xia Shang Zhou 2000). The Erlitou period is further divided into four successive phases, based on changes of ceramic styles, at estimated intervals of around 100 years (Institute of Archaeology 1999:392). Erlitou (300 hectares) (Erlitou Working Team et al. 2001) is the largest among all its contemporary sites in China. Sites containing Erlitou material assemblages have been found over a very broad region, including Henan, southern Shanxi, Eastern Shaanxi, and Hubei (Figure 8.4).

It is difficult to determine whether or not the distribution of Erlitou sites indicates the political sphere of the Erlitou polity. In several cases (discussed below), when the Erlitou material culture spread to the periphery, it appears as intrusive cultural assemblages, replacing much of the local material traditions (Liu and Chen 2001b, 2003). This phenomenon seems to support the correlation between the archaeological remains and political boundaries, at least in some areas.

The operation of the Erlitou political–economic system can be described as a world-system, consisting of a dominant center and several subordinate peripheral regions. World-systems may have as many as four levels of boundary, and incorporation into a world-system is a matter of degree. These boundaries include: (1) information or cultural flows; (2) luxury or prestige goods flows; (3) political–military interaction; and (4) bulk goods flows (Hall 1999). As demonstrated below, these four kinds of boundaries coincide in the Erlitou world-system.

The Erlitou core: sociopolitical and technological innovations

The core area of the Erlitou polity is situated in the Yiluo basin (Figure 8.1). Several marked sociopolitical and technological changes took place when the Erlitou culture

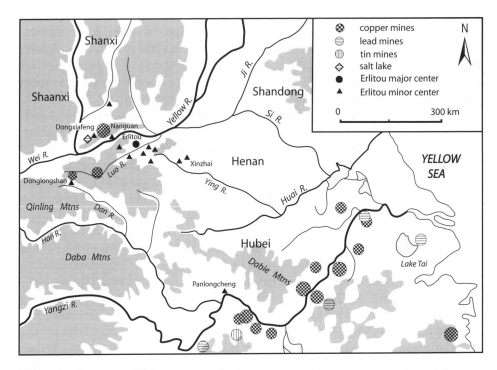

Figure 8.4 Locations of Erlitou major and minor centers and key resources in the periphery

developed. A new form of settlement pattern is characterized by a four-tiered settlement hierarchy centered at Erlitou, densely distributed Erlitou sites in the Yiluo region (Liu et al. 2002–4), and a strong primate curve expressed in the rank-size distribution (Figure 8.3D). Taken together, these indicate the emergence of a politically and economically centralized polity.

The Erlitou site itself, starting from Phase II, developed into a highly stratified urban center. There is a clear social polarization between rich and poor, indicated by burial differences; a large temple–palace complex was constructed, and the site was densely occupied by a population who were involved in agricultural production and various specialized craft manufactures including bronze, bone, and ceramics (Institute of Archaeology 1999; Liu In press).

Bronze metallurgy, using piece-mold techniques for making weapons and ritual vessels, is a new type of prestige-goods production carried out at Erlitou. It is notable that copper and bronze objects first appeared in the Majiayao culture (ca. 3100–2700 B.C.) in the upper Yellow River region (Figure 8.1). Metal objects dating to the second half of the third millennium B.C. are scattered over the Yellow River region (Linduff 1998; Linduff et al. 2000:map 1). These earliest metal artifacts are mainly personal ornaments and utilitarian items including small tools and weapons, which were hammered or cast in simple stone molds. Notably, there is little correlation between the occurrence of early bronze or copper items and the presence of social hierarchy in archaeological records prior to the second millennium B.C. in

China, since few metal items occur in elite burials as status symbol (Liu 2003). At Taosi, for example, a copper bell was found in a small Longshan tomb with no other grave goods, while the prestige goods unearthed from the elite tombs were primarily made of jade, stone, pottery, and wood. It is important to note that this bell was cast in a mold, although the report does not specify if piece-mold techniques were used (Shanxi Team et al. 1984).

It is clear that in the Yellow River region, bronze did not enter the inventory of recurrent types of prestige goods for a long period of time after the technology became available to the Longshan people. That is probably because metallurgical techniques were limited to making small utilitarian objects, which had little value in the existing sociopolitical systems. This situation did not change until ca. 1700 B.C. (Erlitou Phase III) when multi-piece mold casting techniques were used for making ritual vessels as high status symbols at Erlitou (Liu 2003).

At Erlitou the location of the bronze foundry is in close proximity to the pala-tial zone, indicating that bronze metallurgy was extremely important to the ruling elite. The clay molds recovered from the bronze foundry include those used for casting weapons, ritual vessels, and small tools (Zheng 1998:191). No mold for making agricultural implements has been identified. The metal products were closely associated with state political affairs, which centered on warfare and ritual rather than agriculture (Chang 1986:364).

Among its contemporary sites Erlitou is the only locale that yielded evidence for the manufacture of ritual vessels with multi-piece mold techniques. The technol-ogy of casting ritual vessels, therefore, may have been specially controlled by a par-ticular group of craftsmen attached to the Erlitou high elite in the primary center. In contrast, bronze casting was carried out at several sites in the periphery, but only tools and weapons were produced, and with less sophisticated, single or double stone molds (Liu and Chen 2003). Furthermore, Erlitou bronze vessels seem to have been distributed only at the Erlitou site, while pottery ritual vessels of white kaolinitic ware have been found from many major Erlitou sites across a broad region. These phenomena suggest that the Erlitou rulers monopolized the casting of bronze ritual vessels, the production level was low, and the products were exclu-sively distributed among elite members with the highest social status. The white ware vessels may have functioned as an alternative medium to create and maintain a larger political–economic system, including both the core and peripheral regions (Liu 2003).

The multi-piece mold techniques seem to have been either invented or signifi-cantly improved (if the Taosi copper bell was made of such techniques) specifically for making bronze ritual vessels, which became the most important symbols of polit-ical, religious, and economic power throughout the Bronze Age of China (Chang 1983, 1991). This method also marked the divergence of metallurgy at Erlitou from the surrounding regions as well as the rest of the world, where bronze products were predominantly ornamental and utilitarian items. This metallurgical innovation made around 1700 B.C. by the Erlitou artisans later led to the flourishing of the great Shang bronze culture (Bagley 1990; Barnard 1961, 1975; Chase 1983; Gettens 1969).

The multi-piece mold techniques for making bronze ritual vessels may have also been inspired by earlier methods of ceramic production, since white pottery in particular had been partially made with molds. The earliest examples of bronze ritual vessels at Erlitou occurred in four forms: *jue, jia, he* and *ding* tripod, which were used for drinking and cooking. The forms of these vessels, except for the ding, remarkably resemble their white pottery predecessors, which were often used to furnish elite burials in the Yiluo region during Erlitou Phases I and II; these same pottery vessel forms can be further traced back to the Neolithic period (Liu 2003). Large quantities of food vessels in many Neolithic burials may have been related to competitive emulation among elites through ritual feasting (Fung 2000; Underhill 2002). The stylistic continuity of these vessels, as ritual paraphernalia from the Neolithic to Bronze Ages, suggests that similar forms of ceremonies, which involved feasting, had continued, forming a significant cultural tradition. The new metallurgical material was integrated into the existing prestige-goods system only if the new products were meaningful and usable within the traditional ritual framework. This achievement was made in the Erlitou period when the artisans developed new technology capable of rendering sophisticated bronze vessels to imitate traditional pottery vessels.

Piece-mold bronze production requires a high level of division of labor and great control of material resources, knowledge, and people (Franklin 1983). These requirements could only be met within a highly stratified social organization, and in turn may have further stimulated the development of social complexity. The latter point is clearly demonstrated by the political expansion of the Erlitou polity into its periphery.

The Erlitou periphery: procurement of resources

Situated in the flood plain of the Yiluo basin, Erlitou was surrounded by fertile agricultural land with few non-agricultural resources. Several types of resources seem to be the most crucial: a large quantity of timber for constructing palaces and temples at Erlitou; lithic materials for making stone tools; kaolin clay for making elite ceramics (white pottery); copper, tin, and lead for casting bronzes; timber and charcoal as fuel for casting bronzes; and salt for cooking and processing food (Liu et al. 2002–4). Most of these resources were only available in areas peripheral to the Yiluo basin as well as more distant regions. Starting from Phase II and reaching a peak in Phase III, Erlitou material assemblages intrude into the resource-rich periphery, including south Shanxi, east Shaanxi, and the middle Yangzi River region, as the result of population migrations directed by a centralized state in order to procure vital resources (Liu and Chen 2003). At the Erlitou site a marked increase in the number of projectile points occurs in Erlitou Phases II and III, a period coinciding with the Erlitou territorial expansion (Liu In press), suggesting the Erlitou expansion was likely coercive in nature.

Metal and salt were among the most critical resources for the Erlitou state. The nearest copper and salt deposits could have been found around the Zhongtiao

Mountains of southern Shanxi, about 150–200 kilometers northwest of Erlitou. Two regional centers in this region, Dongxiafeng and Nanguan, may have been the outposts of the Erlitou polity for procuring copper and salt (Figure 8.4) (Liu and Chen 2001b). Erlitou material culture also expanded toward other regions, such as Donglongshan in southeastern Shaanxi and Panlongcheng in Hubei (Figure 8.4). Burials associated with stone and jade ritual objects and wasters have been unearthed from the early Erlitou strata at Donglongshan (Yang 2000). The mountainous region near Donglongshan not only possessed jade deposits (Fang 1995:157), but also was rich in copper, lead, and tin deposits (Huo 1993). Similarly, Panlongcheng, which was in close proximity to abundant copper deposits in the middle Yangzi River valley, has yielded evidence of bronze making dating to the Erlitou period (Wang and Chen 1987:74). Copper was likely smelted near the mining areas, and elites in the regional centers may have played the major role in transporting copper ingots to the primary center at Erlitou (Liu and Chen 2003).

As a result of such territorial expansion, ceramic styles changed from diversity in the Longshan period (six variants in Henan and southern Shanxi) to relative uniformity in the Erlitou period (two variants, Erlitou and Dongxiafeng, in the same region). This may suggest an increase in specialization and standardization of craft production relating to the development of political centralization (cf. Longacre 1999; Rice 1981, 1996).

Erlitou also became a far-reaching polity, with direct or indirect contacts with remote places for acquisition of exotic goods. Cowries (*Monetaia moneta* or *Monetaria annulus*) with possible origins in the Indian Ocean region (Peng and Zhu 1999) and some artifacts and decorative motifs with characteristics of Central Asian cultures (Fitzgerald-Huber 1995) found their way to Erlitou elite burials.

The relationship between the core and periphery of the Erlitou polity points to the development of centralized political and economic control, a nucleation of population accompanying urbanism, and political and military expansion of a territorial state. The quest for bronze alloys apparently functioned as a driving force underlying the territorial expansion of the Erlitou polity. Bronze ritual vessels, in particular, were employed as status symbols that constituted social hierarchy, wealth, and power, and were used as the media of ancestral cult ceremonies, which asserted political legitimacy for the elite (Chang 1983). The symbolic power of bronzes may have been much greater than that of traditional prestige materials such as jade and pottery. Not only were the properties of bronze extremely appealing, but the production processes of bronze ritual objects required much more complex technological and managerial skills, greater manpower, and a broader regional scope than was needed for making other types of elite goods. Therefore, greater political, economic, and religious powers were associated with this new type of wealth.

The social–political transition: Erlitou political strategies and world system

Notably, there is a gap of about 100 years between the Longshan culture and the Erlitou culture (ca. 2000–1900 B.C.) in the archaeological record, and the Erlitou site was unoccupied for some 500 years before it emerged as an urban center around

1900 B.C. (Institute of Archaeology 1999). Ceramic types and burial forms of the Erlitou culture seem to have their origins in central Henan (Yuan 1996), where the Xinzhai phase has been identified as a transitional phase between the Longshan and the Erlitou cultures (Zhao 2002). Erlitou and its hinterland in the Yiluo region witnessed a rapid population increase in Erlitou Phase II, which was likely caused by immigration of people from places outside the Yiluo basin (Liu In press; Liu et al. 2002–4). However, the underlying dynamics and processes of such population movement are unclear. More archaeological research is needed in order to understand this important social transformation.

It is clear, nevertheless, that the Erlitou elite adopted political strategies very different from those of its Longshan predecessors in central Henan; the latter may be characterized as "corporate strategies" focusing on group solidarity without conspicuous vertical social stratification among the members of a community. The new Erlitou social system, in contrast, was more inclined to "network strategies," emphasizing social hierarchy, individual status, accumulation of wealth, control of prestige-goods production, and long-distance trade of elite items. What brought about such a dramatic change in leadership strategy is unclear, but the innovation may have been driven more by deliberate decisions of political actors than by an impersonal evolutionary process.

Although many questions remain to be answered, we have begun to understand the political–economic system that structured this first Chinese state. The Erlitou state formed an interregional network focused on production and distribution of prestige goods, especially bronze vessels. This network incorporated two interdependent sectors, core and periphery, which may be referred to as the first world-system in ancient China.

In this system the dominant core controlled the production of prestige items (bronze products, etc.), and the subordinate periphery provided raw material resources (metal ingots) and bulk goods (salt). The Erlitou elite in the core achieved domination through military force by establishing outposts in the periphery to ensure the flows of material and information. The relationship between the core and periphery was asymmetrical. This "world-system" was sustained by a shared ideology centered on ancestral cults that practiced ritual feasting, in which particular types of vessels were used. This cult practice may have in turn helped to form a common cultural tradition.

Conclusion

The sociopolitical transition from the Neolithic to the Bronze Age in the Yellow River valley involved a process through which societies changed from regionalized to centralized, and from multiple loosely related local systems to an integrated core–periphery network which dominated a large part of the region. Since no writing system has been found at Erlitou, it is unclear how the administration of this archaic state managed the flow of information and material between the core and the periphery. Given the large scale of its political–economic undertakings, the Erlitou administrative system must have been complex.

It is notable that Erlitou did not develop in isolation. It emerged from a sea of chiefdoms, and continued to coexist with many societies with different degrees of social complexity spread over the landscape. The rapid expansion of the Erlitou polity however suggests that other regional polities, most likely chiefdoms, were relatively weak and could not compete with the first state. The social organization of the Erlitou state, characterized by large territory and centralized political control, is similar to Egypt but different from Mesopotamia. The Erlitou polity therefore is best described as a territorial state, according to Trigger's definition (Trigger 1999:47–50).

As discussed elsewhere (Liu and Chen 2003), the decline of the Erlitou polity coincided with the rise of the early Shang state (Erligang culture, ca. 1600–1400 B.C.), and the latter appears to have inherited all the political strategies and territorial structure initiated by the Erlitou elite. Erlitou's innovation in the political, economic, and ideological realms marked the first instance of centralized state structure in China.

ACKNOWLEDGMENTS

We are grateful to David Keightley, Miriam Stark, Henry Wright, and Anne Underhill who provided invaluable and constructive comments. We especially thank Wei Ming for his high-quality illustrations, and Thomas Bartlett who edited the manuscript. However, we are responsible for all imperfections in this work.

REFERENCES

Allan, Sarah 1984 The Myth of the Xia Dynasty. Journal of the Royal Asiatic Society of Great Britain and Ireland 2:242–56.
—— 1991 The Shape of the Turtle: Myth, Art and Cosmos in Early China. Albany: State University of New York.
Bagley, Robert 1990 Shang Ritual Bronzes: Casting Technique and Vessel Design. Archives of Asian Art 43:6–20.
—— 1999 Shang Archaeology. In The Cambridge History of Ancient China. Michael Loewe and Edward Shaughnessy, eds. Pp. 124–231. Cambridge: Cambridge University Press.
Barnard, Noel 1961 Bronze Casting and Bronze Alloys in Ancient China. Canberra: Australia National University and Monumenta Serica.
—— ed. 1975 Ancient Chinese Bronzes and Southeast Asian Metal and Other Archaeological Artifacts. Melbourne: National Gallery of Victoria.
Bennett, Gwen 2002 The Organization of Lithic Tool Production During the Longshan Period (ca. 2600–2000 B.C.) in Southeastern Shandong Province, China. Ph.D. dissertation, University of California, Los Angeles.
Billman, Brian R., and Gary M. Feinman 1999 Settlement Pattern Studies in the Americas: Fifty Years Since Viru. Washington and London: Smithsonian Institution Press.

Blanton, Richard, and Gary Feinman 1984 The Mesoamerican World System. American Anthropologist 86:673–82.

Blanton, Richard, with Gary Feinman, Stephen Kowalewski, and Peter Peregrine 1996 A Dual-Processual Theory for the Evolution of Mesoamerican Civilization. Current Anthropology 37(1):1–14.

Brumfiel, Elizabeth, and Timothy Earle 1987 Specialization, Exchange, and Complex Societies: An Introduction. In Specialization, Exchange, and Complex Societies. Elizabeth Brumfiel and Timothy Earle, eds. Pp. 1–9. Cambridge: Cambridge University Press.

Chang, Kwang-chih 1983 Art, Myth, and Ritual. Cambridge MA: Harvard University Press.

—— 1986 [1963, 1968, 1977] Archaeology of Ancient China. New Haven: Yale University Press.

—— 1989 An Essay on Cong. Orientations 20(6):37–43.

—— 1991 Introduction: The Importance of Bronzes in Ancient China. In Ancient Chinese Bronze Art: Casting the Precious Sacral Vessel. W. Thomas Chase, ed. Pp. 15–18. New York: China House Gallery, China Institute America.

—— 1999 China on the Eve of the Historical Period. In The Cambridge History of Ancient China: From the Origins of Civilization to 221 B.C. Michael Loewe and Edward Shaughnessy, eds. Pp. 37–73. Cambridge: Cambridge University Press.

Chase, Thomas W. 1983 Bronze Casting in China: A Short Technical History. In The Great Bronze Age of China: A Symposium. George Kuwayama, ed. Pp. 100–23. Los Angeles: Los Angeles County Museum of Art.

Chen, Xingcan 2000 Zhongguo gudai de botoupi fengsu ji qita (The practice of scalping and other issues in Ancient China). Wenwu 1:48–55.

Childs-Johnson, Elizabeth, ed. 1988 Ritual and Power: Jades of Ancient China. New York: China Institute of America.

—— 1994 Review of The Shape of the Turtle: Myth, Art, and Cosmos in Early China. Journal of Asian Studies 53(1):156–8.

Costin, Cathy L. 2001 Craft Production Systems. In Archaeology at the Millennium: A Sourcebook. Gary M. Feinman and T. Douglas Price, eds. Pp. 273–328. New York: Kluwer Academic/Plenum Publishers.

Du, Zhengsheng 1991 Xiadai kaogu jiqi guojia fazhan de tansuo (Archaeology of the Xia dynasty and the development of state). Kaogu 1:43–56.

Earle, Timothy K. 1987 Chiefdoms in Archaeological and Ethnohistorical Perspective. Annual Review of Anthropology 16:279–308.

—— 1991 Property Rights and the Evolution of Chiefdoms. In Chiefdoms: Power, Economy, and Ideology. T. Earle, ed. Pp. 71–99. Cambridge: Cambridge University Press.

Erlitou Working Team, Institute of Archaeology, and CASS 2001 Erlitou yizhi tianye gongzuo de xinjinzhan (New progress in the fieldwork at the Erlitou site). Zhongguo Shehui Kexueyuan Gudai Wenming Yanjiu Zhongxin Tongxun 1:32–4.

Falkenhausen, Lothar von 1993 On the Historiographical Orientation of Chinese Archaeology. Antiquity 67(257):839–49.

—— 1995 The Regionalist Paradigm in Chinese Archaeology. In Nationalism, Politics, and the Practice of Archaeology. Philip L. Kohl and Clare Fawcett, eds. Pp. 198–217. Cambridge: Cambridge University Press.

Fang, Weizhong 1995 Zhongguo Ziran Ziyuan Congshu – Shaanxi Juan. (The Chinese Natural Resources Series: Shaanxi Volume.) Beijing: Zhongguo Huanjing Kexue Press.

Feinman, Gary 1995 The Emergence of Inequality: A Focus on Strategies and Processes. In Foundations of Social Inequality. Douglas Price and Gary Feinman, eds. Pp. 225–79. New York: Plenum Press.

Fitzgerald-Huber, Louisa 1995 Qijia and Erlitou: The Question of Contacts with Distant Cultures. Early China 20:17–68.

Frankenstein, Susan, and Michael Rowlands 1978 The Internal Structure and Regional Context of Early Iron Age Society in Southwestern Germany. University of London Institute of Archaeology Bulletin 15:73–112.

Franklin, Ursula M. 1983 The Beginnings of Metallurgy in China: A Comparative Approach. In The Great Bronze Age of China. G. Kuwayama, ed. Pp. 94–9. Los Angeles: Los Angeles County Museum.

Fung, Christopher 2000 The Drinks are on Us: Ritual, Social Status, and Practice in Dawenkou Burials, North China. Journal of East Asian Archaeology 2(1–2):67–92.

Gao, Wei, with Xizhang Yang, Wei Wang, and Jinpeng Du 1998 Yanshi Shangcheng yu Xia Shang wenhua fenjie (The Yanshi Shang city and the demarcation between the Xia and Shang cultures). Kaogu 10:66–79.

Gettens, Rutherford John 1969 The Freer Chinese Bronzes. Volume II. Technical Studies. Washington DC: Smithsonian Institution, Freer Gallery of Art.

Gilman, A. 1987 Unequal Development in Copper Age Iberia. In Specialization, Exchange, and Complex Societies. E. Brumfiel and T. Earle, eds. Pp. 22–9. Cambridge: Cambridge University Press.

Hall, Thomas D. 1999 World-Systems and Evolution: An Appraisal. In World-Systems Theory in Practice: Leadership, Production, and Exchange. P. Nick Kardulias, ed. Pp. 1–24. Lanham: Rowman and Littlefield Publishers.

—— 2000a World-Systems Analysis: A Small Sample from a Large Universe. In A World-Systems Reader: New Perspectives on Gender, Urbanism, Cultures, Indigenous Peoples, and Ecology. Thomas D. Hall, ed. Pp. 3–28. Lanham: Rowman and Littlefield Publishers.

—— ed. 2000b A World-Systems Reader: New Perspectives on Gender, Urbanism, Cultures, Indigenous Peoples, and Ecology. London: Rowman and Littlefield.

Hayden, Brian 2001 Richman, Poorman, Beggarman, Chief: The Dynamics of Social Inequality. In Archaeology at the Millennium: A Sourcebook. Gary M. Feinman and T. Douglas Price, eds. Pp. 231–72. New York: Kluwer Academic/Plenum Publishers.

Henan Institute of Cultural Relics 1983 Henan Huaiyang Pingliangtai Longshan wenhua chengzhi shijue jianbao (Brief report on the test excavation of a Longshan cultural town-wall site at Pingliangtai, Huaiyang, Henan). Wenwu 3:21–36.

—— 1992a Dengfeng Wangchenggang yu Yangcheng. (Wangchenggang and Yangcheng in Dengfeng.) Beijing: Wenwu Press.

—— 1992b Yancheng Haojiatai yizhi de fajue (Excavation of the Haojiatai site in Yancheng). Huaxia Kaogu 3:62–91.

—— 1995 Ruzhou Hongshanmiao. (Hongshanmiao in Ruzhou.) Zhengzhou: Zhongzhou Guji Press.

—— 2002 Henan Xinmishi Guchengzhai Longshan wenhua chengzhi fajue jianbao (Brief report of excavations of the walled Longshan site at Guchengzhai in Xinmi, Henan). Huaxia Kaogu 2:53–82.

—— 2003 Henan Lingbao Xipo Yizhi 105 Hao Yangshao Wenhua Fangzhi. Wenwu 8: 4–17.

Huang, Tsui-mei 1992 Liangzhu – a Late Neolithic Jade-Yielding Culture in Southeastern Coastal China. Antiquity 66:75–83.

Huo, Youguang 1993 Shitan Luonan Hongyanshan gutongkuang cai ye di (In search of ancient mining and smelting locations in Mt. Hongyan in Luonan). Kaogu yu Wenwu 1:94–7.

Ikawa-Smith, Fumiko 1999 Construction of National Identity and Origins in East Asia: A Comparative Perspective. Antiquity 73:626–9.

Institute of Archaeology, CASS 1991 Zhongguo Kaoguxue Zhong Tan Shisi Niandai Shujuji. (Radiocarbon dates in Chinese archaeology.) Beijing: Wenwu Press.

—— 1999 Yanshi Erlitou. (Erlitou in Yanshi.) Beijing: Zhongguo Dabaikequanshu Press.

Johnson, Gregory A. 1982 Organizational Structure and Scalar Stress. *In* Theory and Explanation in Archaeology. M. Rowlands, C. Renfrew, and B. Seagraves, eds. Pp. 389–420. New York: Academic Press.

Keightley, David N. 1978 The Religious Commitment: Shang Theology and the Genesis of Chinese Political Culture. History of Religion 17:212–14.

—— 1983 The Late Shang State: When, Where, and What? *In* The Origins of Chinese Civilization. David Keightley, ed. Pp. 523–64. Berkeley: University of California Press.

—— 2000 The Ancestral Landscape: Time, Space, and Community in Late Shang China (ca. 1200–1045 B.C.). Berkeley: Institute of East Asian Studies.

Kohl, Philip 1987 The Use and Abuse of World Systems Theory: The Case of the Pristine West Asian State. Advances in Archaeological Method and Theory 11:1–35.

Lee, Yun Kuen 2002 Building the Chronology of Early Chinese History. Asian Perspectives 41(1):15–42.

Lee, Yun Kuen, and Naicheng Zhu 2002 Social Integration of Religion and Ritual in Prehistoric China. Antiquity (76):715–23.

Li, Xueqin, ed. 1997 Zhongguo Gudai Wenming yu Guojia Xingcheng Yanjiu. Kunming: Yunnan Renmin Press.

Lin, Yun 1998 Guanyu Zhongguo zaoqi guojia xingshi de jige wenti (Issues on the forms of early states in China). *In* Lin Yun Xueshu Wenji. Yun Lin, ed. Pp. 85–99. Beijing: Zhongguo Dabaikequanshu Press.

Linduff, Katheryn M. 1998 The Emergence and Demise of Bronze-Producing Cultures Outside the Central Plain of China. *In* The Bronze Age and Early Iron Age Peoples of Eastern Central Asia. Victor H. Mair, ed. Pp. 619–46. Volume 2. Washington DC: Institute for the Study of Man Inc.

Linduff, Katheryn M., Rubin Han, and Shuyun Sun, eds. 2000 The Beginning of Metallurgy in China. New York: The Edwin Mellen Press.

Liu, Chuanying 1997 Shixi Lutaigang yizhi I, II hao yiji de xingzhi (Analysis of the nature of structures I and II at the Lutaigang site). Jianghan Kaogu 2:45–9.

Liu, Dunyuan 1992 Longshan wenhua ruogan wenti zhiyi (Questions about some issues in the Longshan culture). *In* Shandong Longshan Wenhua Yanjiu Wenji. Fengshu Cai and Fengshi Luan, eds. Pp. 23–40. Jinan: Qilu Shushe.

Liu, Li 1996a Mortuary Ritual and Social Hierarchy in the Longshan Culture. Early China 21:1–46.

—— 1996b Settlement Patterns, Chiefdom Variability, and the Development of Early States in North China. Journal of Anthropological Archaeology 15:237–88.

—— 2000a Ancestor Worship: An Archaeological Investigation of Ritual Activities in Neolithic North China. Journal of East Asian Archaeology 2(1–2):129–64.

—— 2000b The Development and Decline of Social Complexity in China: Some Environmental and Social Factors. Indo-Pacific Prehistory: The Melaka Papers. Bulletin of the Indo-Pacific Prehistory Association 20(4):14–33.

—— 2003 "The Products of Minds as Well as of Hands:" Production of Prestige Goods in the Neolithic and Early State Periods of China. Asian Perspectives 42(1):1–40.

—— 2004 The Chinese Neolithic: Trajectories to Early States. Cambridge: Cambridge University Press.

—— In press Urbanization in China: Erlitou and its Hinterland. *In* Urbanism in the Preindustrial World: Cross-Cultural Approaches. Glenn Storey, ed. Tuscaloosa: University of Alabama Press.

Liu, Li, and Xingcan Chen 2001a China. *In* Encyclopedia of Archaeology: History and Discoveries. Tim Murray, ed. Pp. 315–33. Volume I, A–D. Santa Barbara: ABC Clio.

—— 2001b Cities and Towns: The Control of Natural Resources in Early States, China. Bulletin of the Museum of Far Eastern Antiquities 73:5–47.

—— 2001c Settlement Archaeology and the Study of Social Complexity in China. The Review of Archaeology 22(2):4–21.

—— 2003 State Formation in Early China. London: Duckworth.

Liu, Li, with Xingcan Chen, Yun Kuen Lee, Henry Wright, and Arlene Rosen 2002–4 Settlement Patterns and Development of Social Complexity in the Yiluo Region, North China. Journal of Field Archaeology 29:1–26.

Longacre, W. A. 1999 Standardization and Specialization: What's the Link? *In* Pottery and People: A Dynamic Interaction. J. Skibo and G. Feinman, eds. Pp. 44–58. Salt Lake City: The University of Utah Press.

Luan, Fengshi 1993 Shilun Yueshi wenhua de laiyuan (On the origin of the Yueshi culture). *In* Jinian Chengziyai Yizhi Fajue 60 Zhounian Guoji Xueshu Taolunhui Wenji. Pp. 266–82. Jinan: Qi Lu Press.

Ma, Xiaolin 2003 Emergent Social Complexity in the Yangshao Culture: Analyzes of Settlement Patterns and Faunal Remains from Lingbao, Western Henan, China. Ph.D. dissertation, La Trobe University.

Maisels, Charles 1987 Models of Social Evolution: Trajectories from the Neolithic to the State. Man 22(2):331–59.

—— 1990 The Emergence of Civilization: From Hunting and Gathering to Agriculture, Cities, and the State in the Near East. London: Routledge.

Murowchick, Robert 1997 The State of Sino-Foreign Collaborative Archaeology in China. Orientations 28(6):26–33.

Murowchick, Robert, and David Cohen 2001 Searching for Shang's Beginnings: Great City Shang, City Song, and Collaborative Archaeology in Shangqiu, Henan. The Review of Archaeology 22(2):47–60.

Peng, Ke, and Yanshi Zhu 1999 Zhongguo gudai suoyong haibei laiyuan xintan (New inquiry in the sources of cowries in ancient China). Kaoguxue Jikan 12:119–47.

Peregrine, Peter 1991 Some Political Aspects of Craft Specialization. World Archaeology 23(1):1–11.

Quine, T. A., with D. Walling and X. Zhang 1999 Slope and Gully Response to Agricultural Activity in the Rolling Loess Plateau, China. *In* Fluvial Processes and Environmental Change. A. G. Brown and T. A. Quine, eds. Pp. 71–90. New York: Wiley and Sons.

Railey, Jim 1999 Neolithic to Early Bronze Age Sociopolitical Evolution in the Yuanqu Basin, North-Central China. Ph.D. dissertation, Washington University.

Renfrew, Colin 1975 Trade as Action at a Distance: Questions of Integration and Communication. *In* Ancient Civilization and Trade. Jeremy Sablof and C. C. Lamberg-Karlovsky, eds. Pp. 3–59. Albuquerque: University of New Mexico Press.

Rice, Prudence M. 1981 Evolution of Specialized Pottery Production: A Trial Model. Current Anthropology 22(33):219–40.

—— 1996 Recent Ceramic Analysis: 2. Composition, Production and Theory. Journal of Archaeological Research 4(3):165–202.

Rosen, Arlene M. 1995 The Social Response to Environmental Change in Early Bronze Age Canaan. Journal of Anthropological Archaeology 14:26–44.

Schneider, J. 1991 Was There a Pre-Capitalist World-System? *In* Core-Periphery Relations in Precapitalist Worlds. C. Chase-Dunn and T. D. Hall, eds. Pp. 45–66. Boulder CO: Westview Press.

Shanxi Team, Institute of Archaeology, and CASS 1984 Shanxi Xiangfen Taosi yizhi shouci faxian tongqi (First copper object discovered at the Taosi site in Xiangfen, Shanxi). Kaogu 12:1069–71.

Shanxi Team, Institute of Archaeology, CASS, Shanxi Institute of Archaeology, and Linfen Bureau of Cultural Relics 2003a 2002 nian Shanxi Xiangfen Taosi chengzhi fajue (Excavation of the Taosi walled site in Xiangfen, Shanxi, 2002). Zhongguo Shehui Kexueyuan Gudai Wenming Yanjiu Zhongxin Tongxun 5:40–9.

—— 2003b Taosi chengzhi faxian Taosi wenhua zhongqi muzang (Mid-Taosi phase burials at the Taosi walled site). Kaogu 9:3–6.

Shao, Wangping 1996 Chudi xin wu gui, zhong yinxi shuyuan (In search of the origin of witch-believing and witchcraft in ancient Chu area). *In* Changjiang Zhongyou Shiqian Wenhua ji Dierjie Yazhou Wenming Xueshu Taolunhui Lunwenji. Hunan Institute of Archaeology, ed. Pp. 326–31. Changsha: Yuelu Press.

Shi, Yafeng, with Z. C. Kong, S. M. Wang, L. Y. Tang, F. B. Wang, T. D. Yao, X. T. Zhao, P. Y. Zhang, and S. H. Shi 1992 Zhongguo quanxinshi danuanqi qihou yu huanjing de jiben tezheng (Basic characteristics of climate and environment during the Holocene megathermal in China). *In* Zhongguo Quanxinshi Danuanqi Qihou yu Huanjing. Yafeng Shi and Shaochen Kong, eds. Pp. 1–18. Beijing: Kexue Press.

Sino-American Collaborative Liangcheng Archaeology Team 1997 Shandong Rizhaoshi Liangcheng diqu de kaogu diaocha (Archaeological survey in the Liangcheng area, Rizhao city, Shandong). Kaogu 4:1–15.

—— 2002 Shandong Rizhao diqu xitong quyu diaocha de xin shouhuo (New gains from the systematic regional surveys in the Rizhao district, Shandong). Kaogu 5:10–18.

Sino-American Huan River Valley Archaeology Team 1998 Huanhe liuyu kaogu yanjiu chubu baogao (Preliminary report of regional archaeological research in the Huan River valley). Kaogu 10:13–22.

Song, Xinchao 1991 Yin Shang Wenhua Quyu Yanjiu. (A regional approach to the Shang culture.) Xi'an: Shaanxi Renmin Press.

Southall, Aidan 1993 Urban Theory and the Chinese City. *In* Urban Anthropology in China. G. Guldin and A. Southall, eds. Pp. 19–40. Leiden: E. J. Brill.

Stein, Gil 1999 Rethinking World-Systems: Diasporas, Colonies, and Interaction in Uruk Mesopotamia. Tucson: The University of Arizona Press.

Su, Bingqi, and Weizhang Yin 1981 Guanyu kaoguxue wenhua de quxi leixing wenti (On the issue of the distribution and development of regional cultures in Chinese archaeology). Wenwu 5:10–17.

The Chifeng International Collaborative Archaeological Research Project 2003 Regional Archaeology in Eastern Inner Mongolia: A Methodological Exploration. Beijing: Science Press.

Thorp, Robert 1991 Erlitou and the Search for the Xia. Early China 16:1–38.

Trigger, Bruce 1999 Shang Political Organization: A Comparative Approach. Journal of East Asian Archaeology 1(1–4):43–62.

Underhill, Anne P. 1994 Variation in Settlements During the Longshan Period of Northern China. Asian Perspectives 33(2):197–228.

—— 2000 An Analysis of Mortuary Ritual at the Dawenkou Site, Shandong, China. Journal of East Asian Archaeology 2(1–2):93–128.

—— 2002 Craft Production and Social Change in Northern China. New York: Kluwer Academic/Plenum Publishers.

Underhill, Anne P., with Gary Feinman, Linda Nicholas, Gwen Bennet, Feng Cai, Haiguang Yu, Fengshi Luan, and Hui Fang 1998 Systematic Regional Survey in SE Shandong Province, China. Journal of Field Archaeology 25:453–74.

Underhill, Anne P., with Gary Feinman, Linda Nicholas, Gwen Bennett, Hui Fang, Fengshi Luan, Haiguang Yu, and Fengshu Cai 2002 Regional Survey and the Development of Complex Societies in Southeastern Shandong, China. Antiquity 76:745–55.

Wallerstein, Immanuel 1974 The Modern World-System: Capitalist Agriculture and the Origins of the European World Economy in the Sixteenth Century. New York: Academic Press.

Wang, Jin, and Xianyi Chen 1987 Shilun Shangdai Panlongcheng zaoqi chengshi de xingtai yu tezheng (On the form and characteristics of the early city at Panlongcheng). In Hubeisheng Kaoguxuehui Lunwen Xuanji. Hubei Archaeology Association, ed. Pp. 70–7. Volume 1. Wuhan: Wuhan Daxue Press.

Wang, Lixin 1998 Zao Shang Wenhua Yanjiu. (A study of the early Shang culture.) Beijing: Gaodeng Jiaoyu Press.

Wang, Qing 1993 Shilun shiqian Huanghe xiayou de gaidao yu guwenhua de fazhan (On the changes of the lower Yellow River's course and the development of ancient cultures in prehistory). Zhongyuan Wenwu 4:63–72.

—— 1996 Jujin 4000 nian qianhou de huanjing bianqian yu shehui fazhan (Environmental change and social development in 4000 B.P.). In Dongfang Wenming Zhiguang – Liangzhu Wenhua Faxian 60 Zhounian Jinian Wenji. Huping Xu, ed. Pp. 291–9. Hainan: Hainan Guoji Xinwen Press.

—— 1999 Da Yu zhishui de dili beijing (The geographic background for the regulation of floods by Yu the Great). Zhongyuan Wenwu 1:34–42.

Wang, Tao 1997 The Chinese Archaeological School: Su Bingqi and Contemporary Chinese Archaeology. Antiquity 71:31–9.

Xia Shang Zhou Chronology Project Team, ed. 2000 Xia Shang Zhou Duandai Gongcheng 1996–2000 Nian Jieduan Chengguo Baogao. (Report of the achievements in the 1996–2000 phase of the Xia Shang Zhou chronology project.) Beijing: Shijie Tushu Press.

Xie, Weiyang 1996 Zhongguo Zaoqi Guojia. Hangzhou: Zhejiang Renmin Press.

Yan, Wenming 1982 Jiangou de tougai bei he botoupi fengsu (Skull cap cups from Jiangou and the custom of scalping). Kaogu yu Wenwu 2:38–41.

—— 1987 Zhongguo shiqian wenhua de tongyixing yu duoyangxing (The unity and variability of prehistoric Chinese culture). Wenwu 3:38–50.

Yang, Yachang 2000 Shaanxi Xia shiqi kaogu de xin jinzhan (New progress of the Xia archaeology in Shaanxi). Gudai Wenming Yanjiu Tongxun 5:34–6.

Yates, Robin 1997 The City-State in Ancient China. In The Archaeology of City-states: Cross-Cultural Approaches. Deborah Nichols and Thomas Charlton, eds. Pp. 71–90. Washington DC: Smithsonian Institution Press.

Yin, Da, 1955 Zhongguo Xinshiqi Shidai. (The Neolithic period in China.) Shanghai: Sanlian Press.

Yuan, Guangkuo 1996 Henan Erlitou wenhua muzang de jige wenti (Some issues relating to burials in the Erlitou culture of Henan). Kaogu 12:62–9.

Yun, Xizheng, and Yongkang Mou 1992 Zhongguo shiqian yishu de guibao (Treasures of prehistoric art in China). In Zhongguo Yuqi Quanji. Volume 1. Yongkang Mou and Xizheng Yun, eds. Pp. 23–36. Shijiazhuang: Hebei Meishu Press.

Zhang, Xuehai 2003 Xin Zhongyuan zhongxinlun (The new central plains-centric view-point). Zhongyuan Wenwu 3:7–12.

Zhao, Chunqing 2001 Zhengluo Diqu Xinshiqi Shidai Juluo de Yanbian. Beijing: Beijing University Press.

Zhao, Hui 1999 Liangzhu wenhua de ruogan teshuxing (Some characteristics of the Liangzhu culture). *In* Liangzhu Wenhua Yanjiu. Zhejiang Institute of Archaeology, ed. Pp. 104–19. Beijing: Kexue Press.

Zhao, Qingchun 2002 Xinzhai qi de queren jiqi yiyi (Significance of the confirmation of the Xinzhai phase). Zhongyuan Wenwu 1:21–3.

Zhao, Xitao, ed. 1996 Zhongguo Haimian Bianhua. (Sea level changes in China.) Jinan: Shandong Kexue Jishu Press.

Zhao, Zhiquan 1987 Lun Erlitou yizhi wei Xiadai wanqi duyi (On the Erlitou site as a capital of the late Xia dynasty). Huaxia Kaogu 2:196–204, 217.

Zheng, Guang 1998 Erlitou yizhi yu woguo zaoqi qingtong wenming (The Erlitou site and China's early bronze civilization). *In* Zhongguo Kaoguxue Luncong. Institute of Archaeology, and CASS, ed. Pp. 190–5. Beijing: Kexue Press.

Zhengzhou University 2000 Yudong Qixian Fajue Baogao. (Report of excavations at Qixian in East Henan.) Beijing: Kexue Press.

Zou, Heng 1980 Xia Shang Zhou Kaogu Lunwenji. (Essays on Shang and Zhou archaeology.) Beijing: Wenwu Press.

9

Marks and Labels: Early Writing in Neolithic and Shang China

David N. Keightley

The question must be not only What does the inscription say? but What function did it serve to say it? What did the record keeper think he was doing? (Keightley 1978:154)

The Neolithic Background

The inhabitants of early China, in all likelihood, did not import their logographic writing system from abroad; it would be hard to demonstrate any genetic connection between the signs scratched or painted on Neolithic pots, found usually in burials of higher status (Yang Xiaoneng 2000 provides a pictorial catalog of the evidence) or the oracle-bone graph forms of the Late Shang on the one hand, and Sumerian, Egyptian, or Hittite written forms on the other. Nor is it likely that writing had emerged in China as early as it had done in Mesopotamia (Boltz 1999:108; Keightley 1989:187–99; Xueqin Li et al. 2003:31; Qiu Xigui 2000:29). But the Chinese writing system, once it had developed, was to reign supreme in China right down to the present and was to play a similarly paramount role in the neighboring states of Vietnam, Korea, and Japan.

Turning to the origins of the script, it is possible to identify two major impulses in Neolithic sign making, the naturalistic or realistic (Figure 9.1A) and the diagrammatic or schematic (Figure 9.1B) (cf. Qiu Xigui 2000:30; Yang Xiaoneng 2000:101, 204), and it is, I believe, from the latter tradition, which I associate in particular with the Liangzhu 良渚 (Jiangsu) and Dawenkou 大汶口 (Shandong and northern Jiangsu) cultures of eastern China, that, during the fourth to third millennia B.C., the earliest "characters" started to emerge (Keightley 1989:195–8). How such signs actually functioned is hard to tell. Many were placed on pots, often before firing, that were used as food vessels, and it has generally been supposed that they represented social markers that, when placed in burials, also served some ritual

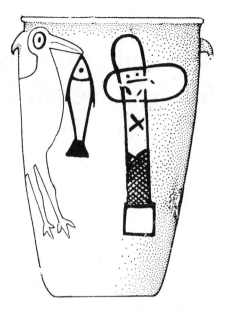

Figure 9.1A Naturalistic heron, fish, and axe design painted on a *gang* urn from Yancun, Henan (ca. 3500–3000 B.C.) (*Zhongyuan wenwu* 中原文物 1981.1:4, Fig. 1.1.)

function (Yang Xiaoneng 2000:71, 80). For the naturalistic tradition, for example, it has been proposed that "the image of the white heron" painted on the urn from Yancun 閻村 in Henan (ca. 3500–3000 B.C.) (Figure 9.1A), "signified a place name or the name of a clan associated with it. The axe likely served as an honorific attribute, indicating rank or status" (Fitzgerald-Huber 1999:64, 66). (Others, however, have proposed that what they see as the *yue* 鉞 axe form was equivalent to *sui* 歲, the word for "year" (Lu Sixian and Li Di 2000:132, 169).) And for the diagrammatic tradition, Wu Hung (1985:34–6; 1995:40–4; see also Keightley 1996:76–87) has proposed that, for example, the sun and bird pictographs found on a small number of Liangzhu jades (ca. 3000 B.C.) should be treated as "emblems" of the *yang niao* 陽鳥 "Sun Bird," the name of a people thought, on the basis of later texts, to have been living in this eastern area between the Yellow River and the Yangzi.

But these pictographs were not necessarily writing, not necessarily characters. As William Boltz has noted, "there is no evidence that these or any other graphs at this time stood for words of any kind, *yang niao* or other" (Boltz 1994:46). That is to say, they have meaning, but it cannot be said with certainty that they are "characterized by a conventionally associated pronunciation" (Boltz 1994:48; 45, Figure 12). Since, moreover, it is not yet certain what language was being spoken in this part of Neolithic China – it has been proposed, for example, that one group would not have spoken "a form of Chinese" but "very likely an Austroasiatic language related to Vietnamese" (Pulleyblank 1996:2–6; cf. Boltz 1999:81–3) – or what it

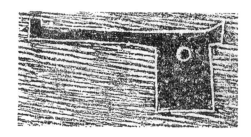

Figure 9.1B Schematic sun, fire, mountain(?), axe, and adze designs incised on pots from the Dawenkou culture (*Dawenkou: Xinshiqi shidai muzang fajue baogao* 大汶口：新石器時代墓葬發掘報告. Beijing: Wenwu chubanshe 1974: p. 118, Fig. 94.1–4.)

would have sounded like, even if it were Proto-Chinese (Boltz 1999:100–3; Takashima 2000:xxii, n. 6) – the difficulty involved in assigning phonetic values to these pictographs is considerable. Nevertheless, one may note that the Liangzhu and Dawenkou peoples, in different parts of China, were already sharing some signs (Cheung Kwong-yue 1983:372–3, Table 12.4; Yang Xiaoneng 1999:102; 2000:73, 197; Xueqin Li et al. 2003:40), an indication of their widespread use. And it may also be noted that a significant number of the Neolithic signs represented ritual implements, such as axes, adzes (Figure 9.1B), and scepters, and that such images may have been ancestral to the pictographic emblems, often taken to be clan-name insignia, distinct from the regular Shang script, inscribed on early Shang bronze vessels (Figure 9.2B). To the extent that one can separate the two functions, such emblems seem to have served as both ornaments and symbols (Boltz 1994:48–50,

Figures 14, 15; Fitzgerald-Huber 1999:66; Yang Xiaoneng 2000:71, 81, 84–102, 112, 117, 144).

Whether, given the inability to attach specific names and phonetic values to such Neolithic marks or signs, one is willing to identify them as proto-writing, on the grounds that they still communicated information if not words, is a matter of theoretical taste (Harris 2000:64–90; Salomon 2001; Sampson 1985:26–30). And, as Sampson (1985:29, 49, 50), commenting on the "ambiguous middle ground between clear semasiography" – involving "systems of visible communication . . . which indicate ideas directly" – and "clear glottography" – systems "which provide visible representation of spoken-language utterances" – has noted,

> given that pre-writing seems to have developed into writing by a slow process of gradual evolution, it may be a rather artificial exercise to decide that the transition to writing has definitely occurred by any particular stage. This point is reinforced by the fact that, when inscriptions are limited to abbreviated jottings rather than full sentences, the distinction between semasiography and logographic writing tends to dissolve.

That some Neolithic signs (Figure 9.2A), however, involving the depiction of a human-and-animal figure, carved into high-status jade axes and *cong* 琮 tubes from elite Liangzhu burials in the Yangzi delta area, seem to have been written both "in clear" (naturalistic; Figure 9.2A, left) and "in code" (schematic: Figure 9.2A, right) suggests that even at this stage the readability of certain signs on ritual objects was to be limited to the initiated, those who could read the "code." The enduring impulse to replace pictures (more naturalistic) with graphs (more schematic, more stylized) was already present (Keightley 1996:76–85; Qiu Xigui 2000:45–8, 64), and this preference for the graph over the picture, for the coded sign over the naturalistic picture, may also have been encouraged by the consideration that the more naturalistic form, although more easily "read" by the uninitiated, would have been more difficult to cut into jade than the more schematic motif, with its simpler lines and circles. If so, it may be that "the schematic version would have been more attractive to artisans, being easier to produce, and more attractive to elites, because it embodied a more esoteric code" (Keightley 1996:81). One needs to consider the role of the craftsmen, the "writers," in addition to the role of the consumers, the "readers," even at this early stage.

The Bronze Age: Shang and Western Zhou

Several signs have been found at the so-called "Early Shang" site of Erlitou 二里頭 (ca. 16th century B.C.) in north Central Henan, generally incised on various pots (Yang Xiaoneng 2000:84–7), but there is, once again, no way to "read" their meaning. A few more symbols and graphs have been found on "Middle Shang" artifacts, from sites like Erligang 二里崗 (16th and 15th centuries B.C.); some of them may have been precursors of oracle-bone graph forms – inscriptions have been found on three bone fragments – but different systems of signs appear to have been involved at different sites (Kwang-chih Chang 1980:268–9, 305–6). And few if any

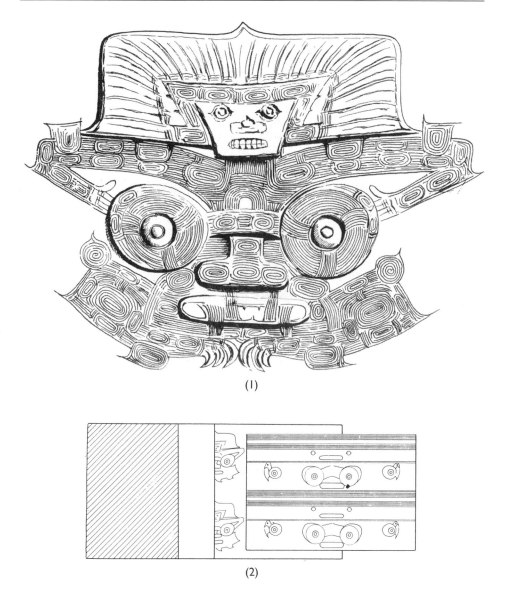

(1)

(2)

Figure 9.2A (1) The more naturalistic, "In Clear" version of the human-and-animal figure incised on a Liangzhu culture jade *cong* (M12:98 from Fanshan); figure is ca. 3 cm high (*Wenwu* 文物 1988.1:12, Fig. 20.). (2) The "In Clear" version in the central track (left), the "Coded," schematic version (opened up, on right) (*Wenwu* 1988.1:12, Fig. 19.)

Figure 9.2B Shang lineage insigne or emblem involving two human silhouettes, back to back, and a dagger-axe, on a bronze *gui* 簋 tureen (early Anyang 安陽 (*Henan Chutu Shang Zhou Qingtonqi*) 河南出土商周青銅器 (1). Beijing: Wenwu chubanshe 1981: p. 219, Fig. 274.)

Erligang ritual bronzes – the new symbols of prestige – were being cast with inscriptions (Bagley 1999:182, n. 92). As Qiu Xigui (2000:42) has concluded, "all the written material from the early Shang discovered thus far is both scant and fragmentary . . . and is of minor value to our study of the formative process of Chinese writing."

Chinese writing, as we see it in its fully developed form in the oracle-bone and bronze inscriptions of the Late Shang, was logographic: it used graphs to record words (Boltz 1994:52–9; DeFrancis 2002; Sampson 1985:148–9; Unger 2004). It was not ideographic, using graphs to record ideas or things without the mediation of language, although a number of Western scholars and commentators have argued that it was (e.g., Hansen 1993; Vandermeersch 1980:473–88). By the time of the oracle-bone inscriptions, moreover, the Shang were not generally writing pictographs; the graphs "show the effects of graphic conventionalization and are not readily recognizable as realistic depictions of anything specific" (Boltz 1994:56; see also Boltz 2000–2001:4–6). The oracle-bone inscriptions thus represent the first large corpus of texts written in a well-developed system whose principles, combining phonetic and semantic elements, we can identify as those of the later script (Boltz 1994:68–9; 1999:110). And it is generally assumed that the writing system came into existence in the previous centuries, probably around the middle of the second millennium B.C. or a little earlier (Boltz 1994:39; Qiu Xigui 2000:44).

The rubbings and drawings of some 41,956 oracle bones (many bearing numerous individual inscriptions) have been reproduced in the *Heji*-合集 corpus; several thousand more have been published in other collections. The oracle-bone inscriptions – modern scholars use the term to refer to inscriptions on both bone (mainly cattle scapulas) and shell (turtle plastrons and carapaces) – employed a vocabulary of some 4,500 to 5,000 individual graphs, about half of which can be deciphered with certainty (Boltz 1999:88–9; Qiu Xigui 2000:49–50). The inscriptions provide much information about the Late Shang world as the kings saw it or, more precisely, as they divined it. The twenty-first Shang king, Wu Ding 武丁 (ca. 1200–1189 B.C.), in particular, divined a wide range of royal topics: sacrifices, military campaigns, hunting expeditions, other excursions, the good fortune of the coming ten-day Shang week, the good fortune of the coming night or day, the weather, agriculture, sickness, childbirth, distress or trouble, dreams, settlement building, the issuing of orders, tribute payments, divine assistance or approval, and requests addressed to ancestral or natural Powers (Keightley 1978:33–5; Keightley [2000] provides translations of 157 oracle-bone inscriptions in context).

It is striking, however, that, with the exception of the generally terse bronze inscriptions, few other Shang documents exist, and that even a majority of the pre-Eastern Zhou 東周 texts (770–256 B.C.) that have come down to us exist only in later redactions. Writing in early China – at least as it has been preserved in the archaeological record – thus appears at first glance to have played a rather different role than it did in early Mesopotamia. We have few if any Bronze-Age Chinese equivalents to, for example, the "inventories of all types and sizes, promissory notes and receipts, deeds of sale, marriage contracts, wills, and court decisions" from Lagash and Nippur (dating from the last half of the third millennium B.C. to the last centuries of the first) (Kramer 1963:23–4; see also pp. 109, 229). Why this should be so is well worth exploring.

Does this comparative scarcity of primary sources mean, as many have supposed, that writing in early China was primarily used in religious or divinatory contexts (e.g., Vandermeersch 1980:289–90, 473–88)? Or does it mean that the "archival fallacy" must be avoided and that the resolutely non-secular nature of the sources that have been preserved on shell and bone reflects primarily, if not only, the perishability of the materials, such as bamboo, wood, and silk, on which other kinds of texts might have been written?

There are reasons to think, for example, that the oracle-bone inscriptions represent a secondary, rather than a primary, record of the rituals performed by the dynasty's diviners and kings. The diviners must, in a significant number of cases, have kept an initial record – presumably written with a brush, on perishable materials such as bamboo strips – of the divinations. The engravers (who were not the diviners) then digested the primary information that had been recorded in these "diviners' notebooks" and carved the final record into the bones and shells, days, if not months, after the pyromantic events they recorded (Keightley 2001). Such primary documents might not have been used in every case, but some inscriptions do indeed suggest that they were copies of texts that have now been lost to us (Venture 2002:303–7).

It is known, furthermore, from traces of writing left on the oracle bones and on pots, that the writing brush already existed and was used for writing characters (Liu

Yiman 1991:546–54, 572; Qiu Xigui 2000:60, 63; Venture 2002:52–3). And the oracle-bone inscriptions alone show that the Shang kept numerical records of military conscriptions, casualties suffered by the Qiang or other enemies, animals offered in sacrifice, animals caught in the hunt, tribute offerings of turtle shells, numbers of days, strings of cowries, measures of wine, and other miscellaneous data (Chen Mengjia 1956:111–13; Keightley 1999c:287). It is probable, therefore, that these records kept by the diviners would have been matched by, and based upon, comparable accounts in the non-oracular sphere where some system of record-keeping would have been needed to coordinate the complex dynastic economy. Given the theocratic nature of the Shang state, the distinction between secular and religious writings is not easy to draw, but it seems likely that a considerable amount of Shang writing would not have been focused primarily on ritual and cult. A small number of non-oracular Shang writings have indeed survived on bone, stone, ceramic, human and animal skull, and jade. These records evidently served as tribute notations, exercises in engraving, labels for ancestral tablets, sacrifice records, genealogies, and potter's or other marks (Venture 2002:136–69). That the marks found on Late Shang pots rarely exceeded one or two in number (Zheng Zhenxiang 1994:248–55) accords with the view that their function was to label the pot in some way; lengthy texts would not have been required.

> In later periods, texts such as ritual manuals, calendars, official regulations or lists of funerary goods are mostly written on wooden or bamboo slips. So it is reasonable to suspect that the Shang people may also have had some sort of documents written on wooden slips, and that they may not have survived, due to the perishable nature of the materials used for such writing. Indeed, actual bamboo or wood strips are attested as early as the fifth century B.C. and support the conclusion that these were probably the materials used for writing everyday documents in earlier times as well. (Postgate et al. 1995:475)

If such perishable materials have not survived (see also Bagley 1999:182; Boltz 1999:108; Postgate et al. 1995:459, 463, 464), then it would seem, on the basis of the records' durability, that the Shang valued ritual, or ritualized, records more than they did secular records. And we can, perhaps, be more specific about the nature of the valuation. It would only have been when the society had become sufficiently differentiated for the ruler to employ specialist engravers who were working with expensive, durable artifacts that long inscriptions on non-perishable materials are found; putting these inscriptions into jade, bronze, or bone, for example, would have required considerable effort on somebody's part.

But more was involved than just value. Early inscriptions in China – whether on bone, bronze, or ceramic – are characterized by the close link between the inscribed object itself and the text, so that the text itself refers to the object (Venture 2002:162, 245–6, 255). Thus, an oracle-bone inscription may be regarded as a "label" informing us that "This is the bone that such-and-such a diviner cracked on such-and-such a day about such-and-such a topic." A bronze inscription is a "label" informing us that "This is the ritual vessel that So-and-so made for (and uses in rituals offered to) his Ancestor Such-and-such" (on this inscription type see von Falkenhausen 1993:153). A pictographic clan insignia cast into a ritual bronze vessel (Figure 9.2B) or other artifact such as a weapon or musical instrument (Yang Xiaoneng 2000:91) would have served a similar function. And even the marks found on Neolithic pots (Figure 9.1A and B), whatever their precise meaning, presumably indicated: "This is the pot belonging to, made by, to be used for, So-and-so or Such-and-such." These inscriptions were all self-referential; they were not independent texts that had an existence of their own. And once again, it seems unlikely that a culture able to label objects in this way with considerable frequency, would have limited itself to writing labels and nothing else. It is hard to believe, in short, that a label-writing culture would not at the same time have produced non-label writings, documents on bamboo or wood, for example, which could have referred to events that had occurred independently of the act and object of inscription. In this view, for example, the numerous divinations about when and where the dependent laborers, mobilized in their thousands, should be conscripted and employed (Keightley 1999c:284–5) would have represented only a fraction of the written orders required to muster and supply the armies and labor gangs. Cultures, such as the Inca, have certainly constructed major works without writing to assist them. But the Shang already had a developed writing system; it is hard to believe that they would not have used it in many non-oracular aspects of their daily lives.

The Oracle-Bone Inscriptions: Who Read Them?

Scapulimancy (divination that uses animal shoulder bones) and plastromancy (divination that uses turtle shells) had undoubtedly been associated with the rise of ritual experts and the increasing specialization and stratification of Late Neolithic society. Such forms of pyromancy would have been one of the techniques by which chieftains and their supporters laid claim to the special knowledge that validated their status. Scapulimancy, which evidently appeared in north China some two millennia earlier than did plastromancy (Li Ling 2000:294, 302–4), may have developed when leaders, making burnt meat offerings of sheep, pig, or cattle to the spirits, claimed that the cracking of the bones in the fire represented the voices or responses of those spirits and, in particular, their acceptance or rejection of the sacrifice (Itô 1962:255, 256; Vandermeersch 1994:249). If offerings were made to the dead – and the richness of the mortuary cult in Neolithic China suggests that early forms of ancestor worship were emerging – then one can see that the practice of divination, even at this early date, could have been associated with sacrifices and an emerging ancestral cult.

The oracle-bone inscriptions of the Late Shang were heirs to this tradition, but they raise a number of questions. Why, for example, did the Shang kings have the divination record incised into the bones? Who incised it? Who was the audience? Were the Shang kings (and their ancestors) literate? And why were these records stored?

There is no doubt that, in some cases, the inscriptional record served to legitimate the king's status as an accurate forecaster; the engravers did not generally record his erroneous forecasts (Keightley 1988:372–3; 1999a:208–10). But why did the Shang engravers bother to carve their inscriptions into the bone? Why did the original notes, the primary documents (see above), not suffice? Why could the king's prognosticatory triumphs not have been written on the bone with a brush, as a few divination records indeed were (Keightley 2001:23–5)? Many aspects of Shang practice will probably never be recoverable, and I suspect that, had they been pressed, different diviners might have provided their own varying rationales for what they did, particularly when it is considered that more than 30 of the 120 diviners whose names are recorded in the divinatory prefaces came from regions that lay beyond the Shang cult center at Xiaotun 小屯 (on the northwest outskirts of Anyang 安陽 in northern Henan) and may well have been influenced by local divinatory traditions (Takashima and Yue 2000:21–3). Nevertheless, the following nine features are worth consideration.

First, it should be noted that the carving of the record was labor intensive. It would have required a special staff of engravers. The "value added" nature of the inscribed bones presumably conferred prestige on their sponsor, the king, quite apart from whether anybody read the inscriptions or not. Uninscribed divination bones – and many have been found (Djamouri 1999:14, 16; Keightley 1978:166; Qiu Xigui 2000:62, n. 3) – might have been cracked by anybody, but only the elites could sponsor the production of divination inscriptions (which is not to say, of course, that they could read them). It is worth recalling that many fine Shang and Western Zhou ritual bronzes carry no inscriptions whatever (von Falkenhausen 1993:167; Venture 2002:277); like the uninscribed divination bones, these bronzes had presumably served an important ritual function, but a function that would have been less evident, less dedicated, than if their makers had labeled them with an inscription. And one may even speculate that many of the Shang bones may have remained uninscribed because the "diviners' notebooks" or the bones to which they referred were never passed on to the engravers; these cases may represent "bureaucratic slippage," perhaps because as an overworked staff might have complained, "Too many bones, too few engravers!"

Second, on occasion, the engravers for some diviner groups also carved out and deepened the *bu* ⼘-shaped pyromantic cracks in the bones themselves (Keightley 1978:53; Venture 2002:48). (The word written with the Shang graph *bu* which appears with great frequency in the divinatory prefaces – 14 *bu* graphs are present in Figure 9.3 – still has the meaning of "to divine.") One may assume, accordingly, that in Shang divinatory theology a homology would have been thought to exist between the cracking and carving of the bone and the carving of the graphs (Lewis 1999:14). That the engravers had cut into the bone both the cracks and the message to which the cracks had responded would have assured that the divinatory results achieved through the making of those cracks would also not lose their visibility, their efficacy (Keightley 1978:22, n. 93). If, as Venture (2002:267) has argued, the principal function of inscriptions on Shang and Western Zhou artifacts was to give a ritual act the possibility of durable existence, in the hope that the makers of the

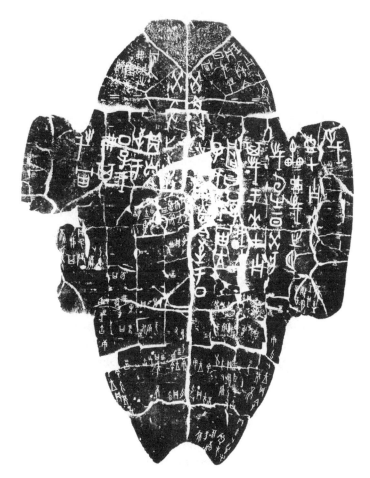

Figure 9.3 Rubbing of a turtle plastron inscribed with Late Shang divination inscriptions that may have spanned a period of fifteen days; their calligraphy varied in size and they were inscribed at different times. Satisfying the requirements of a "display inscription," King Wu Ding forecast in one inscription that the Shang would harm the enemy on the day *jiazi* 甲子 ; the verification confirms that they did indeed do so (bold inscription, center-right). (*Heji* 6834f; plastron is 30 cm long.)

inscription would long benefit from its anticipated blessings, this would again suggest that the creation of the inscription was intended to obtain these benefits; it was not required that a human audience read it.

For the oracle-bone "record," I believe, was meant to mark or label as much as it was meant to document. Nylan (2000:246, n. 90), citing Rosalind Thomas (1992, chapter 3, esp. p. 94) has noted "the crucial distinction between making records [i.e., the oracle-bone inscriptions] and making documents, where [unlike records] there is the expectation that documents will be consulted later." The graphs were a permanent record, a permanent register, placed into the bone like the cracks, that amplified and confirmed what the bone, the cracks, and the ancestors working through those cracks, had already done or were about to do. The graphs were, as suggested earlier, labels, and they were labels that formed part of the particular medium that they labeled. As Harris (2000:87) has reminded us about the reading of books,

> It seems rather obvious that people do not write on paper as they write on soft clay or on wax. But it would be a mistake to conclude that the material is no more than an adventitious or "external" factor . . . in the birth of a writing system. In other words, it is implausible to suppose that the written sign exists from the beginning at a level of abstraction that is independent of its biomechanical realization.

Whoever may have read the oracle-bone inscriptions, they had to, needed to, wanted to, read them in the bone.

Anything written on a bamboo slip, by contrast, would have been merely a written document of no particular efficacy. So far as divinatory texts were concerned, in fact, I would not argue that the Shang court was text-centered; it was "bone-sign"- or "bone-mark"-centered, with the signs or marks sometimes represented by the *bu* ├-shaped cracks, sometimes by the graphs. The link between bone, crack, and graph is also demonstrated by the way in which the right–left orientation of the graph forms might be linked to an inscriptions' placement on the bone, particularly on the plastrons from the reign of Wu Ding 武丁 (?–ca. 1189 B.C.), where the engravers, as in Figure 9.3, often balanced the positive and negative divination "charges" (the term modern scholars use to refer to the divinatory propositions that the diviners submitted to the bone or shell), as they had also balanced the cracks, symmetrically (see below). This provides additional support for the view that the cracks and the graphs were homologous.

Third, there is some tantalizing evidence that a magico-religious impulse may have been involved in the act of inscribing (as opposed to mere "writing"). A small number of scapulas – which were probably not divined by the usual court diviners – were excavated near Xiaotun in 1971. The eight charges on the front of one bone involved offerings, mainly of various kinds of pigs, and exorcisms to various ancestors and ancestresses. Strikingly, the engravers had erased the heads of virtually all (it is hard to be certain in two cases) the various "pig" graphs on the bone, together with the head of the one "dog" graph (also offered in sacrifice), a practice that must have had some significance, possibly magical (Keightley 1999b:184). Perhaps the "erasure" of the head confirmed that the sacrifice had indeed been offered; perhaps it indicated that the animal's head had been removed and offered separately. If the consistent "de-engraving" of the graphs in this way had some symbolic meaning for the Shang, one may suppose that the regular engraving of the graphs would also have done so. And, once again, one notes a lack of interest in making the graphs readable. The erasing of the heads would, in fact, have made the graphs harder to read.

Fourth, some of the inscribing appears to have been performed on a mass-production basis. "In these cases, the engraver first cut all the vertical and sloping strokes for every graph on the bone and then rotated the bone to carve all the horizontal strokes" (Keightley 1978:49). This too suggests that, at least in some cases (see too Yan Yiping 1978:943), the act of "writing *onto*" bone was less important than the act of writing "*into*" bone. The incising of the graphs mattered more than the writing of them. Such mass-produced inscriptions, in fact, can hardly be said to have been "written" at all, but they evidently served a purpose. It is likely, to be sure, that the great majority of the inscriptions were not mass produced in this way (Venture 2002:51 and the scholarship cited there), but the fact that some were does suggest, at the least, that not all inscriptions were created equal, and that different engravers took different approaches to their work.

Occasional evidence of inscriptional insouciance, in fact, can be found in all periods, and by Period V (see Table 9.1) some of the incised records were increasingly perfunctory. (For the five oracle-one periods employed by modern scholars, see Table 9.1 and Keightley 1978:92–4; Shaughnessy 1982–83). That the incising mattered more than the writing is also once again indicated by the fact that strokes were sometimes missing, or graphs were written upside down (see, e.g., Keightley 1978:49, n. 111; Yan Yiping 1978:943–7). This again suggests that the presence of the incised graph may have been more important than its accuracy. Of particular interest are two Period III inscriptions (*Heji* 27382), in which the engraver had twice written the oracle-bone character 天 (for *wang*) 王, ("king") upside down; he had also written the *xin* character upside down in the prefatory day-date, *xinyou* 辛酉. It is hard to assess the significance of these inversions. That the king had twice been inverted on the same bone suggests either that the inversion was intentional or that the engraver was badly trained (the calligraphy is certainly crude). That the oracle-bone *xin* form 辛, was similar in shape to an inverted *wang* form 天, and that the engraver inverted them both, lends support to the view that he might have been having trouble distinguishing certain graph shapes. I doubt, accordingly, that the inverting of the "king" graphic indicates a malcontented engraver, hoping to dishonor the king in this way. The inversion, in any event, whether its origins lay in ignorance or animus, suggests once again that, for the elites who commissioned such work, the value of the inscriptions may have lain primarily in their existence; the engraver might have been confident that his audience would not notice – or, if they were not literate, would not even have known – that the king had been stood on his head. As Venture (2002:270–1) has noted, when Western Zhou elites commissioned artisans to make copies of bronze inscriptions, some of these copies contained numerous wrong characters; he calls the artisans "illiterate" and he likewise concludes that in these cases the integrity of the text mattered little to the elites.

Given the scale of the inscriptional enterprise, such cases in which the incising of inscriptions was perfunctory to one degree or another are hardly surprising. Generally speaking, however, the inscriptions contain remarkably few "typographic" errors of this sort. The engravers appear on the whole to have performed their task conscientiously; presumably, they and their colleagues scrutinized their product and took professional pride in what they produced. At the same time, however, the practice of incising the most routine of divinatory topics into the bone for a period of a century and a half would not only have led to its routinization – as in the "assembly-line" production referred to above – but might well have led to questions

Table 9.1. Oracle-bone periods (Sources: Keightley 1978:203; Loewe and Shaughnessy 1999:25)

Period	Approximate B.C. date	Shang kings
I	1200–1189	Wu Ding
II	1189–1158	Zu Geng, Zu Jia
III	1157–1132	Lin Xin, Kang Ding
IV	1131–1106	Wu Yi, Wen Wu Ding
V	1105–1045	Di Yi, Di Xin

about its necessity. The shrinkage in the scope of divinatory concerns notable in the Period V inscriptions (Keightley 1988:379, 382) could certainly be explained in this way. And it may well be that by the end of the dynasty, the practice of cutting the graphs into the bones was increasingly continued out of traditional inertia rather than deep religious conviction or the need to satisfy a readership.

Fifth, on a good number of the bones – though not all (see, e.g., the discussion of "display inscriptions" below) – the "page design" (as in Figure 9.3) would have given readers no guidance where to begin or what to read next. To be sure, there were certain conventions that would have guided the initiate's eye (Keightley 1978:52; Venture 2001; Yan Yiping 1978:960–1085). But these conventions were often ignored, so that once again, one is left with the impression that many of the oracle-bone inscriptions on plastrons were not designed for easy or consistent reading. The potential Shang reader – and especially the casual uninformed reader, if such existed – would have been confronted with a jumble of notations that would have required, as it has required of modern scholars, considerable effort to negotiate. The inscriptions appear to have been inscribed to leave a record rather than a document; they had not been inscribed for routine reading.

Sixth, I would suggest that the inscribed characters represented, so to speak, the engravers' "rice bowl." That the number of characters would not have been overly large – I estimate, crudely, that the engravers would have carved some 45 to 90 characters per day – may have made it all the more to the engravers' advantage to persuade the king that "The Spirits need these inscriptions. This is hard, creative work, in Your Majesty's service." Part of the impulse to carve the characters may thus have come from the self-interest of the engravers themselves. This possibility again bears on the extent to which the inscriptions actually were read, on why they were needed to be read, after the engravers had done their work.

Seventh, these considerations also bear on the oracle-bone sets, which in Period I consisted of five "carbon copies" of the same inscriptions, with cracks numbered "1" to "5," often on five separate plastrons. It is worth considering why anybody would want to write – let alone read – the same pedestrian charge, 隹父甲"(His Majesty's sick tooth) is due to Father Jia," five different times on the back of the five different plastrons in the same set (as discussed in Keightley 1978:76–90). Any viewers with the plastron in hand could read the inscription once; he or she did not have to read it five times over – unless, of course, the repetitive incising and reading had been part of the ritual. One has the sense in these cases that, from the point of view of both the engravers and the king, it was a matter of "the more ritual writings the better," and that the inscriptions, once again, were not there to be read but to be present. Although the use of such sets declined after Period II (Peng Yushang 1995; Venture 2002:57-9), their prevalence in Period I again strongly supports the view that the Wu Ding inscriptions did not primarily function as documents to be read.

An eighth consideration, already alluded to, suggests the same conclusion. Much of the inscriptional record seems so banal or routine – "In the next ten days there will be no disasters," "The king hunts at X, going and coming back there will be no disasters," et cetera – that the interest of the "reading public" would hardly have been intense or sustained. There would seem to have been little need for most of the court to actually read each routine inscription day after day, week after week. Seeing it on the bone, or, more precisely, knowing it was in the bone, might have been enough. Many of the inscriptions can probably be compared to the "legal notices" that appear in our own newspapers; they are there for the record, there to protect their writers, but only occasionally consulted or invoked by a few interested parties on a "need to know" basis. Once again, I would suggest that the importance of the inscriptions was that they were there, that they existed, not that they were read.

Ninth, the placement of many Shang bronze inscriptions, inside and not infrequently at the dark bottom of tall ritual vessels, would have rendered them virtually invisible and hence unreadable (Venture 2002:282). The placing of the inscriptions *inside* the vessels may have been to provide symbolic contact between the inscription and the sacrificial offering placed in the vessel (Kane 1982–83:14). These considerations, however, again suggest that many Shang bronze inscriptions were not primarily designed to be read, or not, at least, by everybody: it is probable that "the intended recipients of the texts were the ancestral spirits in heaven" (von Falkenhausen 1993:147). It is likely, therefore, that the inscriptions on bone, like the inscriptions on bronze, also participated in a system of symbolic communication that functioned as much through its presence as its readability.

Readers and Reading

The above features – involving the prestige attached to the labor invested, the homology of crack and inscription, the presence of inscribing errors and the mass-production of the graphs, the confusion of the page design, the engravers' vested interest in the engraving, the existence of "carbon-copy" sets of inscriptions, the banality of much of the record, and the way in which Shang bronze inscriptions were not placed for readability – all bear to varying degree on the question of audience. Any conclusions are bound to be speculative, because as Connery (1998:27) reminds us, "Reading leaves no residue of its existence." My sense is that the early inscriptions were intended both for (1) the ancestors or other Powers, whose intentions the divinations were intended to ascertain, confirm, certify, and record, and

(2) the king's immediate supporters at court – at least in the case of the "display inscriptions" of Period I (e.g., Figures 9.3 and 9.4), defined by their bold calligraphy, by the prognostication and verification being written as a single, continuous unit, and by the verification confirming the accuracy of the king's prognostication (Keightley 1978:46, n. 90). But even in these cases it is worth reflecting that the incised version would only have been available some time after the divinatory episode it recorded, when the engravers, working from the primary records of the diviners' notebooks (Keightley 2001; see also Djamouri 1999:16), had finished their task of incision. The inscriptions, in other words, would have been "old news" by the time they "went to print." The time lag suggests once again that many of the inscriptions were not designed to be read, at least for new or current information; they were designed to be present, designed to record, in a religiously charged medium and mode, what had transpired. This does not mean, accordingly, that the king's supporters were necessarily literate; some probably were, some probably were not. For it is possible that the value of the characters lay less in the audience's ability to read them, more in the king's ability to have the inscriptions carved into the bone, causing them to appear just as he had caused the cracks to appear in the bone – cracks that were, like the inscriptions, sometimes cut into the bone themselves. Had the supporters been literate, a brush-written account might have sufficed. But the inscriptions were not just characters; they were characters that the king had caused to appear in the bone!

The engravers of Periods I and II had commonly carved boundary lines (two are visible in Figure 9.4) into the bone to separate one inscription from another (Keightley 1978:53–4). That these readers' aids were virtually never used by Period V (Keightley 1978:112; Venture 2002:64–5) appears to have been related to the increasing order and regularity of the late period inscriptions:

> The order which was introduced into the sacrificial schedule in Period IIb . . . was also reflected in the more systematic placement of the inscriptions on bone and shell. Similarly, the scrambled mix of topics generally found on the Period I bones and shells . . . became less common in Period II, when divinations about just one topic, such as the hunt or the sacrificial cycle, might be clustered on a particular bone or shell over a series of days. Such pure clusters had become the norm by Period V. (Keightley 1978:112)

The conventions for inscribing and placing the oracle-bone inscriptions, in short, evolved over time. A different aesthetic had come into play: bold, assertive display had been replaced by good, routine order. Venture, in fact, has suggested that later diviners, noting the difficulty involved in reading some of the earlier pieces, had resorted to more precision in their work. Whether, however, such good order was achieved in the interests of "readability and intelligibility" (Venture 2002:272), or was simply a result of greater bureaucratic routinization, is hard to determine.

It would appear, in any event, that different diviner groups and their engravers may have had different conceptions of their task in mind. The Bin 賓 -group diviners of Period I (on the diviner groups see, e.g., Shaughnessy 1982–83), for example,

Figure 9.4 Cattle scapula inscribed with series of "display inscriptions." On three occasions Wu Ding forecast that somebody would bring alarming news; on three occasions the verification records that that was what had happened (*Heji* 6057f; scapula fragment is 22 cm long.)

tended to record many of their divination charges as positive and negative charge-pairs (Keightley 1978:37–8, 43, 78–80; 1988:367–8, 373–5), as in "We will receive millet harvest," the positive charge on the right side of a plastron, and "We might not receive millet harvest," the negative charge on the left (*Heji* 9950f). The right–left placement of the inscriptions on plastrons evidently mattered a great deal, with the right side of the shell (both front and back) generally being reserved for the charges, prognostications, and outcomes that the Shang desired. Where the Bin-group diviners had used two complementary charges, however, the approximately contemporary Li 歷-group diviners limited themselves to a single, unpaired charge that focused on the desired or intended consequence; they did not employ a matching charge to address the result that was undesired or unintended. The materiality of the record appears to have played a role here, for the Li-group preference for single charges can be related to their preference for scapulas over plastrons – scapulas lack the central median line and right–left symmetry of plastrons – and to features that were suited to the Bin-diviners' balanced placement of positive–negative charge-pairs. The medium in which the Shang were to make their pyromantic cracks and engrave their inscriptions, in other words, appears to have been influenced by the way they formulated the divinatory charges.

The "one-unit" solution of the Li-group diviners – as in "If (we) pray for harvest to the River Power, we will receive harvest" (*Heji* 33271) – was to be the model that survived. Not only were the divination inscriptions more "efficient" in Period V than they had been in Period I, but the accompanying reduction in the size of the calligraphy suggests that the nature of the intended audience had also changed by the end of the dynasty. The minuscule calligraphy of the Period V inscriptions, no longer for "display," would have made them harder to read – and certainly harder for a large audience to have seen. I find, in a crude test, that I can read the large-calligraphy *ganzhi* 干支 day-dates on the rubbing of a Period I inscription (Figure 9.3) from a distance of 8 feet; I have to be 2 feet 6 inches way from the rubbing of a Period V inscription. And even in the case of the Period I plastron the graphs, engraved at different times, might be large or small (Keightley 1978:85, n. 113, 105, n. 48, 211, Table 19). Even under Wu Ding, not all inscriptions had been rendered equally readable. (These conclusions should also be considered in the context of Rawson's conclusion [1999:44] that the "intricate decoration" on Shang ritual bronzes "implies handling and appreciation from close quarters.")

That the inscriptions were not intended to be read by a wide audience is also indicated by the engravers' frequent "failure" to carve any prognostication and, even more strikingly, any verification into the bone. "Tedious and crude calculations … suggest that the Bin-group diviners recorded only one prognostication for every 83 divinations for a prognostication-per-episode rate of 1.2 percent" (Keightley 1999a:223, n. 30.) As with many other aspects of the divination inscriptions, practice varied here too; some diviner groups recorded prognostications and verifications far less frequently than others. I am in agreement, accordingly, with Venture's conclusion (2002:231, 247) that the desire to register the divinatory ritual was basic to the practice of inscribing the divination records and that that is why the divination charge was recorded far more frequently than the verifications were. The main thing, he concludes, was to make the point that the divinatory act had taken place.

It may seem counter-intuitive to argue that the Shang engravers were recording inscriptions that they did not expect many others to read. Yet such a situation was evidently not unknown in other early cultures. At a 1999 symposium on the origins of writing held at the University of Pennsylvania, "scholars noted that the early rulers could not write or read; they relied on scribes for their messages, record keeping and storytelling" (Wilford 1999:2). In the Shang case, I conceive of the inscriptions as a form of conspicuous cultural capital, in which the Shang elites invested considerable labor resources to produce artifacts whose overwhelming value was ritual. And I would suggest that, with the possible exception of the "display inscriptions" discussed above – and even they may have been "displayed" for the spirits not for humans – the only regular, human audience that eventually read the graphs on a regular basis, and then only as they produced them, is likely to have been the engravers themselves, and, presumably, the officers whose job it was to make sure that the records written in the diviners' notebooks were faithfully incised into the bones.

This view of the matter is supported by the consideration that the concept of unread divination records was not entirely foreign to the political mythology of the Zhou. The record of the Duke of Zhou's divination about the health of King Wu 武 was, according to the "Jin teng 金縢" chapter of the Shangshu 尚書, locked away in the metal-bound coffer, and was not apparently known to the young king Cheng 成 until the coffer was unlocked some two years after his accession. The historicity of this tale is of course problematic; but the impulse to limit the reading of divinatory records was not, evidently, thought to be unusual. That no Zhou text refers to writing an oracle-bone inscription, let alone reading one, also suggests that the writing and reading of these inscriptions was highly esoteric, not widely practiced, or both. The word did not get out.

An Archive? For Posterity?

The tendency to refer to the corpus of oracle-bone inscriptions that has come down to modern times as an "archive" (e.g., Djamouri 1999:20; Postgate et al. 1995:471) should, I think, be resisted. The diviners or their assistants certainly appear to have used some form of filing system for storing and retrieving at least certain shells or bones during the relatively brief period when they were being divined. Thus five plastrons from the reign of Wu Ding were used for one set of charges and were then reused, eleven days later, in precisely the same sequence, for a different set of charges (Keightley 1978:39, n. 54). Other examples reveal the cracking of single bones over periods as long as, in one case, nine months (Keightley 2001:6–7). I think it is likely, however, that, on the death of a king, his old oracle-bones – which might have been stored above ground, in a temple, perhaps, during the course of his reign – were consigned to underground pits (see also Venture 2002:232, 272).

The Western Han historian Sima Qian 司馬遷 (d. ca. 85 B.C.) had heard that the Xia 夏 and Shang threw away their divining stalks and shells after use because they felt that stored plastrons were not spiritually efficacious (1959:3223). It would appear that he was correctly informed about the Shang. The Shang attached little spiritual or historical significance to their divination records after they had served their primary function – to label the divination bone while it was still, as it were, "in play." The bones and shells, after whatever temporary exaltation they may have enjoyed as they were sanctified for divination, cracked, prognosticated, and inscribed, eventually became once again mere bones and shells. The oracle bones come to us from the cellars and refuse pits of the Shang, not from the temple archives. (Venture [2002:222] also rejects an archival function for the inscribed bones.) The variety that we find in the pit contents – some inscriptions of one period, some of several; some all shell or bone, some mixed; some all of one-diviner group, others mixed; one group of plastrons buried with a human skeleton (pit YH 127); some bones dumped in, others arranged more carefully; some plastrons whole, some broken and incomplete; some bones inscribed, some not – all suggests that historical circumstance, such as haste, accident, the need to make room above ground, the need to store reusable bone and shell material, rather than any religio-bureaucratic, or archival principle, dictated the way in which the Shang disposed of their divination bones. I would also note that the bones, by their very nature, would have been difficult to "archive," and particularly in Period I, when the "scratch-paper" approach to recording the inscriptions meant that any plastron or scapula might contain a mix of dates, topics, and diviners. Finding a particular bone five years, or even five months, after the event would have been difficult. (The problem of classification, in fact, has remained to trouble the editors of modern collections of oracle-bone rubbings; see, e.g., Keightley 1990:45–6.) The oracle-bone inscriptions, not much read before they were put into the ground, were not intended to be read after the Shang buried them. And for some 3,000-plus years, until their discovery around 1899, they were not.

Conclusion

The making of oracle-bone inscriptions virtually ceased with the fall of the Shang in 1045 B.C. This suggests that the defeat itself may have discredited such pyromantic practices. Nevertheless, it is worth reflecting that the Shang king, by appealing to the authority of the written word, would also have been ceding some of his own authority to those who were, perhaps, more literate than he was. To the extent that writing would have tended to demystify the mysterious (cf. Djamouri 1999:23, 24), its routine use would have tended to promote the diviners and engravers at the expense of the king, who, in the pre-writing stage, would have embodied the paramount divinatory authority (based on his ability to read the cracks), an authority that he now increasingly shared with his staff.

The association of the script with religious communication, in any event, undoubtedly conferred value on the graph forms – see Sampson (1985:16) on the theme, "script follows religion" – which, by the Bronze Age, were already providing one of the characteristic ways in which the elites ordered and made their mark on Chinese society. The status of the elites, who were to be increasingly associated with literacy, encouraged a general respect for literature and for texts. But the close association between writing and authority that scholars (e.g., Connery 1998; Lewis 1999) have found in the Eastern Zhou and Han was not yet, I suspect, fully developed in Shang and Western Zhou. As Trigger (1998:40) has noted, in early societies such as China's,

> even specialized knowledge remained closely linked to oral traditions, and distinctive literary forms and devices for organizing and conveying knowledge did not develop to any considerable degree until a much later period. For that reason writing's impact on thought in the early civilizations was . . . limited.

Those who were mastering the new skills of writing and reading were no doubt promoting the links between writing and authority as literacy itself was becoming more widespread. But it may not have been until the first century A.D. that written texts were to achieve their paramount cultural role (Nylan 2000:252). The Shang writing that has survived played a powerful role in labeling and recording various ritual activities, including divination, but since most of the writing that I believe existed in the Shang has not survived, the larger extent of its influence is not yet easy to assess.

The written graph forms were to evolve and become standardized over time. And the basic principles and the character forms that the Shang had employed were to endure over the next three-plus millennia. The origins and functions of the first Chinese script, as they may be discerned in the continually expanding archaeological record, are well worth study.

ACKNOWLEDGMENTS

The editor extends special thanks to Tianlong Jiao for technical assistance in preparing this manuscript for publication.

REFERENCES

Bagley, Robert W. 1999 Shang Archaeology. *In* The Cambridge History of Ancient China: From the Origins of Civilization to 221 B.C. Michael Loewe and Edward L. Shaughnessy, eds. Pp. 124–231. Cambridge: Cambridge University Press.

Boltz, William G. 1994 The Origin and Early Development of the Chinese Writing System. American Oriental Series 78. New Haven: American Oriental Society.

—— 1999 Language and Writing. *In* The Cambridge History of Ancient China: From the Origins of Civilization to 221 B.C. Michael Loewe and Edward L. Shaughnessy, eds. Pp. 74–123. Cambridge: Cambridge University Press.

—— 2000–01 The Invention of Writing in China. Oriens Extremus 42:1–17.

Chang, Kwang-chih 1980 Shang Civilization. New Haven: Yale University Press.

Chen Mengjia 陳夢家 1956 Yinxu buci zongshu 殷墟卜辭綜述. Beijing: Kexue chubanshe.

Cheung Kwong-yue 1983 Recent Archaeological Evidence Relating to the Origin of Chinese Characters. *In* The Origins of Chinese Civilization. David N. Keightley, ed. Pp. 323–91. Berkeley: University of California Press.

Connery, Christopher Leigh 1998 The Empire of the Text: Writing and Authority in Early Imperial China. Lanham MD: Rowman and Littlefield.

DeFrancis, John 2002 The Ideographic Myth. *In* Difficult Characters: Interdisciplinary Studies of Chinese and Japanese Writing. Mary S. Erbaugh, ed. Pp. 1–20. Pathways to Advanced Skills Series, 6. Columbus: National East Asian Language Resource Center, Ohio State University.

Djamouri, Redouane 1999 Écriture et divination sous les Shang. *In* Extrême-Orient, Extrême-Occident (Divination et rationalité, en Chine ancienne) 21. Karine Chemla, Donald Harper, and Marc Kalinowski, eds. Pp. 11–35. Paris.

Falkenhausen, Lothar von 1993 Issues in Western Zhou Studies: A Review Article. Early China 18:139–226.

Fitzgerald-Huber, Louisa G. 1999 The Yangshao Culture: Banpo. *In* The Golden Age of Archaeology: Celebrated Discoveries from the People's Republic of China. Xiaoneng Yang, ed. Pp. 54–77. Washington: National Gallery of Art; Kansas City: Nelson-Atkins Museum; New Haven: Yale University Press.

Hansen, Chad 1993 Chinese Ideographs and Western Ideas. Journal of Asian Studies 52:373–99.

Harris, Roy 2000 Rethinking Writing. London: Athlone.

Heji. Guo Moruo 郭沫若 ed., Hu Houxuan 胡厚宣 ed. in chief *Jiaguwen heji* 甲骨文合集 13 vols. N.p.: Zhonghua shuju, 1978–82.

Itô Michiharu 伊藤道治 1962 In izen no ketsuen soshiki to shûkyô 殷以前 血緣組織 宗教 hô gakuuô 東洋學報 32:225–70.

Kane, Virginia C. 1982–83 Aspects of Western Zhou Appointment Inscriptions: The Charge, The Gifts, and The Response. Early China 8:14–28.

Keightley, David N. 1978 Sources of Shang History: The Oracle-Bone Inscriptions of Bronze Age China. Berkeley: University of California Press.

—— 1988 Shang Divination and Metaphysics. Philosophy East and West 38.4:367–97.

—— 1989 The Origins of Writing in China: Scripts and Cultural Contexts. *In* The Origins of Writing. Wayne M. Senner, ed. Pp. 171–202. Lincoln: University of Nebraska Press.

—— 1996 Art, Ancestors, and the Origins of Writing in China. Representations 56:68–95.

—— 1999a Theology and the Writing of History: Truth and the Ancestors in the Wu Ding Divination Records. Journal of East Asian Archaeology 1:207–30.

—— 1999b Shang Oracle Bone Inscriptions from Anyang, Henan Province. *In* The Golden Age of Archaeology: Celebrated Discoveries from the People's Republic of China. Xiaoneng Yang, ed. Pp. 182–86. Washington: National Gallery of Art; Kansas City: Nelson-Atkins Museum; New Haven: Yale University Press.

—— 1999c The Shang: China's First Historical Dynasty. *In* The Cambridge History of Ancient China: From the Origins of Civilization to 221 B.C. Michael Loewe and Edward L. Shaughnessy, eds. Pp. 232–91. New York: Cambridge University Press.

—— 2000 The Ancestral Landscape: Time, Space, and Community in Late Shang China (ca. 1200–1045 B.C.). Berkeley: Institute of East Asian Studies. China Research Monograph 53.

—— 2001 The Diviners' Notebooks: Shang Oracle-Bone Inscriptions as Secondary Sources. *In* Actes du colloque international commémorant le centenaire de la découverte des inscriptions sur os et carapaces (Proceedings of the International Symposium in commemoration of the oracle-bone inscriptions discovery). Yau Shun-chiu and Chrystelle Maréchal, eds. Pp. 11–25. Paris: Èditions Langages Croisés.

Kramer, Samuel Noah 1963 The Sumerians: Their History, Culture, and Character. Chicago: University of Chicago Press.

Lewis, Mark Edward 1999 Writing and Authority in Early China. Albany: State University of New York Press.

Li Ling 李零 2000 Zhongguo fangshu xukao 中國方術續考 Beijing: Dongfang chubanshe.

Li, Xueqin, Garman Harbottle, Juzhong Zhang, and Changsui Wang 2003 The Earliest Writing? Sign Use in the Seventh Millennium B.C. at Jiahu, Henan Province, China. Antiquity 77:31–44.

Liu Yiman 劉一曼 1991 Shilun Yinxu jiagu shuci 試論殷墟甲骨書 辭 Kaogu 考古 1991.6: 546–54, 572.

Loewe, Michael, and Edward L. Shaughnessy, eds. 1999 The Cambridge History of Ancient China: From the Origins of Civilization to 221 B.C. Cambridge: Cambridge University Press.

Lu Sixian 陸思賢, and Li Di 李迪 2000 Tianwen kaogu tonglun 天文考古通論. Beijing: Zijin cheng chubanshe.

Nylan, Michael 2000 Textual Authority in Pre-Han and Han. Early China 25:205–58.

Peng Yushang 彭裕商 1995. Yindai bufa chutan 殷代卜法初探 In Xia Shang wenming yanjiu 夏商文明研究. Luoyang shi dier wenwu gongzuodui 洛陽市第二文物工作隊 ed. Pp. 229–30. Zhengzhou: Zhongzhou guji chubanshe.

Postgate, Nicholas, Wang Tao, and Toby Wilkinson 1995 The Evidence for Early Writing: Utilitarian or Ceremonial? Antiquity 69:459–80.

Pulleyblank, Edwin G. 1996 Early Contacts Between Indo-Europeans and Chinese. International Review of Chinese Linguistics 1.1:1–25.

Qiu Xigui 2000 Chinese Writing. Gilbert L. Mattos and Jerry Norman, trans. Berkeley: The Society for the Study of Early China and The Institute of East Asian Studies, University of California, Berkeley.

Rawson, Jessica 1999 Ancient Chinese Ritual as seen in the Material Record. In State and Court Ritual in China. Joseph P. McDermott, ed. Pp. 20–49. Cambridge: Cambridge University Press.

Salomon, Frank 2001. How an Andean "Writing Without Words" Works. Current Anthropology 42:1–27.

Sampson, Geoffrey 1985 Writing Systems: A Linguistic Introduction. Stanford: Stanford University Press.

Shaughnessy, Edward L. 1982–83 Recent Approaches to Oracle-Bone Periodization. Early China 8:1–13.

Sima Qian 司馬遷 1959 Shiji 史記. 10 vols. Beijing: Zhonghua.

Takashima, Ken-ichi 2000 Foreword. In Chinese Writing, by Qiu Xigui. Pp. xix–xxv. Gilbert L. Mattos and Jerry Norman, trans. Berkeley: The Society for the Study of Early China and The Institute of East Asian Studies, University of California, Berkeley.

Takashima, Ken-ichi, and Anne O. Yue 2000 Evidence of Possible Dialect Mixture in Oracle-Bone Inscriptions. In Yuyan bianhua yu Hanyu fangyan: Li Fanggui xiansheng jinian lunwenji 語言變化與漢語方言：李方桂先生紀念論文集. Ting Pang-hsin and Anne O. Yue, eds. Pp. 1–52. Taibei, Seattle: Zhongyang yanjiuyuan Yuyanxue yanjiusuo, Academia Sinica; University of Washington.

Thomas, Rosalind 1992 Literacy and Orality in Ancient Greece. Cambridge and New York: Cambridge University Press.

Trigger, Bruce 1998 Writing Systems: A Case Study in Cultural Evolution. Norwegian Archaeological Review 31:39–62.

Unger, J. Marshall 2004 Ideogram: Chinese Characters and the Myth of Disembodied Meaning. Honolulu: University of Hawaii Press.

Vandermeersch, Léon 1980 Wangdao ou la voie royale: Recherches sur l'esprit des institutions de la Chine archaique. Tome II: Structures politiques, les rites. Paris: École Francaise d'Extrème-Orient.

—— 1994 Ètudes sinologiques. Paris: Presses Universitaires de France.

Venture, Olivier 2001 Quelques observations au sujet de la mise en page des textes de divination sur plastron. In Actes du colloque international commémorant le centenaire de la découverte des inscriptions sur os et carapaces (Proceedings of the International Symposium in commemoration of the oracle-bone inscriptions discovery). Yau Shun-chiu and Chrystelle Maréchal, eds. Pp. 71–90. Paris: Èditions Langages Croisés.

—— 2002 Ètude d'un emploi rituel de l'écrit dans la Chine archaique (xiiie–viiie siècle avant notre ère): Réflexion sur les matériaux, épigraphiques des Shang et de Zhou Occidentaux. Ph.D. dissertation, Université, Paris 7/Denis Diderot.

Wilford, John Noble 1999 When No One Read, Who Started to Write? New York Times, 6 April, sec. F:1–2.

Wu Hung 1985 Bird Motifs in Eastern Yi Art. Orientations 6.10:30–41.

—— 1995 Monumentality in Early Chinese Art and Architecture. Stanford: Stanford University Press.

Yang Xiaoneng 1999 Pottery *Zun* Urn With Incised Pictograph. *In* The Golden Age of Archaeology: Celebrated Discoveries from the People's Republic of China. Xiaoneng Yang, ed. Pp. 102–3. Washington: National Gallery of Art; Kansas City: Nelson-Atkins Museum; New Haven: Yale University Press.

—— 2000 Reflections of Early China: Decor, Pictographs, and Pictorial Inscriptions. Kansas City: Nelson-Atkins Museum of Art.

Yan Yiping 嚴一萍 1978 Jiaguxue 甲骨學 2 vols. Taibei, Yiwen.

Zheng Zhenxiang 鄭振香 1994 Taowen yu fuhao 陶文與符號 *In* Yinxu de faxian yu yanjiu 殷墟的發現與研究. Zhongguo shehui kexueyuan Kaogu yanjiusuo 中國社會科學院考古研究所 ed. Pp. 248–55. Beijing: Kexue chubanshe.

FURTHER READING

Bagley, Robert W. 1987 Shang Ritual Bronzes in the Arthur M. Sackler Collections. Washington DC and Cambridge MA: Arthur M. Sackler Foundation and Arthur M. Sackler Museum.

—— In press Anyang Writing and the Origins of the Chinese Writing System. *In* The First Writing: Script Invention in Early Civilization. Stephen D. Houston, ed. Cambridge: Cambridge University Press.

Barnard, Noel 1986 A New Approach to the Study of Clan-Sign Inscriptions of Shang. *In* Studies of Shang Archaeology: Selected Papers From the International Conference on Shang Civilization. K. C. Chang, ed. Pp. 141–206. New Haven: Yale University Press.

DeFrancis, John 1991 Chinese Prehistorical Symbols and American Proofreader's Marks. Journal of Chinese Linguistics 19.1:116–21.

Djamouri, Redouane 1997 Ècriture et langue dans les inscriptions chinoises archaiques (xive–xie siècle avant notre ère). *In* Paroles à dire, Paroles à écrire. Pp. 209–40. Paris: Ed. de l'EHESS.

Dorofeeva-Lichtmann, Véra 2001 Spatiality of the Media for Writing in Ancient China and Spatial Organization of Ancient Chinese Texts. Göttinger Beiträge zur Asienforschung 1:87–135.

Keightley, David N. 1990 Sources of Shang History: Two Major Oracle-Bone Collections Published in the People's Republic of China. Journal of the American Oriental Society 110.1:39–59.

Lefeuvre, J. A. 1975 Les inscriptions des Shang sur carapaces de tortue et sur os; aperçu historique et bibliographique de la découverte et des premières études. T'oung Pao 61:1–82.

Porter, David 2001 Ideographia: The Chinese Cipher in Early Modern Europe. Stanford: Stanford University Press.

Pulleyblank, Edwin G. 1996 Zou and Lu and the Sinification of Shandong. *In* Chinese Language, Thought, and Culture: Nivison and His Critics. Philip J. Ivanhoe, ed. Pp. 39–57. Chicago: Open Court.

Schuessler, Alex 1987 A Dictionary of Early Zhou Chinese. Honolulu: University of Hawaii Press.

Shaughnessy, Edward L. 1991 Sources of Western Zhou History: Inscribed Bronze Vessels. Berkeley: University of California Press.

Takashima, Ken-ichi 2001 A Cosmography of Shang Oracle-Bone Graphs. *In* Actes du colloque international commémorant le centenaire de la découverte des inscriptions sur os et carapaces (Proceedings of the International Symposium in commemoration of the oracle-bone inscriptions discovery). Yau Shun-chiu and Chrystelle Maréchal, eds. Pp. 37–62. Paris: Èditions Langages Croisés.

Tsien, Tsuen-hsuin 1962 Written on Bamboo and Silk: The Beginnings of Chinese Books and Inscriptions. Chicago: University of Chicago Press.

Tung Tso-pin 1964 Fifty Years of Studies in Oracle Inscriptions. Tokyo: Center for East Asian Cultural Studies.

Wang Yunzhi 王蘊智 1994 Shiqian taoqi fuhao de faxian yu Hanzi qiyuan de tansuo 史前陶器符號的發現與漢字起源的探索. Huaxia kaogu 華夏考古 3:95–105.

Wang Yuxin 王宇信 1981 Jianguo yilai jiaguwen yanjiu 建國以來甲骨文研究. Beijing: Zhongguo shehui kexue chubanshe.

10

Secondary State Formation and the Development of Local Identity: Change and Continuity in the State of Qin (770–221 B.C.)

Gideon Shelach and Yuri Pines

In his seminal essay "Ancient China and its Anthropological Significance" the late K. C. Chang (1989) first voiced the view that the trajectory leading to the development of state in China and, as a consequence, the Chinese state itself, are fundamentally different from the accepted Western model of state formation and operation. Chang argued that while the Western trajectory is one of "rupture" – a wholesale replacement of a family-based society with new social, legal, and religious systems of the state – in China the process is characterized by continuity of familial institutions and belief systems that were incorporated into the fundamental structure of the state.

Chang's once provocative claim that China (and by extension all East Asian cultures) should serve as a source for a new theoretical model has recently become almost the paradigm among archaeologists of China (e.g. Liu Li 2000; Underhill 2002; Yates 1997). This development is in no small part a reaction against the common practice to exclude the civilizations of East Asia from discussions of state formation. While in the past research on Chinese states and complex societies did inspire the development of general models (e.g. Lattimore 1940; Wheatley 1971; Wittfogel 1957), in those early models Asiatic states were commonly used as the significant other which defined the more advanced and democratic European states (Morrison 1994:184–5). Today, while the formation of pristine states in China is recognized by most scholars, it has become common to omit China altogether from comparative studies (e.g. Feinman and Marcus 1998; see also Morrison's discussion [1994]). It is against this background that we want to propose our study, with the hope of reintroducing China into the general comparativist discourse.

We wholeheartedly embrace Chang's and Morrison's idea that detailed studies of the rich archaeological, epigraphic, and historic data from China can serve to test existing models as well as to formulate new models that can be applied to other case studies. However, our ongoing research into the formation of the Qin state (秦, ca. 770–221 B.C.) leads us to reject (at least for this specific trajectory) Chang's "continuity" model. Our case study suggests, on the contrary, that during the middle to late Zhanguo period (戰國, "Warring States," 453–221 B.C.) the Qin polity underwent comprehensive changes in its structure and in all walks of its life, and that these changes effectively put an end to most archaic features, supplementing them with surprisingly "modern" looking traits, which resemble in many important aspects early modern European states. We believe furthermore that research on the ways such traits were developed, manipulated and combined is fundamental not only for understanding Qin's history but also for purposes of comparison.

We are aware that the trajectory of the Qin is but one of many in ancient China and that different types of states rose and fell in the broader area of East Asia. Rather than attempting to overview all the different trajectories – a task which would have required the entire volume if not more – we decided to focus on one case. Though Qin is not the earliest state in China it is uniquely important, because in the year 221 B.C. it had conquered the entire Chinese world, establishing the first unified empire. While the Qin dynasty lasted for less than fifteen years, its institutions, rites, and functioning norms continued to influence subsequent dynasties for the next two millennia. Moreover, the model of the Qin, modified later by the Han dynasty (漢, 206 B.C.–A.D. 220) and its successors, had profound influence on many of the states that emerged in other parts of East and Southeast Asia.

From a methodological standpoint, Qin is an ideal case study. Rarely does a researcher have in his or her disposal such rich and varied sources to address the process of state formation. Our attempt to synthesize archaeological data, recently discovered epigraphic sources, and traditional (received) texts has been by itself an interesting methodological exercise. Our results, we believe, can be helpful for scholars working in areas that lack such abundance of written sources. Using a variety of sources to address issues of identity formation, particularly analyzing how the members of a group manipulated artifacts and texts to project a new internal and external image of their group, can, as recently pointed by Meskell (2002:280–1), revitalize the field of archaeology and make it more relevant to other academic disciplines and to the general public.

Background: Early Chinese States as a Research Dilemma

The origins of the first state-level societies in the East Asian subcontinent are hotly debated among archaeologists in and outside China. As often happens, political agendas significantly influence these debates. Thus, the traditional identification of the Xia 夏 dynasty, supposedly located at the middle reaches of the Yellow River valley, as the earliest state in China, was used in the past to legitimize the imperial political system; and similar centralizing agendas may stand behind the recently loudly proclaimed Chinese government project to establish an "official chronology" for the Xia and the subsequent Shang 商 and Zhou 周 dynasties (Lee 2002; Li Xueqin 2002), all of which were designated as the forbearers of the "Chinese civilization."

Regardless of such political underpinnings, many serious archaeologists, regardless of whether they accept the historical reality of the Xia dynasty, favor the idea that a state level society was indeed established during the late third or early second millennium B.C. around the middle reaches of the Yellow River basin (Liu Li 1996; Underhill 2002:25). Some scholars place the earliest states in different regions and at earlier periods (Guo 1995), while others push the phenomenon forward to the middle of the second millennium B.C. (Allan 1984). In any case, most scholars agree that by the middle of the second millennium B.C., or during the Shang dynasty according to the Chinese terminology, an elaborate state system existed in the Yellow River basin and perhaps also elsewhere on the territory of China-to-be. However, the nature and extent of these early "Chinese" states is still subject to significant controversies. While some describe the Shang and the Zhou as extensive territorial empires with strong centralized governing systems, the minimalists consider these polities as conglomeration of "city-states" with a weak ruling apparatus having limited control over the hinterland (Shaughnessy 1989; Trigger 1999; Yates 1997).

That the earliest states in East Asia elude clear definition may derive not only from lack of data, but also from the more general problem of the inadequacy of the extant definitions, based as they are on the Occidental experience. For example, while Shang bronze production, most of it in state sponsored workshops, far exceeds anything known from elsewhere in the ancient world (Bagley 1999:137), its political system appears to be insufficiently institutionalized and poorly integrated (Keightley 1999:290). Such apparent contradiction between the strengths and weaknesses of the early Chinese political systems, mirrored in other cases, indicates that the current definitions may be misleading when dealing with the early states in East Asia; a new approach, based on the East Asian experience, may be more appropriate. To develop such an approach we need to focus on specific issues related to political organization, administrative mechanisms, kinship relations and legitimization ideology (Trigger 1999), whether via new archaeological data or improved analysis of extant data.

In this chapter we will not address the early states of the second or the early first millennium B.C. but the second phase of state development, during the second half of the first millennium B.C., when large territorial states emerged in China, eventually giving birth to the Chinese empire. While secondary formations and the evolution of state society is perhaps a less prestigious topic of research than that of the pristine states, it poses fundamental and equally interesting questions. How did the breakdown of a complex state system and the construction of a new one occur? (Baines and Yoffee 1998:256–8; Tainter 1988). What happened during the periods of disintegration: were elements of the old system recombined in the new one, and if so, which elements, and how were they combined? (Van Buren and Richards 2000:4). Is this "secondary" formation an evolution of the old system or a revolution that created a new form of state? (Van Buren and Richards 2000). How does such change affect the rise of new social strata, and how in turn is it affected by it?

(Joyce et al. 2001). What kind of ideology is developed to facilitate and naturalize the sociopolitical changes, and does the ideology itself become an agent of change? (Demarest 1992; Van Buren 2000). Our analysis of processes in the state of Qin addresses some of those issues and suggests ways in which we can advance our concrete and theoretical understanding.

Early Qin: A Zhou Polity

While state-level societies existed in the basins of the Yellow and the Yangzi Rivers at least from the second millennium B.C., prior to 221 B.C. the region was never fully unified. During most of the first millennium B.C. it was nominally ruled by the Zhou house but in reality divided among a number of more or less independent polities. The state of Qin occupied the northwestern corner of the Zhou world, and in the eighth century B.C., following the collapse of the Zhou rule in the Wei river basin, it moved into the lands of the former royal domain. It is from this point of Qin's history that our discussion will begin (Figure 10.1).

As a departure point for our discussion we focus on the much debated topic of Qin ethnic identity and Qin's relations with the rest of the Zhou (i.e. "Chinese") world. This debate began in the 1930s when scholars have suggested that Qin was ethnically and culturally alien to the ancient Xia (also "Chinese") and that it was absorbed into Zhou civilization only on the eve of the imperial unification (Bodde 1938; Meng Wentong 1936; cf. Liu Yutao 1988). This paradigm was based on several passages in Sima Qian's (司馬遷, ca. 145–90 B.C.) Shiji (史記, "Historical Records"), which refer to Qin's similarity to the Rong 戎 and the Di 狄 "barbarians" (Shiji 1997 5:202; 15:685; 68:2234). Later as archaeological and epigraphic discoveries highlighted strong similarities between Qin and Zhou since the earliest stages of Qin history scholars began rejecting the old paradigm, as a result of which the once "barbarian" and remote polity is conceived nowadays as a state which "preserved the practices and inherent values of the Zhou ritual legacy with at least the same eagerness as their eastern neighbors did" (Kern 2000:63; cf. von Falkenhausen 2004 and n.d.).

For many scholars today the textual and archaeological data of Qin history seem to be irreconcilable. We believe, however, that this apparent contradiction between different sources can be resolved if we take into account that Qin identity was not a fixed entity, but one which developed and changed in response to domestic and foreign social and political processes and could be manipulated by the ruling elite. Being a social construct, collective identities, as many recent archaeological studies stressed, are much more fluid and interchangeable than previously assumed (Meskell 2002). Individuals have more than one identity and they change them through their life cycles. Moreover, individuals have different "social skins" which they can put on in different social interactions (Fisher and DiPaolo-Loren 2003). Group identity, so much as it can be identified by analysis of patterns of material remains, is also a social construct (cf. Eisenstadt and Giesen 1995). Such a construct is commonly promoted by the elite to legitimize and maintain their

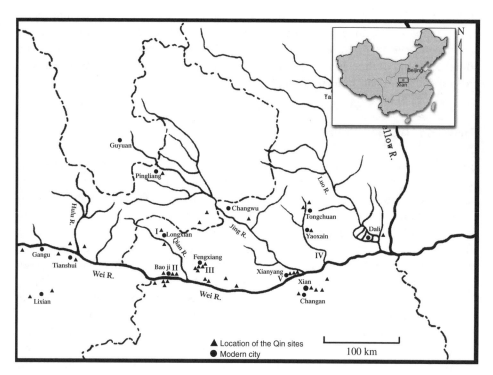

Figure 10.1 Location of Qin capital cities and archaeological sites mentioned in chapter (used with permission from Teng Mingyu). I. Qianwei; II. Pingyang; III. Yongcheng; IV. Yueyang; V. Xianyang

preferential position vis-à-vis the rest of the population (Baines and Yoffee 1998) but it can also serve to enable social negotiation among different strata and regional tradition and naturalize sociopolitical changes (Joyce et al. 2001; Van Buren 2000; Van Buren and Richards 2000:10).

Our study suggests that shifts in the image of Qin in the eyes of its eastern neighbors and in its self-identification are intrinsically linked to the creation of a new type of state during the mid-fourth century B.C. This assumption of dynamic change in Qin identity allows us to elucidate several peculiar aspects of Qin state formation, and raise more broad issues concerning both state building and identity definitions in ancient China and elsewhere. Our study further elucidates the importance of interactions among sociopolitical strata within the political unit and with competing polities from the outside as a factor behind social, political, and economic change.

The archaeological data we use to address the development of the Qin state is far from being complete. Systematic regional surveys have yet to be carried out in this region of China and only a few habitation sites were excavated. Moreover, existing data reflect almost exclusively the life and mortuary rites of the nobles and of the unranked members of aristocratic lineages. This is partly due to a research strategy that focused on the excavation of rich graves and large structures, but, more substantially, this research bias reflects the very basic reality of pre-Zhanguo Qin (and Zhou) society. Prior to the fourth century B.C. members of aristocratic lineages possessed their own residential area and lineage cemeteries, while the commoners remained politically and culturally invisible, leaving few identifiable material remains. These lower strata were not supposed to participate in the ancestral cult and other rites, were militarily inactive, and in all likelihood politically silent (von Falkenhausen n.d.). The state was almost exclusively associated with the dominant elite families. This situation is akin to Baines and Yoffee's (1998:240) model, in which the sociopolitical elite creates a high culture that not only serves to legitimate its prestigious position but almost completely excludes other strata from participation in state affairs. However, in the case of the Qin this situation changed dramatically during the fourth century B.C. when, as we shall show, members of the lower strata entered the sociopolitical arena of the state and the resultant impact of their previously invisible tradition became instrumental in changing the "high culture" of the elite.

In what follows we shall compare aspects of material culture and mortuary practices of Qin elite members with those of their peers from the core Zhou states to the east. We presuppose the existence of the materially identifiable common Zhou ritual culture (von Falkenhausen n.d.; Yin Qun 2001) to which we shall compare Qin cultural traits. The goal of comparison is first to discern the degree of uniqueness of Qin culture within the Zhou world and second, to trace cultural changes in Qin during the period under discussion and their connections to the changes in the nature of the state of Qin.

Our comparison will begin with the capital – a ritual center of the state where the ruling lineage resided and maintained its ancestral temples. As is the case with many other contemporary states, Qin occasionally relocated its capital city. Altogether historical records mention six relocations, each time further to the east (Shiji 1997 5:177–203). We know almost nothing about the first three capitals (Qianyi 汧邑 [776–762 B.C.], Qianwei 汧渭 [762–714 B.C.], and Pingyang 平陽 [714–677 B.C.]), but rich historical and archaeological data is available for the last three: Yongcheng (雍城 677–383 B.C.), Yueyang (櫟陽 383–350 B.C.), and Xianyang (咸陽 350–207 B.C.). Among these three, Yongcheng, which was the capital of Qin for most of its earliest history, is archaeologically the best known. Its remains have been identified at Majiazhuang 馬家莊, in Fengxiang 鳳翔 county, Shaanxi. The city, an imperfect rectangle of about 10 kilometers square, was surrounded by 15 meter-wide walls and ditches 5.2 meters deep and 12.5–25 meters wide (Li Zizhi 1998). Its size and the size of its defensive installations are comparable with other contemporaneous capitals of large polities; actually, Yongcheng, and the next capital, Yueyang, which is estimated to occupy only 6 kilometers square (Wang and Liang 2001), are smaller than such capitals as Linzi 臨淄 of Qi 齊, or Xiadu 下都 of Yan 燕 in the northeast (Li Zizhi 1998:615; Steinhardt 1990:48–9). Yongcheng's defensive installations are dwarfed by the walls of Xinzheng 新鄭, the capital of the states of Zheng 鄭 and later of Han 韓 in Henan, which are as wide as 60 meters, i.e. four times wider than those of Yongcheng (Li Zizhi 1998:21).

The layout of Yongcheng seems to be much less centralized than that of other Chunqiu (春秋, 722–453 B.C.) and Zhanguo capitals. At Yongcheng, remains of palaces and public buildings, such as stamped-earth foundations and bronze fittings for the wooden constructions, have been found over a large area (Li Zizhi 1998; von Falkenhausen 1999), which suggests that the city did not have a single palatial center but rather several clusters of public buildings in different parts of the large walled enclosure. In the capitals of other contemporary states, such as Xiadu and Linzi, political and ritualistic centers were usually much more visible being separated from the rest of the city by walls and a moat (Chen 1994). Thus both the size and layout of Yongcheng, and the lesser-known Yueyang, suggest a relatively conservative and modest approach.

Some of the identifiable buildings within Yongcheng's walls demonstrate Qin's adherence to Zhou ritual norms. For example, ancestral cult, the hallmark of the Zhou ritual system, seems to receive much emphasis. Compound no. 1 at Majia-zhuang, dated to the late Chunqiu period, is probably the best example of an ancestral worship center known throughout China. Its layout is symmetrical, with a large gatehouse in the south; a large walled enclosure measuring 30 meters by 34.5 meters. Inside this enclosure three more or less identical buildings, constructed of wood with tile-covered roofs and raised on low stamped-earth platforms, face a central court in which rows of sacrificial pits are aligned (von Falkenhausen 1999:459; Teng 2002:66–72; Wang and Liang 2001:134–6). These three separate temples are, if anything, less than the number of temples which an overlord was allowed to have under the Zhou code (Wang and Liang 2001:136). Although no comparable ancestral temples of the Western Zhou or the Chunqiu periods are known, the building techniques and the symmetrical arrangement of this complex with its southern entrance are clearly in line with the Zhou tradition.

Nearby is Compound no. 3 in Majiazhuang, which archaeologists have identified as a palace. It is also modest in size and traditional in its arrangement. It contains a succession of five enclosed courtyards arranged from south to north with a total length of 326.5 meters, its width ranging from 86 meters to 60 meters. The main buildings seem to have been constructed at the innermost northern courtyard (Wang and Liang 2001:137). According to Wu Hung (1999:669) this compound and the buildings it housed are typical of the introverted, "two-dimensional and self-contained" style of the Zhou. Thus, like Compound no. 1, the layout and architecture of Compound no. 3 reflect traditional attitudes and esthetic values.

We shall turn later to the last Qin capital, Xianyang, but first let us analyze the graves and mortuary complexes of early Qin rulers. The size and furnishing of these are clearly at odds with the modest and conservative outlook of early Qin capitals. Even the earliest tombs of Qin lords indicate considerable extravagance. The eighth-century B.C. tomb of the Qin lord in Dabuzi 大堡子, Li 禮 county, Gansu, marked as M2, has two tomb passages attached to it from the east and west. The eastern passage is 38 meters long and 6 meters wide. The tomb chamber itself is approximately 12 meters by 12 meters at its mouth and 15 meters deep. Attached to this grave are two pits each containing 4 chariots and 12 horses (Dai 2000). There is reason to believe that the ritual furnishing of the Dabuzi grave greatly exceeded the mortuary rights of the Qin lord. The tomb was badly looted in the 1980s, but Li Chaoyuan (1996:32) estimates that no less than one hundred bronze ritual vessels from this tomb appeared on the Hong Kong antiquities market, a number which by far exceeds that assigned by sumptuary rules to the overlords. In comparison, the largest grave at the roughly contemporaneous cemetery of the Guo 虢 lineage at Shangcunling 上村嶺 (Sanmenxia 三門峽, Henan province) has no tomb passage, is 6 meters by 4 meters in size and 10 meters deep and contains only 57 bronze vessels (von Falkenhausen 1999:471–3; Li Xueqin 1985:80–4).

The Dabuzi tomb is dwarfed in turn by the later burials of Qin rulers from the Nanzhihui 南指揮 necropolis at Fengxiang county, Shaanxi. This cemetery covers an area of more than 20 square kilometers and contains 13 clusters; most of them are walled and each comprises several large and medium size tombs accompanied by sacrificial pits that contain horses and chariots. Altogether 42 tombs have been identified, among them eighteen with two tomb passages, identified as the tombs of Qin rulers from the period of the capital's location at Yongcheng (Teng 2002:55–7). The only large grave so far excavated in this cemetery is M1, identified as the burial of Lord Jing (秦景公, r. 576–37 B.C.). As in the other tombs of similar shape in Nanzhihui the two sloping tomb passages leading to the bottom of the tomb are from the east and the west. The eastern passage is 156 meters long and the western 85 meters long. The burial chamber itself is 60 meters long (from east to west), 40 meters wide and 24 meters deep. The grave was looted in antiquity so its ritual set of bronze vessels and other precious grave goods were not found. However, findings such as the inscribed fragments of chime-stones, 166 human victims each placed in his own coffin, as well as the huge wooden beams used to construct the burial chamber and evidence for a wooden structure which was built above ground (Teng 2002:57), all suggest an extraordinarily rich burial.

The scale of Qin rulers' tombs seems to support von Falkenhausen's (1999:486) observation that it "may well constitute an infraction, in spirit if not in letter, of the sumptuary privileges due to the rulers of a polity." We should remember however that heretofore no tomb of Zhou kings has been found, and that few if any graves of major Chunqiu rulers have been excavated. Tomb no. 5 at Heyatou 河崖頭, although badly looted, is believed to be that of a late Chunqiu lord of Qi. It has only one tomb passage and it is smaller than M1 at Nanzhihui. Even so, huge mortuary consumption is evident here, for the main chamber is surrounded by horse pits, which contain the carcasses of more than 600 horses (von Falkenhausen 1999:502). We still lack an appropriate comparative perspective, but there is no doubt that the lavish burials of Qin rulers and their unique features, such as the east–west orientation instead of the normative Zhou orientation along the south–north axis, challenge the image of a humble and traditional-minded state, as our discussion of Qin capitals suggested.

Epigraphic evidence further demonstrates the conceit of Qin lords. Inscriptions on bronze vessels and chime-stones cast on behalf of Qin rulers from Lord Wu (秦武公, r. 697–78) to Lord Jing proudly state that the founders of the state of Qin received Heaven's mandate (Tian ming 天命), and that the Qin lords rule their state in the name of Heaven (Kern 2000:59–105). This invocation of Heaven's mandate is entirely unparalleled among other Chunqiu rulers (Pines 2002a:57–70), and coupled with other unique ritual activities of the Qin lords, such as worship of Di 帝, the highest god of the Zhou pantheon, it strongly suggests that the Qin rulers considered themselves as ritual peers of the Zhou kings if not their legitimate heirs (Zang 2001).

Remarkably, this aggrandizing tendency of the early Qin rulers and their air of superiority has gone unnoticed by later historians, including such staunch critics of Qin as Sima Qian or Jia Yi (賈誼, 200–168 B.C.). Perhaps the ritual language of self-aggrandizement was designed for a limited circle of Qin top leaders, and was not employed in Qin's contacts with the rest of the Zhou world or in Qin histori- cal records. This careful interplay between the relatively humble capital and the lavish burial sites indicates the Qin rulers' mastery of the subtleties of ritual dis- course – a common language of the Zhou nobility. Rather than confirming Qin's "barbarian" image, its rulers' burials indicate the versatility of its elite in the niceties of the Zhou culture and suggest its belonging to the Zhou ritual milieu.

Mortuary data from the Qin nobility graves similarly indicate the adherence of the Qin elite to the aristocratic tradition of the Zhou, along with certain indepen- dent traits. Our systematic analysis of more than 600 Qin graves from the eighth–third centuries B.C. enables us to discern gradual changes in the Qin elite's adherence to the Zhou rules and the appearance of new cultural traits in the state of Qin. Moreover, this analysis allows us to trace the differences in dissemination of new cultural traits among different social strata.

One of the hallmarks of the Zhou mortuary tradition is a sumptuary system known as *lie ding* (列鼎), in which the number and types of bronze vessels to be buried with the deceased was strictly prescribed according to rank. Though schol- ars are still debating details of the numerical composition of these ritual sets (cf. Hsu and Linduff 1988:173–7; Li Xueqin 1985:460–3; Liu Mingke 2001; Yin 2001:185–7), it is clear that their main components were an odd number of *ding* 鼎 (meat-offering tripods) and an even number of *gui* (簋, grain-offering tureens). Thus, Zhou kings should have, according to this system, nine *ding* and eight *gui*, the overlords (*zhuhou* 諸侯) seven *ding* and six *gui*, the high-ranking nobles (*qing dafu* 卿大夫) five *ding* and four *gui* and so forth, downscaling according to the rank of the deceased. The actual numbers of vessels allowed to each stratum may have changed by the beginning of the Chunqiu period (Yin 2001:202–12), but the strict gradation remained intact.

Several scholars (e.g. Liu Junshe 2000) have argued that the analysis of bronze assemblages from Chunqiu and early Zhanguo Qin elite graves suggests that Qin nobility strictly adhered to the *lie ding* sumptuary system. The actual picture is, however, more complex, mainly because very few intact graves of middle and upper nobility had been excavated (Table 10.1). Among the five early Chunqiu (period 4) graves with ritual sets, four were excavated at the Bianjiazhuang 邊家莊 ceme- tery in Long 隴 county, near the supposed location of the first Qin capital, Qianyi. The ritual sets excavated from these graves are indeed in accordance with Zhou sumptuary rules. Yet already in the mid-Chunqiu (period 5), i.e. by the mid-seventh century B.C., we observe a less rigid usage of the numbered sets. For example, graves

Table 10.1. Qin graves containing bronze ritual vessels (based on data from Teng 2002)

Area	Period	Bronze ding	Bronze gui	Other ritual bronzes	Ceramic mingqi
Chang Long	4	5	4	4	0
Chang Long	4	5	4	4	0
Chang Long	4	5	4	0	0
Bao Ji	4	3	2	4	0
Chang Long	4	3	0	1	0
Bao Ji	5	3	4	4	0
Bao Ji	5	3	4	4	0
Bao Ji	5	3	2	7	0
Bao Ji	5	3	1	3	0
Bao Ji	5	3	0	2	0
Bao Ji	5	2	0	2	0
Chang Long	5	1	0	1	2
Bao Ji	6	3	0	3	4
Bao Ji	7	3	0	1	7
Xi An	7	2	2	7	0
Bao Ji	7	2	0	6	8
Bao Ji	7	1	0	4	10
Bao Ji	8	3	0	8	0
Xi An	8	3	0	8	0
Bao Ji	8	3	0	7	2
Bao Ji	8	1	0	4	0
Bao Ji	8	1	0	3	0
Bao Ji	8	1	0	2	0
Tong Chuan	9	2	1	4	0
Xi An	9	2	0	3	0
Bao Ji	9	1	0	11	0
Chang Long	9	1	0	2	0
Da Li	9	1	0	2	0
Xi An	9	1	0	1	3
Da Li	9	1	0	1	2
Tian Shui	10	2	0	0	2
Bao Ji	10	1	0	4	0
Bao Ji	10	1	0	2	0
Bao Ji	10	1	0	1	0

M1 and M2 from the Yangping Qinjiagou 陽平秦家溝 cemetery in the Baoji 寶雞 region yield sets of three *ding* and four *gui*. It is interesting to note that such numerical transgressions exist even in sets in which real bronze vessels are replaced by ceramic imitations (*mingqi* 明器) (Teng 1992:292). This suggests that violations of the Zhou code became increasingly common among middle and low Qin nobility. However, because no grave of a high-ranking Qin noble has been excavated it is impossible to reach firm conclusions.

Even if Qin nobility were lenient with regard to Zhou sumptuary rules the shapes of Qin's ritual vessels suggest a relatively conservative attitude. While in the states of the Central Plain *gui* vessels had been largely replaced, by the mid-Chunqiu period, by *dui* 敦 or *cheng* 盛 and later by *dou* 豆 vessels (Yin 2001), at Qin graves *gui* vessels – both bronze originals and ceramic *mingqi* – figure prominently well into the Zhanguo period, and disappear only when the entire set of ritual bronze vessels is abandoned (Teng 1992). Moreover, most of the Qin bronze vessel types preserved the Western Zhou shapes long after these were modified in other states (von Falkenhausen 1999:489–93).

After the mid-Chunqiu period, ritual sets become less rigid than before, with almost no grave from period 6 onward containing the prescribed number of *ding* and *gui* bronzes (Table 10.1). In certain cases, however, the lacking bronze vessels are substituted by *mingqi* imitations to make up the complete ritual set. For example, the set excavated from grave M10 at the Fengxiang Gaozhuang 鳳翔高莊 cemetery in the Baoji region contains three bronze *ding* vessels and five other bronze ritual vessels, but no bronze *gui*. However, it does contains two ceramic *gui* imitations (*mingqi*) (Teng 2002:164), which complete the prescribed ritual set.

A systematic survey of all the ritualistic artifacts, bronze vessels, and their ceramic *mingqi* imitations excavated from 626 Qin graves suggests that there was a rapid replacement of real ritual vessels with ceramic imitations in the burials of Qin middle and low aristocracy. Already by the mid Chunqiu period *mingqi* ceramic outnumber bronze vessels, and by the late Chunqiu ritualistic vessels sets are predominantly made up from *mingqi* (Figure 10.2A). This extensive usage of the *mingqi* may indicate either attempts by low-ranking aristocrats to preserve the image of ritual propriety at a lower cost, or, alternatively, introduction of new ideas regarding the afterlife and the separation between the realm of the dead and that of the living (von Falkenhausen 2004). The extensive usage of *mingqi* in Qin predates the eastern states (von Falkenhausen 1999:493), which suggests that while the Qin elite was relatively conservative in their preference of vessel shapes they were innovative in their choice of raw materials and in the quality of the vessels.

The turning point in the furnishing of Qin tombs seems to be the mid-Zhanguo (period 8) when the importance of ritual vessels, both bronze and *mingqi*, rapidly declines. This swift abandonment of the vessels that for centuries had been the hallmark of the aristocratic status indicates beyond doubt sweeping changes in the system of social gradation. Other aspects of the Qin funerary data, surveyed below, also suggest a significant change during the middle and late Zhanguo period.

To show this we shall focus now on unique characteristics of Qin graves. While scholars are still debating what constitute the core elements of Qin culture, and how such elements are related to the Zhou cultural realm (von Falkenhausen 2004; Huang 1991; Liu Mingke 2001; Teng 1993; 2001), they generally identify the following indigenous characteristics of Qin burials: (1) East–west orientation of graves, as opposed to south–north orientation common during the Western Zhou and among the eastern states thereafter; (2) The so-called "flexed burial" as opposed to the extended supine posture of the deceased body common in other states; (3) Small pointed tablets of stone, known as *gui* 圭 are commonly found at Qin graves and

A

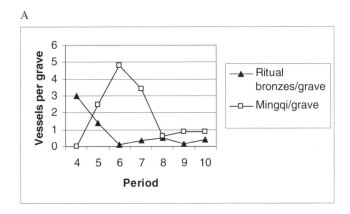

B

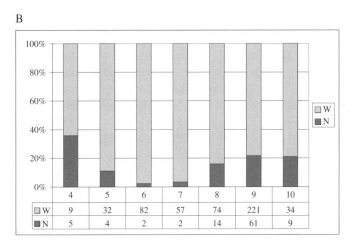

Figure 10.2A and B. A. Average number of ritual bronzes and ceramic *mingqi* in Qin graves of different periods. B. Orientation of Qin graves (W = west–east orientation; N = north–south orientation)

not elsewhere; (4) Catacomb burial, where the deceased is placed in a horizontal chamber adjacent to a vertical shaft, as opposed to a pit (vertical) grave. As a working hypothesis we accepted those traits as markers of Qin local identity and used the sample of 626 Qin graves tabulated by Teng Mingyu (2002:153–82) to analyze the patterns of their distribution during different phases of the Eastern Zhou.

Figure 10.2B clearly shows that during the Chunqiu-Zhanguo period east–west was the dominant orientation of Qin graves. Such orientation is shared by all social strata including the rulers and higher elite members, buried at the Nanzhihui necropolis (Wang and Liang 2001:65–70). It is interesting to note that the proportion of east–west graves reached its peak during the late Chunqiu and early Zhanguo periods (periods 6 and 7) while from the mid-Zhanguo period the number of the south–north oriented graves increases significantly to almost 20 percent of the total. This change is part of an overall drastic process, which occurrs in period 8, marking greater diversification of the Qin culture.

The mid-Zhanguo changes are similarly observable in the distribution of flexed and extended body posture. Both the westward orientation and even more the flexed body posture are burial customs that were widespread in Gansu province and areas further to the north and west (Huang 1991). The paucity of such burials in the core areas of the Shang and Western Zhou cultures – including in the Western Zhou royal domain later occupied by Qin – strongly suggests an indigenous influence. Like grave orientation, the dominancy of flexed burial peaked during the late Chunqiu–early Zhanguo (periods 6–7), and than decreased – though still remaining the most common burial method – during the mid and late Zhanguo (periods 8–9) (Figure 10.3A).

It has been suggested that flexed body position is an attribute of low status (Liu Junshe 2000), but this supposition is not supported by our data. As Figure 10.3B shows, while the extended posture is more common in largest and richest graves (type A according to Teng 2002:19), more than one half of these graves, including some of the richest graves in our sample, contained flexed bodies. While so far we have no information of the burial posture of the Qin rulers and the highest elite, the data currently available suggest that the preference for flexed burial was shared by all strata of Qin society.

Analysis of the use of the two types of graves – vertical pit graves and horizontal catacomb graves – shows a very different pattern. Although catacomb burials are known in northwest China from an early period, our sample of Qin graves shows that in the state of Qin the use of catacomb graves started only during the middle Zhanguo period (period 8) rapidly reaching its zenith by the late Zhanguo (period 9) (Figure 10.3C). As already pointed out by Teng Mingyu (1993), the common use of catacomb graves by the Qin population is a relatively late phenomenon which is associated with change in other cultural and mortuary practices that occurred during the middle and most notably late Zhanguo period. Similar to the flexed posture, catacomb burials are more common among poor graves (C type in Teng 2002:19) but exist also among the richest graves (A type).

The novelty of late Zhanguo Qin graves is paralleled in the structure of the last Qin capital, Xianyang, which was built in 350 B.C. and served as the imperial capital until the end of Qin dynasty in 207 B.C. The overall layout of Xianyang is still unclear although several large palatial buildings were excavated (Shaanxi 2003; Zhao and Gao 2001). City walls have not been identified and it is unclear whether, as some archaeologists argue, Xianyang was more centrist in its organization than Yongcheng (Li Zizhi 1998).

The most salient features of the archaeological remains of Xianyang are monumental palaces built around tall stamped-earth cores. While not true multistory architecture, such "terrace pavilions," which towered above the city skyline, were impressive monuments to the power of the Qin kings. For example, Building no. 1, one of several palatial foundations found on the northern bank of the Wei river, was constructed around a core extending 60 meters from east to west and 45 meters

A

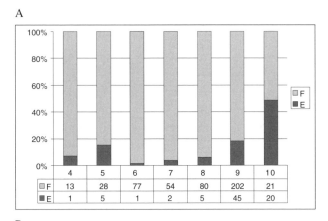

	4	5	6	7	8	9	10
F	13	28	77	54	80	202	21
E	1	5	1	2	5	45	20

B

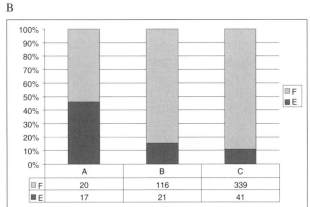

	A	B	C
F	20	116	339
E	17	21	41

C

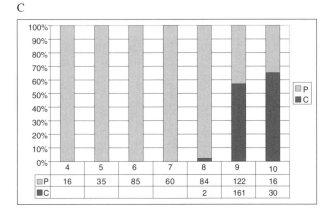

	4	5	6	7	8	9	10
P	16	35	85	60	84	122	16
C					2	161	30

Figure 10.3 A, B, and C. A. Proportion of body posture at Qin graves (F = flexed posture; E = extended posture). B. Proportion of body posture at different type of graves. C. Proportion of pit and catacomb graves (P = pit graves; C = catacomb graves). Periods: 4 = Early Chunqiu (ca. 770–650 B.C.); 5 = Middle Chunqiu (650–560 B.C.); 6 = Late Chunqiu and transition to the Zhanguo (560–470 B.C.); 7 = Early Zhanguo (470–380 B.C.); 8 = Middle Zhanguo (380–290 B.C.); 9 = Late Zhanguo and Qin (290–207 B.C.); 10 = Early Han (206–118 B.C.). All the charts are based on data from Teng 2002:153–82

from south to north (Shaanxi 2003:283–356; Zhao and Gao 2001:8). Archaeologists reconstruct it as a three tiered building that stood 17 meters high (Wang and Liang 2001:71). Such tall buildings represent a transition in esthetic values from the "two-dimensional" and self-contained tradition of the Western Zhou to the "three-dimensional" monumental style of the Zhanguo period (Wu 1999:665–75). Qin was relatively late to adopt this new style form its eastern neighbors, but once it did it apparently took it into a new level of monumentality.

In sum, the archaeological record presents a complex picture of Qin elite identity prior to the fourth century B.C. To understand the meaning of our data we must examine the way in which abstract concepts, such as identity, are "materialized:" to see what materials and methods were selected to transform ideas into a physical reality and which audience were they directed at (De Marrais et al. 1996). Because most of the aspects we were able to analyze, such as the funerary practices of the elite, public buildings, and epigraphic sources, are associated with formal display in the public arena, we assume that the identity we "see" is the one Qin rulers and elite wanted to project to themselves, to their subordinates and to the elite of the other states. This public image is far from being the "barbarous Other;" actually, Qin ruling elite displayed remarkable adherence to many aspects of the Western Zhou tradition, often observing it more closely than their peers from other Zhou states. While our data indicate manipulation of the Zhou sumptuary rules from the mid-Chunqiu period, this was not a unique Qin phenomenon but a process observable in the archaeological record of the eastern states as well (Yin Qun 2001:259–74). In few aspects of its material culture, such as the widespread replacement of bronze vessels with *mingqi*, Qin was more innovative than its neighbors, but the general picture prior to the mid-fourth century B.C. suggests that Qin ruling elite steadfastly adhered to many aspects of the Western Zhou tradition.

Throughout the Chunqiu and early Zhanguo periods Qin graves display remarkable continuity, possibly indicating the strong cultural homogeneity of the elite. During the fourth century B.C. (our period 8), however, a drastic change occurs when many attributes of the Zhou tradition were abandoned and new attributes appeared. This drastic change represents two seemingly contradictory processes: it seems that while the elite accepted during this period many traits associated with the local cultures that predate Qin in this region, such as catacomb graves, it was simultaneously also more open to interactions and cultural contacts with its eastern neighbors. Eastern traits, such as north–south orientation of graves, the use of tumuli at rulers' graves and the type of royal buildings found at Xianyang are clear markers of eastern influence. Noteworthy, this is also a period when Qin cultural traits are more commonly found in the east (von Falkenhausen 2004).

The concomitant presence of indigenous and external influences suggests a period of lesser cultural homogeneity and greater external and internal openness. Whatever the reason for this change, it marked a significant break with the former path of development. As we shall see below, this rupture both reflected and effected deep changes both in Qin identity and in its image in the eyes of the rest of the Zhou world.

The Impact of Shang Yang's Reforms: Qin Against *Tianxia*

The rupture we observed in Qin material culture in the fourth century B.C. may be plausibly related to the overall reforms that occurred in that state during the reign of Lord Xiao (秦孝公, r. 361–338 B.C.) under the guidance of the brilliant reformer, Shang Yang (商鞅, d. 338 B.C.). While it is clear that some of the reforms attributed to Shang Yang were initiated either before or after his life-time, his overall impact on Qin's history is beyond doubt. His reforms have been extensively discussed elsewhere (Lewis 1999; Perelomov 1993; Yang 1998), and we shall not repeat these discussions here; suffice it to say that they had a major impact not only on the military and economic prowess of Qin, but also on its relations with the rest of the Zhou world.

There is little doubt that the major aim of the reforms was to consolidate and strengthen the state of Qin; yet they also had far-reaching consequences for Qin's cultural identity. Changes in social gradation which are partly reflected in the new mortuary practices discussed above undermined major aspects of the aristocratic culture that perpetuated the ties of Qin nobles to their peers in eastern states. While the demise of the aristocratic social order and the parallel decline of the ritual system, initially created by and for this order, were not unique to Qin, the speed and the comprehensiveness of Qin reforms are unparalleled elsewhere. Ranked aristocrats were a major source of cultural unity in the Zhou world (von Falkenhausen n.d.), and the disappearance of this stratum from Qin society meant that this state effectively placed itself outside the pale of the Zhou ritual culture, which was for many equivalent to the Zhou civilization.

Qin's departure from previous ritual norms was sweeping enough to enforce a new image of this state in late Zhanguo texts, the image that later became so pervasive in the *Shiji*. Prior to Shang Yang's reforms Qin was never treated as the Other. Early to mid-Zhanguo texts, such as the *Zuo zhuan* 左傳, *Lunyu* 論語, *Mozi* 墨子, *Guoyu* 國語, and *Mengzi* 孟子 rarely discuss Qin matters, but when they do, Qin is treated as a distant but not culturally distinct state. The situation changes suddenly in the late fourth century B.C. Contemporary texts abound with pejorative remarks about Qin which is either identified as the Yi 夷 "barbarians" (*Chunqiu Gongyang* 1991 22:2319), or, more radically, as a state that "has common customs with the Rong and Di; a state with tiger's and wolf's heart; greedy, profit-seeking and untrustworthy, which knows nothing of ritual, propriety and virtuous behavior" (*Zhanguo ce* 1991 24.8:907). Some of the anti-Qin philippics go to the extreme of designating Qin as "the mortal enemy of All under Heaven (*tianxia* 天下)" (*Zhanguo ce* 1991 14.17:508), an outsider to the civilized world, the cultural Other which exists beyond "the pale of humanity" (Pines 2002c). While these statements may be dismissed as politically tendentious, the evidence suggests that they reflect a broader cultural trend. Curiously, even some Qin courtiers accepted the exclusion of their state from the civilized All under Heaven, which was treated as a mortal enemy to be invaded and annexed (*Han Feizi* 1998 1:2–3; *Zhanguo ce* 1991 3.5:88–91). Whatever is the

historical veracity of such statements attributed to Qin statesmen, they must have
been formulated in accord with the argumentation acceptable at the court of Qin
during the late Zhanguo period. As such they suggest that Qin accepted its unique
position as a state beyond All under Heaven, and a singular enemy of *tianxia*.

Harsh rhetoric notwithstanding, Qin leaders did not opt for complete separation
from the Zhou world. To the very end of the Zhanguo period the rulers of Qin continued to adhere to certain aspects of the Zhou legacy. Of particular importance
was the maintenance of amicable relations with the Zhou house, which remained,
despite its obvious weakness, the major source of inter-state legitimacy. Qin epigraphic sources, such as the so-called "clay document" (*wa shu* 瓦書) and the
recently discovered prayer to Mountain Hua written on the jade tablets, testify
beyond doubt to Qin's ongoing respect to the Zhou kings (Pines In press). Qin official documents furthermore display continuous adherence to the Zhou written tradition, which was preserved in Qin even more than in the core Zhou states (Kern
2000). Similar conservatism is observable in Qin script, as "Qin was the most faith-
ful in carrying on the writing tradition of the Zhou dynasty" (Qiu 2000:78). This
preservation of political and cultural bridges with the Zhou world suggests that significant portions of the Qin ruling elite preferred cultural integration with rather
than separation from their eastern neighbors. Qin rulers' continuous enrolling of
alien statesmen and thinkers to their court suggests their awareness of the need to
preserve cultural bridges with the rest of the Zhou world.

The picture of Qin ties with the Zhou states as obtained from the traditional and
recently discovered texts is therefore not monochromatic, and it may be plausibly
assumed that conflicting views coexisted at the court of Qin with regard to its place
within the Zhou world. It seems, however, that acute interstate conflict between
Qin and its neighbors gradually strengthened the separatist tendency. Thus, by the
late Zhanguo, Qin elites reimagined the history of their state in a way that emphasized its otherness rather than its common roots with the Zhou; hence statements
about Qin's erstwhile "barbarianism" appear even in the texts associated with this
state (e.g. *Lüshi chunqiu* 1990 24.1:1584; *Shiji* 1997 87:2544). These statements
indicate that in the late Zhanguo period not only Qin's image in the eyes of outsiders, but perhaps its own sense of identity had profoundly changed.

Qin's estrangement from the eastern parts of the Zhou realm is further observable from its leaders' reinterpretation of their relations to the Xia (i.e. the traditional "Chinese" world). While in the Chunqiu period Qin lords considered
themselves to be part of the Xia and even its leaders (as in the bronze inscriptions
discussed above), late Zhanguo Qin legal texts convey a different impression. Qin
statutes unearthed in Shuihudi 睡虎地, Hubei, clearly indicate Qin's self-differenti-
ation from the Xia, who are arrogantly designated as vassal states (Hulsewe
1985:170; Shuihudi 2001:134); elsewhere Shuihudi documents pejoratively use the
term "a Xia child" to designate "children born of a vassal state father and a Qin
mother" (Hulsewe 1985:171; Pines In press; Shuihudi 2001:135).Clearly, late
Zhanguo Qin officials distinguished their state from the Xia, which became a different entity, separated by location and by blood and not only by culture. The otherness of Qin in the late Zhanguo cultural landscape is therefore not a post-factum

Han construction, but an outcome of deep cultural and political processes apparently triggered by Shang Yang's reforms. The combination of archaeological data, epigraphy, and classical texts suggest that by the end of the Zhanguo period a new Qin identity appeared, and it was evidently shared by most strata of the Qin society.

Political Perspective: Qin as a Nation-State?

The above discussion has shown that the demise of the aristocratic social order in the state of Qin in the mid-Zhanguo period, and the parallel abandonment of the Zhou ritual system, coincide with the development of a distinct local identity and of a new international image of Qin. Yet as our analysis suggests, Qin leaders of the reform age and thereafter did not try to break away entirely from the Zhou legacy, and it is unlikely that they had ever planned to disaffiliate themselves from the rest of the Zhou world. Was then the emergence of a nascent Qin identity a by-product of the reforms or a result of conscious manipulation by the Qin leaders? Why did the process of formation of unique "Qin-ness" occur? And what role did this identity formation play in the consolidation of Qin's power and the formation of the Qin empire?

Addressing the above questions is crucial in our effort to better understand the negotiation, construction, and manipulation of new identity. We may propose a threefold answer to these questions. First, we should consider the impact of the demise of the hereditary aristocracy, the major source of cultural homogeneity in the Zhou world. The nobles who ruled Zhou states prior to the fourth century B.C. formed a hereditary stratum, effectively closed to outsiders, a stratum that possessed many cultural characteristics common throughout the Zhou world. Aristocrats from different states routinely intermarried (but never married the commoners of their own state), they shared a common ritual and textual culture, they spoke a mutually intelligible language, and routinely communicated during the inter-state meetings. Frequent inter-state and intra-state conflicts did not diminish the sense of belonging to the common culturally unified *tianxia* (Pines 2002c). The hereditary ruling strata perpetuated cultural links throughout the Zhou world long after the demise of the ephemeral unity of the Western Zhou (西周, 1045–771 B.C.) age.

The rule of hereditary aristocracy effectively came to an end during a period of profound political and social reforms of the fifth–fourth centuries B.C. Nowhere was this process as rapid and as thorough as in the state of Qin. The profound changes in mortuary practices observed above are but a partial manifestation of the overall transformation of Qin's social structure. The abolition of hereditary aristocracy and the establishment of a new meritocratic elite, in which ranks were granted for military achievements and high tax yields, blurred the differences between the lower and upper strata of the populace. By the late Zhanguo period Qin achieved remarkable social mobility, as reflected, for instance, in the Almanacs (*Ri shu* 日書) discovered at Shuihudi and at Fangmatan 放馬灘, Gansu, which show an impressive range of career opportunities for a newborn Qin baby (Ri Shu yanjiu ban 2000). The new, popular-based elite came into existence.

The opening of upward mobility routes for commoners had a far-reaching impact on the cultural life of Qin society. The old aristocratic culture, with its roots in the Zhou past, did not disappear entirely, but it was partly submerged by the popular culture which was based on local habits, customs, and beliefs. The changes in Qin mortuary rites surveyed above suggest the ongoing influence of local customs and popular beliefs, an influence which intensified during the fourth century B.C. These are not the only manifestations of the upward dissemination of popular customs. Almanacs, exorcist, and resurrection texts unearthed in late Zhanguo Qin tombs at Shuihudi and Fangmatan all reflect heretofore largely unknown beliefs of the lower strata; these beliefs might have existed for centuries, but their written codification and their presence in the officials' graves reflect a partial merging of elite and popular culture. The impact of lower-strata habits on the new elite culture may explain many of the late Zhanguo cultural changes in the state of Qin, and maybe among its neighbors as well (von Falkenhausen n.d.).

The second major factor that contributed toward the consolidation of Qin (and other states') society was the emergence of the tightly organized Warring State (Hsu 1965; Lewis 1999; Yang 1998). The new state, which sought to mobilize all its population for economic production and warfare, established effective control mechanisms over individuals, and penetrated deeply into society, eliminating or weakening formerly semi-independent units such as the high-ordered lineage or the agricultural commune (Perelomov 1961:66–84), and diminishing thereby former parochial identities. The new state was a highly centralized polity with fixed boundaries, which were often marked by long protective walls. This territorial integration was accompanied by a clear bureaucratic distinction between "us" and "others;" thus, Qin statues clearly distinguish between the native population (*gu Qin min* 故秦民), people from various dependencies, and the subjects of foreign powers who had the status of a guest (*ke* 客 or *bang ke* 邦客). The Shuihudi documents suggest that descent as well as place of birth played an important role in defining belonging to Qin (Hulsewe 1985:171; Shuihudi 2001:135). While speaking of citizenship would certainly be an anachronism, there are undeniable common aspects of Qin in the period of the Warring States and the modern nation-state.

The third, and perhaps the most important, development that had far-reaching impact on the sense of identity of the Qin populace was the appearance of mass conscription. The transformation of the Zhanguo military contributed decisively to the consolidation of the inhabitants of Qin. Prolonged military service, frequent bloody conflicts with rival armies, violent conquest of the neighboring territories and inevitable confrontations between the occupied and the occupiers – all these could not but enhance the sense of common identity among Qin peasant-soldiers (cf. Smith 1981). Widespread hatred of Qin, which is richly documented both in traditional and in recently discovered texts (Pines In press), further fuelled feelings of common destiny among Qin conscripts. The above-mentioned belief of Qin enemies that this state was a singular enemy of the civilized *tianxia* became by itself a powerful means of consolidating the unique Qin identity, political, as well as cultural. Is it possible that during the 3rd century B.C. something akin to modern concepts of ethnic identity and patriotism emerged in Qin only to be abandoned with imperial unification?

The above discussion raises the issue of ideology (in the most general sense) and its role in the formation and consolidation of state authority. This is a controversial issue among archaeologists and anthropologists: was the ideology a by-product of the sociopolitical change? Did it serve as "smoke and mirrors," an elite fabrication designed to naturalize their favorable position and disguise their exploitative actions? Is it merely a post-factum invention by modern scholars? Or was it an active force which determined the local trajectory of sociopolitical change and the type of state apparatuses which emerged from it?

Materialistic views are strongly entrenched in Western anthropological thought and, if only because of the type of data we use, are embedded even more strongly in archaeological theory (Tainter 1988; cf. Earle 1991; Frankenstein and Rowlands 1978; Gilman 1996.) Many archaeologists today would like to see ideology becoming a more independent variable (Shelach 1999:25–30; Yoffee and Sherratt 1993) or at least more fully integrated with other variables (Demarest 1992). As pointed out by De Marrais and her colleagues, the crucial issue is that of "materialization" or, in their words, "the transformation of ideas, values, stories, myths, and the like into a physical reality – a ceremonial event, a symbolic object, a monument or a writing system" (De Marrais et al. 1996:16). However, even with this theoretical framework in mind archaeologists often face situations where without tangible written sources they tend to depend on speculations and subjective interpretations of the archaeological data. We believe that the unique case of Qin, where ideological changes are reflected in the material culture and can be juxtaposed against the written record, is potentially an important source for inter-cultural comparison.

While from the description above it may be supposed that local identity was merely a by-product of political change, we assume that ideology played more than just a passive role in the process. The initial development of elite ideology and exclusive high culture during the Shang period, especially during the Western Zhou, and its maintenance and manipulation by the aristocratic elite, in Qin and in other states, particularly during the Chunqiu period, is akin to the model proposed by Baines and Yoffee (1998). This model, while not without similarities to earlier "exploitative" models, sees the ideology of the dominant elite (expressed in religion, cosmology, prestige items, and art) as an integral part of the development and maintenance of the state rather than one of its by-products.

The emergence on the public scene, as gathered from archaeological, epigraphic, and textual perspectives, of the lower strata and their culture, and the development of a more heterogeneous system, a process not accounted for by the "high culture" model of Baines and Yoffee, should also be seen as an integral part of the sociopolitical process. The new culture was a result of constant negotiation and compromise between the earlier, aristocratic "high culture" and the newly emerging "popular culture." The elite became increasingly open to the lower strata impact, was adopting and adapting itself to the commoners' beliefs, manipulating them to its needs. For instance, the commoners' increasing estrangement from the inhabitants of other states became a useful military asset. Coercion was evidently insufficient to mobilize large peasant armies for a life-or-death struggle. *Pace* Gilman (1996:57), the elite domination over the commoners during the Zhanguo period could not be taken for granted, particularly on the battlefield, when the costs of compliance were immense and the temptation to escape high. Many Zhanguo thinkers and military specialists repeatedly addressed the issue of how to encourage the commoners to fight and how to prevent them from absconding from the field of battle. Clearly, stronger local identity (not to use the too-modern term patriotism), shared by all social strata, increases social cohesion and the motivation of the common people to fight for their state. Moreover, opposing this local identity to that of the enemy reduces the likelihood of defection. It is likely that Zhanguo statesmen were aware of this and manipulated local identity when necessary.

Such a perspective can explain the strong visibility of local cultural traits in the archaeological record of the Zhanguo period. Presumably such traits, like the catacomb tombs of Qin, were not invented *de novo*. More likely, local traits which until this period were submerged under the standard Zhou elite culture were elevated and given expression in order to emphasize local uniqueness. A similar phenomenon is found in other states as well. In Chu 楚, Qin's strongest adversary, it is only during this period that the so-called "southern culture" traits, such as shamanistic religion and depictions of mythological creatures, become archaeologically visible (So 1999; Wu 1999; Xu 1999).

The fact that attributes of these local cultures are most visible in graves of the elite is suggestive. We can argue that once the Qin elite abandoned its claim for legitimacy based on the old Zhou tradition, it actively sought legitimization in the local culture. A complementary process can thus be imagined: local identity was developed from below but it was also re-invented (or re-cast) by the elite to serve its needs for cohesion and legitimization. Rather than viewing ideology and its expression in material culture as a result of elite manipulations (De Marrais et al. 1996), what we see is a kind of ideological dialogue between the sociopolitical strata. Our ability to identify in the archaeological record processes of social negotiation and the participation of lower social strata is also an important issue for archaeologists in other parts of the world (Joyce et al. 2001:345; Pauketat 2000; Van Buren and Richards 2000:10). Further research and analysis of archaeological data related to the Qin state will contribute to a better understanding of this issue. While our data allow only observation of general patterns, in the future more careful excavations and detailed reports may allow for thorough analysis of individual cases and lead to a better understanding of the construction and manipulation of group identities (Fisher and DiPaolo-Loren 2003).

Ideology, the Transmission of Cultural Legacy and Interaction: Concluding Remarks and Theoretical Perspectives

Our discussion thus far may be surprising in light of the well-known historical fact that Qin did not establish a separate entity but became the unifier of All under

Heaven. The apparent contradiction between the processes depicted above and the course of Qin history can be resolved, however, if we take into account that the process of identity-building in the Zhanguo world was extremely complex. Individuals and even groups always have more than a single identity, with different identities that are constructed and recombined, and may overlap or even contradict each other (Eisenstadt and Giesen 1995; Fisher and DiPaolo-Loren 2003; Meskell 2002). In the case of the political self-image of the Qin, tendencies for political and cultural fragmentation were counterbalanced by integrative forces. Among these we may mention economic integration, promulgated by the commercialization of economy and increasing regional interdependence; general fluidity of the boundaries due to frequent conquests and annexations of enemy territory; and, of course, the common cultural legacy of the Zhou, which was never rejected in its entirety, even when some of its aspects were modified or abandoned. The religious factor may also have served as a consolidating force, if, as von Falkenhausen (2004) observes, Qin had spearheaded a new wave of religious beliefs throughout the Zhou world. But perhaps the uniquely important integrative force was the behavior of the educated elite. In sharp distinction from the modern European nation-state practice, Zhanguo statesmen did not develop a sense of "patriotism." Most of the outstanding thinkers, statesmen, and military specialists considered All under Heaven as a huge market of talents, frequently shifting their allegiance from one court to another in exchange for respect, fame, or for more material benefits (Pines 2002b). Instead of promulgating local identity, many leading Zhanguo intellectuals proudly proclaimed themselves "Heaven's subjects" (*tian min* 天民), whose goal was to serve All under Heaven and not the individual state (Mengzi 1992 13.19:308).

"Heaven's subjects" became the most outspoken proponents of political unification of All under Heaven. Qin rulers, like their peers elsewhere, were committed to the goal of unification, and this is a major reason why they never acted decisively to establish a separate Qin identity. In the final account, their field of operation was the entire Zhou realm, not a single state (Pines 2000). Indeed, immediately after conquering eastern states, Qin rulers did their best to create a new synthetic identity, which blended Qin indigenous traits with the local traditions and beliefs of the conquered (Li Ling 2001). The common cultural heritage of the pre-Zhanguo age served again as an important consolidating factor, which may explain the conscious appeal to the patterns of the past in Qin stele inscriptions, the hallmark of imperial propaganda (Kern 2000).

This adaptation of the Zhou legacy to the needs of the newly unified empire is, of course, not unique to Qin. How the legacy of previous periods of political unity was transmitted during times of disintegration and how it was manipulated and recast by the new political actors is a question relevant to many areas of the world (e.g. Baines and Yoffee 1998:252–9; Brumfiel 2000:134; Van Buren 2000). The example of Qin is compelling because it fully embodied the complexity of such processes. Although during the period addressed above the political system changed dramatically, new social strata emerged and new value systems were developed, the legacy of the Zhou – and to a lesser extent of the Shang – has not vanished. Aside from the ideological appeal to a bygone "golden age" (an appeal rejected by the

Qin imperial rulers but which resurfaced during the subsequent dynasty, the Han), many substantive aspects of the Zhou legacy were adopted into the imperial culture. Even the material culture of the Zhou, the hallmark of its "high culture," did not disappear with the demise of the social strata which formulated and used it. For example, throughout the imperial period, bronze ritual vessels, the ultimate material expression of the Zhou, were used in state and religious ceremonies. In form – but not in their decoration – those vessels differ little from their Zhou models. The employment of such bronze vessels in state ceremonies is also reminiscent of their original use even if the ideology embedded in these vessels differed markedly from that of the Zhou age. Such examples are ubiquitous. The more subtle understanding of transmission and change gained from our research of the Qin can, we hope, stimulate similar studies by archaeologists and historians elsewhere in the world.

Interaction among polities has long been at the center of the theoretical discussion of the development of social complexity as a project at times contiguous to the construction of the state (e.g. Renfrew 1986). This approach has attracted some interest among scholars working on similar issues in China (e.g. Chang 1989; Keightley 1983; Shelach 2001) and in other areas of East Asia (e.g. Barnes 1986). We believe that this perspective is crucial for understanding the development of Qin, and of other early Chinese polities. The rise of Qin to power can be seen as an example of a peer-polity process (Renfrew 1986). Changes in Qin (and presumably in other Zhou states) took place in the broader regional context of a shared cultural foundation and political aspirations. Change in the Zhou tradition and even transgressions of it never happened in a vacuum. Qin reacted to developments in other states and affected them in turn. Though this is by no means a new concept, peer-polity can serve as a good framework for the analysis of long-term sociopolitical processes in East Asia, for it allows us to advance beyond traditional concepts which see, for example, the development of states in the Korean peninsula and Japan as merely a secondary manifestation of Chinese culture (Barnes 1986) or labeling Qin as a "barbarian" or rogue state. In both cases the peer-polity framework allows us to look at different socio-geographical dimensions, such as interregional elite spheres (competition as well as emulation and even cooperation), and local interaction among sociopolitical strata. However, if our goal is to use the East Asian data to develop new models of state formation and of state structure (Morrison 1994) we must be more open to integrate current methods and theoretical approaches in our research. For our particular case study we found issues that address the transformation of ideology into material culture and the way such "materialized" ideas are manipulated most revealing (Baines and Yoffee 1998; De Marrais et al. 1996; Fisher and DiPaolo-Loren 2003). Awareness of such issues will, it is hoped, lead archaeologists working in East Asia to look for new kinds of data, for example data related to the human body and to personal adornments, which will allow for more systematic analysis of changing identities (Fisher and DiPaolo-Loren 2003).

In his discussion of the ideology of pre-Columbian societies of the south-central Andes, Kolata (1992:84) identified two models of states: coercive and integrative.

These models are surprisingly close to the traditional explanation of the Qin "paradox:" a state that was able, through the unrestricted use of coercion, to conquer the entire "Chinese" world in a short period of time, and then immediately disintegrated. However, our analysis suggests that prior to unification Qin's achievements were not based on pure coercion but also on ideological integration of its populace. After unification the Qin rulers attempted an even larger ideological integration of "all under Heaven," but with limited success. Qin rulers' skillful presentation of their state as the ultimate outsider perfectly served their goal of internal consolidation before unification, but became a great impediment thereafter. In any case it is clear that Qin never substituted naked force for ideological manipulations, although the latter were not as successful as post-unification Qin rulers might have hoped.

Ethnic identity and its archaeological manifestations is another general issue that is relevant to archaeological research in many parts of the world (Jones 1997; Meskell 2002:285–7). In his paper on the mortuary practices of the Qin, von Falkenhausen (2004) argues that "the defining features of the Qin 'system' were religious ideas that were not essentially linked to ethnic identity or political affiliation." The gist of the argument is that because features that many archaeologists associate with the Qin culture, such as catacomb tombs and flexed burials, are also found outside the political boundaries of the Qin, they are poor ethnic or political markers. We have been making a different, even opposite point – that inter-state interactions are an essential part of creating, recreating, and redefining of what may be called ethnic identity during this period, and that therefore boundary crossing can be a defining aspect of a state's cultural identity and should be expected. For it was precisely when Qin was re-imagined as a barbarian outsider that it also borrowed extensively from the culture of its neighbors. For example, the common practice of rulers and high nobility in states to the east to mark their grave with imposing tumuli was probably adopted by Qin rulers only during the last decades of the fourth century B.C. (Wu 1999:716). Similar trends are seen, as discussed above, in the introduction from the east of new types of public buildings and new esthetic norms.

Our approach to ethnic identity fits well with Jones' (1997:84–105) multidimensional model. However, such a model, because it combines many different aspects that may also represent other types of identity, is necessarily vague (Meskell 2002:286). As pointed out by Ucko (1989:xvi) "there is no necessary one-to-one correlation between material culture and language or art style, nor between either of the former and what a living group may consider the extent of its own culture." Based on our analysis of the Qin data, we suggest that archaeological manifestations of ethnic identity in this type of situation should be seen as quantitative and not qualitative property. In other words, we should not look for the presence or absence of any specific trait in a region but at the prevalence of such traits and their combination with other cultural features. Such an approach has been discussed by Shennan (1989) and we hope that the Qin case, with its unique combination of written and material data, will continue to inspire a more thorough approach to the study of ethnic identities.

ACKNOWLEDGMENTS

We are grateful to Lothar von Falkenhausen and Teng Mingyu who generously shared with us their published and unpublished materials and made insightful comments on earlier versions of this paper. We have also benefited from the comments by Martin Kern, Miriam Stark, and the volume reviewers.

REFERENCES

Allan Sarah, 1984 The Myth of the Xia Dynasty. Journal of the Royal Asiatic Society 2:242–56.

Bagley, Robert 1999 Shang Archaeology. *In* The Cambridge History of Ancient China. Michael Loewe and Edward L. Shaughnessy eds. Pp. 124–231. Cambridge: Cambridge University Press.

Baines, John, and Norman Yoffee 1998 Order, Legitimacy, and Wealth in Ancient Egypt and Mesopotamia. *In* Archaic States. Gary M. Feinman and Joyce Marcus eds. Pp. 199–260. Santa Fe: School of American Research Press.

Barnes, Gina L. 1986 Jiehao, Tonghao: Peer Relations in East Asia. *In* Peer Polity Interaction and Socio-Political Change. Colin Renfrew and John F. Cherry eds. Pp. 79–91. Cambridge: Cambridge University Press.

Bodde, Derk 1938 China's First Unifier: A Study of the Ch'in Dynasty as Seen in the Life of Li Ssu 李斯 280–208 B.C. Hong Kong: Hong Kong University Press.

Brumfiel, Elizabeth M. 2000 The Politics of High Culture: Issues of Worth and Rank. *In* Order, Legitimacy, and Wealth in Ancient States. Janet Richards and Mary Van Buren, eds. Pp. 131–9. Cambridge: Cambridge University Press.

Chang, Kwang-chih 1989 Ancient China and its Anthropological Significance. *In* Archaeological Thought in America. C. C. Lamberg-Karlovsky, ed. Pp. 155–66. Cambridge: Cambridge University Press.

Chen Shen 1994 Early Urbanization in the Eastern Zhou in China (770–221 B.C.): An Archaeological View. Antiquity 68:724–44.

Chunqiu Gongyang zhuan zhushu 春秋公羊傳注疏 1991 He Xiu 何休 and Xu Yan 徐彥, annot. *In* Shisanjing zhushu 十三經注疏. Ruan Yuan 阮元, comp. Volume 2. Pp. 2189–2355. Beijing: Zhonghua shuju.

Dai Chunyang 戴春陽 2000 Lixian Dabuzi shan Qingong mudi ji youguan wenti 禮縣大堡子山秦公墓地及有關問題. Wenwu 5:74–80.

De Marrais E., L. J. Castillo, and T. Earle 1996 Ideology, Materialization, and Power Strategies. Current Anthropology 37.1:15–32.

Demarest, Arthur A. 1992 Archaeology, Ideology, and Pre-Columbian Cultural Evolution. *In* Ideology and Pre-Columbian Civilization. Arthur A. Demarest and Geoffrey W. Conrad, eds. Pp. 1–13. Santa Fe: School of American Research.

Earle, Timothy K. 1991 The Evolution of Chiefdoms. *In* Chiefdoms: Power, Economy, and Ideology. Timothy K. Earle, ed. Pp. 1–15. Cambridge: Cambridge University Press.

Eisenstadt, Shmuel N., and Bernhard Giesen 1995 The Construction of Collective Identity. Archives Européennes de Sociologie 36:72–102.

Falkenhausen, Lothar von 1999 The Waning of the Bronze Age: Material Culture and Social Developments, 770–481 B.C. *In* The Cambridge History of Ancient China. Michael Loewe and Edward L. Shaughnessy, eds. Pp. 352–544. Cambridge: Cambridge University Press.

—— 2004 Mortuary Behavior in Pre-Imperial Qin: A Religious Interpretation. *In* Religion and Chinese Society. Volume 1: Ancient and Medieval China. John Lagerwey, ed. Pp. 109–172. Hong Kong: Chinese University of Hong Kong Press.

—— n.d. Chinese Society in the Age of Confucius: Archaeological Interpretations. Unpublished MS.

Feinman, Gary M., and Joyce Marcus eds. 1998 Archaic States. Santa Fe: School of American Research Press.

Fisher, Genevieve, and Diana DiPaolo-Loren 2003 Embodying Identity in Archaeology: Introduction. Cambridge Archaeological Journal 13.2:225–30.

Frankenstein, Susan, and Michael Rowlands 1978 The Internal Structure and Regional Context of Early Iron Age Society in South-Western Germany. Bulletin of the Institute of Archaeology 15:73–112.

Gilman, Antonio 1996 Comments. Current Anthropology 37.1:56–7.

Guo Dashun 1995 Hongshan and Related Cultures. *In* The Archaeology of Northeast China: Beyond the Great Wall. Sarah. M. Nelson ed. Pp. 21–64. London and New York: Routledge.

Han Feizi jijie 韓非子集解 1998 Wang Xianshen 王先慎, comp. Beijing: Zhonghua.

Hsu Cho-yun 1965 Ancient China in Transition. Stanford: Stanford University Press.

Hsu Cho-yun, and Katheryn M. Linduff 1988 Western Chou Civilization. New Haven: Yale University Press.

Huang Xiao-Fen 黄曉芬 1991 Shin no bosei to sono kigen 秦の墓制とその起源. Shirin 史林 74.6:103–44.

Hulsewe, A. F. P. 1985 Remnants of Ch'in Law: An Annotated Translation of the Ch'in Legal and Administrative Rules of the 3rd Century B.C. Discovered in Yün-meng Prefecture, Hu-pei, Province, in 1975. Leiden: Brill.

Jones, Sian 1997 The Archaeology of Ethnicity. London and New York: Routledge.

Joyce, Arthur A., Laura A. Bustamante, and Marc N. Levine 2001 Commoner Power: A Case Study from the Classic Period Collapse on the Oaxaca Coast. Journal of Archaeological Method and Theory 8.4:343–85.

Keightley, David N. 1983 The Late Shang State: When, Where, and What? *In* The Origins of Chinese Civilization. David Keightley, ed. Pp. 523–64. Berkeley: University of California Press.

—— 1999 The Shang: China's First Historical Dynasty. *In* The Cambridge History of Ancient China. Michael Loewe and Edward L. Shaughnessy eds. Pp. 232–91. Cambridge: Cambridge University Press.

Kern, Martin 2000 The Stele Inscriptions of Ch'in Shih-huang: Text and Ritual in Early Chinese Imperial Representation. New Haven: American Oriental Society.

Kolata, Alan L. 1992 Economy, Ideology, and Imperialism in the South-Central Andes. *In* Ideology and Pre-Columbian Civilizations. Arthur A. Demarest and Geoffrey W. Conrad, eds. Pp. 65–86. Santa Fe: School of American Research.

Lattimore, Owen 1940 Inner Asian Frontiers of China. Oxford: Oxford University Press.

Lee Yun Kuen 2002 Differential Resolution in History and Archaeology. Journal of East Asian Archaeology 4.1–4:375–86.

Lewis, Mark 1999 Warring States: Political History. *In* The Cambridge History of Ancient

China Michael Loewe and Edward L. Shaughnessy, eds. Pp. 587–650. Cambridge: Cambridge University Press.

Li Chaoyuan 李朝遠 1996 Shanghai Bowuguan xin huo Qin gong qi yanjiu 上海博物館新獲秦公器研究. Shanghai Bowuguan jikan 上海博物館集刊 7:23–33.

Li Ling 李零 2001 Qin Han liyi zhong de zongjiao 秦漢禮儀中的宗教. *In* Zhongguo fangshu xukao 中國方術續考. Li Ling. Pp. 131–86. Beijing: Dongfang.

Li Xueqin 1985 Eastern Zhou and Qin Civilization. New Haven and London: Yale University Press.

—— 2002 The Xia-Shang-Zhou Chronology Project: Methodology and Results. Journal of East Asian Archaeology 4.1–4:321–33.

Li Zizhi 李自智 1998 Qin guo yu lieguo ducheng guihua de bejiao yanjiu 秦國與列國都城規劃的比較研究. Zhou Qin wenhua yanjiu 周秦文化研究. Zhou Qin wenhua yanjiu, eds. Pp. 609–23. Xian: Shaanxi renmin chubanshe.

Liu Junshe 劉軍社 2000 Guanyu Chunqiu shiqi Qin guo tongqimude zangshi wenti 關於春秋時期秦國銅器墓的葬式問題. Wenbo 文博 2:37–42.

Liu Li 1996 Settlement Patterns, Chiefdom Variability, and the Development of Early States in North China. Journal of Anthropological Archaeology 15:237–88.

—— 2000 Ancestor Worship: An Archaeological Investigation of Ritual Activities in Neolithic North China. Journal of East Asian Archaeology 2.1–2:129–64.

Liu Mingke 劉明科 2001 Qin guo zaoqi muzang zhong Zhou wenhua yinsu de guancha 秦國早期墓葬中周文化因素的觀察. Qin wenhua luncong 秦文化論叢, 8. Qin Shi huang bingmayong bowuguan "luncong" pianweihui 秦始皇兵馬俑博物館《論叢》編委會, ed. Pp. 378–95. Xian: Shaanxi renmin chubanshe.

Liu Yutao 劉雨濤 1988 Qin yu Huaxia wenhua 秦與華夏文化. Kongzi yanjiu 2:61–7.

Lüshi chunqiu jiaoshi 呂氏春秋校釋 1990 Chen Qiyou 陳奇猷, comp. Shanghai: Xuelin.

Meng Wentong 蒙文通 1936 Qin wei Rong zu kao 秦為戎族考. Yu Gong 禹貢 6.7:17–20.

Mengzi yizhu 孟子譯注 1992 Yang Bojun 楊伯峻, annot. Beijing: Zhonghua.

Meskell, Lynn 2002 The Intersections of Identity and Politics in Archaeology. Annual Review of Anthropology 31:279–301.

Morrison, Kathleen D. 1994 States of Theory and States of Asia: Regional Perspectives on States in Asia. Asian Perspectives 33.2:183–96.

Pauketat, T. R. 2000 The Tragedy of the Commoners. *In* Agency in Archaeology. M.-A. Dobres and J. Robb, eds. Pp. 113–29. London: Routledge.

Perelomov, Leonard S. 1961 Imperiia Tsin' – Pervoe Tsentralizovannoe Gosudarstvo v Kitae. Moscow: Nauka.

—— 1993 Kniga Pravitelia Oblasti Shan (Shang jun shu). Moscow: Ladomir.

Pines, Yuri 2000 "The One that Pervades All" in Ancient Chinese Political Thought: Origins of "the Great Unity" Paradigm. T'oung Pao 86.4–5:280–324.

—— 2002a Foundations of Confucian Thought: Intellectual Life in the Chunqiu Period. Honolulu: University of Hawaii Press.

—— 2002b Friends or Foes: Changing Concepts of Ruler-Minister Relations and the Notion of Loyalty in Pre-Imperial China. Monumenta Serica 50:1–40.

—— 2002c Changing Views of Tianxia in Pre-Imperial Discourse. Oriens Extremus 43.1–2:101–16.

—— In press The Question of Interpretation: Qin History in Light of New Epigraphic Sources. Early China 29.

Qiu Xigui 裘錫圭 2000 Chinese Writing. Gilbert L. Mattos and Jerry Norman, trans. Berkeley: The Society for the Study of Early China.

Renfrew, Colin 1986 Introduction: Peer Polity Interaction and Socio-Political Change. *In*

Peer Polity Interaction and Socio-Political Change. Colin Renfrew and John F. Cherry, eds. Pp. 1–18. Cambridge: Cambridge University Press.

Ri Shu yanjiu ban 日書研究班 2000 Ri shu: Qin guo shehui de yi mian jingzi 日書：秦國社會的一面鏡子. *In* Qin jian Ri shu ji shi 秦簡日書集釋. Wu Xiaoqiang 吳小強, ed. Pp. 291–311. Changsha: Yuelu shushe.

Shaanxi sheng kaogu yanjiusuo 陝西省考古研究所 2003 Qindu Xianyang kaogu baogao 秦都咸陽考古報告. Beijing: Kexue chubanshe.

Shaughnessy, Edward L. 1989 Historical Geography and the Extent of the Earliest Chinese Kingdoms. Asia Major 2.2:1–22.

Shelach, Gideon 1999 Leadership Strategies, Economic Activity, and Interregional Interaction: Social Complexity in Northeast China. New York: Kluwer Academic/Plenum Publishers.

—— 2001 Interaction Spheres and the Development of Social Complexity in Northeast China. The Review of Archaeology. 22.2:22–34.

Shennan, Stephen 1989 Introduction: Archaeological Approaches to Cultural Identity. *In* Archaeological Approaches to Cultural Identity. Stephen Shennan, ed. Pp. 1–32. London: Unwin Hyman.

Shiji 史記 1997 Sima Qian 司馬遷 et al. Beijing: Zhonghua shuju.

Shuihudi Qin mu zhujian zhengli xiaozu 睡虎地秦墓竹簡整理小組 2001 Shuihudi Qin mu zhujian 睡虎地秦墓竹簡. Beijing: Wenwu.

Smith, Anthony D. 1981 War and Ethnicity: The Role of Warfare in the Formation, Self Images and Cohesion of Ethnic Communities. Ethnic and Racial Studies 4.4:375–97.

So, Jenny F. 1999 Chu Art: Link between Old and New. *In* Defining Chu: Image and Reality in Ancient China. Constance A. Cook and John S. Major, eds. Pp. 33–47. Honolulu: University of Hawaii Press.

Steinhardt, Nancy S. 1990 Chinese Imperial City Planning. Honolulu: University of Hawaii Press.

Tainter, Joseph A. 1988 The Collapse of Complex Societies. Cambridge: Cambridge University Press.

Teng Mingyu 滕銘予 1992 Guanzhong Qin mu yanjiu 關中秦墓研究. Kaogu xuebao 考古學報 3:281–300.

—— 1993 Lun Guanzhong Qin mu zhong dongshimu de niandai 論關中秦墓中洞室墓的年代. Huaxia kaogu 華夏考古 2:90–7.

—— 2002 Qin wenhua yanjiu 秦文化研究. Ph.D. dissertation, Jilin University.

Trigger, Bruce G. 1999 Shang Political Organization: A Comparative Approach. Journal of East Asian Archaeology 1.1–4:43–62.

Ucko, Peter J. 1989 Foreword. *In* Archaeological Approaches to Cultural Identity. Stephen Shennan, ed. Pp. ix–xx. London: Unwin Hyman.

Underhill, Anne P. 2002 Craft Production and Social Change in Northern China. New York: Kluwer Academic/Plenum Publishers.

Van Buren, Mary 2000 Political Fragmentation and Ideological Continuity in the Andean Highlands. *In* Order, Legitimacy, and Wealth in Ancient States. Janet Richards and Mary Van Buren, eds. Pp. 77–87. Cambridge: Cambridge University Press.

Van Buren, Mary, and Janet Richards 2000 Introduction: Ideology, Wealth, and the Comparative Study of "Civilizations." *In* Order, Legitimacy, and Wealth in Ancient States. Janet Richards and Mary Van Buren, eds. Pp. 3–12. Cambridge: Cambridge University Press.

Wang Xueli 王學理, and Liang Yun 梁雲 2001 Qin wenhua 秦文化. Beijing: Wenwu chubanshe.

Wheatley, Paul 1971 The Pivot of the Four Quarters. Edinburgh: Edinburgh University Press.

Wittfogel, Karl A. 1957 Oriental Despotism: A Comparative Study of Total Power. New Haven: Yale University Press.

Wu Hung 1999 The Art and Architecture of the Warring States Period. *In* The Cambridge History of Ancient China. Michael Loewe and Edward L. Shaughnessy, eds. Pp. 651–744. Cambridge: Cambridge University Press.

Xu Shaohua 1999 Chu Culture: An Archaeological Overview. *In* Defining Chu: Image and Reality in Ancient China. Constance A. Cook and John S. Major, eds. Pp. 21–32. Honolulu: University of Hawaii Press.

Yang Kuan 楊寬 1998 Zhanguo shi 戰國史. Shanghai: Renmin.

Yates, Robin D. S. 1997 The City-State in Ancient China. *In* The Archaeology of City-States: Cross-Cultural Approaches. Deborah L. Nichols and Thomas H. Charlton, eds. Pp. 71–90. Washington and London: Smithsonian Institution Press.

Yin Qun 印群 2001 Huanghe zhongxiayou diqu de Dong Zhou muzang zhidu 黃河中下游地區的東周墓葬制度. Beijing: Shehui kexue chubanshe.

Yoffee, Norman, and Andrew Sherratt 1993 Introduction: The Source of Archaeological Theory. *In* Archaeological Theory: Who Sets the Agenda? Norman Yoffee and Andrew Sherratt, eds. Pp. 1–9. Cambridge: Cambridge University Press.

Zang Zhifei 臧知非 2001 Qin ren de "shou ming" yishi yu Qin guo de fazhan – Qin Gong-zhong mingwen tanwei 秦人的受命意識與秦國的發展—秦公鐘銘文探微. *In* Qin wenhua luncong 秦文化論叢, 8. Qin Shi huang bingmayong bowuguan "luncong" pianweihui 秦始皇兵馬俑博物館《論叢》編委會, ed. Pp. 243–60. Xian: Shaanxi renmin.

Zhanguo ce zhushi 戰國策注釋 1991 He Jianzhang 何建章, annot. Beijing: Zhonghua shuju.

Zhao Huacheng 趙化成, and Gao Chongwen 高崇文 2001 Qin-Han kaogu 秦漢考古. Beijing: Wenwu chubanshe.

Part V

Crossing Boundaries and Ancient Asian States

11

Frontiers and Boundaries: The Han Empire from its Southern Periphery

Francis Allard

First unified during the short-lived Qin 秦 dynasty (221–207 B.C.; Table 11.1), China experienced a long period of relative prosperity and stability during the following Han 漢 dynasty (202 B.C.–A.D. 220). The period's early years were marked by continued efforts at countering the threat of the Xiongnu 匈奴, a powerful confederacy of mobile pastoralists living beyond China's northern borders (Honeychurch and Amartuvshin, this volume). The rule of emperor Wu Di 武帝 (reigned 141–87 B.C.) brought a measure of political and economic stability to the nation. By 115 B.C., the threat from the north had been significantly lessened and the scene was set for a period of ambitious territorial expansion into new and distant territories, in some cases beyond China's present-day borders (Gernet 1982:120). By 108 B.C., China thus encompassed much of the Korean peninsula in the northeast, the present-day Gansu 甘肅 corridor in the northwest, Yunnan 雲南 in the southwest, Lingnan 嶺南 in the south (corresponding to the present-day provinces of Guangdong 廣東 and Guangxi 廣西), as well as northern and central Vietnam.

Although the Han Empire did not incorporate within it modern China's far northeast, the Tibetan-Qinghai 青海 plateau, and the western Xinjiang 新疆 region, its territory remained a vast one to administer and control, a task accomplished through various means and with varying degrees of success. Policies included the transfer of large numbers of colonizers (for example to the northwest), the establishment of military colonies, as well as small garrisons that protected important routes. The Han empire, including its peripheral regions, was administered from its capitals of Chang'an 長安 during the Western Han dynasty (202 B.C.–A.D. 9), and Luoyang 洛陽 during the Eastern Han (A.D. 25–220). Locally, power was exercised through commanderies, large territories under the leadership of a governor who, although sometimes assisted by a military commandant, was responsible for both civilian and military affairs. Importantly for the outcome of imperial expansion, the Han administrators, settlers, soldiers, and traders living in the peripheral commanderies were often vastly outnumbered by native inhabitants, who on occasion revolted violently against the Han presence. Each characterized by its own set of customs, the many native populations encountered over the course of the expansion fit into a sinocentric worldview with roots in the earlier Zhou 周 dynasty (ca. 1050–221 B.C.) and whose cultural geography recognized a cultural and political core surrounded by increasingly less civilized groups as one moved away from the center. At China's periphery and beyond it, barbarian societies with unusual customs knew little of the Han and were not required to pay tribute to the imperial court as often as those groups living closer to the capital, although they were nevertheless expected to recognize the emperor's suzerainty.

This chapter focuses on the Han expansion toward China's present-day southern and southwestern regions, a process that led to the incorporation in 111 B.C. of Lingnan into China's administrative and political sphere, a fate suffered only two years later by Yunnan (Figure 11.1). Although related through the timing of a coordinated imperial policy, expansion into these two areas involved not only different armies and Han officials, but also different native populations. It is worth noting features common to these two expansions. In both cases, the Chinese faced serious difficulties navigating through a landscape that was ethnically and geopolitically very diverse. The mountainous topography and climate encountered by troops, officials, and other migrants also took a heavy toll. In both the south and southwest, Han officials often managed the newly established commanderies and counties indirectly through native local leaders. In both Lingnan and Yunnan, Han rule was sustained – often precariously – through unending cycles of local rebellions, many of these triggering debates at court regarding the feasibility of maintaining a presence in these distant regions. Archaeology also contributes to knowledge of Wu Di's territorial expansion toward – and incorporation of – these southern regions. Settlement and burial evidence both suggest a process of Sinicization, one initiated during the Western Han period and that culminated, by the Eastern Han, into cultural landscapes that had shed many of their native features to become – at least with regard to elite sectors of society – no more than regional variants of the metropolitan culture present in central and northern China at that time.

This chapter presents, for both Lingnan and Yunnan, summaries of the historical sources and archaeological evidence at the disposal of those interested in gaining a better understanding of imperial expansion into south and southwest China during the Han dynasty. Although the historical and archaeological data available at this moment remain too selective for an appreciation of the details of the expansion, a comparison of these two trajectories – commonalities as well as differences – provides insights into the nature and outcome of Han Wu Di's expansionist ambitions.

Lingnan

Historical sources

Following his victory in 221 B.C. over the last remaining independent state in China, the victorious Qin emperor is said to have dispatched five armies totaling 500,000

Table 11.1. Chronological sequence

Zhou dynasty	ca. 1050–221 B.C.
Qin dynasty	221–207 B.C.
Han dynasty	202 B.C.–A.D. 220
Western Han	202 B.C.–A.D. 9
Wu Di	reigned 141–87 B.C.
Nanyue Kingdom	210–111 B.C.
Zhao Tuo	reigned 210–137 B.C.
Zhao Mo	died ca. 125 B.C.
Dian Kingdom	defeated by Han in 109 B.C.
Eastern Han	A.D. 25–220

men to the south (see also Shelach and Pines, this volume; accounts in English of the Qin, Nanyue 南越, and Han control of Lingnan are available in Wang 1959:1–30; Wiens 1954; Yu 1986:451–5). Four of these armies went directly to Lingnan (represented by present-day Guangdong and Guangxi), a distant and insalubrious region inhabited by various illiterate tribes often known at the time as "Yue" 越 (and sometimes subsumed under the name "Hundred Yue"). The Qin advance into Lingnan was hampered by resistance from the Yue native population, which harassed the Qin troops to such an extent that the latter did not "loosen their armor or unstring their bows" for a period of three years (translation in Wiens 1954:133, original in Huainanzi 淮南子). It was not until 214 B.C., after the troops had been supplemented with "criminals, banished men, social parasites and merchants" (translation in Wang 1959:10, original in Shiji 史記), that the Qin enjoyed some success in subduing Lingnan's native populations and were able to establish the three commanderies of Nanhai 南海, Guilin 桂林, and Xiang 象, each of these staffed by a governor and military commander. The first two commanderies correspond roughly to modern Guangdong and Guangxi respectively, while Xiang encompassed southern Guangxi, western Guangdong, as well as the northernmost portion of Vietnam.

The death of the Qin's first emperor in 210 B.C. was followed by the central government's loss of control over southern regions. Zhao Tuo 趙佗, a successful Qin general in Lingnan, seized the opportunity to establish his authority over the three commanderies, setting himself up as the monarch of the new and independent kingdom of Nanyue (distinguished from Han "kingdoms" in that the latter were governed, unlike commanderies, by members of the imperial line). Zhao Tuo established his capital at Panyu 番禺, situated in the Pearl River delta near the present-day city of Guangzhou 廣州 (also known as Canton) in Guangdong Province. Reigning for over 70 years until his death in 137 B.C., Zhao Tuo is said to have adopted Yue customs, married a Yue woman, encouraged Han men to do the same, and appointed Yue generals and officers. His relationship with the Han monarchs to the north was marked by periods during which he refused to recognize Han suzerainty and even on occasion used military force to expand into Han territory,

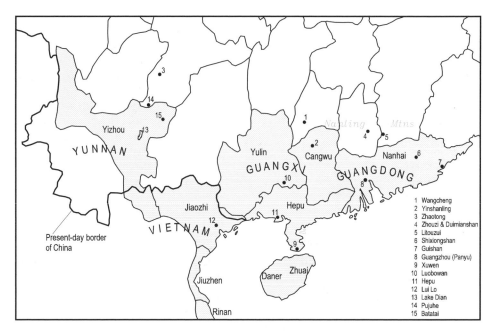

Figure 11.1 South China in 108 B.C., showing selected Han commanderies, the present-day national border, modern provinces, and places mentioned in the text

actions that invariably led to either reprisals or diplomatic missions from the imperial court to Nanyue. Although the two decades prior to and following Zhao Tuo's death were relatively peaceful, in 112 B.C. Emperor Han Wu Di launched a military operation against Nanyue following a Yue revolt. The region was annexed to the Han empire and subdivided into nine commanderies, of which four were in Lingnan (Nanhai, Hepu 合浦, Cangwu 蒼梧, and Yulin 郁林), two on Hainan 海南 island (Zhu'ai 珠崖 and Dan'er 儋耳) and three in northern and central Vietnam (Jiaozhi 交趾, Jiuzhen 九真, and Rinan 日南), possibly as far south as the present-day city of Hue (see Figure 11.1). Some Yue officials who had supported the Chinese were given titles and forced to remain in the Han capital of Chang'an, although some stayed in Lingnan as local officials to help administer the area. Important administrative changes prior to the fall of the Han dynasty included the addition and removal of commanderies at various times, as well as the appointment of an inspector-general who initially resided at Lui Lo (situated in northern Vietnam's Red River delta) and who was responsible for the supervision of all of these southern commanderies.

It is likely that Chinese expansion into Lingnan was from the beginning driven at least in part by commercial motives rather than by a single-minded civilizing impulse (trade between China's southern coast and lands further south is discussed in detail in Wang 1959). The Qin armies, supplemented as they had been by merchants, converged on the area around the city of Guangzhou in the Pearl River delta, a place already known for the many exotic products available there, some of which came from regions south of Lingnan. By the Han dynasty, these products included rhinoceros horns, elephant tusks, cowry shells, kingfisher feathers, pearls, tortoise shells, fruit, cloth, silver, copper, as well as slaves. At the time of the Nanyue kingdom in Lingnan, the Chinese demand for some of these products was signifi-cant enough to cause some advisers to caution against the destabilizing effects of an expanded trade in such goods. Although textual entries point to the presence of sufficiently large Yue ships at the time, it is possible that trade on Chinese vessels did not extend further south than northern Vietnam and that exotic products were carried from distant lands to Nanyue by foreign ships.

Han Wu Di's conquest of Lingnan in 111 B.C. put in place Chinese officials who supervised the overseas trade. Although Panyu remained an important port, the main points of embarkation appear to have been located further south in Hepu (southern Guangxi), Xuwen 徐聞 (southern Guangdong), and along the coast of northern Vietnam. Hepu and Xuwen were also well known for the high quality of their pearls. Importantly, a few references mention the development during the Han dynasty of trading relations with regions as far as India (where even larger pearls could be found), and of tribute missions to China from some of these remote king-doms. What is clear is that Han Wu Di's expansionist policy was associated with an extension of trade relations with ever more distant lands, a development maintained throughout the Han dynasty and one that opponents of such policy were never able to stop.

The texts are mostly mute about Yue culture and political organization. Neither do they provide much useful information about the nature of the relationship between Han officials and Yue peoples. The detailed census of A.D. 2, which pro-vides population figures for each of Lingnan's commanderies, does at least point to some degree of administrative control over local populations and the likely support and participation of local Yue leaders in the task. Interestingly, the census reveals that two thirds of the southern commanderies' 215,448 recorded households lived in Vietnam and only one third in Lingnan, an apparent imbalance that may reflect the fact that the inspector general operated from Jiaozhi commandery and/or that there was a greater density of people living in the agriculturally rich Red River delta, both of which could have facilitated registration (Wang 1959:18). Aside from point-ing to the large populations of the southern commanderies at the time, these dif-ferent figures suggest the possibility that in some regions, large numbers of native inhabitants were able to escape the registration drive and remain independent. Although numbers of different types of Chinese settlers in Lingnan are not known, indirect rule was in part driven by the demographic reality of a relatively small Chinese population base. The region attracted few willing Chinese people as it was generally thought to be a malaria-ridden cultural and political backwater, and a place where criminals were exiled and troops posted. The texts do make clear that Han officials in Lingnan were on occasion forced to rely on imperial and some-times Yue troops to counter local rebellions (especially in the southernmost com-manderies), some of which resulted from dissatisfaction with unscrupulous officials. At court, the policy toward these conquered populations vacillated from appease-ment through the appointment of upstanding officials, to suppression by force.

By the early Eastern Han period, a new policy of Sinicization had been put in place with the hope of altering local customs and rendering the native population more amenable to Chinese control. However, uprisings, which continued until the fall of the Han dynasty, led to the abandonment of the policy. By the second century A.D., the business of administering Lingnan's commanderies had been left increasingly in the hands of local officials, who concerned themselves more with taxing the population and supervising commerce than with "civilizing" the Yue. For hundreds of years following the fall of the Han dynasty, the texts continue to speak of the presence in Lingnan of various unassimilated groups who opposed Chinese rule. Such groups had not amalgamated into a single coherent political and military force, a feature reflecting in part the continued existence of a highly fragmented cultural landscape.

The archaeological record

The archaeological record of Lingnan during the Qin and Han dynasties contrasts sharply with that of the preceding Eastern Zhou period, a distinction witnessed in the amount and nature of the material as well as in its distribution within the region (Allard 1994, 1997; von Falkenhausen 2001). Knowledge of this earlier pre-Qin period is based almost exclusively on burial evidence. Dating from the sixth to the third century B.C., a total of about 200 vertical pit graves – some found singly and others in large cemeteries – have yielded a range of utilitarian ceramics, bronze tools, and weapons, as well as a small number of elaborate bronze vessels and bells that were imports – or copies of objects from – the Chu 楚 or other areas of central and northern China. The presence of these elaborate objects in the wealthier graves, combined with the recovery of local style artifacts, suggests not the presence of Chu officials in Lingnan but rather the existence of local elites who emulated northern styles and may have profited from contacts with the Chu, a possibility supported by the concentration of these graves in the northern half of Lingnan, often along rivers that flow south from the Nanling 南嶺 mountain range.

Han period settlements, buildings, and other non-funerary architecture

Evidence of permanent occupation is present at a number of Han period sites throughout Lingnan, with some marked by substantial architectural remains. The most notable habitation site, named the "Nanyue Palace," is located in downtown Guangzhou city itself (Guangdong sheng wenwu kaogu yanjiu suo 1999:319–20). Excavations have so far identified elements of what appears to have been a palace garden. A cup shaped pool paved with well fitted sandstone slabs covers approximately 4,000 square meters, of which about 10 percent has been excavated so far. A number of collapsed stone columns have been found in the pool, suggesting the presence of buildings both above and alongside the pool. Some of the stone slabs were inscribed with characters, including "pan" 番, the first character in Panyu.

Water from the pool flowed into a shallow canal that wound its way through the area over a distance of over 150 meters, passing over wave-generating "bumps." Other elements of the canal include a flat stone bridge, a water gate, and areas that turtles may have moved in and out of. The 8 × 6 meter crescent-shaped pool into which the canal empties was found to contain large number of turtle shells. Also present was a 9-meter deep well made of bricks, with the small stones and fine sand at the bottom of the well acting as a filtering system. Bricks and tiles are also commonly found at the site. Some of these were decorated (e.g. cord marks and blue glaze on some tiles) and inscribed with characters, including characters for various official titles, indicating a similar administrative system to that of the Han dynasty. Other artifacts include tools, weapons, ceramic vessels (some with impressed place names), and coins, some of the latter dating to the reign of Wendi 文帝 (179–157 B.C.). There is also clear evidence of burning throughout the site.

Although the Nanyue Palace remains by far the most prominent example excavated to date, sites in other regions of Lingnan have yielded evidence of substantial architecture requiring a large labor force to build and surpassing the basic needs of shelter and protection. In eastern Guangdong, we mention two sites of interest. At the early Western Han site of Shixiongshan 獅雄山 (Wuhua 五華 county), archaeologists have identified on a hillside and hilltop the partial remains of a corridor, two small buildings, a 20 meter stretch of a 1.5 meter wide stone paved path, as well as tiles of various types, some of these inscribed with characters (Guangdong sheng bowuguan 1990:223–4; Guangdong sheng wenwu kaogu yanjiu suo 1991). Situated along the coast in Chenghai 澄海 County and dating from the early Western Han to post-Han times, the site of Guishan 龜山 consists of material distributed among a number of terraces dug into the slope of a hill. This material includes the remains of buildings, large numbers of tiles (including floor or paving tiles), ceramic vessels, as well as a few bronze and iron objects (Guangdong sheng wenwu kaogu yanjiu suo et al. 1997).

In northern Guangdong, two sites, each located along an important river that flows south from the Nanling mountain range, deserve mention. At the partially destroyed site of Zhouzi 洲仔, situated along the banks of the Wu 武 river near the town of Lechang 樂昌, archaeologists have identified the remains of a 2 meter wide wall that was at least 50 meters long and whose foundation consisted of river pebbles. Zhouzi has been dated to the early Western Han period. At the site of Litouzui 犁頭嘴, located on the banks of the Zhen 湞 river in Shixing 始興 county, a wall with a perimeter length of 420 meters surrounds a more than 8,000 square meter area that is nearly triangular in shape. An entrance in the wall has also been identified, while the tiles found at the site suggest that Litouzui was occupied during both the Western and Eastern Han (Guangdong sheng bowuguan 1990:224; Guangdong sheng wenwu kaogu yanjiu suo 1999:320). It is worth noting that both Zhouzi and Litouzui were located in commanderies north of Lingnan, although still south of the Nanling mountain range and in present-day Guangdong.

Located along Guangdong's southern coastline in Xuwen County, the sites at the villages of Erqiao 二橋 and Shiwei 仕尾 have also yielded architectural remains, although no distinct building foundations have yet been identified. Some of the tiles, which include floor-paving tiles, are inscribed with characters. The large size of the sites is suggested by the wide spatial distribution of these tiles. A bronze seal with a 4-character inscription has also been found (Guangdong sheng wenwu kaogu yanjiu suo 1999:320). In northern Guangxi, a number of substantial sites that may date to the Han period are located along the uppermost reaches of the Li 漓 river, near the canal that links the Li to the Xiang 湘 river in Hunan 湖南 Province and thus to the drainage basin of central China. Surveys and limited excavation at one such site ("Wangcheng" 王城) located north of Yulin commandery (but presently in Guangxi) have revealed the presence of a wall, gate, defensive moat, and varied architectural remains within the wall. These investigations suggest to the archaeologists that Wangcheng's main function was as a military post (Guangxi Zhuangzu zizhiqu bowuguan 1999:340).

Han period burials

Thousands of Han period burials have been excavated to date in Lingnan, a number representing a very significant increase over the previous Zhou period. Approximately 2,000 of these are located in Guangxi, while 800 or so had been excavated in Guangzhou city alone by the mid 1990s. Concentrations of burials are said to be located in the Pearl River delta in and around Guangzhou, in northern Guangdong and Guangxi along rivers that flow south from the Nanling mountain range, at various points along the coasts of Guangdong and Guangxi (including the counties of Xuwen and Hepu), and along a few inland rivers (Guangdong sheng wenwu kaogu yanjiu suo 1999:320–2; Guangxi Zhuangzu zizhiqu bowuguan 1999:340–1). This distribution points to the importance of riverine and maritime routes of communication, including contact with regions north of Lingnan. It is worth noting that some of the larger cemeteries, such as Yinshanling 銀山嶺 in northern Guangxi and Duimianshan 對面山 in northern Guangdong, contain late Zhou period as well as Han graves, indicating local continuity over an extended period of time.

No comprehensive study of Han period graves in Lingnan has yet been conducted, although one report of 409 Han graves in Guangzhou published in 1981 provides relevant information on changes in funerary practice over time (Guangzhou shi wenwu guanli weiyuanhui and Guangdong sheng bowuguan 1981). This study, combined with knowledge of various published Han tombs in different parts of Lingnan, allows for the following general observations. With regard to tomb type, Western Han tombs are usually vertical pits, with wooden coffins (on occasion subdivided into sections) and ramps sometimes present, all elements found at that time in the graves of regions north of Lingnan. In contrast, features such as waist pits and pebble floors represent local traditions. By the Eastern Han period, an increasingly large proportion of burials are brick chambered tombs of the type found throughout much of Han China, some of these with multiple chambers. Early Western Han ceramic vessels include a number of local types as well as Han-style vessels, a distinction that disappears as later period graves begin to contain mostly northern types.

Beginning especially by the middle of the Western Han, other developments point to a continuing trend toward a funerary practice that is essentially Han in nature. At various points in this development, grave goods begin to include mirrors, censers, lacquered objects, human figurines, ceramic models of stoves, birds, domestic animals, animal pens, houses, granaries, as well as iron tools (Figure 11.2). As in other regions of Han China, some of these grave goods suggest a new focus on the representation at death of the productive and domestic sphere. By the Eastern Han period, Lingnan's funerary landscape thus consists mostly of brick tombs containing northern type grave assemblages.

The general trend toward homogenization should not conceal the fact that funerary practice and grave assemblages in Lingnan display not only some differences with metropolitan Han China to its north, but also variation within the region itself. For example, none of the Eastern Han tombs at Duimianshan are made of bricks or contain models of domestic animals or birds. More significantly perhaps, Han tombs in Guangdong have yielded various artifacts that point to the importance of contacts with areas south of Lingnan. These include ceramic models of pile dwellings, a building method still seen in southeast Asia; ceramic and wooden models of boats and larger ships, some with holding areas; and ceramic lamps whose container sits atop the head of a man with a naked torso and a long nose, features that suggest to some a birthplace in southeast Asia. The ships and the lamps are common finds in Guangzhou's Han period tombs. Artifacts that are likely to have been brought to Lingnan from distant regions include ivory, as well as beads made of glass, agate, and amber (Guangdong sheng wenwu kaogu yanjiu suo 1999: 321–2).

A few important tombs dating to the Nanyue period deserve special mention owing to their scale and usefulness in illustrating some of the trends discussed above. The first, located in Guangzhou city itself, is the tomb of Zhao Mo 趙眜 (Figure 11.3), the second king of the Nanyue kingdom. Over 17 meters long (including the ramp), the tomb was dug from the top of, as well as into, the hill. This, along with its partition into a number of chambers and the use of large stones to line the walls of the chambers, parallels similar but slightly earlier developments in funerary architecture in the north of China. Fifteen human sacrifices were found in the tomb, along with a total of over 1,000 objects, including various jades (the plaques of a funerary suit, a cup, discs, and figurines), gold and jade seals (revealing the identity of the tomb occupant), bronze bells, cooking and serving containers of various types, a silver vessel, and a glass plaque. Aside from the tomb layout itself, many objects and practices (e.g. the jade funerary suit) underscore the importance and impact of cultural links with regions north of Lingnan. In contrast, "Yue style" ding tripods and bronze buckets illustrate the maintenance of local or regional traditions, as do the continuing use of goudiao 勾鑃 bells and the funerary practice of human sacrifice, although the latter two features had in fact originated in regions north of Lingnan but had been abandoned there by then.

Significantly, the silver vessel, glass and ivory objects, and beads of various types indicate contact with distant regions (von Falkenhausen 2001:223–7; Guangzhou shi wenwu guanli weiyuanhui 1991; Guangdong sheng wenwu kaogu yanjiu suo

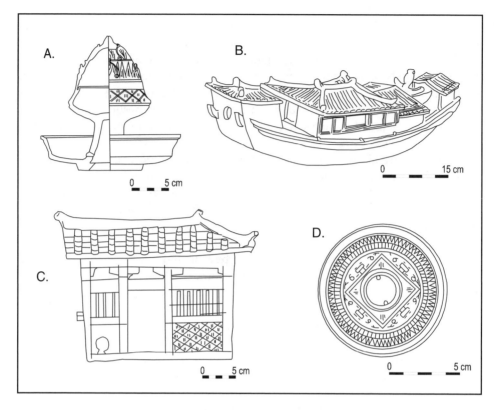

Figure 11.2 Artifacts excavated from various Eastern Han tombs in Guangdong province (A. ceramic censer; B. ceramic boat; C. ceramic house; D. bronze mirror)

1999:320–2). Two other large Nanyue period graves were found at Luobowan 羅泊灣 in southern Guangxi. Both of these were pit graves with a ramp and partitioned wooden coffins. Along with many grave goods reflecting the Sinicization of the region, a number of features at Luobowan illustrate the maintenance of local traditions, including various ceramic vessel types, bronze bells, a bronze drum and pail, as well as the practice of human sacrifice (Guangxi Zhuangzu zizhiqu bowuguan 1988).

Discussion

The archaeological record of Lingnan during the Han dynasty contrasts markedly with that of the previous period. Aside from more substantial settlement evidence, there is a significant increase in the number and average wealth of burials, as well as in the size of the largest burials. Han period graves are also more widely distributed throughout Lingnan. By the beginning of the Han period, the unmistak-

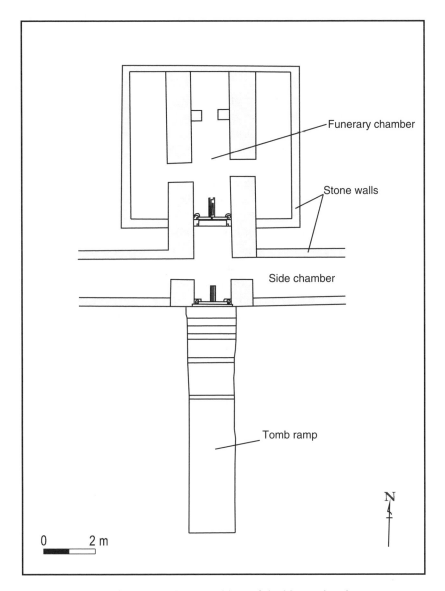

Figure 11.3 The tomb of Zhao Mo, the second king of the Nanyue kingdom

able reorientation taking place in political, economic, and cultural life is under-
scored by both historical and archaeological data, which in fact merge on a number
of fronts. For example, evidence for the historicity of Panyu, the Nanyue Kingdom,
Zhao Tuo, and Zhao Mo have all been located in Guangzhou itself, while inscriptions on tiles and other artifacts found at different locations in Lingnan correspond
to place names and titles mentioned in the texts. Some have suggested that the large
number of burnt artifacts found at the Nanyue Palace confirm a contemporary

textual entry recording its burning by Wu Di's troops. The distribution of graves is itself suggestive. Concentrations of burials are found in Guangzhou as well as along coastlines and major rivers, a distribution that is in accordance with historical references to trade, communication, and defense. Other concentrations occur along the coast in Hepu and Xuwen, both of these locations mentioned in texts as important Han period ports and producers of pearls.

Supported by artisans, architects, and other full- or part-time workers, the process of Sinicization witnessed in Lingnan over the course of the Han period is made evident by changes in funerary behavior, funerary architecture, types and styles of artifacts, as well as by an entirely new sense of aesthetic sensitivity expressed through architectural features such as gardens and ponds. It is interesting to note that, even as Zhao Tuo rebelled against Chinese authority, promoted local customs, and developed an interest in exotic goods from distant regions south of Lingnan, he appears to have in fact hastened the process of Sinicization through his implicit acknowledgment of China's cultural superiority, a fact made clear by the layout and contents of his descendant's tomb, as well as the architectural elements identified so far at the palace. In fact, one should not confuse the presence of exotic traded objects (e.g. glass and precious stones) or other artifacts deriving from local conditions (e.g. models of pile dwellings and boats) with a rejection of Han practices. More indicative of a fundamental change to a new – Chinese – way of thinking is the abandonment of human sacrifice as a funerary practice and the inclusion in graves of ceramic models that are representative of the importance, both in life and in death, of domestic and productive activities. Having said this, we must also recognize that there remains, within Lingnan itself, a certain amount of diversity, some of which may in fact reflect more deep-rooted cultural variation.

Yunnan

Historical sources

The second century B.C. witnessed the gradual but arduous expansion of the Han toward the southwest, a large region that the texts paint as distant, ethnically diverse, and militarily unstable. Textual references to this expansion all postdate the establishment of Han commanderies in the southwest during the second half of the second century B.C. (a chronology of relevant entries translated in English is available in Sun and Xiong 1983). Although not clearly stated in the texts themselves, the reasons for the push toward the present-day provinces of Guizhou 貴州 and Yunnan were certainly varied and included territorial ambitions as well as economic incentives. By the end of the fourth or the beginning of the third century B.C., we read of the Chu general Zhuang Qiao 莊蹻 conquering the tribe known as "Dian" 滇 in present-day eastern Yunnan (the Chu was at the time a powerful state of central China located within the Chinese geopolitical sphere). With his return to the Chu homeland blocked by the victorious Qin armies, Zhuang Qiao "went back and became King of Dian on the strength of his own troops. He changed his dress, adopted the local customs, and so acted as leader" (translation in Sun and Xiong 1983:244, original in Shiji "Account of the Southwestern Barbarians;" see also Allard 1998 for a discussion of the historical record pertaining to the Dian).

References to communication among southwestern tribes during the second century B.C. reveal Han knowledge of – and likely interest in – trading networks. Private trade appears to have linked various tribes of the southwest, including the Ba 巴, Shu 蜀 (both located in present-day Sichuan 四川 Province), and the Dian. At least in the case of the Ba and Shu, such trade involved horses, servants, and yaks. In an entry dated to 135 B.C., we read of the Chinese official Tang Meng 唐蒙 who while in Nanyue was offered citrus paste to eat, a product of Shu that was transported through the territory of Yelang 夜郎 (in present-day Guizhou) and along waterways all the way to its destination in Lingnan's Nanyue Kingdom. Such knowledge not only demonstrated the existence of long-distance communication and trade among the south and southwestern tribes, but also suggested how military campaigns aimed at pacifying the obstinate Nanyue could be conducted from the southwest, a route that would eliminate the difficult crossing of mountain ranges separating central China from the Nanyue while also permitting the recruitment of large numbers of willing warriors from Yelang (translation in Sun and Xiong 1983:245, original in Shiji "Account of the Southwestern Barbarians").

Another passage, this one dated to 122 B.C., reports on the plight of Han envoys who attempted to cross Dian territory in search of an overland trade route to Bactria (a Greek kingdom of the pre-Christian era with its capital in present-day Afghanistan) through India. Detained by the Dian for over one year while Dian scouts were sent ahead to locate such a route – which was found, but blocked by another tribe – the envoys returned to the Han capital, reporting that "Dian is a large state and ought to be bound by closer ties to China. The emperor gave the matter careful consideration" (translation in Watson 1961:294, original in Shiji "Account of the Southwestern Barbarians").

All but surrounded by Han commanderies by the end of the second century B.C., the Dian finally succumbed to a Han military expedition in 109 B.C. – a few years only after the incorporation of the Nanyue Kingdom into the Han empire – at which time the new commandery of Yizhou 益州 was established (see Figure 11.1). At the time of conquest, it is recorded that "the King of Dian had an army number-ing tens of thousands" (translation in Sun and Xiong 1983:246, original in Shiji "Account of the Southwestern Barbarians"). The Dian are also said to have had towns and settlements, with the political center located where the capital of the post-conquest Yizhou commandery was established, in other words close to Lake Dian. It is likely that the commandery incorporated within its territory not only those areas controlled by the Dian, but also the territories of weaker tribes to the Dian's west and south. In general, however, the Han commanderies were organized to reflect the extent of the pre-conquest tribal territories (translation and discus-sion of relevant passages are provided in Tong 1991). The cultural heterogeneity of Yizhou commandery is evident from the texts, which speak of numerous ethnic groups that varied with regard to customs and subsistence activities. The Dian, said to be settled agriculturalists who practiced animal husbandry "wear their hair in the mallet-shaped fashion," while other tribes, located to their west, "braid their hair and move from place to place with their herds of domestic animals, having no fixed homes and no chieftains. Their lands measure several thousand li square" (translation in Watson 1961:290, original in Shiji "Account of the Southwestern Barbarians"). Unfortunately, the texts are mute regarding the social and political organization of the Dian or of the region's other tribes.

Although centrally appointed officials might be present in the commanderies, throughout much of the southwest the Han ruled indirectly through native leaders whose passivity, allegiance, and tribute paid to the court were rewarded with gifts and symbols of authority (such as royal seals) bestowed by the Han. Such indirect rule, which was believed to be the most efficient and least costly method of expanding the empire's territory in such distant regions, reflects a lack of interest on the part of the Han in native life and society, itself illustrated by an absence of textual references regarding such topics. The Shiji records that following the Dian's defeat at the hands of the Han, "because the king of Dian had originally been friendly toward the Han, they were ordered not to execute him . . . he was presented with the seals of the king of Dian and restored to the position of leader of the people" (translation in Watson 1961:296, original in Shiji "Account of the Southwestern Barbarians"). However, the title was eliminated during the reign of Zhao Di 昭帝 (87–84 B.C.) following a rebellion.

Indirect rule through native leaders did succeed in creating an administrative base whose objectives included the establishment of constituent prefectures and the documentation of native population numbers. For example, an entry dated to 109 B.C. records that the newly formed Yizhou Commandery consisted of 24 named prefectures and included 81,946 households and 580,463 inhabitants (Sun and Xiong 1983:247). The administrative reorganization and the recording of precise population numbers in the census, both of whose success depended on the participation of the native leadership, suggest an interest in taxing the native population, who were required to pay their taxes in grain, salt, or a range of other products, depending on the natural resources available in each person's respective region. Yizhou's many attractions are mentioned in one passage in the Hou Han Shu 後漢書, which refers to the region's broad and level plains, exotic birds, fishponds, gold and silver, adding that although "the customs of the people are fierce . . . Han officials who live there become rich" (translation in Xiong 1983:14).

Yizhou's many attractions and economic potential cannot conceal the fact that it remained throughout the Han dynasty a frontier area marked by instability and danger. The texts mention at least seven major native uprisings between 105 B.C. and A.D. 176 in the commandery alone, some of these leading to the death of the governor. For example, an entry dated to 82 B.C. recounts a revolt in Yizhou that involved "beheading or taking prisoner more than 50,000 [native inhabitants] and capturing more than 100,000 head of livestock" (translation in Sun and Xiong 1983:247, original in Han Shu 漢書 "Account of the Southwestern Barbarians"). Even if these numbers are inflated, such accounts point to the shortcomings of a system marked by an absence of a sufficiently large Han presence to control discontented native inhabitants or conflicts among the region's many tribes. Time and time again, we read of military expeditions sent by the Han to quell the uprisings.

The apparent successes of these punitive campaigns is counterbalanced by the frequent recorded debates among Han officials regarding the wisdom of establishing permanent rule in a region whose remoteness and mountainous topography made it difficult to maintain effective communication.

A passage dated to A.D. 84–87 hints at the temporary easing of tensions in Yizhou and the tenacity of Dian customs even after 200 years of rule: "When Wang Fu of Shu Commandery was Governor of Yizhou, his civilizing rule was particularly outstanding. . . . Only now did literary studies prosper and gradually the barbarian customs were changed" (translation in Sun and Xiong 1983:251, original in Huayang Guozhi 華陽國志 "Record of Nanzhong"). While we may question the objectivity of the statement and whether civilizing impulses were at the root of the Han presence in the southwest, the texts do provide evidence for an expansion of Han influence along the southwestern periphery. A number of entries dating to the Eastern Han do in fact speak of tribes living beyond the borders of present-day China who wished to be recognized as tributary states and who were ready to offer the Han gifts of ivory, water buffalos, gold, or yak-hair tassels. Whether driven by hopes of the economic benefits of future trade or fear of Han military occupation, such overtures do not necessarily reflect a respect for Chinese civilization. In the end, neither seals nor bolts of silks offered to native leaders as rewards for support of the Han was sufficient to counterbalance the instability of the system.

The archaeological record

At the time of the Qin's defeat and the establishment of the Han dynasty in China during the late third century B.C., much of eastern Yunnan was inhabited by indigenous peoples belonging to what archaeologists have named "Dian culture," an archaeological culture well known for its wealthy vertical pit burials and strikingly distinctive bronzes (for summaries in Chinese of Dian archaeology, see Yunnan sheng bowuguan 1990:277–9 and Yunnan sheng wenwu kaogu yanjiu suo 1999:405–9; accounts in English include Allard 1999, Higham 1996:142–73, and Rawson 1983). Much of the fieldwork on the Dian has been conducted in the Dian Lake area, where most of the burial grounds and wealthiest graves have been found. The two best-known and wealthiest cemeteries in this central area are Shizhaishan 石寨山 and Lijiashan 李家山. Along the so-called periphery of Dian culture, smaller cemeteries, such as those at Batatai 八塔台 and Pujuhe 普車河, consist of generally poorer burials, although these too have yielded Dian-type material. In part resulting from so much attention being paid to Dian graves, a significant lacuna in Dian archaeology remains the limited amount of available habitation data, which has been located at a few sites in the Dian Lake area but which has yet to provide much useful information to our study of Dian society.

As defined by Chinese archaeologists, Dian culture spans all of the Western Han period and extends to the early Eastern Han. An understanding of the impact of the Chinese conquest of Yunnan in 109 B.C. should therefore consider changes in funerary behavior over the course of the period covered by the Western Han. Although the chronology is still being debated, it is possible to detect general developmental patterns that are relevant to the topic at hand. By the beginning of the Western Han period, wealthy Dian grave assemblages consist mainly of a range of ceramic vessels and bronze objects, the latter of which include a variety of tools and weapons, small figurines, pieces of armor, buckle ornaments, plaques (some displaying "animal combat" scenes), vessels, as well as the well known drums (decorated with various scenes), and impressive cowry shell containers (some decorated with realistic scenes executed in the round).

Although all of these objects are identified as Dian, it is also clear that some (such as weapons and vessels) share generalized features with other parts of China, including central and northern Chinese traditions. There is also evidence of the Dian's likely adoption of Chinese iron and lacquer techniques prior to the Han conquest, knowledge of which could have diffused from China proper through intermediate populations or been carried to Yunnan by merchants and/or adventurers. What the broad chronology makes less clear is whether actual Chinese objects such as mirrors and coins did reach the Dian area prior to 109 B.C. Nevertheless, there is no doubt that the Han conquest was associated with an increase in the number of Chinese artifacts – or copies of such artifacts – in some of the wealthy Dian graves. Along with the above-mentioned mirrors and coins, these include a jade funerary suit, certain types of bronze vessels, and seals (e.g. burial no. 6 at Shizhaishan contained a gold seal whose inscription reads "Seal of the King of Dian"). Therefore, we note the fact that following the Han conquest in 109 B.C., the last century or so of the Western Han period witnessed the inclusion of Han artifacts in funerary contexts that remained fundamentally Dian in nature.

By the early Eastern Han period, however, funerary behavior appears to have witnessed a relatively rapid transition to grave assemblages that consist mostly – or even entirely – of types of artifacts typical of the Eastern Han in other parts of China. These include mirrors, coins, various ceramic and bronze vessels, bronze censers, lamps, as well as ceramic models of humans and of scenes or objects associated with domestic and productive activities (e.g. stoves, cultivation fields, domestic animals and birds, dwellings, and storehouses). The Eastern Han grave assemblages are usually associated with Han-style brick tombs, which come to replace the vertical pit tombs of Dian culture in eastern Yunnan, although some of the latest pit graves (for example at Yangfutou 羊甫頭) have also been found to contain such assemblages. The Eastern Han brick tombs are typically covered by a tall – as much as ten meter high – earthen mound that is typical of the region and are sometimes associated with an inscribed stone stele, the latter suggesting that the tomb owner was Chinese. The interior of these mounded tombs also displays some amount of variation. In the earliest examples, the mound covers a vertical pit grave, while the middle and later portions of the Eastern Han period are characterized by chambered interiors and ramps, features that are clearly derived from funerary practice in metropolitan China. By the late 1990s, more than 400 mounded brick tombs had been identified at a total of 71 burial grounds in eastern, northeastern, central, and western Yunnan (Yunnan sheng wenwu kaogu yanjiu suo 1999:408–9). In the Zhaotong 昭通 area of northeastern Yunnan, a large number of such tombs have been found, although Eastern Han chambered tombs in that area were also sometimes carved into cliff faces. Although their grave assemblages were very similar to those of mounded brick tombs, these cliff burials further support the image of variation in funerary practice during the Eastern Han period.

Discussion

The historical and archaeological records of Yunnan during the Han dynasty merge and complement one another to provide a somewhat consistent – albeit incomplete – picture of the impact of the Han presence on indigenous society. It is interesting to note that, although the historical sources pertaining to Lingnan and Yunnan appear to point to generally similar processes and outcomes in both regions (e.g. indirect rule, economic incentives, native uprisings, civilizing policies, instability), archaeology suggests somewhat different trajectories along the road to increasing homogenization and Sinicization over the course of the Han period. In contrast to Lingnan, where these processes are in evidence even before the Han takeover, Dian-style burials remain in evidence for at least one century after the Han conquest. Thus, we must be careful not to overestimate the impact of acculturation on Yunnan's native leaders, since the wealthy Dian graves contain Chinese artifacts that supplement what continue to be essentially Dian assemblages, while the presence of bronze drums and cowry shell containers suggest the maintenance of traditional belief systems. Because Chinese officials are likely to have preferred a Han-style burial, it is probable that these wealthy Dian graves were those of native leaders who could have profited from the Han policy of indirect rule by associating with Han officials and acting as intermediaries to their own people. The elimination of the rank and position of king by the Han a few decades following the conquest does not necessarily indicate an abandonment of the system of indirect rule, since some of the burials could be those of lower level native leaders.

Although we witness by the end of the Eastern Han period greater homogeneity in funerary behavior, the maintenance of practices such as vertical pit and cliff burials – even as these contain Eastern Han assemblages – illustrates, for some time at least, some adherence to traditional ways. Thus, for all of these reasons – the maintenance of traditional burial customs during the Western Han and an uneven transition to Han funerary behavior during the Eastern Han – we may suggest that the process of Sinicization in Yunnan, at least as witnessed in the burial evidence, followed a more halting path than that in Lingnan. To be sure, although such a contrast may account for what archaeology has revealed so far, it is clear that the identification and recovery of additional settlement and burial data in the future may force us to revisit such views.

Han China's southern peripheries: issues of culture, control, and stability

Whatever its blend of motives and the many reversals it encountered, the expansionist policy adopted and forcefully executed by Han Wu Di carried the Chinese people of central and northern China to what could only then be described as distant lands peopled by natives with unusual customs. It is worth noting a few features of this expansion. First, the size of the Han Empire surpasses even that of the Roman Empire and compares favorably with the empires of the Achaemenid and Alexander the Great. Over the course of much of the Western and Eastern Han dynasty, the Han emperors were able to maintain the geographic integrity of an empire that included portions of Korea and Vietnam, territories separated by over 2,500 kilometers and that are located outside China's present-day borders. Second, China is unusual among world nations in that many of its modern border regions were first reached and administered over 2,000 years ago. Thus, even though the past two millennia have witnessed the periodic partitioning of China's territory, many peripheral regions have been reintegrated in the country's administrative structure once the political and military conditions permitted it. This is certainly true of the south and southwest regions, of which only Vietnam has been lost since the Han dynasty.

The long-term success of China's imperial policies should not conceal the reality of expansionist failures over the shorter term. In fact, one significant feature of the Chinese presence in both Lingnan and Yunnan during the Han period appears to be the apparent inability of centrally appointed officials to establish stable long-term relations with native populations. The histories of both regions speak of regular uprisings and of debates at court regarding the soundness of occupying such distant regions. The cultural landscape remains fragmented and populated by various unassimilated ethnic groups, some of whom at times battle one another and on other occasions inflict losses on the Chinese. How can we explain the fate of successive Chinese administrations along the southern peripheries during the Han dynasty? We begin by noting that the demographics of the occupation never favored the Han Chinese, who were outnumbered by the native inhabitants and whose troops were unable to maintain a firm grip on the many scattered groups living throughout the mountainous landscapes of Lingnan and Yunnan. Although China's expansion toward the south and southwest may have been initially driven by territorial ambitions and economic motives rather than by a zeal aimed at civilizing the distant barbarians, the need to tax and pacify local populations apparently led, after some time, to efforts at making them more "Chinese" through education. Viewed together, the texts suggest that this policy in both Lingnan and Yunnan was at best only partially successful.

In the long run, a successful imperial policy relies not on coercion but rather on the efficacious economic and cultural integration of the native population into the imperial polity, a process that discourages dissidence and thus permits the continued exploitation of such a population. Knowing that continued military pressure on local groups was in any case not successful as a long-term strategy in either Lingnan or Yunnan, we are therefore left asking whether a failure of integration can help explain the instability of these imperial peripheries. What can archaeology contribute to an understanding of the issue of integration? Is there any evidence that a substantial sector of native society reaped the benefits of the Chinese presence?

It is clear that some kings and tribal chiefs in both Lingnan and Yunnan profited from their association with Han officials. However, did such benefits filter down to the lower strata of society?

The burial evidence helps illustrate the Han advance into Lingnan and Yunnan, as well as the processes of cultural homogenization and Sinicization associated with such advance in both regions. However, the picture painted of a region-wide solidarity and common sense of purpose may be misleading. In fact, the absence of detailed comprehensive studies of Han period tombs along the southern and southwestern peripheries precludes the identification of clear spatial and temporal patterning, information that is itself necessary in any attempt to understand how native society was structured and how it changed over time through the period of Chinese occupation. Nevertheless, the available data does permit us to address different relevant scenarios, all of which, it is suggested, support a model of economic and cultural dislocation between commoners on the one hand, and the Chinese and their native agents on the other. The first scenario proposes that the tombs of commoners are seriously underrepresented because of their archaeological near invisibility, as would result, for example, from their small size, the absence of a coffin, and/or a limited number of grave goods. The fact that many large areas in Lingnan and Yunnan have yielded few or no Han-period tombs supports the idea that large segments of the population were buried in a manner that left few traces, which itself helps draw a clear contrast between commoners and the native elite. The second scenario proposes that the tombs identified so far did contain the remains of people representing different sectors of native society. Here again, the evidence points to societal dislocation, since the grave contents of the many poorer burials found to date appear to discount the presence of a redistributive market or prestige-good economy that benefited all sectors of society. A lack of access to the benefits of trade and the Han presence could only have exacerbated emerging feelings of cultural dislocation, as when Han prestige goods began to supplement the grave assemblages of Dian leaders.

Although ideology may sometimes serve as an effective integrating device, the survival of varied ethnic identities along China's southern and southwestern peripheries until today suggests that customs and beliefs divided, rather than united, the many different Chinese and indigenous sectors of the population living there. In this light, we may wonder whether Zhao Tuo's apparently stable rule among Lingnan's many indigenous peoples cannot in part be explained by his insistence on adopting and promoting local customs, as well as his forging among all inhabitants a sense of common identity that opposed Nanyue culture to that of the Chinese to the north. At the very least, we may conclude that any study of the impact of imperial policy on border populations must not only recognize that different segments of society may experience such policies in dramatically different ways, but also that such distinctions do in fact help explain the long-term fate of such policies.

The root of often dramatic instances of culture change in the ancient world, imperial expansion holds undeniable appeal for archaeologists and historians. Initial enthusiasm for scenarios of swift military takeover, effective political restructuring and the subjugation of native inhabitants is now giving way to more nuanced models that recognize a wide range of possible imperial strategies and native responses, as well as spatial and temporal patterning in a process of integration that impacts in different ways on different sectors of society (Parker 2003:525–6, 552–3; Sinopoli 2001). The case of China, with its textual record indicating imperial ambitions and successes, is one such example that points to a highly complex and variable process. In reality, the limitations of both the textual and archaeological – particularly the settlement – records pertaining to the southern expansion of the Han open the door to various scenarios that we are unable to evaluate at present. For example, a lack of knowledge of settlement patterns certainly precludes a real understanding of how native populations were integrated and taxed, although places such as the Nanyue palace and the Han capital of Yizhou indicate the imposition of a visible and some-times effective foreign presence in the native sociopolitical landscape. Furthermore, there is no indication that Han imperial policy did not sometimes encourage the maintenance of a highly dissected ethnic landscape whose divided loyalties posed little threat to the imperial presence. The fact that native uprisings did on occasion manage to shake its foundations does not of course deny the actuality of such a divide-and-conquer policy at various times.

If the analysis presented in this chapter examines the short-term consequences of imperial policies that failed to conquer and effectively integrate the native pop-ulation, the reality is that the imperial periphery became, in the long run, a part of the Chinese state. The rapid growth and decline that is typical of empires through-out history clearly does not apply to southern China's long-term trajectory. Although the early stages of imperial expansion may not result in a stable imperial periphery that effectively manages the cultural diversity which it is forced to deal with, it sets the stage for events and circumstances that can lead to the more gradual cultural and economic integration of the native population, whether such events are rebellions against the occupier or trade links among former adversaries.

Empires do not vanish in thin air following defeat and dissolution. They leave in their former colonial territories an indelible mark that is witnessed in shared cul-tural values between former occupied and occupier and that may lead, in later mil-itary attempts at conquest, to greater success in expanding the empire through the more effective economic integration of different sectors of society. Why this hap-pened in China over the course of two thousand years – and not in other empires, and often gradually and with many reversals of fortune – is difficult to explain, but we may point to a possible coming together of varied conditions, including the appeals of Chinese material culture, as well as a continued highly dissected ethnic landscape which rarely overcame deep seated divisions to maintain a long-term effective military defense and offense. In the end, the imposition of centralized rule combined with the movement of larger numbers of Han peoples to the southern periphery to provide more opportunities at effective integration. Although we witness in Yunnan and Lingnan a process of imperial integration proceeding at dif-ferent rates over the course of the Han dynasty, the ultimate fate of both regions was in the end similar.

REFERENCES

Allard, Francis 1994 Social Complexity and Interaction in Lingnan During the First Millennium B.C. Asian Perspectives 33:309–26.

—— 1997 Growth and Stability Among Complex Societies in Prehistoric Lingnan, Southeast China. Papers from the Institute of Archaeology 8:37–58.

—— 1998 Stirrings at the Periphery: History, Archaeology and the Study of Dian. International Journal of Historical Archaeology 2:321–41.

—— 1999 The Archaeology of Dian: Trends and Tradition. Antiquity 73(279):77–85.

Falkenhausen, Lothar von 2001 The Use and Significance of Ritual Bronzes in the Lingnan Region During the Eastern Zhou Period. Journal of East Asian Archaeology 3(1–2): 193–236.

Gernet, Jacques 1982 A History of Chinese Civilization. Cambridge: Cambridge University Press.

Guangdong sheng bowuguan 1990 Guangdong Kaogu Shi Nian Gaishu (A brief account of ten years of archaeology in Guangdong). In Wenwu Kaogu Gongzuo Shi Nian 1979–89 (Ten years of archaeological work 1979–89). Wenwu Bianji Weiyuanhui, ed. Pp. 217–28. Beijing: Wenwu Chubanshe.

Guangdong sheng wenwu kaogu yanjiu suo 1991 Guangdong Wuhua Xian Shixiongshan Handai Jianzhu Yizhi (Han Dynasty architectural remains at the site of Shixiongshan, Wuhua County, Guangdong). Wenwu 11:27–37.

—— 1999 Guangdong Sheng Kaogu Wushi Nian (Fifty years of archaeology in Guangdong). In Xin Zhongguo Kaogu Wushi Nian (Fifty years of archaeology in China). Wenwu Chubanshe, ed. Pp. 312–29. Beijing: Wenwu Chubanshe.

Guangdong sheng wenwu kaogu yanjiu suo, Shantou shi wenwu guanli weiyuanhui, and Chenghai shi bowuguan 1997 Chenghai Guishan Handai Yizhi (The Han Dynasty site of Guishan in Chenghai). Guangzhou: Guangdong Renmin Chubanshe.

Guangxi Zhuangzu zizhiqu bowuguan 1988 Guangxi Guixian Luobowan Han mu (The Han Dynasty tombs at Luobowan, Guixian, Guangxi). Beijing: Wenwu Chubanshe.

—— 1999 Guangxi Zhuangzu Zizhiqu Kaogu Wushi Nian (Fifty years of archaeology in Guangxi). In Xin Zhongguo Kaogu Wushi Nian (Fifty years of archaeology in China). Wenwu Chubanshe, ed. Pp. 330–46. Beijing: Wenwu Chubanshe.

Guangzhou shi wenwu guanli weiyuanhui 1991 Xi Han Nanyue wangmu (The Western Han tomb of the king of Nanyue). 2 vols. Beijing: Wenwu Chubanshe.

Guangzhou shi wenwu guanli weiyuanhui, and Guangdong sheng bowuguan 1981 Guangzhou Han Mu (Han Dynasty tombs in Guangzhou). 2 vols. Beijing: Wenwu Chubanshe.

Higham, Charles 1996 The Bronze Age of Southeast Asia. Cambridge: Cambridge University Press.

Parker, Bradley J. 2003 Archaeological Manifestations of Empire: Assyria's Imprint on Southeastern Anatolia. American Journal of Archaeology 107:525–57.

Rawson, Jessica, ed. 1983 The Chinese Bronzes of Yunnan. London: Sidgwick and Jackson in association with Beijing: The Cultural Relics Publishing House.

Sinopoli, Carla M. 2001 Imperial Integration and Imperial Subjects. In Empires: Perspectives from Archaeology and History. Susan A. Alcock, Terence N. D'Altroy, Kathleen D. Morrison, and Carla M. Sinopoli, eds. Pp. 195–200. Cambridge: Cambridge University Press.

Sun, Taichu, and Xiong Xi 1983 Chronology. In The Chinese Bronzes of Yunnan. Jessica

Rawson, ed. Pp. 243–52. London: Sidgwick and Jackson in association with Beijing: The Cultural Relics Publishing House.

Tong, Enzhen 1991 Chiefdoms in Southwest China: The Dian Culture as an Example. Paper presented at the conference High Bronze Age of Southeast China and South China, Hua Hin (Thailand), January.

Wang, Gungwu 1959 The Nanhai Trade. Journal of the Malayan Branch of the Royal Asiatic Society 31, part 2 (182).

Watson, Burton 1961 Records of the Grand Historian of China: Translations from the Shih Chi of Ssu-ma Ch'ien. New York: Columbia University Press.

Wiens, Herold J. 1954 China's March Toward the Tropics. Hamden CT: The Shoe String Press.

Xiong, Taichu 1983 Preface to the Chinese Edition. In The Chinese Bronzes of Yunnan. Jessica Rawson, ed. Pp. 12–18. London: Sidgwick and Jackson in association with Beijing: The Cultural Relics Publishing House.

Yu, Ying-shih 1986 Han Foreign Relations. In The Cambridge History of China. Volume 1: The Ch'in and Han Empires, 221 B.C.–A.D. 220. Denis Twitchett and Michael Loewe, eds. Pp. 377–462. Cambridge: Cambridge University Press.

Yunnan sheng bowuguan 1990 Shi Nian Lai Yunnan Wenwu Kaogu Xin Faxian Ji Yanjiu (New discoveries and research in archaeology in Yunnan over the past 10 years). In Wenwu Kaogu Gongzuo Shi Nian 1979–89 (Ten years of archaeological work 1979–89). Wenwu bianji weiyuanhui, ed. Pp. 272–82. Beijing: Wenwu Chubanshe.

Yunnan sheng wenwu kaogu yanjiu suo 1999 Yunnan Sheng Wenwu Kaogu Wushi Nian (Fifty years of archaeology in Yunnan Province). In Xin Zhongguo Kaogu Wushi Nian (Fifty years of archaeology in China). Wenwu Chubanshe, ed. Pp. 401–14. Beijing: Wenwu Chubanshe.

12

States on Horseback: The Rise of Inner Asian Confederations and Empires

William Honeychurch and Chunag Amartuvshin

Genghis Khan, founder of the largest contiguous land empire ever known, was once thought to have said that an empire can be conquered on horseback, but cannot be ruled from horseback. This would have been a surprising statement for a leader who ruled both a steppe polity and a growing empire entirely from horseback and very much in control of the territories coming under sway of the 13th century medieval Mongols. Upon his death in 1227, the sons and grandsons of Genghis Khan pursued the expansion and consolidation of an empire that eventually stretched across Eurasia from the coasts of China to the fringes of Eastern Europe. Mongol warriors set out to do battle with Japanese samurai on one side of the earth and Egyptian Mamluk slave armies and Polish armored knights on the other. Ruling such an expanse from horseback or otherwise would have been difficult and perhaps for that very reason, the Mongol Empire was one of the larger and shorter-lived empires known to historians. By 1260, succession disputes and rivalry between the descendants of Genghis Khan led to withdrawal from a unified imperial structure along the lines of regional successor states such as the Golden Horde of Russia, the Il-Khanate of the Middle East, and the Yuan dynasty of China.

The sheer immensity of the Mongol empire is worth pondering to investigate questions that have beset scholars of empire since the dissolution of Mongol Eurasia. Simply put, how and why did a relatively small group of nomads from the Eurasian steppe manage to conquer much of the contemporary known world? Was this, as some have argued, an historical accident in which Mongol armies consistently encountered weakened or declining states as they advanced? Was their rapid territorial expansion simply the result of superior military capabilities that nomadic peoples brought to the field? If military conquest was the specialty of the Mongols, what political, economic, and cultural infrastructure was devised to articulate and consolidate conquered regions? To what degree was the construction of the empire based on pre-existing organization and institutions among incorporated states and

what, if any, were the contributions of steppe traditions in which the Mongols originally constituted themselves as a political and economic force?

Such questions echo those asked of other pre-modern imperial states, and
because the medieval Mongols had a very different background as mobile agro-
pastoralists, a better understanding of their empire and its political traditions
promises an important comparative perspective. If indeed imperialism is an organizational approach to the management and exploitation of diversity, as Thomas
Barfield has suggested (2001a:29), then understanding how spatially extensive
steppe polities integrated different cultural, linguistic, and economic groups should
help to answer the questions posed above. In this chapter, we examine explanations
for the emergence of steppe polities and the expansive empires that followed in their
wake using two archaeological case studies: the development of the Xiongnu confederation at the end of the first millennium B.C. and the rise of the medieval
Mongol empire during the 13th century A.D. Our discussion raises three topics that
help to contextualize steppe imperialism within the broader study of imperial states:
(a) alternative approaches to political control made possible by mobility, transport,
and long-distance communication; (b) interrelations between imperial polities over
time in the form of traditions of statecraft and political ideology; and (c) amalgamation of diverse political models as an important aspect of organizational growth
within an expanding imperial polity.

Geography and Culture of the Northeastern Steppe

Inner Asia, Central Asia, the Central Eurasian steppe, and a patchwork of alternative labels have been used to describe the swath of heartland stretching between
Europe and Asia. As the Greek historian, Herodotus, pointed out over 2,400 years
ago, this region is distinguished by broad expanses of grasslands and by the nomadic
peoples who live there, driving their herds on horseback. On the other side of
Eurasia, a Chinese historian writing at the end of the first millennium B.C. described
these steppe peoples as those who ". . . move about in search of water and pasture
and have no walled cities or fixed dwellings" (Watson 1993:129). While these two
early reports seem to be describing the same region and similar groups of people,
the steppe zone has had a greater diversity of environments and cultures than was
usually recognized by the historians of sedentary civilizations. The eastern end of
the steppe zone comprises the territories of Mongolia, South Siberia, and Inner
Mongolia which form the core areas of development for the steppe polities
described in this chapter (Figure 12.1). The region contains a wide variety of steppe
vegetation, lake and river systems, mountains and deserts, distributed across the
high Mongolian plateau.

North of the central steppe region of Mongolia are the forest-steppes of southern Siberia extending up along the Selenge River to the shores of Lake Baikal. We
discuss archaeological sites in the Buriat Republic (Buriatiia) of South Siberia
(Figure 12.2) which has a landscape of forested mountains interspersed with steppe
valleys and is commonly referred to in Russian as *Zabaikal'e*. Far to the south is

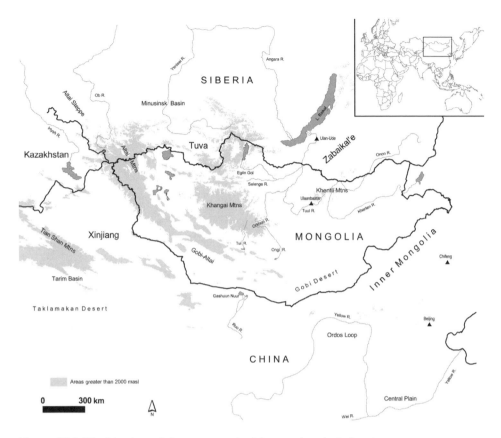

Figure 12.1 The Northeast Asian steppe and adjacent archaeological regions

Inner Mongolia, containing stretches of the Gobi desert in the west and low mountains and rolling steppe lands stretching east and northeast. The archaeology of
Inner Mongolia has been studied independently from that of Mongolia and Siberia
and the relationships between these areas, especially during the earliest periods, are
still unclear, but nevertheless essential to understanding steppe development, especially in relation to early state processes in northern China.

Surrounding Mongolia, Zabaikal'e, and Inner Mongolia are regions that share
in the long history of steppe political formations. These include the grassland fringes
of eastern Kazakhstan, the Russian Altai mountains, the Sayan mountain-steppe
and upper Yenisei river of Tuva, and the far eastern forest zone of Manchuria. Southwest of Mongolia is the Tarim basin of Xinjiang province where the Tian-shan
mountains slope down to meet the arid Taklamakan sand desert. It is through this
formidable region of small oasis polities that the most famous sections of the Silk
Road caravan route once passed over 2,000 years ago. The final region of importance for our discussion of steppe societies is north central China, or what is often
called *Zhongyuan*, the Chinese "Central Plain." The Central Plain region comprises

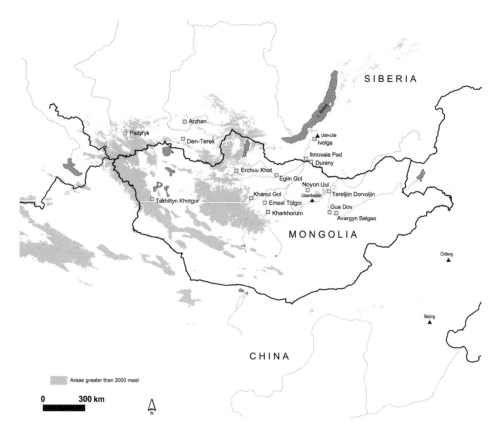

Figure 12.2 Archaeological sites of the Northeast Asian steppe

the low mountain chains, fertile loess valleys, and major river courses of the Yellow and Wei rivers that make up the heartland of ancient China's agricultural and urban core.

The historical geographer, Owen Lattimore, once described the Inner Asian frontier between the early states of China and the nomadic confederations of Mongolia as, ". . . one of the most absolute frontiers in the history of the world" (Lattimore 1992[1940]:21). For Lattimore, this frontier was as much socio-cultural as political and it marked the division between pastoral nomadic and sedentary, agricultural societies, often referred to as the opposition of "the steppe and the sown." The socio-cultural adaptation to grassland environments involving spatial management of animals constitutes a highly specialized body of knowledge. Mobile herding developed over thousands of years beginning with the initial use of animal species in food-producing economies, followed by an increasing dependence on varieties of herd animals. The conditions that favored this long-term trend across the western, central, and eastern Eurasian steppe were in many cases variable compositions of environmental, social, and political factors occurring at different times.

Groups dispersed across the diverse ecological zones of Mongolia, South Siberia, and Inner Mongolia adopted higher degrees of mobility and livestock dependence through different processes. By the third millennium B.C., the northeastern steppe was already characterized by a great deal of diversity in subsistence production. The range of subsistence pursuits at this time included small-scale mixed economies with agricultural production and specialized hunting, groups with broad spectrum hunting–gathering and fishing economies, and still other groups inhabiting fully sedentary villages with developed agriculture and animal husbandry (Novgorodova 1989:56–9; Shelach 1999:73–87; Weber et al. 2002).

During much of the second and early first millenniums B.C., domestic herd animals became a staple subsistence resource across the northeast Asian steppe. This gradual transformation involved not only increased pastoralism and mobility, but also investment in more diverse techniques for animal exploitation, including dairying, traction, riding, and more specialized uses of animal resources such as wool and hides. The material evidence for more mobile forms of herding are: (a) the occurrence of particular species compositions, especially combinations of small stock (sheep, goats) and horses; (b) household mobility and seasonal campsite use showing little structural investment in habitation locales; and (c) technologies related to pastoral production and horseback riding.

The presence of horses is of particular importance to arguments for the emergence of mobile pastoralism on the northeastern steppe. Horses are a source of meat and dairy products, but also facilitate mobile forms of herding through horseback riding and traction. Furthermore, the grazing patterns of horse herds complement and facilitate those of smaller stock in two important ways. Horses normally consume the upper portions of grasses leaving the lower stems that smaller stock favor. Horses also locate and uncover pasture beneath accumulated snow that makes winter grasses accessible for sheep and goats. Since late winter and early spring are the seasons of greatest productive risk on the northeastern steppe, this complementary relationship between horses and small stock sustains herd numbers and increases carrying capacity overall.

In the forest-steppe zone extending southwards from Lake Baikal and into central Mongolia, excavations at large-scale, ceremonial monuments known as *khirigsuurs* suggest evidence for increased domesticated horse use. Khirigsuur stone mounds usually have rectangular or circular stone enclosures around them, as well as smaller stone heaps beyond their enclosures in the form of "satellite" features. These smaller stone mounds sometimes contain domesticated horse crania and vertebrae and occasional fragments of ceramics or bronze items (Erdenebaatar 2002:213; Tsybiktarov 1998:140). The central mounds of khirigsuurs may also contain faunal fragments of domestic herd animals; however, the chronological range of artifacts retrieved from these contexts suggests that the intrusion of later materials from episodes of re-use is problematic. Recent radiocarbon dates on horse bone and charcoal samples excavated from undisturbed satellite features have dated to the middle of the second and beginning of the first millennium B.C.

We should emphasize that increased animal dependency and mobility did not entail an abandonment of other productive strategies like hunting, gathering, and fishing (Volkov 1967:93). Despite some arguments that late Bronze and early Iron Age groups across the Eurasian steppe rapidly adopted a highly specialized form of horse nomadism, the most recent archaeological research argues for long-term change and geographical diversity in subsistence mixtures of agriculture, pastoralism, and hunting–gathering and fishing. The occurrence of higher stock dependency probably did not result in a "pure" pastoral nomadism; rather, the peoples of the northeastern steppe seem to have maintained a tradition of multi-resource pastoralism which included the flexibility to emphasize or de-emphasize subsistence pursuits relative to local environmental, social, and political conditions.

By the late Bronze and early Iron Age (eighth century B.C.) archaeological cultures of the northeastern steppe having multiple lines of evidence for mobile pastoralism, a particular weapon or tool set, and decorative craft goods with "animal style" designs, are often described as "Early Nomadic" cultures by Russian and Mongolian archaeologists. This period is associated with increasingly asymmetric political and economic relationships. Differentiated mortuary assemblages and the elaborate monumentality of burial construction at sites such as Arzhan and Pazyryk lead many researchers to conclude that during the early to mid first millennium B.C., northeastern steppe societies were organized as small-scale groups having hereditary transfer of status and elite control over labor and resources (Griaznov 1980; Hiebert 1992). Archaeologists working on the Upper Xiajiadian societies of eastern Inner Mongolia (early first millennium B.C.) have also found that greater mobility and emphasis on herd animal production was accompanied by more pronounced marking of individual political status (Shelach 1999:173–6).

By the end of the first millennium B.C., these distinctive small-scale societies scattered across the northeastern steppe transformed into a novel organizational form by way of sociopolitical processes that are still poorly understood. From 200 B.C. onwards, what are described in the Chinese historical records as large-scale, hierarchically organized, and integrated polities of pastoral peoples, or "states on horseback," become the defining feature of steppe history. The rise and fall of these polities was closely observed by Chinese writers from whom we have a detailed textual record of individual leaders, tribute negotiations, and warfare. Systematic archaeological study has provided an independent record of material evidence that, when combined with the indigenous and external historical records, makes up an impressive body of information for understanding early steppe polities and later empires. The chronological periods for northeastern steppe archaeology are listed in Table 12.1, according to the names of the major centralized polities that occupied and controlled the core territory of Mongolia (Tseveendorj et al. 2003).

Models for Steppe Polities

Steppe polities emerged under conditions characterized by agro-pastoral economics, mobile and dispersed populations, and marginal environments, all features commonly associated with more egalitarian groups. Understanding the political technologies through which such societies were constructed, financed, and stabi-

Table 12.1. Chronology of steppe polities

Xiongnu	3rd century B.C. to 2nd century A.D.
Turk	6th–8th centuries A.D.
Uighur	8th–9th centuries A.D.
Khitan	10th–12th centuries A.D.
Mongol	13th–14th centuries A.D.
Manchu/Buddhist	17th–early 20th centuries A.D.

lized helps anthropologists to more fully understand the range of variability and points of structural difference between societies considered to be "complex." The political approaches of steppe leaders had to overcome a variety of problems including that of economic support, since pastoral production tends to be unstable over time and has low surplus yield (Khazanov 1994). Perhaps even more challenging was the problem of integrating, centralizing, and maintaining a political organization across a population that was decidedly centrifugal in character. Broadly dispersed resource zones and mobile groups that were ethnically and linguistically differentiated as well as militarily capable of resistance made factionalization a threat to any centralized authority and a major source of instability for large-scale integration (Fletcher 1986).

In order to explain how large-scale and highly organized confederations and empires arose on the steppe, a variety of models have been suggested and supported using mainly historical evidence. Many current models of steppe political organization share the proposition that nomadic polities emerged through forms of economic and political dependence on the Chinese states to the south (Barfield 2001a; Kradin 2002). The core–periphery framework employed by these models predicates much of the change that occurred in peripheral regions on processes operating within a mature state. In the case of steppe societies, such models suggest that the low productivity of pastoral nomadism required steppe groups to obtain agricultural products and finished goods from the neighboring Chinese states through border trade. When strong, centralized administration emerged in China in the form of a new dynasty, border trade was often curtailed by the state elite in an attempt to control resources and exchange. Steppe groups therefore organized large-scale, weakly integrated military confederations to coerce and negotiate subsidies from the Chinese state. The organizational structure of the steppe polity was therefore organized for the purpose of external interactions, but internally it was decentralized, consensual, and loosely structured.

A second approach to explaining steppe polities challenges the core–periphery model and instead attributes the development of steppe polities to actions taken by and among steppe groups themselves. Regions adjacent to mature states, in this case, are viewed as agentive and actively define the conditions and processes of interregional interaction (Stein 2002). The key factors in this model are regional social disruption brought about by internal or external events, military consolidation around a charismatic leader and the structuring of an elite hierarchical core, followed by rapid military expansion and the mobilization of political finance combining tribute, taxation, and trade revenue (Di Cosmo 2002). According to this model, the steppe economy is diverse and self-sufficient, but incapable of supporting a large-scale political organization without external income. These polities therefore seek access to sources of political finance through interregional interaction, often encompassing immense territories and maintaining far-flung relationships.

While both models make valid points for understanding steppe polity consolidation, for the purpose of a comparative discussion of steppe empires, two valuable insights have emerged from the various competing explanations. First is the recognition that the steppe cultural emphasis on mobility and the technologies of horse riding and horse-based warfare provided steppe peoples with experience in organizing activities, resources, and peoples over substantial spatial distances (Barfield 2001b). This body of experience facilitated long-distance interactions and exchange and most importantly, promoted approaches for effectively managing diverse peoples, languages, and cultures. By developing the ability to effectively project their spatial reach, steppe groups already had in place strategies for controlling the logistics and diversity that are characteristic of many large-scale imperial polities. Such experience is often lacking in smaller, more insular states without developed transport technologies.

A second point is the importance of diachronic political traditions among steppe groups that created organizational continuities between different confederations and empires. These have been described as "traditionary" institutions and represent the long-term repertoire of techniques by which steppe polities were organized and financed and which were passed down, selected, employed differentially, and elaborated over successive periods of regional organization (Di Cosmo 1999). It was this developing body of statecraft and the political legitimacy endowed by invoking such a tradition that allowed for more centralized and integrated steppe polities over time, despite the centrifugal character of what were mobile and dispersed agro-pastoral populations. We now turn to the archaeology of the steppe to examine these two points further and to suggest ways that an understanding of steppe empires clarifies general processes of political growth and consolidation over large-scale territories.

The Archaeology of the Xiongnu Period

The Xiongnu polity is the prototypical example of regional political organization on the northeastern steppe. The Xiongnu was a mounted, nomadic group contemporary with the Qin (221–07 B.C.), Western Han (202 B.C.–A.D. 8), and Eastern Han (A.D. 25–220) dynasties of China and commonly thought of as the group against which the early Qin portions of the Great Wall were erected. As with many steppe peoples, the historical reputation of the early Xiongnu is primarily associated with the destruction and havoc they instigated along the Chinese frontier. The Xiongnu polity is historically dated from 209 B.C. to A.D. 93 inclusive of several major political and territorial transformations. At their height, the Xiongnu are reported to have directly or indirectly controlled territory from Manchuria to Kazakhstan, from southern Siberia to Inner Mongolia, and the Tarim Basin states of southeastern Central Asia (present-day Xinjiang). Chinese historical accounts from the *Shiji* and the *Han shu* have been the major sources of information concerning the society, culture, and politics of the Xiongnu, though the origins and development of this group remain obscure.

The political organization of the regional polity is reported in the histories as based upon a decimal system of administrative–military units. The decimal system is described in the *Shiji* (Watson 1993:163) as predicated on the number of warriors a leader could call up for battle. Positions included leaders of 10 warriors, 100, 1,000, et cetera, and this leadership hierarchy extended over the spatial area containing the number of families needed to contribute the requisite number of horsemen. During the Xiongnu period it is not entirely clear the degree to which these positions represented both military and administrative responsibilities, nor how closely or directly tied they were to higher levels of leadership. The administrative weight of these positions has been a major point of contention in the on-going debate over the nature of "statehood" among the Xiongnu. Based upon historical accounts, positions within the upper levels of the decimal system intersected with the elite hierarchy of the central court. These positions were filled by members of the royal clans or by members of the immediate family of the polity leader, known as the *Shanyu*. This uppermost hierarchy was also geographically divided into a central, a far eastern, and a far western section, the latter two of which were known as the "left" and "right" kingships respectively. Typically, the Shanyu and the royal court controlled the central district directly while the left and right kingship positions were appointed to sons or brothers of the Shanyu.

The process of matching groups mentioned in historical texts to material cultures is hardly ever straightforward; however, a good case has been made, based on geographical, chronological, and descriptive features, for a "Xiongnu" material culture distributed over much of South Siberia, Mongolia, and Inner Mongolia (Dorjsuren 1961; Rudenko 1962; Wu 1990). The association of a specific archaeological culture with the historical Xiongnu polity was first proposed towards the end of the 19th century based upon the burial excavations of Tal'ko-Gryntsevich in the Zabaikal'e region of Siberia. In the 1920s, mortuary research carried out by the Kozlov expedition at the Noyon Uul (Noin Ula) cemetery of central Mongolia and by G. P. Sosnovskii at Il'movaia Pad of Zabaikal'e helped to strengthen the hypothesis that a specific set of well-documented burial types and their associated material culture could be related to the Xiongnu nomads of the Chinese histories (Konovalov 1976; Rudenko 1962:6). Later excavations at walled settlement sites by Davydova in Siberia (1995) and Perlee in Mongolia (1961:17–39) recovered artifacts similar to those known from Xiongnu burial grounds and began to add a much needed settlement perspective for this period.

Problems with translation, communication, and travel between Russia, Mongolia, and Inner Mongolia have hampered efforts to share ideas and data on Xiongnu archaeology, though understanding the early sociopolitical dynamics across this broad and differentiated area is essential. Consistency in the material culture of the

Xiongnu period exists across southern Siberia and Mongolia and to a lesser degree in the regions of Inner Mongolia and northern China (Wu 1990). Such geographical variation is interesting and one major task facing archaeologists on both sides of the Gobi desert is to discover developmentally significant links between the Xiongnu archaeological evidence as known from Inner Mongolia and the substantial Xiongnu material culture of Mongolia and Zabaikal'e. We focus mainly on sites in Mongolia and South Siberia that represent elite mortuary practices, large-scale settlement, and local spatial patterns during the Xiongnu period.

Mortuary research is a major part of Xiongnu archaeology and the evidence assembled over the past 100 years provides an image of Xiongnu society as having a sophisticated social hierarchy. Patterns of differentiation in mortuary treatment reveal that interment of political elite involved massive labor expenditures, large-scale ritual activities, the deposition of local and long-distance prestige objects, and probably human sacrifice. By far the best-known Xiongnu mortuary sites are those containing the elite burial mounds that were first discovered and excavated at the Mongolian cemetery of Noyon Uul in the 1920s (Dorjsuren 1961; Rudenko 1962). Noyon Uul is located in a region well known for gold deposits, and exploration by Russian mining concerns first brought the burial ground to the attention of archaeologists. The site is dispersed among the three valleys of Sujigt, Khujirt, and Zuramt that are inter-connected by passes and extend along the upper reaches of mountain ridges approximately 80 kilometers northwest of Ulaanbaatar. The contemporary environment at Noyon Uul consists of low lying steppe valleys with agricultural fields and upper mountain slopes that are forested with larch, pines, and birch, and natural springs that water the main Sujigt valley. Burial features totaling 212 have been located in eight locations and include both large aristocratic mounds as well as smaller ring-shaped stone features marking the more common Xiongnu interments. In the surrounding area, cemeteries of the preceding Bronze and Early Iron Age have been recorded as well as a settlement 45 kilometers to the west of Noyon Uul with evidence for ceramic workshops dated to the Xiongnu period.

The elite burial mounds recorded at this site are oriented north–south and have associated clusters of common burials around them. The elite burial surface constructions consist of a low rectangular or slightly trapezoidal earth and stone mound ranging in dimension from approximately 16 to 22.5 meters on a side with a height of 0.5 to 1.95 meters above the modern surface. On the south side there often appears a sloping entryway as much as 22 meters in length that accesses the central burial chamber. The burial pits of these tombs reach 10 meters or more in depth and the construction work overlying the chamber consists of soil, stone, and wood layers. The burial chamber itself includes an inner and outer wooden construction of hewn logs and wooden planks usually made of larch (*Larix sibericus*). Within the innermost chamber, a wooden coffin holding the interred individual is sometimes found, though disruption from pillaging has often destroyed the internal contexts of these sites (Dorjsuren 1961:24–40). The Noyon Uul burials were pillaged in antiquity, though remaining organic materials were extraordinarily well preserved by the anaerobic conditions caused by water seepage into burial chambers. The artifact assemblage from Noyon Uul is the best example so far recovered of the diverse material culture of the Xiongnu elite. These tombs were richly furnished with large ceramic vessels, felt and woven carpets, silks, jade items, bronze mirrors, and Chinese lacquer ware. A wide range of horse-related equipment was also recovered, as was faunal evidence for cattle, Bactrian camel, deer, and quantities of domestic grain.

The burial assemblage provides evidence that long-distance contacts were oriented not only towards the Chinese states to the south but also included significant relationships with groups far to the west. Chinese goods were sent to the Xiongnu elite in the form of tribute payments from the rulers of the Han dynasty and Chinese goods appear in a wide range of elite and intermediate elite mortuary and settlement contexts. However, material and textual evidence suggest that the Chinese state was only one flank of a spatial network of exchange and tribute developed by the Xiongnu elite (Barfield 2001b). Analyses of bronze artifacts as well as stylistic and weave studies of tapestry fragments recovered from Noyon Uul suggest a Bactrian origin in Central Asia. This material evidence is matched by the identification of beads, glass, and semi-precious stones chemically provenanced to the western regions of Central Asia, recovered from common Xiongnu burials at the Ivolga cemetery.

Elite mortuary treatment differs significantly from the smaller ring-shaped burials which also have structural variations associated with differences in social status. The Noyon Uul cemetery is only one location in the northeastern steppe at which elite burial mounds of the Xiongnu appear. Elite cemeteries that have recently been studied include the Tsaram burial site near the border town of Kiakhta in South Siberia, sites in the Khanui Gol basin of central Mongolia, and Takhiltyn Khotgor in the far western Altai Mountains. Monumental sites occur less often in the western and eastern provinces of Mongolia and have not been discovered in Inner Mongolia. Such elite contexts provide insight into steppe social organization and imply a high degree of social differentiation within the mature Xiongnu polity and elite control of human and material resources. Perhaps the clearest evidence for both extreme differences in status and degree of elite control has recently been exposed by excavations at the Tsaram cemetery. To the south of a massive elite burial (number seven) eight smaller ring-shaped burials were studied and found to contain the skeletons of individual males arranged north to south according to their age at the time of death, suggesting to the excavators a potential pattern of human sacrifice (Miniaev and Sakharovskaia 2002).

The mortuary record of the Xiongnu period argues for a society in which the political leadership had a higher degree of authority and more sophisticated external contacts than predicted by some models. Likewise, archaeological evidence for fully sedentary, agricultural settlements from the Xiongnu period on the Ivolga river just south of Lake Baikal suggests that economic production within the Xiongnu polity was more complex and differentiated than might be expected. The Ivolga site is located on a terrace above an older course of the Selenge river in the forest-steppe environment of southern Buriatiia, only 16 kilometers from the modern city of Ulan-Ude. Excavated intermittently since 1928 and intensively from 1950 to the 1980s, this settlement is the most comprehensively studied Xiongnu site in the steppe region (Davydova 1995).

The settlement has a series of four earthen ramparts alternating with three ditches and a wooden stockade on the north, west, and south sides, enclosing an area of 7.5 hectares. Internal to the surrounding wall and ditch system is a series of low rises that were discovered to be the remains of dwellings. The site has a smaller enclosure immediately to the south and a large Xiongnu period cemetery to the north. Broad horizontal excavation units were used to expose a sample of 7,000 square meters in the interior of the settlement in order to explore the habitation structures and their spatial arrangement. These were discovered to be semi-subterranean dwellings of which 51 were excavated and studied. The pit houses consisted of an oblong or rectangular pit probably covered by a pitched roof supported by wooden posts and having a sophisticated fireplace system with heating flues. Many structures have connecting pen areas probably for domestic animals during the winter months. Some dwellings differ dramatically from others in terms of size, artifact assemblage, and design that may have been related to the differential status of the occupants (Davydova 1995:17). Excavations recovered an extensive artifact assemblage providing chronological evidence that the settlement was occupied from the third to first centuries B.C. Fire eventually consumed the settlement under conditions about which we know very little, but potentially related to a hostile local setting which would also explain the need for fortifications.

Ivolga economic activities are particularly important for assessing models of steppe organization and interregional interaction. Ivolga inhabitants cultivated and stored grain (millet, barley, wheat), they engaged in iron and bronze metallurgy, and they manufactured ceramics locally (Davydova 1995:43–6). Agriculture was practiced in conjunction with livestock herding of sheep, horse, cattle, camel, and yak. According to Davydova, the comprehensive evidence from Ivolga for developed agriculture and craft production within the Xiongnu territory suggests a radically different model of political economy. Based on the perspective from Ivolga, the Xiongnu polity may have been organized around a complex and differentiated regional economy with internal exchange or redistribution of a variety of subsistence and craft resources supported by a system of sedentary centers and mobile groups. In support of this hypothesis, other Xiongnu settlement sites in Buriatiia, such as that of Dureny I and II, have produced similar evidence for diversified productive capabilities. There is also evidence for the internal transport of ceramics between Xiongnu population centers in Buriatiia and the Russian Altai based on chemical composition analysis of ceramic samples for five different sites, including Ivolga.

Several walled Xiongnu period settlements are also known from Mongolia, such as the sites of Gua Dov and Tereljiin Dorvoljin. The Mongolian archaeologist, Perlee, conducted a countrywide survey of settlements in the 1950s and lists nine walled sites that are of the Xiongnu period, most of which are dated on the basis of diagnostic ceramics (Perlee 1961). These sites have earthen rectangular ramparts enclosing areas ranging in size from 2 to 13 hectares with traces of internal structures, surface scatters of artifacts including fired clay roof tiles, and occasional cemetery sites located nearby. Previously unknown Xiongnu walled sites are still being discovered and reported in Mongolian archaeological journals, such as the

three walled settlements found in the vicinity of the Emeel Tolgoi Xiongnu cemetery of west central Mongolia in 2001.

Xiongnu walled settlements in Mongolia are still little studied beyond size estimates and chronological designation based on surface collections and some test
excavations. However, the presence of such sites lends support to Davydova's argument for a more complex form of regional political economy involving mobile and
sedentary sectors. Based on the material evidence at hand, a revised model for the
Xiongnu economy suggests that when organized at the level of a regional polity,
steppe peoples practiced multiple and diverse forms of economic production,
mobility, and sedentism. Recent research on the Wusun period (contemporary with
the Xiongnu) in southeastern Kazakhstan supports this view. Wusun period deposits
at the habitation site of Tuzusai on the Talgar plain show a shift in the relative mix
of agro-pastoral investment towards a greater emphasis on agriculture. Excavations
at the site produced features containing phytolith silicates of agricultural plants
including millet, wheat, and even rice. This period of more intensive agricultural
production was not only the result of change in climatic conditions towards a
warmer and more humid environment, but was likely related to processes of political consolidation and the need to control critical resources such as grain production (Rosen et al. 2000).

Archaeological evidence has expanded the historical understanding of regional
steppe economic systems, but the question of internal political organization has also
come under scrutiny, particularly with respect to centralized integration among
steppe groups. The dominant view argues that the local political unit is stable and
confederates with other units in a modular fashion without a great deal of internal
transformation. Our final Xiongnu archaeological example provides a measure of
the stability of a given local area as political changes occurred at the regional scale.
A survey of the Egiin Gol valley in the forest steppe zone of northern Mongolia
recovered settlement and surface feature distributions for the late Bronze and early
Iron Age and the Xiongnu period. Spatial data for these two phases at Egiin Gol
allow us to compare continuities and differences in landscape organization in
order to assess how this particular local area was integrated into the first regional
steppe polity and whether stability or reorganization characterized that process
(Honeychurch and Amartuvshin 2003).

An examination of site patterns for the two periods reveals that a substantial restructuring did in fact take place over time. First, the Xiongnu period at Egiin Gol
shows a different locational pattern from that of the preceding phase. The most dramatic transformation is a shift of the majority of habitation and mortuary sites from
the upper tributary valleys to locations in the main Egiin Gol valley. Associated with
this shift in location is a five-fold increase in the mean size of habitation sites, from
0.25 hectares during the early Iron Age to 1.47 hectares in the Xiongnu period. In
addition, the size distribution of habitations greatly expands to include three distinct tiers with the largest site in the valley measuring slightly greater than four
hectares. Furthermore, the locations of the top tier settlements during the Xiongnu
period occurred along major pathways of movement through the valley suggesting a strategy of spatial control on mobility. These patterns represent the kinds of

change we might expect from either the destabilization of the local elite or the promotion of a single elite segment over others to facilitate more centralized control of an area within a regional integrative framework. This study, along with the Ivolga and other settlement data, suggests that the Xiongnu polity was founded on a more developed system of statecraft than is generally supposed. Given the long-term stability of this first polity, the Xiongnu political system seems to have been quite adept at integrating and managing mobile and dispersed populations.

The principal archaeological sites discussed above provide evidence for substantial status differentiation between the Xiongnu elite and commoners, interregional contacts that are multi-lateral involving trade and tribute extraction, a complex and differentiated economic system involving mobile and sedentary sectors, and centralized integration of local areas with an emphasis on spatial strategies of control. These characteristics are indicative of an independent tradition of complex regional organization that emerged within a particular social and environmental setting and which addressed organizational problems inherent to steppe conditions. The Xiongnu polity may not be considered an empire per se (Barfield 2001a:28), but it was certainly a spatially extensive organization that incorporated significant diversity within its territory. As the first regional steppe polity, the Xiongnu devised a series of political emphases and techniques that would eventually serve as a foundation for the later medieval Mongolian imperial state. In order to better understand the transmission of this political tradition over time we turn to an examination of Mongol medieval period archaeology, dating approximately one thousand years after the rise of the Xiongnu.

Archaeology of the Mongol Empire

Between the years A.D. 1206 and 1368, the Old World was shaken by the conquests and empire building of the medieval Mongols. A review of the archaeology of the empire could conceivably cover China, the Middle East, Central Asia, and much of Russia, however for the questions we attempt to answer, the perspective from the core polity of the empire, the steppe polity, is most important. Was the Mongolian medieval empire the culmination of a long tradition of statecraft and military technique passed down from the time of the Xiongnu and subsequent polities, or was the emergent empire an aberration in which the military prowess of steppe peoples far outpaced their administrative and political capabilities? Different conceptions of what a steppe polity was and how such polities related to their sedentary neighbors give contrasting answers to this question. Research on imperial states in other parts of the world has directed attention to the logistical and ideological reorganization that imperial core regions undergo in support of large-scale expansions. The Mongolian empire has often been explained as a protracted military foray that met with outstanding success in conquest but achieved little in terms of political restructuring and consolidation. This has been attributed to a lack of administrative tradition in steppe politics and the basic incompatibilities between large-scale nomadic organizations and sedentary states founded on intensive agriculture and taxation.

According to this view, the steppe region was a resource deprived and underdeveloped imperial core that rapidly became peripheral as major sedentary territories were incorporated. Other scholars view the steppe region as having experienced complex transformations during the rise and expansion of the Mongol polity involving both organizational precedent and innovation.

The imperial period begins with the emergence of a Mongol-led steppe polity consolidated in A.D. 1206, when the victorious steppe leader, Temujin, was renamed Genghis Khan. External expansion proceeded rapidly once the steppe was united and the Eurasian empire emerged within a time span almost too brief for the range of chronological control in most archaeological contexts. Knowledge of the imperial steppe region is growing, but research on the Mongolian empire is still biased toward historical records from conquered regions. A small number of indigenous historical texts, such as the *Secret History of the Mongols* (Cleaves 1982), a few travel reports (Dawson 1980), and medieval inscriptions discovered on the territory of Mongolia provide important textual information about conditions within the imperial heartland. To characterize the period's archaeology we describe research results from three major settlement sites: Avargyn Balgas in northeastern Mongolia; the medieval capital city of Kharkhorum in central Mongolia; and a garrisoned outpost in Tuva. We then consider mortuary evidence for the Mongol period from the Egiin Gol valley to explore the kinds of local changes that this world empire produced for steppe inhabitants.

The site of Avargyn Balgas is located in the northeastern Gurvan Gol or Three Rivers region of Khentii province, Mongolia. The region is historically important and still revered today as the homeland of Genghis Khan and the Mongol royal lineage. The settlement is located on an open plain northwest of the Avarga river and was excavated in the 1960s and more recently by a Mongolian–Japanese archaeological team (Shiraishi et al. 2001). The total extent of the site occupies an area of 4.5 square kilometers with a 60 hectare area containing evidence for extensive architecture including building foundations, fired clay roof tiles, tiled floors, and roadways. To the north of the architectural areas, earthworks and canal systems are present. The largest building foundation is surrounded by double walls and is located on top of an earthen platform that has proven to be the remains of an earlier foundation. This large, central building is described as a palace or ceremonial temple while the group of ruins to the east of the central building is believed to be elite residences.

Other sectors of the settlement were used for economic activities and an associated Mongol period cemetery lies 20 kilometers to the northwest. These may well be burials of intermediate elite within the core polity structure, though none as of yet have been excavated and studied. Field investigations at Avargyn Balgas have yielded a wide range of glazed and earthenware ceramics, coins, iron working debris, evidence for extensive agricultural production, and a faunal assemblage primarily characterized by cattle, horse, sheep, and goat. Numismatic evidence and radiocarbon dating suggest the site was in use from the end of the 12th through the 14th century A.D. References in the historical documents of the Mongol dynasty of China, the Yuan (A.D. 1260–368), indicate that the site was probably one of the earliest settlements constructed by the medieval Mongols and contained the main palace of Genghis Khan, known as Ikh Ord.

Avargyn Balgas is therefore an important example of early Mongol infrastructure and investment in the political and economic consolidation of the steppe-imperial polity. Excavations at Avargyn Balgas in 2003 have provided evidence for changes in the faunal composition of the site over time, from a subsistence-based assemblage to one comprised mostly of specific horse bones known to have had ritual significance. This preliminary pattern suggests to the excavators a potential shift in the function of the site from an administrative center to what later became a ceremonial center; perhaps for periodically consolidating the factions that comprised the imperial elite (Kato et al. 2004:10). If so, this material evidence would correspond nicely to the historical reports which describe Mongolian khans making ritual offerings annually at important sites within their ancestral homeland. Such activities in the Mongol place of origin suggest the importance of exercising control over groups that were able to mount political challenges to an increasingly distant central authority. Similar practices were in use by the leadership of the early medieval Turk polity 600 years prior to the rise of the Mongols and very likely these represent a continuing steppe tradition of political technique (Allsen 1996:129).

A further example of Mongol utilization of past political traditions was the process of selecting the site of the imperial capital. While Avargyn Balgas functioned as an effective center early on, as the steppe polity grew rapidly to immense size through successful military campaigns, a more central area of administration was required. Genghis Khan's original decision to create an imperial capital in the Orkhon river valley of central Mongolia had both ideological and functional implications for the creation and maintenance of the expanding empire. The Orkhon valley had been the site of major Turkic political monuments and the site of the Uighur capital city, Ordu Balik. Constructing the Mongol capital in this location therefore appropriated the traditional authority associated with these polities. Geographically, Kharkhorum's location also provided access to key trade routes between south-central and northern Mongolia and between eastern and western Mongolia. Finally, the two river systems that represent the southernmost extensions of surface water into the Gobi desert, the Ongi and Tui rivers, have their headwaters in the mountains above the Orkhon valley. Both rivers are jump-off points to southern trade routes, one of which passes through the Gashuun Nuur corridor and into China. Kharkhorum therefore controlled several major routes of long-distance and large-scale movement across the northeastern steppe and represented a highly functional point of spatial control relative to the larger steppe region.

Following the Yuan dynasty's decline in China (A.D. 1368), Kharkhorum became the center of the Mongol Yuan elite who fled Dadu (Beijing). The following 100 years saw the city sacked a number of times in conflicts with the Ming dynasty of China and during periods of internecine warfare between steppe rivals. In 1585 building materials were scavenged from the city precincts in order to construct the Lamaist monastery of Erdene Zuu that now occupies the southern end of the site. The ruins of Kharkhorum were first mapped in the 19th century and again in the mid 20th century and two modern mapping projects were undertaken in the 1990s.

Excavations at the city center by Russian, Mongolian, and German archaeologists have been undertaken intermittently since 1949, and have concentrated on the city's agricultural system and the palace structures.

The city's period of major construction dates from A.D. 1220 to 1260 and included the erection of a semi-rectangular, pounded-earth wall that is now much deteriorated but once may have stood as high as five to eight meters (Roth and Erdenebat 2002:34–5). The perimeter of the wall encloses an area of approximately 10 hectares, and two main avenues divide the city into four sections. Most architectural remains of Kharkhorum cluster around the two main roads with the imperial palace located in the southwest section of the city. Beyond the wall, two cemeteries have been discovered to the southwest and northwest with evidence for burial practices from diverse parts of the empire. Specialized sub-districts of the city have been identified that include craft specialist enclaves and administrative offices, and artifact finds have included objects from regions stretching across Central Asia and as far away as North Africa.

While some researchers have considered Kharkhorum to be a low-infrastructure, non-productive, and dependent center, archaeologists have argued to the contrary that the unprecedented investment in infrastructure and large population residing at the city required massive transport of resources from multiple regions of the steppe core and beyond (Kiselev 1965:180; Kyzlasov 1969:159). As an imperial capital Kharkhorum was well positioned to integrate the various economic and strategic outlying regions of the empire; not only because of its location along major travel routes and between the resource zones of Siberia and China, but also due to the great ideological significance of its geography. The positioning, arrangement, and function of the capital city shows concern for balancing the requirements of steppe politics with the dynamics of a far-flung imperial system. Striking this balance properly was a matter of great concern to the Mongol elite and is revealed, for example, in the Mongol approach to urbanism. While the plan of Kharkhorum drew upon sedentary models for urban and administrative centers, the steppe elite used their capitals as tethering points for mobile courts. The circulation of elite leadership around an urban center allowed direct monitoring of the urban hinterland and was a strategic practice in use as early as the Xiongnu period. Such practices reflect an approach to centralized space that exploits the fluid and mobile setting in which steppe politics were conducted while maintaining an imperial city that was indeed the center of the medieval world.

While the city of Kharkhorum is a relatively well-studied urban site of the Mongol period, there are numerous urban sites distributed along medieval trade routes and major river valleys across central and eastern Mongolia and southern Siberia. Some are elite seasonal palaces, such as Erchuu Khot in Khovsgol province of northwestern Mongolia where an inscribed stele associates the site with Monkh Khan (A.D. 1251–9) (Perlee 1961:104–5). Such secondary and tertiary walled centers have been reported, but most have not been thoroughly studied by archaeologists. One important exception is the medieval period settlements of Tuva, where the organizational reach of the emerging Mongol empire has been analyzed at six urban sites, of which Den-Terek is one of main outposts.

From his extensive excavations at Den-Terek, Kyzlasov (1969:159) explains the appearance of large urban centers in Tuva as garrisoned colonies meant to secure resources for transport back to the Mongol imperial elite. These colonies both stabilized the northern frontier of the Mongol core polity and engaged in intensive agriculture, mining, and specialized craft production for re-circulation back to Mongolia. The site of Den-Terek is located on an island system in the Elegest river covering an area of 30 hectares and having a number of low mounds which when excavated revealed the stone foundations of dwellings. There are 120 such mounds at the site though the recovery of some wooden foundations suggests there were probably more buildings originally. Excavations in 1956 and 1957 revealed evidence for intensive agriculture involving large-scale horse drawn millstones, canal systems, and remains of wheat, barley, and millet. Craft production at the site took the form of specialized iron working, stone carving, and textile production (Kiselev 1965:118). Herding was also practiced, evidenced by finds of cattle, horse, camel, sheep/goat, in addition to a number of local wild species. Kyzlasov (1969:169) argues that Den-Terek was probably the main administrative center of the Tuvan region and may have been an important point on the massive trade networks that linked the Mongol center to the northwest Altai and the Yenisei river basin.

The urban sites of the imperial period provide an image of the steppe core as having substantial organizational and administrative investment. In short, the steppe was indeed transformed and restructured as a sociopolitical landscape by the formation of the Mongolian empire, but what of local areas and the herders that made up the majority population of the core polity? The mortuary sites of medieval period commoners have received substantial attention from archaeologists and are easily recognized by their distinctive surface features found across the territory of Mongolia and southern Siberia. Mongol burials typically have slightly mounded, oval shaped, stone features made up of medium sized local stones, oriented north–south or northeast–southwest, and are almost always located on moderate slopes in small enclosed valleys or on the banks of erosion cuts. One of the most thoroughly studied samples of these features comes from the Egiin Gol valley where 28 burials of the medieval Mongol period have been excavated from among 110 burials discovered by systematic survey (Torbat et al. 2003). Nine radiocarbon dates have been published on samples from among these excavated mortuary contexts supporting their periodization.

Below the stone surface features, the Egiin Gol burials consist of an earthen pit of between 0.45 and 1.4 meters in depth and having an interred supine individual placed in a birch bark wrapping, a wooden coffin, or a stone sided pit. Associated mortuary materials include iron scissors, knives, and arrow points, small ceramic vessels, birch bark containers and arrow quivers, stone beads, earrings, and bones from sheep, goat, and deer. Non-local artifacts were very few in number and consisted of cowry shells, Chinese-style bronze mirrors, and a few exotic bead types. The Egiin Gol Mongol period burial sample shows a decided lack of distinction between individual interments (Torbat et al. 2003:128, 131). The absence of burial differentiation in the valley during the imperial period is also reflected in the small number of external luxury or status items with the exception of the few instances noted above, none of which appear in especially large or elaborate burial contexts. The spatial distribution of burials during the imperial period is dispersed instead of consolidated and the majority of burials are grouped into small clusters of two or three with a maximal group of 18 burials. The Mongol burial distribution at Egiin Gol is difficult to describe as a cemetery pattern and shows little emphasis on spatial marking within the valley. This suggests a less formal process of burial area selection, probably involving small-scale family groups instead of larger corporate group participation.

Historical sources mention the forest steppe zone in which Egiin Gol is situated as critical to the support of Mongol expansion due to its agricultural resources, but expansion to the north in the form of trade, agricultural, and specialized craft settlements was dependent on the maintenance of networks of movement that may have regularly traversed intermediate areas like Egiin Gol (Kyzlasov 1969:138, 169). The valley, therefore, may have been organized in relation to a larger administrative unit that shifted the effective scale of organization to a level far above a single valley. This might explain the lack of differentiation among burials, especially in contrast to the differentiated and spatially consolidated Xiongnu cemetery patterns in the valley. A shift in organizational scale is one major difference between Xiongnu and Mongol integration at Egiin Gol and is evidenced by the extent of organizational investment observable within the valley during the Xiongnu period and the complete lack of such investment in evidence during the Mongol period.

The historical sources for the Mongol empire are so extensive it is not often the case that archaeological data enters into discussions of imperial organization or development. Just as in the case of the Xiongnu, however, the agendas of those writing histories must be taken into account, even in the case of indigenous texts. The bulk of records related to the Mongol expansion outward from the northeastern steppe were recorded by the historians of vanquished states, many of whom had little appreciation of the Mongolian background nor a favorable predisposition toward the intrusive nomadic elite. The archaeology of the steppe during the imperial period provides a more balanced impression of events there, indicating that the steppe region was not a passive or isolated "backwater" but rather a region organized as an expansive steppe polity that later transformed into the heartland of a Eurasian empire.

The archaeological examples of urban centers that we have discussed show a pattern of strategic consideration for the growth of a large-scale polity, including attention to sub-regional factionalism, control of long distance movement, ideological legitimation related to former empires, and organized resource extraction from distant territories. From the medieval mortuary data we infer not only the diversity of populations and traditions evident from the cemeteries near the medieval capital, but also a level of differentiation between commoner and aristocracy that is no longer detectable at the local sub-region, such as the Egiin Gol valley. These are patterns that are in part, unique to the Mongol polity but that also arise from the long tradition of steppe polities, from the Xiongnu onward, whose legacy the imperial Mongols inherited and expanded upon.

Conclusions

The medieval Mongols succeeded in uniting a substantial geographical area that included diverse linguistic and cultural groups having a variety of economic practices and distinctive political traditions. Our discussion of steppe archaeology highlights some of the unique characteristics of the Xiongnu and Mongol polities and of the steppe political tradition in general, but also reveals variables that are useful for comparing different large-scale, imperial organizations. These include the degree to which imperial polities effectively balance spatial expansion and internal consolidation and the ways in which political techniques are received and processed with attention to prior imperial traditions and the political models of groups integrated within the expanding empire.

In the first case, one of the distinctive practices of the steppe approach to empire is an innovative use of space, mobility, transport, and communication. As our discussion of the Xiongnu record demonstrates, spatial strategies for political control were both a fundamental part of maintaining a steppe polity in the face of factional challenge and necessary for accessing distant sources of political income, whether through exchange, tribute, or plunder. As a steppe polity expanded through military conquest, the importance of long distance interactions had to be balanced by internal, local, and small-scale political organization in order to support and effectively channel spatial investment. Very often these strategies were opportunistic instead of comprehensive and included tactics as simple as controlling primary and secondary pathways of movement across the landscape. In other cases, strategies were subtler, such as the tendency for steppe elite to be mobile across their administrative territories, even when sophisticated urban centers had been constructed. Elite mobility is a practice found in other imperial states and in the steppe context it provided one way of monitoring and controlling a population that had the ability to move out from under elite authority.

While the logistics of maintaining organization over great distances is a major challenge for most empires having sedentary traditions, for steppe groups with experience in long-distance horse-based transport, the internal organization that supported spatial reach was often the primary organizational hurdle. This underscores one of the essential problems in consolidating large-scale imperial states: innovating a balance of integrative strategies that both projects and maintains control over geographical space while simultaneously supporting the stability of the imperial core region. The political statecraft of non-imperial, pre-modern states favors techniques for internal consolidation and control of production while the projection of political influence over great distances generally requires an innovation in statecraft. Often the process of imperial expansion relies upon a preliminary mobilization of the core polity for support (e.g., Bauer and Covey 2002:847). In contrast, steppe empires tended to expand spatially as a way to facilitate consolidation and control of their core regions.

The important role of innovative statecraft cannot be overestimated in this process of imperial expansion and consolidation. In many cases, such statecraft can be adopted through knowledge of past imperial models or from interaction with polities having higher degrees of spatial expertise and technologies. One of the important processes of imperial consolidation, therefore, is accessing and employing diverse political technique; whether by remodeling past forms of political organization or by studying and recasting techniques already in use by contemporary polities (Sinopoli 2001:460–1). The consolidation of the Mongol empire is an excellent example of both processes being pursued quite consciously by members of the political elite. This observation is in distinct contrast to much historical research viewing the Mongol state as a process of conquest by superior military forces, followed by the adoption of local administrative techniques as a result of Mongol inexperience with political administration. The Mongol imperial elite were in fact particularly adept at investigating and utilizing statecraft and forms of legitimation from past steppe polities and from those peoples incorporated into the Mongol imperial sphere.

As discussed above, an example of this first process is evident in the selection of the site of the Orkhon valley of central Mongolia for the construction of the Kharkhorum capital. Historical sources comment on the lengths to which Mongol advisors researched the political and ritual geography of the former Turk and Uighur polities in order to decide upon a site for the capital city (Allsen 1996:126–7). The search for information on past traditions even involved excavations in the vicinity of the Orkhon Uighur capital in order to confirm that the site was indeed that of Ordu Balik. The Mongol elite had good reason to investigate the statecraft of past steppe polities. Not only was the Orkhon valley proclaimed by the Turkic elite as the only place from which the peoples of the steppe could be consolidated, but just as important was the political legitimation bestowed upon the new Mongol elite by associating themselves politically and ceremonially with the imperial Turks and Uighurs. This was an extremely prudent measure on the part of the Mongols since the vast majority of peoples of the growing Eurasian empire were of Turkic descent (Allsen 1996:128).

Throughout the construction of the empire, the Mongol elite pursued not only the political past, but the political present as well, in the form of contemporary expertise on diverse approaches to political organization. Uighur and Khitan steppe political knowledge was accessed by the Mongol elite through the epics and oral histories of the time, but also by integrating the cultural descendants of these polities into the empire and promoting a cadre of Uighur and Khitan advisors to influential positions. Groups of skilled political consultants were often recruited and transported between different regions within the empire to assist in organizational efforts. This interest on the part of the Mongol elite in differentiated approaches to political systems, new sources of ideas, and advisors with diverse experience, explains the readiness with which a foreigner like Marco Polo was able to enter into administrative service of the Yuan dynasty.

Finally, study of the Mongol empire informs us of yet another critical variable involved in imperial consolidation. From the Xiongnu confederation onward, steppe polities emphasized synthesis and amalgamation over the imposition of a standardized political culture. The Mongol elite were primarily interested in a broad spectrum of information resources, belief systems, and technologies due to the benefits that accruing such diverse knowledge contributed to administering the empire. For that reason, the political culture of the empire was synthetic and accommodating rather than exclusive. While some researchers argue that these techniques reflected an impoverished steppe political culture, we argue that the ability to tolerate, synthesize, and exploit diversity is a technique that is at the core of imperial statecraft. There is some evidence to suggest that the opposite approach of creating "self-similar" standardized units from conquered groups in order to facilitate integration is a less stable strategy. An example of the difficulties of imposing a uniform political culture is provided by the Chinese Han empire which attempted to integrate differentiated groups through a process of Sinicization (Allard, this volume). In contrast, the Mongol imperial state was masterful at effectively exploiting diversity, projecting legitimacy, and organizing large groups of people and resources over the extent of their immense territory. Such expertise helps to explain the success of the imperial nomads, not just in conquering, but also in linking together for the first time peoples and cultures at opposite ends of the earth.

REFERENCES

Allsen, Thomas 1996 Spiritual Geography and Political Legitimacy in the Eastern Steppe. *In* Ideology and the Formation of Early States. H. J. M. Claessen and J. G. Osten, eds. Pp. 116–35. New York: E. J. Brill.

Barfield, Thomas 2001a The Shadow Empires: Imperial State Formation along the Chinese-Nomad Frontier. *In* Empires: Perspectives from Archaeology and History. Susan E. Alcock, Terence N. D'Altroy, Kathleen D. Morrison, and Carla M. Sinopoli, eds. Pp. 10–41. Cambridge: Cambridge University Press.

—— 2001b Steppe Empires, China, and the Silk Route: Nomads as a Force in International Trade and Politics. *In* Nomads in the Sedentary World. Anatoly Khazanov and André Wink, eds. Pp. 234–49. London: Curzon Press.

Bauer, Brian, and Alan Covey 2002 Processes of State Formation in the Inca Heartland (Cuzco, Peru). American Anthropologist 104:846–64.

Cleaves, Francis 1982 The Secret History of the Mongols. Cambridge: Harvard University Press.

Davydova, Antonina 1995 Ivolginskii arkheologicheskii kompleks: Ivolginskoe gorodishche (The Ivolga archaeological complex: Ivolga settlement). Saint Petersburg: AziatIKA.

Dawson, Christopher 1980 Mission to Asia. Toronto: University of Toronto Press.

Di Cosmo, Nicola 1999 State Formation and Periodization in Inner Asian History. Journal of World History 10:1–40.

—— 2002 Ancient China and Its Enemies: The Rise of Nomadic Power in East Asian History. Cambridge: Cambridge University Press.

Dorjsuren, Tsogdanzan 1961 Umard Khunnu (The Northern Khunnu). Ulaanbaatar: Academy of Sciences.

Erdenebaatar, Diimaajav 2002 Mongol nutgiin dorvoljin bulsh, khirigsuuriin soel (Slab burial and Khirigsuur culture of Mongolia). Ulaanbaatar: Academy of Sciences.

Fletcher, Joseph 1986 The Mongols: Ecological and Social Perspectives. Harvard Journal of Asiatic Studies 46:11–50.

Griaznov, Mikhail 1980 Arzhan: tsarskii kurgan ranneskifskogo vremeni (Arzhan: a royal kurgan of the early Scythian period). Leningrad: Nauka.

Hiebert, Fredrik 1992 Pazyryk Chronology and Early Horse Nomads Reconsidered. Bulletin of the Asia Institute 6:117–29.

Honeychurch, William, and Chunag Amartuvshin 2003 An Examination of Khunnu Period Settlement in the Egiin Gol Valley, Mongolia. Studia Archaeologica 21:1:59–65.

Kato, Shinpei, Noriyuki Shiraishi, Damdinsuren Tseveendorj, and Batmonkh Tsogtbaatar 2004 Preliminary Report on the Japan–Mongolia Joint Archaeological Expedition "New Century Project" 2003. Ulaanbaatar: Institute of Archaeology.

Khazanov, Anatoly 1994 Nomads and the Outside World. Madison: Wisconsin University Press.

Kiselev, Sergei, ed. 1965 Drevnemongol'skie goroda (Ancient Mongolian cities). Moscow: Nauka.

Konovalov, Prokopii 1976 Khunnu v Zabaikal'e (The Khunnu of Zabaikal). Ulan-Ude: Nauka.

Kradin, Nikolai 2002 Nomadism, Evolution, and World-Systems: Pastoral Societies in Theories of Historical Development. Journal of World-Systems Research 8:368–88.

Kyzlasov, Leonid 1969 Istoriia Tuvy v srednie veka (The history of Tuva in the medieval period). Moscow: Moscow University.

Lattimore, Owen 1992[1940] Inner Asian Frontiers of China. New York: Oxford University Press.

Miniaev, Sergei, and Lena Sakharovskaia 2002 Soprovoditel'nye zakhoroneniia "tsarskogo" kompleksa No. 7 v mogil'nike Tsaram (Accompanying burials of royal complex No. 7 at the Tsaram cemetery). Arkheologicheskie Vesti (Archaeological news) 9:86–118.

Novgorodova, Eleonora 1989 Drevniaia Mongoliia (Ancient Mongolia). Moscow: Nauka.

Perlee, Khodoo 1961 Mongol Ard Ulsyn ert, dundad ueiin khot suuriny tovchoon (A brief history of ancient and medieval period settlements in the Mongolian People's Republic). Ulaanbaatar: Academy of Sciences.

Rosen, Arlene, Claudia Chang, and Fedor Grigoriev 2000 Palaeoenvironments and Economy of Iron Age Saka-Wusun Agro-Pastoralists in Southeastern Kazakhstan. Antiquity 74:611–23.

Roth, Helmut, and Ulambayar Erdenebat, eds. 2002 Qara Qorum City (Mongolia) I: Preliminary Report of the Excavations 2000/2001. Bonn: Bonn University.

Rudenko, Sergei 1962 Kul'tura khunnov i Noinulinskie kurgany (Khunnu culture and the Kurgans of Noin Ula). Moscow: Nauka.

Shelach, Gideon 1999 Leadership Strategies, Economic Activity, and Interregional Interaction: Social Complexity in Northeast China. New York: Plenum Press.

Shiraishi, Noriyuki, Damdinsuren Tseveendorj, and Batmonkh Tsogtbaatar 2001 Preliminary Report on the Japan–Mongolia Joint Archaeological Expedition "New Century Project." Ulaanbaatar: Institute of History.

Sinopoli, Carla 2001 Empires. In Archaeology at the Millennium: A Sourcebook. Gary Feinman and T. Douglas Price, eds. Pp. 439–71.

Stein Gil 2002 From Passive Periphery to Active Agents: Emerging Perspectives in the Archaeology of Interregional Interaction. American Anthropologist 104:903–16.

Torbat, Tsagaan, Chunag Amartuvshin, and Ulambayar Erdenebat 2003 Egiin Golyn sav nutag dakh' arkheologiin dursgaluud (Archaeological monuments of Egiin Gol valley). Ulaanbaatar: Mongolian Institute of Archaeology.

Tseveendorj, Damdinsuren, Dovdoi Bayar, Yadmaa Tserendagva, and Tseveendorj Ochirkhuyag 2003 Mongolyn Arkheologi (Mongolian archaeology). Ulaanbaatar: Academy of Sciences.

Tsybiktarov, Aleksandr 1998 Kul'tura plitochnykh mogil Mongolii i Zabaikal'ia (Culture of the slab burials of Mongolia and Zabaikal'e). Ulan-Ude: Nauka.

Volkov, Vitalii 1967 Bronzovyi i rannii zheleznyi vek severnoi Mongolii (The Bronze and early Iron Age of Northern Mongolia). Ulaanbaatar: Academy of Sciences.

Watson, Burton 1993 Records of the Grand Historian of China: Han Dynasty II. New York: Columbia University Press.

Weber, Andrzej, David Link, and M. Anne Katzenberg 2002 Hunter-Gatherer Culture Change and Continuity in the Middle Holocene of the Cis-Baikal, Siberia. Journal of Anthropological Archaeology 21:230–99.

Wu, En 1990 Lun Xiongnu kaogu yanjiu zhong de jige wenti (Some questions on the archaeological study of the Xiongnu). Kaogu Xuebao 4:409–37.

13

Historicizing Foraging in South Asia: Power, History, and Ecology of Holocene Hunting and Gathering

Kathleen D. Morrison

From the sparsely-populated worlds of the Palaeolithic when all humans relied on gathering and hunting for their sole subsistence, to the contemporary postcolonial world in which a small but significant number of people still gather wild plants and hunt wild animals as part of shifting and diverse regimes of production, foraging strategies have had a continuing salience across much of Asia, as elsewhere. Why have hunting and gathering, along with the apparently simple extractive technologies they employ, had such an enduring significance in Asia, especially South and Southeast Asia? We should also consider the long-term importance of this phenomenon – is the existence of Holocene hunter-gatherers simply a curiosity, or might it instead imply something more fundamental about the trajectory of both foragers and their neighbors? Although a complete answer to these questions is beyond the scope of this chapter, I will suggest here that far from representing the rather exotic activity of a series of marginal peoples, gathering in particular has played a far greater role in the development of several South and Southeast Asian states than is generally acknowledged.

This chapter addresses some aspects of the complex history of foraging in Asia, focusing on the South Asian Holocene and the integration of foraging strategies with agriculture, wage labor, trade and tribute relations, and pastoralism. Rather than adopting the widespread but problematic view of Holocene hunter-gatherers as enduring remnants of more ancient groups or as representatives of pre-agricultural lifeways, I contextualize hunting and gathering in terms of its historical political ecologies. Gathering, fishing, and hunting involve particular relations of humans to the natural world; at the same time, those who deploy these strategies are virtually always involved in relations of power, affect, and sometimes interdependence with others. Although the contexts of foraging – here I use the term foraging as a general gloss for all gathering, fishing, and hunting activities without any necessary assumptions about the goals, strategies, or constraints of those activities – have, in places, changed radically since the advent of agriculture, hunting and gathering have never died out but remain important strategies of resource acquisition and of social and political action. Using three examples from South Asia, this chapter works to extract hunting and gathering from their traditional roles as place markers within a presumed cultural evolutionary sequence, analyzing them instead in terms of historically-situated tactics deployed within contexts of specific local ecologies, polities, exchange networks, and cultural frameworks.

Perspectives on Agriculture and Foraging

In early archaeological views of agriculture that saw agriculture as a self-evident good, both the initial development of plant domestication and cultivation and its subsequent expansion could easily be accommodated as inevitable outcomes of the growth of knowledge. In this view, the existence of peoples who, for one reason or another, failed to adopt agriculture constituted a puzzle. Whether noble or depraved, those who continued to hunt and gather evidently failed to progress in some fundamental way. Hunting and gathering, in this perspective, were identified with an early stage in cultural evolution and the continuing existence of these extractive strategies could only be viewed in terms of persistence of earlier forms or of "reversion" to such forms in an episteme that equates "early" with "simple" and hunting and gathering with both. Once the knowledge of agriculture came into being, foragers verging on the brink of subsistence disaster were free to expand their populations, begin to discriminate among categories of people, and ultimately to develop social "complexity" and civilization.

With the destruction of the Hobbesian view of hunter-gatherers in the late 1960s, foragers lost some of their negative taint, if not their academically marginal status among scholars, becoming, conversely, easy-going egalitarians enjoying a life of relative ease. Instead of wondering why domestication and agriculture had not been "invented" before, the transition to the arduous life of an agriculturalist now became the puzzle to be solved. A key work in this intellectual transition was Boserup (1965), which posited that population growth leads to the intensification of agricultural production and thus to increases in overall production rather than, following Malthus, increased production itself allowing population growth. Although Boserup did not consider hunting and gathering, extending her model to the beginnings of agriculture constituted only a short intellectual leap (e.g. Cohen 1977).

Even though this shift – from poor foragers and rich farmers to leisured foragers and harried farmers – was enormous, in many ways the basic scaffolding supporting views of change continued to be one of step-wise progressive cultural evolution in which the stages of change, though usually defined politically, continued to be powerfully associated with modal economic strategies. Thus, band societies were seen to be built on a base of hunting and gathering, tribes on simple agriculture, and chiefdoms and states on more intensive forms of agriculture. The simple power of these associations has meant that, even now, it may seem contrarian to suggest that in some parts of Asia, state economies required the existence of foraging as

well as agriculture; at some times and in some places hunter-gatherers were critical to state formation, specialization, and even colonial expansion.

Although, at this time, the ethnographic literature on hunter-gatherers was dominated by several "classic" ethnographic cases of small, mobile, egalitarian groups,
archaeological examples of non-agriculturalists with large populations, sedentary
lifestyles, or stratified social organization were disconcertingly common. The rum-
blings in the archaeological literature found voice in the "complex hunter-gatherer"
concept. Price and Brown (1985:8) defined this complexity in terms of "increases
in societal size, scale, and organization," with indices such as new technology,
specialized production, occupational and status differentiation, sedentism, and low
mobility (1985:10–12) playing a key role in marking complexity archaeologically.
In some respects, I would suggest that their delineation of the realm of complex
hunter-gatherers did not go far enough, partly because of its focus on within-group
dynamics. Many apparently egalitarian groups are, in fact, enmeshed in relationships of unequal power when seen in regional context, a situation probably not
uncommon for much of the Holocene. Within these larger (and longer) frames,
then, even small-scale groups might usefully be characterized as "complex,"
enmeshed with (and within) larger polities, economies, and cultural orders. The
conceptual problem here is certainly one of scale and is complicated by difficulties
in drawing boundaries between cultural groups, but where foragers have had long
histories of interaction with differently-organized others it seems shortsighted at
best to excise those others from general considerations of their organization.

Why Foraging?

Why have hunting and gathering persisted and, at times, even replaced agriculture
not only as basic strategies for survival but also, for some groups, as culturally-
central activities? Anthropologists from the 1970s onward developed what we may
call the basic energetic argument: this view grew out of a demographic perspective
combined with least-cost assumptions and suggests that hunting and gathering is
easier and more reliable than agriculture. Thus, people will always cling to foraging if they can. Certainly, this insight is critical and continues to have much
analytical value. However, it is also clear that human subsistence strategies can be
considerably more complex than such models assume. First of all, they may involve
what are, from the perspective of economic efficiency, seemingly perverse cultural
logics that make least-cost assumptions problematic. In addition, as Price and
Brown (1985) implicitly recognized and I emphasize here, the answer to this question does not lie solely within the realm of internal-group dynamics, but requires
a larger and longer view. Questions about the persistence or (re)emergence of
hunting and gathering require supra-regional and at times even global answers. For
much of the later Holocene and up to the present, many groups did not have the
luxury of selecting subsistence activities without any reference to outsiders. Post-
Palaeolithic hunting, gathering, agriculture, craft production, and other activities

all took place within widely varying regional relations of power. Even among egalitarian societies, external relationships may involve degrees of coercion, allure, and even downright oppression so that ignoring power relations in the study of hunter-gatherers seems seriously misguided.

Here the insights of the revisionists (see Morrison 2002a) are particularly germane to the study of Holocene foraging in Asia where so many groups have long been involved with agriculturalists, states, and even world markets – we might consider the many degrees of engagement between Asian foragers and differently-organized others as so many more modes of complex hunting and gathering. In fact, the view from Asia places the early revisionist assertion of a qualitative break between archaeology and ethnography (that is, the argument that because of the long histories of engagement of foraging groups with the rest of the world, the ethnographic record is of dubious utility for archaeological reconstruction) in a rather ironic light. On the contrary, the ethnographic record of this region is extremely helpful for seeing how people might hunt and gather in and around a world of agriculture, states, markets, and money, and how foragers might conceive of and organize those activities.

But why have hunting and gathering remained so important, especially in South and Southeast Asia? There seem to be many reasons and I make no claims to a full account here. However, three of the salient factors needed to explain this situation involve aspects of occupational history, geography, and resources. I take up each of these in turn, though a general account would require more elaboration and empirical support than can be provided in the brief case studies presented here. In general, it is possible to isolate conditions more favorable to what might be called "classic" forms of foraging (self-sufficient subsistence extraction) as well as those conducive to the development and maintenance of what I have termed "forager-trader" forms (Morrison and Junker 2002). Although these are by no means mutually exclusive modes of existence, the point I want to make here is that the relative importance of hunting and gathering across much of tropical and monsoon Asia (even after the development of agriculture) cannot be understood without reference to both "modes" of hunting and gathering. Although individuals and groups could and did shift between subsistence foraging and foraging for exchange, the conditions allowing forager-traders to exist are somewhat different than those facilitating "classic" gathering and hunting and it may be that more "commercial" forms of extraction worked to underwrite the continued existence of subsistence foraging in many places.

Occupational History: Irrigated Lowlands, Forested Uplands, and Beyond

Differential occupational histories not only build on local and regional ecological contexts and possibilities, but they also create historical consequences, some more easily reversible than others. To take a simple example, the extension of intensive agricultural practices such as the construction of irrigated, terraced rice fields and the massive translocations of soil, vegetation, wildlife habitat, and water that such constructions entail, would require substantial changes in foraging practices of people who use a landscape containing such transformed contexts. To be sure, not all anthropogenic environments involve such stark modifications of flora, fauna, topography, and hydrology, but even more modest changes alter the possibilities for hunting and gathering. This can be seen either in a more conventional way, where the extension of agriculture, animal husbandry, urbanism, and/or industry destroy the conditions necessary for subsistence foraging or in a more opportunistic light in which the expansion of specialized economies makes forager-trader strategies possible.

This first factor, then, relates to the oft-cited fact that contemporary hunter-gatherers typically live in environments that are less than hospitable to agriculture. I would add an historical dimension, however, in insisting that occupational history, more than simply raw potentiality, is at issue. For example, in parts of island Southeast Asia, large-scale landscape transformation of the sort that seems to have happened quite early in comparable parts of the west coast of India took place relatively recently (e.g. Boomgaard et al. 1997). In some regions of southwest Borneo (Knapen 2001), and elsewhere in Indonesia (Boomgaard 1997:16), even swidden agriculture faced recurrent problems and the scale and scope of agriculture and thus of anthropogenic landscape transformation appears to have been slight until New World crops such as maize (*Zea mays*) became available. Perhaps it is not surprising, then, that hunter-gatherers, albeit ones oriented toward exchange as well as subsistence foraging, have been able to maintain themselves in these places, in light of these occupational histories.

In general, the scope and historical precociousness of landscape change in the large deltas of South and East Asia have indeed meant that hunting and gathering, both as strategy and identity, have tended to disappear through time. In India, areas with the longest histories of agriculture, especially intensive agriculture, tend to have the fewest foragers and it is certainly no accident that contemporary "tribal" groups who practice at least some hunting and gathering are differentially concentrated in the tropical northeast, the uplands of the semi-tropical southwest, and the hilly regions of central India where dense deciduous monsoonal forests still exist. For "classic" hunter-gatherers it is perhaps sufficient that landscapes that are forested, hilly, poorly-drained, or otherwise hostile to agriculture may have few others competing for space, but for foragers adjusted to exchange it is also necessary that such locations contain resources desired by outsiders.

Thus, both competition and cooperation with differently-organized others as well as the material constraints of altered conditions of biota, territorial freedom and mobility, and perhaps even cultural understandings of the world consonant with variable ways of making a living (cf. Barnard 2002), work to shape the possibilities of different places and different times. One advantage of insisting on the importance of occupational history rather than simply environmental context is that it highlights the role of human action, not only in making physical environments (and making them meaningful), but also in terms of the regional power dynamics. The occupational histories that impinge on the lives of foragers are not only their own, but also those of expanding agriculturalists, miners, prospectors, royal courts, foresters, and others. As I illustrate below, these histories create both problems and opportunities for foraging peoples; the continued importance of hunting and gathering in tropical and monsoonal Asia represents, in part, evidence of widespread response to these opportunities.

Geography: islands, narrow mountain chains, and transport by land and water

To a certain extent, the continuing importance of hunting and gathering in parts of Asia has required a fine balance of proximity and distance between foragers and others. Although one tends to think of hunter-gatherers as being isolated people living far from the fields of agriculturalists and the seats of political power (and indeed this is sometimes the case), the long occupational histories and flexible environmental possibilities of much of Asia have led to many situations where true remoteness is rare. Where desired resources (below) are clustered, especially in areas of difficult access and perhaps less hospitable to agriculture, and where their exploitation requires developed local knowledge, it may not be too surprising that specialists in resource extraction emerge. If these specialists are able to survive (even periodically) away from a regular supply chain, so much the better. As I have discussed elsewhere (Morrison 2002c), the real difficulty is convincing locally knowledgeable people to commit to regular exchange relations, especially when those relations create conditions of insecurity related to, for example, global market shifts; this is often achieved through coercion as well as local desires for exotic goods.

Although exceptions to this pattern certainly exist, many of the ethnographically and historically-known forager-trader groups of Asia live either on islands or in relatively narrow mountain chains surrounded by state-level agricultural societies. Thus, while there are real possibilities of communication between differently organized others, these others also face some difficulty of access. Too far away, and regular relationships cannot be maintained, too close and foragers are threatened by landscape transformation and competition from other would-be gatherers.

Resources: Forest Products, Manufactures, and Cultigens

Although the known range of human subsistence strategies is large and many foraging groups are able to subsist under very harsh conditions, it is clear that some environments are more conducive to human survival than others. There exists some controversy about the viability of subsistence foraging in tropical forest environments (Bailey et al. 1989; see discussion by Junker 2002a), and while there is evidence suggesting that Bailey et al.'s formulation is too absolute and that subsistence foragers have, in some cases, managed to exist in tropical forest settings, at the same time, the small number of such exceptions does point to the difficulty of foraging-based subsistence in these kinds of environments. In fact, the co-occurrence of both classic subsistence foraging and forager-traders forms in Holocene South and Southeast Asia may be seen as highlighting the salience of resource distributions for hunter-gatherer lifeways. On the one hand, foraging-based subsistence might have been difficult in certain forest environments as well as in many of the anthropogenic environments of Asia. At the same time, critically, many of these forests were also home to plant, animal, and mineral resources desired by outsiders. It was the existence of these latter resources, along with the incentive for reciprocal exchange, which made forager-trader lifestyles possible.

It hardly needs to be noted that resources, as such, are always culturally defined. Historically, we see major shifts in the resources exploited by hunter-gatherers for the use of others – metal ores, for example, had no utility whatsoever before the development of smelting technology, and even afterwards the effective exploitation of metal ores required not only knowledge of their presence and distribution, but also the means to extract and transport them to processing locales. This is illustrated graphically in the case of Bangka (Sumatra); on this island forest products such as rattans and a scented wood obtained from diseased *Gonstylus bancanus* trees had long been involved, somewhat sporadically, in international trade networks, but neither local upland groups nor the coastal Orang Laut, famed as ocean-going raiders (Andaya 1993; Virunha 2002) mined or used Bangka's rich tin deposits. Tin mining here began only in 1710 (Colombijn 1997:316), after the takeover of Bangka by the Palembang state and, not coincidentally, along with declining revenues from the environmentally-degrading production of pepper (Andaya 1993). Extraction of lucrative tin ores, traded to the Dutch, was initially small in scale, but the migration of skilled Chinese miners (only partially state-sanctioned) quickly led to the adoption of more efficient extraction techniques. In the subsequent boom, both mining and charcoal production for smelting led to dramatic deforestation and environmental degradation (Colombijn 1997).

Similarly, sappan wood (also known as Brazil-wood, *Caesalpinia sappan*), which grows across much of tropical South and Southeast Asia, was much in demand in Europe and Asia until the late nineteenth century. Sappan harvesting between the 14th and 19th centuries on the island of Sumbawa, Indonesia (de Jong Boers 1997) led to dramatic reductions in the local occurrence of this species. This, along with the development of artificial substitutes for the red dye obtained from this wood caused the collection of sappan wood from Sumbawa to cease entirely (de Jong Boers 1997:267). Similar accounts could be given for other forest products, many of which were not used locally at all or which had very limited utility to local people. The list of such items is very long, including bird's nests, sea slugs, bird of paradise feathers, benzoin gum (*Styrax sp.*), camphor (*Dryobalanops sp.*), sandalwood (*Santalum album*), and many of the other aromatics, gums, dyes, and resins obtained from upland forests (Cooper 2002; Cribb 1997; Potter 1997). Other products, such as hunted animals, honey, and medicinal plants and spices were potentially more useful to their gatherers, but in any case local people would have needed only a tiny fraction of the quantities actually harvested for exchange.

In other cases, plants once under the primary control of local forest peoples became so important that they were transplanted to other contexts. Many of the spices such as pepper, cardamom, ginger, cinnamon, clove, and nutmeg, which were among the most important forest products traded out of and across South and

Southeast Asia, originated in specific locales as gathered wild plants. Pepper in southwest India, cinnamon in Sri Lanka, cloves and nutmeg in Maluku – although these spices were traded outside their areas of origin for centuries, most of this commerce involved the exploitation of wild stands. While this gathering activity continued well into the 19th century, these same plants were increasingly grown in gardens and swidden fields and thus the organization of their production shifted dramatically along with the transition from wild plant to cultigen (Morrison 2002c).

All the examples above relate to forest products desired by outside groups – indeed I would suggest that this external interest, along with a concomitant organizational ability to mobilize and exchange these resources, is central to the development and maintenance of relationships between hunter-gatherers and others. Boomgaard (1989:378) goes so far as to suggest that state structure (to mobilize gathering) was necessary in order to attract foreign merchants, who needed reliable flows of goods. While this may be true for the larger-scale forms of extraction and exchange characteristic of both southwest India and island Southeast Asia after the sixteenth century, it is also clear from the examples of the Harappan borderlands and the Andaman Islands (see below) that commercial exchange can thrive even in the absence of state structures on both sides.

Beyond the important issue of political control, it is also worth considering what goods were traded back into the forests as these resources, too, had to be culturally defined as desirable in order to lubricate trade relations. Briefly, forager-traders and others involved in the exploitation of wild forest products were virtually always the recipients of significant quantities of foodstuffs, usually grains such as rice. The development of a taste for rice and a cultural preference for rice over more energetically-efficient foods such as sago is a critical and little-studied component of the historical development of the trade in forest products across South and Southeast Asia (cf. Knapen 2001:214–26) and, concomitantly, of the persistence of hunting and gathering in these same regions. Other products obtained by forager-traders often include textiles and tools (Morrison 2002c) as well as sumptuary goods including, in Southeast Asia, Chinese porcelains (Bellwood 1985:141; Junker 2002b) and other exotica.

Holocene Foraging in South Asia

The long Palaeolithic record of Asia lies beyond the scope of this paper, though it should be noted that in many areas occupational histories map the record of both modern and premodern humans, creating a record of astonishing depth. In other areas, human occupation is relatively recent. Agricultural histories are similarly variable, and clearly these have influenced the extent to which foraging remained a viable possibility. Allied changes such as the differential development of social and political inequality, state formation, and forms of economic specialization also created both opportunities and constraints for would-be foragers. Although all these conditions varied from place to place across Asia, there are some common features of the cases discussed in this chapter, most notably their participation in long-distance exchange networks that, prior to European colonization, eventually reached as far as the Mediterranean and East Asia and, afterwards, encompassed nearly the entire globe. In all the three cases considered here – the Indus valley and its peripheries, southwest India, and the Andamans – people identified as hunter-gatherers not only have long histories, but these groups (or others like them) also still exist, pointing to the contemporary salience of historical analyses.

Curiously, the non-arctic peoples of Asia who gather and hunt have had only a small impact on the anthropological literature. In his foreword to a reader on hunter-gatherers, Lee (1998:xi–xii), for example, writes, "Hunter-gatherers in recent history have been surprisingly persistent. As recently as A.D. 1500, hunters occupied fully one-third of the globe, including all of Australia and most of North America, as well as large tracts of South America, Africa, and northeast Asia." Lee must have known that both South and Southeast Asia boast numerous hunter-gatherer groups (Lee and Daly eds. 2000), yet somehow these groups (and a vast stretch of the earth's surface) disappeared in his enumeration. As I have argued before (Morrison 2002a), this invisibility seems to stem from the complex entanglements of South and Southeast Asian hunter-gatherers in worlds outside the forest – while other foragers have only recently been "exposed" as being more connected and less isolated than previously presumed, many South and Southeast Asian groups have clearly long maintained foraging lifeways in the face of substantial interaction with others. The degree and nature of this interaction varied substantially, as did, presumably, the ability of foraging groups to persist as cultural groups increasingly surrounded by farmers, traders, and others. In spite of this and although connections between foragers and others were (and are) often marked by deep ambivalence, even exploitation, non-foragers, from colonial governments to local elites, were not always bent on assimilating hunter-gatherers. On the contrary, the products of Asian forests often constituted critical state resources and their exploitation often required considerable local expertise. One of the many ways in which this exploitation was effected historically was through relationships with foraging groups; thus we cannot fully account for many state economies and polities without reference to hunting and gathering.

The following sections consider Holocene foraging in three places, each with different occupational histories: I begin with what is now northwestern India and Pakistan, where human histories are extremely long and where agriculture was adopted early in the Holocene, looking at interaction between hunter-gatherers and others on the fringes of the Indus civilization in the semi-arid environment of western India. Moving then to peninsular India, where a long record of hunting and gathering in low-lying areas is matched with a relatively late adoption of agriculture, I consider the regional context of the Western Ghat Mountains. These steep peaks are cloaked in tropical and semi-tropical forests that presented both challenges to and opportunities for human subsistence. Finally, I consider the Andaman Islands, with their relatively brief record of human habitation. Prior to the establishment of a British penal colony in the late 19th century, the Andamans could boast both tropical evergreen and monsoonal deciduous forest cover and were occupied only by hunting and gathering groups. All of these areas, while evincing complex local histories, were integrated to some extent by international networks of exchange from at least the first few centuries A.D. and all felt the effects of European colonial expansion from the 16th century onward. The degree to which local people were integrated into larger worlds and the importance of hunting and gathering for local or colonial states also varied tremendously. In all cases, however, it is possible both to point to the importance of external forces on the changing strategies and identities of local foraging groups and to consider the importance of foragers and of gathered products for those external groups.

There are a large number of different hunting and gathering groups in South Asia today, a situation mirrored throughout the Holocene. Although particular ethnic groups may have moved in and out of foraging, have expanded or contracted in size, or have reformed their boundaries, it is clear that foraging has been important on the subcontinent from the beginnings of human history. The earliest written records mention gathering and hunting groups – inscriptions commissioned by the North Indian Mauryan emperor Ashoka during the third century B.C. note the presence of undefeated forest "tribes" on the borders of the state in Central India (Kulke and Rothermund 1990) while other Mauryan texts mention the existence of taxes on both timber and on hunters "who maintained a livelihood from the animals of the forest" (Thapar 1997:118) – suggesting state interest in forest products as well as the presence of distinct categories of people incorporated into that polity. Later inscriptional records from South India make references to hill peoples and note their role in the specialized procurement of forest products such as spices, gums and resins, honey, and medicinal and aromatic plants. Many of these gathering and hunting peoples in southwest India had regular tribute relationships with lowland rulers, supplying them with gathered and hunted forest products. While historical notices of foragers are consistently present, if sporadic and brief before the 16th century A.D., they become abundant by the nineteenth century A.D., with the advent of European record-keeping. Around this time it becomes possible to identify by name particular foraging groups, many of whom still exist today.

Harappan cities, traders, and hunter-gatherers

In South Asia, the rich archaeological record of the Paleolithic gives way around the beginning of the Holocene to assemblages usually labeled Mesolithic (Korisettar and Rajaguru 2002). Early Holocene lithic assemblages are generally based on a microlithic flake-blade technology (while still including larger tool types) and are thus characterized as "microlithic." While Mesolithic assemblages do typically contain microliths, microliths did not disappear with agriculture and are associated (Misra 1976:45) with Chalcolithic, Early Historic, and finally Gupta ceramics (fourth to seventh centuries A.D.). Late use of flaked stone and glass tools has also been documented into the 16th century A.D. in southern India (Lycett and Morrison 1989). Malik (1959:50), too, found a core chipped from the base of a molded beer-bottle near Mahabaleswar in the Western Ghats. Cooper (2002:93) notes that such containers were not made until the 17th or 18th century A.D., citing

Malik's conclusion (1959:50) that this find indicates the late survival of a "microlithic" industry. In the "Mesolithic" site of Adamgarh Cave, too, microliths of bottle glass were found alongside specimens made on chalcedony, jasper, and other fine-grained lithic material (Khatri 1964:759). Cooper (2002:83) notes that in this case, "No pottery was found in association with the microliths, thus confirming the existence of a foraging economy in isolated areas, contemporaneous with urban settlements in the adjoining valleys."

Although some scholars in South Asia use terms like Mesolithic and microlithic to describe contemporary peoples, despite their lack of stone tools, microlithic or otherwise, such terms obscure more than they illuminate. Here I use the term Mesolithic only to refer to a time period that begins with the Holocene and ends (somewhat arbitrarily) as early as the seventh millennium B.C. in the northwest and as late as the beginning of the third in the south, when local Neolithic periods began (Korisettar et al. 2002). I use the term microlithic to refer only to a miniature blade-based lithic technology (and see Morrison 2000).

All this terminological confusion means that the specifically archaeological evidence for Holocene hunting and gathering is difficult to assess. In the absence of absolute dates, many temporal assignments in the literature based solely on lithic technology must be considered suspect. Clearly, many archaeological sites described as "Mesolithic" were formed during the later Holocene, and if the distributions of published radiocarbon dates for sites with (what are called) microlithic artifacts are plotted, the results show a very broad range of dates with a distribution across the entire Holocene, a pattern not evident for the Neolithic or Chalcolithic (Lycett and Morrison 1989).

Despite the small body of research on subsistence and mobility during the Mesolithic, it is clear that there was significant regional variation across the subcontinent. Although many foraging groups were small and mobile, others were sedentary or semi-sedentary, particularly along the southern coasts where they engaged in fishing as well as gathering and hunting terrestrial game. Many of the major excavated caves and rock shelters of Central and Western India occupied during the early Holocene (Bagor, Langhnaj, Adamgarh, Bhimbetka) were exploited only seasonally, some filling with aeolian sand in the dry season. Both Adamgarh and Bhimbetka contain faunal remains of domesticated animals, suggesting that they were occupied by people not totally dependent upon wild taxa. Langhnaj is discussed below.

Evidence for interaction between hunter-gatherers and state societies in South Asia begins during the Chalcolithic, almost as early as states themselves. As is well known, the Indus Valley, a broad alluvial plain with five major rivers fed by both monsoon rains and Himalayan snowmelt, was the home of the one of the world's first urban societies. By the middle of the third millennium B.C., the so-called Mature Phase of the Indus boasted several large cities with well-planned streets and drainage, complex differentiation of space and public architecture, systems of weights and writing, and a high degree of occupational specialization (Kenoyer 1997). Even before this period, in the Early Harappan, there is considerable evidence for large, fortified settlements, writing or record-keeping, specialized production, and other indications of a politically and socially stratified society. Mature Phase Indus cities, towns, and villages were integrated into an as-yet poorly understood political structure consisting of either a single state or, perhaps more likely, a series of smaller polities linked by extensive and well-organized trade networks.

The rich floodplains of the Indus and its tributaries were friendly to agricultural production, supporting large nucleated population centers. However, like Mesopotamia, resources such as water, silt, and clay, while useful for ceramic production, construction, and farming, did not meet local needs for tools, groundstone, ornaments, and the raw material needed to make specialized objects such as seals and weights. Although some of these materials were obtained more locally – the Indus cultural sphere was extremely large, more than one million square kilometers (Possehl 1999); thus even what I am calling local exchange might involve significant distances – raw materials and some finished goods clearly flowed into the Indus heartland from great distances. The organization of long-distance trade followed a variety of strategies, including what seems to be direct procurement by Harappans moving into culturally and politically alien terrain. For example, the settlement of Shortugai in what is now Afghanistan appears in most respects to be a standard Harappan town; only its location, far from the Indus plain and near sources of lapis lazuli indicates its possible role as an outpost for trading and/or extraction of this valued stone. Other goods were obtained through exchange relations with other urbanized groups, for example, those in the Gulf region and Mesopotamia (Ratnagar 1981).

It is also clear, however, that there were regular, well-organized exchanges between Harappan urbanites and peninsular pastoralists and hunter-gatherers. The evidence for this relationship was first discussed by Possehl (1976, 2002; Possehl and Kennedy 1979), and both recent excavations and bioarchaeological research (Lukacs 1990, 2002) have expanded the picture somewhat. Archaeological evidence of these connections comes from both sides of the relationship, from specialized Harappan towns such as Lothal and Kuntasi, both located on or beyond the southeastern margins of the Indus world in what is now Gujarat, India, to "Mesolithic" sites such as Langhnaj which show evidence of both local and exotic artifacts in the context of an occupation history that appears to be both small-scale and intermittent. The open-air site of Langhnaj, in Gujarat, was excavated for more nearly twenty years by Sankalia (1965). Lying some 160 kilometers north of the Harappan city of Lothal, it appears to have been occupied by small, semi-mobile groups of people in contact with Harappan peoples, probably those at Lothal itself. Local environments contrasted sharply with those of southwest India discussed below; here semi-arid monsoon forests and dry scrub associations provided both opportunities and challenges to farming and foraging. Pastoralism was an important economic strategy and forest resources other than wood seem not to have been of great interest to outsiders.

Sankalia (1965) identified three discrete occupational phases at Langhnaj, all containing some ceramics, though sherds in the lower two levels were highly fragmented, apparently the result of being poorly fired (Possehl 2002:71). In addition to these fragmentary ceramics, Phase I contained microliths, bones of wild animals including wild cattle (*Bos indicus*) and water buffalo (*Bubalis bubalis*), groundstone fragments, and dentalium shell beads. Phase II deposits also contained microliths and had a faunal assemblage similar to that of Phase I. In addition, however, a quartzite ringstone, steatite disk beads, two miniature ground schist axes, and a long copper knife were recovered in Phase II. The only radiocarbon date for Langhnaj comes from mixed Phase I/II deposits; this date (2440–2160 B.C. [calibrated], Possehl 2002:71) is contemporaneous with the Mature Harappan. The copper knife is morphologically similar to Harappan forms and was probably obtained in trade from the nearby Kutch Harappans of Gujarat (Possehl 2002:71). Several other sites in this region such as Kanewal (Mehta et al. 1980) and Oriyo Timbo (Rissman and Chitalwala 1990) show what Possehl (2002:70) calls an "interdigitation" of habitation by hunter-gatherers and Harappans – alternating strata that indicate the contemporaneity of distinct modes of existence. In these sites, the hunter-gatherers appear to be represented by strata with microliths, no architecture, and either no or very few ceramics. Certainly it is possible that these artifact associations represent special-purpose locales made by settled farmers, though if this were the case we might expect to see more overlap in lithic technology (cf. Selvakumar In press). Given the broad range of dates for "Mesolithic" sites in India, the notion that foragers and Harappans were interacting is not difficult to accept.

Although the presence of technologically sophisticated artifacts such as ceramics and metal, and especially the appearance of domestic animals in "Mesolithic" sites might seem to suggest that local hunter-gatherers were the primary beneficiaries of exchange and were perhaps dependent on city-dwellers, in fact the opposite is probably true. Some of the most valued raw materials in the Indus realm appear to have come from areas primarily occupied by mobile foragers. The modern-day state of Gujarat lies at the far edge of the Harappan sphere and contains both non-Harappan settlements (called Sorath Harappan by Possehl [1992] in recognition of their relationship to Indus urbanism) as well as cities and towns such as Dholavira, Lothal, and (the much smaller) Kuntasi that conform in most ways to the "classic" Harappan pattern and which would not seem out of place in the Indus heartland. As early as 1976, Possehl suggested that the urban site of Lothal was a "gateway community" located to take advantage of the specialized procurement of raw materials by hunter-gatherers for manufacture by urban artisans. Dhavalikar et al. (1995) argue for a similar role for the small Harappan port and manufacturing site of Kuntasi, in Kutch. Both Lothal and Kuntasi have evidence for a high degree of craft specialization, especially bead-making, suggesting that locally-obtained raw materials were being worked into finished or semi-finished goods before being transported north. Among the goods procured by non-Harappan locals were agate, carnelian, rock crystal, steatite, shell, and ivory, along with wood, including teak from the Western Ghats (Possehl 2002:73). If this list is accurate, then there must have been not only connections with local, Gujarat-area hunter-gatherers, but also (perhaps less direct) connections to groups further south and east as well.

Finally, biological evidence also points to sustained connections between hunter-gatherers and others in South Asia. Based on a multivariate analysis of metric variables from skeletal populations, Kennedy at al. (1984) have grouped specimens from Langhnaj and Lothal together, making the case for substantial gene flow between these two places. Further, Lukacs and Pal (1993, and see Lukacs 2002) have shown that the residents of Langhnaj have a much higher rate of dental caries than other hunter-gatherers, suggesting a diet containing a significant quantity of grain or other carbohydrate. They argue for exchange relationships involving food, a pattern consistent with later historically-known cases from southern India (Morrison 2002c).

Although much more remains to be learned about relationships between non-Harappan foragers and Indus craftspeople, traders, consumers, middlemen, and others, at present there is little reason to see these relationships as stratified or as coercive in any way. Perhaps the fact that Harappan settlements like Lothal and Kuntasi were in some sense on alien ground, distant from the centers of the Indus state(s) is relevant here; it would have been difficult to coerce mobile groups in a sparsely-populated landscape to engage in unwanted exchanges. Perhaps, then, the primary incentive for local foragers and pastoralists was the appeal of exotic manufactures, domesticates, and cultigens. One missing element in this speculative equation is the non-Harappan agriculturalists. The residents of Lothal and other "classic" Harappan settlements were greatly outnumbered by villages and towns only minimally integrated into Indus cultural and political spheres. Evidence for biological relatedness between populations of Lothal and Langhnaj and for a starchy, caries-inducing diet at the latter do suggest that Harappan trade relations with local hunter-gatherers were simply an extension of already-existing and ongoing connections between foragers and others.

Based on regional archaeological patterns, it seems probable that settled farming populations at this time were still sufficiently small so as not to seriously threaten the habitat of foraging peoples and, whatever the nature of the relationships, it is clear that this region supported a range of economic strategies from farming to pastoralism to foraging. The resources desired by urban-dwellers seem to have been high-value and (with the exception of wood) relatively portable materials that were available in only limited contexts and whose exploitation required some local knowledge. Like the other cases discussed here, transportation by sea was an essential component in moving goods collected by hunter-gatherers (and local farmers) to distant consumers; this form of technology as well as the social organization required to exploit regional differences in resources seems to be critical to the maintenance of such relationships. It is impossible at present to know how important the semiprecious stones and other raw materials collected by hunter-gatherers were to the Indus state(s) itself. Certainly, the beads and especially the seals and weights made out of these materials would have been very important economically and socially, but it is too soon to say if Harappan elites depended in any fundamental way on these goods.

The Western Ghats and the trade in forest products

South of the Harappan sphere, the hills of both Central and Eastern India, many still covered in dense dry monsoonal forests, have provided refuge for such ethnographically-studied groups as the Chenchus. Although this group, and others like them, have been described by anthropologists as isolated, archaic, and primitive, historical data paint a different picture. The assessment of ethnographer von Fürer-Haimendorf (1982:4–5), for example ("Until two or three generations ago, the Jungle Chenchus seem to have persisted in a life-style similar to that of the most archaic Indian tribal populations, and their traditional economy can hardly have been very different from that of forest dwellers of earlier ages."), can be contrasted with the work of Murthy (1994), who used historical documents to describe the wealth of the Chenchus, the existence of Chenchu royalty, and the ways Chenchus served various governments in eastern India from about the fifth century A.D. (and see Guha 1999; Skaria 1999).

In southern India, patterns of rainfall and vegetation are powerfully structured by the Western Ghat range that towers just beyond the west coast of the peninsula. This mountain chain traps a significant part of the southwest monsoon, creating both a narrow high-precipitation coastal strip and a larger rainshadow across the semi-arid peninsula. The orographic effect of the Ghats also accounts for a distinctive vegetation pattern in which upland tropical and semi-tropical forests, with their rich resources, lie relatively close to the west coast while interior vegetation types consist of deciduous monsoon forest and open scrub. Like other tropical forests, the resources of the Ghat uplands are not always those useful to foraging groups, but include products desired by lowland agriculturalists and states, including gums and resins, dyes and aromatics, and herbs and spices (Morrison 2002c). Even though these products may not have been widely used by foraging groups, in many cases their effective exploitation required significant local knowledge. Some tree-derived products, for example, included timber such as sandalwood (*Santalum album*) and teak (*Tectona grandis*) which had only to be located, identified, and harvested, while others required locating products derived only from diseased trees or involved extracting substances such as camphor, a crystallization from either *Dryobalanops camphora* or *Cinnamomun camphorum*. Both camphor and sandalwood were (and are) widely used for ceremonial purposes in South Asia and thus may be considered essential items of ritual and state.

Of all the forest products of southwest India, the most important historically was pepper (*Piper nigrum*), a vine of mid-elevation forests indigenous to the Malabar coast. Pepper and other forest products were traded far beyond South Asia as early as the first few centuries A.D., and it may be the case that local hunter-gatherers were involved in this exchange (Morrison 2002c). Although little archaeological research has been conducted in the Ghats, at present archaeological (Zagarell 1997, 2002; Noble 1989) and paleobotanical (Caratini et al. 1991) evidence point to the period around the first few centuries A.D. as the time when human impact on upland forests first began to be evident, the period when we also have archaeological and historical evidence for large-scale exchange connecting the Mediterranean, South, and Southeast Asia (Morrison 1997; Ray 2003). Pepper was clearly one of the goods leaving South Asia, movement dramatically represented by the recovery of peppercorns from North Africa (Phillips 1997). That South Asia's role as a node in Indian Ocean trade networks predated even this period seems likely, as indicated by, for example, the occurrence of cloves (a gathered wild plant product) from

Maluku in eastern Indonesia (Reid 1998:112) in the Mesopotamian site of Terqa dated to 1700 B.C. Although Southeast Asian products such as cloves could have been moved overland, perhaps with the assistance of some of the same mobile groups already involved in exchange with Indus urbanites, the presence of cowrie shells from the Maldive Islands (off the west coast of India) in Egypt as early as the late third millennium B.C. (Phillips 1997:424–6) does suggest the presence of very early ocean-going trade.

From as early as we have information, then, forest-dwelling groups of southern India have been integrated into lowland states and empires, usually through periodic payment of tribute and gift exchanges (Morrison 2002c). Even in these early centuries we have evidence that the most important goods moving into the forests were manufactured products such as textiles and iron, as well as cultigens such as rice. These exotic goods may have quickly become basic subsistence items; by the 18th century it is clear that upland groups relied heavily on rice, textiles, and iron tools from the lowlands.

The impetus for developing reciprocal relationships with non-foragers, then, may have related in part to the desire of hunter-gatherers in semi-remote locations for the domesticated and manufactured products available from settled agriculturalists, but it is also clear that, at least since the mid-Holocene, coercion also played a role. In South India not only were taxes or other official obligations sometimes levied on forest groups as well as agriculturalists, but equally importantly, relations of debt were developed which kept foragers perpetually in hock to intermediaries who supplied them with advances of lowland goods and collected from them pepper, cardamom, dyes and resins, honey, and other forest products (Morrison 2002c). Many of these intermediaries were licensed by indigenous and, later, colonial governments in a system of tax farming analogous to forms of extraction also employed against agriculturalists (Morrison 2001). Like upland groups, many South Asian farmers, too, were mired in debt that could last generations, caught in a cycle of repeated loans, high interest rates, and misinformation. Oppression was not reserved only for foragers, nor were its forms entirely unique; the common bonds of consumption and debt that bound farmer and forager alike attest to their shared participation in historically- and culturally-specific forms of power. Thus, in the later Holocene many upland groups in South India with primarily egalitarian social relations were simultaneously caught up in unequal power relations with neighboring farmers, with government-licensed or entrepreneurial brokers, and/or with government officials, relations of inequality that continue to this day (cf. Béteille 1998). Calling such groups egalitarian provides only a partial picture of their lives – at the very least we should employ the label of complex hunter-gatherer – better yet would be to consider these foragers, too, a "complex society."

The forest products collected by upland groups in southwestern India were clearly essential to the local and international trade of many of the small polities of India's west coast (cf. Boomgaard 1989, in which he argues that gathered forest products were essential to the development of many Southeast Asian trading states), as they also were to Portuguese trade from the 16th century onward (Morrison 2002c). Furthermore, the complex networks of production and exchange that brought manufactured goods and food crops inland and upland, and pepper and other forest products down to coastal entrepôt cities ensured that forest dwellers, some of whom operated primarily as hunter-gatherers, were critical partners in the development and maintenance of indigenous and colonial states, even when their home territories were not officially part of those polities (Morrison 2002c). Thus, later Holocene hunter-gatherers in South India, far from being isolated people marginal to the development of complex societies or to colonialism, were in fact essential players in that development.

With the massive expansion of the spice trade in the 16th and 17th centuries A.D. and the more direct involvement of Europeans in this trade following Portuguese (and later Dutch and English) colonial expansion into Asia, it becomes much easier to detect the activities of local foragers, agriculturalists, and others in these long-distance networks. In these centuries, we have some evidence that groups who formerly practiced a range of subsistence activities, including agriculture, military service, raiding, and wage labor, may have begun to specialize in the extraction of forest products; these same groups would later appear in the ethnographic literature represented as "timeless" exemplars of an earlier way of life (Morrison 2002b, 2002c). This intellectual history has had the unfortunate consequence of erasing foraging groups from the mainstream political and economic history of South Asia, a position they are only now coming to reclaim.

The Andaman islands

In Chalcolithic Western India, foragers, pastoralists, and other mobile groups had the advantage of occupational histories and local environments that left them room to expand and, if necessary, flee the attentions of urban-dwellers. Given the existence of numerous archaeological sites of the Mesolithic, local monsoon forests clearly provided an adequate resource base for subsistence foraging (though as noted, many of these are difficult to date precisely). In southwestern India, forest-dwellers in the tropical and semi-tropical evergreen forests of the Western Ghats had the advantage of local knowledge of this steep and difficult mountain terrain, but throughout the second millennium A.D., they seem to have been increasingly squeezed by the expansion of lowland agriculture (Morrison 2002c) as well as by the desirability of local forest products to nearby agriculturalists and faraway empires alike. Certainly, the differences between these two cases are significant, but in both we see the development of forms of engagement between hunter-gatherers and others that, although marked by inequities, also allowed mobile foragers to maintain their cultural distinctiveness and way of life. In both cases, subsistence foraging and foraging for exchange may have coexisted, with strategies of groups, families, even individuals probably shifting between these modes as well as between other options such as cultivation, wage labor, military service, and banditry (see Morrison 2002c). The Andaman Islands present a rather different situation, one with similarities to parts of island Southeast Asia, where coastal environments with abundant marine resources fringe upland tropical forests and where oceans both isolate and, through their ease of transport, unite far-distant areas. In the Andamans, where hunting and gathering have, until recently, been the primary mode of subsistence, the islanders were famous for their fierce avoidance of out-siders (Cooper 2002) while at the same time Andaman products circulated in Indian Ocean trade networks.

The Andamans, now part of India, lie to the southeast of the subcontinent only about 300 kilometers from Burma and 120 from the Nicobar chain (Cooper 2002:18), right along a sea route between South and Southeast Asia. Mentions in textual sources as early as the second century A.D. consistently describe the Andaman Islanders as hostile, even as cannibals, a characterization markedly dif-ferent from that of the Nicobarese, major suppliers of ambergris to the 16th-century port city of Melaka on the Malay peninsula (Cooper 2002:12–14) and where, by this time, the language of commerce was Portuguese. While archaeological finds of Chinese ceramics are reported for the Nicobars, no such evidence has been found in the Andamans where an (undated) excavated shell midden containing several 17th-century Sumatran gold coins is the primary material evidence for long-distance exchange (Cooper 2002:2). In her recent review of Andaman history and report on new archaeological research, Cooper (2002:17–25) describes how Andaman Islanders were consistently victimized by slave raiders, convincingly attributing some of their xenophobia as a reaction to this threat.

At the same time, several local resources drew outside attention, but like many such products, neither was used by local people. Malay, Burmese, and even Chinese ships regularly visited the coastal caves and rockshelters containing nests of the white-nest swiftlet (*Collocalia fuciphaga inexpectata*), considered a delicacy in China and parts of Southeast Asia. Similarly, sea slugs caught in coastal waters made their way to eastern consumers. Although Cooper notes (2002:22) that in the Mergui archipelago near southern Burma the indigenous Moken people were employed to collect these same products for Malay and Chinese traders, she posits that this was not the case in the Andamans (and see Mann 1883). Although iron objects are con-sistently found in both lower and upper levels of excavated midden sites, Cooper argues (2002:22–3) that this highly coveted material could have come entirely from shipwrecks. Certainly, with the takeover of the islands by the British and the estab-lishment of a British penal colony there in 1858, islanders were forced to interact with others – their transfer of chipped stone technology to molded bottle glass pro-vides a forceful material record of this engagement.

In contrast to the very long occupational history of the greater Indus region, where hunting and gathering coexisted with agriculture from the early Holocene, and the intermediate-length record of southwest coastal India where the uplands appear to have been occupied year-round only since the first few centuries A.D. while the lowlands show a longer record of settlement, the occupational history of the Andamans is relatively short. Cooper's recent excavations provide the only absolute dates – her earliest radiocarbon assessment (BS–599, 2002:156), from the base of the 4.45-meter deep Chauldhuri midden, dates to between A.D. 162 and 290 (calibrated using Stuiver and Reimer 1993 [version 4.4] with delta R [marine reservoir] value of 7+/34 after Dutta et al. 2000). The presence of both pig (*Sus scrofa*) bones and a small number of ceramics from the earliest levels of this site suggest that the Andaman islanders brought some of the accouterments of settled agricultural life with them at the time of initial colonization (Cooper 2002:7, 83–93).

That the earliest dates (at present) for the colonization of the Andamans fall around the same time as the well-documented expansion in Indian Ocean trade in the first few centuries A.D. (Morrison 1997) may be no coincidence. In spite of the well-documented fierceness and aloofness of the Andaman foragers, they have clearly been involved in relationships with others throughout their history. Living on the "stepping stones between Burma and the Nicobars" (Cooper 2002:166), the islanders were not only victims of slave raids and occasional pillagers of shipwrecks and unwary visitors, but they may also have been involved in the gathering of birds' nests and sea slugs for external exchange. Following British colonization, many were forcibly settled and lifeways were radically altered (Cooper 2002; cf. Radcliffe-Brown 1922). In the face of virtual extinction Andaman islanders continued to innovate, adapting lithic technology to manufactured glass and hunting techniques to accommodate newly-introduced domestic dogs. While the income from the pepper and other forest products of the Western Ghats and many of the high islands of Southeast Asia provided critical support to local exchange-oriented polities, the bird nests, sea slugs, and human slaves of the Andamans never propped up a local elite. Still, their value in Malay and Chinese societies is evident in the distance and effort traders were to brave in order to obtain them.

Discussion

Why is the continuing existence of hunting and gathering important? Although agriculture and its concomitant package(s) of landscape change and social and political reorganization were taken up at different times and in different ways across Asia, foraging strategies both persisted and evolved. Far from being an outmoded, primitive, or archaic form of subsistence, foraging has proven to be a resilient (cf. Barnard 2002), appealing, and persistent way of life equally at home (though not always thriving to the same degree) in the context of early territorial states, trade-based states and empires, colonial empires, and modern global capitalism. Asian hunter-gatherers, perhaps more than most, exemplify this flexibility. Historically, we can trace their deployment of both subsistence foraging and forager-trader forms as well as, at times, involvement in agriculture, wage labor, military service, and extra-legal activities such as raiding and piracy. Here the fact that the categories of hunting and gathering, pastoralism, agriculture, and other forms of occupational specialization can not always be analytically separated (Morrison 2002a), far from decreasing the importance of Holocene foraging, actually makes it more compelling. Firstly, cultural strategies this complex and resilient certainly merit our attention as alternate ways of living in the contemporary world. Secondly, all of our ethnographic and historical models and understandings of hunting and gathering are based on the experience of Holocene foragers. If the very categories of, for example, forager and agriculturalist, seem to be too sharply drawn, to say nothing of more problematic distinctions such as simple and complex, and archaic and modern, then surely we will need to reconsider our delineation and deployment of such categories.

My primary concern in this chapter is not the relevance or irrelevance of the study of recent hunter-gatherers for understanding a world prior to the development of agriculture. Hunter-gatherers have been part of the archaeology and history of Asia from the beginning, and they remain so today. The analysis in this chapter of a few examples of Holocene hunting and gathering in South Asia has shown, not only that foragers in this region have always been "part of history," as proponents of the revisionist camp would have it, but more than this, that they have often been integral parts of regional networks of exchange, political and social forms, and relations of kinship. Although I have stressed the importance of unequal power relations, it is worth pointing out that foragers have not always been at the mercy of their neighbors. Although South Indian foragers have been subjected to debt peonage and Andaman Islanders to slave raiding, displacement, and pauperization, foragers in South and Southeast Asia can not be seen solely as victims of external power relations. Instead, hunting and gathering peoples have also been raiders, warriors, pirates, and (no doubt apocryphally) "cannibals."

In considering the distinct occupational histories, geographies, and resources of South Asia (and Asia in general), it is clear that the continued existence of hunting and gathering represents much more than simply the stubborn cultural conservatism of a few small groups. On the contrary, it is impossible to appreciate the operation of many South and Southeast Asian states without an understanding of the role of local foragers. In many places, particularly the smaller polities of southwest coastal India and island Southeast Asia, gathered forest products constituted the most valuable goods in regional spheres of exchange and were the primary economic support for local states, propping up elite lifestyles and enriching local and foreign traders. Foragers, along with other groups, made possible the dissemination and perpetuation of culturally-valued products in Europe and East Asia, fashion fads such as bird of paradise feathers, exotic spices such as pepper that moved from luxury to necessity and from wild plant to cultigen, and items of elite consumption such as birds' nests, ivory, sandalwood, ebony, and teak. In general, polities built on the labor of hunting and gathering were smaller, trade-oriented states rather than large, land-based agrarian states, but even in some of the latter such as the 14th- to 16th-century A.D. Vijayanagara empire of southern India, trade in forest products was economically significant, with hill peoples also playing important military and cultural roles as buffer communities, members of the armed forces, and royal hunting guides (Guha 1999; Morrison 2002c).

South and Southeast Asian Holocene foragers have been notoriously problematic in hunter-gatherer ethnography, primarily because of their long histories of engagement with others and because such studies have generally been oriented either toward providing models for the Palaeolithic or context-free general models of behavior. If we however discard the possibility of acontextual models of this sort and embrace the complexities of the actual historical trajectories of Asian foragers, it is then, perhaps paradoxically, this engagement that makes them so interesting and important. Hunting and gathering, sometimes in conjunction with other subsistence forms and sometimes alone, have been part of the workings of many South and Southeast Asian societies since at least the third millennium B.C., societies with and without state-level governance and, in most cases, societies deeply involved in long-distance exchange, specialization, and unequal power relations. Analyses of state formation, trade, and colonialism that leave out gathering and hunting thus leave out key actors and key resources in these processes – Holocene foraging is thus an issue of general concern for the archaeology and history of large parts of Asia rather than the domain of a small group of specialists.

REFERENCES

Andaya, Barbara Watson 1993 To Live as Brothers: Southeast Sumatra in the Seventeenth and Eighteenth Centuries. Honolulu: University of Hawaii Press.

Bailey, Richard C., Genevieve Head, Mark Jenike, Bruce Owen, Robert Rechtman, and Elzbieta Zechenter 1989 Hunting and Gathering the Tropical Rainforest: Is it Possible? American Anthropologist 91:59–82.

Barnard, Alan 2002 The Foraging Mode of Thought. In Self- and Other-Images of Hunter-Gatherers. H. Stewart, A. Barnard, and K. Omura, eds. Pp. 5–24. Senri Ethnological Studies 60. Osaka: National Museum of Ethnology.

Bellwood, Peter 1985 Prehistory of the Indo-Malaysian Archipelago. Honolulu: University of Hawaii Press.

Béteille, Andre 1998 The Idea of Indigenous People. Current Anthropology 39(2):187–91.

Boomgaard, Peter 1989 The VOC Trade in Forest Products. In Nature and the Orient: The Environmental History of South and Southeast Asia. Richard H. Grove, Vinita Damodaran, and Satpal Sangwan, eds. Delhi: Oxford University Press.

—— 1997 Introducing Environmental Histories of Indonesia. In Paper Landscapes: Explorations in the Environmental History of Indonesia. Peter Boomgaard, Freek Columbijn, and David Henley, eds. Pp. 1–26. Leiden: KITLV Press.

Boomgaard, Peter, Freek Columbijn, and David Henley, eds. 1997 Paper Landscapes: Explorations in the Environmental History of Indonesia. Leiden: KITLV Press.

Boserup, Esther 1965 The Conditions of Agricultural Growth. Chicago: Aldine.

Caratini, Claude, Jean-Paul Pascal, Colette Tissot, and G. Rajagopalan 1991 Palynological Reconstruction of a Wet Evergreen Forest in the Western Ghats (India) ca. 1800 to ca. 1400 Years B.P. Journal of Palynology 1990–91:123–37.

Cohen, Mark N. 1977 The Food Crisis in Prehistory. New Haven: Yale University Press.

Columbijn, Freek 1997 The Ecological Sustainability of Frontier Societies in Eastern Sumatra. In Paper Landscapes: Explorations in the Environmental History of Indonesia. Peter Boomgaard, Freek Columbijn, and David Henley, eds. Pp. 309–40. Leiden: KITLV Press.

Cooper, Zarine 2002 Archaeology and History: Early Settlements in the Andaman Islands. Delhi: Oxford University Press.

Cribb, Robert 1997 Birds of Paradise and Environmental Politics in Colonial Indonesia, 1890–1931. In Paper Landscapes: Explorations in the Environmental History of Indonesia.

Peter Boomgaard, Freek Columbijn, and David Henley, eds. Pp. 379–408. Leiden: KITLV Press.

Dhavalikar, M. K., M. R. Raval, and Y. M. Chitalwala 1995 Kuntasi: A Harappan Emporium on West Coast. Pune, India: Deccan College Postgraduate and Research Institute.

Dutta, K., R. Bhushan, and B. L. K. Samayajulu 2001 Delta R Correction Values for the Northern Indian Ocean. Radiocarbon 43:483–8.

Fürer-Haimendorf, Christophe von 1982 Tribes of India: The Struggle for Survival. Berkeley: University of California Press.

Guha, Sumit 1999 Environment and Ethnicity in India 1200–1991. Cambridge: Cambridge University Press.

de Jong Boers, Bernice 1997 Sustainability and Time Perspective in Natural Resource Management: The Exploitation of Sappan Trees in the Forests of Sumbawa, Indonesia, 1500–1875. In Paper Landscapes: Explorations in the Environmental History of Indonesia. Peter Boomgaard, Freek Columbijn, and David Henley, eds. Pp. 261–80. Leiden: KITLV Press.

Junker, Laura L. 2002a Southeast Asia: Introduction. In Forager-Traders in South and Southeast Asia: Long-Term Histories. Kathleen D. Morrison and Laura L. Junker, eds. Pp. 131–66. Cambridge: Cambridge University Press.

—— 2002b Economic Specialization and Inter-Ethnic Trade Between Foragers and Farmers in the Prehispanic Philippines. In Forager-Traders in South and Southeast Asia: Long-Term Histories. Kathleen D. Morrison and Laura L. Junker, eds. Pp. 203–41. Cambridge: Cambridge University Press.

Kennedy, Kenneth A. R., John Chimet, Tod Disotell, and David Meyers 1984 Principal-Components Analysis of Prehistoric South Asian Crania. American Journal of Physical Anthropology 64(2):105–18.

Kenoyer, Jonathan Mark 1997 Trade and Technology of the Indus Valley: New Insights from Harappa, Pakistan. World Archaeology 29(2):262–80.

Khatri, A. P. 1964 Rock Paintings of Adamgarh (Central India) and their Age. Anthropos 59:759–71.

Knapen, Hans 2001 Forests of Fortune? The Environmental History of Southeast Borneo, 1600–1880. Leiden: KITLV Press.

Korisettar, Ravi, and S. N. Rajaguru 2002 Understanding Man-Land Relationships in Peninsular Deccan: With Special Reference to Karnataka. In Indian Archaeology in Retrospect, Volume I: Prehistory. S. Settar and R. Korisettar, eds. Pp. 243–96. Delhi: ICHR and Manohar Press.

Korisettar, Ravi, P. C. Venkatasubbaiah, and Doreen Q. Fuller 2002 Brahmagiri and Beyond: The Archaeology of the Southern Neolithic. In Indian Archaeology in Retrospect, Volume I: Prehistory. S. Settar and Ravi Korisettar, eds. Pp. 151–238. Delhi: ICHR and Manohar Press.

Kulke, Hermann, and Diethmar Rothermund 1990 History of India. London: Routledge.

Lee, Richard B. 1998 Foreword. In Limited Wants, Unlimited Means: A Reader on Hunter-Gatherer Economics and the Environment. John M. Gowdy, ed. Pp. ix–xii. Washington DC: Island Press.

Lee, Richard B., and Richard Daly, eds. 2000 Cambridge Encyclopedia of Hunters and Gatherers. Cambridge: Cambridge University Press.

Lukacs, John R. 1990 On Hunter-Gatherers and their Neighbors in Prehistoric India: Contact and Pathology. Current Anthropologist 31(2):183–6.

—— 2002 Hunting and Gathering Strategies in Prehistoric India: A Biocultural Perspective on Trade And Subsistence. In Forager-Traders in South And Southeast Asia: Long-Term

Histories. Kathleen D. Morrison and Laura L. Junker, eds. Pp. 41–61. Cambridge: Cambridge University Press.

Lukacs, John R., and J. N. Pal 1993 Mesolithic Subsistence in North India: Inferences from Dental Attributes. Current Anthropology 34(5):745–65.

Lycett, Mark T., and Kathleen D. Morrison 1989 Persistent Lithics: Post Iron Age Lithic Technology in South India. Paper presented at the Annual Conference on South Asia, Madison, Wisconsin, Nov. 3–5.

Malik, S. C. 1959 Stone Age Industries of the Bombay and Satara Districts. Baroda: Maharaja Sayajirao University.

Mann, Edward H. 1883 On the Aboriginal Inhabitants of the Andaman Islands. Journal of the Anthropological Institute of Great Britain and Ireland 12:69–175, 327–434.

Mehta, R. N., K. N. Momin, and D. R. Shah 1980 Excavation at Kanewal. Baroda: Maharaja Sayajirao University.

Misra, V. N. 1976 Ecological Adaptations During the Terminal Stone Age in Western and Central India. In Ecological Backgrounds of South Asian Prehistory. K. A. R. Kennedy and G. L. Possehl, eds. Pp. 28–51. Ithaca: South Asia Occasional Papers, Cornell University.

Morrison, Kathleen D. 1997 Commerce and Culture in South Asia: Perspectives from Archaeology and History. Annual Review of Anthropology 26:87–108.

—— 2000 South Asia: Prehistory. In Cambridge Encyclopedia of Hunters and Gatherers. R. B. Lee and R. Daly, eds. Pp. 238–42. Cambridge: Cambridge University Press.

—— 2001 Coercion, Resistance, and Hierarchy: Local Processes and Imperial Strategies in the Vijayanagara Empire. In Empires: Perspectives from Archaeology and History. Susan Alcock, Terence D'Altroy, Kathleen Morrison, and Carla Sinopoli, eds. Pp. 253–78. Cambridge: Cambridge University Press.

—— 2002a General Introduction: Historicizing Adaptation, Adapting to History. In Forager-Traders in South and Southeast Asia: Long-Term Histories. Kathleen D. Morrison and Laura L. Junker, eds. Pp. 1–20. Cambridge: Cambridge University Press.

—— 2002b Introduction: South Asia. In Forager-Traders in South and Southeast Asia: Long-Term Histories. Kathleen D. Morrison and Laura L. Junker, eds. Pp. 21–40. Cambridge: Cambridge University Press.

—— 2002c Pepper in the Hills: Upland-Lowland Exchange and the Intensification of the Spice Trade. In Forager-Traders in South and Southeast Asia: Long-Term Histories. Kathleen D. Morrison and Laura L. Junker, eds. Pp. 105–30. Cambridge: Cambridge University Press.

Morrison, Kathleen D., and Laura L. Junker, eds. 2002 Forager-Traders in South and Southeast Asia: Long-Term Histories. Cambridge: Cambridge University Press.

Murthy, M. L. K. 1994 Forest Peoples and Historical Traditions in the Eastern Ghats, South India. In Living Traditions: Studies in the Ethnoarchaeology of South Asia. Bridget Allchin, ed. Pp. 205–18. New Delhi: Oxford and IBH.

Noble, William A. 1989 Nilgiri Prehistoric Remains. In Blue Mountains: The Ethnography and Biogeography of a South Indian Region. P. Hockings, ed. Pp. 102–32. New Delhi: Oxford University Press.

Phillips, Jacke 1997 Punt and Aksum: Egypt and the Horn of Africa. The Journal of African History 38(3):423–57.

Possehl, Gregory L. 1976 Lothal: A Gateway Settlement of the Harappan Civilization. In Ecological Backgrounds of South Asian Prehistory. Kenneth A. R. Kennedy and Gregory L. Possehl, eds. Pp. 118–31. Ithaca: Occasional Papers No. 4: Cornell South Asia Program.

—— 1992 The Harappan Civilization in Gujarat: The Sorath and Sindhi Harappans. Eastern Anthropologist 45(1–2):117–54.

—— 1999 Indus Age: The Beginnings. Philadelphia: University of Pennsylvania Press.

—— 2002 Harappans and Hunters: Economic Interaction and Specialization in Prehistoric India. *In* Forager-Traders in South and Southeast Asia: Long-Term Histories. Kathleen D. Morrison and Laura L. Junker, eds. Pp. 62–76. Cambridge: Cambridge University Press.

Possehl, Gregory L., and Kenneth A. R. Kennedy 1979 Hunter-Gatherer/Agriculturalist Exchange in Prehistory: An Indian Example. Current Anthropology 20(3):592–3.

Potter, Leslie M. 1997 A Forest Product Out of Control: Gutta Percha in Indonesia and the Wider Malay World. *In* Blue Mountains Revisited: Cultural Studies on the Nilgiri Hills Explorations in the Environmental History of Indonesia. Peter Boomgaard, Freek Columbijn, and David Henley, eds. Pp. 281–308. Leiden: KITLV Press.

Price, T. Douglas, and James A. Brown, eds. 1985 Prehistoric Hunter-Gatherers: The Emergence of Cultural Complexity. Orlando: Academic Press.

Radcliffe-Brown, Alfred Reginald 1922 The Andaman Islanders. Cambridge: Cambridge University Press.

Ratnagar, Shareen 1981 Encounters: The Westerly Trade of the Harappa Civilization. Delhi: Oxford University Press.

Ray, Himanshu Prabha 2003 The Archaeology of Seafaring in Ancient South Asia. Cambridge: Cambridge University Press.

Reid, Anthony 1998 Humans and Forests in Pre-Colonial Southeast Asia. *In* Nature and the Orient: The Environmental History of South and Southeast Asia. Richard H. Grove, Vinita Damodaran, and Satpal Sangwan, eds. Pp. 106–26. Delhi: Oxford University Press.

Rissman, Paul C., and Y. M. Chitalwala 1990 Harappan Civilization and Oriyo Timbo. New Delhi: Oxford and IBH.

Sankalia, H. D. 1965 Archaeological Excavations at Langhnaj: 1944–63, Pt. 1. Pune, India: Deccan College Postgraduate and Research Institute.

Selvakumar, V. In press Hunter-Gatherer–Agropastoralist Interactions During the Iron Age–Early Historic Period in the Upper Gundar Basin, Tamil Nadu. *In* Recent Research on the Archaeology of Southern India. V. V. Rami Reddy and K. D. Morrison, eds. Delhi: Munshiram Manhoharlal.

Skaria, Ajay 1999 Hybrid Histories: Forests, Frontiers, and Wilderness in Western India. Delhi: Oxford University Press.

Stuiver, Minze, and Paula J. Reimer 1993 Extended 14C Database and Revised CALIB Radiocarbon Calibration Program. Radiocarbon 35:215–30.

Thapar, Romila 1997 Asoka and the Decline of the Mauryas. Rev. edition. Delhi: Oxford University Press.

Virunha, Chuleeporn 2002 Power Relations Between the Orang Laut and the Malay Kingdoms of Melaka and Johor During the Fifteenth to Seventeenth Centuries. *In* Recalling Local Pasts: Autonomous History in Southeast Asia. Sunait Chutintaranond and Chris Baker, eds. Pp. 143–66. Chiang Mai: Silkworm Books.

Zagarell, Alan 1997 Megalithic Graves of the Nilgiri Hills and the Moyar Ditch. *In* Blue Mountains Revisited: Cultural Studies on the Nilgiri Hills. Paul Hockings, ed. Pp. 23–73. Delhi: Oxford University Press.

—— 2002 Gender and Social Organization in the Reliefs of the Nilgiri Hills. *In* Forager-Traders in South and Southeast Asia: Long-Term Histories. Kathleen D. Morrison and Laura L. Junker, eds. Pp. 77–104. Cambridge: Cambridge University Press.

14

The Axial Age in Asia: The Archaeology of Buddhism (500 B.C.–A.D. 500)

Himanshu Prabha Ray

The middle of the first millennium B.C. saw several new developments in the religions of South Asia and is best known for the emergence of Buddhism and Jainism as well as for changes within the sacrificial and philosophical doctrines of the Vedas. The German philosopher Karl Jaspers (1883–1969) proposed the idea of Axial Age as a theory to describe the coincident appearance of several major world religious and philosophical founders from 800 to 200 B.C. From the beginning of the sixth century B.C. to the end of the fourth century B.C., a drastic change is said to have occurred in religious traditions, which brought about several new religions including Hinduism, Buddhism, Confucianism, Taoism, and Zoroastrianism. These religions, though unique in their own way, are said to share general aspects of the Axial Age religious transformations, i.e. that having strong, positive ethics and morals was very important. More recently, scholars have critiqued Jaspers' hypothesis of Axial Age, which they suggest is no more than a convenient entry point for further observations and comparisons and should not be taken as a law of human history but as a helpful observation of the founding of ancient philosophy and religions (Eisenstadt 1986).

In this chapter the focus is on Buddhism, since, although both Buddhism and Hinduism expanded into several regions of the Indian Ocean world, this aspect of Buddhism is the least studied. What was the agency for the spread of religious doctrines across the Indian Ocean? Was it the ruler and the state or was it the Buddhist clergy, thus creating an autonomous religious network that cut across political boundaries? In this expansion across the Indian Ocean how did Buddhism transform itself and adapt to the local environment?

This chapter documents this expansion and religious transformation based on archaeological data from South and Southeast Asia. It also highlights the larger than life role of the Mauryan ruler Asoka, whose close association with the spread of Buddhism is a memory that continued to be invoked in the subsequent centuries. The dissemination of languages such as Pali, Sanskrit, and Tamil, and use of the

Brahmi and Kharosthi scripts marked by local variations provides another dimension to this maritime network. The shared culture that traversed the Indian Ocean was part of a larger literate tradition, but by no means was controlled by the ruler or the Brahman, as has been traditionally suggested. Writing facilitated the storing of information and cumulative knowledge promoted a new genre of cultural and artistic expression (Goody 2001:144).

There are three traditions about the date of the death of the Buddha placing it ca. 543 B.C., ca. 486/3 B.C. or ca. 370 B.C. The first is based on the Sri Lankan Chronicles, the second coincides with Chinese records, while the third or shorter chronology is derived from the Chinese and Tibetan translations of the *Vinaya Pitaka*. Bechert (1995) has made a case for the shorter chronology in recent years, though others have argued for sixth-fifth centuries B.C. as the lifetime of the Buddha (Chakrabarti 2000:377; see also Erdosy 1993).

The traditional approach to the study of Buddhism in South Asia, especially with reference to its introduction into Sri Lanka has been to discuss it as expanding "from court to court, a product of state patronage" during the Mauryan period (317–186 B.C.) (Gombrich 1994:145). Nor is Gombrich alone in this formulation. Tambiah (1976) acclaims Buddhism as an efficacious ideology of pacification, political stability and security, which Asoka propagated. Thapar on the other hand makes a distinction between the ruler's personal and official religious affiliation and refers to Asoka's endorsement of Buddhism arising out of imperial needs, namely acculturation of a diverse populace (Thapar 1997:309). Another common assumption is that by the end of the reign of Asoka in the second century B.C., Buddhist monks and nuns were established in monasteries throughout the Indian subcontinent and that these monasteries, located near cities relied on state support (Lopez 1995:4).

There is, similarly, no unanimity regarding the communities that adopted Buddhism as a result of Asoka's propagation. Tambiah proposes that it was the category of people located on the "margins of civilization" and variously described as forest people, frontier people, and hill tribes who converted to Buddhism (1976:64). Thapar, on the other hand, states that the ethical teachings of the Buddhists and Jainas were "more appropriate to richer agriculturists and urbanites rather than to pastoral and hunting tribal people" (2000:884).

One of the related issues with regard to the emergence and spread of Buddhism has been the question of identity of the lay Buddhist, i.e. was Buddhism a religion of the community at large or was it restricted to those who renounced the world, i.e. the monks and nuns? It has been suggested that the Buddha prescribed a path to salvation and was not interested in expounding a ritual or communal religion. While this may by and large be valid, there is no denying the fact that the Buddhist canon makes a concerted attempt to inculcate a sense of moral and ethical values among the laity based on Buddhist ethics and loyalty to the Triratna, viz. Buddha, Dhamma, and Sangha.

At the same time there was emphasis on a distinctive identity based on the outward appearance of the monks and nuns (Brekke 1997:7–32). Lists of rules of personal conduct were drawn up and all monks and nuns had to recite these at the fortnightly ceremony. The image of early Buddhist monks and nuns as professional salvation seekers who distanced themselves from the world is also being increasingly questioned (Schopen 1988–89), especially with regard to their role in innovation and social change. It is then evident that in this chapter Buddhism is discussed not merely as a religion for ascetics and monks and nuns, but as a social religion with a lay following. Buddhism also expounded distinct notions of kingship and in certain periods and regions achieved close links with the ruling elite. The Buddhist political *dhamma* concept is a theory of royal conduct, which states that *cariya* or *vidhana* (procedure or method) makes the king a moral being, and this provided uniqueness to early Buddhist political theory.

Why did Buddhism spread so successfully? Gombrich suggests that the major factor was that it filled a void in Sri Lankan and Southeast Asian societies, which had no soteriology and no literate culture of their own. Buddhism offered "both a coherent, universalistic ethic and a way to salvation from suffering" (1997:151). Reginald Ray (1994:404), on the other hand, argues that it was the institutionalization of the classical monastic tradition, which allowed Buddhism to expand into newer areas and to newer cultures. This institutionalization has traditionally been attributed to the Buddha, though recent scholarship has emphasized that it was a far more complex process involving a more gradual development.

The archaeological map of Buddhist sites in India was drawn as a result of the surveys conducted by Alexander Cunningham largely in north India in the 19th century. Cunningham (1871–2, 1961, 1962) argued that an enquirer into Indian archaeology should retrace the steps of the Chinese travellers Faxian and Xuanzang. As a result his exploration extended mainly across modern Uttar Pradesh and Bihar, though his search for Pundravardhana took him briefly to Bengal in 1879–80 leading to the discovery of the site of Mahasthangarh (Imam 1966). These pioneering investigations were primarily aimed at documentation and cataloguing and were neither comprehensive nor analytical, but nevertheless they provided much of the basis for subsequent interpretation. Heitzman (1984) documented and analysed archaeological data vis-à-vis the location of early Buddhist sites in India, though within the dominant paradigm of political power as an agent of change. The locational analysis of sites indicated that there is little archaeological evidence to suggest that Buddhist centers had any political or economic role. Writing in 1987, Schopen argued that if the history of religions, which was textbound, had instead been archaeology of religions "it would have been preoccupied *not* with what small, literate almost exclusively male and certainly atypical professionalized subgroups wrote, but rather, with what religious people of all segments of a given community actually did and how they lived" (Schopen 1987:193).

Insoll (2001), who approaches the theme at a more general level, suggests that archaeology can help uncover changes in ritual practices and disposal of the dead, as well as transformations in food habits and dietary alterations and modifications in the utilization of sacred space and religious architecture.

Another volume of significance to this discussion is the special issue of *World Archaeology* devoted to Buddhism (1995), especially the papers by Chakrabarti, Morrison, and Coningham. Chakrabarti (1995) identifies three stages in the development of Buddhism in north India between the sixth century B.C. and the 13th century A.D. and distinguishes pre-Buddhist archaeological cultures in different regions of the Ganga valley. Thus while human occupation in the Ganga-Yamuna *doab* began with metal-using Late Harappan cultures representing a continuity from the preceding Mature Harappan stage, this was not the case elsewhere in the region. In the middle and lower Ganga valley for example, early settlement dates to the Mesolithic hunting–gathering tradition and it is in the fitness of things that Buddhism emerged in this region. Morrison (1995), on the other hand, sees agricultural expansion as a precondition for commercial expansion in the Deccan and argues for an agricultural base prior to the emergence of Buddhist monastic sites in the region. Following Tambiah's (1984:54) early work on forest monks, Coningham (1995) proposes that the form of early Buddhism that came to Sri Lanka was very similar to that practiced by modern forest monks dwelling within the island.

A recent micro-study based on archaeological surface survey at the monastic site of Thotlakonda in coastal Andhra highlights the role of ritual in early Buddhism. The survey of the hills surrounding Thotlakonda revealed roughly 200 stone cairns, which were carefully recorded and mapped. All were constructed of natural boulders, easily available in the fields dotting the hilltops, and ranged between one and three meters in diameter, with a few larger ones being more than 10 meters in diameter. It is difficult to state the exact function of these cairns, but similar finds elsewhere in South Asia have been interpreted as memorials entombing the ashes of devout Buddhists. From the pattern of distribution of the cairns it is clear that the monastery served as the focus of a large mortuary landscape (Fogelin 2003).

The spread of Buddhism into peninsular India and across the Bay of Bengal, and the interaction between Buddhism and other religious groups, are issues that have been discussed elsewhere (Ray 2003; Ray and Sinopoli 2004). The central argument in this chapter is that the role of the state both in providing patronage and in the expansion of Buddhism to different regions has been exaggerated. Instead we need to highlight the diverse communities that owed allegiance to the Buddhist faith, in addition to the monks and nuns. Certainly the lay community played a key role both in providing patronage and in the maintenance of the monastic establishments. A comparative study of monastic sites in India, Sri Lanka, and Thailand highlights not only their diverse contexts, but also different patterns of adaptation and appropriation. Besides, an important factor in this expansion relates to the study of routes and communication networks that made voyages across the Indian Ocean possible. In most cases these routes were avenues for trade and it was along these that religious preachers traveled, though there was a clear separation between economic activity and religious proselytization.

It is similarly important to make a distinction between state intervention as opposed to appropriation and reinvention, especially in the context of the Indian Ocean realm. Historically, several rulers in Sri Lanka and Southeast Asia invoked the legacy of Asoka in their relations with the Buddhist Sangha and the lay community. The fourth–fifth century *Mahavamsa*, which has traditionally been used for a history of the island of Sri Lanka, not only credits Asoka with the spread of Buddhism, but also refers in glowing terms to the envoys sent by him to the consecration of the Sri Lankan monarch Devanampiya Tissa. No doubt the historical memory of Asoka was strong enough well into the first millennium A.D. to posit such linkages. Tambiah (1976:6) argues that notions of kingship crystallized in Thailand from the 12th century onwards and significant inputs in this process came from the Sinhalese tradition, which accorded an important role to the king in the guardianship and purification of the Buddhist Sangha.

Maritime Networks

The beginnings of the Indian Ocean maritime system may be traced to the prehistoric Mesolithic period when communities first settled along the coasts of South and Southeast Asia from 10,000 B.C. onwards. Perhaps the earliest evidence of fishing communities in South Asia as evidenced by the finds of beads on shell comes from the Batadombalena Caves in Sri Lanka dated to circa 28,500–16,000 B.P. (Deraniyagala 1990:215). Located on the northwest coast of Sri Lanka Mantai has provided evidence for exploitation of marine resources such as various molluscs, fish, sea turtles, dolphin, and so on in the prehistoric Mesolithic phase dated to the beginning of the second millennium B.C.

Comparable dates of 23,050 ± 200 B.C. are available from late prehistoric sites in western India. Around 10,000 B.C. there was an increase in the number of sites in the Indian subcontinent as well as occupation in a range of diverse ecological niches by communities using microliths, generally defined as small lithic implements of less then one to five centimeters length (Chakrabarti 1999:91).

Coastal shell midden, open, and cave sites with marine shell deposits dating from after 8,000 years ago have been identified in northern Sumatra, western peninsular Malaysia, and north Vietnam dating from 6000 to 1500 B.C. At present, many of these sites are found inland – for example in Sumatra, on an old shoreline 10–15 kilometers away from the coast – thereby reflecting the higher sea levels during the middle Holocene (Bellwood 1992:87).

These fishing and sailing communities, in addition to exploiting the resources of the sea, were agents for the transportation of passengers and commodities in their cargo carriers and thus formed the bedrock of maritime travel (Ray 2003:30–54). By the second–first centuries B.C., coastal sites were well integrated into inland systems and the trading network was well established across the Bay of Bengal, incorporating a variety of overland and coastal routes (Glover 1990).

The distribution of a range of ceramics at archaeological sites indicates several regional and trans-oceanic circuits. The distribution of Rouletted Ware, a fine textured pottery with rouletted decoration on the base, indicates that the coastal system had expanded to include the entire stretch of the east coast of the Indian subcontinent and across the Bay of Bengal to sites in Southeast Asia. Wheeler had identified this ceramic in his excavations at Arikamedu and dated it to the end of first century B.C.–beginning of first century A.D. (Wheeler 1946:45). Begley, on the other hand, has argued for tracing its beginning to the third–second century B.C. based on a re-analysis of the archaeological data from the site. In the 1950s only a few sites were known to have yielded Rouletted Ware and these included the sites of Chandravalli and Brahmagiri in Karnataka and Amaravati in Andhra (Wheeler 1946:48). Since then the number of sites yielding Rouletted Ware sherds has increased and the distribution map of the Ware now extends from Mahasthangarh and Chandraketugarh in Bengal to Tissamaharama (Weisshaar et al. 2001:199) in Sri Lanka. Across the Bay of Bengal Rouletted Ware sherds have been found at Buni culture sites in Java, and Sembiran on the north coast of Bali (Ardika and Bellwood 1991). Thus the Bay of Bengal trading system is clearly established by these results and it is also apparent that sites in Sri Lanka and mainland and island Southeast Asia formed an integral part of it.

The commodities involved in maritime trade in the Indian Ocean may be divided into various broad categories such as: aromatics, medicines, dyes, and spices; food-stuffs, wood, and textiles; gems and ornaments; metals; and plant and animal prod-ucts. These categories find mention in a range of textual sources from the first century A.D. *Periplus Maris Erythraei* to the Geniza documents of the 11th–13th cen-turies, Chinese accounts, and medieval Arab writings.

Textiles covered a wide range of types, from coarse cottons to fine silks. Furni-ture in Asia consisted mostly of various types of carpets, cushions, canopies, and draperies – all of these being produced by the textile industry. The cloths traveling to Southeast Asia were stored or ceremonially displayed as signs of wealth. It is not surprising then that the first European accounts of life in Arab and Asian ports invariably mention the presence of trading craft that carried large quantities of textiles.

This is not to suggest that weaving was unknown in Southeast Asia. On the con-trary, local weaving tradition in the Indonesian archipelago has existed for nearly 4,000 years, but Indian textiles were nonetheless considered special and continued to be imported. These imports included double-ikat silk *patola* and block-printed cotton textiles, which were traded to the region on account of their status and ritual significance (Bühler 1959:4–46).

Together with carnelian, beads of glass traveled long distances along the Indian Ocean network. These small (generally under 6 millimeters in diameter) mono-chrome drawn beads, termed "Indo-Pacific beads," were made from glass tubes cut into short segments and were the most ubiquitous from South Africa to Korea between the third–second centuries B.C. and A.D. 1200 (Francis 1996:140; Glover and Bellina 2001). Several centers for the production of these beads have been iden-tified in South and Southeast Asia (Bellina 2003). These include Arikamedu on the Tamil coast (third century B.C. to third century A.D.), Mantai in Sri Lanka (first century to tenth century A.D.), Khuan Lukpad in south Thailand (second to sixth–seventh centuries A.D.) and Oc Eo in Vietnam and Angkor Borei in Cambodia (second to sixth centuries A.D.).

In Southeast Asia, Neolithic sites largely produced beads in locally occurring substances such as shell and stone. From the Metal Age around 500 B.C. to A.D. 1500 a variety of facetted carnelian and etched agate beads are dominant in archae-ological assemblages (Bellwood 1979:228–31). The most distinctive, however, are the etched carnelian beads, and more than fifty were found in burials during the three seasons of excavations at the Metal Age site of Ban Don Ta Phet in central Thailand (Glover 1990:18). Other commodities such as cloves, sandalwood, gold, metal, et cetera are referred to in textual sources, but are more difficult to locate in the archaeological record. It is within this maritime network that religious beliefs and knowledge of languages and scripts traversed the seas.

The Archaeology of Early Monastic Centers in South Asia

Literary references record that within the lifetime of the Buddha as many as twenty-nine sites and buildings had been donated to Him: eighteen in Rajagriha, four in Vaisali, three in Kosala and four in Kosambi (Lamotte 1958:19, 22). Further support for the early association of some of the sites with the life of the Buddha comes from one of the earliest Buddhist texts, i.e. the *Mahaparinibbana Sutta* (V.16–22), which mentions four places to be visited and revered by the devotee. These include places where the Buddha was born (identified with Lumbini); where he attained enlightenment (Bodh Gaya); where he preached the first sermon (Sarnath); and where he passed away (Kusinagara).

These textual references, however, do not match the archaeological data, since a majority of the structures associated with early Buddhism are shrines rather than residential monastic complexes, which date from the Mauryan period (fourth to third centuries B.C.) onwards. Perhaps the only example of a pre-Mauryan religious structure is the clay stupa from Vaisali dated to the pre-Mauryan period by the excavators (Mitra 1971:75). The Mauryan date is particularly valid for sites associated with the life of the Buddha such as Kusinagara, Bodh Gaya, Sravasti, Rajagriha, Sarnath, Kausambi, Vaisali, Lumbini, and Kapilavastu (Haertel 1995:141–59).

Thus the role of the Mauryan ruler Asoka in the delineation of the sacred landscape of Buddhism is obvious, but it would be simplistic to expect its uniform application on a pan-Indian level or to view the ruler as the agency of dissemination of Buddhist principles. No doubt, Asoka provided a new lease of life to spots associated with the life of the Buddha by identifying and marking these with stone pillars. Buddhist tradition incorporated in the somewhat later text the *Asokavadana* ascribes the role of identifying the sacred spots to Asoka's spiritual advisor, the monk Upagupta from Mathura. Many of these visits are referred to in Asokan inscriptions as well; for example, Rock Edict VIII dates Asoka's pilgrimage (*dharmayatra*) to Sambodhi, i.e. Bodh Gaya ten years after his coronation, though there is no epigraphic reference to Upagupta.

Asoka visited Lumbini 20 years after his coronation and set up a stone pillar at the site, while the Nigalisagara pillar inscription refers to a stupa in the Nepalese *terai* dedicated to the Buddha's mythical predecessors and enlarged and embellished by Asoka (Sircar 1975:61). Asoka is also credited with the setting up of the Dharmarajika stupa at Sarnath with an inscribed pillar in front. The inscription on the Asokan pillar does not mention Sarnath as the location where the first sermon was delivered, unlike the record at Lumbini, but it assumes the presence of monks and nuns in the region. Indeed considering that Sarnath is almost 240 kilometers

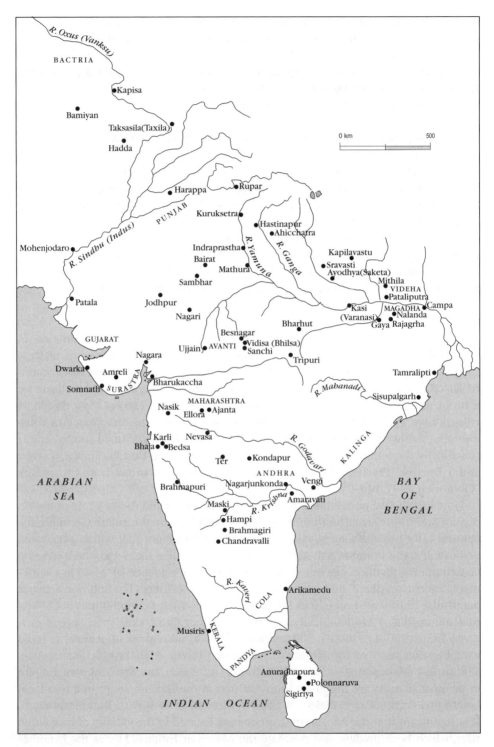

Figure 14.1 Major sites in South Asia (after Indrawooth 1999: Map 1; drafted by Ms. Uma Bhattacharya)

from Bodh Gaya, the site of the Buddha's Enlightenment, its identification as the spot where the Buddha delivered his first sermon needs careful reconsideration (Karetzky 1995:127–148).

In addition to questions of identification of sites associated with the life of the Buddha visited by Asoka and marked by pillars, there are sites, such as that of Sanchi, which had little association with the Master. Sanchi lies ten kilometers from the ancient urban center of Vidisa, strategically located along the river Betwa on a pivotal route connecting the urban centers of the Ganga basin with those located further south across the Vindhyas. The monastic complex is located on top of a hill, with a cluster of monastic sites in the vicinity at Sonari, Satdhara, Bhojpur, and Andher, which date from the second–first centuries B.C. It was already home to a large community of monks and nuns, as evident from the minor pillar inscription of Asoka (MPE III), generally referred to as the schism edict, which warns monks and nuns against creating schisms in the Sangha. The schism edict is located in the vicinity of a brick apsidal caitya dated to the Mauryan period and is similar to the one at Sarnath (Allchin 1995:244). Copies of the schism edict are also known from Sarnath and Allahabad. It is significant that as at Sarnath, no monastic residence of the Mauryan period has so far been unearthed in archaeological excavation at Sanchi.

The active participation of monks in the emergence and dissemination of stupa–relic cult has been convincingly shown on the basis of inscriptions and the suggestion made that it was both monastically controlled and monastically domi- nated (Ray 1986:100–6; Schopen 1997:34). Interesting parallels for patterns for transformation may be drawn with present practice in Sri Lanka. Most Sinhalese villages have a local temple with a resident monk – in fact the temple begins when a monk establishes his residence or *avasa*. An avasa is transformed into a temple (*vihara*) by the addition of objects of worship such as the Buddha image, a stupa and a Bo tree. Traditionally the function of the monk is to teach and to preach (Gombrich 1997:146–7).

How then do we understand the spread of Buddhism and Asoka's role in it? Was this an attempt at acculturation of a diverse populace by the ruler? Certainly the cultural milieu of the Ganga valley was very different from that which permeated peninsular India in the fourth–third centuries B.C. Unlike the north, there were no contemporary fortified centers in the south and no evidence of Mauryan settle- ment, except scattered finds of ceramics at coastal centers. The interior areas of peninsular India were home to iron-using megalithic village communities in the first millennium B.C. Chronologically, the Iron Age megalithic sites span several cen- turies from 1200 B.C. to A.D. 300 and extend across all regions of peninsular India with the exception of the western Deccan or present Maharashtra (Ray 1994). Within this cultural milieu, the sole indicators of Asoka and the Mauryan Empire in peninsular India are the inscriptions written in the Brahmi script in a non-local language, i.e. the eastern dialect of Prakrit, often in proximity to Buddhist caityas. It is significant that the Asokan inscriptions are located in the vicinity of megalithic sites, which both predate and postdate the Mauryan Empire. Hence the hypothe- sis of acculturation of a diverse population is not supported by archaeological evidence.

In contrast to the scattered shrines of the Mauryan period, large inter-connected monastic complexes emerged in the second–first centuries B.C. Sanchi and its neighbouring sites such as Sonari, Satdhara, Bhojpur, and Andher provide a good example of this phenomenon. A study of the inscriptions on relics and reliquaries shows that these were all linked to the person of Gotiputa and formed a tightly knit monastic community owing allegiance to the Hemavata school (Willis 2000:22). Archaeological survey conducted in Raisen and Vidisha districts led to the recovery of 120 settlements and 35 previously unrecorded sites and an impressive database incorporating finds of 15 embankments within about 400 square kilometers around Sanchi (Shaw and Sutcliffe 2001:55–75). It is suggested that the extensive water system around the monastic establishment at Sanchi may have been associated with irrigation and rice cultivation, rather than as a source of domestic supply to the monasteries.

Nor are these examples limited to India. Inscriptions from Sri Lanka indicate that as early as the second century B.C. land and irrigation works were transferred to the Buddhist Sangha. In some cases arrangements for irrigation were also made along with the transfer of land, but in other cases the monastery enjoyed privileged access to irrigation facilities. Fiscal rights and administrative and judicial authority that the king had traditionally enjoyed were transferred to the monastic authorities. The autonomy that these religious institutions enjoyed changed the nature of interaction between them and the lay community.

How does one explain the discrepancy between monastic rules, which disallowed practice of agriculture to monks, and the presence of clearly identified structures used for agrarian purposes in the vicinity of monastic sites? The dichotomy between theory and practice was easily resolved by employing several lay people for undertaking and supervising various jobs in the monasteries. In addition some of them were placed in charge of irrigation reservoirs belonging to the monasteries to collect the water dues (Gunawardana 1979:99). While this may have resolved functional issues, the philosophic and doctrinal aspects of this change still needed to be addressed and internalized.

From the fifth century A.D. onwards an interesting development in architecture, epigraphy, and literary texts was the unambiguous notion that the Buddha himself was the legal head of the monastery and donations to these were conceived as gifts to the Master. The language used in the inscriptions suggests the personal presence and permanent residence of the Buddha in Indian monasteries, further corroborated by changes in plans indicating that specific accommodation was being provided for in the monastic sites. For example, while in the early monasteries there was separation between the residence of the monks and the shrine, the later monasteries combined the two. These changes correspond with another development – the most abstract theories regarding the person of the Buddha were beginning to take definitive shape (Schopen 1997). This provides a stimulating example of the intertwining of diverse strands associated with factors as varied as agrarian expansion and management and abstruse philosophical discussions. We now move across the Bay of Bengal in an attempt to understand the expansion of Buddhism along the sea-lanes and its adoption by a range of communities including both the royalty and the laity.

Sri Lanka and the Expansion of Buddhism

Archaeologically, the change from the Mesolithic to the Iron Age in Sri Lanka is dated to between 900 and 600 B.C. with no intervening Copper–Bronze Age. Practice of paddy cultivation and the introduction of the horse and domestic cattle mark this transformation. The earliest known protohistoric settlement at Anuradhapura extended over 10 hectares by 800 B.C. (Deraniyagala 1990:260). The second period is dated to between 510–340 B.C. and indicates a more permanent occupation of the site. A pit burial from this period yielded four sherds bearing portions of Brahmi inscriptions, though no skeletal remains were found associated with it (Coningham et al. 1996:73–97).

Archaeological excavations in the citadel area at Anuradhapura have provided evidence for change in the nature of the structures between 360 and 190 B.C. It was at this time that a rampart and ditch were constructed around the settlement. The faunal record showed a high proportion of seashells and material finds included several imports from India, such as a fine grey ware, carnelian, and lapis lazuli. Coins were in evidence for the first time. Another five sherds with portions of Brahmi inscriptions were also recovered. Of interest is the clay sealing from Anuradhapura (pit in period H) with the legend: "Magaha, the Purumaka, son of Tissa." The same name appears in the Mihintale cave inscription dedicated to the Buddhist Sangha and dated to the third–second century B.C.

The finds of inscribed sherds at Anuradhapura in a well-dated sequence has led the excavators to suggest mercantile involvement in the rise of the Brahmi script or at least in its introduction into Sri Lanka (Coningham et al. 1996:73–97). An analysis of the inscribed sherds from Anuradhapura indicates that the legends were inscribed on lids and on ceramic vessels and that many of these vessels may have been dedicated to Buddhist religious establishments. During excavations of the northern and southern *ayakas* of the main Buddhist stupa at Jetavana at Anuradhapura, 17 vessels were found containing conch shells, ivories, over two thousand beads, hundreds of fragments of semi-precious stones, and so on (Coningham et al. 1996:90).

As with other regions of the western Indian Ocean, trade was an important component in the economy of ancient Sri Lanka; important coastal settlements on the island were those of Mantai in the north and Kirinda and Godavaya in the south. While the former served the northern region of Anuradhapura, 110 kilometers inland, the latter provided an outlet for Tissamaharama or ancient Ruhuna located 12 kilometers from the coast in a flat coastal plain. The earliest occupation of Mantai dates to the Mesolithic period. After a hiatus, the site was reoccupied in the third century B.C. and continued in occupation until the 13th century A.D. Trade contacts with India are evident in the ceramic inventory from the site dated between the third and seventh centuries, such as sherds of the Red Polished Ware. Contacts with India are further corroborated by a fourth-century Brahmi inscription from Jetavanarama, which records the donation of 100 *kahapanas* by two merchants from Andhra to a monastery (*Ancient Ceylon* VI 1990, no. 12).

The visible ruins of Tissamaharama are located around a tank (Tissawewa) built in the second century B.C. and excavations at the site have revealed a sequence dating from the fourth–third centuries B.C. to eighth century A.D. (Weisshaar et al. 2001:280). On the eastern shore of the lake lies the citadel area on the settlement hill known as Akurgoda, and outside the citadel area are monasteries and four stupas. The area to the south of the Akurugoda Hill yielded iron slag, bronze fragments, and crucibles indicating its use as a workshop.

Further south along the coast were the centers of Kirinda, on the Kirinda Oya, and Godavaya, located close to the mouth of the Walawe Ganga. Twelve kilometers upstream is the old gem mining area of Ridiyagama. Stray discoveries and finds of about seventy-five thousand late Roman coins in earthen vessels from Godavaya led to systematic exploration in the area, which yielded 119 sites, further supporting the importance of the southern coast for maritime contacts (Weisshaar et al. 2001:291–306). Archaeological excavations at the site have yielded three stone pillars of grey-banded gneiss and a fourth structural member identified as a transom, in addition to large quantities of coins and pottery. It is suggested that these stone pillars formed part of a structure – a building of comparable construction is the stone bridge across the Malwatu Oya, north of Jetavana – perhaps to facilitate loading and unloading (Kessler 1998:30). Thus several units may be identified around Godavaya, viz. a monastic complex, the landing site, and a huge settlement area (Weisshaar et al. 2001:324–6).

Three rock inscriptions from the site of Godavaya provide valuable information on the relationship between the *patana* or market center of Godapavata, the monastic center, and the ruler Gajabahu Gamani Abhaya (A.D. 174–96). While the first inscription contains a few meaningless characters, the second text records the transfer of regular and minor duties of the patana to the Buddhist vihara by the ruler. The third epigraph documents the donation of a park (*arama*), three *karisa* of land "of those public fields called Uvanakava" and a plot called "Sati" for the caitya by Ahalaya, an official of the king, together with his brother and mother (Weisshaar et al. 2001:327–34). This is perhaps the sole evidence for the transfer of duties from trade by the king to a monastic site in the second-century world of the Indian Ocean; the records from India largely refer to revenues from agriculture being transferred.

In addition to the east coast network indicated by Rouletted Ware finds in which centers in Sri Lanka participated, a second system incorporating centers in south India is also evident from the presence of inscribed sherds with legends in Sinhala-Prakrit at Kodumanal, Arikamedu, and other coastal sites (Mahadevan 1996).

Finally it is also evident that a distinctive Buddhist architecture evolved in Sri Lanka, as distinct from that which prevailed at sites in the Deccan. In contrast to peninsular India where the earliest evidence of Buddhist presence is generally provided by shrines, in Sri Lanka the first phase of Buddhist activity was associated with the donation of caves as residences for the Buddhist clergy in the large granite outcrops in the north and east. A majority of these are slightly enlarged natural caves and incised just below the drip ledge is the record of donation. The development of Buddhist monastic architecture in Sri Lanka has, nevertheless, to be seen in response to local social and political demands. Thus with the consolidation of political power and religious authority at Anuradhapura in the early centuries of the Common Era, the plan of the metropolitan monasteries around the city changed from acentric to monocentric, with a ritual structure dominating the center of the monastic structure (Bandaranayake 1989:184). This consolidation of political and religious authority in Anuradhapura is further documented in the large corpus of inscriptions from Sri Lanka.

Of the 1,300 inscriptions in Sinhalese collected from 269 different Buddhist sites on the island dated between the third century B.C. and the first century A.D., the *parumaka*s are mentioned in nearly thirty percent of the inscriptions published so far (Paranavitana 1970: vol. I:lxxiv–lxxxvi). The parumaka inscriptions do not add their ancestry, but do indicate matrimonial alliances with other chiefs, but with the emergence of Anuradhapura, there is no further reference to parumakas after the second–third centuries A.D.

Buddhism Across the Bay of Bengal

As is the case with Sri Lanka, several centers in mainland and island Southeast Asia also participated in Indian Ocean maritime activity and archaeological evidence for this has been recorded at a large number of sites (Glover 1990). It is apparent that notions of Buddhist and Hindu kingship, worship of Indic deities, and the use of Indian languages and scripts spread across Southeast Asia from the second–first centuries B.C. onwards. Scholars have long debated the agents and the process of this transformation with "Indianization" and "localization" presenting two ends of the academic spectrum.

In this chapter the focus is on Buddhism, which has seldom been discussed in secondary writing, it being generally assumed that notions of kingship derived from Hinduism. It is suggested here that there can be no one explanation, and the nature and causes of transformation, as well as cultural influences, varied in different regions of Southeast Asia. It is crucial to emphasize that the communities that traveled across the Indian Ocean were diverse, including sailors, traders, craftsmen, pilgrims, religious clergy, adventurers, minstrels, and so on. The epigraphic record indicates the presence of several Indic languages in Southeast Asia, from the early legends in Prakrit and Sanskrit on carnelian seals dated to the first–second centuries A.D., to Pali inscriptions of the sixth–seventh centuries A.D. A Tamil inscription of the third–fourth century A.D. was identified on a small flat rectangular stone in the collection of Wat Khlong Thom in south Thailand, and read, "perumpatan kal" or "this is the touchstone of Perumpatan." The scripts used also varied from Brahmi and Tamil-Brahmi to Kharosthi. Given this wide range, it would be simplistic to expect neat categories in terms of language, caste, or religious affiliations.

A cluster of fifth-century inscriptions of unequivocal Buddhist affiliation has been found in Kedah on the west coast of the Malay Peninsula. This includes engraving of the Buddhist formula "ajñanac-ciyate karmma" on stone – a feature that does not occur among contemporary records from the Indian subcontinent,

though the formula is found on terracotta seals. Three of these inscriptions are made
of local stone and bear similar illustrations of Buddhist stupas. Texts very similar
to these inscriptions have been found on the island of Borneo and on the coast of
Brunei (Christie 1995:256). The most interesting of these inscriptions in Sanskrit
is that of Buddhagupta, which refers to the setting up of the stone by the mariner
Buddhagupta, resident of Raktamrttika, on the successful completion of his voyage
(Chhabra 1965:23–4).

The Sarvastivadins are one of the sects of Buddhism who are known to have
developed missionary activity outside India, and one of the missionaries who stayed
for many years in Indonesia, as described in the Chinese sources, was Gunavarman
(A.D. 367–431). About one and a half centuries after Gunavarman's visit, the
Chinese monk, I-Tsing, confirmed that the Sarvastivada school was flourishing in
the lands of the South Sea.

Scholars have suggested that in the context of early Indonesia certain features of
the older Indonesian civilization were, to a large extent, due to the activity of pilgrims from the Indonesian islands visiting sacred sites in India to take instructions
from teachers there. An important text for the study of pilgrimage in early
Buddhism is the *Gandavyuha*, which dates back in all probability to the early centuries of the Common Era. It describes the travels of Sudhana who is inspired to
travel by Manjusri and advised to visit fifty-three "spiritual friends" in order to learn
bodhicarya or "the Bodhisattva practice." The *Gandavyuha* forms a part of the
Avatamsakasutra, which is thought to have issued from different hands in the Indian
cultural sphere in the first–second centuries A.D. Comprehensive renditions of the
text were made in China in the early fifth and late seventh centuries A.D. from versions of the text obtained from Khotan (Cleary 1993:2). It became one of the pillars
of East Asian Buddhism and a major school of Buddhist philosophy developed
based on its teachings. An Orissan king generally accepted to be a member of the
Bhaumakara dynasty is said to have presented an autographed manuscript of the
Gandavyuha to the Chinese emperor in A.D. 795. This text and a letter were
entrusted to the monk Prajna who was asked to provide a translation into Chinese
(Levi 1919–20:363–4).

One of the monuments that holds an important position in the context of pilgrimage is that of Borobodur. On the basis of the palaeography of the fragmentary
inscriptions covering the base, the monument has been dated to the late eighth or
ninth century A.D. The monument is elaborately carved with 1,460 sculpted panels,
a majority of these depicting scenes from the life of the Buddha.

What is interesting is that not only did Borobodur spread the message of acquisition of knowledge and merit, but it also became a center of pilgrimage itself. In
the ninth century central Java had acquired a reputation of being a treasure house
of sacred learning, as evident from an inscription from Champa (Wolters 1999:49,
62). An indication of the importance of the site of Borobodur for pilgrimage is provided by the finds of more than 2,000 unbaked clay votive stupas (2,397 in total)
and 252 clay tablets to the southwest of the Borobodur hill. These were found acci-
dentally under a Bodhisattva image together with five pots, fragments of potsherds,
and four rolled silver plates. One of the silver plates found on the surface carried a

one-line inscription of a Buddhist *dharani* in the Old Javanese script. The votive stupas, dated to the ninth century, may be divided into two categories. The first type resembles the stupas of Borobodur, some of which have an inscription "om ye te svaha" – an abbreviated version of the Buddhist creed – at the base, while the second type has eight small stupas around a central one. Similar votive stupas with Buddhist formulae have also been found in Bali and Sumatra and are well attested from the Indian subcontinent as described by Xuanzang. Since the script on these is by no means uniform, they seem to have been written by a diverse group of devotees and monks.

Another manifestation of this network of travel and Buddhist pilgrimage is discernible in the centers that developed in the river valleys of the Irrawaddy and the Chao Phraya. While both these shared in the allegiance to Buddhism, they also evolved distinctive local features (Stargardt 1990:191–228). Here we shall focus on the Dvaravati culture that developed in central Thailand from the sixth to 11th centuries A.D.

Dvaravati culture

Early Chinese sources refer to the state of *To-lo-po-ti* in the Chao Phraya river basin, and conventionally this term has been translated as "the kingdom of Dvaravati," also known from coins inscribed with the legend "sri dvaravati." Traditionally historians have viewed Dvaravati as a politically unified state with a well-defined territory encompassing a largely homogenous Mon population. On the basis of similarity in form of the cultural materials rather than their content, Dvaravati art was seen as representing the power of the state radiating from the center. In secondary literature, there has been an overemphasis on art and architecture, with little attention to settlement pattern and material culture (Vallibhotama 1986:233–6).

Archaeological research during the last few decades has challenged this notion of a unified superimposed state. Instead it is apparent that there were several competing centers dating between 2000 and 200 B.C. based on rice agriculture and bronze and iron production. During the Iron Age large settlements with extensive inland and trans-oceanic exchange and trade networks are known from central and northeast Thailand. It is significant that several aspects of the material culture present similarity across the Irrawaddy, Chao Phraya, and Mekong river valleys. This uniformity is paralleled by the use of artifacts obtained from India and China. Many of the sites provide evidence of burials with an impressive array of grave goods, followed by large settlements, which have in the past been termed as urban centers leading to the emergence of the state. Subsequent scholarship has suggested that the Thai term "muang," literally "coming together of communities," best describes these economically, socially, and politically self-contained units (Saraya 1999:30), and that the connection between them may be defined by the term heterarchy (White 1995:101–23; Wolters 1999:122–5). Heterarchy refers to the relation of elements that possess the potential of being ranked in a number of ways. For example, three cities important for diverse functions such as military,

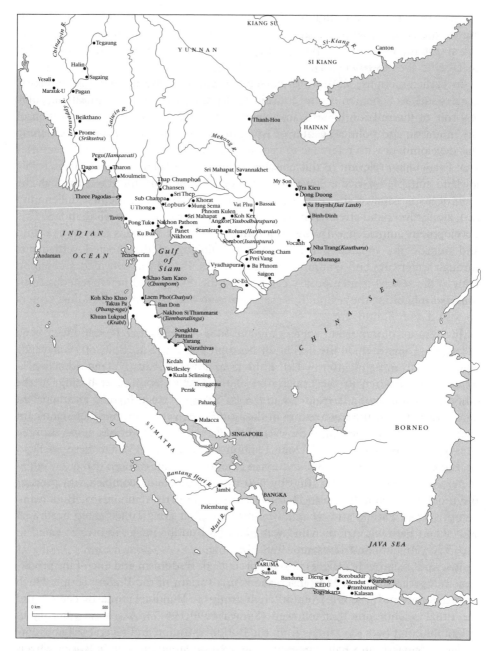

Figure 14.2 Important sites during the Dvaravati period (after Indrawooth 1999: Map 6; drafted by Ms. Uma Bhattacharya)

manufacturing, and education may be ranked in different orders of priority depending on the context. White suggests that religious centers formed a parallel hierarchical system, which served to ideologically and financially support the local landed social elite (White 1995:114).

In earlier sections, we have discussed the participation of Buddhist monastic centers such as Sanchi in central India in agrarian expansion, and the unifying political role of the religion in Sri Lanka as evident from the predominant position of the monastic and political center of Anuradhapura. It would be worth examining this development with reference to central Thailand from the sixth to 11th centuries A.D. Particularly relevant to this chapter is the Chao Phraya valley, the large fertile lowland suitable for rice cultivation and accessible to maritime travel through the Gulf of Siam. Moated sites developed here from the middle of the first millennium A.D. along rivers and streams that also supplied water to the encircling moats. This development coincided with the establishment of large religious sites both within and outside the moated perimeter and the linking of the moated settlements through waterways and communication networks. Buddhism provided a common faith to the several contemporary centers and the diverse and heterogeneous communities inhabiting the region. It is also significant that as in India, Buddhist centers coexisted with Hindu shrines.

Five groups of important ancient moated sites of the Dvaravati period have been identified. These include the U-Thong–Nakhon Pathom–Khu Bua complex on the coast to the west of the Chao Phraya basin and Khu–Muang–Chansen–U Taphao–Dong Khon in the upper part of the Chao Phraya river basin. On the Khorat plateau, the Si Thep group in the Pa Sak river basin formed an important center matched by the Lavo group in the Lop Buri river basin. Another significant group of towns was located to the east of the Chao Phraya river basin, for example sites such as Si Mahosot and Dong Lakhon (Saraya 1999:33). Of these the first, i.e. the U-Thong (1,690 by 840 meters in extent)–Nakhon Pathom (3,700 by 2,000 meters in extent)–Khu Bua (200 by 800 meters in extent) complex was perhaps the most important. It is also in this area that the early remnants of Buddhism, comprising of a stupa and *vihara*, were recognised at Pong Tuk, located northwest of Nakhon Pathong. Another find was that of a Buddha image in bronze dated to A.D. 550 (Higham and Thosarat 1998:178).

Inscriptions provide insights into the practice of Buddhism and one of the prominent categories includes Mon inscriptions in a variant of the Brahmi script, which record donations by people from different groups to Buddhist monastic centers and the ritual celebrations that followed (Saraya 1999:196–7). A second category of epigraphs comprises of extracts from the Buddhist Canon and several religious formulae in Sanskrit and Pali. These are engraved on stone *dhammacakkas* or wheels of law, octagonal pillars, stone slabs, clay tablets, and reliquaries, and are dated between the sixth and eighth centuries A.D. This practice is well attested in both Thailand and Myanmar, but no contemporary canonical inscriptions have been found in Sri Lanka. In contrast, religious formulae and extracts from canonical texts occur at several Indian sites from the fifth century A.D. onwards (Skilling 1997:94). Nevertheless there are marked variations between the two, the most prominent being the large and ornate stone *dhammacakkas*, the plans of stupas and caityas, the style of Buddha images, and several unique images, such as that of Banaspati. Banaspati is a composite animal with horns like Siva's vehicle Nandi, wings like Visnu's vehicle Garuda, and a beak like Brahma's vehicle the swan.

In conclusion it is evident that Buddhism was receptive to the spiritual and material needs of the lay community and Buddhist monks and nuns developed close links with both settled villages and trading groups. In addition to trading commodities, the watercraft of the Indian Ocean also transported pilgrims and religious clergy. It is significant that this traffic was bilateral and included pilgrims traveling from Sri Lanka and parts of Southeast Asia to visit sites associated with the life of the Buddha as well as those traveling out from India. The close association between trading groups and the clergy, or gifts and donations made by the rulers and other elite groups by no means affected the autonomy of the religious institutions. It is important to understand that as Buddhism expanded to other parts of the Indian Ocean world, it created its own network of communication and identity and that this network cut across political frontiers and boundaries. Participation in this network also facilitated integration in the literate Indian Ocean world.

REFERENCES

Allchin, Frank Raymond 1995 The Archaeology of Early Historic South Asia: The Emergence of Cities and States. Cambridge: Cambridge University Press.

Ardika, I. Wayan, and Peter Bellwood 1991 Sembiran: The Beginnings of Indian Contact with Bali. Antiquity 65:221–32.

Bandaranayake, Senake 1989 Monastery Plan and Social Formation: The Spatial Organization of the Buddhist Monastic Complexes of the Early and Middle Historical Period in Sri Lanka and Changing Patterns of Political Power. *In* Domination and Resistance. Daniel Miller, Michael Rowlands, and Christopher Tilley, eds. Pp. 179–95. London: Unwin Hyman.

Bechert, Heinz, ed. 1995 When did the Buddha Live? New Delhi: Satguru Publications.

Bellina, Bérénice 2003 Beads, Social Change and Interaction between India and South-East Asia. Antiquity 77:285–96.

Bellwood, Peter 1979 Man's Conquest of the Pacific. Auckland, Sydney, New York: Oxford University Press.

—— 1992 Southeast Asia Before History. *In* The Cambridge History of Southeast Asia. Nicholas Tarling, ed. Pp. 56–136. Cambridge: Cambridge University Press.

Brekke, Torkel 1997 The Early Sangha and the Laity. Journal of the International Association of Buddhist Studies 20(2):7–32.

Bühler, Alfred 1959 Patola Influences in Southeast Asia. Journal of Indian Textile History IV:4–46.

Chakrabarti, Dilip K. 1995 Buddhist Sites Across South Asia as Influenced by Political and Economic Forces. World Archaeology 27(2):185–202.

—— 1999 India: An Archaeological History. New Delhi: Oxford University Press.

—— 2000 Mahajanapada States of Early Historic India. *In* A Comparative Study of Thirty City-State Cultures. Mogens Herman Hansen, ed. Pp. 375–91. Copenhagen: C. A. Reitzels Forlag.

Chhabra, Bahadur Chand 1965 Expansion of Indo-Aryan Culture During Pallava Rule, As Evidenced by the Inscriptions. New Delhi: Munshiram Manoharlal.

Christie, Jan Wisseman 1995 State Formation in Early Maritime Southeast Asia: A Consideration of the Theories and the Data. Bijdragen tot de Taal-, Land- en Volkenkunde 151(2):235–88.

Cleary, Thomas 1993 The Flower Ornament Scripture. Boston and London: Shambhala.

Coningham, Robin A. E. 1995 Monks, Caves and Kings: A Reassessment of the Nature of Early Buddhism. World Archaeology 27(2):222–42.

Coningham, Robin A. E., Frank Raymond Allchin, C. M. Batt, and D. Lucy 1996 Passage to India? Anuradhapura and the Early Use of the Brahmi Script. Cambridge Archaeological Journal 6(1):73–97.

Cunningham, Alexander 1871–72 Annual Report. Archaeological Survey of India 3:13–46.

—— 1961 Inscriptions of Asoka. Varanasi: Indological Book House (reprint).

—— 1962 The Stupa of Bharhut. Varanasi: Indological Book House (reprint).

Deraniyagala, Siran 1990 The Prehistoric Chronology of Sri Lanka. Ancient Ceylon 12(6). Colombo: Archaeological Survey Department of Sri Lanka.

Eisenstadt, Shmuel N., ed. 1986 The Origins and Diversity of Axial Age Civilizations. Albany, New York: State University of New York Press.

Erdosy, George, 1993 The Archaeology of Early Buddhism. In Studies on Buddhism in Honour of Professor A. K. Warder. Narendra Kumar Wagle and Fumimaro Watanabe, eds. Pp. 40–56. Toronto: University of Toronto.

Fogelin, Lars 2003 Ritual and Presentation in Early Buddhist Religious Architecture. Asian Perspectives 42(1):129–54.

Francis, Peter Jr. 1996 Beads, the Bead Trade and State Development in Southeast Asia. In Ancient Trades and Cultural Contacts in Southeast Asia. Pp. 139–60. Bangkok: The Office of the National Culture Commission.

Glover, Ian C. 1990 Early Trade Between India and Southeast Asia. 2nd rev. edition. Hull: University of Hull.

Glover, Ian C., and Bérénice Bellina 2001 Alkaline Etched Beads East of India in the Late Prehistoric and Early Historic Periods. Bulletin de l'École Française d'Extrême Orient 88:191–215.

Gombrich, Richard Francis 1994 Theravada Buddhism: A Social History from Ancient Benares to Modern Colombo. London and New York: Routledge.

—— 1997 How Buddhism Began: The Conditioned Genesis of the Early Teaching. New Delhi: Munshiram Manoharlal.

Goody, Jack 2001 The Power of the Written Tradition. Washington and London: Smithsonian Institution Press.

Gunawardana, R. A. L. H. 1979 Robe and Plough: Monasticism and Economic Interest in Early Medieval Sri Lanka. Tucson: University of Arizona Press.

Haertel, Herbert 1995 Archaeological Research on Ancient Buddhist Sites. In When Did the Buddha Live? Heinz Bechert, ed. Pp. 141–59. New Delhi: Satguru Publications.

Heitzman, James 1984 Early Buddhism, Trade and Empire. In Studies in the Archaeology and Palaeoanthropology of South Asia. Kenneth A. R. Kennedy and Gregory L. Possehl, eds. Pp. 121–37. New Delhi: Oxford and IBH.

Higham, Charles F. W., and Rachanie Thosarat 1998 Prehistoric Thailand: From Early Settlement to Sukhothai. Bangkok: River Books.

Imam, Abu 1966 Sir Alexander Cunningham and the Beginnings of Indian Archaeology. Dacca: Asiatic Society of Pakistan.

Indrawooth, Phasook 1999 Dvaravati: A Critical Study Based on Archaeological Evidence. Bangkok: Rongphim 'Aksonsamai 2542.

Insoll, Timothy 2001 Archaeology and World Religion. London and New York: Routledge.

Karetzky, Patricia Eichenbaum 1995 The First Sermon. East and West 45:1–4:127–48.

Kessler, Oliver 1998 The Discovery of an Ancient Sea Port at the Silk Road of the Sea – Archaeological Relics of the Godavaya Harbour. *In* Sri Lanka: Past and Present. Manfred Domroes and Helmut Roth, eds. Pp. 12–37. Weikersheim: Margraf Verlag.

Lamotte, Etienne 1958 Histoire du Bouddhisme Indien. Louvain: Université de Louvain.

Levi, Sylvain 1919–20 King Subhakara of Orissa. Epigraphia Indica 15:363–4.

Lopez, Donald S., ed. 1995 Buddhism in Practice. Princeton: Princeton University Press.

Mahadevan, Iravatham 1996 Old Sinhalese Inscriptions from Indian Ports: New Evidence for Ancient India–Sri Lanka Contacts. Journal of the Institute of Asian Studies XIV(1):55–65.

Mitra, Debala 1971/1980 Buddhist Monuments. Calcutta: Sahitya Samsad.

Morrison, Kathleen D. 1995 Trade, Urbanism and Agricultural Expansion: Buddhist Monastic Institutions and the State in the Early Historic Western Deccan. World Archaeology 27(2):203–21.

Paranavitana, Senerat 1970 Inscriptions of Ceylon, Volume I. Colombo: Department of Archaeology.

Ray, Himanshu Prabha 1986 Monastery and Guild: Commerce Under the Satavahanas. New Delhi: Oxford University Press.

—— 1994/1996 The Winds of Change: Buddhism and the Maritime Links of Early South Asia. New Delhi: Oxford University Press.

—— 2003 The Archaeology of Seafaring in Ancient South Asia. Cambridge: Cambridge University Press.

Ray, Himanshu Prabha, and Carla Sinopoli, eds. 2004 Archaeology as History in Early South Asia. New Delhi: Indian Council for Historical Research and Aryan Books International.

Ray, Reginald A. 1994 Buddhist Saints in India. New York: Oxford University Press.

Saraya, Dhida 1999 (Sri) Dvaravati: The Initial Phase of Siam's History. Bangkok: Muang Boran Publishing House.

Schopen, Gregory 1987 Burial Ad Sanctos and the Physical Presence of the Buddha in Early Indian Buddhism: A Study in the Archaeology of Religions. Religion 17:193–225.

—— 1988–89 On Monks, Nuns and "Vulgar" Practices. Artibus Asiae 49:153–68.

—— 1997 Bones, Stones, and Buddhist Monks. Honolulu: University of Hawaii Press.

Shaw, Julia, and John Sutcliffe 2001 Ancient Irrigation Works in the Sanchi Area: An Archaeological and Hydrological Investigation. South Asian Studies 17:55–75.

Sircar, Dinesh Chandra 1975 Inscriptions of Asoka. 3rd edition. New Delhi: Government of India.

Skilling, Peter 1997 The Advent of Theravada Buddhism to Mainland Southeast Asia. Journal of the International Association of Buddhist Studies 20(1):93–107.

Stargardt, Janice 1990 The Ancient Pyu of Burma. Cambridge: PACSEA and The Institute of Southeast Asian Studies.

Tambiah, Stanley J. 1976 World Conqueror and World Renouncer. Cambridge: Cambridge University Press.

—— 1984 The Buddhist Saints of the Forest and the Cult of Amulets. Cambridge: Cambridge University Press.

Thapar, Romila 1997 Asoka and the Decline of the Mauryas. New Delhi: Oxford India Paperbacks.

—— 2000 Cultural Pasts. New Delhi: Oxford University Press.

Vallibhotama, Srisakra 1986 Political and Cultural Continuities at Dvaravati Sites. *In* Southeast Asia in the 9th to 14th Centuries. David G. Marr and Anthony C. Milner, eds. Pp.

229–38. Singapore and Canberra: Institute of Southeast Asian Studies and Australian National University.

Weisshaar, Hans-Joachim, Helmut Roth, and W. Wijeyapala, eds. 2001 Ancient Ruhuna. Mainz am Rhein: Verlag Philipp von Zabern.

Wheeler, R. E. Mortimer 1946, 1947–48 Arikamedu: An Indo-Roman Trading-Station on the East Coast. Ancient India 2:17–124.

White, Joyce 1995 Incorporating Heterarchy into Theory on Socio-Political Development: The Case from Southeast Asia. *In* Heterarchy and the Analysis of Complex Societies. Robert M. Ehrenreich, Carole L. Crumley, and Janet E. Levy, eds. Pp. 101–23. Arlington VA: American Anthropological Association.

Willis, Michael 2000 Buddhist Reliquaries from Ancient India. London: The British Museum Press.

Wolters, Oliver W. 1999 History, Culture, and Region in Southeast Asian Perspectives. Rev. edition. Ithaca and Singapore: Cornell University and the Institute of Southeast Asian Studies.

15

Imperial Landscapes of South Asia

Carla M. Sinopoli

South Asian history is often portrayed as a sequence of great empires – Maurya, Satavahana, Gupta, Rashtrakuta, Delhi Sultanate, Chola, Mughal, Vijayanagara, Britain, among others. These polities, and the many other regional states and empires recorded in historical sources, were indeed important political forces in South Asia for more than 2,000 years, from the mid–first millennium B.C. through the late second millennium A.D. They varied in duration, geographic extent, political and economic structures and impact, and in their legacies, as manifest both in the physical landscape of South Asia and in subsequent political configurations and historical memory. For present purposes, I define empires broadly, as large states with heterogeneous ethnic and cultural composition that are formed through the incorporation of less powerful polities and regions by conquest or coercion (Sinopoli 2001a; also Alcock et al. 2001).

Although many dozens of polities with imperial claims existed in South Asia, in this chapter I limit my attention to those that have been the focus of extended historic and archaeological research, and I largely confine my chronological focus to the Early Historic period. This is a more restricted group, constrained by the uneven history of archaeological work, by the differential visibility of various imperial polities, and by the challenges of scale posed by the archaeological study of empires (Sinopoli 1994, 2001a).

Overall, there has been far more art historical and numismatic research on South Asian empires than strictly archaeological work. This has resulted in attributions of objects and artistic styles (usually of sculpture) as "Kushana," "Gupta," "Maurya," etcetera, though often with limited understanding of how, or if, their production was associated with the ruling dynasties after which they are named. Similarly, research on surviving imperial monuments has focused on identifying architectural styles associated with particular periods or dynasties. Archaeological surveys and excavations throughout South Asia have examined imperial sites, primarily centers of empires, and their most monumental remains. Systematic regional research and studies of imperial economies, political and social structures, and infrastructure have, however, been rare.

Along with the need for more systematic and sustained archaeological research, equally fundamental intellectual challenges must be addressed if archaeology is to make significant contributions to the study of South Asian empires. These include a rethinking of the contributions that archaeological data can make to the study of the historic past (see Ray and Sinopoli, eds. 2004). Historic period archaeology in South Asia (and all of the empires discussed here are associated with written sources) has long been characterized by a privileging of texts over material evidence (Trautmann and Sinopoli 2002; also Lape 2003; Li 2003; Moreland 2001 for discussion of similar issues in other regions). Literary sources, inscriptions, and travelers' reports have been seen as providing the necessary historical accounting of South Asia's past. The material sources – mainly coins, monuments, and sculptures – have served primarily to provide visual illustration of what is already known from documents. Archaeological evidence is not considered an independent source of information that could in itself contribute to historical knowledge: it can only make what is already known visible and tangible. There is thus relatively little motivation to conduct long-term archaeological research on historic period sites, and most of the best and most sustained archaeological projects of the last eight decades have focused on prehistoric, pre-imperial, periods.

In addition to being guided by written sources, archaeologists who have worked on South Asian empires have tended to use the sources narrowly. Interpretive efforts in historic period archaeology in South Asia have, in general, lagged behind the dramatic changes that have occurred over the last several decades within both prehistoric archaeology and historiography (see also Allchin 1998; Dhavalikar 1999; Ray and Mukherjee, eds. 1990; Ray and Sinopoli, eds. 2004). Nineteenth- and early twentieth-century historians focused largely on political or dynastic history, dividing the South Asian past into a succession of "periods" associated with dominant polities (e.g., The Mauryan Period, The Gupta Period, etc.) or religions (e.g., Buddhist, Hindu, Muslim periods). Over the last five decades, historians have moved away from these problematic perspectives to explore a broad range of intellectually diverse and sophisticated approaches to social, economic, and political history (see discussions in Kulke 1995; Mukhia 2000; Thapar 2000). They have engaged in wide-ranging debates concerning the nature and organization of pre-colonial South Asian states and empires and have drawn on diverse theoretical frameworks, from Indian feudalism to segmentary states, among others (see Kulke 1995; Sinopoli 2003).

Within historic period archaeology, in contrast, an emphasis on linear and dynastic history has remained dominant, with little effort to address broader anthropological or historic questions. This is problematic on multiple grounds, not least the challenges in precisely linking material remains, whether architecture or artifacts, with specific rulers and dynasties, and the dangers of assuming that material changes directly parallel political ones.

While other shortcomings could no doubt be added to this list, it is not my purpose here to chronicle the problems of South Asian archaeology. Nor would it be appropriate to do so. There have been tremendous accomplishments over the last ca. 200 years of archaeological research in South Asia. Enormous numbers of sites have been recorded and a great deal of evidence is available to address a wide range of issues. In the remainder of this chapter, I employ archaeological and written evidence to discuss specific empires and to address broader patterns, processes, and methodological and theoretical concerns in archaeological research on South Asian empires.

I limit my discussion to four important case studies dating to the "Early Historic" Period (ca. 500 B.C.–ca. A.D. 300), a period that witnessed the formation and expansion of complex societies – states and empires – in both northern and southern regions of mainland South Asia and Sri Lanka. I begin with earliest empires documented in South Asia: the Achaemenid and Seleucid empires (from ca. 500–322 B.C.) and the Mauryan empire (ca. 322–187 B.C.). The bases of Achaemenid and Seleucid power lay outside of South Asia, in Persia and Syria, while the Mauryans were South Asia's first indigenous empire. I maintain this external–internal focus in the next two case studies: the Satavahana empire (ca. 100 B.C.–A.D. 200) of peninsular India and the northern Kushana empire (ca. 35 B.C.–A.D. 300), whose ruling dynasty traced its origins to Central Asia. Leaving the Early Historic, I then jump forward by more than a millennium to briefly consider some recent research that I have been involved with on the south Indian Vijayanagara empire (ca. A.D. 1350–1650). This case is used as a jumping off point from which to address broader theoretical and methodological issues in archaeological approaches to the study of empires at a general level and South Asian empires more specifically.

Empires from Outside; Empires from Inside

The history and sequence of South Asian empires is complex, made more so by the fact that South Asia, like other areas of the Old World, has never been isolated from developments beyond its borders. Throughout South Asian history, empires both arose internally and were introduced by conquering powers, predominantly coming from the north and west. Further, conquest was not the only kind of relation that linked South Asians to the rest of the Old World. Numerous other kinds of external contact also occurred with regions to the north, west, and east – including trade, pilgrimage, migration, and diplomatic exchanges (see Ray 2003; this volume). Understanding relations between internal and external political, economic, and social dynamics of South Asia's historic empires is essential to the study of the South Asian past, and is, as in many areas, a thorny topic, intertwined with both contemporary and colonial political ideologies.

Many (though certainly not all) colonial period historians and archaeologists looked to external sources to account for documented historical changes in South Asia. In the dominant colonial historiographic discourse, South Asia was viewed as a region where internal progress was made impossible by its combination of tyrannical despots (the "Oriental Despot") and isolated caste-ridden villages (see Inden

1990; Sinopoli 2003). When change came, it therefore had to come from outside the region (usually from the west) – whether from invading Iron Age Aryans or 18th- and 19th-century British merchants and colonists. Migration and conquest thus became the dominant idiom for explaining South Asian history.

This early focus on external explanations began to be challenged during the Independence struggle of the late 19th and early 20th centuries, as nationalists turned to internal accounts of South Asia's past that demonstrated the region's ability for self-rule. In particular, the third century B.C. Mauryan empire (discussed below) and its legendary ruler Asoka became important symbols of a past when India was both united and independent. Jawaharlal Nehru, independent India's first prime minister, frequently invoked Asoka as providing proof of India's strength and potential when united under a just, noble, and tolerant indigenous rule. Even today, a carved Asokan column capital is illustrated on India's currency.

More recently, the inward focus in the study of the past has taken a more ominous turn within India, as religious conservatives have sought to reconfigure Indian history and indeed its archaeological landscape by denying the existence and/or contributions of external contacts to the region's history (a trend that some well meaning archaeologists have unwittingly contributed to). In 1992, mobs destroyed the Babri Masjid mosque in Ayodhya, a protected monument constructed by the first Mughal emperor Babur in the early 16th century. Hindu nationalists argued that the mosque overlay an earlier temple marking the birthplace of the god Rama (Mandal 1993). In the rioting that followed, thousands lost their lives. While the mosque is now destroyed, the fate of the site where it once stood remains a contentious and politically charged issue, which will ultimately be decided by India's Supreme Court.

The Babri Masjid–Ram Jhanmabhoomi dispute shifted the role of archaeology in India from a marginal intellectual pursuit to a central player in debates about India's past and the nature and future of the contemporary Indian state. Numerous publications have explored this conflict and its broader implications (e.g., Guha Thakurta 1997; Rao 1994; Shaw 2000a). Here, I merely note that the Babri Masjid case and similar struggles in Sri Lanka (Coningham and Lewer 1999) and Afghanistan (Cruickshank 2002; Lawler 2002; Manhart 2001; Meskell 2002) are powerful examples of an internally-focused religious nationalism that employs archaeological sites and monuments in efforts to rewrite the past and shape the future.

The changing emphasis from external to internal explanations for cultural change currently being played out in unique ways in the South Asian context has broader parallels in the history of archaeology in many regions of the world, where migration and diffusionism have been replaced by models that emphasize internal processes of change (see Trigger 1989:149–55, 224–7, 296–7). This is, overall, a positive trend, forcing scholars to examine how individuals and communities shape and transform their societies and the natural and cultural environments in which they live. However, while it is dangerous to assume that all changes result from external contacts and sources, it is equally problematic to treat past societies as isolated or closed communities and to ignore the fact that the cultural landscapes that past societies responded to often included peoples, ideas, and objects that originated in distant areas. In the study of historic South Asia, the politicization of archaeological and historical discourse has made nuanced explorations of the complex relations between external contacts and internal processes both increasingly difficult and increasingly important.

Empires at the Beginning of History (ca. 500 B.C.–A.D. 300)

Achaemenid and Seleucid presence in northwest India

The earliest historical evidence for imperial states in South Asia is of polities originating outside the region that expanded into the northwestern portions of South Asia, from Afghanistan to the Indus Valley of modern Pakistan. The first of these is the Persian Achaemenid empire, which under Darius I (522–486 B.C.) extended its territories into eastern Afghanistan and northwest Pakistan (Allchin 1995:130; Kuhrt 2001). Three administrative districts, or satrapies, are documented in Achaemenid written sources – Arachosia (modern Afghanistan), Gandhara (northwest Pakistan), and "Hindush" (Sind or Indus), though both texts and archaeology provide relatively little information on their extent or structure.

The largest South Asian political formations that the Achaemenids encountered were organized as small territorial polities, centered on sizeable sites that may have been the centers of emergent city-states (Erdosy 1995; Kenoyer 1997; Thapar 1984, 1995). Their strongest cultural and economic connections were with the Ganges Basin to the east where similar processes of state formation were occurring. Based on knowledge of Achaemenid imperial strategies elsewhere and the limited textual record for the eastern empire (Kuhrt 2001), it is likely that existing centers – Kandahar in Afghanistan, and Charsada (Puskalavati) and Taxila in Gandhara – became the administrative seats of the eastern satrapies (Ali et al. 1997–98:3; Allchin 1995:131), and that local elites were incorporated into Achaemenid imperial administration. However, direct material evidence of Achaemenid presence at these sites is scarce, limited to a single tablet excavated at Kandahar and coin hoards containing Achaemenid and later coins from several locations at Taxila (Erdosy 1990:664–5).

Although, and perhaps because, evidence is limited, it does not appear that major changes occurred in the South Asian regions claimed by the Achaemenids after conquest. Perhaps the most striking evidence for Achaemenid influence in the region is the use of Aramaic, the main Achaemenid administrative language, in the third-century B.C. inscriptions of the Mauryan emperor Asoka at Kandahar and Taxila (see below; Allchin 1995; Mac Dowall and Taddei 1978:192). The introduction and forms of coinage in northern portions of South Asia at this time also likely has much to do with expanding interactions with western polities (Bopearachchi and Pieper 1998:59).

The Achaemenid empire collapsed in ca. 330 B.C., aided in no small part by the expansionist mission of the Macedonian conqueror Alexander the Great. Alexander's short-lived empire left even less direct evidence in South Asia than did the Achaemenids, although his presence in the region is well documented by the biographers who accompanied his army (e.g., Arrian 1981). Following Alexander's death in 323 B.C. his empire was divided among his generals. South Asian territories fell to the control of Seleucus, first ruler of the Seleucid empire. Unlike the earlier Achaemenid rulers, the Seleucids were no longer the sole claimants to empire in the region and their attempts to retain and expand Alexander's South Asian territories were met with resistance from the forces of Chandragupta, ruler of the Magadha kingdom centered in the Ganges Basin. Seleucus was forced to cede the Indus Valley, Gandhara, and, eventually, Arachosia, to Chandragupta and his successors, rulers of South Asia's first internally based empire: the Mauryans (Sherwin-White and Kuhrt 1993:chapter 4).

While South Asia's first contact with imperialism came from the outside, it is important to emphasize that the direct impact of these early imperial states was limited. Geographically, it was restricted to the northwest region of the subcontinent, not extending east of the Indus Valley. This region was also closely linked with broader developments in northern South Asia: particularly the Ganges Valley, and it is in this direction the greatest material and historical connections are evident archaeologically. Much of peninsular India and Sri Lanka lay outside of the sphere of both foreign and northern South Asian polities until at least the Mauryan period.

The Mauryan empire (ca. 322–187 B.C.)

The polity forged by the military conquests and political treaties of Chandragupta expanded under his successors, particularly the Maurya's most famous and effective king, Asoka (ca. 273–232 B.C.). The empire did not long outlast Asoka's reign, collapsing within 40 years of his death. The Mauryan core lay in the Gangetic heartland of the Magadha state; at its maximal extent, Mauryan territories extended to the northwest regions described above and south into peninsular India (Figure 15.1).

The Mauryan capital at Pataliputra (modern Patna) on the Ganges River has been the subject of sporadic excavation since the late 19th century. Documented remains include traces of a wooden palisade and a large columned structure (Allchin 1995; Spooner 1913). Excavations have been relatively limited at the site, which lies beneath a modern city, and our primary material evidence for the Mauryans derives from the lithic inscriptions that record Asoka's words or edicts in Prakrit (a vernacular form of Sanskrit), Aramaic, and Greek. These are the earliest inscriptions found in South Asia, and provide some of the first evidence for writing in the region. Asoka's inscriptions were engraved on stone columns in urban centers in the Ganges basin and on rock outcrops across the territories over which the empire claimed sovereignty. Some three-dozen unique Asokan texts, termed the major and minor rock edicts and pillar edicts, have been identified at approximately 50 sites (Figure 15.1; Allchin 1995:199; Chaudhary 1983:44–5). The inscriptions are written in the king's voice and span roughly 20 years of his reign, following his

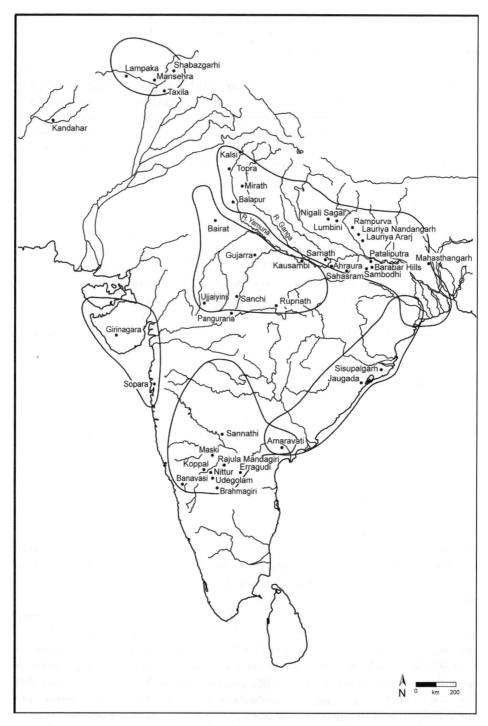

Figure 15.1 The Mauryan empire: major sites and possible territorial boundaries (after Sinopoli 2001b)

conversion to Buddhism in his eighth regnal year. As recorded in the thirteenth major rock edict, Asoka's conversion took place after Mauryan conquest of the Kalinga state of eastern India:

> A hundred and fifty thousand people were deported, a hundred thousand were killed and many times that number perished. Afterwards, now that Kalinga was annexed, the Beloved of the Gods [Ashoka] very earnestly practiced Dhamma [right behavior according to religious principles], desired Dhamma, and taught Dhamma. On con-quering Kalinga, the Beloved of the Gods felt remorse, for, when an independent country is conquered the slaughter, death, and deportation of the people is extremely grievous to the Beloved of the Gods, and weighs heavily on his mind . . . (13th Major Rock Edict, Thapar 1997:255)

As a key source of primary data, Asokan inscriptions have been essential in inter-pretations of the Mauryan polity. Along with information on Asoka's religious values and behavioral proscriptions, they contain insights into imperial political structures, including mention of border states, administrative offices, and revenue collection. Their locations have been used to map imperial geography (Figure 15.1; Fussman 1988; Habib and Habib 1990). At the very least, the presence of inscriptions iden-tifies areas where the Mauryans claimed hegemony. The extent to which those areas were actually under effective imperial domination is less clear, especially in the southern part of the peninsula where there is relatively little additional evidence for the Mauryan presence (Sugandhi 2003).

Other archaeological evidence of the Mauryans is far less definitive. Coins and sculptures can be reasonably securely dated to the Mauryan period, but it is more difficult to associate long-lived ceramic wares and other archaeological evidence from Early Historic archaeological sites with the Mauryan polity. Many major arti-fact types (particularly ceramics) and architectural styles were produced and con-sumed for far longer than the 135-year period of Mauryan hegemony and cannot be directly tied to the imperial period. And although Asoka is reputed to have spon-sored the construction of hundreds of Buddhist monuments or stupas, none survive intact from his reign.

Both early scholarship and nationalist rhetoric about the Mauryans portrayed the empire as a highly centralized and homogenous polity that unified a vast region into a single monolithic imperial state. Recent writings have, in contrast, empha-sized the discontinuous geography of the empire and internal variability in its administration (e.g., Fussman 1988; Sinopoli 2001b; Thapar 1987, 1997; though see Chakrabarti 1997:203–6). While the Mauryans may have had effective territo-rial control in their northern heartland, imperial territories in peninsular India were restricted to areas near important mineral resources and trade routes, suggesting discontinuous territories and limited presence in many areas of the peninsula. Other than the inscriptions and some rare artifacts, areas distant from the imperial core contain relatively little direct evidence of the Mauryan presence, and no evidence of the form that presence may have taken (Sinopoli 2001b). Thus, while the Mauryan empire was certainly far more extensive and complexly organized than any previous South Asian state, claims for its universal status and highly central-ized political structure appear to have been overstated.

The Early Historic period after the Mauryans (ca. 200 B.C.–A.D. 300)

Even during the seemingly centralized Mauryan period, the South Asian political and social landscape is best understood as a complex mosaic of diverse polities and social groups. This pattern continued in the centuries following Mauryan collapse, with numerous small and large states, empires, and non-state societies documented in the inscriptional, textual, and archaeological records. Such societies emerged in the context of broader social and economic changes of the Early Historic period that had begun in previous centuries. These included economic intensification in agricultural and craft economies, expanding trade and commerce within and beyond South Asia, and the spread of Buddhism (see Ray, this volume), Jainism, and Brahmanical religious communities and practices.

Archaeologist Dilip Chakrabarti (1995:274–8) has outlined some of the major polities dominant in South Asia between ca. 200 B.C. to A.D. 320 (Figure 15.2). Between ca. 200 and 1 B.C., these included the Indo-Greeks and Indo-Parthians in areas formerly controlled by the Seleucids and Mauryans, the Sungas in the Ganges Basin, the Satavahanas in the Deccan, and the Cholas, Cheras, and Pandyas in the far south (Abraham 2003). From ca. A.D. 1–320, the Kushanas were dominant in the northwest and Ganges and the Western Shakas in western India. The Satava-hana dynasty and the Cholas, Cheras, and Pandyas remained important in penin-sular and southern India.

Even this complicated list greatly oversimplifies the large number of polities (state and non-state) of this span, and the political and social history of many areas of South Asia remains poorly understood. Below, I limit my discussion to only two of the many known imperial states of the later Early Historic period: the Satavahanas of peninsular India and the Kushanas of the north.

The Satavahana empire (ca. 100 B.C.–A.D. 200)

Like the Mauryans, the Satavahana empire is known from both textual and mate-rial sources. Also like the Mauryans, scholars have viewed the Satavahana polity as a centralized imperial state (albeit smaller and more fractious). However, evidence for Satavahana history and political structure is complex and, at times, contradic-tory, and there remains considerable debate about the empire's chronology, geo-graphic extent, and political and economic organization (see Dehejia 1972; Parasher-Sen 1993; Ray 1986; Shastri 1987, 1991; Sinopoli 2001b).

Our best evidence for the Satavahanas comes from sources that are simultane-ously material and textual: coins and inscriptions. By the first century B.C., both were widespread in the Deccan region of peninsular India. Several hundred inscrip-

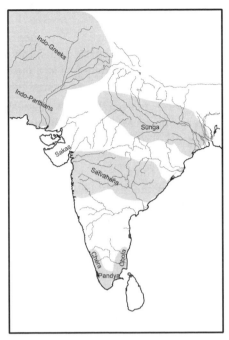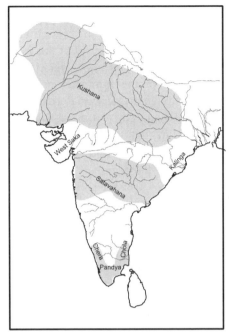

A. ca. 200–1 B.C.E.   B. ca. 1–300 C.E.

Figure 15.2 A and B. Major polities in South Asia: A. from ca. 200–1 B.C.; B. from ca. A.D. 1–300

tions have been documented, most in Prakrit, with a smaller number in Telugu and Tamil. The majority record gifts to Buddhist and Jain monastic institutions from monks and nuns, laymen and women, and merchant and artisan guilds. Fewer than three-dozen inscriptions refer explicitly to Satavahana rulers (Burgess 1964[1881], 1970[1883]; Burgess and Indraji 1976[1881]; Mirashi 1981). All record royal donations and a small number include royal genealogies or information on rulers and the territories they governed.

Coins constitute the most abundant evidence of Satavahana rulers (Bopearachchi and Pieper 1998:37–41; Dutta 1990). Thousands of lead, copper, and potin (an alloy of copper, zinc, lead, and tin; Goyal 1995:89) coins, and smaller numbers of gold and silver coins have been recovered from sites and hoards throughout the Deccan and south India. They were often inscribed with the names of rulers, including some 16 to 20 Satavahana kings. The precise number is impossible to determine because many coins list names or titles common to several rulers (Dutta 1990:18), and because rulers' names varied regionally. Additional written references to the Satavahanas include various king lists provided in the Puranas, a group of 18 sacred Sanskrit historical texts whose earliest written versions date to the mid–first millennium A.D. (though they are believed to have been composed as oral texts much earlier; Thapar 1993). These lists also differ. It is thus not possible to identify all of the empire's rulers or create a linear narrative of Satavahana dynastic history.

The inconsistencies in the written record are probably not just a consequence of limited extant sources, but are instead indicative of political turmoil, including contested kingship and/or cycles of fragmentation and consolidation. Combined evidence from the numismatic, inscriptional, and textual sources indicates two periods of relative imperial strength (from ca. 100–25 B.C. and from ca. A.D. 86–187) separated by a more than century-long period of political fragmentation (see Bopearachchi and Pieper 1998:40; Sinopoli 2001b). Except for coins, we lack the refined archaeological chronologies necessary to document these relatively brief (by archaeological standards) phases.

Along with providing textual information, inscriptions and coins are artifacts, with material and spatial dimensions. They are found in a broad band across northern peninsular India, extending from the west coast (modern Maharashtra) to the east (Andhra Pradesh). Dated inscriptions and coin hoards produce contradictory evidence on where the earliest Satavahana kings emerged, and scholars continue to debate a western versus eastern origin for the rulers (e.g., Goyal 1995; Krishnasastry 1983; Parasher-Sen 1993, 1996; R. Reddy and S. Reddy 1987:58–60). Additional archaeological evidence on Satavahana political geography includes hundreds of contemporary sites found throughout the Deccan. These include monasteries, settlements, agricultural features, and craft production locales (Parasher-Sen 1993; Ray 1986). Few have been carefully excavated and in most cases, their chronological sequences and their positions in local and regional political and economic structures are poorly understood. Both the poor archaeological resolution and the empire's fluctuating political fortunes make Satavahana geographic boundaries difficult to ascertain.

Royal and non-royal inscriptions provide some information about imperial structure, particularly during the period of imperial florescence from A.D. 86–187. Geographic districts called *aharas* were under the control of officials appointed by the king. Three distinctive types of settlements – *nagara* (city or palace), *nigama* (market town), and *gama* (village) – point to a hierarchy of spatial and functional organization. While limited, this evidence does point to efforts to develop durable administrative frameworks under the centralized control of the state.

Much remains to be learned about the history and the organization of the Satavahanas. Available textual sources have been studied in considerable detail and are unlikely to provide significant new information. Scholars must turn to the rich archaeological resources of the Deccan to better understand the nature and organization of the empire and the dynamic between local and imperial economic, social, and political practices and structures. Many important sites of the period have had at least some excavations, though more and better excavations are certainly needed. Systematic survey is critical to permit examination of the infrastructure and hinterland of the emerging urban sites and trade centers of the period and to better understand agricultural economies. In addition, archaeological chronologies must be further refined and common typological and analytical frameworks developed to permit comparisons across sites and regions.

The Kushana empire (ca. 35 B.C.–A.D. 300)

Best known for its striking gold coinage and the spectacular Gandhara and Mathura sculptural traditions, the Kushana empire extended from Central Asia, across Afghanistan, Pakistan, and northern India in the early centuries A.D. (Figure 15.3). Included in Kushana territories were major segments of the Silk Road, and rulers and subjects were participants in and beneficiaries of the extensive trade networks linking the Roman empire with China. Much remains debated about Kushana history, including the broad chronology of the dynasty and its rulers (see Basham 1968; Mukherjee 1988; Rosenfeld 1967). Although numerous sites are known and have had some excavation, there has been relatively little focused research on the period in the last few decades. In part, this is because many important early Kushana sites are in Afghanistan where work has not been possible since the late 1970s. More than mere neglect, from the 1990s until the present the archaeological record of Afghanistan has been decimated: by deliberate destruction and widespread looting of sites and museums (Cruikshank 2002; Lawler 2002; Manhart 2001).

Nonetheless, the Kushana empire provides a valuable case for this chapter. It was contemporary with the Satavahanas and provides another example of an empire originating outside of South Asia with significant impacts in the subcontinent. In addition, Kushana territories incorporated regions of Asia that researchers now treat as distinct cultural areas: Central Asia, eastern Iran, Afghanistan, and northern South Asia. Study of this empire obliges scholars to transcend these geographic boundaries and reminds us that we need to be cautious in essentializing culture areas and applying modern geopolitical constructs to our study of the past. Finally, there are suggestive indications that Kushana hegemony may have penetrated further into local political, economic, and social structures and practices than did many other South Asian empires, allowing us to consider differing strategies and consequences of individual imperial states.

The Kushanas did not leave their own written histories and are little mentioned in contemporary Indian texts (Rosenfeld 1967:8). Instead, much of what we know about Kushana history has been reconstructed from Han dynastic histories and other Chinese sources. Central Asian and Tibetan Buddhist texts discuss the contributions of the Kushana ruler Kanishka to the spread of Buddhism beyond South Asia (Thakur 1999:48–56). Chinese sources allow us to trace the dynasty's origins to the early second century B.C. Yuezhi (Yueh-chih) nomads, who were reportedly defeated by the expansionist Xiongnu empire (see Barfield 1989, 2001; Honeychurch and Amartuvshin, this volume) and pushed from their homes on the southern edge of the Gobi desert. By ca. 135 B.C., the chronicles place them in Bactria near the Oxus River, an area with a longstanding urban tradition under the Seleucids and succeeding Hellenistic–Bactrian states, with major urban centers at Balkh, Ai Khanum, Begram, and Kandahar (Mac Dowall and Taddei 1978; Sidky 2000).

At around 35 B.C. an internal struggle began among the five Yuezhi "tribes" or "lineages." Kujula Kadaphasa, head of the Kuei-shang (Kushan) lineage, emerged

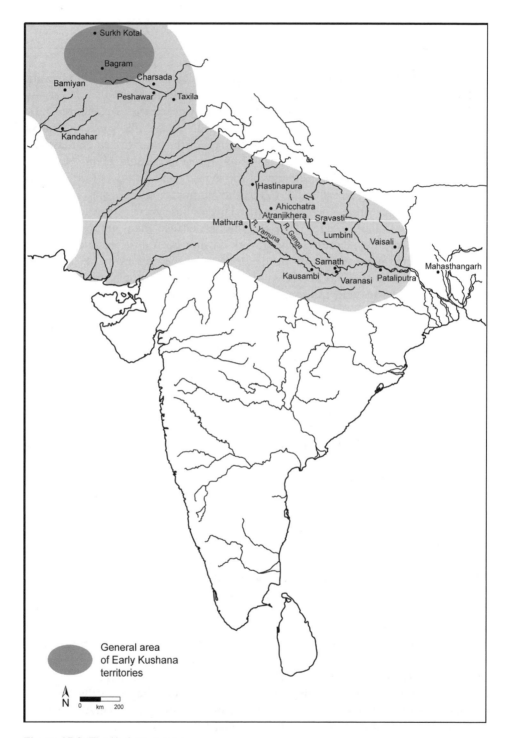

Figure 15.3 The Kushana empire

victorious. Under Kujula and his successor, the Kushanas solidified control over Bactria and expanded west into Afghani territories of the Parthian empire and east into the Gandhara region of northwest Pakistan. During the reign of the third and most famous Kushana ruler, Kanishka (Mukherjee 1988; Rosenfeld 1967), the empire reached its maximal extent, expanding into the Ganges Valley. Major administrative centers are believed to have been Peshawar in northwest Pakistan and Mathura in the Ganges Basin (Sharma 1984; Srinivasan 1989; Thakur 1999). Other South Asian sites that have yielded Kushana remains include Taxila (Marshall 1951) and Charsada (Dani 1965–6; Wheeler 1962) in the northwest, and Hastinapur (Lal 1955), Atranjikhera (Gaur 1983), Kausambi (Sharma 1960), Sravasti (Venkataramayya 1981), Ahicchatra (Agrawala 1985), and Varanasi (Narain and Roy 1976), in the Ganges Basin (Figure 15.3).

Although excavations have been conducted on Kushana period sites in Afghanistan, the former Soviet Union (Gafurov et al. 1970), Pakistan, and India, there is no single synthesis of Kushana period archaeology. In a valuable contribution, Shrava (1993) has compiled more than 200 dated Kushana inscriptions found on structures, boulders, Buddhist and Jain images and architectural complexes, portrait sculptures, and seals. Most record non-royal donations to religious institutions. However, unlike comparable Deccani inscriptions, many contain references to the reigning king (Shrava 1993). The frequent reference to rulers may be simply a rhetorical device, but may also indicate that the authority and visibility of the state was far more pervasive in Kushana territories than in the contemporary Deccani region. The epithets appended to the names of the Kushana kings in both inscription and coins illustrate the rulers' success in asserting universal sovereignty, and include maharaja (great king), *rajadiraja* (king of kings), *kaisara* (Caesar) (Shrava 1993:159), and *devaputra* (son of god).

Imperial ideologies are also materialized in the abundant royal portraiture of the Kushana period, occurring in coins and sculpture. In general, portraiture is rare in South Asia. It is, however, quite common in the Kushana period (e.g., Schlumberger 1983) and, in the coinage at least, bears strong relations to contemporary Greek and Roman practices. Copper portrait coins appear in the reign of Kujula, and gold currency, in standardized weights, appears under the empire's second king, Vima. This standard remains constant for more than two centuries, suggesting a high degree of control of currency (Rosenfeld 1967:20). Along with royal portraits and titles, the coins depict numerous Greek, Persian, and Brahmanical deities, further supporting a universalist ideology (Gupta and Kulashreshtha 1994; Rosenfeld 1967).

Administrative and economic structures of the Kushana empire are in general poorly understood. Virtually nothing is known about taxation and revenue; and despite depictions of soldiers in sculpture and iconography and references to military outposts, we know little about Kushana military strategies, or how and when various territories were incorporated into the empire. Titles on coins and inscriptions record the existence of numerous administrative ranks or offices, though it is difficult to discern the precise tasks performed by various office holders or how imperial organization changed over time (Chattopadhyaya 1975:96–151; Mukherjee 1988). Several titles indicate that the empire was organized into provinces or administrative districts (satraps). The rulers of these districts were referred to as "kshatrapas" or "mahakshtrapas" (suggesting a possible hierarchy of provinces); other regional rulers have the title "raja," or king. The last title may refer to local elites who retained or were granted authority over their territories even after they were incorporated into imperial domains (Chattopadhyaya 1975:114: Mukherjee 1988). The titles "dandanayaka" and "mahadandanayaka" refer to important imperial administrators, perhaps military leaders (Mukherjee 1988:338).

The titles documented in the inscriptional record indicate that both geography and functional roles structured Kushana administration. Less clear are the hierarchical and horizontal connections among these various office holders, and the extent to which such administrative structures were relevant to diverse regions of the empire over time.

Early Historic Empires: Discussion

The brief overviews presented above point to the wealth of archaeological and historical evidence available for the study of early South Asian empires. These four cases also make clear that much remains to be learned. Archaeological research has resulted in the identification of major sites and sacred monuments, with a particular focus on elite material culture. The site focus has meant that there has been relatively less emphasis on placing these major centers in the broader regional and environmental contexts, and considerable research is necessary to better understand the lives of imperial subjects and the social, political, and economic activities and relations that supported and constituted these large territorial polities. In many cases, archaeology can provide the only route to exploring these issues, which are not addressed in the limited textual sources available from South Asia's earliest empires.

Rather than wade through other examples of South Asian empires where we face similar challenges and limitations (and there are many), in the remainder of this chapter I move forward in time to briefly discuss a much later case: the South Indian Vijayanagara empire (ca. A.D. 1350–1650), which has been a focus of much of my archaeological research. Vijayanagara provides several advantages over the previously discussed polities. First, the period is characterized by a much larger and more diverse corpus of written sources than earlier empires, and these sources have been systematically catalogued and studied by a number of historians and epigraphers. Second, major sites of the Vijayanagara period, particularly its first capital, are both easily accessible to archaeological research (that is, they do not lie beneath or within modern cities), and have been the focus of long-term problem-oriented archaeological research. As such, Vijayanagara provides both a more optimistic note on which to conclude this chapter and a starting point from which to pose some suggestions for future research on South Asian empires.

Vijayanagara

The Vijayanagara empire emerged in the mid-14th century in the semi-arid inlands of South India. The empire took form after a period of dramatic political transitions in peninsular India in the wake of the collapse of the northern Delhi Sultanate and the southern Kakatiya, Chalukya, Hoysala, and Chola imperial states (see Sinopoli 2003:chapter 3; Stein 1989). Vijayanagara's founders, rulers of the Sangama dynasty (the first of four ruling lineages), began their expansion from a small base on the Tungabhadra River in modern Karnataka, and through effective military techniques and diplomacy, rapidly extended their territories southwards to encompass much of the peninsula (Figure 15.4). The first Vijayanagara capital grew to one of South Asia's largest cities, and was a major commercial, sacred, and political center until its abandonment in A.D. 1565 (when the imperial capital successively shifted southwards to Penukonda, Chandragiri, and Vellore). Textual sources of the Vijayanagara period include tens of thousands of inscriptions as well as literary and historical texts, poetry, and the accounts of foreign visitors to the empire (Sinopoli 2003:chapter 5). Archaeological evidence for the period is also abundant, though systematic archaeology has largely been restricted to the region of the imperial capital.

Although there is a long history of scholarship on Vijayanagara (e.g., Heras 1927, 1929; Nilakanta Sastri and Kallidaikurichi 1966; Sewell 1900), contemporary interest in the period can be traced to the 1980 publication of *Peasant State and Society in Medieval India* by historian Burton Stein. Stein proposed that Vijayanagara and the earlier South Indian Chola empire are best viewed as segmentary states, employing a model of political organization derived from the writings of the Africanist cultural anthropologist Aidan Southall (1956). In his initial formulation, Stein argued that Vijayanagara was comprised of multiple, semi-autonomous, redundant segments, linked primarily through their acknowledgment of the ritual sovereignty of the king. Stein's formulation of Vijayanagara state structures inspired some (e.g., Dirks 1987) and was soundly criticized by others (Champakalakshmi 1981; Palat 1987), and Stein himself rethought and revised his approach in subsequent publications (Stein 1985, 1989, 1995). What is important here is that his writings initiated a period of theoretically informed research on Vijayanagara that moved beyond dynastic history to consider a range of political, economic, ideological, and social questions. From a rather different theoretical direction, that of feudal models of Indian states and empires, historian Noburu Karashima's (1984, 1992, 2002) careful analyses of inscriptions have explored Vijayanagara economy, taxation, and political structures and further contributed to expanding interest in the period.

While historians were developing new approaches to Vijayanagara, three new archaeological projects were initiated at the first imperial capital. In the late 1970s, the Archaeological Survey of India and Government of Karnataka Department of Archaeological and Museums (Nagaraja Rao 1983, 1985) began separate excavation projects in the administrative heart of the capital. The third project, directed by architectural historian George Michell and anthropological archaeologist John

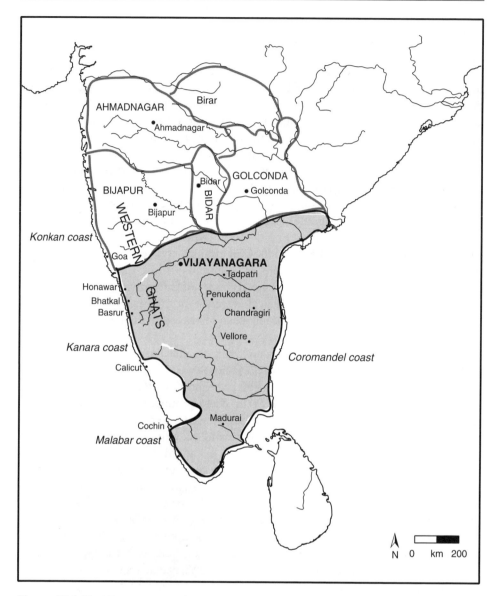

Figure 15.4 The Vijayanagara empire

Fritz, focused on comprehensive surface documentation of the 25 square kilometer core of the imperial capital, with an eye to examining relations between urban form and political and ideological structures (Fritz, Michell and Nagaraja Rao 1985). In the late 1980s, a fourth project was added to this mix, the "Vijayanagara Metropolitan Survey," directed by Kathleen D. Morrison and Carla M. Sinopoli, a ten-year systematic regional survey of the ca. 450 square kilometer fortified hinterland of Vijayanagara (Morrison 1995; Sinopoli and Morrison 1995, In press, In prep.). This project moved beyond areas of elite settlement to examine agriculture, regional settlement, craft production, and defensive and transport networks in the metropolitan region of the imperial capital. The ca. 750 sites identified provide information on a complex and changing landscape, inhabited by the non-elites whose labor and activities constituted the foundation on which the capital and empire were constructed.

Recent work on Vijayanagara by historians and archaeologists has intersected in a variety of formal (Dallapiccola and Zingel Ave-Lallemant 1985) and informal contexts, with considerable cross-fertilization of ideas and research perspectives. As a result, archaeology has moved beyond merely illustrating what was already known from written sources, to providing new and important evidence that allowed scholars to address a variety of research questions. Fritz's (1986) work on the sacred landscape of the Vijayanagara capital and its role in the constitution of royal ideologies was influenced in part by Stein's early emphasis on the ritual authority of Vijayanagara kings but created new understandings of the kinds of sacred claims that rulers made to legitimize their rule. Michell's (1992a, 1992b, 1995) research on Vijayanagara courtly architecture, and its creative merger of elements from southern and northern traditions (also Sinopoli 2000), has been echoed in research by historians Philip Wagoner (1993, 1996, 2000), and Cynthia Talbot (2001) on relations between Vijayanagara and the contemporary Deccani sultanates, who were simultaneously Vijayanagara's major enemies and peers. Morrison (1995, In press) and Sinopoli's (1988, 1998, 2003) research has focused primarily on social and economic structures and transformations in the Vijayanagara period. In its emphasis on political economy, the organization of production, social dynamics, and the relations between local and imperial communities, structures, and processes, this work has intersected with that of historians David Ludden (1985), Sanjay Subrahmanyam (1990a, 1990b, 1995), Vijaya Ramaswamy (1985), and Noburu Karashima (1992).

Archaeological research on Vijayanagara differs in significant respects from the cases discussed earlier. Because of the rich historical sources for the Vijayanagara period, there is relatively little debate about the sequences of kings and ruling dynasties or the changing territorial extent of the empire. Archaeologists have moved beyond the documentation of monuments and sculptures to consider the full range of archaeological evidence, and beyond their temporal and spatial contexts to examine a broad range of political, economic, social, and ideological issues. Morrison and Sinopoli's regional survey allowed Vijayanagara to be placed in its broader environmental and cultural setting and allowed an examination of non-elites. Although the metropolitan region constitutes only a very small portion of the empire and much work remains to be done, this is a step in the right direction and a valuable illustration of the contributions that can be made to the study of South Asian empires by sustained and systematic regional research.

Conclusions

In this chapter, I have presented information on several South Asian empires that have been studied by archaeologists. I have excluded many periods and polities –

including the Gupta (Altekar 1957; Jayaswal 2001; Williams 1993), Chola (Dehejia 1990; Swaminathan 1998), Delhi Sultanate (Jackson 1999), and Mughal (Asher 1992; Petruccioli 1988; Richards 1993) empires, to name but a few. To cover archaeological research on all South Asian empires in even minimal detail is impossible in a single chapter, nor is the inevitable catalogue of sites and discoveries that would emerge from such an approach likely to be of interest to most readers of this volume. Nonetheless, I hope that this chapter has demonstrated the potential that archaeological research on historic empires has in the South Asian context, both in enhancing understandings of particular polities and periods and in addressing issues of interest to archaeologists working in other regions of the world.

The cases discussed here also illustrate the challenges to making substantive contributions that can extend beyond the historical particularities of individual cases. I have argued that a necessary requirement to do so is a fundamental rethinking of the relations between archaeological and textual evidence to allow us to move beyond the use of archaeological evidence merely to illustrate prior knowledge derived from written sources. There are additional practical and theoretical challenges to the archaeology of South Asian empires, and indeed of all early empires. Empires are by definition large, encompassing vast territories and multiple ethnic and social groups with diverse political, social, economic, and ideological practices and organization. Understanding the full complexities of any imperial system requires multiple scholars and coordinated efforts. There is need to pay greater attention to rural sites, agricultural and craft production remains, environmental history, transport and trade routes, and the military infrastructures that are crucial to the existence and success (or failure) of imperial states. The compilation of detailed gazetteers of site distributions, generated by multiple surveys and research projects is important (see Chakrabarti 2001; Erdosy 1985; Mughal 1997; Shaw 2000b for additional examples of regional survey projects), perhaps especially so for empires that extended across the territories of more than one contemporary nation-state. The potential of such broad-based scholarship can only be reached if we develop and refine common terminologies for material forms (architecture, artifacts) and chronological schemas.

Perhaps most important, we need to carefully consider our object of study and what we mean by an "archaeology of empire." Empires are political systems, imposed by warfare and coercion, with potentially enormous impact on social, ideological, economic, and political structures and activities of peoples and regions in their territories. All of these realms are potentially accessible through problem-oriented archaeology. However, empires are often fragile polities, easily fragmented by internal stresses and external threats, whose fortunes can rise and fall with those of individual rulers or dynasties. Short-lived dynastic chronologies can seldom be precisely matched to our longer archaeological chronologies, and much archaeological data may in many contexts be better suited to examining the broader consequences of imperial transformations and incorporation, rather than specifics of political history.

As a final note, the politicization of archaeology in the contemporary South Asian context, discussed at the beginning of this chapter, looms ominously over much contemporary archaeological research in the region, affecting both the questions being asked and the status of the archaeological record itself. Archaeology has come to play a central role in discussions about the present and future of South Asian nations. The subject of "empire" has not been the main focus of the current culture wars that are playing out particularly publicly in India, but empires and their study are implicated in these debates in significant ways – and archaeologists ignore them at our peril.

REFERENCES

Abraham, Shinu A. 2003 Chera, Chola, Pandya: Using Archaeological Evidence to Identify the Tamil Kingdoms of Early Historic South India. Asian Perspectives 42:207–23.

Agrawala, V. S. 1985 Terracotta Figurines of Ahichchhatra, District Bareilly, U.P. Varanasi: Prithivi Prakashan.

Alcock, Susan E., Terence N. D'Altroy, Kathleen D. Morrison, and Carla M. Sinopoli, eds. 2001 Empires: Perspectives from Archaeology and History. Cambridge: Cambridge University Press.

Ali, Taj, Robin Coningham, Mukhtar Ali Durrani, and Gul Rahim Khan 1997–98 Preliminary Report of Two Seasons of Archaeological Investigations at the Bala Hisar of Charsadda, NWFP, Pakistan. Ancient Pakistan XII:3–33.

Allchin, Frank Raymond 1995 The Archaeology of Early Historic South Asia: The Emergence of Cities and States. Cambridge: Cambridge University Press.

—— 1998 The Interface of Archaeology and History. Man and Environment 22:19–35.

Altekar, Anant S. 1957 The Coinage of the Gupta Empire and Its Imitations. Banaras: Banaras Hindu University.

Arrian 1981 Alexander the Great: Selections from Arrian. J. G. Lloyd, trans. Cambridge: Cambridge University Press.

Asher, Catherine 1992 Architecture of Mughal India. Cambridge: Cambridge University Press.

Barfield, Thomas 1989 The Perilous Frontier: Nomadic Empires and China, 221 B.C.E. to A.D. 1757. Cambridge MA: Blackwell.

—— 2001 The Shadow Empires: Imperial State Formation along the Chinese-Nomad Frontier. In Empires: Perspectives from Archaeology and History. Susan E. Alcock, Terence N. D'Altroy, Kathleen D. Morrison, and Carla M. Sinopoli, eds. Pp. 10–41. Cambridge: Cambridge University Press.

Basham, Arthur, ed. 1968 Papers on the Date of Kaniska. Leiden: E. J. Brill.

Bopearachchi, Osmund, and Wilfried Pieper 1998 Ancient Indian Coins. Turnhout, The Netherlands: Brepols.

Burgess, James A. 1964[1881] Report on the Buddhist Cave Temples and Their Inscriptions. Archaeological Survey of Western India IV. Delhi: Indological Book House.

—— 1970[1883] Report on the Elura Cave Temples and the Brahmanaical and Jaina Caves in Western India. Archaeological Survey of Western India V. Delhi: Indological Book House.

Burgess, James A., and P. Bhagwanlal Indraji 1976[1881] Inscriptions from Cave Temples of Western India. Archaeological Survey of Western India. Delhi: Indian India.

Chakrabarti, Dilip K. 1995 Post-Mauryan States of Mainland South Asia (ca. B.C. 185–A.D. 320). *In* The Archaeology of Early Historic South Asia: The Emergence of Cities and States, Frank Raymond Allchin, ed. Pp. 274–326. Cambridge: Cambridge University Press.

—— 1997 Colonial Indology: Sociopolitics of the Ancient Indian Past. New Delhi: Munshiram Manoharlal.

—— 2001 Archaeological Geography of the Ganga Plain. Delhi: Permanent Black.

Champakalakshmi, Radha 1981 "Peasant State and Society in Medieval South India:" A Review Article. Indian Economic and Social History Review 18:411–26.

Chattopadhyaya, Bhaskar 1975 Kushana State and Indian Society: A Study in Post-Mauryan Polity and Society. Calcutta: Punthi Pustak.

Chaudhary, Radhakrishna, ed. 1983 Inscriptions of Ancient India. New Delhi: Meenakshi Prakashan.

Coningham, Robin, and Nick Lewer 1999 Paradise Lost: The Bombing of the Temple of the Tooth – a UNESCO World Heritage Site in Sri Lanka. Antiquity 73:857–66.

Cruickshank, Dan 2002 View from Kabul. The Architectural Review 212:32–4.

Dallapiccola, Anna L., and M. Zingel Ave-Lallemant, eds. 1985 Vijayanagara: City and Empire. Weisbaden: Franz Steiner Verlag.

Dani, Ahmad Hasan 1965–66 Shaikhan-Deri Excavations. Ancient Pakistan 2:17–124.

Dehejia, Vidula 1972 Early Buddhist Rock Temples: A Chronology. Ithaca: Cornell University Press.

—— 1990 Art of the Imperial Cholas. New York: Columbia University Press.

Dhavalikar, M. K. 1999 Historical Archaeology of India. New Delhi: Books and Books.

Dirks, Nicholas 1987 The Hollow Crown: Ethnohistory of an Indian Kingdom. Cambridge: Cambridge University Press.

Dutta, M. 1990 A Study of the Satavahana Coinage. New Delhi: Harman Publishing House.

Erdosy, George 1985 Settlement Archaeology of the Kausambi Region. Man and Environment 9:66–79.

—— 1990 Taxila: Political History and Urban Structure. *In* South Asian Archaeology, 1987. Maurizio Taddei, ed. Pp. 657–74. Rome: Istituto Italiano per il Medio ed Estremo Oriente.

—— 1995 City States of North India and Pakistan at the Time of the Buddha. *In* The Archaeology of Early Historic South Asia: The Emergence of Cities and States. Frank Raymond Allchin, ed. Pp. 99–122. Cambridge: Cambridge University Press.

Fritz, John M. 1986 Vijayanagara: Authority and Meaning of a South Indian Imperial Capital. American Anthropologist 88:44–55.

Fritz, John M., George A. Michell, and M. S. Nagaraja Rao 1985 Where Kings and Gods Meet: The Royal Center at Vijayanagara. Tucson: University of Arizona Press.

Fussman, Gerard 1988 Central and Provincial Administration in Ancient India: The Problem of the Mauryan Empire. The Indian Historical Review 14:43–72.

Gafurov, Bobodzhan Gafurovich, M. Asimov, G. M. Bongard-Levin, B. Ya. Stavisky, B. A. Litvinsky, and others 1970 Kushan Studies in U.S.S.R. Calcutta: Indian Studies Past and Present.

Gaur, R. C. 1983 Excavations at Atranjikhera: Early Civilization of the Upper Ganga Basin. Delhi: Motilal Banarsidass.

Goyal, Srirama 1995 The Dynastic Coins of Ancient India. Jodhpur: Kusumanjali Prakashan.

Guha Thakurta, Tapati 1997 Archaeology as Evidence: Looking Back from the Ayodhya Debate. Calcutta: Center for Studies in the Social Sciences.

Gupta, Parmeshwari Lal, and Sarojini Kulashreshtha 1994 Kusana Coins and History. New Delhi: D. K. Print World.

Habib, Irfan, and F. Habib 1990 Mapping the Mauryan Empire. Proceedings of the Indian History Congress 1989–90:57–79.

Heras, Henry 1927 The Aravidu Dynasty of Vijayanagara. Madras: B. G. Paul.

—— 1929 Beginnings of Vijayanagara History. Bombay: Indian Historical Research Institute.

Inden, Ron 1990 Imagining India. Cambridge MA: Blackwell.

Jackson, Peter 1999 The Delhi Sultanate: A Political and Military History. Cambridge: Cambridge University Press.

Jayaswal, Vidula 2001 Royal Temples of Gupta Period: Excavations at Bhitari. Aryan Books: New Delhi.

Karashima, Noburu 1984 South Indian History and Society: Studies from Inscriptions, A.D. 850–1800. Delhi: Oxford University Press.

—— 1992 Toward a New Formation: South Indian Society Under Vijayanagara Rule. Delhi: Oxford University Press.

—— 2002 A Concordance of Nayakas: The Vijayanagar Inscriptions in South India. Oxford: Oxford University Press.

Kenoyer, J. Mark 1997 Early City-States in South Asia: Comparing the Harappan Phase and Early Historic Period. In The Archaeology of City-States: Cross-Cultural Approaches. Debra L. Nichols and Thomas H. Charlton, eds. Pp. 51–70. Washington DC: Smithsonian Institution Press.

Krishnasastry, K. V. 1983 The Proto and Early Historical Cultures of Andhra Pradesh. Archaeological Series 58. Hyderabad: Government of Andhra Pradesh.

Kuhrt, Amelie 2001 The Achaemenid Persian Empire (ca. 550– ca. 330 B.C.E.): Continuities, Adaptations, and Transformations. In Empires: Perspectives from Archaeology and History. Susan E. Alcock, Terence N. D'Altroy, Kathleen D. Morrison, and Carla M. Sinopoli, eds. Pp. 93–123. Cambridge: Cambridge University Press.

Kulke, Hermann, ed. 1995 The State in Premodern India 1000–1700. Delhi: Oxford University Press.

Lal, Braj Basi 1955 Excavations at Hastinapura and Other Explorations in the Upper Ganga and Sutlej Basins. Ancient India 11:5–151.

Lape, Peter V. 2003 On the Use of Archaeology and History in Island Southeast Asia. Journal of the Economic and Social History of the Orient 45:468–91.

Lawler, A. 2002 Then They Buried their History. Science 298:1202–3.

Li, Min 2003 Ji'nan in the First Millennium B.C.: Archaeology and History. Economic and Social History of the Orient 46:88–126.

Ludden, David 1985 Peasant History in South India. Delhi: Oxford University Press.

Mac Dowall, D. W., and Maurizio Taddei 1978 The Early Historic Period: Achaemenids and Greeks. In The Archaeology of Afghanistan from Earliest Times to the Timurid Period. Frank Raymond Allchin and Norman Hammond, eds. Pp. 187–232. New York: Academic Press.

Mandal, D. 1993 Ayodhya: Archaeology After Demolition. Hyderabad: Orient Longman.

Manhart, Christian 2001 The Afghan Cultural Heritage Crisis: UNESCO's Response to the Destruction of Statues in Afghanistan. American Journal of Archaeology 105:387–8.

Marshall, Sir John 1951 Taxila, an Illustrated Account of Archaeological Excavations Carried Out at Taxila Under the Orders of the Government of India Between the Years 1913 and 1934. Cambridge: Cambridge University Press.

Meskell, Lynn 2002 Negative Heritage and Past Mastering in Archaeology. Anthropological Quarterly 73:557–74.

Michell, George A. 1992a The Vijayanagara Courtly Style. New Delhi: Manohar Book Service and American Institute of Indian Studies.

—— 1992b Royal Architecture and Imperial Style at Vijayanagara. *In* The Powers of Art: Patronage in Indian Culture. Barbara Stoler Miller, ed. Pp. 168–79. Delhi: Oxford University Press.

—— 1995 Architecture and Art of Southern India: Vijayanagara and the Successor States. The New Cambridge History of India I:6. Cambridge: Cambridge University Press.

Mirashi, Vasudev Vishnu 1981 The History and Inscriptions of the Satavahanas and the Western Kshtrapas. Bombay: Maharashtra Board for Literature and Culture.

Moreland, John 2001 Archaeology and Text. London: Duckworth.

Morrison, Kathleen D. 1995 Fields of Victory: Vijayanagara and the Course of Intensification. Contributions to the Archaeological Research Facility, No. 52. Berkeley: University of California.

—— In press Oceans of Dharma: Landscape History in Southern India. Chicago: University of Chicago Press.

Mughal, Mohammad Rafique 1997 Ancient Cholistan: Archaeology and Architecture. Rawalpindi: Ferozsons.

Mukherjee, Bratindra Nath 1988 The Rise and Fall of the Kushana Empire. Calcutta: Firma KLM.

Mukhia, Harbans, ed. 2000 The Feudalism Debate. New Delhi: Manohar.

Nagaraja Rao, M. S., ed. 1983 Vijayanagara: Progress of Research 1979–83. Mysore: Department of Archaeology and Museums.

—— 1985 Vijayanagara: Progress of Research 1983–84. Mysore: Department of Archaeology and Museums.

Narain, Abodh Kishor Narain, and Tribhuna Nath Roy 1976 Excavations at Rajghat, 1957–58, 1960–65. Varanasi: Banaras Hindu University.

Nilakanta Sastri, and Kallidaikurichi Aiyah N. 1966 A History of South India from Prehistoric Times to the Fall of Vijayanagara. Madras: Oxford University Press.

Palat, Ravi 1987 The Vijayanagara Empire: Re-Integration of the Agrarian Order of Medieval South India, 1336–1569. *In* Early State Dynamics. Henri J. M. Claessen and P. Van de Velde, eds. Pp. 170–86. Leiden: E. J. Brill.

Parasher-Sen, Aloka 1993 Introductions – Problems of Interpretation. *In* Social and Economic History of Early Deccan: Some Interpretations. A. Parasher-Sen, ed. Pp. 1–65. New Delhi: Manohar.

—— 1996 The Archaeology of Regions: Existing Perspectives and Challenges. *In* Indian Archaeology since Independence. H. R. Shrimali, ed. Pp. 19–23. Delhi: Association for the Study of Archaeology and History.

Petruccioli, Attilio 1988 Fathpur Sikri: Città del Sole e delle Acque. Rome: Carucci.

Ramaswamy, Vijaya 1985 Textiles and Weavers in Medieval South India. Oxford: Oxford University Press.

Rao, Nandini 1994 Interpreting Silences: Symbol and History in the Case of Ram Janmabhoomi/Babri Masjid. *In* Social Construction of the Past: Representation of Power. George C. Bond and Angela Gilliam, eds. Pp. 154–64. London: Routledge.

Ray, Amita, and Samir Mukherjee, eds. 1990 Historical Archaeology of India. New Delhi: Books and Books.

Ray, Himanshu P. 1986 Monastery and Guild: Commerce under the Satavahanas. Delhi: Oxford University Press.

—— 2003 The Archaeology of Seafaring in Ancient South Asia. Cambridge: Cambridge University Press.

Ray, Himanshu P., and Carla M. Sinopoli, eds. 2004 Archaeology as History. Delhi: Indian Council For Historical Research.

Reddy, D. Raja, and Suryanarayana Reddy 1987 Kotalingala Coinage. Satavahanas and Other Local Rulers: A Profile. Hyderabad: Numismatic Society of Hyderabad.

Richards, John F. 1993 The Mughal Empire. Cambridge: Cambridge University Press.

Rosenfeld, John M. 1967 The Dynastic Art of the Kushans. Berkeley: University of California Press.

Schlumberger, Daniel 1983 Surkh Kotal en Bactriane. With contributions by Marc Le Berre and Gérard Fussman. Mémoires de la Délégation Archéologique Française en Afghanistan, vol. 32. Paris: Diffusion de Boccard.

Sewell, Robert 1900 A Forgotten Empire (Vijayanagar). London: Swann Sonneschein.

Sharma, Govardhan Raji 1960 The Excavations at Kausambi (1957–59). Allahabad: University of Allahabad.

Sharma, Ramesh Chandra 1984 Buddhist Art of Mathura. Delhi: Agam.

Shastri, Ajay Mitra 1987 Early History of the Deccan: Problems and Perspectives. Delhi: Sundeep Prakashan.

—— 1991 Satavahana Silver Coinage. In Studies in South Indian Coins, vol. 1. A. V. Narasimha Murty, ed. Pp. 45–60. Madras: New Era Publications.

Shaw, Julia 2000a Ayodhya's Sacred Landscape: Ritual Memory, Politics and Archaeological "fact." Antiquity 74:693–700.

—— 2000b Sanchi and Its Archaeological Landscape: Buddhist Monasteries, Settlements, and Irrigation Works in Central India. Antiquity 74:775–6.

Sherwin-White, Susan, and Amelie Kuhrt 1993 From Samarkhand to Sardis: A New Approach to the Seleucid Empire. Berkeley: University of California Press.

Shrava, Satya 1993 The Dated Kushana Inscriptions. New Delhi: Pranava Prakashan.

Sidky, Homayun 2000 The Greek Kingdom of Bactria from Alexander to Eurcratides the Great. Washington DC: University Press of America.

Sinopoli, Carla M. 1988 The Organization of Craft Production at Vijayanagara, South India. American Anthropologist 90(3):580–97.

—— 1994 The Archaeology of Empires. Annual Review of Anthropology 23:159–80.

—— 1998 Identity and Social Action among Craft Producers of the Vijayanagara Period. In Craft and Social Identity. Cathy L. Costin and Rita P. Wright, eds. Pp. 161–72. Archeological Paper No. 8. Washington DC: American Anthropological Association.

—— 2000 From the Lion Throne: Political and Social Dynamics of the Vijayanagara Empire. Journal of the Economic and Social History of the Orient 43:364–98.

—— 2001a Empires. In Archaeology at the Millennium. T. Douglas Price and Gary M. Feinman, eds. Pp. 439–71. New York: Kluwer/Plenum.

—— 2001b On the Edge of Empire: Form and Substance in the Satavahana Dynasty. In Empires: Perspectives from Archaeology and History. Susan E. Alcock, Terence N. D'Altroy, Kathleen D. Morrison, and Carla M. Sinopoli, eds. Pp. 155–78. Cambridge: Cambridge University Press.

—— 2003 The Political Economy of Craft Production: Crafting Empire in South India, 1350–1650. Cambridge: Cambridge University Press.

Sinopoli, Carla M., and Kathleen D. Morrison 1995 Dimensions of Imperial Control: The Vijayanagara Capital. American Anthropologist 97:83–96.

—— In press The Regional Landscapes of the Imperial City of Vijayanagara: Report on the Vijayanagara Metropolitan Survey Project. In South Asian Archaeology 1999. Karel R. van Kooij and Ellen Raven, eds. Groningen: Egbert Forsten Publishing.

—— In prep. The Vijayanagara Metropolitan Survey: Monograph Series, vol. 1. Anthropological Monographs. Ann Arbor: Museum of Anthropology, University of Michigan.

Southall, Aidan 1956 Alur Society. Cambridge: W. Heffer.

Spooner, Dave B. 1913 Mr. Ratan Tata's Excavations at Pataliputra. Annual Report of the Archaeological Survey of India 1912–13. Pp. 53–86. Calcutta: Archaeological Survey of India.

Srinivasan, Doris Meth, ed. 1989 Mathura: The Cultural Heritage. New Delhi: Manohar and American Institute of Indian Studies.

Stein, Burton 1985 Vijayanagara and the Transition to Patrimonial Systems. In Vijayanagara: City and Empire. Anna L. Dallapiccola and Marie Zingel Ave-Lallemant, eds. Pp. 73–87. Weisbaden: Franz Steiner Verlag.

—— 1989 Vijayanagara. The New Cambridge History of India, I:2. Cambridge: Cambridge University Press.

—— 1995 The Segmentary State: Interim Reflections. In The State in Premodern India 1000–1700. Hermann Kulke, ed. Pp. 134–61. Delhi: Oxford University Press.

Subrahmanyam, Sanjay 1990a The Political Economy of Commerce: Southern India 1500–1650. Cambridge: Cambridge University Press.

—— 1990b The Portuguese, the Port of Basrur, and the Rice Trade, 1600–50. In Merchants, Markets and the State in Early Modern India. Sanjay Subrahmanyam, ed. Pp. 17–47. Delhi: Oxford University Press.

—— 1995 Of Imârat and Tijârat: Asian Merchants and State Power in the Western Indian Ocean, 1400 to 1750. Comparative Studies in Society and History 35:750–80.

Sugandhi, Namita 2003 Context, Content, and Composition: Questions of Intended Meaning and the Asokan Edicts. Asian Perspectives 42:224–46.

Swaminathan, S. 1998 The Early Cholas: History, Art, and Culture. Delhi: Sharada Publishing.

Talbot, Cynthia 2001 Precolonial India in Practice: Society, Religion, and Identity in Medieval Andhra. Oxford: Oxford University Press.

Thakur, Manoj J. 1999 India in the Age of Kanishka. 2nd rev. edition. Delhi: World View.

Thapar, Romila 1984 From Lineage to State: Social Formations in the Mid-First Millennium B.C. in the Ganga Valley. Bombay: Oxford University Press.

—— 1987 The Mauryas Revisited (S. G. Deuskar Lectures on Indian History 1984). Calcutta: Centre for Studies in Social Sciences and K. P. Bagchi and Co.

—— 1993 Society and Historical Consciousness: The Itihara-Purana Tradition. In Interpreting Early India. Romila Thapar, ed. Pp. 136–73. Delhi: Oxford University Press.

—— 1995 The First Millennium B.C. in Northern India. In Recent Perspectives on Early Indian History. Romila Thapar, ed. Pp. 80–141. Bombay: Popular Prakashan.

—— 1997 Asoka and the Decline of the Mauryas. New rev. edition. Delhi: Oxford University Press.

—— 2000 Cultural Pasts: Essays in Early Indian History. Delhi: Oxford University Press.

Trautmann, Thomas, and Carla M. Sinopoli 2002 In the Beginning Was the Word: Excavating the Relations between Archaeology and History in South Asia. Journal of the Economic and Social History of the Orient 45:492–523.

Trigger, Bruce G. 1989 A History of Archaeological Thought. Cambridge: Cambridge University Press.

Venkataramayya, M. 1981 Sravasti. 2ⁿᵈ edition. New Delhi: Archaeological Survey of India.

Wagoner, Phillip B. 1993 Tidings of the King: A Translation and Ethnohistorical Analysis of the Rayāvācakamu. Honolulu: University of Hawaii Press.

—— 1996 "Sultan among Hindu Kings:" Dress, Titles, and the Islamicization of Hindu Culture at Vijayanagara. Journal of Asian Studies 55:851–80.

—— 2000 Harihara, Bukka, and the Sultan: The Delhi Sultanate in the Political Imagination of Vijayanagara. *In* Beyond Turk and Hindu: Rethinking Religious Identities in Islamicate South Asia. David Gilmartin and Bruce B. Lawrence, eds. Pp. 300–26. Gainesville: University Press of Florida.

Wheeler, Sir Mortimer 1962 Charsada: A Metropolis of the North-West Frontier. Oxford: Oxford University Press.

Williams, Joanna 1993 The Art of Gupta India: Empire and Province. Princeton: Princeton University Press.

Index

Note: page numbers in italics refer to figures or tables